Praise for Competing Like a Pro

"Competing Like a Pro is an insightful look into the world of a competitive ballroom dancer. It's filled with the useful details everyone should really know before they begin competing, whether it be just for the passion or a full-blown career. I would have liked to have had this book myself when I was starting out!"

- LOUIS VAN AMSTEL, THREE-TIME WORLD DANCE CHAMPION AND EMMY-NOMINATED CHOREOGRAPHER. LOUIS IS ALSO THE CREATOR OF THE INTERNATIONAL BALLROOM DANCE FITNESS WORKOUT SENSATION "LABLAST" (LABLASTFITNESS.COM) AND HIS NEW WOMEN'S LIFESTYLE CLOTHING LINE 'LVA' IS NOW AVAILABLE AT SEARS.COM

"Competing Like a Pro offers a magical combination of dancing and life skills to help the reader dance with greater joy and happiness. Jammed packed with stories and examples of dancers who have overcome obstacles to achieve their goals on and off the dance floor, it inspires us to reach for the stars and follow our dreams."

- GREG HICKS, BESTSELLING CO-AUTHOR OF, HOW WE CHOOSE TO BE HAPPY: THE 9 CHOICES OF EXTREMELY HAPPY PEOPLE – THEIR SECRETS, THEIR STORIES

"Nike says Just Do It. I say Just Read It! I recommend this book for competitors of all levels who want to shine on the ballroom floor and make judges take notice."

- BILL SPARKS, JUDGE, COACH, ORGANIZER, AND FOUR-TIME UNITED STATES LATIN CHAMPION

"This book is a great kick start to an enjoyable competitive journey. What takes years to discover are spelled out in advance. An important read for both students and newer teachers in the world of DanceSport!"

- EDWARD SIMON, JUDGE, COACH AND UNITED STATES PROFESSIONAL AMERICAN BALLROOM CHAMPION. EDWARD IS ALSO THE ORGANIZER OF THE NEW YORK DANCE FESTIVAL AND THE AMERICAN STYLE CONGRESS

"Jessika's experience as a dancer, competitor and Master Level Executive Coach has given her the insight needed to guide the new competitor through the process of preparing for what to expect at their first Ballroom Dancesport Competition as well as giving the seasoned competitor the information necessary to help them take their dancing to the next level. Newcomer to Open Amateur, first competition or fiftieth. You will benefit from Jessika's hard work and dedication."

- WAYNE ENG, FOUNDER & OWNER OF DANCE VISION ORGANIZER OF THE EMERALD BALL DANCESPORT CHAMPIONSHIPS COMPETITION DIRECTOR OF THE UNITED STATES DANCE CHAMPIONSHIPS

More Praise for Competing Like a Pro

"Inspiring, unique and practical - the wisdom and insights Jessika shares in this book will give you the skills, confidence and courage you need to enjoy greater success and satisfaction - on the dance floor and beyond. Don't wait for the 'right time' to read it. There has never been a better moment for you to take a giant leap toward the future you've always wanted."

- MARGIE WARRELL, MASTER COACH AND BESTSELLING AUTHOR OF FIND YOUR COURAGE (WILEY) AND STOP PLAYING SAFE (MCGRAW-HILL)

"I wish this book was available when I first started competing. It took me more than five years of competing to finally understand all that Jessika has revealed in this valuable book. It's especially helpful to understand the fundamentals of successful competing in ballroom competitions from various perspectives – judges, ballroom teachers, pro-am dancers, etc. Jessika's book is a 'must-read' for anyone who is considering competing and even those who are already competing."

- PATRICE TANAKA, AUTHOR, BECOMING GINGER ROGERS...HOW BALLROOM DANCING MADE ME A HAPPIER WOMAN, BETTER PARTNER AND SMARTER CEO, AND CO-CHAIR, CHIEF CREATIVE OFFICER, CRT/TANAKA

"Jessika has written an informative and comprehensive book about what it takes to compete with grace and success as a Pro/Am student. I recommend it to any level competitor who wants to be their personal best."

- WENDY JOHNSON, JUDGE AND CO-ORGANIZER OF THE HOLIDAY DANCE CLASSIC CHAMPIONSHIPS AND KIWI DANCE CLASSIC DANCE COMPETITION

"Coaching from top ballroom judges is one of the very best ways you can spend your ballroom budget. Jessika's interviews with several outstanding coaches will give you insights into what they are looking for when they judge. When you compare the cost of coaching with the cost of a book, this is a huge bargain!"

- ELIZABETH SEAGULL, AUTHOR OF BALLROOM DANCING IS NOT FOR SISSIES. ELIZABETH IS ALSO AN EXPERIENCED PRO/AM AND AM/AM COMPETITOR

Competing Like a Pro: Spotlight Strategies To Help You Shine On and Off the Ballroom Floor

Editor: Nancy Flynn, Nancy Flynn Public Relations, Inc.
Book design and layout: Matthew Ryan
Cover photography: Stephen Marino Photography
Dancing costume on cover is by Doré Designs

This publication is designed to provide information with regard to the subject matter covered. It is published with the understanding that the publisher and author are not engaged in rendering medical, psychological, financial or other professional advice. If medical, psychological, financial or other professional advice is required, the services of a competent professional should be sought.

Limit of Liability/Disclaimer of Warranty: While the publisher and author have used their best efforts in preparing this book, they make no representations or warranties with respect to the accuracy or completeness of the contents of this book and specifically disclaim any implied warranties of merchantability or fitness for a particular purpose. This book is designed to be used as a guide, and the advice contained herein may not be suitable for your situation. Neither the publisher nor the author shall be liable for any loss or other damages arising from or in any way connected with the contents of this book.

First edition
ISBN-13: 978-0-9833700-3-1
Library of Congress Control Number: 2013945399
Printed in the United States of America

How to order:
Copies may be ordered by contacting Next Level Dancing, LLC, or visiting nextleveldancing.com

Quantity discounts available by calling 614-441-8972 or emailing books@nextleveldancing.com

In Loving Memory of My Two Mothers,
Monica Magnusson and Judith Turchetta.
You always saw the light in others and
encouraged me to shine through grace.
Thank you for continuing to guide me
from above.

Acknowledgments

I have truly loved every moment of writing this book and have been amazed at the flow and ease from which it emerged. At one point I had to just stop and say, "I'll cover that concept in the next book," or I would still be writing.

Okay, there were a few times when I doubted that I would meet the deadline and struggled to set aside time to write while managing my leadership-coaching business, ballroom competing, practicing, and life. While writing this book, I sold my condo, stored my belongings, moved in with a friend, bought a house, moved into my new house and a new office (in the same month), acquired seven new business clients, and doubled my ballroom competition schedule. I also decided to add a new consignment/rental division to my ballroom-related business, Next Level Dancing, LLC, and bring on a new employee and a summer intern.

For those of you who know me, this seemingly insane schedule will come as no surprise. For those of you who don't know me yet, it's okay to think that I'm slightly nuts. I wonder myself at times.

The truth is that in order for me to operate at "warp speed," I rely on amazing people who support and cheer me on. I am blessed to have extraordinary people in my life, and while I can't thank all of you by name, please know that I see you, hear you, and I'm here for you, just as you are here for me.

There are, however, a few people who were instrumental in creating this book, and I'd like to acknowledge their help and support. First, I'd like to thank my team (Laura Benton, Franny Lazarus, and Jenny Semprun) at my companies, J.Ferm, LLC and Next Level Dancing, LLC. You keep me sane, and I appreciate everything you do, from anticipating my need to eat to making sure our clients feel supported when I'm away from the office. You are flexible and nimble and never utter a word of complaint. I truly couldn't do this without you.

I also want to offer a special thank you to my editor Nancy Flynn who took on this massive project thinking it was half the size and didn't adjust the invoice accordingly. Without you and your generosity and professionalism, I would have a big manuscript— but no book.

Thank you Diane Jarmolow for seeing the dancer in me and supporting me with your guidance and expertise. I love you, all the doggies, Peter, and your beautiful home. I plan to spend a lot more time enjoying the views for years to come. Thank you for being a strong and powerful female role model for me in the ballroom world.

I also want to acknowledge my "soul sisters," Sophia Österberg, Barbara Wayman, Michelle Ladd, Molly Luffy, Annette Franks, Beth Wittman, Victoria McMahon, and Sally Curley for reminding me to trust my intuitive guidance and balance my body, soul, and spirit. Without your unwavering support and encouragement to ground myself and take time for me, I certainly couldn't have completed this book with grace and ease.

There are several "dance sisters" out there whom I would also like to acknowledge. You understand me like no one else can, and I deeply value our friendships on and off the floor. Thank you Christina Diaz, Aiyesha Dey, Rachel Halversen, Rebecca Klinger, Kristine Reimer, Pamela Conn, Christina Donelson, and Janet Simsic, for being part of my journey. Here's to us competing, as long as it serves our "inner princesses," for years to come. If I missed listing your name, I hope to thank you in person instead. I appreciate and love you all.

A special thank you to all the dancing girls/guys out there who continue to share your unsolicited feedback about how my books, tips, and tools are helping you dance with greater joy. It makes my day every time you seek me out. I wrote this book and my earlier title, *The Ballroom Dance Coach*, so we all can embrace our inner dancers. I believe that one of my life's missions is to be a conduit to help others connect with their deepest source and to live, work, and dance from a place of pure joy. Thank you for letting me be a part of your lives and dancing journeys.

Thank you Bonita Brockert for offering additional detail for the gentlemen competitors. It's easy for us ladies to think that they just put on a pair of pants and head out there, which is far from a true or good idea. I know the gentlemen reading this book will benefit greatly from Bonita's years of experience. Thank you also for sharing your invaluable insight as a judge at Am/Am events and your knowledge of the USADance rulebook. My limited experiences as an Am/Am competitor certainly wouldn't have been expansive enough.

I'd like to take a moment to acknowledge the amazing coaching team I work with. Without you, I would be lost and limited. Thank you from the bottom of my heart for pushing and challenging me to be the best dancer I can be. I also feel blessed to serve as a business and "mental" coach to several amazing professional and amateur dancers. It's an honor to work with you and I love seeing you reach your goals and dreams through our work together.

Lastly, I'd like to thank Jeffrey Goltiao, my instructor and friend with whom I have been able to walk this journey with such joy, passion, and grace. From the very first lesson to our debut competition and several wonderful accomplishments on the competitive floor, I am forever blessed to have met you.

Table of Contents

A Note from the Author ix

The Book is Designed for. xi

Chapter 1: To Compete or Not to Compete 1

    First Blush Competition Readiness Inventory 3
    The Four Key Questions You Must Answer to Determine Your Readiness Level 5
    Setting Realistic Expectations for Your Dancing and Competing 21
    Your "Non-Negotiable" Ballroom Principles 22
    Important "Ballroom Lingo" 24
    Reviewing the Highlights and Challenges of Competing 29
    Chapter Summary 31
    Chapter Takeaways 32
    Interview Insights:
        Patrice Tanaka 33
        Aiyesha Dey 36
        Michelle Ladd 38
        Carly Booth 41
        Glenis Dee Creger 43
        Giovanni Fortezza 45

Chapter 2: Yes I Want to Compete. Now What? 49

    How Ballroom Competing Works 51
    Determining Your "Competition Type". 59
    Aligning Your Dancing and Competing Goals 62
    Picking the Right Competition 67
    Tapping into Your Strengths and Embracing Your Weaknesses While Competing 70
    Getting Your Mental Game On. 73
    Chapter Summary 81
    Chapter Takeaways 82
    Interview Insights:
        Marianne Nicole and John DePalma 83
        Toni Redpath. 86
        Kasia Kozak 92
        Michael Mead 94
        Shalene Archer 98

Chapter 3: How Do I Deal With All These Emotions? 103

    Understanding the Emotional Roller Coaster of Competing 105
    Common Feelings and Emotions Before, During, and After a Competition 108
    Dealing With Performance Anxiety. 113
    Chapter Summary 116
    Chapter Takeaways 117
    Interview Insights:
        Tony Scheppler. 118
        Connie Marshall 120
        Beverly Moore 122

Chapter 4: Bring on the Bling: Hair, Make-up, Dresses, Jewelry, and More 125

    The "Top Ten Appearance Musts" That Give You a Competitive Edge 128

The "Appearance Musts" Checklist 136
Chapter Summary 138
Chapter Takeaways 139
Interview Insights:
   Sharon Savoy 140
   Pat Traymore 142
   Maria McGill 145
   Lisa Bentley DeBevec 148
   Kimberley Mitchell 154

Chapter 5: Preparing for Competition 157

What You Need to Know Before You Leave and When You Get to the Competition 159
Your Competition Checklist 163
What Experienced Competitors Wish They Had Known When They Started 172
The Dos and Don'ts of Ballroom Dancing: What You Must Know Before Competing 175
Chapter Summary 177
Chapter Takeaways 178
Interview Insights:
   Yolanda Vargas 179
   Andrea Ringgold 182
   Forrest Vance 184

Chapter 6: Competing On a Budget 187

How to Maximize Your Competing Dollars 189
Chapter Summary 199
Chapter Takeaways 200
Interview Insights:
   Rhonda Lee 201
   Gene Brockert 204

Chapter 7: Competing Like a Pro, Every Time 207

Debriefing Strategies That Propel Your Dancing 210
Getting Ready for the Next "Go Around" 212
Your Dancing, Your Responsibility 213
Communication Strategies That Strengthen Your Dance Partnership While Competing 215
When You Know It's Time to Let Go 221
Embracing Grace On and Off the Dance Floor 226
The Balanced Ballroom Dancer: Strategies for Continuing Your Development On and Off
the Dance Floor 230
Chapter Summary 245
Chapter Takeaways 246
Interview Insights:
   Peter and Alexandra Perzhu 248
   Diane Jarmolow 251
   Christina Diaz 254
   Slawek Sochacki and Marzena Stachura 256

Chapter 8: Your Dancing and Competing Resources 259

Books 260
Online Resources 262
Costumes, Accessories, Shoes, and Competition Prep 264
Ballroom Dancing Exercise Plan by Michelle Ladd 266
Annual Goal Planning Worksheet 269

A Note from the Author

Photo by: Tom Wehrung

*If you ask me what I came into this life to do,
I will tell you: I came to live out loud.*

– EMILE ZOLA

In 2009 my world changed forever. I walked into a ballroom dance studio near my office on a dare and something magical happened. I found myself. I began to reignite the passion and joy I had been missing for years.

Many of my fellow ballroom dancers share similar experiences. It's as if the act of dancing allows us to reconnect with our deepest selves and taps into a powerful internal source. One way to amplify this feeling is to enter the magical world of ballroom competition. This book is tailored to first-time competitors eager to do their best, as well as experienced competitors who desire to get more from the experience.

I recognize that for true "ballroom competing newbies," this book may be a bit intimidating or overwhelming. More experienced or advanced dancers may feel as though they've "been there, done that." Regardless of your experience, I encourage you to read the sections that call to you and leave those that may not be a fit for you for another time. I hope this book will be with you for years to come and help you dance and compete with greater joy and success.

I have to be honest. When it came to deciding what information to include, I struggled at times. Sometimes I worried about not including enough, and other times I was concerned that I had included too much. I feared that sharing certain information would upset some people, while others would be offended if I didn't share. After careful and considered time editing, I'm pleased to share the concepts that I think are most essential to those who want to maximize their competitive journeys.

Whenever I had doubts, I thought about the reader and asked myself, "Would readers benefit from this information?" "Would they dance with greater joy, grace, and success if they had this information available to them?" If I excluded a section, I asked myself if it was because it truly didn't add something essential, OR if I were afraid to upset people who may not want "insider" information to be readily available. It was not always an easy choice, but I know, without a shadow of a doubt, that the information I have shared in this book is accurate, truthful, and comes from a deep place of caring for my fellow dancers.

When I began to dance and compete (for me, they came hand-in-hand), I had difficulty finding resources that were uniquely tailored to me as an amateur dancer and combined the mental, emotional, and technical aspects of ballroom competing. After reading almost every book available on ballroom dancing, I realized that no one had yet collected the information I so desperately needed to help me take my dancing to the next level.

To help fill this void, I decided to write a series of books that would help the amateur dancer enjoy the process of dancing and competing, while learning from the best in the ballroom business. This is the second book, in what I hope will be a series of several more. My first book, *The Ballroom Dance Coach: Expert Strategies to Take Your Dancing to the Next Level*, helps you understand the stages of learning in order to coach yourself through the emotional stages of dancing as a social or competitive dancer.

This new book is tailored to the dancer who wants to compete with greater joy, grace, and success. Both books merge my experiences as an amateur competitive ballroom dancer with the expertise of some of the most accomplished professional and amateur dancers in the United States, esteemed judges, talented ballroom professionals, and competition organizers. This book is a gem for anyone who wants to reach competing goals. I also incorporate my unique perspective and expertise as a Master Level Executive Coach in the competitive business world to help the reader shine and "on and off the dance floor."

Competing is a separate skill from dancing. This concept often surprises even the most experienced dancer. If you want to compete successfully, you will need to sharpen your technical dance skills, as well as your competing skills. This book helps you get ready by offering tactical strategies that yield immediate results. While I can't guarantee that you will place better, I know that if you use the tools and tips in this book, you will feel better and enjoy your competing journey for years to come.

I look forward to seeing you on and off the competition floor!

Embrace Grace,

Photo by: Tom Wehrung

This Book is Designed for...

This book has been carefully laid out and written to serve a wide range of readers from the soon-to-be competitor to intermediate or experienced competitors. While it is geared mostly to Pro/Am (Professional/Amateur) competitors and includes my perspective and experience in this segment of competing, I have also included (where appropriate) references to those who dance and compete in Am/Am (Amateur/Amateur).

While I competed in Am/Am for a year, I cannot hold myself out as an expert in this area; I have included references for Am/Am where they differ from Pro/Am to the best of my ability. I've also received tips from established judges who work the Amateur competing circuit and also compete with their students in Pro/Am. With this unique mix, I believe both audiences are served in one book. If you are a pure Am/Am competitor, substitute the word "instructor" for "coach" or "dance partner" as you read. At times, I have made references to Junior competitors and younger (mostly for dressing and attire), but the book is designed for the adult competitor.

If you have never competed before and have limited knowledge of the ins and outs of the competitive ballroom world, this book may appear a bit overwhelming at first. In my desire to share as much information as possible and ensure you don't miss anything, I have included more details than you will need to get started. Please don't let this mountain of information deter you from competing! My suggestion: if you have never competed before or are thinking of doing a local competition or show dance, first ask your instructor what you can expect—before diving into this book. Let your instructor guide you through the first couple of experiences. It will build confidence and you will have a wonderful time. When you are ready to explore competing in more detail, this book will serve as your trusted guide.

This book is a response to comments I often hear from fellow competitors: "Why didn't anyone tell me that when I started?" Or "I wish I had known that before I…." I happen to be one of those competitors who, right from the start, wanted as much information as I could get my hands on because I felt that I was missing what I needed in order to be my personal best. That is why this book is tailored to students who are (or believe themselves to be) ready to compete and eager to learn as much as possible about how to do it well.

If you are a newer competitor, the initial five chapters are specifically designed for you. If you are an intermediate to experienced competitor, you may find that chapters six, seven, and eight contain invaluable tools and strategies that help you compete with greater success and joy.

My recommendation, however, is to read each chapter, regardless of your level. While the newer dancer may feel a bit overwhelmed reading about the emotional aspects of competing or learning about how the judging process works, the information will be invaluable in the future. For the intermediate to advanced competitor, you may be tempted to skip the chapter on "should I compete or not" or strategies for determining your competition style, but I encourage you to read these sections anyway. I know you will find powerful "nuggets" that can become the missing puzzle pieces to creating a comprehensive competition picture for you.

Because the book is designed to meet a broad range of competitors, some information shows up in several different chapters. If you find yourself thinking, "Didn't I already read this?" chances are you have, but trust me, you will want to hear certain things more than once, as they may become keys to your success.

Each chapter has a "Chapter Takeaway" section, where you can summarize your key "ahas" and indicate the action steps you are going to take to move closer to your competing goals. Remember, nothing will happen if you don't do something with the information you have learned.

At the end of each chapter, you will also find interview insights by each ballroom expert. Never before have so many experts been interviewed and included in one comprehensive book, and you don't want to miss their amazing stories, advice, and tips.

I'm an avid reader of all types of information, and as you will see, I've incorporated concepts from dancing, sport psychology, personal development, and business to offer you a comprehensive tool kit to improve your dancing and competing success. All resources referenced throughout the book can be found in the resource section in Chapter 8, where I've also recommended several favorite books that I believe you will find helpful on your ballroom dancing and life journey.

Please note that I do not receive any financial reward for promoting the resources in this book, including the ballroom vendors mentioned in Chapter 8. On the contrary, I've worked with several vendors to negotiate savings for you. Please refer to our website nextleveldancing.com/discounts.html to download the most up-to-date offers.

You'll find all of the recommended books at most retail or online bookstores. If you opt to buy books from my company website, nextleveldancing.com, please be aware that we receive a minor commission for books sold to compensate for the expense of marketing and selling them.

Enjoy the fantastic journey of competing! It has brought immeasurable joy to millions of ballroom dancers around the world, and I hope that you will be able to connect with your deepest self and explore all the wonderful things that ballroom dancing and competing bring. I also hope that, by avoiding some of the pitfalls many of us had to experience because resources like this book weren't available when we first started, you will be able to "compete like a pro" in no time!

1

To Compete or Not to Compete

The starting point of all achievement is desire.

- NAPOLEON HILL

Photo by: Ryan Kenner Photography

To transition from good social dancer to great competitor requires significant introspection, contemplation, and planning. In this chapter, you will take a deep personal inventory to determine if you are ready—emotionally, mentally, physically, and financially—to put your dancing out for the world to see (and judge).

This chapter is specifically designed for the soon-to-be or newer competitor. If you have done a few show dances or medal exams at the studio or have participated in one or two local competitions and are ready to consider competing more seriously, you will find this chapter especially helpful.

If you are already competing, but are having doubts or questions about how well it suits you, this chapter can become invaluable in helping you gain clarity and direction. Don't skip this chapter on the assumption that you won't learn anything from it. It can serve as an important reminder for even the intermediate to advanced competitor to ensure that you are getting the most from your competition experience. You especially don't want to miss the powerful expert insights in this chapter, including tips from successful Pro/Am competitors, World Professional Champions, esteemed judges and coaches, and fitness specialists.

Most competitive ballroom dancers don't start off competing. They begin by taking lessons because they love to dance and only later feel competition calling them. Patrice Tanaka, Silver-level Pro/Am competitor and author of *Becoming Ginger Rogers: How Ballroom Dancing Made Me a Happier Woman, Better Partner, and Smarter CEO* was one of those dancers, and you can read her story in her insight on page 33. While Patrice "fell into" competing and did so successfully for almost ten years, she realized a few years ago that competing sometimes took away from her joy of dance, and she now competes sparingly and only if it feeds her soul.

As you read this chapter, consider what competing may or may not do for you. Check in with your gut, heart, and head to determine if it evokes feelings that you want to explore. There are no right or wrong answers, and only you will know if competing will serve you. Some of what you learn may push you a bit outside your comfort zone, and you may feel hesitant or scared. If you do, don't worry. These are natural feelings, and they will either dissipate or remain as you learn about the amazing benefits of ballroom competing and how you can participate with great joy and personal satisfaction.

Before we dive into the details of competing, let's conduct a quick initial inventory to establish your competing baseline. It's called the "First Blush Competition Readiness Inventory" because, for most new competitors, it is truly their first time even considering these questions. Don't worry about making right or wrong choices. The more honest you are, the more helpful the results will be.

First Blush Competition Readiness Inventory

ⁿⁿ *The only competition worthy of a wise man is with himself."*

- WASHINGTON ALLSTON

This exercise is for your eyes only. Check "yes" only if you are able to do so without hesitation. Check "no" if you know in your heart that you can't answer yes. Use the "not sure" for all other answers.

	Yes	No	Not Sure
I'm ready to challenge myself and take my dancing to the next level.			
I want to gain perspective on my dancing and see how I stack up against other dancers at my age and skill level.			
I enjoy the camaraderie of ballroom competing and would like to compete alongside my team/studio.			
I know that competing requires me to have the right mental game plan, and I have, or look forward to having, the tools to help me compete with joy and grace.			
I enjoy competing.			
I have competed in other sports or areas of my life and know how I respond emotionally to winning and losing.			
My instructor/coach/partner has encouraged me to compete.			
I have a great relationship with my instructor/coach/partner and trust his judgment about my readiness, even if I don't feel ready myself.			
When I commit to doing something, I stick with it and rarely give up when things get hard.			
I'm ready to get feedback from judges about what I do well and what I need to improve.			
I can handle setbacks gracefully.			
I have a support system of dancers who also compete to ask questions of and gain positive feedback from.			
I have a solid understanding of the financial commitment needed to compete.			
I know how much time I will need to set aside in addition to my current dance schedule to get ready for a competition.			

Take a moment to review the questions you checked "no" or "not sure" to. It may be helpful to highlight them for now. At the end of this chapter, we will revisit this page to see if you have been able to move some of your "no" or "not sure" answers to "yes." Or you may have designed a few new action steps to help you gain more clarity about your decision to compete. It's not important to have all the answers at this time. It is, however, essential that you prepare yourself as much as possible, so you can answer "yes" to the majority of these questions before you commit to your first competition.

In the next section, we will explore the four key questions you must ask yourself to determine your competing readiness level. When I first started to compete, I dove in headfirst and didn't consider a single one of them. I was enamored with ballroom dancing and made some decision that I wouldn't make again based solely on intense passion and initial enthusiasm. I wrote this book because I don't recommend taking this approach. Throughout the book I will refer to being a "BBD." That stands for "Balanced Ballroom Dancer." When we take this approach, we can allow ballroom dancing and competing to fuel our passions for years to come instead of going in full-speed only to burn out half-way and quit (to learn more about how to become a BBD, see Chapter 7).

Most importantly, don't let this chapter discourage you from deciding to compete. Think of it instead as a checklist to make sure that you have all the facts and information to allow competing to feed your soul, passion, and joy for dance.

The Four Key Questions You Must Answer to Determine Your Readiness Level

> **❝❝** The secret of getting ahead is getting started."

> - AGATHA CHRISTIE

By now, you may find yourself thinking, "Am I really ready for this?" or "What makes me think I can do this?" If you are, know that almost all beginners ask themselves similar questions when they start. I still ask myself the week before I head out to compete, "Why did I sign up for this competition again?" And I have competed close to 30 times at this point. I have learned that it is just my fear rearing its ugly head, and once I'm on the floor dancing, I know exactly why I compete, and why I chose to do it over and over again. It's important to acknowledge your fears, but don't let them stand in the way of exploring something you have a desire to do.

The next section will help you determine your "competition readiness" level. Think of it as establishing your competing baseline. It is not important to be 100 percent ready or have all the answers to the next set of questions. Actually, if you are hoping for that, chances are you will never compete. The idea is to get as close to ready as you can. If you find that your answers to the following questions give you severe anxiety, chances are you are not yet ready. If they make you slightly uncomfortable and a little nervous, you are probably more ready than you think.

There are four key questions you must ask yourself in order to determine if you are ready to compete. They include:

1. **What is my available time commitment?**

2. **Am I physically ready?**

3. **Do I have the right support system?**

4. **Do I have the financial resources?**

Let's start by looking at your time commitment. All the top Pro/Am competitors interviewed for this book set aside a significant amount of time to invest in their dancing, and I hope you will be inspired by their stories. If you are an Am/Am dancer or couple, you are already used to significant personal and partner practice, as you don't have the luxury of relying on the help of an instructor to lead you through the steps as much as a one-on-one student would.

1. Making Time

TAKING MORE LESSONS

Depending on your level of dancing (Bronze, Silver, or Gold), you will probably need to increase your regular dance lessons by 50-to-100 percent. If you currently take one or two lessons a week, you may want to consider increasing them to two or four per week to get ready for a competition. The average serious competitor (at any level) takes three-to-ten lessons per week in preparation for a competition. Depending on your competitive goals, financial resources, and time availability, you will need to find a path that works best for you. You can still compete taking only one lesson a week, but your progress may be slower and the results take longer to achieve.

As an Am/Am partnership, you will need to consider adding extra coaching lessons instead.

You may find it helpful to read successful Open Gold-Level Pro/Am Competitor Aiyesha Dey's insight on page 36, in which she describes the process she designed to take herself to the next level. Keep in mind that her story illustrates how she went from Bronze to Silver and not from brand new competitor to her first competition. Even so, her story is truly inspiring, and it illustrates the need to make time to take extra lessons and practice by yourself in order to meet your goals. Remember, competing is different from social dancing. To get you ready, your instructor will need to spend more time focusing on technical details and showmanship strategies to help you become successful.

ADDING TIME FOR COACHING SESSIONS

Your instructor may also want you to work with a dance coach for a few sessions prior to your competition, in order to receive objective feedback about your dancing and your connection as a partnership. Most experienced coaches are also judges, and the benefit of working with a coach is that he gets to see and know you prior to the competition—and will look for you on the floor. It is a great way to get noticed, especially if your first competition has semi- or quarter- finals. There is, of course, no guarantee that your coach will judge your competition or individual heat (or that your coach will like your dancing). Should your coach, however, watch or judge you, he can offer invaluable feedback after the competition about your improvements and the need for continued development. While we will discuss this in more detail in later chapters, please note that many coaches recommend that you not take coaching lessons too close to the date of your competition. For many newer competitors, the information a coach offers can be difficult to implement quickly. And in an effort to please the coach or challenge yourself to do too much too soon, your dancing is likely to suffer, which can be reflected negatively in your results.

PRACTICING BY YOURSELF

Almost all serious competitors spend a significant amount of time practicing by themselves. When I first started to compete, I became almost dependent on my instructor and had six-to-eight hours of lessons each week. I was so attached to him that I forgot to sharpen my dancing skills on my own between lessons. At one point, he told me I couldn't have another lesson until I practiced what he had taught me for at least one hour prior to our next session. I remember feeling scared at first, but the more I practiced by myself, the more my confidence grew.

Again, as an Am/Am dancer you already have a leg up on the competition on this one, but you can still practice more by yourself without your partner in order to take your dancing to the next level.

In preparation for a competition, you want to set aside at least one-to-three hours a week to practice on your own. When Slawek Sochacki, undefeated World and U.S. Professional Smooth Champion, first started to dance, one of his coaches told him that, for every hour-long lesson he took, he needed to practice by himself for two hours. You can read more of his tips in the insight in Chapter 7, page 256. Quality practice makes you better, but remember: always check with your instructor/coach to receive specific direction on what to work on. It doesn't matter how many hours you practice, if you practice something incorrectly.

It doesn't matter how many hours you practice, if you practice something incorrectly.

I would also recommend that you get instructor/coach-approved videos from companies like DanceVision, featuring ballroom dancing experts and champions. You can peruse them by visiting dancevision.com. My personal favorites for beginner practice are DVDs by Professional Smooth Champion Toni Redpath, who helps you learn how to warm up and better understand American Smooth variations and styling. I also like Professional Latin Champion Kasia Kozak's videos on body strengthening and arm awareness or turns and arm styling for International Latin and American Rhythm. The DanceVision website is easy to browse, and you can sort by instructor to find some of your favorites.

Another recommendation is Diane Jarmolow's and Kasia Kozak's *Move Like a Champion* program, which includes a workbook and DVD illustrating powerful warm-up techniques and easy-to-implement exercises that help you understand your body in order to "move like a champion." You can purchase these resources and get information on upcoming workshops at movelikeachampion.com.

In Chapter 7, we will discuss several other strategies for developing your skills on and off the dance floor as you advance in your dancing and competing experience. The resources listed in the current chapter are selected for your early dancing journey.

Remember, while the Internet is a great place to get information, you want to make sure your instructor or coach has approved what you are watching and trying to emulate. When we begin dancing, we are not experienced enough to decipher good from bad technique, as it relates to the competition floor. A great street salsa is very different from the structured and organized patterns of competition salsa or mambo.

Another great tip is to record your lessons at the studio, using a video camera or phone. That way, you can review your steps and techniques at your leisure and then practice portions of your routine by yourself (assuming your instructor offers set routines). If your instructor does not have set routines, practice each figure separately to raise your awareness and skills.

If you decide to compete, I highly encourage you to buy a professionally recorded video of your dancing at your first competition, so you can see what you look like on the floor. A mistake many newer competitors make is assuming they look exactly the way they feel, which is rarely the case—for better or worse. It's important to begin collecting tapes of yourself as early as possible, so you can track your own progress and use your videos as development tools. For more information ordering competition videos, see Chapter 5, page 161.

TAKING TIME AWAY FROM WORK, FAMILY, AND NON-DANCING FRIENDS

There are many different types of competitions to consider when starting out. There are local one-day competitions, which tend to be held on Saturdays or Sundays, and there are local and national competitions that last anywhere from two days to a week. The benefit of starting off with local one-day competitions is that you won't have to be away from family and loved ones for very long, nor will you have to take time away from work. During these competitions, all four styles of dance are conducted on the same day. For longer competitions, locally or out-of-state, you may dance American Rhythm on a Tuesday and American Smooth on a Thursday, or you may dance International Latin on a Friday and International Standard on a Saturday. It's important to realize that you need to arrive a day early. So, for most competitions, you should plan to be away for at least three days. Prepare yourself, your work, and your family for your absence while competing. If you live by yourself and have children or animals, then arranging for care is an important part of the planning process. For more information on picking the "right" competition, please see Chapter 2, page 67.

Checklist: Let's Take A Look At Your Time-Readiness

Give yourself a score from 1-5 (1 is "not at all" and 5 is "absolutely") on the following questions. Then tally your points at the bottom.

	1	2	3	4	5
I'm willing and able to increase my lessons by one to two per week to get ready.					
I'm willing to work with and pay for a few coaching sessions prior to my first competition should my instructor think it's a good idea.					
I'm willing and able to set aside at least two-to-three hours per week to practice on my own.					
I am willing and able to take time off from work/family/friends to compete.					
Total Score					

Scoring Guide:

4-8: Now may not be the right time for you to compete. It doesn't mean you won't be able to do so in the future, but at this time, you don't have the available time to devote to competing seriously. If you want to compete and just enjoy the camaraderie and dance for fun, absolutely do so!

9-12: You are probably ready to compete, but may need to sit down with your instructor to map out where and how to maximize your available time. It may be that a smaller, local one- or two- day competition is the answer for your first competition.

13-20: You are ready to go! You have the time and commitment to "go big or go home." If you are competing for the first time, you may be ready for a medium-sized three-day competition or a large competition where the best of the best come to compete.

Just remember, if you don't have the time to put into your dancing, you won't improve. There is a misconception that dancing is all about natural talent. This is far from true. Yes, talented dancers have a leg up on the competition, but talent alone will not make you a great dancer. High-quality practice, practice, practice will. You may find it inspiring to read the insights of top Pro/Am competitors Carly Booth, Aiyesha Dey, Christina Diaz, Giovanni Fortezza, Rhonda Lee, and Beverly Moore, who all attribute their success to consistent practice, tenacity, and an unwavering commitment to do whatever it takes to be their personal best.

2. Getting Physically Ready*

Please note that I'm not a professional trainer, dietician, or healthcare provider. These are my personal tips, and they may not be best suited for you. Please consult a trained professional before engaging in any of these recommendations.

STAMINA

The difference between social dancing and competing is the amount of dancing you do in close succession. When you social dance, you dance a few dances, and then you can opt to sit down. When you compete, you have to dance all your dances in your style in one swoop. For example, if you compete in American Rhythm, you dance five dances in a row for 1.10 minutes each. That means you will dance for over five and a half minutes straight, with very short breaks between each dance. Often you are asked to dance your five dances twice, so it's not uncommon to dance for 10-to-15 minutes straight. You dance most of the day, depending on how many dances and styles you signed up for. In short, you need to increase your physical stamina and prepare your body with nutrition and hydration to keep going. For tips on how to manage your stamina, and to see the exercise program that Michelle Ladd, my personal trainer and I have designed, see pages 38 and 266. You may also find top Amateur Competitor Carly Booth's insight on page 41 inspiring, as she shares her cross-training strategies for keeping in top ballroom shape. Finally, you may want to consider an exercise program like Zumba or LaBlast to make sure you've got the stamina you need. The LaBlast program is designed specifically for ballroom dancers and was created by Dancing With The Stars professional, Louis van Amstel. See Chapter 8 for additional details.

BONES, JOINTS, AND TENDONS

When you increase your dancing in preparation for competition, you will also increase the wear and tear on your body. It's important to conduct a physical audit to make sure you aren't over-using certain muscles or positioning yourself in ways that create pain in your body. If you have issues with your feet, knees, back, or other key dancing areas, inventory yourself and learn what you may need to do more or less of in order to be in the best physical shape you can. Since I started to seriously dance and compete, I have added a cadre of support people who help me stay in shape, including a chiropractor, massage therapist, and acupuncturist. While this is by no means a requirement for competing, it is important to keep a close eye on your body and listen as it tells you what it may need to help you perform at your best.

DIET

As you prepare for competition, you will dance and exercise more, and it becomes increasingly important that you prepare nutritious and healthy food for your body. I find it hard to eat while I compete, and I have had to learn to prepare my body well in advance of the competition date in order to maintain a steady flow of energy. For example, leading up to competition, I drink at least 64-to-90 ounces of water a day. The ballroom is often dry and cold, and you may not realize that you are sweating and losing a lot of body fluids while you dance. I also make sure I have the right vitamins and snack food during the competition to keep me going. It is a great idea to avoid overly salty or sugary foods for two weeks to one month before you compete. On our dance team, we also avoid alcohol before and during the competition to make sure we don't become sluggish or dehydrated. For more tips on what to eat and how to pack for your competition, see Chapter 5, page 170.

Checklist: Let's Take A Look At Your Physical-Readiness

Give yourself a score from 1-5 (1 is "no" and 5 is "absolutely") on the following questions. Tally your answers at the bottom.

	1	2	3	4	5
I can easily dance for 10-15 minutes in a row at high intensity with only a few short spurts of low-intensity pausing.					
I am able to practice my routines with my instructor without becoming overly winded.					
I don't have any physical limitations or ailments at this time that need extra-care and attention.					
I drink at least 64 ounces of water a day.					
I eat a balanced diet and avoid salt, sugar, alcohol, and artificially flavored or processed food.					
Total Score					

Scoring Guide:

5-10: Now may be the perfect time to make some changes in order to live and dance with greater ease and joy! Look at any areas in which you scored a 1 or 2, and create an action step for improving that score over the next couple of weeks or months. Even if you are not ready now, it doesn't mean you won't be ready when the competition arrives.

11-19: You are in overall good shape and probably know that, with some minor tweaks here and there, you can be in tip-top shape in no time. Make that commitment now. Create a few action steps to get you ready to compete with greater joy and efficiency.

20-25: Congratulations! You are in fabulous physical shape and are ready to compete right now.

3. Having The Right People On Your Bus

YOUR FAMILY AND LOVED ONES

Not everyone outside the ballroom world will understand your desire to dance and compete. While trying to be helpful, they may dissuade you from putting yourself out there. In the beginning, we may even be a bit confused by this budding passion inside of us, and it's possible that we send mixed-messages to those around us about what we want to do.

One minute, we may be excited and exuberant about our dancing, and the next we feel insecure and deflated. It may make sense to us, but loved ones are not always able to understand these frequent emotional highs and lows; consequently, they believe that competing won't be good for us.

The husband of one of my dancing friends was thoroughly confused by her intense excitement and emotional lows, appearing out of nowhere. He just couldn't see the point of her continuing to dance and compete, if it made her cry so often. She had a difficult time explaining to him that the times she felt great completely overshadowed the times she came home from practice in tears. She had not been prepared for the emotional ups and downs of ballroom dancing, nor for how deeply it would touch her heart (a topic we will discuss in detail in Chapter 3). The more we help our loved ones understand the whole range of emotions that may show up in the early stages of our dancing, the more supportive they can be.

If they believe you are following your bliss, they are more likely to support you.

The important thing is that you are reading this book and considering competing, because something about it seems important, interesting, or rewarding to you. The time leading up to your first competition can be confusing and filled with uncertainty, and it is essential that you have the right people around you during this time, people who will encourage you to follow your vision and dreams. Remember to share your passion with them. If they believe you are following your bliss, they are more likely to support you. Set aside some time to share why you love to dance and what your goals are for competing. Perhaps you are interested in seeing how far you can push yourself, or maybe you simply want to increase your joy by sharing the experience with others who are as excited about dancing as you are. The more clarity you have, the easier it will be for others to support you.

YOUR INSTRUCTOR

Pro/Am students must remember that instructors are not mind-readers or therapists. They will not intuitively know what we want and need. They may, however, see our desire, talent, and capabilities before we do, and they may then encourage us to compete in order to explore our dancing fully. Sadly, there are also instructors out there who encourage us to compete for their own personal benefit. While this is rare, it is important to check in with ourselves and our instructor about our competing goals.

Your instructor should be able to tell you what he or she believes you can accomplish, and how competing matches up with your overall dancing goals. An instructor should know which competitions are best suited for you, and which may be too far outside your comfort zone. Certain competitions like the Ohio Star Ball or Emerald Ball, with thousands of competitors competing over an entire week, can be overwhelming for beginners. Alternatively, a local one-day competition with a few hundred competitors can leave a beginner feeling encouraged and excited. Until you have developed this type of open relationship with your instructor, competing should probably be put on hold.

When we compete the first time, we may feel vulnerable and sensitive. It is imperative that you believe your instructor has your best interest at heart. You may find it helpful to read avid Judge and Four-Time Undefeated World and U.S. Professional Smooth Champion Michael Mead's insight on page 94, in which he mentions that one of the three key factors to competing success is to pick the right partner or instructor. He also offers some great tips for creating a long-lasting teacher-student partnership for competing students, which you don't want to miss.

YOUR COACHES

As mentioned under the time commitment section, having a coach or several coaches will help improve your dancing and give you increased confidence to compete. It is essential that the coach you decide to work with is a fit for both parties in the Pro/Am relationship. If you trust your instructor's judgment, you will be happy with her selection of a coach. As you become more experienced, you may also want to offer feedback on the coaches with whom you would like to work. I select coaches based on my dancing goals and their personality and experience. For me, it is absolutely essential that I trust their expertise and authenticity. Other dancers choose to work with coaches because they meet their goals faster or with greater flair. There is no right or wrong way to select a coach. It just has to work for you and your instructor. For more tips on how to select a coach, read the insight of experienced Coach and Judge Glenis Dee Creger on page 43.

For an Am/Am couple, it is important to decide if the coach is a fit for both of you. If one of you is excited and connects well with a coach, but the other doesn't, the dancing may suffer. Sit down and explore the characteristics you both want in a coach and make a dream list to screen coaches against. Pick a coach that fits most of the characteristics on your list.

YOUR DANCE FAMILY

My favorite part of competing is the community feel of the competition scene. It allows me to meet women and men from all over the world who share my passion for dance. It often feels like they "get me" in ways that my friends outside the ballroom world can't. With them, I can be completely absorbed in my dancing, and they instantly know how I feel. Pro/Am Open Gold Rhythm Champion Giovanni Fortezza shares in his insight, page 45, that while he still loves his "non-dancing friends," his closest relationships are with other dancers and his teacher Jolanta Mosteika. When you spend most of your time outside work and family at the studio or on the competition floor, you form close and unique relationships that often last a lifetime.

I have also been blessed with an amazing studio. Everyone who walks through its doors, competitive or not, instantly is part of a family that is extremely loving toward one another. When you first start to compete, this "dance family" will be extremely important.

One of the most unique and wonderful parts of ballroom competing for me is the random acts of kindness I often experience and witness from fellow dancers. It is not uncommon to have someone come up to you and offer an unsolicited compliment or sweet remark about your dancing, dress, or attitude. Ballroom dancing is a supportive and encouraging sport unlike any other. Simply by competing or putting yourself in the competitive landscape, you are an instant member of the extended ballroom family.

You can also connect with dancers at studios other than your own. Some of my best "dancing buddies" don't dance at my studio, and others aren't even located in my hometown. While certain studios may have rivalries, you don't have to get caught in the middle. It is very important to have close personal friends when you embark on your competition journey, as we will discuss in later chapters.

If you don't have or "feel the love" from your own studio, reach out to dancers in other locations to connect. Join online groups such as Dance Forums (dance-forums.com), subscribe to the online dance magazine *DanceBeat* (dancebeat.com), follow people on Twitter, and connect on Facebook. Many ballroom dancers are glad to accept your invitations if you do so respectfully. For additional resources see Chapter 8.

Once a female dancer reached out to me by writing a beautiful message on Facebook and asking if I would accept her friendship request. I loved her approach and instantly accepted. She took the time to write a message and share why she wanted to stay in touch. That approach motivated me to welcome someone I hadn't met in person, but who belongs to our dancing community. Please be courteous and avoid "stalking" professional dancers or judges on Facebook. Connecting with them is a great idea, but excessive posting on their walls is not appropriate.

Checklist: Let's Take A Look At Your Support-System-Readiness

Give yourself a score from 1-5 (1 is "no" and 5 is "absolutely") on the following questions. Tally your answers at the bottom.

	1	2	3	4	5
My family and loved ones understand and support my desire to compete.					
I trust my instructor's/coach's encouragement to compete. I believe it when I'm told I'm ready to compete.					
My instructor/dance partner and I communicate very well, and I feel I can be honest about my desires, needs and wants.					
I/we either have a trusted coach or would be willing to look for a coach in order to prepare for a competition.					
I feel connected to my extended dance family and can lean on them for support while I plan to compete.					
I have at least one other dance friend who competes or who intends to compete, with whom I feel comfortable speaking about challenging emotions.					
Total Score					

Scoring Guide:

6-12: This score indicates that you have some significant gaps in your support system. This can become especially challenging if your low scores relate to your relationship with your instructor. If this is the case, consider talking openly about your fears. If your scores relate to a lack of support from family and loved ones, do the same there. Sit down to share with them how important dancing is to you, and how it fuels the other areas of life. If you are missing or lacking dance friends/community, reach out and connect in-person or online. Ask a competitor you know for a quick phone call or coffee date to ask questions. Most dancers will be happy to do so.

13-24: You have the support you need to "compete like a pro." Keep building your dancing support network, and remember to share your passion for dance with others. The more they understand your desire, the more supportive they will be.

25-30: You've definitely got the right people on your bus, and you will have a team of supporters cheering you on to success.

4. Allocating Fun(ds)

YOUR LESSONS

Deciding to compete will affect your finances (both in Pro/Am and Am/Am). You will increase the amount of lessons you take, and you want to consider the financial issues that come with this decision. If you are competing in Pro/Am, you may want to talk to your instructor about payment options. At our studio, we receive a discounted rate if we buy lessons in bulk. If you know you are going to increase your lessons, it may be smart to buy a series of lessons up front. Michael Mead suggests creating a business plan with your instructor before competing, so you don't get surprised or caught off guard when the bill arrives. To learn more about his advice on competing, see page 94. Pro/Am Open Gold Competitor Rhonda Lee offers additional tips on how to compete within a budget and with greater efficiency. You can read her insight in Chapter 6, page 201.

If you are competing in Am/Am, you may be able to negotiate a special floor- fee plan with the studio, in which you take lessons to see if they offer a "pay in advance" discount for buying floor fees in bulk.

YOUR COACHING

Coaches' rates vary, and you want to consider if working with a local coach is more cost-effective than a working with a traveling coach for whom the studio has to pay hotel and travel expenses, which are passed on to you. You may want to determine the maximum number of sessions you will take with a coach before committing to working together prior to a competition. Most coaching fees range from $100-to-$300 per session and do not include the fee your instructor charges for his time during the coaching session.

YOUR COSTUMES AND JEWELRY

While we will get into the selection of costumes and jewelry in detail in Chapters 4 and 5, it is important to consider whether you want to rent or buy a costume. Rentals for quality dresses range from $150-to-$300 per dress. Professionally made costumes retail from $1,000-to-$7,000, depending upon the dressmaker or seller. Inexpensive costumes can be bought on Ebay and abroad, but the quality can be a concern. As with any service, you usually get what you pay for. You may also consider buying a dress from another dancer on websites like ballroomdancers.com. Please note that buying anything online comes with a set of risks. I bought one of my Standard dresses online from another dancer who didn't offer a try-on. It was a big risk, because if it didn't fit, there was no way to return in. I was fortunate that it worked out, but my advice is to only "gamble what you are willing to lose." You may also opt to compete in what is called a "practice dress." These range in price from $150-to-$500 and are great options for beginning competitors. For now, simply consider what your financial resources are, so you can decide if competing will fit your plan.

While you can certainly wear any jewelry that sparkles well on the dance floor, there are vendors who sell jewelry specifically designed for ballroom dancing. They are custom-made to fit you perfectly as you move and dance and are designed from carefully selected fabrics to feel light and seamlessly blend with your skin. Remember, you will be moving around a lot, and your jewelry must stay in place. The lights on the floor pick up Swarovski crystals very well, and the sparkle they emanate will help call attention to your dancing. At first, you may feel that ballroom jewelry is a bit "over the top." If that is the feeling you get, good! It's supposed to be. Ballroom jewelry ranges from $50-to-$300, depending on its style and stoning. Most earrings range from $50-to-$90. Bracelets from $40-to-$200 and necklaces from $79-to-$300. Hair accessories range from $15-to-$200. As you consider jewelry for your dress and style, discuss your options with your instructor or dance friends. Some friends will be happy to lend you jewelry, if they are not using it at the same time.

As you consider competing, please know that jewelry is one of the things that can go farther down on your list of necessities, but it's good to know what to consider for the future. For more information about vendors and to view pictures of ballroom jewelry, turn to Chapters 4 and 5.

YOUR SHOES

Competing shoes must be clean and well-kept. It is usually a good idea to keep a pair just for competing. Almost all of the judges who were interviewed for this book mentioned the fact that dirty or worn-out shoes on the competition floor are pet peeves. Remember, you don't want to give the judges any unnecessary reasons to mark you down. A pair of quality competing shoes will range from $75-to-$200. For more information on how and where to buy a pair of competing ballroom shoes, see Chapters 5 and 8.

YOUR COMPETITION INVESTMENT

Depending on your studio and instructor, the entries (the number of dances you will do) vary. Some instructors and studios offer a package price, and some charge per dance. It is important that you ask your instructor or studio for the costs associated with the competition prior to committing—to learn what those costs include. You will be paying for your entries, hotel, travel, and food. You will also pay for your instructor's package and fees. If your instructor or studio is vague about what the actual charges are, be firm and insist on an explanation of service charges. It is important to know what you are paying for. Avoid comparing your competition costs with another dancer. Most studios and instructors have different ways of charging for their services, and you may be comparing apples to oranges. The most important thing is that you feel comfortable with the cost and believe you are getting value for your money.

For Am/Am competitors, your competition investment at USADance events varies by organizer. But it tends to be significantly less than Pro/Am events, since you pay for entries only and don't have to pay for your instructor's fees or expenses. Each person in the Am/Am relationship pays his own entry fees and travel expenses. Some organizers charge a one-time fee that allows you to dance as many entries as you would like, and others charge per-entry. Please note that multi-dances are counted as one entry, and "fun dances" are counted as single entries. Some events include the door charge in the entry fee, and some don't. Familiarize yourself with all the details on the organizer's website or entry form before you decide if competing is for you. Am/Am entry fees at National Dance Council of America (NDCA) events are the same as Pro/Am entries; however, since partners split entry expenses, it is easier on the wallet.

MISCELLANEOUS EXPENSES

To get ready to compete, there are always minor costs that tend to be forgotten when considering how to allocate funds. They include professionally applied spray tans, hair, makeup, nails, pantyhose, etc. We will review all these details in Chapters 4 and 5, but for now, keep your financial situation in mind, as you begin to consider the expenses associated with competing.

Over the years, I have created a basic spreadsheet that lists expenses associated with competing. I am happy to share a copy of that spreadsheet with you if you email me at info@nextleveldancing.com (please include "competition spending plan" in the subject line). It can serve as a great baseline for talking with your instructor about competition expenses and building a competition business plan.

In many circles and family systems, discussions about money are taboo. If you enter the ballroom competing world afraid to speak about money and your unique financial situation, you may find yourself in financial trouble in no time. If this is the case, consider doing some personal development in this area before deciding to compete. I highly recommend the book *The Energy of Money: A Spiritual Guide to Financial and Personal Fulfillment* by Maria Nemeth (New York: The Ballantine Publishing Group, 1997). She reminds us that,

> "How you do money is how you do life. Our relationship with money is a metaphor for our relationship with all forms of energy: time, physical, vitality, enjoyment, creativity, and the support to friends. These energies empower our lives. Without any one of them, life becomes difficult. But improving the flow in any one of these forms of energy usually makes our lives easier" (p.18).

Checklist: Let's Take A Look At Your Financial-Readiness

Give yourself a score from 1-5 (1 is "no" and 5 is "absolutely") on the following questions. Tally your answers at the bottom. If you are a pure Am/Am competitor, check N/A (Not Applicable) for answers that don't apply and count that as a 5 in your overall score.

	1	2	3	4	5	N/A
I am able to increase my lessons by one or two a week in order to get ready for the competition.						
I am able to allocate funds for working with a coach, should we choose to.						
I have the budget to invest in or rent a dress and a pair of competing shoes for the event.						
My instructor has offered or will offer me a range or a detailed plan, outlining the general expense of my first competition.						
I feel comfortable or excited about making this financial investment in my dancing.						
I have considered miscellaneous expenses for which I need to budget.						
Total Score						

Scoring Guide:

5-10: You may not be ready financially to compete at this time. Waiting until you are ready makes a big difference. Ask your studio or instructor about options that require less financial commitment, such as showcases, medal exams, or show dances at your local studio. They can be extremely rewarding and will get you ready to compete.

11-19: While you are ready to go financially, you may need to have a few more clarifying conversations with your instructor about how to allocate your funds in order to get the most from your competing adventures.

20-25: Great work. It looks like you are ready to allocate funds and start the fun!

I remember the first conversation my instructor and I had about what the competing experience was going to cost me. I asked him straight-up how much money I should expect investing if I wanted to meet the aggressive goal I had set. He came back with a number that was completely out of my spending plan. I was devastated at first, because I thought it meant I would have to give up competing entirely.

A few numbers-crunching evenings later, I realized that if I re-prioritized how I spent my money, I could commit to half the competitions we had originally planned. I drastically reduced the amount I spent on restaurants and clothes. In the end, I was able to invest more than my instructor's initial number, and I met all the goals that I had set for myself. While some dancers have unlimited budgets, most don't. For those of us who need to be careful about how we spend our competing dollars, there are numerous ways to save money that allow you to compete and be a Balanced Ballroom Dancer (BBD). For "competing on a budget" tips, see Chapter 6 and page 187.

Setting Realistic Expectations for Your Dancing and Competing

" *Don't judge each day by the harvest you reap but by the seeds that you plant."*

- ROBERT LOUIS STEVENSON

One of the major pitfalls I see newer (and sometimes experienced) dancers making is that they have unrealistic expectations when it comes to competing. If you expect to win your first competition, dancing against more experienced dancers, you are likely going to be disappointed. Or if you take one lesson a week and still expect to accomplish the same results as ladies or gentlemen who take 10 lessons a week, you may be in for a letdown. Also, if you compete in more than one style, then your progress is likely to be slower than a person who commits to one style only.

The important thing to remember is that your first couple of competitions are learning experiences. If you enter them assuming or expecting to learn the dos and don'ts of ballroom competing, you will be much happier and enjoy the process more. You will also have an important "edge," because you are open to learning and absorbing information that later will help you reach your competing goals. At the end of this chapter, on page 32, you will have a chance to write down your "new" first competition expectations, which will serve as an important reminder to help keep your expectations in check.

Renowned Ballroom Judge and Undefeated World and U.S. Professional Smooth Champion and Coach Toni Redpath states in her insight on page 86 that we tend to perform at competition just as we did two months earlier in practice. When nerves and excitement hit, we revert back to what we know intuitively and through muscle memory. The wonderful new routines or elaborate arm styling you practiced so well at the studio two weeks before the competition, tend to fly out the window, especially the first couple of times you compete.

One of my competing friends worked tremendously hard in preparation for her first major competition. She took six-to-eight lessons a week, practiced five-to-eight hours a week by herself, and felt ready to blow the competition out of the water. When she didn't place as well as she expected, she was defeated and almost gave up competing all together. Thankfully she only took a quick break. When she returned to the competition scene a few months later, her results were amazing! She realized that all the hard work she put into her dancing two months earlier was now paying off; she learned the "two-month-delay" principle.

It's imperative to set realistic expectations for competing. The more you plan and prepare, the better equipped you will be, and the more you will enjoy your dancing journey.

Your "Non-Negotiable" Ballroom Principles

" " *If you get the inside right, the outside will fall into place."*

–ECKHART TOLLE

We have already discussed the four questions "What is my available time commitment?" "Am I physically ready?" "Do I have the right support system?" "Do I have the financial resources?" Do that and you will enjoy your ballroom competing journey for years to come, should you choose.

Through my competing experiences, I have also learned to identify what I call my "non-negotiable" ballroom principles. They are my guiding lights and help me make healthy decisions for my life and dancing. I run all decisions through these principles or questions:

1. **Will it jeopardize my financial stability?**

2. **Will it damage my emotional health?**

If the answer to either one of these questions is yes, then I either don't do it, or I renegotiate the commitments I have made. The important thing to remember is that dancing and competing should enhance your life and bring you joy. Accepting a small financial setback for a greater gain, may be something I'm happy to do. Or pushing myself outside of my emotional comfort zone to get better is perfectly okay. When my decisions for my dancing jeopardize my long-term financial stability or begin to leave emotional scars, I know it's time to end or change things immediately.

Take a moment to consider what your non-negotiables may be. While it's not necessary to identify them right now, it is important that you begin to consider them early on your competing journey. The world of ballroom dancing can be intoxicating and enthralling. The more grounded and balanced you are, the less likely you are to get sucked into something that isn't sustainable or may hurt you in the long run. At the end of this chapter, you'll find "Chapter Takeaways," which will give you a chance to record what may become your non-negotiables. Please note that it may take you a bit of time to formulate what they are. Sometimes we discover them through "lessons learned." For now, simply sit with the concept and begin to jot down a few ideas. When you've "got 'em," you'll know.

Congratulations on staying with me this far! This chapter may appear to take some of the "fun" out of the process at first, but it is designed to help you determine if dedicated competing is really for you.

If you've discovered through these exercises that competing isn't a fit for you, congratulations. You just saved yourself a lot of time and money. Most people cannot arrive at this conclusion before competing the first time, because they simply do not know what questions to ask themselves or their instructors. But now you do. The more information you have, the better decisions you can make.

Before we leave this section, let's look at some of the common "ballroom lingo" you need to become familiar with if you decide to compete.

Important "Ballroom Lingo*"

> **"** Language is a living thing. We can feel it changing. Parts of it become old: they drop off and are forgotten. New pieces bud out, spread into leaves, and become big branches, proliferating."

– GILBERT HIGHET

The ballroom competition world has its own language. If you are a new competitor, you will find these descriptors helpful.

The following descriptions have been interpreted by the author and are written in a language best suited for readability. For a complete listing of the rules of ballroom dancing or more information about appropriate terminology, please visit the National Dance Council of America at ndca.org/ and read the NDCA rule book. You can also find the NDCA sanctioned competitions and event details on this website. If you compete on the Amateur circuit, you also want to review the USADance rule book at usadance.org. Please note that some rules differ between NDCA and USADance. If you are an amateur competing in both Am/ Am and Pro/Am events, you want to make sure you know the difference between the two rule books.

9- and 10-Dance Events	Some dancers choose a path where they compete in events called American Style 9-Dance (a combination of Smooth and Rhythm dances including Cha Cha, Rumba, East Coast Swing, Bolero, Mambo, Waltz, Tango, Foxtrot, and Viennese Waltz) or International Style 10-Dance (a combination of Latin and Ballroom dances including Cha Cha, Rumba, Samba, Paso Doble, Jive, Waltz, Tango, Viennese Waltz, Foxtrot, and Quickstep).
Age Group	All dancers have to dance in their age group or below. Age ranges are determined by competition and will vary. Sample age groups are "A" (16-25), "B" (36-50), "C" (51+). Dancers are not allowed to "dance up" into an age group with dancers older than their group. You may, however, "dance down" if the competition allows for it. Your instructor will place you in the appropriate age category when preparing the entry form.
Am/Am	When two amateur dancers compete together. You may also think of this as Student/Student.
Amateur	An amateur ballroom dancer is someone for whom dancing is a hobby. In order to maintain their amateur status, amateur dancers are not permitted to teach or take money from teaching. For rules specific to amateur status at USADance events, please refer to the USADance rule book.

Category	You can dance in several categories during a competition. Each competition has its own rules on the categories you are allowed to enter. There are three different levels, Bronze, Silver, and Gold. Within each level are categories including: Newcomer (first time you compete in a particular competition) Pre-(Bronze, Silver or Gold) Intermediate (Bronze, Silver, or Gold) Full (Bronze, Silver, or Gold) Open (Bronze, Silver or Gold) These categories are also referred to as level 1, 2, and 3 (Bronze 1, Bronze 2, etc.).
Chairman of Judges	The chairman of judges keeps track of how many people are allowed to dance in a particular heat and makes sure the event runs as listed on the program. The "boss" of the judges during the competition, the chairman makes sure all judges' scores and the scruitineer's recordings are accurate.
Closed and Open Figures Category and "Out of Category" remarks	Closed figures are the steps listed in any syllabus. When competing in closed categories, only those steps and variations are allowed to be danced. The invigilators of competitions ensure that couples who compete in closed categories only dance closed figures. If they don't, the invigilators will warn the couple that they are dancing "out of category." If not corrected, the student's scores may be affected. Open figures are less restrictive and allow for additional freedom in choreography. When competing in open categories, competitors may be more creative and use steps that are outside the syllabus. For additional information on allowable steps in closed and open figures/categories, please visit the NDCA website and review the NDCA rulebook or your studio's syllabus.
Championships:	Some competitions offer championship events. As with scholarships, these event categories tend to involve broaderage groups and are highly competitive. Placements are awarded to the couples who place in the final. Unlike scholarships, there are no financial awards for these events, but there often are medals or certificates awarded to the final winners.
Comp	Short for competition.

Competitions Within the Competition Scene	These are competitions within the competition circuit. Several of these qualifiers culminate at one of the larger competitions at the end of the ballroom calendar year, and the winners are announced and rewarded at the award ceremony of the last competition in the circuit. For more information about each event, please visit the websites listed. Best of the Best Dancesport Challenge: bestofthebestdancesport.com/ World Pro/Am Dancesport Series: dancesportseries.com/ Global DanceSport Series: globaldancesport.com/ Dancer's Cup Tour: dancerscup.com/
"Dance Well"	The phrase that most ballroom dancers use to cheer each other on. It's similar to the phrase "break a leg," which you may hear in other artistic professions.
Entries	The times you dance during a competition. For example, if your instructor entered you in one age category and one level, and you danced American Rhythm, you would have five entries. If you danced in one age category, but danced two levels (pre-Bronze and intermediate Bronze,) you would have ten entries (five times two).
Entry Forms	These are the forms the instructor submits to let the organizers know in what levels and categories you will be competing. There are deadlines associated with entry forms, and it is the instructor's responsibly to submit your entry forms before the deadline. If entries are submitted late, you may be charged a late fee. It is the student's responsibility to review entry forms and submit payment well in advance of the deadline, to ensure an accurate listing in the competition program.
Floor Crafting	The delicate skills of maneuvering around other couples on the dance floor while competing or social dancing. For tips on how to prepare to "maneuver like a pro," see Toni Redpath's insight on page 86.
Heat	Think of it as a round or one dance. Most heats are a dance, say Heat 45, the Cha Cha. Multi-dances are counted as one heat and combine several dances together. You may dance several heats in a row, or you may dance one heat and then get off the floor.
Invigilators	Most competitions have several invigilators. They tend to be judges who ensure that teachers are dancing in the correct category in each heat. For example, if a teacher entered a student in closed pre-Bronze, then only the first few figures of the syllabus are allowed. If a teacher dances steps from the full-Bronze syllabus, the teacher may be invigilated and jeopardize the scores of the student. Most invigilators give the teacher a warning before penalizing a student's scores.

Multi-dances	All competitions offer events called multi-dances. Here the competitors dance three of their dances in a particular style (five in open styles) without a break. For example, you would dance all five of your International Latin dances in one set. As with championships, there are no cash awards for multi-dances, but there often are medals or certificates awarded to the final winners.
Newcomer	This is a category for students who attend a competition for the very first time. The next time the student attends the same competition, he may only enter the next category up (for example pre-Bronze). Students can attend newcomer categories in several different competitions, as long as they only do so once per competition.
Night Club Dances	These dances include Hustle, West Coast Swing, Samba, Salsa, Merengue, and they are often danced on the same day as American Rhythm.
Novice	Competitors attending Amateur events can enter a category called "Novice." While the word may indicate a newer student, the category is much broader for USADance events. Competitors must carefully review the USADance rule book to determine the appropriate category (you can find the rule book here usadance.org/dancesport/forms-and-resources/rules-policies-and-bylaws/). Please note that Novice on the Amateur circuit is an open category and is not the same as Newcomer or Novice at Pro/Am events (which is almost always a closed category). Again, please check your rules carefully.
On-Deck Area	This is the area in the ballroom where you enter the dance floor. It is usually located at one of the corners of the ballroom and at larger competitions it may be highlighted with a banner or awning.
On-Deck Captain	There are usually one or two on-deck captains per competition. They stand by the on-deck area and make sure that the right couples go out on the floor at the right time. Always make it a habit to check in with the on-deck captain when you get close to your heat. To learn more about how to approach the on-deck area and the on-deck captains, please see Chapter 5, tips from professional On-deck captains Andrea Ringgold and Yolanda Vargas. You can find their insights on pages 182 and 179.
On or Off Package	When you sign up for a competition, you will be either on or off package. This means that depending on the number of heats you do at a competition, you will receive a discount if you are on package. On package pricing often includes hotel rooms, entry tickets, and dinners. Please check each entry form or competition guidelines for additional detail.
Organizer	This is the owner or owners of the ballroom competitions you attend.

Pro/Am	When a professional dancer is teamed up with an amateur dancer in competition.
Program	Each competition has a program in which all dancers are listed by their individual heats. It is tremendously helpful to purchase a program for your first couple of competitions, so you can see when you dance and who you compete against.
Professional	A professional ballroom dancer is someone who declares in action (teaching or competing with students) or by word to be a professional.
Registrar	The registrar enters all the competition details and accepts entries submitted by teachers.
Rounds, Quarter, Semi, and Finals	At larger competitions, you may have up to 40 or 50 couples competing for the top six spots. In this case, the competition will do first or second rounds to get the number down to a quarterfinal round, which includes the top 24 couples. The next cut is semi-finals, where they pick out 12 of the 24 couples to see again. From the semi-final round, the top six competitors are chosen. For individual heats, only the top three couples receive verbal placements. For scholarship or championship rounds, all six couples are announced and placed in order on the podium from sixth place to first place.
Scholarships	Most competitions offer events called scholarships. Dancers are placed in age categories with wider brackets such as A, B, and C (instead of A1, A2, or A3). It's not uncommon to have quarter-finals in the scholarship events, as there are more people competing within each grouping. The top six or seven couples are called back to the final and are announced by name as they enter the floor. Final placements are announced by position, from sixth to first. For the final three placements, individual results are often announced as "placing first in the Waltz, second in the Tango, second in the Foxtrot, and first in the Viennese Waltz." There usually are cash awards for the scholarship finalists.
Scrutineer	The scrutineer enters the scores from the judges after each heat and is in charge of making sure the scores are accurately recorded.
Syllabi	Each studio has its own syllabus from which they teach dance steps. Based on the syllabus, each figure or pattern may vary slightly. Franchise schools like Fred Astaire and Arthur Murray use their own syllabus. Many independent studios use the DVIDA® syllabus, and the most commonly used syllabus for the International Style is the Imperial Society of Teachers of Dancing (ISTD) syllabus.

Before we move on to Chapter 2 and dive into the next layer of competition, let's review the insights and challenges of ballroom competing.

Reviewing the Highlights and Challenges of Competing

" I'd rather regret the things I've done than regret the things
I haven't done."

- LUCILLE BALL

Highlights	Challenges
• It challenges you to take your dancing to the next level.	• It highlights what you need to develop and work on.
• You get feedback from experts in the field about how you can get better.	• You receive feedback that is sometimes hard to hear about your dancing.
• It pushes you to increase your stamina, physical health, and emotional well-being. And it pushes you to stay in shape.	• It can increase the stress on certain body parts.
• It expands your network of people from all over the world who have the same passion for dance that you do.	• It can push you financially to the point where you may sacrifice your basic needs in order to dance and compete.
• It helps you deal with stressful and emotional situations with greater skill.	• It can bring out the "darkest sides" of your personality, thanks to increased stress and pressure.
• It helps you take an honest look at your skills and abilities and set realistic expectations.	• It can bring on performance anxiety and cause you to experience emotions you may not want to explore.

For me, the highlights overwhelmingly exceed the challenges, which is why I continue to compete. I also believe it's important to acknowledge a few "brutal facts" before we move on.

YES...

• Ballroom competing is an expensive hobby (so is golf, horse dressage, and car racing). You have to consider where you want to spend your money, and what it gives you in return. I have learned how to balance my passion for competing with the other interests in my life. Several of my ballroom competing friends have exchanged country club memberships and vacations for competing. Top Pro/Am Competitor Giovanni Fortezza cut down on his "going out for dinner budget" in his hometown, New York City. Instead invests that money in competitions. It's all about the choices you are willing to make.

- It is easy to get wrapped up in the glamour of this hobby and lose sight of reality. That is why having a support network is so important. You need people in your life who will call you out if you go too far or become overly engulfed in the sport. One of my dancing friends jokes that it is only slightly less addictive than cocaine, so proceed with caution!

- You will probably invest more in building an effective partnership with your instructor/ dance partner than with most other people in your life. And that partnership can, at times, be REALLY frustrating. Remember, you are building a long-term relationship, and it requires the same investment and attention as a romantic or business partnership. With time and patience, it can blossom into a rewarding experience for both of you.

- You will go through various stages of emotions (some you wish you never had to experience), and you will have to look at yourself from all angles, and that is what helps you grow as a person.

- If you are not careful, you can get drawn into the drama that is ballroom or the "political game" that some people speak of. Remember, you dance for YOU, not anyone else.

- You can throw yourself in headfirst and hope for the best (which is what I did my first year), but the consequences of that type of behavior can be costly and leave scars. I wrote this book to help others approach their competing journey wisely and strategically, in order to make it last for a lifetime.

For some, the desire to compete is like a personal life calling. My friend John Schuster begins his book *Answering Your Call: A Guide for Living Your Deepest Purpose* this way, "Only by discovering, and then somehow creatively deploying, our unique combination of gifts, can we ever feel the deep satisfaction of a life well lived" (San Francisco: Berrett-Koehler Publishers, Inc., 2003, p.1).

What I personally love about dancing is that I don't have to be the best at it to enjoy it and share my passion with the world. I simply have to live a life where I creatively express my calling to dance, and competing is one venue to do so.

If you decide that competing is right for you, you will learn through the concepts in this book to do so within your available time, physical abilities, and budget. And with the help of a support network. As you embrace the idea of competing, remember: it has to bring something special to your life and enhance your joy for dancing and life.

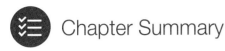 Chapter Summary

- To move from social dancing to competing requires a different mindset, commitment, and approach.

- Some ballroom dancers decide to compete in order to challenge their dancing or to reach personal goals. Some decide not to compete and instead enjoy the process of being a great social dancer. There are no right or wrong options. Competing has to feel right for you.

- At "first blush," you may feel a bit overwhelmed by the prospect of competing, but by reading this chapter and checking in on your readiness, you may find yourself more relaxed and excited.

- By carefully considering the four questions—What is my available time commitment? Am I physically ready? Do I have the right support system? Do I have the financial resources?—you are able to approach the possibility of competing with increased clarity and focus.

- By embracing the concept of the Balanced Ballroom Dancer (BBD), you will enjoy the wonderful world of competing for years to come, without burning out or straining yourself financially or emotionally.

- All the top Pro/Am and Am/Am Champions emphasize the importance of quality personal practice in addition to lessons.

- It's important to get your body ready to compete.

- Having people around who support your decision to compete makes a world of difference.

- Developing a financial or business plan helps you be financially responsible and prevents you from amassing large unexpected expenses related to your competing.

- Managing your expectations early in your competing process will help you compete with greater ease and joy. It will also help you stay open to new information that will take your dancing to the next level.

- Identifying your non-negotiable ballroom principles helps you stay grounded and prevents you from making detrimental impulsive decisions related to your competing journey.

- By learning the most frequently used ballroom lingo, you are able to speak fluently and understand terminology that will help you compete with greater ease.

- Ballroom competing has its own unique pros and cons. It's important to consider both before deciding to embark on this unique journey.

Chapter Takeaways

Take a moment to summarize your takeaways from this chapter. These notes will come in handy as you reflect on whether competing is right for you. If you are encouraged, excited, or interested, you will find that Chapter 2 has some great tips and tools for getting ready to compete.

After reading this chapter I feel:

_____

My most valuable takeaway was:

_____

I realize that in order to compete, I need to:

_____

My most significant concern about competing is:

_____

I will take the following action step to reduce my hesitation:

_____

After reviewing my answers to the First Blush Competition Readiness Inventory on page 3, I realize that I am ready to:

_____ and I still need to: _____

My "new" first competition expectation is:

_____

One of my potential non-negotiable competing principles is:

_____

In summary, I believe that I am:

◯ Ready   ◯ Still Considering   ◯ Not Ready to compete.

Interview Insight: Patrice Tanaka

Photo by: Karol DuClos

EXPERIENCED PRO/AM SILVER SMOOTH AND RHYTHM DANCER.

She is also the author of *Becoming Ginger Rogers: How Ballroom Dancing Made Me a Happier Woman, Better Partner, and Smarter CEO* and co-chair and chief creative officer of CRT/Tanaka. She resides in New York, NY.

Jessika Ferm: *You are the author of the book Becoming Ginger Rogers, in which you share your journey into ballroom dancing and how it changed your life and work. What is it about dancing and competing that makes you keep doing it?*

Patrice Tanaka: I dance because it brings me joy. I took my first dance lesson at age 50 and had never had any formal dance training prior, but I discovered right away that dancing fed my soul like nothing else, and it brought me unimaginable joy.

It took me almost 10 years of taking lessons and competing to realize that I love to dance, but I don't really like to compete. The stress of having to memorize and execute set routines robs me of the joy of dancing in the moment and just following my teacher's lead. Initially, competitions provided me with tangible milestones for improving my dancing in a way that lessons alone probably wouldn't have. Today, I'm still focused on improving my dancing, but I no longer want to be constrained by pre-set routines in competition. To that end, my instructor, Emmanuel Pierre-Antoine, and I have decided to compete without set routines in any of our six dances. That way, I can experience the joy of dancing in the moment, without over-focusing on figures and routines. It allows me to dance from a place of pure, unfettered joy.

What I still love about the competition scene is that it gives me an opportunity to cheer on my dancing friends and my teacher when he and his professional partner, Liana Churilova, compete in the evening. I love going to competitions and taking a weekend break from the "real world" to enjoy the glitz and glamor of the "ballroom world." Let's be honest, how awesome is it that you can wear rhinestones and a ball gown for breakfast and fit right in?

Jessika Ferm: *What were some of the important memories you have of your early days competing?*

Patrice Tanaka: I was fascinated to discover the dazzling, underground world of ballroom dance competitions. When I started dancing 10 years ago, shows like Dancing With The Stars weren't on the air yet in America, and if you weren't part of the ballroom world, you had no idea about competitions.

I remember my very first ballroom competition, which was the New York Dance Festival. Prior to competing in it, I had only performed in a small showcase dance event at my dance studio. I was amazed at the difference between the two events. Even though the New York Dance Festival was just a one-day competition back then, I quickly realized that a ballroom competition is a whole different ballgame from a studio showcase. I liken it to emerging from a cocoon into a dazzling world of exquisitely costumed dancers competing non-stop from 7:00 A.M. to 1:00 A.M., with everyone as passionate about dancing as you are. I actually found it hard at times to re-enter the "real world" after a weekend at a ballroom competition. I often wore a pair of rhinestone earrings or a cuff to work on Monday to keep a part of "dancing me" in the business world.

Jessika Ferm: *What other gifts have ballroom competing offered you?*

Patrice Tanaka: As a young girl, I loved playing dress up. I had a drawer full of tiaras, and I cherished the time I spent with my girlfriends, changing into our "make-believe" princess ball gowns, adorned with all of our moms' glittering jewelry, and wearing makeup applied heavily by our little hands. Ballroom competing lets me reconnect with these wonderful childhood memories and provides an opportunity to embrace femininity and beauty.

The ballroom world also offers me an "alternate reality," a place where I can indulge the "other side" of me and feed my soul at these incredibly rich "make-believe" weekends. Ballroom dancing and competing has helped me reconnect with my personal power by integrating the two parts of me that make me so unique. I actually love it when I wear one of my heavily stoned cuffs with a business suit, and it sparks fascinating conversations with colleagues and clients alike.

Jessika Ferm: *You danced both American Smooth and Rhythm. What is your favorite dance or style?*

Patrice Tanaka: My first love was the Samba because of the irresistible music and the bounce in the movement. For me, it is the dance of joy. But, because my then-teacher, Tony Scheppler, was (and still is) a fabulous Smooth dancer, I did mostly Smooth early on. After a few years, the Latin beat kept pulsating through my body, and I knew I wanted to explore more of the Rhythm dances. At that time, I began dancing with Emmanuel Pierre-Antoine, one of the best rhythm dancers in the world, and I felt that this style was more me. Today, I have to say that Mambo is my dance of joy. But as a true dancer, I love all my Rhythm dances, and I actually miss my Smooth quite a bit, especially when an irresistible Foxtrot starts playing.

Jessika Ferm: *What tips would you offer new competitors to help them dance and compete with joy?*

Patrice Tanaka: It's important to remember that ballroom competing can be intoxicating, and it can sometimes make you do foolish things. I once bought a peach-colored, fox stole at a competition because it seemed like just the thing to keep my shoulders warm in the chilly ballroom. It was beautiful and expensive, and I've only worn it that one time. You need to carefully consider what you can afford and what you are willing to invest in competitions. Once you are in the "ballroom bubble," it's easy to float away, lifted up by the energy and excitement of the comp. But you could easily get into emotional or financial trouble if you aren't careful. My advice to new dancers is to carefully consider what you can afford and create a budget or plan. It's so easy to get carried away and spend more than you really want to. Increased lessons, competition, travel expenses, ballroom costumes, hair, and makeup—it all adds up.

Interview Insight: Aiyesha Dey

Photo by: Park West Photography

PRO/AM SILVER/GOLD AMERICAN AND INTERNATIONAL STYLE DANCER.

Among the prestigious titles Aiyesha holds are Silver World Rhythm, Smooth, Latin, and 9-Dance Champion at USDC and Ohio Star Ball.

Outside the ballroom Aiyesha is an assistant professor of accounting at the Carlson School of Management at the University of Minnesota. She resides in Minneapolis, MN.

Jessika Ferm: *You are one of ballroom's most accomplished Silver/Open Pro/Am competitors. What are the secrets to your success?*

Aiyesha Dey: I've been dancing with Eric Hudson for two years. The first year I was mostly confused and not sure what I wanted to do. Then, when I came to the Silver level, I had a desire to discover how far I could push myself. Like most amateur competitors, I have a full-time career. I needed to figure out how to align my dancing goals with the amount of time I had available to prepare to compete at a higher level.

When Eric and I sat down and mapped out our goals, I knew that I wanted to place in the top-three in Silver at Ohio Star Ball. I remember that it sounded ridiculous when I said it out loud at first, but I figured I'd shoot for the stars.

Then I asked myself what I needed to do to get there. At the beginning of 2012, Eric and I developed a plan that I could stick with for the year. We took into account my limitations—financial, time, and other variables—and we worked every angle to maximize our chances of accomplishing our goal.

Once we set our goal, I determined that I could afford four lessons a week. I travel a lot for work, so I had to be willing to make up any missed sessions. I also committed to doing more if needed prior to a competition.

Once I checked-off that box, Eric asked how many coaching sessions I could afford, and I had to pin that down. I also needed to consider how many hours I could set aside for my own practice in order to implement what I was learning. No matter what, I was willing to remain after each lesson to practice on my own. That resulted in another two-to-three hours during the week. I also put in another two-to-three hours on weekends.

If I could allocate four-to-six hours weekly for my own personal practice time, then I felt I had a chance to meet my goals. I actually don't like practicing. But every time I started to waiver, I thought of my goal and what it would feel like to meet it. That is what I needed to push myself through. I didn't want to look back and realize that the reason I didn't accomplish my goal was because I didn't practice hard enough.

To summarize, there are three main secrets to my success: a fantastic teacher, a great plan, and lots of practice.

Jessika Ferm: *What was it like to meet that goal?*

Aiyesha Dey: It felt amazing. I had dreamt about it many times before it happened. It was really exciting, and I almost couldn't believe it when it happened.

Jessika Ferm: *So what is next for you?*

Aiyesha Dey: I want to continue to work hard and make the final in Gold/Open next year. It's going to be an incredible experience to be able to dance with people I have always looked up to.

Interview Insight: Michelle Ladd

CO-OWNER OF THE HUMAN FORM, A HOLISTIC PERSONAL TRAINING STUDIO IN COLUMBUS, OHIO.

Michelle has a B.S. in exercise physiology and is a National Academy of Sports Medicine certified trainer.

Jessika Ferm: *You have trained several world champion ballroom dancers, including Sam Sodano and Bill Sparks. What tips do you have to help ballroom dancers who are considering getting ready to compete increase their stamina?*

Michelle Ladd: My advice for anyone getting ready for a competition or race is to both strengthen the entire body and specific muscles that help execute a particular sport in the most efficient way possible. Many athletes or performers believe that regular activity such as dancing or running is sufficient. Consequently they don't have a plan to strengthen their bodies or develop a unique cardio system that helps them perform at maximum capacity. This misconception often leads to unnecessary injuries or burn out.

For our ballroom dancers, we design a unique system that closely mimics what they ask their bodies to do while dancing or competing. Ballroom dancing demands bursts of high-intensity work with very short periods of rest in between dances. So, we model our cardio routines after this to include 60-to-90-second bursts of activity, followed by 20-to-30 seconds of rest. We couple this with exercises geared toward the muscles used most in dancing. The deep core, upper back, and glutes, as well as stabilizers of the knees and ankles are all important for proper dancing posture and injury prevention.

Doing more traditional "steady-state cardio," where you might do 30-to-40 minutes of activity on a bike or elliptical, doesn't crossover to the type of endurance you need for a competition. Some of our clients want to "fit into the dress" or feel physically good, which we encourage, but they often overdo this type of cardio because they think it will help them lose weight. Instead, they tend to wear their bodies out, which can lead to injury and less-than- optimal performance on the dance floor.

Remember that you are asking your body to do a lot when you prepare it to compete. Take a proactive approach by giving your body plenty of TLC in the form of stretching, hydration, clean eating, and regular body work (like massage). Taking care of your body inside and out is just as important in advance of competition as increased ballroom lessons.

My biggest recommendation: think of preparing your body for competition as a goal that is just as important as performing your best. Without your body's help and support, you won't be able to meet any of your competing goals.

Jessika Ferm: *What are some dietary recommendations to keep dancers feeling great as they prepare for competition?*

Michelle Ladd: We utilize a very individualized approach to nutrition with our clients. But I have my top five rules that anyone interested in improving their health, physique, or athletic performance can follow:

1. Eat every three-to-four hours, no matter what.

2. Eat fruits or vegetables with every meal and snack.

3. Eat a protein and a fat with each meal.

4. Eat a whole-foods-based diet, cutting out processed foods like pasta, cereal, bread, baked goods, etc.

5. Drink mostly water. Avoid calorie- or chemical- containing beverages.

Jessika Ferm: *What are some of the most common mistakes you see people making when they begin to increase their exercise to get ready for a competition?*

Michelle Ladd: One of the big mistakes is isolating certain muscle groups. It is what I call the "body-building approach." For example, people may go to the gym and work their legs one day, chest and back the next day, arms and shoulders another day. The challenge with this approach is that you are training the body one muscle group at a time. This works great for body builders who want to gain mass and flex their muscles while standing still. In ballroom competing, you are using almost every muscle while moving and dancing. The body needs to be able to coordinate these muscles simultaneously, or it won't be able to support you fluidly on the dance floor.

My recommendation is that you combine multi-joint exercises to work your entire body at each workout, like you do when you compete. Having a certified personal trainer design a program for you would be ideal, but if you don't have access to that, you can refer to the exercises on page 265.

Another major mistake is cutting calories and fat in an effort to lose weight, instead of eating a good clean diet based on high-quality whole foods. Good fats, such as olive oil, butter, nuts, avocado, and full-fat dairy, are important for keeping the body fuller longer, as well as maintaining beautiful skin, hair, and nails. Cutting calories can slow down your metabolism, making it harder to lose weight in the future. And it may not provide you with the proper fuel to support your body during practice and help you perform your best during competition.

Interview Insight: Carly Booth

Photo by: Park West Photography

PRO/AM OPEN GOLD DANCER, LATIN, AND SMOOTH.

Among the prestigious titles Carly holds are Open U.S. and World Latin and Smooth Champion at USDC and Ohio Star Ball. She is a full-time student at Grand Canyon University, where she studies business management and hopes to debut as a professional 10-dancer in the near future. She resides in Tempe, AZ.

Jessika Ferm: *You won the highest titles in both International Latin and American Smooth styles at a very early age. Tell us more about how you got into ballroom, and share some of your secrets to success.*

Carly Booth: I've been dancing jazz and ballet since I was two. Both my mom and grandmother own dance studios. When I was 16, my grandmother, Wanda Manville, a successful Pro/Am competitor, encouraged me to take ballroom lessons. She set out to find me a great teacher and encouraged me to dance with Radomir Pashev. The only challenge was that his studio was 90 minutes from my home, so I had to decide if I loved ballroom enough to commute three times a week for about three hours a day. The answer was a resounding "yes," and I've been commuting ever since.

As far as secrets to success, I believe it comes down to a having a strong work ethic. I work on my technique daily and often do, for example, nothing but rumba walks—over and over again. I also cross-train, which has been instrumental in making me a stronger dancer. I work out at the gym and stretch every night just to keep myself physically strong.

It's also about giving yourself and your dancing time. When I first started to compete, I was in the youth category and didn't have a lot of competition. Then, when I moved up to the A category, it was really hard for me to place. Sometimes placements can be confusing. I've competed for four years, and only now are judges starting to know who I am. I actually didn't make the finals at USDC last year, and that really spurred me on to work even harder. I used to say that it was the best thing that ever happened to me.

Jessika Ferm: *Who is a ballroom person or icon you admire or look up to?*

Carly Booth: For me it is Boriana Deltcheva. She is one of my coaches and mentors, and I look to her for advice and feedback. I also love watching her dance. And, of course, I also look up to Yulia Zagoruychenko and Anna Melnikova.

Jessika Ferm: *What do you like most about your teacher?*

Carly Booth: Radomir is dedicated and really enjoys teaching. He is deeply committed to all his students, and his joy for dancing is contagious. For me, finding the right teacher made all the difference.

Jessika Ferm: *What are some of the hardest things emotionally about ballroom?*

Carly Booth: The pressure to keep doing well, place at the top, and dance well. It's hard to balance going to college with my commitment to dancing. I want to be at the studio all day every day. Competitions also can be emotionally draining. Even so, ballroom makes me happy. I couldn't picture doing anything else with my life.

Jessika Ferm: *What tips would you give a brand-new student or competitor?*

Carly Booth: Take the time to find the right teacher. It will play a big role in the joy you experience from your dancing.

Photo by: Ryan Kenner Photography

Interview Insight:
Glenis Dee Creger

JUDGE, COACH, AND ORGANIZER OF THE POPULAR
MARYLAND DANCESPORT CHAMPIONSHIPS. SHE
RESIDES IN CENTREVILLE, MD.

Jessika Ferm: *You travel around the country judging competitions and coaching professionals and amateurs to dance their personal best. What tips do you have for new competitors and teachers who are looking to find the right coach?*

Glenis Dee Creger: If you are looking to break through to the next level, you and your instructor may want to work with a coach. In selecting a coach, consider the coach's personality, teaching style, and experience. Remember that selecting a coach in order to "win" his or her favor may backfire, because what can be hidden or missed on the competitive floor is sure to be highlighted during one-on-one coaching. Avoid working with a coach too close to a major competition, as it may provide too much new information that can be difficult to implement.

Jessika Ferm: *What tips do you have for students who are buying a dress for the first time?*

Glenis Dee Creger: Wear a dress or costume that is appropriate for your level of dancing. If you are in pre-Bronze, avoid a dress with too many layers in the skirt or one that is overly embellished. When you put a "big" dress on the floor, judges expect your dancing to match your dress. Similarly, if you are in Silver or advanced levels, your dress may need to be more sophisticated to match your dancing. This is a good time to invest in a more "serious" dress. But remember, judges evaluate your dancing and are not easily fooled by fancy dresses that attempt to hide or distract from your lack of experience!

Jessika Ferm: *What are some of your pet peeves as a coach?*

Glenis Dee Creger: When professionals or amateurs aren't open to working on the basics. I once had a professional couple who wanted to coach with me, and after reviewing their routine, I told them we needed to work on a fundamental step that they weren't executing correctly. They were offended by my feedback because they didn't think they needed help on a Bronze figure. Because they weren't open, I decided not to continue working with them. The fact is that all dancers, professional and amateur, need to consistently fine-tune their basics.

Jessika Ferm: *I know you were trained in England by some of the top ballroom legends. What important lessons did you learn from them that you continue to share with your students today?*

Glenis Dee Creger: I was fortunate to coach with the great Peter Eggleton, and his style of coaching was deliberate and focused on understanding how the body moves. He is infamous for tapping the sides of his legs to remind students of the movement we must make from side to side in the Smooth and Standard dances. Because I was taught how to move first, and how to execute steps second, I emphasize this with all my students (professional and amateur). Without understanding how the body moves, it's impossible to dance well or dance with the greatest ease and efficiency. For all styles of dance, I remind my students that their legs start at the beginning of their ribcage. If they think of making their movement from this position, they will move almost effortlessly and engage all the right muscles.

Photo by: Ryan Kenner Photography

Interview Insight: Giovanni Fortezza

PRO/AM OPEN RHYTHM DANCER.

Among the prestigious titles Giovanni holds are Open World Rhythm Champion and U.S. Open Rhythm Champion.

Outside of ballroom Giovanni is a director of user experiences at one of the largest advertising agencies in the world. Giovanni resides in New York, NY

Jessika Ferm: *You are the top Open Rhythm dancer in the U.S., and it's impressive to have accomplished it as a gentleman competitor. How did you get started in ballroom dancing?*

Giovanni Fortezza: I had taken a few Argentine Tango lessons, but I never really did much with it. It was something most New Yorkers were into at that time. Then I started to date a girl who loved to dance. After we had gone out a few times, she told me she loved my enthusiasm for dance, but I needed to take some lessons. I kept walking by a ballroom studio on my way to work, and one day I decided to go inside and try a lesson. I took my introductory packet and then bought a package of five lessons.

My first teacher wasn't a good fit for me. Then I met Jolanta Mosteika, and everything changed. I remember seeing Darius (Jolanta's husband) and her on PBS, and I was intrigued by their quality of dancing. When she took me on, I was honored. I started by coming in once a week, then a few days a week. Fast forward to today, and I now take lessons five days a week.

Jessika Ferm: *What makes your partnership with Jolanta so unique, and what do you appreciate about her?*

Giovanni Fortezza: A big part of it is that she teaches the way I learn. I'm not good with too many steps or complicated routines. She is all about learning the basics and doing them well before moving on. Luckily I don't get bored with repetitive tasks, because it isn't unusual for us to spend hours on side-together steps or Cuban motion alone. The first six months, it seemed like that was all we did. One time at a two-hour lesson, I stretched out on the floor in the middle of the lesson because I was exhausted physically and mentally. I learned that side-together steps can be really challenging if you strive for perfection.

I also enjoy the fact that Jolanta does not get distracted by anything else that is going on in the studio. She is extremely focused and pushes me to not make any excuses. She believes that everyone should dance to the best of their abilities, and she treats everyone with the same level of respect and attention.

Jessika Ferm: *When did you do your first competition, and how many competitions do you do on average now?*

Giovanni Fortezza: We did a small and super-friendly Fred Astaire competition about nine months after I started taking lessons. There were only three couples, and we got second, which felt great. It was a nice way to enter the competitive arena. Then we began competing more. Now I do between 18 and 22 competitions a year. We only do Rhythm, so it's a bit easier to manage my work schedule with the competition calendar.

Jessika Ferm: *That is ambitious! How you do manage your time between your professional job and your dancing career?*

Giovanni Fortezza: I'm a creative director for an advertising agency, so I have more flexibility than most other executives. Aside from my one-week vacation with my daughter every year, all other holidays or time off is spent competing or practicing. Most of my friends are also dancing, so when I am at the studio or at a competition, I'm hanging out with the people I really love. It's easy to manage time with my friends because they are passionate about the same things I am.

Jessika Ferm: *How often do you take lessons or practice each week?*

Giovanni Fortezza: I average eight lessons a week. When combined with my competing schedule, I pretty much spend all my spare time outside of work at the studio. I also take coaching with whomever comes to the studio, so that adds a few additional hours a week.

Jessika Ferm: *You mentioned that some of your friends or fellow competitors ask you how you manage all those lessons and competition expenses. How do you balance it all?*

Giovanni Fortezza: Dancing is my passion, and I prioritize my life around it. My friends spend a lot of money going out for dinner and drinks, but I don't. Every extra penny I have (aside from the money I spend on my daughter) goes to my dancing. It's not a sacrifice; it's an easy choice.

Jessika Ferm: *How has ballroom dancing affected your life?*

Giovanni Fortezza: When I first started to dance, I was 180 pounds with a visible belly. I remember sitting with my Italian father, who is 5'2" and a bit round, and he told me that I was fatter than he was. That was the turning point for me. Over the next three years, I lost over 30 pounds, thanks to ballroom dancing. I feel healthy now, and I enjoy working out. I take mostly cardio exercise classes like body sculpting, because being lean and having excellent stamina helps my dancing. When I compare my lifestyle to that of friends my age, I feel and look amazing.

Jessika Ferm: *What are some of the traits you possess that you think contribute to your success?*

Giovanni Fortezza: I'm ultra-confident. Sometimes Jolanta makes fun of me, and other times she admires my "blind" confidence. I follow through on all my commitments, and because I have Jolanta's confidence in me, it's easy. I'm also a really friendly person. Philip Widlanski, Jolanta's other student, and I make friends with anyone we dance with.

Jessika Ferm: *Share an "aha" moment that you've had while working with Jolanta.*

Giovanni Fortezza: Once, in the middle of a coaching session, Jolanta asked me to do something that she had asked me to do—unsuccessfully—many times before. I just couldn't do it. A few minutes later, using different words, she told me to do the same thing—and I did it without effort. I quickly realized what had happened and burst out laughing. Jolanta was just happy that I finally had a breakthrough. This type of scenario happens often, and I really admire her patience.

Jessika Ferm: *Now that you have won the top titles, what are your goals for this year?*

Giovanni Fortezza: I know that I have much to improve upon this year. I really want to grow as a dancer and keep the titles. I don't want a close win. I know there are some great girls coming up the ranks who are also going for the titles, and I'll have to continue to work hard to reach my goals.

2

Yes I Want to Compete. Now What?

My father used to say that it's never too late to do anything you wanted to do. And he said, You never know what you can accomplish until you try.

- MICHAEL JORDAN

Photo by: Ryan Kenner Photography

So you have decided to compete or are at least still interested in coming on this part of the journey with us. Wonderful! Let me be the first to welcome you to the fabulous and rewarding world of ballroom competing. It has been a tremendous exploration of growth for me and has helped me develop into the person I am today. Competing has allowed me to explore my emotional intelligence, patience, and compassion. I can't wait to see what it does for you.

This chapter will help you take a deeper dive into how ballroom competing works, identify what type of competitor you are, establish and align your dancing and competing goals, and brainstorm ideas for the types of competitions that best fit you. We will review your potential competing strengths and weaknesses and help you get your "mental game" on.

How Ballroom Competing Works

> **"** Luck? I don't know anything about luck. I've never banked on it and I'm afraid of people who do. Luck to me is something else: Hard work - and realizing what is opportunity and what isn't."

– LUCILLE BALL

Ballroom competing is a world in itself. You may find that as you begin to take your dancing more seriously and move from social dancer to competitor, this new world can be confusing and difficult to understand. This section is designed specifically to help you understand some of the important ins and outs and prepare intellectually, mentally, and emotionally for the journey.

The first concept you must embrace is that, when you compete, your scores and placements are at the mercy of the judges. That is how this sport/art works. It is a highly subjective process, and each judge has individual opinions, philosophies, and tastes when it comes to the competitive floor. It is best to accept this fact, rather than trying to figure out the judges' inner-workings in too much detail. Let's take a look at the basic process first: how placements work.

The Mystery of Placements

Depending on the size of the competition, the individual heats, or categories, you may have a mix of three-to-11 judges marking you. For competitions sanctioned by the National Dance Council of America (NDCA), all judges must pass a comprehensive adjudicator exam. All judges are former dancers and have extensive experience dancing, teaching, and coaching. For USADance events, all judges are either NDCA or World DanceSport Federation (WDSF) certified and are members of the USADance organization.

They stand around the floor with clipboards and rank the dancers in order, from highest to lowest. The numbers gentlemen wear on their backs are used to identify which couples the judges wish to see again or place in a certain order.

As a dancer, you are evaluated against the other couples on the floor. If you have a heat with very experienced dancers, you may score lower than you would in a heat with less experienced dancers.

In larger competitions, you may experience dancing in first rounds, quarterfinals, semifinals, and finals. If you have first rounds, it means the judges select 24 couples to make the quarterfinal, choosing from as many as 50 couples competing in several heats. At that level, the judges are picking the dancers who stand out the most. It is very hard for them to evaluate technique when picking from a large number of couples, so confidence, good posture, and impeccable grooming goes a long way (we explore these concepts in detail in Chapters 4 and 5). The next cut usually selects the 12 who make the semifinal.

At this stage, judges are looking more at each dancer and make decisions about styling and technique. When it gets down to the final six–to-eight, the judges are looking for the couples who really stand out and are the top dancers for the style and level. It is not uncommon to see consistency in the judges' picks for the final. When they get to the order of the final couples (first through sixth place), the judges tend to be less consistent. This is where their own personal styles and preferences kick in. While "good dancing is always good dancing," as Sam Sodano, the legendary organizer of the Ohio Star Balls says, judges will pick the dancers they most enjoyed for the coveted placements in the final.

At the end of the day, or sometimes at the end of the competition, you are able to see where each judge placed you in comparison to the other dancers in your heat. Most scores are available on the organizer's competition website. But before you run off to check your scores, please continue reading. I'm a theoretically and intellectually driven dancer, and I found the judging process to be extremely frustrating at first. It was confusing to me that some judges liked my dancing and some didn't—even though I was doing exactly the same movements. And sometimes when I changed a movement or step, some judges liked it and others didn't, but there didn't seem to be a logical reason for their preferences.

It was confusing to me that some judges liked my dancing and some didn't—even though I was doing exactly the same movements.

Welcome to the world of competitive ballroom dancing! Even more frustrating was the experience of seeing my scores and discovering that four judges liked my dancing (placing me one-to-three in all dances), and one just didn't like it at all (placing me six in all dances). I just couldn't fathom what would make each judge see the same picture so differently. I often got stuck trying to figure out what I needed to do in order to change someone's opinion. Please note that over-focusing on why a certain judge places you in a particular position is unnecessary. Avid Judge, Coach, and Competition Co-organizer of Capital DanceSport Championship, Marianne Nicole, sheds some light on this issue on her interview insight on page 83.

In short, she encourages all dancers (especially newer ones) to keep their competing choreography to a few basic steps and do them well. The more flawlessly you dance, the more consistent your judging results are likely to be. Remember, not all judges look at you at the same time. So if you do one step in front of one judge really well, he or she may mark you high. If you do another step poorly in front of another judge, that person may mark you low.

To avoid confusing yourself early in your competing journey, my recommendation is to avoid looking at your scores altogether. If you really want to know, ask your instructor to share themes that may be helpful to your dancing. For example, "We made finals in all dances," or "We need to still work on our Samba. The judges' scores were all over the place." Not all instructors will look at your scores or share them with you. If you want to look at your own scores, do so with caution. You can often access your scores a few hours after your heats in a competition score binders in the registrar's area or on the competition website a day or so after the competition ends. One big word of caution: do not look at the names of specific judges. This is tremendously tempting, but doing so may make you:

- Become upset or hurt if one of your favorite judges didn't like your dancing.

- Over-focus on scores and dance to please judges; thereby missing out on the joy of dancing just for you.

- Try to overcompensate in order to please a particular judge, making your dancing look forced or tense.

- Mistakenly assume that your dancing isn't good enough, and you weren't as good as you felt you were.

I know how detrimental these reactions can be, because I speak from experience. I also recommend that you don't look at other dancers' scores. While the information is available online, be a gracious dancer, and let others have their privacy.

There are, however, times when seeing your scores from a particular judge can be helpful. In my case, it was the feedback from the esteemed judge and undefeated World and U.S. Professional Smooth Champion Toni Redpath that most affected me.

When I started to dance I bought several DVDs from DanceVision, including Toni's entire Smooth series. I had seen her husband and partner Michael Mead and her dance on numerous YouTube videos, and their dancing mesmerized me. I knew immediately that I wanted to know what she knew. A few months later, at my very first competition, I walked out on the floor and couldn't believe my eyes when I saw Toni and her clipboard right in front of me. I was amazed that she was going to judge me, and I couldn't wait to see my scores!

Nothing could have prepared me for my disappointment. Not only did she not call me back to the final, but she didn't seem to like my dancing at all. I was devastated! So back to the studio we went, working really hard on our Smooth. The next year at the same competition, there she was again. This time, I was sure she would like the changes we had made. We first danced our Rhythm dances, and when I ran into Toni in the hallway she said, "I really liked your Rhythm." My Rhythm! Who cares about my Rhythm? I wanted Toni to like my Smooth!

After our Smooth heats, I anxiously ran back to look at our scores. This year, she picked us for the final, but barely. I couldn't figure out what she didn't like, so I asked my instructor if we could get some coaching with Toni. Several months later, she agreed to take us. After learning her philosophy and key concepts of Smooth, it was obvious to me what we were missing. I never even had to ask her why she hadn't liked our Smooth at the beginning. To learn more about the top three things Toni looks for when she judges, read her interview insight on page 86.

This doesn't mean that you should try to please every judge on the floor. What I hope this story illustrates is that there may be judges out there whom you and your instructor/dance partner admire and would like to learn from. If so, take coaching from that judge, as it can truly take your dancing to new heights.

Some judges are happy to share what you can do to improve, but a word of caution here. For example, Toni Redpath will offer feedback to those who coach with her, as she shares in her interview on page 86. Going up to judges and asking for their "random feedback," however, may put them in an uncomfortable position. They spend such a short amount of time watching and judging you that they may not be able to offer thoughtful feedback. If you do want to ask a judge for feedback, my advice is to approach someone you have worked with in coaching, or someone who has watched you several times, and ask for one correction that you can make over the next few months to improve your dancing.

Don't approach judges who don't seem to like your dancing and score you low consistently. There is a judge (or two) out there who just doesn't seem to like my dancing. That is okay. Remember, you dance for yourself, not for scores or the judges' approval.

If you weren't concerned with placing well, you probably wouldn't compete. As you will hear me say consistently throughout this book, ballroom dancing is emotional. There is something in us that leads us to the competitive floor. Later in this chapter, you will have a chance to identify your "Competition Type," the reasons you dance. It may be that you are internally or externally competitive or that you like to challenge yourself to see how good you can get. Or you may just enjoy the positive energy that comes from being around other dancers or the glitz and glamour of the ballroom industry. Regardless, placements have an important role on our dance journeys, and managing the emotions that come with this experience is important.

In the beginning, it is difficult to understand how the scoring system works. I used to think that if I didn't make finals or place where I had hoped, my dancing was somehow bad. Let me stress one more time: don't let placements get in the way of your joy for dance! You have very little control over your placement in a competition or heat. As you will learn in this section, there are several factors that contribute to your score. While placements and scoring can offer you important insights into how to improve your dancing, they should never become measuring sticks for your own self-worth. You know you have "arrived" when placements are just the icing on the cake, and your true joy is in knowing that your dancing has improved, and you have met the small measurable goals you set for yourself for each competition. We will review effective goal-setting shortly.

The Most Common Placement Pitfalls

ASSUMING THAT PLACING FIRST MEANS YOU WILL FEEL GREAT

Many top dancers who consistently place first, suffer from the, "Yeah, but…" syndrome. When you congratulate them on their wins, they respond with something that seems to diminish their accomplishments. They may say, "Thank you, but it wasn't a very competitive heat," or "I can't believe I won. I made so many mistakes." If you are fortunate to place first, embrace it. Say "Thank you" when someone congratulates you. I don't care if you were uncontested. Enjoy your accomplishments and celebrate your wins. You won't always place first. Some competitors who consistently win are often unable to enjoy their placements because they are so scared they will come in second. There is a lot of pressure "at the top" to stay on a winning streak. Celebrate every win and take it in. Kasia Kozak, World and U.S. Professional Latin Champion and judge, warns competitors about being overly focused on winning. In her interview insight on page 92, she encourages competitors to "embrace the tiger within" AND balance the desire to win with appreciating and enjoying the journey.

ASSUMING THAT PLACING SECOND OR THIRD MEANS YOU SOMEHOW FAILED

While I'm not a big fan of the "everyone gets a medal" philosophy, I am in favor of celebrating and enjoying every placement (no matter where you place). Placing anywhere, especially in the top three spots, is fabulous! There are many closet-ballroom dancers who wish they shared your courage to compete, but they don't. Measure your worth by your courage to go out there and compete. Remember to congratulate the winner. Being a good sport is always appreciated.

GIVING UP IF YOU DON'T MAKE THE NEXT CUT

When you dance at very competitive and large competitions, you are probably going to have first rounds, quarterfinals, and semifinals. If you don't make it to the next cut, embrace where you are on your dancing journey. While you may feel disappointed, don't wallow in it. Breathe it in then breathe it out. There is always the next year or the next competition. Sometimes judges just can't see you, and they missed your awesomeness. Too bad for them. Get back out there and show them again!

ASSUMING THAT, BECAUSE YOU PLACE BETTER THAN SOMEONE ELSE, YOU ARE ALWAYS GOING TO DO SO

When you compete in Bronze, you will start with a large group of competitors. You pretty much start off at the same level and will become friends with many of them. Very soon, depending on each person's unique journey, skill, and abilities, some dancers will separate from the rest and move faster or slower in their process. You may have consistently placed higher than a certain person when you started, but all of a sudden that dancer is passing you on the scoreboard. Remember, do not compare yourself with others. If someone consistently places higher than you, it simply means that individual is advancing faster than you. That's all. It doesn't mean you aren't a good dancer, or you don't have what it takes to be great. You are on your own journey and may pass that person at a different part of your path.

THINKING YOU CAN MANIPULATE YOUR WAY TO BETTER SCORES

While the competing ballroom world can be political for professional dancers, for most amateur dancers, this is not the case. In one of Michael Mead's (undefeated World and U.S. Professional Smooth Champion and judge) lectures, he addresses the issue of seeking out a judge for private coaching in order to win favor. He says, "Be very careful. What I may miss as a judge when you compete because I have limited time to observe you, I will surely find if you hire me for a private session." Glenis Dee Creger, esteemed judge, warns against hiring a judge as a coach close to an upcoming competition in order to be on the judge's radar. She says, "Most people who try this approach are not able to implement what they learned in the coaching session and end up trying to do too much in order to please the judge. What happens instead is that they confuse their choreography and appear unfinished. It usually ends up being a mistake." Another strategy some amateur competitors try is to do multiple entries at several key competitions in order to seduce judges who are also competition organizers. They may assume that, by contributing to the judge/organizer's bottom line, they have a leg up on the competition. On the contrary, however, most judges are not for sale! They are smart and passionate about their craft and are absolutely impeccable in their professional ethics.

THINKING YOU NEED A "GOOD" JUDGING PANEL TO WIN

As you compete more frequently, you will find that some judges consistently mark you in a favorable way. They may like your dancing and your progress and reward your efforts. It also works the other way. Some judges won't like your style or technique, and it may be close to impossible to change their perception of you. I made a key mistake early in my dancing. I always reviewed how each judge scored me and began making assumptions about who liked my dancing and who didn't. One year I learned that the panel I thought would judge me well, didn't. And the one I assumed wouldn't, did. That was the year I gave up focusing on wanting the "good" panel to walk out on the floor. I remind myself that I am where I am in my dancing, and what I show on the floor is my best, for now. If they like it, great. If they don't, I'll work harder to get better, not to please judges.

ASSUMING THAT, IF YOU WIN OR MAKE THE FINAL IN ONE COMPETITION, YOU WILL DO SO IN ALL COMPETITIONS

Even though I have competed for over four years, I am regularly amazed at how inconsistent some competitions are. When you begin to compete, it is hard to understand why, if you have placed well in most competitions, suddenly you don't place well in another. As you become more experienced, that tends to change. But until you get to Silver or Gold, this process is fairly confusing. It's important to take the following factors for placement discrepancies into consideration:

- **Who shows up:** You may have been competing at smaller local competitions, where the level of dancing is lower than it is at larger national competitions. Or you may be used to competing on the East Coast or Midwest. If you suddenly attend a competition on the West Coast you will dance against competitors you have never seen before, and you may not get the results you are used to. Ask your instructor/coach, prior to signing up for a competition, what you can expect.

- **Who the judges are:** If you compete in your region, chances are the judges have seen you dance before, as they tend to stay local as well. They may know your dancing abilities and automatically score you for callbacks or placements, because they know how you dance. If you compete in a different region with judges who have never seen you before, they may score the dancers they know first, missing you for callbacks. Remember, judges spend about 10 seconds on each couple before deciding to bring them back or place them.

- **How you danced that day:** Some days are just better than others. Sometimes you don't place because you didn't dance well, compared to the other dancers. Chuck it up as a loss, collect your "lessons learned," and move on.

- **Who dances up or down:** At most competitions, dancers can dance down one age category and compete in three skill levels. For example, if you are in pre-Bronze and are used to competing with pre-Bronze dancers, you may be surprised to find a "new" person competing in your category, even though she is a full Bronze dancer in an age category above you. Remember, you are judged against the other dancers on the floor, not how well you dance against everyone who has danced as long as you have.

How the Music Works

Each competition has a music director who is in charge of selecting and playing the music for each heat. The songs are carefully selected, and all music directors make sure songs are a mix of old familiar tunes and the latest on the billboards. If you watch shows like Dancing With The Stars or have had the pleasure of seeing segments from the Blackpool Dance Festival in England, you may have noticed that they dance to a live band. At Pro/Am and Am/Am competitions in the United States, we dance to recorded music managed by the music director.

You may want to join ballroomplaylist.com where, for a small monthly fee, you can download pre-arranged playlists for each style of dance. These are great for practicing and learning to identify music. See the resource section in Chapter 8 for more details.

It's important to know that you don't get to select the music unless you are doing a solo or show dance. Learn to count music, so you can understand how the bars and beats work.

According to former U.S. Professional Smooth Champion and Judge David Hamilton, if all else is equal, the most musical couple will win. It is the job of your teacher/coach to teach you how to best express the music through your dancing; however, there is a lot you can do to educate yourself.

As competitors, we do not enter this sport with an equal amount of musical understanding. We bring our musical experience, nil or profound, to the dance floor. Those who have had years of music lessons will have a keen ear for musical beats, measures, phrasing, moods, and highlights. Others may not know the difference between a beat and a beetle. Some hear music intuitively without any formal education in music, while others need a great deal of training to truly dance to the music. To the extent "knowledge is power," addressing your musical understanding can only help you. Take every opportunity to count beats, bars, and phrases when listening to music. This will help tune your ear to the rhythm and feel of each piece of music.

For basic information about how music relates to ballroom dancing, pick up a copy of Diane Jarmolow's *Teach Like a Pro: The Ultimate Guide for Ballroom Instructors*. The exercises outlined in Chapter 4 will help improve your musical awareness.

A word of caution. When you compete, avoid getting caught up in a good song. Once, when one of my favorite songs was played in an important heat, I began to sing along. A few bars into the song, I had lost count and was off timing. While it is tempting to get wrapped up in the music, avoid doing so. It may make you overly emotional, which can lead to a discombobulated heat. World and U.S. Latin Champion and Judge, Kimberley Mitchell, is famous for saying, "It's not the music in your head that we hear and judge. It's the song that is playing in the ballroom."

It's important to remember that art and science are both involved in ballroom competing and scoring. The more you focus on your own enjoyment, improvement, and happiness, the less you will be driven by placements. Instead let's focus next on what type of competitor you are and how you can tap into your driving motivators to dance your best.

Determining Your "Competition Type"

> ❝ Competition can be the most nerve-racking experience. Some people just thrive on it."
>
> – ITZHAK PERLMAN

While we all compete for different reasons, there are two main types of competitors. Michael Mead defines them as "professional amateurs" and "pure amateurs" (learn more in his interview insight on page 94). Both types thrive in the competitive arena, but they tend to take a different approach to competing.

Take a moment to checkmark the characteristics that best describe you. Remember, there are no good or bad answers.

		Mostly describes me
1.	I don't care so much about placing first. My main priority in competing is to have a good time and enjoy the process.	
2.	I compete because I want to see how good I can get. Placements matter to me, even if I don't always place first.	
3.	I go, or would consider going, to a competition just to support my friends who compete. I love the community of dancing and being part of it.	
4.	I want to win.	
5.	I love going to the studio to hang out with my dancing friends. It makes my day to connect with others who share my passion.	
6.	I am committed to doing whatever it takes to meet my dancing goals.	
7.	I'm happy for others, even when they place better than I do. In the end, it's all about having a good time.	
8.	I want my instructor to push the limits to help me get better.	
9.	While I want to improve my dancing, it's more important to me that I have a good time during my lessons and that my instructor helps me enjoy my dancing journey.	
10.	I believe that "quality practice makes perfect," and I commit a significant amount of time outside lessons to improve and push my dancing to the next level.	

11. Getting help and advice from experts is important to me because it helps me develop my dancing quicker and more efficiently.

12. I love taking coaching lessons with top coaches or professionals. It gives me a chance to get to know them better and experience something new.

13. I enjoy competing in different cities all over the U.S. It gives me a chance to tour and enjoy some vacation time.

14. I watch how professional dancers practice and compete, and I emulate them as much as I can.

15. When it's all said and done, I want to look back at my competing experience and think of all the wonderful people I have met. How I did competitively is secondary to me.

16. Socializing at a competition is secondary to me. My primary goal is to dance and perform.

If you checked mostly numbers 1, 3, 5, 7, 9, 12, 13, and 15, your type is most likely "pure amateur."

If you checked mostly numbers 2, 4, 6, 8, 10, 11, 14, and 16, your type is most likely "professional amateur."

Some important differences between each type of competitor:

Pure Amateurs...

Compete for the joy of the experience. They love to dance because it allows them to share their passion with others and be part of other people's dancing journeys. For them, it's less about placing first and more about having fun. They are a breath of fresh air and cheer others on from the sidelines. Pure amateurs enjoy coaching lessons because they offer a chance to experience something new. While they very much enjoy winning, it's not their driver. It is just as important for them to strive to be their own personal best, as they define it.

Professional Amateurs...

Compete and prepare for competitions like "mini-pros." They are motivated to win and be their own personal best in almost everything they do. Competing for them provides structure, milestones, and motivation to improve. They tend to excel faster on their competition journeys, because they practice more intensely and take their dancing very seriously. It's not uncommon for some professional amateurs to train as hard as professional dancers. They seek out the best coaches, who often treat their instructors and them as they would professional couples

Most competitive dancers will fall somewhere on this continuum. You may not fit perfectly into either category at this stage of your journey. For now, it is more important to consider which type you most identify with, because it will help you choose a dancing and competition goal that is best-suited for your type. It will also help you determine which instructor is the best fit for you.

For example, if you are a "professional amateur," and your drive and desire is to "compete like a pro," then you'll want to make sure your instructor/coach can take you there. Likewise, if you are more of a "pure amateur," you'll want to select an instructor/coach who understands that competing has to be fun for you. Pressuring you into making placements or attending multiple competitions may demotivate you, instead of moving you forward.

It is the same for Am/Am relationships. If one of the parties is a "pure amateur" and the other is a "professional amateur," then the relationship will be tense and strained. My advice is to find a partner who either is the same type as you, or is close to you on the continuum.

Depending where you are on your competing continuum, you may go back and forth between these types. It's neither "good" nor "bad" to be either type; it's just information to help you create a competing experience that is the best fit for you.

Successful dancer Patrice Tanaka (see her interview insight on page 33) most identifies with the "pure amateur," whereas Beverly Moore (see her interview insight on page 122) personifies the "professional amateur." Both dancers are successful and have found a way to compete that help them meet their goals and dreams.

Aligning Your Dancing and Competing Goals

> **"** When it is obvious that the goals cannot be reached, don't adjust the goals, adjust the action steps."

- CONFUCIUS

The next step is to review your dancing goals. There are many competitions to choose from. If you have already worked your way through the checklists in Chapter 1, you'll find this process is a great deal easier.

We know that having powerful and well-articulated goals helps us stay focused, motivated, and encouraged.

When asked how to set effective goals, Daniel Coyle, author of *The Talent Code: Greatness Isn't Born. It's Grown. Here's How*, advises, "Choose a goal just beyond your present abilities; to target the struggle. Thrashing blindly doesn't help. Reaching does" (New York: Bantam Dell, 2009, p.19).

The following steps will help you determine your goals and map out a plan for reaching your next level of performance. It is also a great opportunity to develop your partnering and communication skills with your instructor/dance partner. I encourage you to do these steps together. It allows you to review successes and disappointments and offers you a chance to develop goals that you are both committed to.

STEP 1: CONDUCT AN AUDIT OF YOUR PREVIOUS YEAR'S DANCING SUCCESSES AND DISAPPOINTMENTS. *(IF THIS IS YOUR FIRST YEAR DANCING, SKIP TO STEP 2.)*
Take out a piece of paper and divide it into two columns (or use the Annual Goal Planning Worksheet on page 269, Chapter 8). On one side, list all the things that were "wins" or successes last year. It may be that you were able to move from Bronze to Silver, or perhaps you added a new style of dance. It may be as simple as figuring out how to style your arms, or it may have been your first year of lessons. If you and your partner (either Pro or Am) have overcome any communication challenges, list these in the success column.

In the second column, list any disappointments or failures you have experienced. If you find yourself staring blindly at this column, you may not have danced long enough to record any. Trust me, they will come, and they will bring about tremendous opportunity for growth. For example, you may not have placed where you had hoped at a particular competition. Or you may be at a transitional point in your dancing, where everything feels challenging, and your attitude is negative.

Once you have material in both columns, take a look at what successes you can build from, and identify the disappointments you want to learn from or avoid. These become important aspects in your goal-setting process. You may want to summarize both columns at the bottom of the page. Then pick the one thing you are most proud of and the one thing that was most disappointing.

End this step by thanking yourself and your partner for a great year, and give yourself a quick virtual (or literal) hug. Let the negative feelings and disappointments be a thing of the past. The new competition plan starts with your fresh attitude and determination to succeed.

STEP 2: MAKE A LIST OF WHAT YOU REALLY WANT AND BELIEVE YOU CAN DO, AND WHAT YOU DREAM OF ACCOMPLISHING

This exercise is broken up in to two sub-steps. Again, take out a piece of paper and make two columns. Name the first one, "What I Really Want and Believe I Can Do" and name the second, "What I Dream of Accomplishing."

In the first column, make a list of at least six things you really want and believe you can do. For example, you may list that you really want to take three lessons a week, or you may want a new dress for a particular style. It may be that you really want to dance with a particular partner, or you really want to let go of someone you are currently dancing with. If you are doing this exercise with your partner, you may want to keep the "change of partner" wish to yourself. In this column also list the things you really believe you can accomplish this competing year. For example, you may believe (and have good reason to believe) that you can place in the top three at your next competition. Or you may believe that you could push through a certain obstacle in your dancing, if you practiced twice as hard. Focus on identifying at least six things that are within your control, and reach for them this year.

In your second column, list the dreams you have for this year. It may be helpful to also list dreams that aren't attainable this year, but may be within your reach in the future. One of my goals for 2011 was to become the Top American Style Student in full Bronze at the Ohio Star Ball. When I set it, it felt particularity BIG, as I had to really push my skills to a whole new level. My instructor and I worked hard, were lucky, and accomplished our goal. We know that we wouldn't have done it without having listed it in our dream column.

In my goal planning sheet, I also keep my REALLY BIG goal. This is one that I created when I had danced for only two months and was in pre-Bronze. The goal I established (and am still committed to) is to be one of the top- three American Style dancers by 2015. That's a big dream for someone just starting out dancing, but I knew then, and I know now, that with continued commitment, dedicated training, and a passion for this sport, I have a shot at it. When we dream BIG, it's important to develop a goal that is within your capacity, and like Daniel Coyle says, just a bit beyond your present abilities. We will discuss the importance of dreaming big in detail later in this chapter.

Once you are finished writing, review your columns and start looking for a pattern or theme. For example, is this the year that you want to focus on communicating more effectively with your partner? Or is this the year you kick your lessons up a bit, in order to reach greater heights more consistently? Each year tends to have its own organic theme. Listen to what matters most to you and design goals that bring you joy and a sense of accomplishment.

STEP 3: CREATE SMALL STEP-BY-STEP GOALS THAT LEAD TO AN OVERALL GOAL

When we begin to compete, it is easy to make our goals or milestones about placements. By now, you know that this can be a big mistake. If you want to really enjoy your competing journey, stop doing this immediately. It is a lot harder than it seems, because we often associate placing first with being good and placing second with not being good enough. Remember, unlike other sports or artistic forms of athleticism, in ballroom you are competing against a set number of dancers and are being judged against how well you dance compared to them at that particular moment.

It may be helpful at this point to go back to pages 59-61 to review which type of competitor you feel you are. The goals of "professional amateurs" tend to be more performance-based; those of "pure amateurs" tend to center around having a great experience. There are no right or wrong goals.

If you want to make placement a goal, I highly encourage you give yourself a range, like Aiyesha Dey did when she decided to place in the top three in Silver. Or make "feeding my soul" a goal, like Patrice Tanaka did when she decided to compete only if it made her feel good.

Once you reconnect with your competing type and have identified the goals you really want to achieve, create small attainable goals that you and/or your partner are in control of, and which move you closer to a bigger goal. One effective goal-setting tool is called Specific, Measurable, Attainable, Relevant, and Timed, or SMART. When we use this acronym to design our goals, we have a higher likelihood of accomplishing them, AND we know when we've reached them because we can measure the result.

Toni Redpath lists effective goal-setting as one of the key elements to "competing like a pro." She recommends identifying one big goal and then breaking that one down into smaller goals. Her advice is to structure action steps in two-month segments to help you stay focused and energized. You can learn more in her interview insight on page 86.

An example of a larger SMART dance goal might be, "I want to learn Latin (Specific) and consistently place in the top six (Measurable) in pre-Bronze and intermediate Bronze (Attainable) while competing this year (Relevant and Timed)."

An ineffective version of this goal would be, "I want to be a great Latin dancer." While that may be a goal, it's not easily measured, and goals that aren't SMART enough tend to be forgotten or ignored.

Breaking the SMART Latin goal down into smaller steps may look something like this:

In the next two months I will:

- Increase my lessons by one a week to dive deeper into the technique of Latin.

- Seek a Latin coach to work with my partner and me for the next six months.

- Attend at least one dance camp and go to sessions that focus on Latin techniques.

- Increase my practice time by two hours a week to review my figures and routines.

- Compete with my Latin routines at a one-day competition to work out the kinks in the new routine.

The key to effective goal setting is to keep the goals SMART and short.

One of my goals in 2012 was to improve my American Rhythm technique in all five dances, in order to have a chance at winning the U.S. Bronze Rhythm title at United States Dance Championships (USDC). While I really, really wanted to win, my goal was to improve my dancing, so I had the best chance of winning. I knew that I had no control over whether we would win or not, but I believed that if I did everything I could to improve my own dancing, including increased lessons, top coaching, and lots of practice, we had a chance at it.

I still remember when they announced us for first place. I looked at my instructor, and we shared a special moment because it meant that all the hard work had paid off, and the placement ended up being a delicious icing on the cake.

Remember, setting goals is a great way to get focused and stay motivated. If they don't happen this year, you may just have made your goal too big or unattainable—or it just wasn't the year for you to reach it. Don't be discouraged. If you have gone through Steps 1-to-3 with careful thought and assessment, chances are you are well on your way to accomplishing your dancing goals soon.

STEP 4: REVIEW YOUR GOALS WITH YOUR INSTRUCTOR/DANCE PARTNER AND CHECK IN ON EXPECTATIONS

In order to have support from your instructor/dance partner, remember to discuss and review your goals together. You may also find it helpful to share your goals with your significant other, if he isn't dancing with you. The more support and encouragement you have for your goals, the easier it will be to jump over hurdles and avoid any obstacles that appear. It also offers you an opportunity to celebrate your successes with others. I find that sharing my goals with my network of dancers gives me tremendous support and encouragement. Once I have shared my goals and have been fortunate to know the goals of others, we cheer each other on and find strength in our mutual passion for ballroom dancing.

As an Am/Am couple, it is especially important to have the same goals. My Am/Am relationship ended because, while I very much enjoyed dancing with my Am partner, and he was extraordinarily committed to our dancing, I loved Pro/Am more. And I only have so much time to allocate to my dancing. I still miss dancing Am/Am, but my goal was to be the best dancer I could be, and that required me to focus my attention on one area of my dancing in order to meet it. I highly recommend the "Partner Compatibility Questionnaire" in the book *Ballroom Dancing is Not for Sissies: An R-Rated Guide for Partnership*, if you want to learn if you are truly compatible with your dance partner.

Top Pro/Am Teacher and Coach Shalene Archer reminds newer competitors in her interview insight on page 98 to set realistic expectations once goals have been established. She reiterates that the competing experience is unique in itself, and it is a separate skill from dancing. Frequent competing helps students sharpen their competing and dancing skills in ways that practice alone can't. If students only do one or two competitions per year, their competing skills will take longer to develop. If that is all they can afford or have time for, then they have to make sure their goals and expectations are realistic.

Picking the Right Competition

" If you can dream it, you can do it."

– WALT DISNEY

Now that you have a clearer picture of how competing works, what your competition type is, and what your dancing and competing goals are, it's time to figure out which type of competition and schedule will best fit your goals and budget.

Each year, my instructor and I select the competitions we definitely will go to, and we also keep a few "fun" or "if we can make it" competitions on the list. One of my challenges is that I own my own business and don't get paid on a regular schedule. As a result, some years I have more financial resources than others. I make sure to adjust my competing schedule with my cash flow, and my instructor knows that I may have to make adjustments along the way. The key is to communicate with your instructor and plan for as many "unforeseen circumstances" as possible to avoid dramatic shifts to your plan that may affect both you and your instructor/dance partner.

My advice is to always start with your dancing goals and then match or align the competitions accordingly. I highly recommend mapping out an annual competition plan to avoid getting bamboozled by last-minute competitions and big financial commitments, unless time and money are not a concern for you.

Start with your dancing goals and then match or align the competitions accordingly.

If your goal is to get your feet wet and see what you can do for your first time, you may enjoy a smaller one- or two- day local competition. This is a great way to experience the competition scene without getting overwhelmed.

If your goal is to see how you match up with the best in North America, then sign up for one-week competition such as United States Dancesport Championship (USDC) in Orlando, Florida or the Ohio Star Ball in Columbus, Ohio, where the best dancers compete for titles and prestige in Bronze, Silver, Gold, and Open Professional. For a comprehensive list of the NDCA-sanctioned competitions in the United States, go to ndca.org. If you compete or hope to compete in pure Am/Am events and dance among the best, you must first attend a qualifying event in order to dance at the National DanceSport Championships. For more information about this event and the process for qualifying, please visit usadance.org.

The three most-common types of competitions are one-day, two-to-three day, or weeklong. Most one-day competitions are local or regional and offer all four styles of dancing (American Smooth, American Rhythm, International Standard, and International Latin) on the same day. If you compete in all four styles, it makes for a busy day. If you only compete in one or two styles, it is a wonderful way to focus your dancing and then relax once you are done. Almost all Am/Am USADance events (especially qualifying ones) last two days. There is also an amateur national event run by Brigham Young University. Please visit byudancesport.com for more information.

Mid-sized local or regional competitions tend to range from two-to-three days, and they have more competitors than one-day competitions. You will most likely have semi- or quarter- finals in some of your heats, and the competition-level tends to be more intense. It's not because one-day competitions aren't high-quality; it's simply that there are more high-level competitors at longer competitions.

The national competitions tend to last six or seven days and are located all over the U.S. There are several competitions at which you can win a title in your category or dance level, and these events are extremely competitive. The best of the best in ballroom at every level, from Bronze to Professional, compete here. And it makes for an intense experience.

Most first-timers compete in local one-day or two-to-three-day competitions to get their feet wet. I'm lucky to be based in Columbus, Ohio, where we have several high-quality local and regional small- to mid- sized competitions. Plus, we have the prestigious Ohio Star Ball, which is one of the largest competitions in the U.S. and takes place just a few blocks from my home.

My very first competition, just three months after my first dance lesson, was the three-day Cleveland DanceSport Challenge. My second competition was the Ohio Star Ball, two months later. I didn't know I was competing at one of the largest and most competitive competitions in the U.S., and I'm glad I didn't know! I loved every second of it and wasn't nervous at all. The second year we did the Ohio Star Ball was a completely different story. This time I knew it was a big deal. Consequently I had to learn to manage both my dancing techniques and my nerves.

Remember, you have to trust your instructor's judgment and believe that he won't steer you wrong. The truth is that I would have never felt ready if my instructor had told me just how big a deal the Ohio Star Ball is. But he knew my goal was to compete among the best, regardless of where I placed, and I trusted his guidance.

Instructors may invite you to dance at a particular competition because they have several other students going, and the event may be less expensive that way. While this may be a great option if you are on a budget, avoid dancing at competitions simply because they are cheaper. They will still be a significant investment, and you may be disappointed in the end, because the competition or experience didn't help you meet your goals. As you become more experienced in the competitive arena, you may want to make choices to compete only if other students come and share the expenses.

The following checklist will help you decide which type of competition best matches your competing goals right now. Put a check mark in the "That's me!" section. Then determine which type of competition may be your best fit.

That's me!		Local/ regional one-day comp	Mid-sized regional 2-to-3-day comp	National highly competitive comp
	I want to get my feet wet and see if competing is for me.	X		
	I want to have fun and not experience too much stress for my competitions.	X		
	I like to dance everything in one day and then sit back and enjoy the rest of the competition.	X		
	I don't want to, or can't be, away from home/ work for too long.	X		
	I'd like to do a lot of entries and dance as much as I can.	X	X	X
	I want to compete as much as possible, and I have the financial and physical abilities to do so.	X	X	X
	I prefer to dance one style of dance each day.		X	X
	I'd like to do a competition where I have mostly finals or semi-finals.		X	
	I would like to combine my competing with some sightseeing.		X	
	I have tough skin, and I'd like to see how I rank among the top in my category.			X
	I want to see if I can win a title in my category.			X

Remember, your competing plan has to work for your dance partner and you. You may start off with some local one-day competitions, and then add a two-to-three-day competition mid-year. Or you may opt to go full-speed ahead and do one a month, not worrying about the length or competitiveness of them. Once you have planned your next competition or annual competition plan, make sure you mark your calendar to avoid scheduling mishaps or mistakes.

Tapping into Your Strengths and Embracing Your Weaknesses While Competing

> **"** Know yourself. Don't accept your dog's admiration as conclusive evidence that you are wonderful."

- ANN LANDERS

Each dancer and competitor brings a unique set of strengths and weakness to the competing journey. This section is meant to assist you in maximizing your strengths and minimizing your weaknesses.

The first step is to list at least three key strengths that you believe help you compete with joy, grace, and personal success. Take a moment and brainstorm any characteristics, behaviors, skills, talents, or attitudes you possess that make you especially well-suited for competing. Don't worry about doing it right. Just write them down for now. If you are doing this exercise with your instructor/dance partner, ask her to share what she sees as your potential competing strengths.

When asked in his interview about his biggest strengths, Top Pro/Am Competitor Giovanni Fortezza said, "I'm ultra-confident. Sometimes my partner Jolanta makes fun of me, and other times she admires my 'blind' confidence." It's imperative that we know what we do well and embrace our strengths.

For example, some of my competitive strengths include my unwavering desire to improve, drive to be my own personal best, openness to critical feedback, and a true passion for ballroom dancing.

When I compete and go through some challenging times, I remind myself of these strengths and always find a renewed determination to push forward. At the end of this section, I will ask you to write down the top-three strengths from your list and develop strategies for tapping into them as you compete.

Competing husband and wife team Elizabeth and Arthur Seagull wrote the fabulous book *Ballroom Dancing Is Not For Sissies: An R Rated Guide for Partnership*, which offers wonderful tips on how to dance and partner more effectively. The title really does hits home a key point. Ballroom dancing is not for the softhearted and neither is ballroom competing. It can bring out the best and the worst in you and your partner. Someone likened ballroom dancing to opening your own emotional "Pandora's box." On this journey, you are likely to experience some of your most powerful highs and possibly some of your lowest lows. At these moments, you'll need to lean on your strengths and remind yourself that you have what it takes to continue growing. We will review the "emotional rollercoaster" of ballroom dancing in more detail in Chapter 3.

The next step is to acknowledge and embrace your weaknesses. This is a bit harder at first, mostly because we are so unaccustomed to talking about them. We somehow believe that if we don't mention them, no one will know they exist. As your husband/wife/significant other/parents/siblings/ friends would tell you if you asked them, your weaknesses aren't secrets to them!

Take a few moments to jot down a few weaknesses that could affect your dancing if they aren't managed or addressed. Write down at least three, so we have something to work with.

Mine include that I tend to be impatient with my instructor and myself, overly blunt, and have a tendency to over-commit. As you can imagine, all these weaknesses can affect my dancing and my competing goals if I'm not careful. At the very least, they are likely to affect my relationship with my instructor/dance partner.

The key to this exercise is to become comfortable saying, writing, and looking at your weaknesses. They are really nothing more than another side of you. The more we are able to connect with our strengths and embrace our weaknesses, the more self-aware we will be, and the smoother and more enjoyable our dancing will be.

Take a moment to record your discoveries here.

My top three competing strengths are:

1.

2.

3.

During my practice, dancing, and competing, I will maximize them in the following way:

My top three competing weaknesses are:

1.

2.

3.

During my practice, dancing, and competing, I will minimize or manage them more effectively by:

The more self-aware you are, the easier it will be for you to improve your own "mental game" and reach the goals you want with greater ease.

Getting Your Mental Game On

 The most important attribute a player must have is mental toughness."

- MIA HAMM

Before we dive into the importance of managing your emotions, picking the right costume, and learning about dos and don'ts of ballroom dancing, let's explore the most importance tool in your competition tool box: your mind.

Many beautifully skilled dancers fall under the pressures of ballroom competing and find that all their wonderful preparation falls apart because their minds get in the way before, during, or after the competition.

In this section, we will only scratch the surface of the ballroom mental game necessary to compete like a pro. (It really warrants a separate book, which I hope to write next). For now, I'm sharing strategies that I know will help you better understand your own mental game and tap into your hidden strengths to maximize your competition edge right away.

For the serious amateur competitor, especially those who identified themselves as "professional amateurs," I highly recommend getting the book *Dance to Your Maximum: The Competitive Ballroom Dancer's Workbook,* by Maximiliaan Winkelhuis. Please see the resource section in Chapter 8 for details on how to purchase a copy. While it is mainly tailored to the professional competitor, competitors of all levels (Pro or Am) will greatly benefit from its tips. Please note that if you are newer to dancing, you may need your instructor's/dance partner's help in working your way through some of the concepts. It is written mostly for an audience dancing International Latin and Standard, so you may not be familiar with some of the terminology. Consider it one of your "must-haves" as you explore your dancing and work to maximize your competitive presence.

There are three cornerstones to making sure you've got a strong mental foundation:

1. **Mental Toughness**

2. **Optimism**

3. **Courage**

Don't worry if you don't have all three yet. The great news is that all cornerstones can be taught! While some people have a natural propensity for optimism, others don't. Some may have plenty of courage, but are not optimistic by nature. Fear not. In this section, you will learn which cornerstone is your strongest and which you need to develop in order to maximize and enjoy your competitive experience.

1. Mental Toughness

The concept was first introduced to me in the book *Mind Gym: An Athlete's Guide to Inner Excellence*, by Gary Mack and David Casstevens (New York: McGraw Hill Professional, 2002). They define a mentally tough person as someone who "looks at competition as a challenge to rise up to rather than a threat to back down from" (p.25).

Please note that almost all competitors have a sense of fear or doubt about competing. The difference is that they meet the challenge head on anyway. I love the book *Feel the Fear and Do It Anyway: Dynamic Techniques for Turning Fear, Indecision, and Anger into Power, Action, and Love*, by Susan Jeffers. Having mental toughness is not about being a "tough guy" and pretending you don't have fears. The difference is that people with mental toughness acknowledge their fears AND don't let them stand in the way of doing what they love. Let's take a look at the seven Cs that Mack and Casstevens share in their book.

1. **Competitive:** If you choose to engage in competition, you must have an internal drive to be your personal best. Let's not confuse it with always wanting to win. True competitors compete within and strive to reach their own personal best at all times. Take a moment to score yourself on your competitiveness:

Not Very High									Very High
1	2	3	4	5	6	7	8	9	10

2. **Confident:** Mentally ready competitors find something in their game that they are confident about. Remember, all competitors aren't confident all the time, but they find inner strength and believe they can do anything they put their minds to. They have an acute sense of self-awareness about their strengths and weaknesses and gain confidence from repetitive practice. I love Wendy Palmer's quote in her book *The Intuitive Body: Aikido as a Clairsentient Practice* (Berkely: North Atlantic Books, 1994, p.22). "Confidence comes from doing something over and over to the point where we feel we can do it naturally." Take a moment to score yourself on your confidence:

Not Very High									Very High
1	2	3	4	5	6	7	8	9	10

3. **Control:** The name of the competing game is control. Successful competitors know how to control their emotions and behaviors. We will review how to do so in detail in the next chapter. For now, simply score yourself on your ability to control emotions, feelings, and thoughts while you compete.

Not Very High									Very High
1	2	3	4	5	6	7	8	9	10

4. **Committed:** Top competitors focus their attention on their game and dreams. They are intensely committed to sharpening their skills and are highly motivated to succeed. How committed are you to dancing, improving, or being your own personal best?

Not Very High									Very High
1	2	3	4	5	6	7	8	9	10

5. **Composure:** Competitors with mental toughness know how to deal with setbacks and adversity. They have realistic expectations and can stay calm under pressure. Give yourself a score on how highly you rate your ability to keep cool.

Not Very High									Very High
1	2	3	4	5	6	7	8	9	10

6. **Courage:** We will discuss courage in more detail in step 3. For this part of the exercise, we define courage as your willingness to take risks to reach your goals.

Not Very High									Very High
1	2	3	4	5	6	7	8	9	10

7. **Consistency:** Top competitors are able to consistently perform at a high level and don't make excuses. Rate yourself and your dancing on your ability to perform consistently.

Not Very High									Very High
1	2	3	4	5	6	7	8	9	10

Take a moment to review your answers to the seven Cs above. Which of the Cs do you want to develop and grow? Which are your natural strengths? It may be helpful to turn to the Chapter Takeways section on page 82 and identify at least one action step you can take to improve your mental toughness before we take a look at the second powerful mental capacity.

2. Optimism

Before I began my research, I had no idea that optimism can be learned! I thought people were either optimistic by nature or not. While this may be true in some cases, optimism also can be learned. It is one of the foundational building blocks to your competing success. Henry Ford is famous for saying, "Whether you think you can, or you think you can't—you're right." Nothing is as destructive to your competing success as negative thinking. It takes you in only one direction—down! While there are thousands of resources on the topic, I highly recommend three key books. One is called, *Learned Optimism: How to Change Your Mind and Your Life,* by Martin E.P. Seligman. Another is *Ask and It is Given: Learning to Manifest Your Desires,* by Esther and Jerry Hicks. And the last is *How We Choose to Be Happy: The 9 Choices of Extremely Happy People–Their Secrets, Their Stories* by Rick Foster and Greg Hicks. I've taken a few key concepts from each book to provide tactical tools for tapping into your optimism to develop your mental game.

The first concept we will look at is the difference between pessimism and optimism as shared in *Learned Optimism* by Martin E.P. Seligman (New York: Vintage Books, 1996).

According to Seligman, "the defining characteristic of pessimists is that they tend to believe bad events will last a long time, will undermine everything they do, and are their own fault" (p.4). If you have a more pessimistic disposition as you compete in ballroom, you are likely to believe that if you don't achieve the desired placement in a given event, then you never will. Or you may feel your placements are your own "fault." As you can imagine, neither thought pattern will help you compete with grace and joy.

> **There are going to be times when you don't place where you would have hoped, and it's imperative that you remain positive and optimistic about your ability to improve.**

On the other hand, optimists, "who are confronted with the same hard knocks of this world, think about misfortune in the opposite way. They tend to believe defeat is just a temporary setback, that its causes are confined to this one case. The optimists believe defeat is not their fault....Confronted by a bad situation, they perceive it as a challenge and try harder" (p.4-5). Just reading the definition of optimism, it's easy to see how important this trait is to being a successful ballroom dancer. Many times you will have setbacks and will need to bounce back quickly. There are going to be times when you don't place where you would have hoped, and it's imperative that you remain positive and optimistic about your ability to improve.

I'm not suggesting that you should assume it is always within your control to change something or to improve yourself. I'm simply suggesting that an optimistic outlook will help you reach your competing goals and is one of the cornerstone skills you must learn if you want to compete well and enjoy the journey. To learn more about your natural disposition in either direction, I highly recommend buying Seligman's book and taking the self-assessment listed. This book also has several fabulous techniques for increasing your optimism, which you don't want to miss.

While you compete, practice staying optimistic. Avoid using self-deprecating language, assume you will do better in each round, and focus on thinking positive thoughts about yourself and others. Each time I'm lined up for awards, I assume I've won. This is of course not always the case, but I've learned to stay positive and to think that it is possible.

The next concept we will dive into is the power of manifestation from the book, *Ask and It Is Given: Learning to Manifest Your Desires,* by Esther and Jerry Hicks (New York: Hay House, 2004). You have probably heard of the "Law of Attraction," which gained mainstream popularity by the book *The Secret,* by Rhonda Byrne. But the law of attraction is a powerful concept discussed through literary history for hundred of years. The Hicks define it as, "That which is like unto itself is drawn" (p.25). Think of it as a giant magnet. They go on to say, "Whatever you are giving your attention to causes you to emit a vibration, and the vibrations that you offer equal your asking, which equals your point of attraction" (p.26).

Avoid using self-deprecating language, assume you will do better in each round, and focus on thinking positive thoughts about yourself and others.

If we assume the law of attraction works, the more optimistically we look at our lives and dancing, the more positive energy we vibrate and attract. If you commit to thinking and saying only positive things to yourself and others while you dance, more positive energy will flow to you. Whether you believe in the concept of the law of attraction doesn't matter. Thinking and active positively won't hurt anyone, so you may as well try it.

Ways to maximize your positive vibrational energy while competing include doing and saying nice things to others, thinking and praying for positive things to come to you, assuming good things have already happened, and being a positive force at all times while practicing and competing. If you are struggling with self-doubt or challenging emotions like the ones we will discuss in Chapter 3, remember these principles. I promise you that your dancing and joy for competing will change dramatically if you choose to use the lens of optimism and consider the law of attraction.

The final concept we will discuss is offered by Rick Foster and Greg Hicks in the book *How We Choose to Be Happy: The 9 Choices of Extremely Happy People* (New York: The Penguin Group, 2004). They spent over three years studying what happy people have in common, and they uncovered nine key choices that all happy people make. The interesting part of their research is that these unusually happy people have very little else in common. They live in different parts of the world, have varying degrees of education, come from different racial, socio-economic, and religious backgrounds, and have experienced various hardships in life. But somehow they had found ways to stay extraordinarily happy. Let's take a deeper look at how happiness makes a difference in your ballroom competition journey. In this section we will review three of the happy subjects' nine choices: intention, recasting, and appreciation. I highly recommend reading this book and learning about all nine traits when you have a moment.

- **Intention:** In order to increase our "happiness quotient," we need to have a desire and intention to be happy. Being happy is different from being positive. Happiness is a deep feeling of well-being that resides in our hearts. Positive thinking is a state of mind. Both are essential. One powerful way to increase your happiness is to set a daily intention as soon as you wake up. Decide to be happy, no matter what happens throughout the day. There is plenty to be grateful for and happy about. It may be as simple as deciding to be happy that you are alive and able to get out of bed. You may be grateful for the opportunity to be able to head over to the studio to practice. Practice setting daily intentions to be happy, and your disposition will shift, and your natural optimism will flow. Judges want to see you being happy on the dance floor. They don't care if you are technically perfect, unless you also exude a love for dance.

- **Recasting:** Life and dancing don't always go as we would like or hope. All of the people interviewed in the book had experienced deep loss, financial, and/or emotional hardships. That is just life. What they were able to do was to recast the experiences. Here are two unique parts to recasting. First, happy people dive into negative and difficult feelings head-on, experiencing them deeply. They mourn and grieve. They don't censor difficult emotions, but instead they make room for them to be noticed and felt. The second step is transforming challenges with new insights and reactions. Happy people ask themselves, "What lessons can I learn?" "What opportunities can I create from this experience?" Even through the most difficult situations, they search for insight and meaning.

One year, a week before Ohio Star Ball, my mother unexpectedly passed away in Sweden. I flew home to help with her arrangements, unsure if I would return in time to compete. After a few days, my brother encouraged me to fly back to the U.S. and compete. He said there was nothing more I could do, and our mother would have wanted me to dance. I did fly back, and as I entered my first round, I deeply felt the presence of my mother. I smiled and pure happiness filled me. I knew deep within my soul that my mother, who had been struggling with a life-long illness, was now at peace. She was with me in sprit, beaming with joy and pride. I chose to let her joy fill me, even as I was grieving from the loss. Today, several years later, I still recall that precious moment. I know my ability to recast helped me heal and continue to live a life of happiness, in spite of the fact that my mother is not here to share it with me.

- **Appreciation:** I love how Foster and Hicks define appreciation, "It's the way we open our emotional floodgates and let our happiness flow into the world. And appreciation is our way of living fully in the moment" (p.316 of 554 on iBook). By being continuously grateful and showing our appreciation to others, we make ourselves and others happy. Happy people appreciate the little things in life. They take time to notice the details and stop to breathe in the moment. We will discuss strategies for doing so in Chapter 7, but for now, consider how you may be showing or experiencing your appreciation. For example, when was the last time you thanked your instructor/dance partner for being there for you? When did you reach out to say or do something nice for someone unexpectedly? The more you give, the more happiness you will gain.

Take a moment to pause here and identify one area that you wish to develop in order to amp up your optimism. You may want record at least one action step on page 82 to remember your commitment.

3. Courage

My dear friend Margie Warrell is the author of *Find Your Courage: 12 Acts for Becoming Fearless in Work and Life* and *Stop Playing Safe: Rethink Risk. Unlock the Power of Courage. Achieve Outstanding Success.* She is also is a courage expert. Not only because she writes about it, but she has lived and continues to live a courageous life. She has experienced a myriad of highs and lows in her life including losing her brother, traveling the world by herself, raising four wonderful children, and living on several different continents. In her first book, *Find Your Courage: Unleash Your Full Potential & Live the Life You Really Want* (Austin: Synergy Books, 2007), she speaks about several different types of courage. For our purposes, let's look at the concepts, "The Courage to Dream Bigger" and "The Courage to Be Yourself."

- **The Courage to Dream Bigger:** As you begin to compete or consider competing, it's easy to become a bit scared. Even after you've made your decision to do it, you may experience feelings of doubt, regret, or confusion. Dreaming of being more or thinking bigger is risky. What if you dream big, and it doesn't come true? Will you feel silly, uncomfortable, doubtful? What if others make fun of your dreams or challenge them? As Margie reminds us, everyone who has ever dared to dream bigger, goes through a stage of fear, but they do it anyway. She shares, "Those who go on to follow their dreams do so not because they have some genetic immunity to fear, but because they find within themselves the courage to risk the possibility that their dreams will not become realty. They pursue their dreams anyway, despite their doubts and despite the many challenges that line the path they have dared to travel" (p.66). As you begin to compete and formulate your goals, remember to have a column or list for BIG dreams. Be courageous. Share your big goals with a dance friend you trust. Let your friends support you along the way. It's imperative to surround yourself with others who dream bigger and cheer one another on. Consider what you are doing outside the ballroom world to dream bigger also. Life may be short. How are you spending your time? What dreams may you be putting off in favor of safely remaining the same?

- **The Courage to Be Yourself:** I know it sounds silly, but most of us are deeply afraid to be ourselves. As we start off in ballroom dancing, we may believe that we need to be like someone else in order to be successful. After all, there is a certain ballroom look that most serious competitive dancers strive to emulate, and there are acceptable rules of conduct that you are expected to adhere to. While this is true, on and off the dance floor, the trick is to display the persona of elegance and grace without changing who you are. Consider Margie's question, "Why be you?" Well, who else can you be? I love watching most young and old people approach life. They tend to be themselves and don't worry about what others think of them or how they spend their days. I guess the really young ones just trust their instincts and haven't yet been programmed to "be" a certain way. And older people have learned from experience that life is short, and they are done trying to please others. Being yourself doesn't mean you don't work on improving and becoming a better version of who you are. It means having the courage to shine and to let your light and uniqueness affect others positively. Think of how you can bring the positive aspects of your personality to the competition floor and how you can share your gifts while competing. To learn more and to assess areas in your life where you may not be aligned with your "inner you," I highly recommend reading Margie's books.

In what area would you like to have more courage? Consider one action step you want to take and record it in the Chapter Takeaway on page 82. Making a commitment to your own personal growth in order to be your authentic self is tremendously rewarding.

As you may have noticed, all the resources and concepts listed in this section weave into one another. That is because they originate from the same place: love for self and others. As you begin to compete, remember to keep working on your own personal development in addition to your dancing. What sets truly amazing competitors apart is not just their dancing, but also how they show up in the ballroom world. There is goodness about them; they radiate positive energy. Choose to be that force in this world, even as you experience the difficult and challenging emotions that are sure to surface as you compete.

Before we dive into Chapter 3, let's sum up this chapter.

Chapter Summary

- Your scores and placements are at the mercy of the judges' subjective opinions. Avoid making your goals about winning, and you will dance with greater joy and ease. Think of placements as the "icing on the cake."

- Judges' scores are not always consistent. They bring their subjectivity to the judging process, and sometimes it works in your favor and sometimes it doesn't. Avoid getting hung up on each judge's opinion of your dancing.

- As you start competing, avoid looking at your marks. Simply enjoy the process and embrace all the wonderful aspects that make up ballroom dancing.

- Avoid making assumptions about placements and your dancing. The more you avoid the common pitfalls, the more you will enjoy the process.

- You don't get to pick the music for your heats. Learn to count music, so you are prepared for whatever song comes your way.

- There are two types of competitors: the professional amateur and the pure amateur. Each type of dancer enjoys different aspects of competing. There are no good or bad types. Knowing which type you are will help you align your competing goals, select the right teacher, and map out a competition plan that is best suited for you.

- Powerful dancing goals are designed around what you most desire and dream of accomplishing. They are then broken down into smaller SMART goals that are easily measured and can be celebrated along your dancing journey.

- When designing a competition plan, first consider the goals you have set for your dancing and competing. Then match the best type of competition to your goals.

- Powerful dancers are self-aware. They know what strengths they need to lean on and what weaknesses they must manage in order to compete with joy and grace.

- Your "mental game" is sometimes more powerful than your ability to produce impeccable technique. By maximizing your mental toughness, optimism, and courage you will experience tremendous success and joy in competing.

Chapter Takeaways

Take a moment to summarize your takeaways from this chapter. These notes will come in handy as you take the next important steps in dealing with the emotional aspects of ballroom dancing.

After reading this chapter I realized that:

_____

My most valuable takeaway is:

_____

I learned the following about how judging and placements work:

_____

My "competition type" is:

◯ Professional Amateur   ◯ Pure Amateur

As a result of recognizing my type, I need to:

_____

My competition goal-setting can use the following improvements:

_____

In order to design a tailored competition plan that aligns with my goals, I need to:

_____

I know that the following strengths will serve me well as I compete:

_____

I will design strategies for addressing the following competition weaknesses:

_____

I will take the following action steps to improve my:

1. Mental Toughness: _____

2. Optimism: _____

3. Courage: _____

Interview Insight: Marianne Nicole and John DePalma

Photo by: Ryan Kenner Photography

MARIANNE IS AN AVID JUDGE AND COACH. JOHN CO-OWNS THE METROPOLITAN DANCE CENTER IN STAMFORD, CT. HE AND MARIANNE ARE ORGANIZERS OF THE POPULAR CAPITAL DANCESPORT CHAMPIONSHIPS.

They are a ballroom power couple. John has been in the ballroom business for 40 years and is known as "The Voice of Ballroom." He emcees most competitions in the United States.

Jessika Ferm: *As a couple, professional dancers, coaches, and judges, you offer a unique perspective on how to shine on and off the floor. What tips do you have for newer competitors to help them enjoy the competition process?*

Marianne Nicole: Remember that even though you may be competing with others, you are really only competing against yourself. Set a goal prior to attending a competition. For example, you may decide that, for your first competition, you are going to focus on foot placement or posture. For the next competition, you might opt to focus on partnering skills. That way you are basing your success on your progress, not placements.

John DePalma: Work with your instructor to set small attainable goals that fit into your broader long-term dancing plan. Use competitions as opportunities to focus on specific areas for development. For example, preparing for a competition can help you work on perfecting your technical and partnering skills. That is a perfect short-term goal if your desire is to be a great social dancer. If you are an internally driven and competitive person, signing up for a competition can help you maintain your motivation and elevate your dancing skills.

Jessika Ferm: *It is often hard for new competitors to understand the judging process. Sometimes you may score well against a certain group of competitors, and at the next competition, with almost the exact same group and judging panel, you place differently. What insights would you offer to help newer-to-intermediate competitors better understand the process?*

Marianne Nicole: Some students get a bit "step happy" and end up doing too many patterns. There is a misconception that the more steps you do, the more advanced you are. Remember,

I may be looking at you doing the step that you are completely comfortable with, and if the technique and artistry are there, I mark you high. The next judge may catch you at a time when you are doing a step that you are not as comfortable with, and your technique and comfort level are lower, so the scores will reflect what is seen at that moment. The more consistent you are in your routines, the more consistent the scores will be. My feeling is that less is more. Quality has to be your number-one priority. I suggest that newcomers do between three and four patterns, no more.

John DePalma: Some instructors teach using a syllabus. They focus on patterns and steps first, then add partnership, continuity, and styling. They tend to teach one step at a time and produce limited steps for students for each level of their dancing. In contrast, other instructors are more focused on choreography, and their teaching approach tends to include a large variety of steps and artistic expressions. Regardless of a student's level of ability, students need a methodical and progressive form of instruction, so the quality of the dancing will not be negatively affected. As judges, we look for quality, not quantity. I recommend that, if you are new to dancing or competing, make sure you research your selected studio or instructor. Ask for the studio's syllabus and teaching approach to make sure you find the right fit for you.

Jessika Ferm: *What recommendations do you have for students who want to advance their dancing, learn more, or get faster results?*

Marianne Nicole: We believe that group classes enhance your individual lessons. If your studio offers group classes, take them. Learn the steps and the patterns in a group, so you come better prepared to work with your instructor on technique and partnering skills. That way, you don't have to spend your precious time dealing with things you could learn in a group setting.

John DePalma: Group lessons teach you how to dance from the waist down. They give you the mechanics: patterns, footwork, timing, and rhythm. Group lessons alone will not teach you how to dance or prepare you for competition though. Private lessons will teach you everything you need to know. But if you take private lessons alone, it will take you longer to accomplish the same goal as with group and private lessons combined. Most competitors start as social dancers. The students who walk into the studio and say "I want to compete" are few and far between. Group classes serve as a great bridge for those who love to dance. When combined with private instruction to perfect partnership, continuity of steps, and the natural characteristics of the dance, confidence will grow, and the student may consider competing as a result.

Jessika Ferm: What are some of your competition pet peeves?

Marianne Nicole: One of my pet peeves is inappropriate costuming. Competitors should consider what looks good on them, not necessarily what looks good on someone else. Newcomers are not expected to wear expensive gowns, as they may not know if competing is for them at that early stage. There are some good practice-wear options that look great on the floor when matched with nice jewelry. It is important that you look prepared in both appearance and dancing skill. If your teacher isn't able to offer you guidance, ask a coach or a trusted dressmaker to give you feedback. I often help the students I coach pick or look for dresses. I sometimes even have a discussion with a dress designer prior to the student's meeting with the designer. I have the designer sketch something up for the student to look at.

John DePalma: One if my pet peeves is when teachers don't offer their students honest feedback about what they are wearing on the dance floor. Sometimes they aren't concerned about their students' costuming choices, and they aren't giving feedback that will help the student create a successful image in the long run. At our studio, all dresses are approved by us before students hit the competition floor. Most of our instructors are so well trained that the process has become seamless. Marianne and I are not shy about offering our solicited and unsolicited feedback on costuming. We want students to enter the floor feeling beautiful and looking appropriate.

*Jessika Ferm: **Would you share some ballroom "Dos and Don'ts" to help professionals compete with success?***

John DePalma: Marianne and I are "old school" when it comes to professionals projecting their "public" image on—and off—the floor. Aim to look well-groomed and presentable at all times when you're competing. Think of yourself being on the floor the moment you leave for the airport or get in your car to drive to the competition. Do the same when you show up for practice at the studio. You can never go wrong looking well-groomed. I believe in the saying, "Dress for Success." In some cases, how you present yourself publicly can be an inspiration to the student who desires a better public image. The student may turn to the instructor for guidance and suggestions. Who doesn't want a little bit of glamour in one's life?

Marianne Nicole: Please wear fishnets or panty house when you compete. I don't care how nice you think your legs are. You are still flashing bare skin in the faces of the judges. Consider it a mandatory part of costuming.

Interview Insight: Toni Redpath

Photo by: Deena Ensworth

JUDGE, COACH, CHOREOGRAPHER, AND FOUR-TIME UNDEFEATED U.S. BALLROOM CHAMPION

Toni and her husband Michael Mead are regular choreographers on the popular Fox TV Show, *So You Think You Can Dance.* Toni resides in San Diego, CA.

Jessika Ferm: *I have always admired your strong opinions and advice. As a judge and coach, what key advice would you offer dancers of all levels to help them take their dancing to the next level and compete with greater success?*

Toni Redpath: There are three key elements that I know work: effective goal setting, structure, and personal accountability. They really go hand-in-hand. Once you have your goals identified, you need to create disciplined actions in order to meet them. While your instructor is a big factor in your success, it ultimately comes down to how hard you are willing to work.

I recommend that you start by identifying what you want to accomplish, and create a plan for reaching those goals. Begin by meeting with your instructor and identifying one big goal that you want to accomplish. Then break that goal into smaller, more attainable ones. Map out what you want to achieve in two-month blocks. Remember, there can only be one champion at a time. If you make your goals about placement, you may be setting yourself up for disappointment. This process will help you stay focused, on course, and in charge.

For your practice sessions and lessons, create a structured process for warming up. Show up early to prepare, and stay late to record your accomplishments or obstacles. Remember, it is your responsibility to maximize your sessions.

During competitions, create a structured process for everything from warming up to showing up in the ballroom. This will assist with managing your mental game, nerves, and stress.

After each competition or practice, review your progress, audit yourself, and ask for your instructor's feedback. Consider what is working—what is helping you get closer to your goals—and what you still need to work on. For example, if you bought a video of yourself competing, sit down and slowly watch each of your dances. Then identify what you can do to "self-medicate" or fix any problems. If necessary, make a checklist and work your way through it.

Don't wait for your instructor to point out your mistakes or flaws. Take personal responsibility for your dancing. Evaluate and correct the things that you know you can fix yourself. When you have reached your limit, ask your instructor or coach for help.

Jessika Ferm: Tell the reader a bit more about what you recommend to help create a structure for warming up and getting ready to compete.

Toni Redpath: The more structure you have in your warm-up process, the easier it is to remember what to do and be consistent when competing. I'm a big believer in mimicking success. If you want to be successful at something, copy someone who has already done it. Look at someone who is where you want to be, and copy that person. Don't make it any harder for yourself than necessary.

For example, I use a five-step process for getting ready to dance and compete. As you can see, it involves a set structure that helps me stay focused and organized. I recommend this process for anyone from "Baby Bronzer" to Professional.

Step 1: Physical Warm Up: To get started, I do anything that gets the whole body warmed up. I once did a Paula Abdul workout video to get warmed up, but it can be anything from cross training to yoga or treadmill.

Step 2: Dance-Specific Warm Up: Once you are warmed up, it's time to get your dance body ready. For example, if you are dancing Rhythm or Latin, you want to make sure your hips are loose and stretched. If you are doing Standard or Smooth, make sure your back and neck have been adequately warmed up. [There are several great warm-up videos available from DanceVision, featuring Toni's dance warm ups. You can access them here: dancevision.com. Type in Toni Redpath and look for the American Style Smooth Solo Smooth Exercises.]

Step 3: Stretching: Make sure each muscle is warmed up by stretching carefully.

Step 4: Mental Warm Up: Your mental warm up should not be underestimated. I used to do three visual rounds before I competed (if you are new to dancing, one of these rounds may be plenty).

I closed my eyes and considered my dancing from the audience's point of view. I asked myself, "How do they perceive me?" Then I saw myself from my own perspective, and I asked, "How do I feel in my own body?" The last point of view was from Michael, my dance partner. I asked myself, "How do I feel to him?" When I looked at myself from Michael's perspective, I had to picture Michael's steps and figure out how he moved. This really helped me appreciate his position in the dance relationship. I always saw myself better than I was. The beauty of doing so is that sometimes I danced that well, and sometimes I didn't. Either way, I always visualized the best version of myself and my dancing.

Step 5: Connection Exercises With My Partner: The last step is to connect with your partner. The first four steps are your responsibility. It's not until this stage that you check to see how you flow together. If both parties have done the first four steps, the last step is a lot more productive and sets you up for greater success.

Jessika Ferm: *Many new-to-intermediate competitors are often confused by the judges' scores and how the judging process works. Would you shed some light on how you judge, and what goes into your process?*

Toni Redpath: I can understand that the judging process is confusing at times. As a judge I have one key principle. I judge or mark what I see in the moment, no matter what I know a particular couple is capable of or how well I have seen them dance in the past. I never deviate from that. If you make a significant mistake as I'm judging you, that is what I have to mark. That is why I sometimes mark a couple a certain way in one heat, yet mark them totally differently the next time I see them. The more consistently a couple dances, the more consistent my scores will be.

When I judge I look for three specific things:

1. **Technical ability** (including posture, footwork, frame, etc.)

2. **Dynamics** (how you physically connect with your partner, what the couple does dynamically to the music, what kind of energy they exude, how they interact with each other, etc.)

3. **Intent** (how you interact emotionally with your partner, what story you are telling, how the couple is able to project their message to the audience and each other, etc.)

For Bronze dancers, I'm not looking for the third one. I may not even be looking as much at the second one. Instead I look at their technical ability and the confidence they are exuding. Smiling is a big part of confidence. Also, it's important to keep your eyes up and engaged, not glossed over. I know that when a dancer is connecting with the audience visually, he or she isn't counting any more, and the dancing flows nicely.

You can often tell before the music even starts how a person is going to dance. The attention to detail that students put into their dancing, from their grooming to the way they carry themselves on the floor, says a lot about their training and coaching. If someone looks impeccable, I know that the instruction or coaching has been good.

Jessika Ferm: *Tell the reader more about your opinions on costuming and appearance. What advice do you have for competitors of all levels on stage presence?*

Toni Redpath: There is a lot to say about costuming and appearance, but these three categories will help any level dancer look and feel his or her best.

1. **Physical fit:** The costuming has to be age-appropriate. Avoid showing too much skin, especially as you get older. Look as much at the back as the front. See if anything gets caught when you are in dance position. You need to know what your body looks good in. Don't worry about what looks good on the hanger or mannequin.

2. **Aesthetics:** A good rule of thumb is "simple is better." It doesn't have to be bright to get our attention. Avoid the "kitchen sink." Too much "stuff" just makes it look like you are trying too hard. I love it when a dress is beautifully cut, and I would consider wearing it to a really nice party. A good rule of thumb: ask yourself if you would wear the dress to the Oscars. Consider whether or not a champion at Blackpool would wear it. It doesn't have to be really expensive; it just has to be classy.

3. **Ask an expert:** When buying your first three-to-five dresses, either bring a coach along, or text a photo to your coach for his or her opinion. Remember, most coaches are also judges. They know what looks good on the floor and on you.

Jessika Ferm: *What are some of the key tips you would share to get someone ready to compete and to help set realistic expectations?*

Toni Redpath: Before you even get to the first competition, build into your practice all the things that may go wrong. For lady competitors, this may mean practicing trust-building exercises, such as dancing a portion of the routines with their eyes closed. For gentlemen competitors, it may be preparing a routine for a smaller floor with chairs placed in awkward positions in order to improve floor crafting skills. Other great tips are to make the music beat too fast or too slow, or dance the routine in the studio when there are several other couples present. These strategies will help you feel in advance what it is like to respond to interruptions and distractions on the competition floor. The more skilled you are at handling these situations, the more confident and relaxed you will be.

While you sometimes dance and perform with great flow and are able to execute routines almost flawlessly, other times you're just not able to show up on the floor the way you did in practice. Nerves and people get in the way, and it isn't uncommon to go back as many as two months in your skill level once you hit the competition floor. Most often, you are dancing what you practiced two months ago. Remember that all the great things you learned over the past two months have not been stored into muscle memory yet. When you compete, your body will naturally respond and produce what you have memorized. That is why I recommend that teachers underwhelm the student at the first competition. Students will often ask the teacher for more steps or more complicated moves right before a competition, because they think this will get the judges' attention or help them look more competitive. The exact opposite is actually true. If you can do five steps, only use three on the competitive floor. You want to go out there feeling as though you could do so much more, yet doing the basics really well. That builds confidence, and you get a feeling like, "I've got this." If you do a round in the studio, and it overwhelms you even one bit, it's too much. Scale it back. The stress will show, and you won't fool anybody. One of my pet peeves is seeing people doing material outside their skill set.

Jessika Ferm: *Please share some of your other pet peeves as a judge.*

Toni Redpath: I get annoyed and sad when I see people overwhelmed for no good reason. I get frustrated at the teacher and upset for the student. I also get peeved when people are not spending the time they should on the fundamentals. My other pet peeve is when a dancer looks beautiful technically but is missing the emotion and partner dynamics. The opposite is also true—when a person is into the music and feeling of the dance but has lost the technique. I guess my pet peeve is when the three areas I judge (technique, dynamics, intent) are out of balance.

Jessika Ferm: *What "Dos and Don'ts" would you offer competitors of any level to help them compete with grace and joy?*

Toni Redpath: Don't ask me about your dancing if you don't work with me. If I don't have time to watch a video or really look at your dancing up close, I can't offer insightful information. I work mostly with professional dancers, so this would apply more to them. For amateur dancers, please know that I don't like to engage in long conversations with specific people while at a competition. Though I may enjoy your company or dancing, I don't want it to look like I favor one student over another.

Don't watch fellow competitors if they are dancing in heats prior to yours. This can produce unnecessary "head trash," and you may become overly focused on their dancing or abilities and forget to focus on your own journey. If you catch yourself, try to reconnect with why you dance and what you are at the competition to accomplish. How they dance, you have no control over. How you perform, you do.

Do practice in your dress prior to wearing it on the competition floor. Always do a test run, preferably in full hair and makeup. You don't want to discover that you get caught up in your dress or jacket while you are out on the floor.

Do find a professional makeup artist to prepare for competition. They are readily available on competition organizers' websites. If you can't find one, I know many dancers who have had excellent makeup help from drag queens. No one seems to know more about makeup and femininity than a man who strives to look like a woman.

Interview Insight: Kasia Kozak

WORLD AND U.S. CHAMPION LATIN DANCER, JUDGE, COACH, FOUNDER OF KASIA'S HIGH HEELS BOOT CAMP, AND CO-AUTHOR OF *MOVE LIKE A CHAMPION*. SHE RESIDES IN SAN DIEGO, CA.

Jessika Ferm: *You have had an amazing amateur and professional ballroom competing career. What lessons did you learn along that way that you believe would help students compete with greater joy and grace?*

Kasia Kozak: My first tip would be to avoid over-focusing on winning. You have to want to win and be ready to "embrace the tiger within," but if you make it all about winning, your natural driver will come from an intense and often-negative energy. It may make you win, but it won't make you embrace and enjoy the journey.

My second tip is to stick to what you know. If you are competing for the first time, don't try to change too many things at once. You won't be able to process everything, so stick to a few basic strategies like "shoulders down" and "connect with your partner." Adding too many goals will only confuse you.

My last tip would be to exaggerate the details. For advanced dancers, we are looking for expression, technique, and precise movement. Ask yourself, "What do I want to highlight?" and "How clear are my movements and steps?"

Jessika Ferm: *What are some of your pet peeves as a judge?*

Kasia Kozak: While I'm not big on pet peeves, I don't like seeing dancers settle for average or not try their hardest to be the best they can be. I realize they may not always be able to push their limits in every heat, but I do want to see them try to do their best.

Jessika Ferm: *What made you create Kasia's High Heels Boot Camp, and what benefits do students get from taking it?*

Kasia Kozak: The idea behind my boot camp was to help women become strong, independent female dancers and give them exercises and drills that they could use to improve their dancing on their own. I also wanted to give them a sense of control and confidence in their dancing by preparing them for the performance aspects of dance competition.

The most common feedback I get from ladies who participate in my boot camp and other workshops is the feeling of empowerment. I love the fact that they take what they learn in my dance workshop and use it to enhance all aspects of their lives.

Photo by: Deena Ensworth

Interview Insight:
Michael Mead

JUDGE, COACH, CHOREOGRAPHER, AND FOUR-TIME
UNDEFEATED U.S. BALLROOM CHAMPION.

Michael and his wife, Toni Redpath, are choreographers on the
popular Fox TV show, *So You Think You Can Dance*. Michael
resides in San Diego, CA.

Jessika Ferm: *Toni and you have been my mentors throughout
my dancing journey. I still use several of the key concepts that
you taught me when I first started dancing. What tips or strategies would you share with soon-to-
be or newer competitors to help them dance with greater ease and joy?*

Michael Mead: There are certain attributes that are desirable and expected of a professional or a
high-level amateur dancer. A dancer who is new to competition will not necessarily be aware of
these things. The instructor of new competitors is responsible for advising them on grooming,
performance on the floor, and conduct both on and off the floor. As a new competitor, you
should look for an instructor who will focus not just on getting you ready technically, but also
will offer the detailed advice necessary to produce a comprehensive product "package."

Let's look at two types of competitors. First there is the "pure amateur" dancer who competes
for the love of dancing and for whom placements are secondary. These dancers tend to be
more emotionally driven, and their primary focus is to enjoy the process of competing and
connecting with other dancers throughout the event.

Then there is the "professional amateur," for whom competing is more goal- oriented. They
prepare, practice, and often perform like professionals. They use competitions as a measuring
stick to gauge their improvements or accomplishments. During the event, they tend to be more
focused on the elements that will help them produce a better performance. That can sometimes
sideline their socializing with other dancers while competing.

There is no good or bad type. You may start as a "pure amateur" and find that you love it so
much that you increase your commitment and focus as you go along. Or you may find that you
really enjoy the competitive side of placing better, and then want to explore what it takes to get
there.

The same can also be true in the reverse. You may begin competing as a "professional amateur" and discover that the pressure of placing well or being constantly judged takes away the joy for you.

Here are three important things to consider in evaluating if competing is right for you: *(1) know yourself; (2) pick the right partner; and (3) create a (business) plan to lay out a step-by-step path for reaching your goals.*

First, you need to know a bit about yourself, why you currently dance, how that relates to your motivations to compete, and what type of competitor you are. Ask yourself what it is about ballroom dancing that makes you want to participate in it. Then figure out what added-value you expect to gain by competing versus just dancing socially. This is important because the motivations and drivers of each individual are very different. If your heart is not in it, competing may feel like a chore.

The next thing you need to do to compete effectively is to pick the right partner/instructor. This is a partner sport, and you can't do it by yourself. You are literally attached to another person who is as much a part of your success as you are.

When you know what drives you to compete and what type of competitor you are, it will be a lot easier to select the right partner. For example, if you sense that you may be a "professional amateur," but your partner is more connected to the joy of dance and doesn't share your drive for placement or accomplishments, you will be mismatched. Similarly, if you are a "pure amateur" at heart, and your professional partner is a hard-core competitor, chances are you will lose your joy for dancing, and the partnership will be a challenge. When you understand yourself and what type of competitor you are, you will have more success selecting the right partner for you and your goals.

Most dancers start with the person they were matched with when they first walked into their studio. As your dancing progresses and you consider competing, you will need to make sure he or she is still the right fit.

Do your research to find the partner who best matches your goals. Just because they look good competing with their professional partners doesn't mean they are the right fit for your goals. Watch how they dance with their amateur students. See how they treat them on and off the floor. Consider what kind of reputation they have and what styles of dancing are they strong in. Ask them about their work ethic and share your goals with them. Make sure they are open to listening to what you want to accomplish. Remember, any time you take up a new competitive hobby or sport, you want to work with the best possible person in your area, who will give you the best information.

Once you begin dancing together, make sure you have or develop mutual respect and trust. In the Pro-Am relationship, an effective professional will understand, support, and champion the amateur's goals. He or she should not lose sight of the fact that it is a business relationship, in which the professional is the service provider, and the amateur is the client. The amateur's goals should always be uppermost and should guide the professional's approach. At the same time, the amateur must understand and trust that the professional has the experience and wisdom to suggest effective strategies for reaching competitive goals. If you don't have respect and trust, the partnership is likely to fail.

It takes a certain degree of maturity from both sides to build a powerful partnership. Professionals sometimes need to sublimate their own desires to dance and perform at the highest level they are capable of, and instead focus on being a great teacher and partner in order to further the amateur's goals. The amateur must also work hard on managing emotions while competing and remember that it is not the professional's job to make sure your every need is met. It's not a bad idea for both parties to remember that neither party is irreplaceable. Relationships change over time, and both parties can chose a different path at any time.

The last tip is to create a business plan together. If you have identified your dancing goals and found the right partner, you need to develop a plan that is feasible and attainable. Consider what you are willing to invest, in terms of your finances and time. Review your goals and decide if the resources you are able to allocate to the sport will make you happy and fulfilled. A business plan will allow you to carefully review your financial and time allocations and map out a plan to accomplish the most with the resources you have available. It helps both sides with goal-planning if you are honest with your partner and share what you are prepared to invest in your hobby.

Jessika Ferm: *You have some great tips for measuring whether you have had a successful competition or not. Would you please share some of your favorite ones?*

Michael Mead: Absolutely. Here are a few that would help a competitive dancer at any level:

1. Get a video of at least one round at every competition. This gives you an objective view of your dancing, and you can identify the areas you need to improve and work on before the next competition.

2. Review the video with your coach. Identify small achievable improvement goals that are within your control. When you assign a small goal for each competition, you can easily assess if you are improving. This is why competing is so helpful. It provides you with constant opportunities to improve and get feedback.

3. Ask yourself, "Did I execute the material I've been working on in practice on the competitive floor?" If the answer is yes, be happy with your accomplishments; you have achieved your goal of improving your performance. If not, consider what you need to change or improve on to make it happen next time.

4. Focus on what you can control. We tell the professional couples we work with that competition placement or marks should not be your primary focus. You have no control over who else turns up to compete, how they dance, or who the judges are. Your results will fluctuate, depending on variables that are totally outside of your control. The only thing you have control over is what you present on the floor, so focus on that and don't open yourself up to being jerked around emotionally by a results roller coaster. Remember, when you improve as a competitor, the results will change as well. Better results are almost always a byproduct of hard work between competitions.

5. Make the judges believe that you aren't making mistakes. Judges will believe whatever you tell them. Couples who react obviously and negatively when things go wrong tell judges that something went wrong, even if the judges didn't see it. For newer competitors, remember, it's not how good you are, it's how well you hide your errors. For judges, a couple who broadcasts weakness makes the job of selecting a loser (and thereby a winner) much easier.

Jessika Ferm: *What are some of your pet peeves as a judge?*

Michael Mead: Showing that something went wrong or being upset with your partner. When you compete, you have to prepare for how you are going to react when things go wrong. Reacting negatively on or off the floor may be momentarily emotionally satisfying in a self-indulgent way, but it disturbs the storyline you are presenting and downgrades the effectiveness of your presentation.

Another pet peeve is when a lady's hair falls out. Professionals and amateurs are expected to look well-groomed. A careless approach to your grooming and attitude is a distraction and can impact a judge's marks. Don't give a judge an easy reason to mark you down.

Interview Insight: Shalene Archer

Photo by: Alliance Video & Photography

WORLD AND U.S. PROFESSIONAL AMERICAN SMOOTH AND 9-DANCE CHAMPION, TOP PRO/AM TEACHER, AND COACH. SHE RESIDES IN NASHVILLE, TN.

Jessika Ferm: *You are not only a former World and U.S. Professional Smooth Champion, but also one of the most respected top teachers in the United States. What are some of the unique aspects about competing with gentlemen ballroom dancers?*

Shalene Archer: I feel so fortunate to work with and coach gentlemen dancers. There is something unique about ballroom dancing that blends together the physical, intellectual, and emotional aspects. Most men have participated in competitive sports or activities prior to dancing, but by the time they meet me, they're not in high school or college anymore, and their competitive outlets have dwindled. The truth is that, even if they have done competitive sports, they have rarely merged the intellectual and emotional aspects in ways they do while dancing. Dancing also becomes a huge pressure release from work, family, and other obligations that need their attention. It is a chance for them to have a moment of time when it is all about them AND they get to incorporate their mind, body, and emotions, which they find particularly challenging in a good way.

Very few of my gentlemen come to the studio knowing they want to compete. Instead, they usually want to take lessons because they don't want to look silly at social functions, or their significant others "made" them go. But as they start to dance and build confidence in their abilities to lead and learn music, it seems to tap into something deep within them. They start to remember that they love certain songs and how much dancing moves them. When they realize that they can compete in something they have a deep emotional connection to, which also requires intellectual rigor and stamina, it seems to be a perfect match. I feel blessed to be a part of this journey with them and see that spark ignite.

Jessika Ferm: *You have a structured approach to your lessons and a unique method for tapping into each student's unique strengths and learning style. What have you found to be especially helpful in producing a consistent track record of high-quality students?*

Shalene Archer: First, I would say it is structure and preparation. I am a left-brained individual, and it's one of the reasons I'm so uniquely tailored and fortunate to work with gentlemen who tend to be more left-brained or sequential in their learning. It's easy and natural for me to teach that way. I have found that my gentlemen are more eager to engage in the competitive journey if the path is clearly laid out for them. If they are under the impression that we are "flying by the seat of our pants," it makes them uncomfortable and resistant. While this can be true of many female dancers, it seems to especially true for my gentlemen.

I also believe that being an organized and flexible teacher helps my students succeed. I have lesson plans for each person and take notes from every lesson with highlighted key words that resonate for them. No student learns the same way, and I believe as teachers we need to be flexible and adaptable in order to meet each person's needs. Some students are visual learners, while others are auditory. It's my job to figure out what works best for them and find whatever way (even if it requires 100 different approaches) to teach them a specific concept or step. Once I find the "magic" word or phrase that resonates, I write it down in their folder. That way I can create truly individualized plans for each student. I bring this folder or list of key words to competitions and repeat them as we dance. It is a powerful teaching and learning tool because each student's word resonates with him, and he can adapt or adjust in the moment without us having a long conversation.

Finally, I would suggest setting realistic expectations. Each student has a different competing goal. Prior to starting a competing year or deciding to join a competition, we establish a goal and review our expectations. I remind them that what they may be able to produce in the studio while practicing may feel and look different on the competitive floor. I don't expect them to be perfect. If we can get to about 80 percent of what we are able to do in practice, I'm happy. This sometimes surprises my newer competitive students who often have unrealistic expectations of what they will be able to produce on the floor. The key is to make small changes each time and build up to big improvements.

Jessika Ferm: *These are such great points. What tips would you share with newer competitors to help them manage expectations and become their personal best?*

Shalene Archer: The competitive landscape can be confusing to newer competitors, and they don't always understand that there is a process that helps them become successful in the long run. There is a drastic difference between competing once or twice a year and competing consistently (six to 12 times a year). It's not realistic for newer dancers to achieve the results that the more frequent competitors experience, if they don't have opportunities to practice. Competing is a separate skill from dancing, and the more you compete, the more you fine-tune your skills. Frequent competing also helps you stay focused and challenged, which in turn pushes you to get better. I can't recreate the unique pressures and heightened awareness in practice that the competition experience offers. When students are intensely focused and their adrenaline is running, they learn faster and more deeply. There are actual studies that support this phenomenon. The more my students compete, the deeper their learning becomes, and the more successful they tend to be. It's always shocking to me how much better they are after a competition, and they often tell me that they get as much out of one competition as they do from 10 lessons.

I also train my newer competitors not to focus on placements. Instead we go back to their goals and evaluate how much of our routine we were able to get through or how well they felt they remembered their key words. Then placements become the icing on the cake. I help my gentlemen set realistic goals, like being in the final or in the top three, as opposed to winning first place.

It's often confusing for newer competitors to realize that, even when they dance their routines flawlessly and are on time and do their very best, they may not win. It's up to us teachers to explain that, while they did their very best, someone else may have done the same, and the judges picked the other person for a higher placement. It's important to remember that the judges are comparing the couples on the floor, and your best may not be enough to place in the top. That makes effective personal goal-setting so much more important, because you have to create goals that you are in control of accomplishing.

Jessika Ferm: *What is a non-negotiable that you share with students who want to compete?*

Shalene Archer: They have to check in to see if they are having fun. If they don't have fun competing, I recommend they do something else with their dancing. It doesn't mean that every single moment has to be fun, but the overall experience has to add to their increased happiness and fulfillment.

Jessika Ferm: *What one piece of competition advice will help competitors of any level get the most from their competitive experience?*

Shalene Archer: You need to dance for yourself and be present with your partner, not to win or make judges happy. When I competed as a pro with Ben Ermis we had several years when we kept getting second place and were stuck in the mode of "chasing" the top spot. One day, when I viewed our video after a major competition, I saw how tense I looked. It was obvious to me that I was trying too hard to be something that I thought I needed to be in order to win. At that moment, I decided to give up the chase and just dance for me and be totally present with Ben. That was the year we broke through to first place.

Jessika Ferm: *What advice do you have for getting re-energized and ready for the next competition after you have come back to the studio?*

Shalene Archer: I recommend you get a video after each competition (especially as you start to compete). If you don't want to record every dance, pick a round, so you have something to review with your teacher when you get back to the studio. The videos are important for both the student and the teacher, because while your teacher can feel you as you dance, teachers don't know what you look like to the judges.

Watching videos can be brutal, so I recommend doing so a few days after the competition and preferably with your teacher. I also tell my students that for every mistake they see, you have to point out something good. Videos are great teaching tools, but over-focusing on the negatives isn't healthy.

Lastly, enjoy the journey. All small positive changes add up to great results. Slow and steady wins the race.

3

How Do I Deal With All These Emotions?

I am consumed with the fear of failing. Reaching deep down and finding confidence has made all my dreams come true.

- ARSENIO HALL

photo by: Mark Halverson Photography

In this chapter, we will take a look at one of the most challenging aspects of ballroom dancing: managing your emotional game. My first book, *The Ballroom Dance Coach: Expert Strategies to Take Your Dancing to the Next Level*, is designed to help coach you along the emotional journey that all dancers, professional and amateur, go through as they develop their dancing. In it, we talk about the four stages of learning:

Stage 1: Unconscious Incompetence: You don't know what you don't know, and you feel great!

Stage 2: Conscious Incompetence: You know what you don't know, and you begin to experience a series of challenging emotions and thoughts.

Stage 3: Conscious Competence: You know what you know and don't know, and you feel increased confidence and less confusion.

Stage 4: Unconscious Competence: You no longer think about what you are doing or how you are doing it because it has become second nature.

Stage 2 is the most challenging stage, and it happens over and over again. Each time you learn a new style of dance, or as you move from social dancer to competitor, you'll go through it. It happens when you have to learn new routines or when you step up a level, from Bronze to Silver or Silver to Gold. Remember, this stage is important and necessary. It is where you grow and evolve. The trick to moving to Stage 3 with greater ease is to manage the mental and emotional process. In short, there is no skipping Stage 2. You can, however, learn to move through it quicker. This chapter will teach you several key strategies for doing so.

Most successful dancers have (often through experience) learned how to manage the emotional roller coaster that comes with this sport. They have sharpened their mental game to ensure that they project confidence and power on the floor, even when they may not feel those emotions. Jerry Lynch, the author of *The Way of the Champion: Lessons from Sun Tzu's The Art of War and other Tao Wisdom for Sports & Life* (Tokyo: Tuttle Publishing, 2006) shares:

> "How far you go, how great you become in athletics and life, depends on how strongly you become connected–body, mind, heart–to the situation, the arena the, relationship, the task. Champion athletes are like great actors, who, while on stage, project their deep energy, love, passion, courage, feelings, by 'acting as if' they truly are the character. It's not their technical skill that makes them stand out, but their presence, their ability to connect with true emotion" (p.59).

It's virtually impossible to manage emotions without having your "mental game" in order. If you skipped that part of Chapter 2, I highly recommend you take a few moments to read the section titled "Getting Your Mental Game On," to make sure you have learned the foundational mental tools that will assist you in managing your emotions.

Understanding the Emotional Roller Coaster of Competing

> **"** The one thing I've learned in the last ten years is that successful artists don't get paid to write and sing songs, they get paid for the psychological roller coaster they're going to have to ride. That's the hard work."

> — ENRIQUE IGLESIAS

Ballroom competing can bring out the best and worst in you. Many of us who compete are intensely passionate about our dancing. Under increased pressure, emotions and behaviors that we would otherwise hide or manage, may show up unexpectedly.

I had no idea, when I started to compete, that I would be forced to confront some of my most challenging behavioral traits—giving me the chance to develop better communication skills, patience, and self-awareness. I had little awareness of the emotional ups and downs that come with competing, and I certainly hadn't prepared in advance. The good news is that you are reading this book and have the tools you need to prepare to compete and manage challenging emotions with more grace and ease.

As much as this sport is about technical expertise and artistry, it is very much an emotional and mental sport as well. I have watched several friends start to compete, and then give it up because they couldn't handle the pressures that come with being continuously judged, criticized, or evaluated.

Any insecurities or baggage you carry will likely show up on and off the floor during your competition. Some of my "shadow behaviors" under stress include being judgmental, angry, dictatorial, and blaming others (mostly my instructor). Shadow behaviors are our "dark sides." We can't always see them, but others can.

When we compete and the pressure is on, our shadows often appear too quickly for us to manage effectively in the moment. If we don't have advance strategies for handling them well, they can trigger emotional fistfights that may significantly damage our partnerships. I have learned, through some painful experiences, to set up some basic "rules for competing" in order to keep my emotions in check.

One of my rules is not to offer my instructor feedback about our dancing until several hours after the heats or when the competition is over. We do offer each other small corrections that we know we can implement immediately, like "give me more connection here" or "lift your side up." But for issues that require more work or help, we wait until after the competition.

I'll never forget how I learned this difficult lesson and established this particular communication rule. It was at Millennium Dancesport Championships, and the incident almost ended my dance partnership.

My instructor Jeffrey Goltiao and I were doing International Standard for the first time. We had agreed to be kind and supportive of one another our first time out. As the competition moved along, the pressure kept building, but I felt positive and excited—until they decided to remove the rope barrier that divides the ballroom in half. I suddenly realized I had to do our routine on the big floor.

Up to this point, we had only practiced our routines on a half-floor, as that is all our studio allows for. This small, last-minute change of plans really threw me for a loop. The style and all the figures were new to me, and I wasn't comfortable switching-up the routine at a moment's notice. But ready or not, we headed out onto the floor.

Any insecurities or baggage you carry will likely show up on and off the floor during your competition.

We danced our heats without any major hiccups, but as we exited the floor, I felt my anger swell up. I began feeling irate. Why hadn't Jeffrey prepared our routines for a large floor? How could he have been so careless? I paid a lot of money for this competition! If we didn't place well, it would be because we didn't prepare enough, and that just wasn't acceptable! We made it into the area just outside the ballroom before I exploded. We had a short and intense conversation before both of us headed in opposite directions, hoping to not bump into each other again for several hours.

Looking back, I realize that I completely over-reacted, and that I, in fact, had broken our agreement to be supportive of one another. In truth, I was angry at myself and felt stupid for not knowing how to adjust to a larger floor. My emotions got the best of me, and I took it all out on Jeffrey. I lost my composure in front of other competitors and any judges who happened to be walking by at the time of our heated discussion (a big no-no in ballroom dancing). Luckily the incident didn't break-up our partnership. Until now, I don't think anyone, other than Jeffrey and me, even knew it took place.

The point is that challenging emotions will surface if you compete. The difference between being a successful or happy competitor versus an angry or frustrated competitor resides in your ability to deal with emotions, so they don't affect you negatively.

Remember, you are dancing in a partnership sport. While your partner may be your professional ballroom instructor, he also is a human being with emotions, feelings, needs, and wants. As a student, it isn't necessarily your job to help manage your instructor's or dance partner's emotions, but you can certainly help by learning how to manage your own.

Toni Redpath and Michael Mead list this great remind in their "Elite Competitor" program:

- If you have health problems, see a doctor.

- If you have relationship problems, see a counselor.

- If you have competition performance issues, see a sports psychologist or a life coach.

- If you are overwhelmed with stress, anxiety, or depression, see a psychiatrist.

- If you have weight or energy issues, see a nutritionist or fitness professional.

- If you have troubles with any aspect of your *dance training* or competition planning, see your instructor or dance coach.

Your dance instructor, coach, or partner is not trained or equipped to help you deal with all the emotional aspects of dancing and competing. While they may be great partners and help us through difficult times, it is not their job or responsibility to hold us together emotionally. It is our job to address our emotional issues and seek appropriate resources to help us dance and compete with fewer bumps in the road.

Please note that the previous list is meant to prove the point that your instructor/coach can't serve every need you have. There are plenty of professional resources available to help you with the various aspects of your competition preparation. There are also many free and inexpensive resources online and in the bookstore to help you get your mental and emotional game on. Please see Chapter 8 for additional resources.

An accomplished Pro/Am teacher, Tony Scheppler and his student Connie Marshall have learned to overcome several challenging emotions while dancing together for almost five years. Both Tony's and Connie's interview insights share some great tips for overcoming obstacles and building a long-term partnership based on mutual trust and respect. You can find their insights on pages 118-121.

One of Tony's tips for newer competitors is to "shake it off" when things don't go as planned, or when you don't place where you would like. We all make mistakes. It's important to be able to quickly move along before unproductive emotions take hold.

The next section is designed to help you identify some of the most common, challenging emotions you may encounter and prepare strategies for dealing with them ahead of time. I hope they help you avoid some of the painful experiences I have had to deal with along the way. If not, they may offer your partner and you a chance to discuss feelings in advance and design strategies or communication rules that will help you dance with greater joy and build a partnership of respect and trust.

Common Feelings and Emotions Before, During, and After a Competition

 Feelings come and go like clouds in a windy sky. Conscious breathing is my anchor."

- THICH NHAT HANH

Dancing is emotional. It allows us to experience the spectrum from deep joy to extreme disappointment. Those dancers who learn to manage their emotions while competing have a heads up on the competition. Undefeated World and U.S. Pro/Am Open Gold Lady C Champion Beverly Moore discovered that feeling terrified, extremely nervous, and almost sick came with the territory on her beginning competition journey. You can discover more about how she and her teacher learned to handle these challenges in her interview insight on page 122. The important point is to know that every competitor goes through a series of emotions that are difficult to manage at first.

Next I will share will a list of the common emotions you may experience before, during, and after a competition. You'll also find counter-strategies to help you minimize the negative consequences of these emotions.

According to several etymological dictionaries, the word emotion is derived from the French word émouvoir, which is based on the Latin emovere, meaning to "move" or "stir up." As we begin to physically move to music, it is almost impossible not to activate a host of emotions, some positive and some more challenging. To clarify, emotions are feelings about and reactions to something or someone specific, and they usually involve our ego. Emotions are felt in the body. A feeling is the inner-body experience that results from an emotion. In short, we may be angry (an emotion), and we may feel our heart beating faster (a feeling). To make it easier, we will combine emotions and feelings, as they are often difficult to separate. Just remember, while we may say "I feel (inadequate, angry, defeated, etc.)" we may actually be describing an emotion.

INADEQUATE OR "NOT GOOD ENOUGH"

Feeling inadequate or "not good enough" goes with the territory in DanceSport. The beauty of ballroom dancing is that we will never "arrive" or complete our journeys. There is always something more to learn or discover. And because this is a partner sport, we have twice as many opportunities to grow. How we respond to our challenges is what truly matters. If we fall into the trap of beating ourselves up or comparing ourselves to others, we lose. We may find ourselves questioning why we can't do something other people can do, or why we don't have the look or abilities that other dancers have, and then we lose track of all the wonderful things we already know and can do.

Counter-Strategy: Comparing ourselves to others is never a good idea. If you find yourself not feeling "good enough," make a commitment to stop comparing yourself. Period. Honor where you are in your dancing by remaining positive and supportive of your talents and abilities. The truth is that most of the time we "compare our insides to other people's outsides," and we have no idea what goes on for them. We tend to assume that what we observe is the truth, and it oftentimes isn't. Remember to reward yourself and recognize the talents you have. As you begin to do so, the feeling of inadequacy will dissipate or even disappear, and you will embrace and enjoy exactly where you are on your dancing journey.

EMBARRASSED

Some dancers are not extroverts by nature and feel embarrassed being in the spotlight. Others are perfectionists and have learned somewhere along the way that they should do things perfectly, and when they don't, they feel embarrassed. Other dancers are private and become uncomfortable trying to produce a "sexy" or "serene" look while dancing or performing. In discussing the emotion of embarrassment, we aren't referring to having an unexpecting dress malfunction or an unchoreographed fall on the floor; we are referring to an ongoing feeling of embarrassment while dancing.

Counter-Strategy: Learning to let go of control and be completely present will ease the feeling of embarrassment. Remember that most dancers are slightly nervous or uncomfortable when they try a new dance or look. The most important lesson to learn is to not take yourself too seriously. Being gentle and allowing yourself to "just be" can significantly reduce the fear of looking foolish or not meeting your own high standards.

FRUSTRATED

Some of us lack the gift of patience! We want to get it now, and we tend to be overly hard on ourselves if we aren't able to accomplish or learn something. When we don't understand a step or a new move, we may start feeling frustrated and begin to block our ability to learn. If we aren't careful, we may take our frustrations out on our dance partners, which rarely leads to positive results. Unmanaged frustrations can cause debilitating results and can significantly hurt your partnership. If we get stuck in frustration mode, we limit our ability to access the real emotions that tend to linger just below the surface. We may use frustrations to mask feelings of insecurity, fear of success/failure, or inability.

Counter-Strategy: Give yourself a "timeout." When you start feeling frustration bubble up inside, tell yourself and your partner that you need a minute. Go to the restroom or sit down somewhere in the studio or outside the competition floor, uninterrupted. Take 10 long breaths, and remind yourself that your frustrations are just physical manifestations of your own insecurities. You may find it helpful to say to yourself, "It's okay that I don't know or understand how to do this right now. Someday I will." Or "I'm not perfect, and I'm in a new learning phase. I will get through this." One time at a competition, I had to give myself a timeout for several minutes. I retreated to a separate room and actually stomped my feet and acted like a two-year-old. I just needed to release my frustrations physically. (Should you feel the need to do so, please make sure you are alone! No one needs to see us acting like immature kids, especially our dance partners.) When I calmed down, I spoke to my partner about what I was feeling. I was afraid our coach (who was also judging us) wouldn't be pleased with our performance. I was acting out at my partner instead of addressing my feelings with our coach.

ANGRY

Depending on your unique makeup, genes, and experiences, you may find that anger is a frequent emotion that rears its ugly head during times of increased stress. It may be anger directed at self or others. Either way, the emotion is extremely powerful and if unmanaged can leave negative consequences in its wake. Displays of anger are usually extreme frustrations and inabilities to express emotions in constructive ways.

Counter-Strategy: Anger management is serious business. If you are naturally programmed (through nature or nurture) to ignite anger, you will need to work hard and be unwaveringly committed to managing this powerful emotion on your dancing journey. If the anger is directed inward, stop hurting yourself! Beating yourself up isn't going to make you a better dancer. It's going to make you an angry dancer, and no one wants to watch that. I know it isn't as easy as it sounds, but as with any endorphin- or addiction- related activity, you must stop doing it in order to get better. Most people who beat themselves up have low self-esteem. They are so used to berating themselves that they believe this is the only way to act. It's not the case, and it's extremely debilitating.

Make a commitment to yourself and your dance partner: no negative self-talk or self-deprecating language. If you are more likely to express your anger at others, your dance partner may be taking the brunt of your unmanaged anger. When you become angry and are ready to unleash on the next person you see, practice giving yourself a timeout. Remove yourself from the situation. As with managing frustrations, find a space to release your emotions (first ensuring you are alone). Another effective strategy is to breathe deeply and count to 100. This strategy seems deceptively simple. The power of breathing is that it increases the level of oxygen in our bloodstream, and our heart rate goes down. It sends messages to our brain that we are relaxed, and our anger is sure to dissipate. Remember, it is your responsibility to manage your anger. It is never okay to take your anger or unprocessed emotions out on others.

DEFLATED OR UNMOTIVATED

In practice and on the competition floor, it's easy to feel deflated or unmotivated. We may have tried over and over to learn a certain move or step. Or we may be trying our hardest to dance well, but everything seems to work against us. That's when we can begin to feel deflated or unmotivated. We may begin to seriously doubt our abilities to overcome the obstacles we see in front of us and may lose steam, pass judgments, or begin negative thinking. While feeling these emotions during short times in our dancing can be helpful, leaving us more focused and energized, wallowing in them can be seriously detrimental.

Counter-Strategy: When these feelings creep up, acknowledge them. Say to yourself, "I'm just feeling down or upset right now." Remind yourself that you know strategies to re-energize and to rediscover what motivates you to push through challenging times. Ask your dance partner to share positive feedback with you about your dancing or progress. Speak to a dance friend who understands the peaks and valleys of ballroom dancing. The most powerful way to handle these challenging emotions is to reach out and connect with others who understand what you are going through. Having a close-knit dance community is key in helping you through these powerful emotional stages.

DEFEATED

Some of us move from feeling deflated or unmotivated to defeated. We may have been programmed to think that, when things get hard, we should give up or stop trying. The truth is that dancing is difficult at times, and we have to consistently push ourselves beyond what we currently think we can do. Giving in to defeat will leave us feeling incomplete and inadequate.

Counter-Strategy: The feeling of defeat leaves us unempowered and victimized. It strips away the knowledge that we can rise up from any challenging situation. The good news is that the feeling of defeat is just our mind tricking us into thinking that we have to give up, when we don't. The next time the feeling of defeat descends upon you, repeat any of the following affirmations:

- I can do this, even though I know it's hard.

- I have the skills to overcome challenging situations; I have before.

- I don't give up.

- This time I will push through.

- I'm not a victim of my circumstances.

- I'm in charge, not my old programming.

- I can change anything about me that I want.

- I'm done feeling defeated.

PANIC

Under extreme pressure like competing, debilitating panic may set in. You may find yourself going blank or freezing in your tracks. Or you may have a strong physical response, including feelings similar to that of a heart attack or nausea. According to Scientific American and the Diagnostic and Statistical Manual (DSM), panic (or panic attacks) happens when stress builds up to a critical level. It is defined as "an abrupt and discrete experience of intense fear or acute discomfort, accompanied by symptoms such as heart palpitations, shortness of breath, sweating."

Counter-Strategy: To avoid moving from being excited or nervous to panicking, remember to take deep breaths often during stressful times. If you are spiritual, pray. Let go of your belief that you can affect or change the outcome of the situation you are in. Sometimes giving the situation up to a higher power takes the pressure off. Repeating positive affirmations such as "I can do this" or "I'm safe" can help relax your fears and bring your heart rate down. Remember to avoid isolation. Speak about your fears to your instructor or dance friends. Keeping fears hidden only amps up the feeling of panic.

DEPRESSED, SAD, OR "BLUE"

After a competition, it's not unusual to feel sad or a bit depressed. We call this the "competition blues," and most dancers experience it. I find that, even if I've have a successful competition, the day I return home, I feel a bit blue. When you compete, your body is at an all-time high, with "pleasure chemicals" such as dopamine, serotonin, and adrenaline flushing through your system. When you stop, your body needs to find its way back to homeostasis. It does that by reducing the "feel-good" chemicals. As a result, you may feel slight depression, moodiness, or sadness. If you haven't had a chance to compete yet, you may relate to the same emotional let-down if you've ever come back from a fantastic vacation and felt listless or apathetic the next day. If you'd like to learn more about this phenomenon, I recommend Loretta Graziano Breuning's *Psychology Today* article, "What a Let-Down! When Your Happy Chemicals Dip your Brain Concocts Failure," and Dean Hebert's blog post, "Post Race Depression" (coachdeanhebert.wordpress.com). Trust me, your brain is playing tricks on you, and almost all athletes experience it! You can find a direct link to it in Chapter 8.

Counter-Strategy: Plan for the "blues" and set up a time to meditate or pray when you get back from a competition. I find that taking a long walk with my dog or slowing down in general really helps me flush the sadness from my body. I also love snuggling up on the couch and watching a movie as a great antidote for the blues. The good news is that it rarely lasts more than a day, so don't worry. You will be back to your normal self in no time. If you find that the blues linger a bit longer, you may need to take a week off from practice or the studio. I have done this and find it tremendously helpful. Once I'm feeling great again, I get even more out of my lessons and the atmosphere at the studio.

Dealing with Performance Anxiety

> ❝ Anxiety is love's greatest killer. It makes others feel as you might when a drowning man holds on to you. You want to save him, but you know he will strangle you with his panic."

— ANAÏS NIN

Another key challenge is dealing with performance anxiety while competing. While it may manifest differently for different people (including but not limited to increased perspiration, heart palpitations, nausea, vomiting, frequent urination, jitters, excessive talking, hyper-activity, and memory loss), ballroom competing is sure to stimulate your nervous system. It's important to map out a plan to prepare for these emotions and feelings in advance, so they don't overwhelm or throw you off your game while you compete.

I've learned how to do so the hard way. My third competition was the Atlanta Open. We were doing a show dance for the first time, and I wasn't terribly comfortable with the routine. I was especially nervous as we were the third heat out of the entire competition, and I was still getting my competition sea legs. Our song was a slow, continuously rhythmical melody without words. As the music started, I was all set to go—at least for the first eight counts. After that, everything went blank. I had no idea where I was or what I was doing. I experienced a complete "blank out."

A few bars into the music, I saw my intructor's panicked face and realized I somehow had to find my way back into the song and finish the dance. After what seemed like an eternity, the song ended, and I was mortified. I remembered one of our coaches telling us never to show our mistakes on our faces, so I smiled broadly and took a deep bow. Then I went through the service area to my room and dealt with my feelings of utter defeat.

I didn't have more than 30 minutes to feel sorry for myself because after that fiasco, I had to go back down to dance Smooth. With renewed determination, I was sure that I would do well, which I did— until we weren't called back to finals in any of our dances. At that point, I was close to giving up and going home, but after a few minutes of indulging in my own personal pity-party, the competitor in me woke up. I had invested a lot of time and money in this competition, and I wasn't about to give up before it was over! The next day, for our Rhythm heats, nothing could stop me from brining my A-game, and I danced my heart out.

That was the year we won the "Best of the Best" Rhythm qualifier, which allowed us to compete in a show dance at the Ohio Star Ball, along with the best dancers in the United States. Back to the show dance—my performance anxiety was all too fresh after the Atlanta Open fiasco, and now I had to compete with the best Bronze dancers in the country, doing another show dance! To say I was nervous was an understatement.

To help manage my anxiety, my instructor and I sat down to identify areas were we could minimize the trigger points I had experienced in Atlanta. We changed the song to a fun and flirty Cha Cha/Rumba combo to create a sense of ease and flow. We picked a song that had words, so if I got lost again, I could easily find my way back. And we set a goal. The goal for our first Best of the Best show dance was to execute it without any major mistakes. That year, we placed seventh out of 13 couples, and I was so relieved. We met our goal! I also recognized that show dances are just not my thing. Some dancers absolutely love them, but apparently I'm not one of them, at least not yet. The point is that the better you know yourself, the better you can prepare, minimizing the triggers that cause performance anxiety.

Take a moment to write down what you know to be (or think may be) your responses to increased pressure or the need to perform. For example, you may need to visit the bathroom frequently, or you become quiet and withdrawn. You may get butterflies in your stomach or dry mouth. Take a moment to write them down here.

When I compete or think of competing, I tend to:

_____

_____

_____

Next, list what you will do to manage your nerves BEFORE they escalate. You may create a mantra that keeps you focused and in the-moment. Or you might practice deep-breathing techniques in the on-deck area. Or you may need to position your instructor and yourself close to a bathroom if you need to use it frequently. The key is to think it through before it happens, and design a strategy that will help you manage your emotions more effectively. If you are not sure at this moment, return to this exercise after your first competition and complete the answers below.

_____

_____

_____

While this "before, during, and after" emotional list isn't all-inclusive, it is designed to help you prepare mentally and emotionally in advance of your competition. To be a successful competitor, you must learn to manage emotions with grace. It may be helpful to remember that this skill is just as important as the skill of doing technically flawless routines. If you don't practice or prepare in advance, you won't achieve the results you want. As Kimberely Mitchell's mom used to remind her when she competed, "You can collapse off the floor!"

Let's take a moment to reflect on the emotions that you most need to work on.

- List at least one emotion that tends to show up before you compete or consider competing:

  _____

- What counter-strategy will you use to manage it while preparing for your next competition?

  _____

- List at least one emotion that tends to show up while competing or one that you may be afraid will show up:

  _____

- What counter-strategy will you use to manage it while dancing in your next competition?

  _____

- List at least one emotion that tends to show up after competing or one that you may anticipate will appear:

  _____

- What counter-strategy will you use to manage it after your next competition?

  _____

- What "competition communication rule" might your instructor and you want to create to avoid pushing one another's buttons while competing?

  _____

Remember, there are no "accidental champions." All top amateur and professional competitors prepare physically, mentally, AND emotionally for success.

 ## Chapter Summary

- Ballroom dancing can be an emotional roller coaster. The better you prepare to handle your emotions in advance, the less bumpy the ride will be.

- "Shadow behaviors" are the dark sides of our personality that tend to amplify during increased stress or pressure. We often have more difficulty seeing them than others do.

- Ballroom dancing is a partnership sport. Both your instructor and you have emotional triggers. Be kind and gentle with yourself and your partner.

- Your instructor is not your therapist. YOU are responsible for managing your own emotions. While he or she can help by not pushing your emotional triggers, in the end you are the only person responsible for how you feel and act.

- All top amateur and professional competitors experience a variety of emotions while competing. The difference is that they sharpen their "emotional game" just like any other skill and recognize that in order to be their personal best, they need to manage their emotions with grace.

- The more self-aware you are, the easier it will be to manage your emotions. You can't "fix" what you don't know is flawed.

- Most ballroom dancers experience some form of performance anxiety. They strategize in advance to ensure that their emotional triggers aren't activated unnecessarily.

- If you are aware of your emotional triggers, your partner and you can design "competition communication rules" to help manage the pressure more effectively while competing.

Dancing American Rhythm at my very first competition, the Cleveland DanceSport Challenge, in 2009. My dress was rented from Rhinestone Rentals, and hair and makeup were done by Lisa Bentley DeBevec.

Photo courtesy Alliance Video and Photography

"Dream" coaching with Dancing With The Stars celebrity Karina Smirnoff after a few weeks of dancing. I think all we did was work on my foot placements and posture. I had no idea what a "New Yorker" or "Alemana" was.

Photo courtesy of Barbara Wayman

Dancing American Smooth also at Cleveland DanceSport Challenge in 2009. My dress was rented from Rhythmic Rentals, and hair and makeup were done by Lisa Bentley DeBevec. Notice Toni Redpath judging us in the background.

Photo courtesy Alliance Video and Photography

The infamous "blank out" show dance at Atlanta Open in 2009. I look like I know what I'm doing, but I am completely lost. All I remembered was to smile. My dress was purchased from a vendor in Asia. Notice the lack of fishnet pantyhose. A mistake I won't make today.

Photo courtesy of Park West Photography

Beautiful "glamour shot" by Stephen Marino. I'm wearing my very first "big dress," which I bought from Designs to Shine. I still remember how "grown up" I felt. This photo was taken at the First Coast Classic Dancesport Championship in St. Augustine, FL in 2010.

Together with my dear friend Rebecca Klinger at our very first Ohio Star Ball in 2009. We met that year while dancing American Smooth and have been friends ever since. Never underestimate the friendships you may make in the on-deck area. My dress was rented from Rhythmic Rentals. I was so impressed when they told me that Jane Seymour had worn it on the first season of Dancing With the Stars.

Photo courtesy of Park West Photography

Award coins from Ohio Star Ball in 2009. I was so excited about these placements in pre-Bronze American Rhythm.

Photo courtesy of Barbara Wayman

Other competitions give out ribbons or paper tickets for the top-three spots. Here is Sophia D'Angelo accepting her placements at Maryland DanceSport Championships in 2013.

Photo courtesy Ryan Kenner Photography

My beautiful friend Helen Leach with her Amateur partner Jim Blakeslee at the Columbus DanceSport Classic 2013. Helen is wearing a gorgeous practice dress with matching jewelry. She exemplifies elegance and grace without an expensive gown. She had her hair and makeup professionally done.

Photo courtesy of Tom Wehrung

This is the Paso Doble in International Latin. I was surprised by how much I liked this dance. The beauty of trying different styles of dance is that you may find a particular dance that you really like and would like to explore more. I am wearing a dress by Doré Designs.

Getting into dance position for International Standard. There were 48 couples competing for the coveted top spots in several heats. We were blessed to make it to the final and place fourth. I'm wearing a Doré Designs dress.

In 2012 we competed in all four styles of dance for the first time at the Ohio Star Ball. It was an enormously challenging goal. I'm glad I did it and truly admire my fellow dancers who consistently do so.

One of the most precious moments of my early dancing journey. Placing first in American Rhythm Bronze. I'm wearing a Vesa dress I bought from a professional competitor.

American Smooth Tango in serious promenade position. This is one of my favorite Smooth dresses from Designs to Shine.

Gentleman competitor, Eric Leininger receives his top student award together with his professional instructor, Katt Baumgartner at the Columbus DanceSport Classic 2013. He worked hard and looks like he is enjoying his reward!

Top Teacher Diego Semprun with his competing ladies at the Columbus DanceSport Classic in 2013.

Professional ballroom instructor Katt Baumgartner with her student Rick Hoffman. He is displaying a great example of a well-groomed and dressed gentleman competitor dancing International Latin.

Jeffrey and I meet our new ballroom friend Cindy Ronveaux at Maryland Dancesport Championship in 2013. Make it a habit to stop and chat with your fellow dancers. You will be amazed at the wonderful people you will get to know.

Photo courtesy of Ryan Kenner Photography

Top Teacher Forrest Vance tracks his students' successes during the award ceremony. Many teachers keep a careful eye on the placements for each heat by bringing the heat list and a pen.

My friend Marcy Garson accepting her first-place awards from Judge Chuck Danza at Maryland DanceSport Championships. I love the happiness she exudes.

Nervously awaiting our scores at Emerald Ball Dancesport Championships 2013. When awards are announced, all who have competed in the previous heats line up to receive their placement awards. My beautiful turquoise dress is by Doré Designs.

One of the thrilling moments of competing. This time we were lucky enough to earn the Silver 9-Dance Championship title at Emerald Ball Dancesport Championships. It's not always easy for the judges to manage the intricate hair creations of ballroom competing. Experienced Judge, Edward Simon is doing his best.

One of the best parts of competing—hanging out and competing with my dancing BFFs. Here I am with Christina Diaz at the Emerald Ball Dancesport Championships. We both had a great competition and were fortunate enough to walk away with first-place medals.

Judges hard at work at Emerald Ball Dancesport Championships 2013. Judges will carry clipboards to make their marks and will continue to watch until they have made their selections. Some judges save their marks until the very end and others pick their favorites early.

The final seven couples of American Smooth
scholarships are lined up for their photo at
the Columbus DanceSport Classic, 2013.
The wining couple stands next to the judges.

Photo courtesy of Tom Wehrung

Linda Gieseke and Diego Semprun
dance a fierce International Tango at the
Columbus DanceSport Classic. Linda is
wearing an International Standard dress
and you can tell by the floats.

Photo courtesy of Tom Wehrung

Don't forget to practice your bowing skills. It is a great exercise to do on your own and each dancer has his or her unique style of expressing audience appreciation. Bows range from wide expressive gestures to humble curtseys. If you are in pre-Bronze, start with something a bit more reserved. As your dancing skill and success expand, try something more elaborate. I'm wearing a beautiful dress from Designs to Shine.

Photo courtesy of Ryan Kenner Photography

Lisa Bentley DeBevec making sure Coralli So's hair is tight and neat in preparation for her Smooth dancing. Notice the cans of hairspray behind Lisa. Ballroom hairstyles require significant hairspray!

Each year, Next Level Dancing, LLC awards a scholarship to a deserving person who otherwise may not be financially able to compete. This is Emily Meinert, our 2012 award recipient. She attends Otterbein University and hopes to become a ballroom instructor.

Dancing With The Stars celebrity Louis van Amstel has designed a fabulous program to increase your ballroom stamina called LaBlast. It incorporates familiar ballroom steps with fun and engaging music. I was fortunate to meet Louis and Pamela Conn, one of his Master Trainers, during the Columbus Health and Fitness Expo. To learn more about LaBlast, visit LaBlast.com.

Photo courtesy of Yarrington Studio Photography & Design

Chapter Takeaways

Take a moment to summarize your takeaways from this chapter. These notes will come in handy as you take the next important steps in preparing to compete.

After reading this chapter I realized that:

_____

My most valuable takeaway is:

_____

I learned the following about how I need to manage my emotions while dancing and competing:

_____

My most challenging emotion while dancing and competing is:

_____

My counter-strategy for managing this emotion is:

_____

I will commit to doing the following in preparation for my next competition to make sure I manage my emotions with grace:

_____

I will speak to my instructor/partner about my most challenging emotions relating to my dancing and/or competing on _____ (day).

I'd like to establish the following "competition communication rule" to ensure that I don't push his/her buttons or trigger mine as we compete:

_____

Photo by: Ryan Kenner Photography

Interview Insight: Tony Scheppler

U.S. RISING STAR SMOOTH CHAMPION, THIRD PLACE
BLACKPOOL FINALIST IN THEATER ARTS, AND WINNING
PRO-AM TEACHER

Tony also acts in movies and commercials. He resides in
Canton, OH.

Jessika Ferm: *I know that you have some great tips for helping
your competitive students reach their goals. Please share how
you help elevate your students' skills.*

Tony Scheppler: Many students get excited about competing, and we begin by identifying their
goals. Then we look at how many lessons they are able to take per week to ensure that they are
setting themselves up for success. Once they have clarity about their goals and are committed to
the plan, we begin preparing.

Competing students must be able to take at least three or four lessons a week. I ask all my
students to be in the studio 10-to-15 minutes before their lessons. I want to see them warming
up, so we don't waste time.

Most experienced judges look at legs and feet to make sure that the competitor has a good
grasp of the basics. It is extremely important to me that my competing students understand the
fundamentals of dancing before we do more advanced movements.

I use a concept I call "PAR," which stands for Prepare, Action, Recover. It helps students
understand how to maximize each movement. First they need to show their preparation, then
they move into action, and finally they need to recover before preparing again.

I always encourage my competitive students to objectively look at their dancing. The best way
to do so is to get a video of their dancing. Then review the recording five times, each from a
different perspective. The first perspective is looking at the video without the volume on. Ask
yourself if you can identify which dance you are doing, and observe your own movements. It's
helpful to count from the very first step and check if you "commence to rise at the end of one,
continue to rise on two and three, lower at the end of three" in the Waltz. Keeping the volume
off will enable you to see your strengths and flaws much more clearly.

The second time, look at the other competitors and the judges. Are they rising and falling to the music, or are they on or off timing? Reviewing others is helpful because you may be able to pick up correct and incorrect movements more objectively by looking at someone else. Thirdly, observe what the judges are focusing on. Some judges look at feet, and others look at top line. The fourth time, look at how your teacher moves. This can give you valuable insight into where he or she is placing you or where you aren't in sync. The last time, look at the video as a whole and take in the complete experience. By reviewing the dancing experience from five different perspectives, you will be able to self-correct and adjust your dancing more effectively.

I also use a five-step concept to help my students improve their posture and movement. Five is the core right around the pelvis area; four is just above the belly button; three is in the middle of the chest; two is the throat; and one is the neck. Because my students use this in practice and on the competing floor, it gives us a powerful and instant language. I may say "one" in between dances, and my students know what they need to correct. Or they can say to me, "I need help strengthening my five," and I know right away what they mean.

Some of my students live out of state, and it forces us to be creative. We use Skype, phone, and email to communicate about routines, changes, and exercises to help them compete more effectively. My commuter students do not work on steps between lessons; they work on strengthening and posture exercises, so when we get together, they already have the stamina and movements down. When we get together, we work on flow and partnering.

Jessika Ferm: *What tips do you give your students to help them deal with challenging emotions during practice and on the competition floor?*

Tony Scheppler: I know students work really hard to reach their goals, and sometimes the results don't align with the amount of work they put in. I encourage them to believe in themselves and in me as their teacher. If we are aligned and are developing and growing, results are not as important.

It's also important not to dwell on the past. If you have a bad heat, shake it off and move on. You can only control yourself and how you respond to the emotions you feel.

Jessika Ferm: *Do you have any non-negotiable behaviors that you won't put up with from your students?*

Tony Scheppler: Yes, I don't put up with prima donnas. A person who thinks he or she is above the team isn't a fit for me. If that is what they want, they'll have to find a teacher who puts up with that. I'm not one of them.

Interview Insight:
Connie Marshall

Photo by: Decadance

BRONZE STANDARD AND SMOOTH DANCER.

Outside the ballroom world, Connie is the owner of Wild About Birds and resides in Ocean View, DE.

Jessika Ferm: *How did you get started in ballroom dancing, and when did you know you wanted to compete?*

Connie Marshall: I run a store called *Wild About Birds* in a small beach community in Delaware, where there are no opportunities to dance locally. Ever since I was a little girl, I was mesmerized by the movies of Fred Astaire and Ginger Rogers. I fell in love with ballroom dancing right then and there, but it never occurred to me that one day dancing would be an option for me.

One day, at age 48, I started talking to a customer who said he was taking rhythm group lessons in a small house locally, and I knew instantly that I wanted to give it a try. A few months later, the main teacher said that I would probably enjoy competing. I realized that I needed to take one-on-one lessons with a teacher who had competition experience. Since there was no one for me to dance with locally, I ventured out to northern Delaware to try out a studio that my group instructor recommended.

Jessika Ferm: *How did you meet Tony Scheppler, and what is it about him that made it feel like the right fit for you?*

Connie Marshall: While taking lessons with another teacher at the Delaware studio, I met Tony. He was tall, commanding, and moved with grace and ease. Because he looked the part of a quintessential Smooth/Standard dancer (not unlike my childhood hero, Fred Astaire), he caught my eye. I'm six-feet tall, and Tony is 6'4, so he matched me in height and shape, which was necessary to produce a great match and not easily found.

I specifically watched how he interacted with the other students, and I liked how he patiently led each student to find his or her path. Now that I know him better, I admire his sense of fairness. He treats all his students respectfully and doesn't let us beat ourselves up unnecessarily. He can be stern and demanding, yet he is fair. I also appreciate the fact that Tony and I have a relationship based on mutual respect. While we don't speak on the phone all the time or keep in constant contact, we have developed a strong and loyal partnership.

Jessika Ferm: *You and Tony have danced together for four years, and you commute to dance together. What makes you do that, and how do you make it work?*

Connie Marshall: Just a few months into our dancing, Tony told me he was moving to Ohio, and I burst into tears. He assured me that he would be back often to visit his other students in New York, and we began a long-distance dance relationship. Most of the time, I take a bus to meet him in New York City. I will be making my first trip to Ohio this month to work with him at his current studio.

Since we compete fairly often, we also schedule time before competitions to practice and do lessons to ensure that we are in sync. I know that Tony is the right teacher for me at this stage in my dancing, and I'm willing to invest in our partnership. It is hard to find the right fit out there. Since I have it with Tony, the commuting and distance are just par for the course.

Photo by: Stephen Marino

Interview Insight: Beverly Moore

OPEN GOLD PRO/AM COMPETITOR IN INTERNATIONAL STANDARD, INTERNATIONAL LATIN, AND AMERICAN SMOOTH

Beverly competes in a variety of age categories. She is a five-time Ladies C and two-time Ladies B International Standard and World Champion. Since 2009, Beverly has been the undefeated Ladies C American Smooth and International Latin Champion. She resides in Verdun, QC, Canada.

Jessika Ferm: *You have danced for many years and compete in three of the four styles of dance for an average of 20 competitions a year. Describe your dancing journey and the steps you took to get to where you are today.*

Beverly Moore: I began dancing in 1996 and took a few years off when I was transitioning between teachers, so all together I've danced for about 15 years. When I began dancing, I lived in Saskatoon in the Saskatchewan province in Canada, and there weren't a lot of ballroom studios in the region. I started to dance with a teacher who taught mostly beginners. When the studio owner saw me dance, he mentioned that I would probably enjoy competing, so I began to dance and compete with him. My first competition was at the Ohio Star Ball as a newcomer.

As my passion for dance grew, I knew I needed to find a teacher who could take me to the next level. I also knew I had to look outside Saskatoon to Alberta to find my next teacher. That worked for a while, but then the teachers I danced with began to move around to different studios. Consequently I lost the consistency I needed to improve my dancing. That is when I called Alain Doucet and asked him to take me as a student. That was not exactly protocol at that time in ballroom, but I knew he was the teacher for me. That was eight years ago.

The choice to work with Alain came with its own set of challenges. Because I was located in Saskatoon, and Alain was in Quebec, I had to fly almost four hours each way to take lessons with him. For a year and a half, I stayed at a hotel and rented a car because I wanted to make sure it was the right fit. When my husband recently retired, we bought a condo in Quebec, so I can be closer to Alain and my dancing. It's a decision I've never regretted.

Jessika Ferm: *What is it about Alain that makes the two of you a great fit?*

Beverly Moore: What I love most about Alain is that he is fiercely competitive and extremely knowledgeable and talented. I never stop learning from him. He challenges me to improve all the time. He has a great height and look for me, and he is a former World Champion. All these factors played into my decision to dance with him. He is a hard worker, and so am I. I take three lessons a day, five days a week, in addition to competing on-average twice a month. So I need to work with someone who has the desire, passion, and stamina to consistently perform.

I also love the fact that Alain is open to new information and always welcomes feedback on how to better himself. He is a former World Champion, yet he consistently seeks out new information. We are fortunate to be able to receive coaching from his wife and former partner, Anik Jolicoeur, which is a true blessing.

Jessika Ferm: *What emotions have you had to learn to deal with or master on your competing journey?*

Beverly Moore: The first emotions I remember were being absolutely terrified, extremely nervous, and feeling almost sick. It occurred just when I started to dance with Alain, and I have never forgotten how he helped me deal with it. Instead of trying to fix it or talk me off the ledge, he simply stopped practicing with me in between dances or before going out on the floor. We just went out there and danced what we had, and all of a sudden my emotions started to dissipate. I guess I just didn't have time to think about how nervous I was.

The truth is, I still feel a bit anxious before I go out on the floor. But as soon as I start moving, it goes away. I think it is just part of being a competitor. You have little butterflies in your stomach because you are going to compete, and you hope to put your best out there. If you aren't at least a little nervous, I'm not sure you are truly challenging yourself.

Jessika Ferm: *You are at the top of your game in the most advanced dance category. How do you keep yourself motivated to grow and avoid becoming complacent?*

Beverly Moore: I have to continue to push myself each time I compete. It can be stressful at the top, because there is always someone chasing you or looking to come up from behind. I'm a competitor at heart, and I'm mostly internally competitive. So I always strive to grow and become better for my own satisfaction. I love dancing with all my heart, and I can't imagine doing anything else. My primary quest is to become better than I was yesterday. Since I have no plans to stop dancing anytime soon, I have to continue growing and learning new ways to dance the best I can.

4

Bring on the Bling: Hair, Makeup, Dresses, Jewelry, and More

I'm attracted to people who make this effort in knowing what suits them—they are individual and stylish.

- VIVIENNE WESTWOOD

Photo by: Stephen Marino Photography

For many female ballroom competitors, this chapter is what makes this sport and art such a joy. We get to dress up in beautiful gowns, have our hair and makeup done, and sparkle like mad. As Sharon Savoy, four-time Blackpool Exhibition Dance Champion and author of *Ballroom! Obsession and Passion inside the World of Competitive Dance*, states in her interview insight on page 140:

> "Dance is a gift…it helps you feel physically, intellectually, emotionally, mentally, and spiritually fit. Consider that you get to dance with a person of the opposite sex to beautiful music wearing glamorous dresses instead of sweating at the gym in worn-out sweatpants in order to stay in shape physically and mentally."

I love Patrice Tanaka's interview, in which she states, "Let's be honest. How awesome is it that you can wear rhinestones and a ball gown for breakfast and fit right in?"

While most gentlemen competitors don't get too wrapped up in the bling part of the sport, it's not uncommon to see them get excited about costumes for show dances and special events. While most of this chapter is geared toward the dos and don'ts for lady competitors, there are some important tips that gentlemen should be aware of as well.

Let's be honest. How awesome is it that you can wear rhinestones and a ball gown for breakfast and fit right in?

In this chapter, we will review how to prepare your ballroom look and discuss the ways in which you can set yourself apart from the competition. World and U.S. Professional Smooth Champion Marzena Stachura stresses in her interview insight (page 256) that it's never too early for beginners to make a good first impression.

> "Even as a beginner, make sure you have a look that is presentable and shows that you are taking competing seriously. You don't have to have an expensive gown, but you need to get your hair done and look clean and well put together."

The interview insights in this section provide you with detailed tips from top judges, hair and makeup professionals, and costume dressmakers. Almost all judges and coaches who were interviewed for this book offer specific ideas on grooming and dress, so don't skip any of the interview insights in each chapter.

We will go into extensive detail in Chapter 5 on how and where to "get the goods." This chapter, however, is designed to give you the top-ten "musts" for competing with style. They are called "musts" for a reason. These are not "nice to have" or "good to know" suggestions. If you plan to compete, make sure you can check off each of the 10 musts before heading out onto the competitive floor. There is a checklist on page 136 to help you identify areas that may need to be addressed before your next competition.

Judges appreciate competitors who have taken the time to learn the "rules of the game" and project a professional and appropriate image. Don't forget that you are entering their professional domain. If you were going for a "dream job" interview or meeting your future in-laws for the first time, you would probably put your best foot forward, wouldn't you? It's the same here.

The "Top-Ten Appearance Musts" That Give You a Competitive Edge

> Your appearance, attitude, and confidence define you as a person. A professional, well-dressed golfer, like a businessperson, gives the impression that he thinks that the golf course and/or workplace and the people there are important."

— LORII MYERS

The most important first step is to look the part. The following section offers tips and tools for both lady and gentleman competitors. Before you take one step unto the dance floor, judges will scan you to see if you have created the appropriate "ballroom look." Judges and coaches look for you to have:

1. **An appropriate costume that highlights your assets (including fishnets for ladies):** For new competitors, the costume issue is usually a biggie. While most judges agree that you don't need to make a major investment in a dress or costume for your first competition, you do need to wear something that is appropriate to compete in. Gentlemen have an easier time because their outfits are more streamlined and less expensive at first. For gentlemen who dance International Standard, costumes become a more significant investment as you advance.

   Each style of dance has a distinct "look," and there are several important "rules" to be aware of prior to selecting the right costume. For example, ladies dancing International Standard will wear a long dress with floats attached to the arms or the dress itself. This produces an elegant look. Since the couple is in closed position at all times while dancing, the floats are meant to draw attention to the lady, while not interfering with the dance flow. On the contrary, ladies competing in American Smooth, where there is dramatic movement and shaping throughout the dance, do not wear floats. Instead they often wear eye-catching arm or wrist jewelry to grab the judges' attention. Gentlemen competing in International Standard wear a black tuxedo tail suit. For American Smooth, gentlemen wear a long-sleeved shirt and a waist coat/dinner jacket or custom-tailored suit. Ladies competing in International Latin or American Rhythm usually wear a shorter dress with fringe, feathers, or beading, but longer straight styles are also appropriate. Gentlemen wear tight trousers and shirts. We will dive into additional tips for selecting the right costume shortly.

   Now that you know what style of costume you need to wear, let's discuss the most important dos and don'ts.

   A costume should fit you well, highlight your best features, and hide any imperfections. They can also cleverly minimize any potential dancing flaw if executed well. No dress will hide poor footwork or bad posture, but some dresses actually extenuate them, so pick your dress carefully.

The beauty of ballroom dresses is that they stretch. It's not uncommon for both a size four and an eight to fit nicely into the same dress. That doesn't mean it will look good on you as you move and dance. During the fitting process, it is important to move around in a dress to make sure you can breathe in it while dancing. Remember, you will be dancing in it, not going to the Oscars, where you would simply stand and walk. If you try a dress on and begin to fidget or pull it to "make it fit," it may not be the right dress for you—or you may need to have it altered. Dresses should fit perfectly and feel comfortable as soon as you put them on.

Always consider what you look like from behind. Use a full-length mirror to look at your back and the back of your legs. If your dress creates funny "bumps" or folds, it may not be the right dress for you. I find that even people with almost-perfect figures have body parts that are better off covered.

The wonderfully opinionated judge and coach Pat Traymore has seen it all over her 55-year career in ballroom. In her interview insight on page 142, she speaks about her pet peeves with a passion. She jokes about creating a workshop titled "What we (the judges) see that you aren't aware of."

If you are a woman over 30, it is strongly advised (really, really important) to wear dark or light-brown fishnets.

There is such a thing as "age appropriate" dresses. One of my fellow competitors is in her 60s and insists on wearing long-sleeved dresses for Rhythm and Smooth. As she puts it, "No one wants to see my jiggly arms." If you are under 18, you also are advised to wear an age-appropriate costume. Avoid showing too much skin; wear a dress that is youthful, not overly sexy. You want to highlight your dancing and figure without looking like a seductress. There are specific rules for Junior or Youth competitors. If your instructor hasn't already shared the rules with you, please take a moment to look up the NDCA rule book, which you can find by visiting ndca.org.

If you are a woman over 30, it is strongly advised (really, really important) to wear dark or light-brown fishnets. You can buy these at dance stores or most competitions. Unless you have the perfect legs of a 19-year-old, always wear fishnets. They should match the color of your shoes (not your body color) to create an elongated look. The idea is to blend your shoes with your legs. Avid judge Marianne Nicole (and almost all of the judges interviewed for this book) considers fishnets a mandatory part of your costume. You can read more of her tips on page 83.

Bonita Brockert, a popular judge and avid Pro/Am competitor, offers the following advice for Am/Am couples who compete in USADance events:

> "Competitors will need to check the costume rules for amateur events. Rules are strictly enforced in Junior through Adult (under 35) age divisions. Senior events (over 35) do not have the same restrictions. Although more of the rules will apply to the ladies' costumes, men also have rules they must adhere to. For instance, men must wear a white shirt in the ballroom/standard syllabus levels. No personal jewelry is allowed. You can access the adult men's regulations on page 33 of the rule book. Here is the link to the USADance website: usadance.org/dancesport/forms-and-resources/rules-policies-and-bylaws/."

For additional help selecting a dress or working with a professional ballroom costume maker, see Designs to Shine Owner Maria McGill's interview insight on page 145.

While it is a wonderful personal choice to wear tattoos, they are not embraced in the competitive ballroom world. If you have tattoos, cover them with your outfit or body paint.

Gentlemen are encouraged to wear black pants or trousers with matching shirts for American Rhythm and International Latin. Wear the same ensemble with a vest or custom-tailored jacket for American Smooth and International Standard. It may be tempting in the beginning to wear a pair of casual pants when competing, but remember, you must look neat and put together. An overly casual look does not display the professional image of ballroom competing.

Bonita offers the following advice for newer gentlemen when it comes to selecting a costume and shoes:

> "Use discretion in your choice of shirts for Rhythm/Latin and consider your physique honestly. Few men look their best in the stretchy, tight- fitting shirts pros often wear. Whether you are very very slim or carry last night's lasagna around your waist, the effect can be less than pleasing. Likewise big, loose-fitting and billowing shirts are sloppy and distracting. A classic look that works for any body type is a black dress shirt with a dance vest and black tie. A tie with some color is fine, but you cannot go wrong with all black. Pin the shirt into the trousers, so you have room to move but do not have the concern of your shirttails flying out or creating a balloon of fabric about your waistline. Get yourself a well-fitted dance vest with a full back for Smooth or Latin. Many vendors carry shirt styles with a leotard-type attachment to keep the shirt inside the trousers. There are other shirt options, but this commentary should give you better guidelines when you are shopping. Never wear casual t-shirts or shirts with the armpits exposed.

"If your pants require a belt, wear an unobtrusive classic belt to produce a finished look. Avoid rhinestone belts, large buckles, or any other belt that distracts the eye or could be offensive or hazardous to your partner's dress.

"As far as shoes go, be sure to have a Latin shoe for Rhythm and Latin dances and black patent shoes for Smooth and Standard dances. Your daily leather practice shoe is not dressy enough for competing, and a flat shoe is inappropriate for the Latin dances. Some beginners are surprised to find themselves headed for the floor face-first when they premiere their patent shoes! They will stick together; seasoned dancers carry a bit of petroleum jelly in their dance bags to grease the inside of the shoe on each wearing to avoid this issue. Much better idea than keeping your feet a mile apart when you should be neatly closing! While we're discussing footwear, remember that glimpses of your socks are not unheard of. It may seem more than obvious that dark socks are the rule of the day, so no one notices them.

"Lastly, a word about your number. Pin it neatly, and make sure it is straight and not too high on your back. Place it at the bottom of the shoulder blade."

As gentlemen competitors advance in level, a special tuxedo suit is advised for International Standard. Experienced ballroom tailors attend competitions and can help you select the best suit option. They are also tremendously helpful in tailoring pants to the right length. A common mistake is for gentlemen's trousers to be too short. Remember, you will be rising and falling as you dance. Jonathan S. Marion, author of the book *Ballroom: Culture and Costume in Competitive Dance*, offers a great summary of ballroom dress codes, "Elaborated Costuming Trends, By Ballroom Style and Gender" on p.126 of his book (Oxford: Berg, 2008). Please see Chapter 8 for gentlemen costuming resources.

2. **Hair professionally done:** Your hair should be done in a manner appropriate for your style of dance. For Smooth and Standard dances, hair should be in a tight up-do with absolutely no "fly-away" stands of hair. For Rhythm and Latin, the hair can be up or down, but it should be well-coiffed and not serve as a distraction to you or your instructor/dance partner. If you choose to wear your hair down, do a test run to make sure it doesn't wrap around your face— or the face of your instructor.

I highly recommend that you have your hair done by a professional ballroom hair stylist. If you are on a budget, or there isn't a professional ballroom hair stylist available at your competition, you may opt to do your own hair. If this is the case, keep your hair in an up-do that is slicked tight to your skull. Many "non-ballroom" hair stylists believe they can style your hair for competitions, but I promise you they are not prepared for the amount of hairspray needed to keep ballroom hair in place. To save money when I compete in different styles over a period of days, I sleep in my "done" hair, and it doesn't move from one day to the next.

That should tell you how well structured and heavily sprayed it is! For more information about ballroom hair, see professional ballroom hair and makeup artist Lisa Bentley DeBevec's interview insight on page 148.

Gentlemen's hair should be neat and freshly cut (if it's been more than two weeks since your last hair cut, it's time to get it trimmed before you go out on the competition floor). The back of the neck needs to be above the collar of your shirt. A great check point is to see if the hair touches the collar. If it does, have it trimmed. While it may seem like an easy thing to do yourself or have someone do for you, you should have a professional barber trim your hair right before your competition to create the sharpest look possible. If you wear long hair, keep it in a tight bun at the base of your neck or in a very tight and neatly coiffed ponytail to avoid fly-aways.

3. **Appropriate ballroom makeup:** I also recommend having your makeup applied professionally for your first competition. It is hard to fathom the amount of makeup you need to wear on the floor. One of my coaches used to say, "If you would go out in public, you don't have enough on." It's not just about slapping on a bunch of makeup. There is a specific look that professional ballroom makeup artists know how to create. You may want to have it done once, and then learn how to do it yourself after that. There is a fine line between looking like a ballroom competitor and a drag queen. For more information on the specifics of ballroom makeup, please see professional ballroom stylist Lisa Bentley DeBevec's interview insight on page 148. She shares valuable tips, from eye shadow dos and don'ts to selecting the right brush for the right application. If you are competing on a budget, please see Chapter 6, page 165 for additional tips.

    Makeup for men is a big "no-no." It is okay to wear some foundation or bronzer, but avoid using a color that doesn't match your natural skin tone. Bonita shares the following tips for gentlemen competitors who may want to add some color while competing:

    > "It is fine to wear a little bit of a base for championship-level dancers. Choose a shade closest to your natural skin color. It produces a poor impression when gentlemen wear dark shades as if trying to changes their skin color. An appropriate base evens out skin tones and imperfections without looking made up. Makeup is not to be seen."

    A word of caution. If you are not used to applying bronzers, it is best to ask an experienced person or professional makeup artist to assist with the first couple competitions. Gentlemen, skip the eyeliner, mascara, and lip liner/lipstick (yes, a few men have been seen wearing them).

4. **Toes and fingernails painted and styled:** Most ballroom dancers wear acrylic nails, which produce a professional and finished look. Personally, I either have my nails done at a salon with a gel cover if my nails are strong and long, or I wear press-on French manicured nails that work just as well. If you prefer this option, make sure that the nails sit tight and don't fly off during your dancing. I use a brand called Kiss, which you can buy at any drugstore or large grocery store. While there are no "rules" for toe colors that I know of, pick a color that stands out or matches your dress if you are dancing Latin or Rhythm. For Standards and Smooth, no one will see your toes, so feel free to leave them nude if you wish.

    Gentlemen, make sure your nails are short without harsh edges. It's not a bad idea to bring a nail file or keep a set of clippers handy at the competition, in case your nails need a last-minute trim. Ladies are not amused by scratching fingernails while dancing.

5. **A spray tan or appropriate body coloring:** Ballroom lights will wash out most of your natural color. Getting a spray tan or tanning naturally prior to a competition makes you look like you have a glow and highlights your muscle tone nicely. While this is not an absolute must, it is highly recommended. I remember the first time I had a spray tan done. I was amazed at how dark I looked, but my coach took one look at me and sent me back to the salon to get re-sprayed. A "ballroom tan" is much different from the natural glow you may prefer for a nice evening out. You can also use an at-home self-tanner, but remember to start early to ensure that the tan gives you the darkest color possible.

    Because most of the gentleman's skin is covered by the outfit, spray tans are optional. Most professional competitors wear one or use a bronzing cream for areas that are visible (face, chest, and hands). If you opt to wear a bronzing gel or color, make sure you don't get it on your partner's costume—they tend to rub off while perspiring.

6. **Eye-catching ballroom jewelry:** Ballroom jewelry must sparkle. There are no ifs, ands, or buts about it. Most ballroom competitors buy jewelry that is specifically designed for ballroom competing and can be purchased online or at the competition. Popular jewelry includes bracelets, necklaces, earrings, and hair pieces. It's unusual to see rings, ankle bracelets, or belly button rings/piercing jewelry on the competitive floor. Earrings for American Smooth can include smaller hoops or posts. Women competing in International Standard avoid hoops and mostly use traditional earrings with prongs that fit tightly to the ear. American Rhythm or International Latin can include larger hoops or posts. The color of the jewelry should match your dress. Most professional dressmakers will help you select the jewelry that goes best with your dress. If you opt to sell your dress, it is customary to sell it with the matching jewelry. While there are a myriad of colorful crystals to choose from, the most commonly used one is referred to as "AB," which stands for "Auroras Borealis," after the beautiful Northern Lights that cast a myriad of colors in the night sky. These crystals pick up a variety of colors, which make them uniquely suited for almost any dress.

Custom-made ballroom jewelry is more expensive than the jewelry you buy at the local mall, and for good reason. I once made the mistake of buying inexpensive bracelets that ended up ripping my instructor's competing shirt to shreds. I didn't know that "regular" jewelry uses a prong setting, which can easily attach to clothing. Ballroom jewelry does not. What seemed like a brilliant $6 bracelet, ended up costing me $200 in replacement costs for his shirt. If you choose to use "regular" jewelry, make sure it is attached securely and can withstand the rigorous movements of a Cha Cha or Tango. It's always best to practice before using specific jewelry for a competition.

Gentlemen are not encouraged to wear ballroom jewelry. Sometimes, the gentleman may match his tie to his partner's dress or may stone the tie for eye-catching effect, but remember your job is to make the lady shine!

7. **Clean and neat competing shoes:** When asked about pet peeves, several of the judges interviewed for this book mentioned amateurs and professionals wearing dirty dance shoes on the competition floor. It's important to remember that judges are looking for you to present a total package. You don't want to draw their attention to something negative like dirty shoes. For each style, I keep a pair of dance shoes that I only use for competition. That way, they can last a year or more.

Same rules apply for gentlemen competitors.

8. **A smile on your face:** Dancing is supposed to be fun. Remember, you are performing for the audience and the judges. They don't care if you are nervous, afraid, upset, or scared. They want to see you put on a show, and the easiest way to do that is to wear a smile. Practice smiling during your run-throughs at the studio. If you think smiling will come naturally on the competition floor, you may be surprised when you look at your videos after the event. Most newer competitors are not used to performing while they dance, and smiling tends to be the first thing to get lost. As Pat Traymore states in her interview insight on page 142, "If you love to dance, remember to tell your face." Make it a point to practice smiling, but avoid over-using mouth manipulations. Sharon Savoy lists this as one of her pet peeves while judging. You can read more of her great tips on page 140.

Same tips apply for gentlemen competitors.

9. **Confidence:** This "skill" or trait goes hand-in-hand with the smile. Judges don't care if you feel confident. They judge what you look like. As British Professional Rising Star Champion and Popular Judge Kimberley Mitchell shares in her interview insight on page 154, "I look at you as soon as you walk out on the floor, before the first beat of music has started. I love to see students walk out with confidence and embrace the concept of feeling and looking like a Champion."

   Confidence does not discriminate; it is a must for both lady and gentlemen competitors.

10. **A positive attitude.** You may get nervous or scared, but displaying a positive attitude in the ballroom at all times is essential. Judges walk around, and they see you on and off the dance floor. Be courteous to everyone you meet, and go out of your way to be nice to other dancers. Stay close to the on-deck area when your heats are about to start, so the on-deck captain doesn't have to come looking for you.

    Again, the same tips apply to ladies and gentlemen.

Trust me, these 10 "musts" are not merely "nice to have." All of the judges and professionals interviewed for this book mentioned these 10 items in their interview insights. If you take nothing else away from this book, please make sure you implement these right away.

The "Appearance Musts" Checklist

> " I don't mind making jokes, but I don't want to look like one."
>
> - MARILYN MONROE

Before we leave this chapter, take a moment to see if you have all of the "appearance musts" necessary to stand out on the floor. If you check "no" or "will have," then make a note in the "action steps" column to indicate what action you need to take in order to convert it to a "yes."

Do you...	Yes	No	Will have	Action steps
Have an appropriate costume that flatters your body and highlights your features for each of the styles in which you compete?				
Know a professional ballroom hair stylist, so you can get your hair done for each style of dance?				
Know someone who can create your "ballroom makeup look," or feel confident that you can produce the right look by yourself (ladies only)?				
Know where you can go to have your fingers and toes polished or manicured?				
Know where you can get a "ballroom spray tan" applied or otherwise tan to get a significant glow, so you look good on the competition floor?				
Have eye-catching ballroom jewelry to highlight your dress (ladies only)?				
Have a pair of clean shoes, with no visible marks or scuffs, that you can use on the competition floor?				
Have practiced smiling while dancing at the studio, so you don't need to think about smiling at the competition?				
Have experience walking on to the floor and projecting confidence or joy even if you don't feel it?				
Have a positive attitude and approach others with grace and joy?				

In Chapter 5, we will review your competition checklist and share ways that you can easily transform "no" or "I will" responses to "yes." For now, just consider which of the categories above are current strengths, and which you need to develop. Remember, there are no good or bad answers. Your number-one priority right now is to make sure you have the information necessary to take appropriate action and fix any shortcomings before your next competition.

Chapter Summary

- Being able to dance is a gift. To compete is even more precious. Treat your competition with honor and grace by working as hard on your appearance as you do your dancing.

- Your costume should highlight your best features and hide any imperfections.

- Hair must be neatly arranged in a tight up-do or in a manner that keeps it away from your eyes and face. Gentlemen's hair must be freshly cut with sharp edges.

- Ballroom makeup closely resembles stage makeup, but be careful. More is not always better. Have a professional ballroom makeup artist do your makeup the first couple of times, if you are able. Gentlemen, skip the makeup all together or use only a foundation or bronzer that highlights your skin without discoloring it.

- Hands and feet are important extensions of your dancing. Make sure they are carefully manicured.

- Get a spray tan or self-tanner in preparation for your competition. The lights on the competition floor will wipe out any natural color you have; as a result, the judges may not notice you on the floor.

- Bring on the bling! Make sure your ballroom jewelry is appropriate and easy to wear. You don't want anything flying off while dancing.

- Keep a pair of competing shoes if possible. Or make sure your shoes are nice and clean before hitting the floor. Remember, judges pay attention to the smallest details.

- Practice smiling! When we get nervous or tense, we tend to forget to smile, and our appearance points will go down!

- Walk with confidence. Practice in the grocery store, at the mall, or anywhere you walk. You don't have to feel confident to project it, and judges mark what they see, not what you feel.

- Being prepared is the key to succeeding and competing like a pro. Make every detail count and leave nothing to chance.

Chapter Takeaways

Take a moment to summarize your takeaways from this chapter. These notes will come in handy as you prepare for your next competition.

After reading this chapter I realized that:

_____

My most valuable takeaway is:

_____

I learned the following about the "top 10 appearance musts":

_____

I need to take the following action steps to ensure that I can say "yes" to all "top 10 appearance musts" before my next competition:

_____

_____

_____

_____

Interview Insight: Sharon Savoy

Photo by: Len de Pas

AUTHOR OF *BALLROOM! OBSESSION AND PASSION INSIDE THE WORLD OF COMPETITIVE DANCE*, JUDGE, THREE-TIME WORLD EXHIBITION CHAMPION, FOUR-TIME BLACKPOOL EXHIBITION DANCE CHAMPION, AND THREE-TIME STAR SEARCH WINNER. SHARON RESIDES IN LOS ANGELES, CA.

Jessika Ferm: *What is important for a new-to-intermediate amateur dancer to embrace or know?*

Sharon Savoy: Every level of dancer needs to embrace the process and the journey. Enjoy the little "aha" moments that go off on the competition floor and in practice. Each increment of expertise that you add to your technique arsenal is part of the journey and will help you feel more competent. The more you learn to improve your technique, the more joy you will experience from your dancing.

The purpose of technique is to produce greater efficiency, which leads to increased fluidity. This is why perfecting your technique is so important. Once you have the basic elements, and they are beyond muscle memory, then the freedom to express emotions and musicality evolves more naturally. It's important to recognize that you are always on a journey to increase your skill level. You will never "arrive," so enjoy the learning process. If you stop being curious about your dancing and your experiences, you stop growing.

Remember, dance is a gift. Dancing helps you stay physically, intellectually, emotionally, mentally, and spiritually fit. Consider that you get to dance with a person of the opposite sex to beautiful music wearing glamorous dresses—instead of sweating at the gym in worn-out sweatpants—in order to stay in shape physically and mentally.

If you are hard on yourself or don't meet the goals you desire right away, remember the overall picture and the gift you are given. Then a bad mark or challenging feedback is not negative; it is just part of the experience that moves you closer to your dancing goals. Dance elevates your spirit and soul and feeds you artistically.

Jessika Ferm: *As a judge, what do you look for in a new-to-intermediate competitor (Pre-Bronze)?*

Sharon Savoy: I look at technique, which is the biggest indicator of skill level. First I look at posture and frame, and then I look at footwork. I find that if dancers look comfortable in their own skin, then there is a sense that they know what they are doing. If they look nervous or have strange contortions on their faces, then they may be pushing the limits of what they are capable of. The brain is trying to catch up with what they are doing, and the ease is gone. Ease tells me, as a judge, that they feel competent and know what they are doing.

Jessika Ferm: *What is one of your judging pet peeves?*

Sharon Savoy: Too much mouth manipulation. It indicates that they are using the face to try to replace a feeling that should be felt in the body. The face then becomes distorted. I am also passionate about competitors using correct arm, hand, and finger styling, especially in Smooth. Too often, competitors are unaware of how to use their hands or arms appropriately. It is distracting. There is a history of technique for arm styling. For example, the Waltz and the Viennese Waltz typically use a more balletic styling; Tango has the element of Spanish dance and Flamenco; and Foxtrot interpretation opens the door to Broadway and Jazz styles because of the music. Most people understand the concept of passing their feet; however, proper arm movement passes through the gateway of our core.

Interview Insight:
Pat Traymore

JUDGE, COACH, AND BALLROOM CONSULTANT.

Pat has 55 years of ballroom experience and has performed on the Johnny Carson, Merv Griffin and Harry Belafonte shows. She speaks five languages fluently and has written numerous ballroom training manuals. She resides in McLean, VA.

Jessika Ferm: *You have been in this industry for over 50 years and traveled to studios all over the country to coach. What tips or strategies would you give newer competitors to help them compete successfully?*

Pat Traymore: It doesn't really matter if you are a professional or amateur, the same tips apply to any level dancer. Start with the basics. It's like baking a cake. Make sure you have all the right ingredients to bake a tasty cake. Then add the frosting to make it look pretty. Too many dancers focus on getting the frosting right, and then the cake or the foundation is a mess. Don't worry about arm styling until you have figured out your feet. Using your feet correctly is essential to good-quality dancing. They express the story of the dance, and when I see a dancer who understands how to use his or her feet, I know the quality of dancing and the instruction is good. Remember, arms and hands are the extensions of your body. They are not artificial appendices that you choreograph into a routine. If you were a tree and the branches were your arms, they would move with the breeze. If there isn't a breeze, they don't move. It is the same with your arm styling. If you are in motion, your arms will naturally flow with your body. The only time arms should not move is if you are in closed dance position.

Make sure you understand the character of each dance. Sometimes it is helpful to think of each dance using a different metaphor. For example, the Waltz resembles a pendulum swinging from one side to another. Foxtrot resembles ice dancing or Fred Astaire and Ginger Rogers. Tango resembles a panther stalking its prey. Rumba resembles dancing on the beach, digging your toes into the sand.

I advise new competitors to learn their Bronze syllabus completely before moving on to Silver or advanced steps. Silver is like the frosting on the cake, but if you don't have your basics or foundation from Bronze, your cake will start to wobble and eventually fall apart, even if it looks pretty at first. Don't be in a hurry to compete. Instead learn the basics, and then put what you are proud of out on the competitive floor.

Jessika Ferm: *Those are excellent points to keep in mind. What else would you add?*

Pat Traymore: Everyone makes mistakes. Without them you don't learn or grow. Don't be afraid to ask questions or share what you want help with. You wouldn't go to the doctor and not share what ails you. If you work with a coach, discuss what you want help with. You have to be honest with yourself, so you can improve the issues you're facing.

Students often forget that becoming a great dancer requires the same commitment as losing weight or preparing for a marathon. You need to put in the time at the studio to get the results you want. If all you do is work out one day a week, you will feel sore for the next couple of days. But if you work out several days a week, your body will become used to the increased pressure and adapt. You need to practice or work out at least two or three days a week to allow your body to store into muscle memory what you want it to do for you.

When it comes to costumes, I have a few important pointers. If you are a bigger woman, wear a dress that elongates your body. Don't wear a short dress that makes you appear shorter or rounder. If you are over 50, please consider wearing dresses with mesh or closed backs. Your skin, no matter how skinny you are, begins to sag. When the gentleman puts his hand on your back, it will wrinkle your skin. Always wear pantyhose! Even if you are young and your legs look nice, get used to wearing fishnets to mask any imperfections you may have. Judges don't want to see your bare skin flashed in our faces. I'd love to do a lecture titled, "What we see that you aren't aware of."

Don't wear your dirty or worn practice shoes on the competition floor. Have a pair of competing shoes that you only wear for competition, so they are in pristine condition. This goes for all amateur and professional dancers. One of my pet peeves is when I see a professional lady teacher dancing in worn shoes. There is no excuse for being sloppy when you are representing your students at a competition.

You have to get your hair done. Many women who insist on doing their own hair forget to look at the back. They look fine from the front, but the back looks like a bird's nest. The only hairstyle that does not need to be arranged is the short bob with wispy bangs. All others should be worn up without random flyaway strands.

Please use a bronzer or consider spray-tanning yourself. White skin just doesn't look good on the floor. Make sure you have a manicure and pedicure. You are expected to look impeccable when you compete. Remember you are representing not only yourself but also your instructor.

Don't forget to show your love for dance when you are on the floor. Your body may seem to love to dance, but if you don't tell your face, you are missing an important part of performing.

This tip is more for professionals, but it goes for any serious amateur competitor, as well. Dress up at all times when you are at a competition or when you meet a coach. It's not just how you look when you are competing, but also how you show up in the ballroom when you aren't dancing. This is an elegant sport, and you want to look like to take your profession or hobby seriously.

Photo by: Joe Eberts

Interview Insight:
Maria McGill

OWNER OF DESIGNS TO SHINE, THE PREMIERE LUXURY
BALLROOM DANCEWEAR DESIGNER. SHE RESIDES IN
TAMPA, FL.

Jessika Ferm: *You started as a professional dancer when you were 19 and designed all your own costumes. How has your dancing career influenced your ballroom dancewear business today?*

Maria McGill: Because I am a former professional ballroom dancer, I know what fits and looks good on the floor. I can relate to my clients because I've been in their shoes. My unique style is based on what will accentuate dancers' bodies while they move. Our draping techniques have become our trademark, and we often hear "That's a Designs to Shine dress." People know our quality and look on the floor.

Jessika Ferm: *What else makes Designs to Shine so special?*

Maria McGill: We are a family. Almost all my team members have been with me for more than seven years and some as long as 18. All of our dresses are designed and made right here in the U.S. The women who buy our dresses become part of our family and call themselves the "Designs to Shine Girls." That means the world to me because it speaks of a long-term relationship that is built on mutual trust and respect. We pride ourselves on our customer service and our ability to help you find a dress that enhances your dancing. The truth is that our dresses sell themselves, and we are not a high-pressure sales team. Come in, browse, and let us know if you need help. We want you to have an exceptional experience from the moment you walk into our booth to when you enter the dance floor in your beautiful gown.

Jessika Ferm: *What tips do you have for newer-to-intermediate competitors when it comes to buying their first "big" dress?*

Maria McGill: Start by trying on dresses. Go to different dressmakers and see what style of dresses you like the best. Remember to focus on fit and design first. My staff will gladly sit down with you and ask you a series of questions in order to get to know what you like and what you envision for your look. If you don't find something on the rack, we will happily design a dress for you. Many of our dresses are custom-made for clients. We listen to your ideas and produce a sketch for your approval. The absolute best way to design a dress is to come to our studio in St. Petersburg, Florida. You can see samples of fabrics, and we can drape dress ideas for you. It also gives you uninterrupted time away from the hustle and bustle of the busy ballroom. If you aren't able to come and see us, we can design a dress for you at a competition. The best second option: come to a competition when you are not dancing and spend time shopping for your dress. Remember that your first dress is a precious experience, and you want to cherish it.

It is also helpful to go to our website and browse through the dresses we currently have and those in the archive. Print out the ones you like and share them with us, so that we can see what details and styles you gravitate toward. It is also a great idea to bring pictures of high-fashion dresses. It is fun for us to create something that you would love to wear on the red carpet, modifying it to fit the ballroom floor.

Jessika Ferm: *What are some of the most common mistakes you see students make when it comes to buying dresses?*

Maria McGill: They forget to consider what they look good in, and they get mesmerized by a certain color. Not everyone can wear acid green or hot pink. It may look beautiful on the floor, but it isn't a good fit for everyone. If you are willing to consider color alternatives, my team will find the best possible color that will highlight your skin tone and hair color and make you stand out on the floor.

I also see students making the mistake of selecting a dress style they like because they have seen a pro or someone else wearing it. They want that dress and don't consider whether it is a good fit for them. I prefer to take the concept of a dress they like and design something that has that look and feel, but is customized for a particular fit. Right now, everyone loves our sponsored pro dancer Lianna Churilova, and they come and say, "I want to buy her dress." They forget that she is short and tiny. The dress she wears will not look right on a 5' 8" woman who is a size 8.

Jessika Ferm: *What are some other tips that would be helpful for newer clients?*

Maria McGill: If you buy a dress from us, and you want to change your style later, we gladly will take your Designs to Shine gown on consignment. You'll receive a credit toward the purchase of your next dress when your gown sells. Sometimes that credit is as high as 70 percent, so your initial purchase is an investment. We don't, however, accept dresses from other designers.

When you come out of the dressing room in a gown, you want to have the "Oh, my goodness" response from those around you—and yourself. If you feel "okay," keep looking. You want to look and feel amazing in your dress, because it becomes an important part of your dancing experience.

If are looking for a high-quality dress but can't afford to pay for a premiere gown, you want to look at dressmakers' webpages for special sales or clearance dresses. We often post great deals in the clearance section on our webpage and have special sales that offer great options.

Interview Insight:
Lisa Bentley-DeBevec

Photo by: Foschi Photography

FORMER U.S. 9-DANCE FINALIST, NDCA, AND NADTA
CERTIFIED INSTRUCTOR AND ADJUDICATOR.

Lisa is the owner of GlamourPuss, Inc. She resides in Bear, DE.

Jessika Ferm: *You are one of the premier hair and makeup artists in the ballroom business. What advice would you offer competitors who may be newer to ballroom or who want help creating the "ballroom look" by themselves?*

Lisa Bentley-DeBevec: Let's start with makeup. If you've never had your ballroom makeup done, go to M.A.C., which you can find at almost any large department store. M.A.C. stands for Make-up Art Cosmetics. Their cosmetics are of a theatrical quality, highly pigmented, bright, and vibrant. Their artists are usually young professionals who are not afraid to put color on your face. When you dance, the lights on the floor are bright, and you have to wear much more makeup than you are accustomed to. In short, when you look in the mirror after putting on your makeup and think you look like a floozy, you're on the right track! Once you are in the makeup artist's chair and your makeup application begins, take a picture with your smartphone or camera at each step, so you can reconstruct it later. When you are finished, go home, take the makeup off one side of your face only and try to duplicate the look, referring to your photos and the other side of your face and using the products you have purchased. Remember to practice several times a few weeks or months prior to your competition. It is a skill and an art, and you need to practice to make it look good.

Brushes: If you are going to do your own makeup, invest in a good set of brushes. They make a world of difference in how the makeup is applied. You can purchase them at M.A.C., and while they may be a bit pricy, it's worth the investment. Again, take pictures of the brushes while the artist is working on you to remember which brushes go with which product. Questions are never a bad thing. Makeup artists enjoy taking the time to impart their knowledge to you.

Eye shadow: If you are going to do your makeup yourself, use neutral colors like browns. You can always go darker later, but starting with a softer palette is usually a great idea. If you are in your 20s to early 40s you can wear the shimmery shadows. If you are over 50, avoid anything that glitters on your eyes. It doesn't highlight your features; instead it just amplifies wrinkles and any other flaws we may be trying to conceal. Avoid using too much white eye shadow all around the eye. You don't want to look like a raccoon! Draw a thin line directly under the eyebrow to help pop the eye. Remember to blend your colors to avoid harsh lines between shades.

Eyeliners: Eyeliners are important to help define the eye. The area of application will determine whether the eye is made to appear bigger or smaller. Kohl eyeliners are quite dark and have great staying power. You can also dip a small brush in a bit of water and create a paste with a dark eye shadow. Experiment to see what will last longer on your skin.

Eyelashes: Visit a Sally's Beauty Supply store and purchase their eyelashes. They are as good as the $15 to $20 eyelashes that you wear once or twice. Practice putting them on. A pair of tweezers with an angled edge (Revlon makes a good pair) is a big help. Apply a thin coat of glue to the lash, and make sure the glue has a chance to set before you apply the lash to the lid. It should only take a few seconds for the glue to become tacky. If the lash is too wet, it has a tendency to move around before it can adhere. Use a Q-tip to dab off the excess glue. If you need to cut the lashes to fit your eyes, cut them from the outside (the part closest to your ears). The shorter end of the lash goes closer to your nose (just not too close to the corner; it will poke you all day long). Place the longer end closer to your ear. I prefer a type of lash called "wispies" by Ardell. They are pretty and look natural and full. They aren't too heavy on the eyelid or uncomfortable to wear (especially if it is your first time using lashes). Don't over-do it if you are a beginner. Lashes are meant to open your eyes to viewers who see you from afar. You don't want the lashes to be so heavy that they make your eyes appear to be closed from the floor.

Avoid lashes with rhinestones for your first couple events. They can produce a "sleepy" eye effect on the floor. You can try a pair as you become more experienced at wearing lashes. If you plan to re-use your lashes, peel them gently from the outside of your eye toward your nose. They should come off fairly easily. Do so before cleaning your face. If you get them wet, you will need to toss them. There is no need to wash them; just put them back in the case they came in and reapply them with glue the next time. I recommend re-using your lashes no more than two or three times. Most competitors wear one pair per competition, or they may stretch one pair over two competitions, but no more.

Eyebrows: Don't forget to fill in your eyebrows with an eyebrow powder or very fine brow pencil that matches the color of your eyebrows. You want to make sure your brows are clearly visible on your face and frame the eyes. Have them waxed or threaded a week before the comp. A well-groomed brow opens your eyes and allows more space for color and definition.

Blush: When applying blush, stay with brighter colors. After application, stand back about 10 feet and look at yourself in the mirror. If you can't see your cheekbones, you need more. If it looks like you have "clown cheeks," you need to blend. The biggest issue with girls who do their own makeup is they don't blend enough. You want to look like a Rembrandt not a Warhol. Blend, blend, blend!

Lipstick and lip gloss: Get a lipstick and liner that flatters your skin color and the color of the dress you will be wearing. The softer the color you apply, the less visible your lips will be on the floor, so go for stronger colors that aren't too harsh. Pink or wine-colored lipsticks work really well. Avoid intensely dark colors that may call too much attention to your lips. If your lips are dry, exfoliate them with a sugar scrub. Applying foundation to your lips during the initial makeup process and then powdering them will help the lipsticks' longevity. If your lipstick tends to "bleed" onto your face, Guerlain has a wonderful product called Lip Lift. Apply around the outer edge of your lips then follow with liner and color. Using a lip brush to apply the color will help blend the liner. Applying a layer of gloss can either enhance the color (darker gloss) or soften the color (lighter gloss). Using a straw to drink through during the day will also help keep that pretty pout.

Spray tan: Almost all competitors use a spray tan or body bronzer when competing. Remember that the lights are bright on the floor, and you will look washed out if you have no color. The more skin that is exposed, the more important color becomes. If your costume covers most of your body, it's not quite as necessary. My best advice is to have it professionally applied the first time, and NEVER spray your face. Ask the person tanning you to finish just under the jaw line. It will be easier to blend your makeup from that point. Most of us have dry patches, hyper pigmentations, or dark spots on our faces from sun damage. Spray tan will be drawn into those areas and accentuate them. It can also lead to break outs, so leave the spray tan to your body and use makeup to match your face. A helpful tip: after your spray tan is applied, stop by M.A.C. and have them select a foundation to match your freshly tanned body.

Hair: Ballroom hair is different from any other hairstyle in the world. You may want to Google "ballroom dancing hair styles" to get an idea of what ballroom hair looks like before having your hair done the first time. You can also go to competition websites and look at pictures of other competitors.

If you want to stand out on the floor, have your hair done by a professional ballroom stylist for your first couple competitions. Your hair must be neat and stay put while you dance. It is hard to imagine the amount of hairspray required in order to make sure it stays during a full day of head snapping and back bends. Most competitors wear their hair in a tight up-do for all dance styles. For Rhythm or Latin, you may wear part of your hair down or use a longer hairpiece like a ponytail, but the front of your hair should stay out of your eyes and lipstick. It's not unusual for a competitor to have her hair done once for a two- or three- day competition and sleep on it overnight. If you decide to do so, bring a silk scarf or satin pillowcase to sleep on to prevent your hairstyle from becoming disheveled overnight. Again, look at the other competitors and ask the ones you like who did their hair. You could also ask if they mind letting you take a picture of their coif. I don't think they will say no.

As with makeup, bring a picture or share a preference with your stylist, and then let the stylist do her job. You will be amazed at what we can create if you just let us work our magic. It is not in our best interest to send you out of the room looking awful. It may be helpful to know that most ballroom hairstyles are designed to give you height and volume, so they may appear a bit unnatural at first. While it may look odd upfront or in the mirror, it looks stunning on the floor.

You don't need hair accessories, but they can add an extra touch. You can buy them at the competition from a vendor, or you can purchase them at the mall. Avoid over-investing in accessories of a certain color that you may only wear with one dress. If you pick an AB crystal (stands for Aurora Borealis), you can use it with almost any dress as it picks up several different colors.

For hairspray, I prefer the Sebastian brand, which works well because it isn't too sticky. To set a style, I follow up with Got2b Blasting Freeze Spray by Schwarzkopf, which is probably one of the best products out there to finish off a hairstyle.

When you use hairpins and bobby pins to hold a style, always cross the pins for maximum hold.

If you want to use a hairpiece, get one made from human hair. If you use a synthetic piece, just remember that you can't use a straightening iron on it as it will melt the hair. To find quality hairpieces for less, visit any store that sells wigs or extensions. I favor what I call a "sister-girl shop," and most African American women have one they visit frequently. You can find a wide range of styles from curly to straight and colors from platinum blonde to jet-black. When attaching a hairpiece by yourself, make sure it is securely fastened. Always practice dancing your routines while wearing it prior to the competition. It is not unusual to see poorly attached hairpieces fly off in the middle of a heat, and the judges are not amused by this lack of attention to detail. Make sure your hairpiece matches your hair color when it is up. Your hair may be one color at the tips or at the top of your hair and another underneath. Your hair will look wet from all the hairspray, and it will appear much darker than you are used to. Opt for matching the more prominent tones of your hair.

Jessika Ferm: *What are some "Dos and Don'ts" for newer competitors who are working with you or other stylists at competitions?*

Lisa Bentley-DeBevec: I've danced and competed for 28 years, and I've been in your shoes. I know what it is like to have someone you don't know do your hair and makeup. It is essential that you trust your stylist, so before you decide to work with someone, ask for references. Identify a few women who look great competing and ask them who did their hair or makeup. Once you find the right stylist, allow the professional to do her job.

I book up very quickly, so you will need to contact me a few months prior to your competition to set an appointment. You can do so by contacting me directly at lisa@glamrpuss.com. Visit the competition website for more information. When you book your appointment let me know the competition you are attending and the level at which you dance (Bronze, Silver, Open, etc.). Once the heat sheets are out, I will contact you to confirm your appointment. When you get to the competition, ask the front desk to call my room, and I'll tell you where I'm located in the hotel. I usually keep a towel in the door, so it is easy to spot. No need to knock, just come right in and have a seat. For more information about how I work, visit my website: glamrpuss.com/Rules.aspx

If there is something you are allergic to, please tell me during our initial phone conversation.

It's a great idea to invest in a travel alarm clock as a backup or set your phone to wake you up on time for your appointment. If you are new to dancing (in Newcomer or Pre-Bronze) you may have an appointment as early as 4:00 a.m. If you oversleep, I may not be able to get you in. Please arrive at your appointment with a clean, moisturized face and clean, dry hair (no mousse, gel, or hairspray in it).

Please don't call me the day before to ask if I'm running on time. I won't know how the schedule will flow until I get into my day. Each appointment (for hair or makeup) is approximately 30 minutes long and an early arrival is appreciated. Every effort is made to maintain punctuality. Just know that I may sometimes run a bit over if I have to accommodate last-minute emergencies. If you are going to be late, call me on my cell phone or text me. (Don't leave me a message on my office phone; I won't be there or get the message.) If you are going to be significantly late, I may not be able to take you, but I will try to work you in as soon as I can, schedule permitting. If you don't show up for your appointment, you will be charged.

Once you are at the appointment, share any preferences you may have, like "I want a smoky eye," or "I prefer some softness around my face." Then let me do my job. It becomes difficult when clients are too involved or try to control every step I take. I just get bogged down, and I lose creativity. I want to make you happy, and I know that my experience and skill will make you look beautiful. If you have a picture of something you like, bring it. I work better with pictures, and while I can't promise it will look exactly like the photo, I have a much better idea what you are expecting.

If you are a more advanced competitor and would like to change your look, start talking to me about the changes you are contemplating well in advance. It's helpful to try out a new look or style at a smaller competition. At a larger competition like Ohio Star Ball or USDC, I don't have a lot of time during your appointment to creatively brainstorm ideas with you.

Jessika Ferm: *Is it customary to tip the stylists at the competition?*

Lisa Bentley-DeBevec: Tips are at the client's discretion as with any service provider. Most of my clients do tip, and I greatly appreciate it.

Interview Insight: Kimberley Mitchell

HOLDS SEVERAL U.S. AND INTERNATIONAL TITLES INCLUDING BRITISH PROFESSIONAL RISING STAR, FIFTH IN THE WORLD INTERNATIONAL LATIN, TWO-TIME INTERNATIONAL CHAMPION, AND TWO-TIME UNITED STATES LATIN CHAMPION.

Kimberley judges competitions all over the United States and also coaches and competes with her Open Gold amateur students. She resides in Columbus, OH.

Jessika Ferm: *You began your dancing career at age two and became a professional at 18. How did you get started in ballroom dancing?*

Kimberley Mitchell: Both of my parents competed as amateurs when they were kids and began dancing as professionals as they got older. Somewhere in there, they married and opened a ballroom studio. Then, all of a sudden, I came along. I used to say I came out dancing. My mother taught a lesson on Thursday night and delivered me on Friday morning. I grew up at the studio, and both my parents and their students kept me busy dancing, in order to keep me out of trouble.

I had my first dance partner at age five and won my first international championship at eight. I competed as an amateur in Britain until I moved to the U.S. at the age 18 and began a professional partnership with Bill Sparks. We had a great career together and produced some amazing results.

Jessika Ferm: *What tips were most instrumental to you early in your ballroom dancing journey, helping set you on the path to success?*

Kimberley Mitchell: My mum was my first teacher, and like many well-meaning mothers, she kept nagging me about my posture. "Keep your shoulders down and head up," she kept saying. She didn't stop giving me that advice until I retired from professional dancing! The truth is, it definitely shaped me into having exceptional posture on and off the dance floor.

My mother also used to say, "You can collapse off the floor," meaning don't let your emotions rule you on the dance floor. When all the heats are done, you can fall apart all you want, just do it away from the ballroom.

I also learned that judges can't feel your feelings; they can only see your performance. So no matter how much I may enjoy or embrace a certain feeling as I'm dancing, I have to be able to project it through my movements.

Jessika Ferm: *As a professional competitor, what one event or situation stands out as a pivotal moment, and what did you learn from it?*

Kimberley Mitchell: Bill and I were invited to a special event in England called "The Night of a Hundred Stars," where the top six couples in each category are invited to do a show dance. Bill and I had a West Coast Swing routine that we felt great about. What I didn't expect was that the whole floor would be pitch black, except for two spotlights that followed us along the floor. At one point, Bill and I were separated, and the spotlight was blinding me, so I had no idea where he was. Luckily he found me, and I was able to finish the routine without most of the judges noticing. What I learned is that, no matter what, you have to be able to work around obstacles without letting them throw you off your game.

Jessika Ferm: *What are some of your pet peeves as a judge?*

Kimberley Mitchell: My big pet peeve is when the student or the teacher is off timing. Remember, it's not the music you hear inside your head that matters. Dancing to the beat of the music is a foundational principle in ballroom dancing. If the teacher is off, and the student is talented enough to get back on track, I will mark the student fairly. Even when a student is uncontested, I will mark her second if the timing is off. When uncontested students who receive second placements approach me and ask me about my marks, I tell them my reasons. Don't be afraid to ask me if this happens to you, so you can improve. Just approach me off the dance floor, away from other students and judges. I really don't mind. The more information you have and seek, the better chance you have of improving.

Jessika Ferm: *Who do you look at first?*

Kimberley Mitchell: I look at you as soon as you walk out on the floor, before the first beat of music has started. I love to see students walk out with confidence and embrace the concept of feeling and looking like a "champion." Just know that there is a fine balance between being confident and having an "over-the-top" attitude that doesn't match up with your dancing skill.

I'm drawn to anything that stands out, both good and bad. My positive attention gets drawn to students who wear clean shoes, have their hair professionally done, and show up in beautiful well-fitting costumes. Students who exude appropriate confidence also get my attention. On the negative side, if your grooming or costuming is off, I will notice you. And if I do, your dancing better be exceptional. In short, don't ever make me question your dancing by missing the important details like grooming and costuming.

Jessika Ferm: *You have two successful Open Gold Latin gentlemen students who compete with you. What tips do you offer them and other gentlemen competitors to compete with grace and joy?*

Kimberley Mitchell: Both Jacob Neal and Joe DiRosario, my amateur competitive guys, were already competing at the Open Gold level when I met them, so they had experience. What I tell them, and would tell any competitor, is to work on performing on the competitive floor they way you do in practice. A mistake many students make is that they try too hard to produce something on the competition floor, which ends up throwing the partnership off balance. It is easy for the amateur gentleman to feel the need to "compete" with the "big pros," even though they are being judged against the ladies in their heats. Instead, focus on your partnership, and remember to dance with your partner. When you are relaxed and confident, you will attract the judges' attention and enjoy your dancing even more.

5

Preparing for Competition

Dancing's not always stressful, but I always make sure that I'm prepared as I can be, both physically, mentally, and practically.

- DEBORAH BULL

Photos by: Stephen Marino Photography

This chapter is designed to offer tips and strategies for brand-new to newer competitors in order to "prepare like a pros" for competitions; however, most intermediate- to- experienced competitors will benefit from reading this chapter as well.

You may not know, for example, that the on-deck captains want you to check in with them before you take a restroom break between your heats, or that they can help you manage especially tight heats to make sure you don't miss a dance. The highlight interviews by professional On-deck Captains Yolanda Vargas and Andrea Ringgold on pages 179 and 182 offer powerful nuggets of information that you don't want to miss. You also don't want to skip "Your Competition Checklist" on page 163 to make sure you have packed all the necessary items before your next competition.

The key to any successful competition is preparation. The first time you compete, the process can be a bit overwhelming. Each competitor has experienced the "first time," and for most, the experience resembles a whirlwind (for some, a tornado).

This chapter will help prepare you and assist in minimizing any unnecessary stress or anxiety. Believe me. Competing will be plenty nerve-wracking all on its own.

What You Need to Know Before You Leave and When You Get to the Competition

> **"** I've always considered myself to be just average talent, and what I have is a ridiculous insane obsessiveness for practice and preparation."
>
> - WILL SMITH

Consider yourself on the competition floor from the moment you leave your house. Remember, judges can see you anytime before you enter the dance floor. The more professional you appear, the more they will view you in a positive light. As John DePalma, prominent emcee and co-organizer of the Capital DanceSport Championship, states in his insight on page 83:

> "Aim to look well-groomed and presentable at all times when you're competing. Think of it as being on the floor the moment you leave for the airport or get in your car to drive to the competition. Do the same when you show up for practice at the studio. You can never go wrong looking well groomed."

I have a certain outfit that I wear for travel, which is both comfortable and stylish. I typically have a freshly applied spray tan and can't wear a bra, because it will create lines in places that my competing dresses can't hide. So the outfit I wear needs to cover-up the fact that I'm not wearing a bra. While you will see competitors in all types of clothes, from pajama-like outfits to stylish Louis Vuitton ensembles, my recommendation is to wear something in-between that highlights your assets and gets you noticed in a positive way, should you bump into a judge on your way to the competition.

Once you walk through the doors of the hotel, you have officially entered the competition (which means you want to mind your posture, appear confident, and greet everyone with a smile). Top teacher and organizer of the prestigious People's Choice competition, Forrest Vance, reminds us in his insight on page 184 that we can never go wrong by embracing formal etiquette. Addressing someone as "sir" or "ma'am" never goes out of style. For the evening portion of his competition, he stresses that the dress code is formal. Forrest expects attendees to wear a ball gown or tuxedo/suit, because he wants to make sure that everyone is having a first- class experience. After all, ballroom dancing is an elegant and glamorous sport.

When you first arrive at the competition venue or the hotel, you may feel slightly overwhelmed. You may bump into judges, professionals, fellow competitors—and everything and everyone seems to sparkle and glitter. The following tips will help you stay centered and enjoy the experience, from the moment you enter to the time you leave.

- If you are staying at the hotel, check in and go to your room.

- Unpack your dresses or suits and make sure everything arrived in good condition. It's not a bad idea to iron or steam your competing clothes right away, so you don't have to do so first thing in the morning. Personally, I lay out each outfit with the matching jewelry and pantyhose, so I know I have all the pieces I need. Several times, I thought I had brought a piece of jewelry only to learn I left it at home. You don't want to discover these things shortly before you have to dance the next day.

- Check in with your instructor or partner, and confirm that you arrived safely if you are traveling separately. This will reduce any stress any one may have about your safe arrival.

- If you have plans to practice, meet your instructor/dance partner in the ballroom or practice room. Don't forget to bring your dance shoes with you.

- Familiarize yourself with the hotel:

  ○ **Locate the ballroom:** It's important to know where you will be dancing, so you can visualize yourself dancing there. If the floor is up, you may be able to practice on it the night before. Sometimes the floor is slippery, and other times it's a bit tacky. You want to know how the floor feels prior to entering it for your heats. It can make a world of difference in how you modify your shoes or routine to accommodate it. Always ask the organizer or event planner if you can use the floor before doing so. You don't want to be in the way of them preparing for the competition.

  ○ **Locate the bathroom nearest to the ballroom:** While this may seem odd at first, bathrooms become hot commodities when you compete. At some competitions you need to exit the ballroom to visit the restroom, and at others they are located nearby. Again, don't let the restroom search increase your stress or keep you from dancing a heat.

  ○ **Find the practice room:** There is usually a separate room with a smaller practice floor, where you and your instructor can prepare for the competition. You may also visit the practice room to warm up yourself. One "perk" of using the practice room is that you often get to dance next to some of the amazing professionals and top amateurs who also use the room. It's like getting an up-close-and-personal view of their dancing, which can serve as great inspiration. Avoid approaching them as they are practicing. Be courteous and let them have their space and time to get ready.

- **Find the registration desk:** At almost all competitions, the registration desk is open the night before or very early the next morning. Your instructor may have already checked in and received your competing number, heat sheets, and program. If not, meet at the registration desk to finalize any last minute details.

- **Find the nearest restaurant and convenience shop:** You may need to eat quickly between heats or grab an emergency power bar or drink while you dance. Knowing where you can get quick food helps relieve potential stress. It's a good idea to know what the convenience store at the hotel offers in case you need extra Band-Aids, deodorant, or breath mints.

- **Review your heat sheets and program:** It's important to remember that your heat sheet is a guideline for when you will be dancing. Don't assume you will be dancing exactly the way it's listed on the heat sheet. The rule of thumb is to be in the ballroom one hour to 45-minutes prior to your heats. Competitions can run up to 30-minutes early or late, and you don't want to miss your chance to shine on the floor. Familiarize yourself with the program. In it, you will learn who you will be dancing with and see if you have finals, semi-finals, or quarterfinals in each heat. You can go nuts trying to figure it all out if you are just starting out. But a program is extremely helpful in determining when you will be dancing and how the heats are organized. Avoid over-focusing on the program, however. Please remember that there aren't any refunds if you miss a heat. It's your responsibly (not your teacher's) to be in the right place at the right time.

- **Order your competition video:** Many new dancers assume that they are automatically taped, and when they approach the videographer for their videos, they are disappointed to learn that they needed to pre-order them. As soon as you have your heat sheets and program, fill out the video-recording form (usually located on the tables in the ballroom, or you can approach the videographers in the ballroom and ask for a form).

If this is your first time competing, ask your instructor to help you fill it out. You will need your instructor's competing number and your heat numbers in order to complete the form. Remember to hand it to the videographer BEFORE your first heat. You may opt to record each heat or just pick a few to help manage your competing budget. When I first started to compete, I taped each heat including scholarships/championships to get as much of my dancing on tape as I could. Now, I tape only my scholarships/championships because I consider my first few heats as practice or warm up. To learn why it's important to have a video of your dancing and for more tips on how to view your video see Michael Mead's tips on page 94 and Tony Scheppler's on page 118. If you are competing on a budget or need advice on how to decide which heats to tape, you may find the tips on page 198 in Chapter 6 especially helpful.

- **Be in the ballroom at least 45-minutes-to-one-hour prior to your first heat:** While we've already gone over this it bears repeating: You don't want to miss a heat or a chance to compete just because you were late getting to the ballroom. And remember, there are no refunds for missed heats. The organizers aren't responsible for your lack of planning.

- **Give yourself a break (or a few) throughout the competition:** The ballroom is extraordinarily stimulating. You have music playing 24-7, sparkles and dresses as far as the eye can see, and you engage with others while watching or dancing. It's not uncommon to feel completely wiped out, even before you dance, by the stimulation and movement of the ballroom alone. Take breaks after your heats are done or between dinner and the evening session. It's important to have time to process and recharge. Going back to your room for an hour or two can help a great deal. Trust me. This is a lot harder than it may seem at first. Most competitors are cheering others on when they aren't dancing, and they don't want to miss a thing. This is a surefire way of burning yourself out, so be careful.

Once it's your turn to compete, make sure you arrive early in the ballroom, and, if you are new, introduce yourself to the on-deck captains. To learn more about them and their jobs, please refer to page 27 in Chapter 1. Professional On-deck Captains Yolanda Vargas and Andrea Ringgold share in their insights on pages 179 and 182 that they want you to know if you are new. That way, they can help guide you along and ensure that you are on the floor for the right heats. I highly recommend that you read both of their highlights to prepare adequately for your first competition. They also share great tips for interacting with others while in the on-deck area and for making your first couple of competitions run smoothly.

These preparation tips will help you avoid some of the most common pitfalls, and they provide ideas for making your transition from social dancer to competitor a smooth one. In the next section we will review your competition checklist and go through the important timelines that help you get ready.

Your Competition Checklist

> " I write everything down. I email the second I think of something, or I write notes in my BlackBerry calendar. I set up reminder alerts on my phone. And I have a notebook by my bedside so I can write down any last-minute ideas."

> — GIADA DE LAURENTIIS

As promised in Chapter 4, it's time to get down to the nitty-gritty and review the action steps you indicated you needed to take in the "Appearance Musts Checklist" on page 136. Take a moment to review your list before reading the next section. Consider expanding your list with additional details you gain here, to make sure you have crossed all your Ts and dotted all the Is.

The checklist below is outlined by weeks to help you get organized. If you are reading this book and are closer than eight weeks to your next competition, don't worry. You still have time to catch up. The timelines are meant as general guidelines to help you stay on track. It may be helpful to put the tips on your calendar to ensure you don't forget any of the steps.

Eight-to-12 Weeks Prior to a Competition

CONSIDER VISITING A COMPETITION AS AN AUDIENCE MEMBER FIRST
- Prior to attending my first competition, my instructor encouraged me to visit a competition to get a feel for what to expect. I was on a business trip in New York City and decided to attend the Empire State Dance Sport Championship. It was a great experience, and I had a chance to take in the whole ballroom scene. I learned some important language, and I was able to try on a few dresses. It also helped me see other dancers at my level and encouraged me to move forward.

BEGIN SEARCHING FOR A DRESS
- **Renting:** If you are renting a dress, I recommend going with a reputable rental company such as Rhythmic Rentals, rhythmicrentals.com or Encore Ballroom Couture, encoreballroomcouture.com. Professional ballroom rental companies have an easy process and are extremely helpful in selecting the dress that works best for you. Visit the company's website, select a few dresses to try on, and they will ship them to you. After you are done, ship the dresses back, reserving the one you want for your competition. A week or so prior to your competition, they will send the dress back to you. After you are finished competing, you ship it back to them. If you are in the Columbus, Ohio area, you can to rent from my company Next Level Dancing, nextleveldancing.com. While we offer limited try-on services, you are welcome to make an appointment to try on dresses at our offices. For an extensive list of costume resources, see page 264, Chapter 8. Gentlemen buy their outfits, which are not as

expensive as ladies' dresses. For a beginner, a nicely ironed pair of black trousers and a black shirt and tie will suffice.

- **Buying consignment dresses online:** There are several online sites on which competitors sell their dresses directly. A site I highly recommend is ballroomdancers.com. Remember the rule "buyer beware," and be careful from whom you buy. I have bought dresses from this site and have had great luck. Avoid sending payments to persons abroad, unless you know them or have spoken to them. Don't wire money abroad. Instead insist on sending a certified check, bank check, PayPal, or a similar method that enables you to get your money back should things go awry. I encourage gentlemen to buy their costumes from the dress vendors at competitions. There are several vendors who specialize in gentlemen's costumes exclusively and I highly recommend Don Cheng at Star Dance Shop (stardanceshop.com). You can find additional details in Chapter 8.

- **Buying new dresses online:** It can be overwhelming to search for dresses online. There are several sites that sell inexpensive dresses, and they are often located in Asia. While these dresses can be great options to start off your competing journey, the quality can be an issue. Remember, you get what you pay for. If you are looking for your first Rhythm/Latin dress, this can be an excellent option. For a Smooth/Standard dress, the quality tends to be lacking since there is more fabric and dress needed to cover you. This is where the gentlemen have an advantage. Inexpensive dance costumes can be bought online or custom-made to order at very reasonable prices. The quality may not be as good as a tailor-made outfit, but for the price it's worth ordering a few options and hoping one of them fits.

- **Buying new or consignment dresses from ballroom competition dressmakers:** Buying new or consigned dresses from dressmakers is a wonderful option. They tend to range from $1,500-to-$7,000. Most judges and coaches recommend that you get a dress that is appropriate for your dancing level. If this is your first competition and you are dancing in Bronze Newcomer, you want to pick a dress that is less elaborate and more understated than someone who is dancing Open Gold. If you show up in a dress that looks like it was made for a professional, the judges will expect your dancing level to match. Experienced judge Glenis Dee Creger shares her ideas on selecting the right dress for your level on page 43.

A professional dressmaker like Designs to Shine, (designstoshine.com) or Doré Designs, (doredesigns.com) will guide you into the best dress for this stage in your dancing. For great tips, please read the interview insight of Designs to Shine's founder Maria McGill's on page 145. As you become more advanced in your dancing, you can sell your dress and "trade up," without having to make the same investment again. Most professional dressmakers will sell your previous gown on consignment and offer up to 60 percent credit toward the purchase of a new dress. Other companies like Encore (encoreballroomcouture.com), offer cash back for dresses sold. They do collect a minimal upfront fee to photograph and list a dress on their website.

When considering buying your first dress, avoid over-spending. If you are competing in Pre-Bronze you may want to invest more of your available cash in lessons. No dress will make up for a lack of technique or skill. As you advance in your dancing, your dress will need to match your skill level, and it may be a better time to spend the money on an appropriate costume. A great tip is to visit the website of the competition you plan to attend to see what vendors will be attending. You then can make an appointment to meet with a dressmaker for additional help.

BOOK YOUR HAIR AND MAKEUP APPOINTMENT

- **Hair and Makeup:** Most larger competitions have at least one hair and makeup professional onsite. Because most serious competitive dancers get their hair and makeup done professionally, there is usually a waiting list to get an appointment. I recommend Lisa Bentley DeBevec and Linda Doyle. You can read more about Lisa's fabulous tips for hair and makeup in her interview insight on page 148. Both Lisa and Linda are extremely professional, reliable, and organized. You want to call them as soon as you know where you will be competing and what style and level you are signed up for. Lisa or Linda will put you on the list and let you know when you are slotted for your appointments the week of the competition. Please remember that if you are doing Newcomer or Pre-Bronze, you are one of the first people out on the floor in the morning, which means you will need to get your hair done the night before or really early in the morning. It is not unusual for appointments to start at 4:00 A.M. Please be respectful of your stylists' time and show up five-to-ten minutes early for your appointment. You can expect to pay about $70-to-$100 for each service, which average about 30 minutes each. If you are doing hair and makeup, you will have a one-hour appointment. Please consider tipping your stylist in addition to their quoted fees. For contact information for Lisa and Linda, please see Chapter 8.

MAKE SURE YOU HAVE A CLEAN PAIR OF COMPETING SHOES

- **Competing Shoes:** As you know by now, many judges are particular about amateurs and professionals wearing clean and neat dance shoes while competing. It is a great idea to keep one pair of shoes that you use only to compete in for each style. You can buy shoes online, but most people buy them at the competitions. There are usually several vendors whose prices range from $50-to-$200 for a pair of quality shoes. For recommended shoe retailers, please see Chapter 8, page 264.

MAKE A SPRAY TANNING APPOINTMENT OR BEGIN EXPERIMENTING WITH SELF-TANNERS

- **Tanning Options:** While tanning, spray tanning, and self-tanning are not required to compete, it is highly recommended that you consider adding some color to your body when competing. Some lucky dancers have natural coloring; unfortunately I, like most Caucasian women, don't have enough natural Latina in me to make myself stand out. A bit of added color helps me look like I have a glow under the unforgiving ballroom lights.

  Consider doing a tanner test run to see how the product wears on you prior to having it done in preparation for the competition. I found that some spray tans don't work well with my skin, so I needed to test a few before finding the right fit. If you are competing in Smooth or Standard only, a self-tanner on the chest, arms, and back may be all you need. There are also products such as creams and spray-on-tans that can be used, but be careful. They may stain your dresses or hotel room when applied.

MAKE SURE YOU KNOW YOUR ROUTINES BY YOURSELF

- **Your Routines:** Practice your routines physically and mentally. It is essential that you feel comfortable about your routines, so you won't experience "mental freeze" right before you go on to the floor. For more tips on how to avoid performance anxiety, see page 113 in Chapter 3. For your first competition, you should have a simple routine with figures that you can easily repeat with or without your instructor. I practice my routines as much in my head as I do physically. That way, I can practice wherever I am. If your instructor does not have set routines, practice your figures one at a time. For additional warm-up tips and strategies for getting your "mental game" on, see Toni Redpath's interview insight on page 86. Another great tip is to create playlists with the songs in which you compete. I have a list for each of the four styles titled by style (American Rhythm, American Smooth, International Latin, International Standard), so I can run through each dance without stopping to find the right song.

PRACTICE DANCING IN YOUR COSTUME BEFORE THE COMPETITION

- **Run-throughs:** You don't want to discover that your dress unzips, moves too much, or falls off your shoulder at the competition. Always do a run-through in your dress and with your instructor before you leave for the competition. I once had a gorgeous Rhythm dress with a very heavy skirt. Thankfully we did a practice run, and I learned that the skirt was so heavy it threw me off balance. That "aha" may have thrown me off my game had I discovered it on the competition floor. For active dances such as Jive and Swing, it's easy to get caught with your heel in your dress, which can have disastrous results. Several of my friends have had the misfortune of flashing the judges a bit too much skin after their dresses were pulled down by a heel stuck in the bottom of a dress or a skirt that flared out too much.

- Another great tip is to spend a lesson running through your dances as you would in a competition. Ask your instructor to prepare a heat with all your dances in the order and timing in which you will compete. That way, you become accustomed to the flow and stamina that is required to complete your routines.

PURCHASE AND PACK YOUR BALLROOM NECESSITIES

- **The Ballroom Checklist:** Over the years, I have compiled a checklist that I use to ensure I'm prepared before, during, and after a competition. You may want to create your own checklist, borrowing items that make sense for you from my personal list below:

  - **Self-tanner or tanning spray:** I always bring a self-tanning spray or cream such as Sexsymbol or Aery Jo, in case my spray tan has gaps. You can buy these online or from a vendor at the competition.

  - **Press-on nails (when I use them):** I bring several packages in case I need to reapply nails during the competition. I love the brand Kiss, which you can by in any major supermarket or drug store.

  - **Acetone:** Don't forget to bring pure Acetone to ensure press-on nails are applied properly.

  - **Satin pillowcase or satin scarf:** I most often sleep with my hair already made up, and I tie a silk or satin scarf around my head to prevent breakage or fly-aways. Some professional ballroom hair stylists sell them; pick one up when you get your hair done.

  - **Lashes:** I always bring several sets of fake eyelashes, in case I need to change them. If you opt to do your own makeup, please wear lashes! They make a big difference on the floor.

- **Robe/Studio Jackets:** Most dancers wear a silk robe or similar cover-up over their ballroom dresses while walking to and from the ballroom and inside the ballroom to keep warm. It is notoriously cold in the ballroom to keep competitors from getting over-heated while dancing. A pashmina scarf or beautiful throw is another great option. Some studios have studio jackets that their dancers wear, which tell you where they dance. If you'd like a matching jacket, ask your studio if they have them.

- **Sewing kit:** I bring a sewing kit that includes safety pins and scissors. I always keep thread that matches the color of all my dresses, just in case.

- **Headphones that connect to iPhone or recording device:** If you are your teacher's only student, you may get lucky and have a run-through of your dances. But if you are one of many students, then you may not have that luxury. I always bring my headphones and iPhone with the songs I am dancing to pre-recorded, so I can warm up by myself.

- **Ballroom jewelry:** I buy all my dance jewelry from vendors at the competition. My favorite vendor is Ann Liew from DanzAnn. She is extremely helpful and stands by her jewelry for years to come. Don't make the same jewelry mistake I did, when I inadvertently destroyed my instructor's dance shirt (see page 134). I always double-check to be sure I have packed the right jewelry, including bracelets, earrings, and necklaces, for each style/dress.

- **Soft shoes, flip-flops, slippers:** When you are dancing in high heels all day, it feels wonderful to take your dance shoes off and put on comfortable shoes that let your feet rest a bit. I prefer a soft ballerina shoe or slippers. If you decide to bring flip flops or thong sandals, remember that you will most likely be wearing fishnet pantyhose, and they don't work well with these types of shoes.

- **Semi-formal and formal outfits:** If you dance at a larger competition that spans three days, you will have the opportunity to watch professional couples dance. These evening events tend to be dressy. For a three-day competition, you may want to bring a cocktail dress or similar. For a large competition like USDC or Ohio Star Ball, the Saturday event is formal, so bring your ball gowns.

- **Comfortable and fashionable outfits:** Most serious competitors think of their ballroom competition like an "all inclusive event," and they embrace it as if it were an important business meeting. Remember, the judges see you at breakfast, lunch, dinner, in the practice room, trying on dresses, and at the airport. Watch your dress code, posture, and manners during the entire competition. Amp up your overall presence, in other words.

- **Practice wear:** If you will be practicing with your instructor, don't forget to bring your practice wear and practice shoes.

- **Pack an "emergency ballroom kit:"** In addition to your prepped items, add a small kit that you can carry into the ballroom (so you don't have to run up to your room to grab emergency items). In my kit, I keep:

  - Band-aids
  - Breath mints/gum
  - A compact mirror
  - Deodorant
  - Double-sided tape/fashion tape
  - Eyelash glue
  - Hairpins
  - Hairspray
  - Heal-stoppers for dance shoes
  - Nail file/clippers
  - Nail or super-glue
  - A pen
  - A small sewing kit
  - Safety pins
  - Sanitary wipes for freshening up
  - Shoe brush
  - Tissues
  - A towel

Because of popular demand, my company has begun selling what we call the "Saving Grace Case," which includes most of the items listed above—and more. You can buy a "starter kit" or the "full kit" at our website, nextleveldancing.com, if you want one already prepared. Otherwise, just use this checklist and prepare your own.

BUY AND PACK YOUR SNACKS

- **Competition Snacks:** I have found it absolutely essential to bring healthy and nutritious snacks for in-between munching. I am rarely able to eat lunch or dinner due to my dancing schedule, and I need replenishment throughout the day. Because I prefer to eat only organic food, I always locate the closest Whole Foods, Trader Joe's, or large grocery store. I'll travel by taxi if I don't have a car handy. I've found that having access to the right type of food is key. You may not have any special dietary needs, but it's always helpful to know where you can get food and snacks if you aren't able to pack them.

  Power bars, water with electrolytes, nuts, shredded coconut, kiwis, and almond butter are a few of my favorites. You will need high-protein, high-fat foods to hold you over, and don't forget to drink plenty of water. It is usually best to bring your own water, even though most competitions have water stations in the ballroom. On average, I drink about four large bottles of water a day (134 ounces), so having my bottles handy, instead of running to the water station between heats, is especially helpful. Bring a small cooler or bag to store your goodies. Remember to bring enough for your instructor as well. Depending on how much your instructor dances throughout the day, he will greatly appreciate it if you bring along his favorite snacks, too.

MAKE SURE YOU HAVE CASH

- **Cash is king:** Almost all ballroom competitions accept cash only (no checks, debit, or credit cards). Make sure you bring enough for last-minute tickets, entries, or programs. I always bring at least $300, just in case.

DOUBLE-CHECK YOUR PACKING

- **Dresses and shoes:** If you are flying to a competition, always pack your dresses in a carry-on bag. I have heard horror stories of competitors who packed several dresses in checked bags, only to arrive at the competition with empty bags or no bags at all. I have an extra practice dress that I always pack for a worst-case scenario—should a dress tear or if someone else is in desperate need of one. This practice came in handy for me when I arrived at a competition only to realize that I had left my dress bag at the rental car office—four hours away! My dear friend lent me her extra dress, enabling me to dance. I always pack my dresses and shoes together, so I have everything in one place. Remember to double-check your ballroom jewelry, as well.

PREPARE TO COMPETE

- **Print and bring copies of your heat sheets:** Most competitions will post heat sheets (the order in which you dance) online a day or so before the competition. While your instructor will share them with you at the competition, I always like to print and bring my own. That way, we have an extra set just in case. It also helps me mentally prepare if I know the order in which I will dance. Please note: initial heat sheets may change by the day of competition, so always double-check for accuracy.

- **Confirm or double-check your hair and makeup appointments:** If you decide to work with a ballroom stylist at the competition, confirm your appointment time and location. Most stylists arrive a day early to set up.

Armed with the checklists above, and a greater awareness of what to expect when you arrive at the competition, let's take a look at some of the things other dancers wish they had known before they began competing.

What Experienced Competitors Wish They Had Known When They Started

> " Wisdom is nothing but a preparation of the soul, a capacity, a secret art of thinking, feeling and breathing thoughts of unity at every moment of life."

- HERMAN HESSE

My experienced competitive friends often say, "Oh, I wish I had known that when I started." Here are some of their great tips to help you avoid pitfalls and embrace opportunities.

I wish I had known that:

When I'm competing, and we are not on package, my teacher expects me to pay for his food during the competition. I didn't know this, and it created an awkward moment between us.

The dresses have body suits. The first time I tried on a ballroom gown, the dressmaker gave it to me and led me to the ladies' room. I did what I would with any dress and tried to put it on over my head. It took me 10 minutes to figure out that I had to step into it like I would a bathing suit. When it finally dawned on me, I laughed out loud. The woman in the stall next to me asked if I was okay. I still chuckle when I think about it.

You can use a smooth dress for standard if you are on a budget. Before I decided to do so, I asked a neutral judge/coach for honest feedback. I just wanted to make sure the dressmaker's opinion matched that of the judge.

The dress you pick has to be comfortable and fit you perfectly. It should highlight your best assets and hide anything you don't wish to show. It's easy to get mesmerized by a pretty dress on a mannequin or another dancer. Remember, just because it fits someone else, that doesn't mean it will fit you perfectly. Comfort and fit are far more important than sparkles and flair.

I shouldn't wash my hands right after getting a spray tan. The first time I got one, it looked like someone had chopped off my hands. They were bright white, and the rest of my body was really dark.

When traveling to a competition, I should carry on my dresses, not pack them in my checked luggage. I was devastated when I realized that my competition dresses had been stolen from my checked luggage. Always bring your dresses and competing shoes as carry on items!

I wouldn't recognize myself in the mirror the first time I turned around in ballroom makeup. I remember thinking, Who is that staring back at me?

I could have rented dresses at first and not invested all my available resources in my first dress.

This sport is amazing. I wish I had started earlier.

Most competitions are cash only and won't accept personal checks or credit cards. For a non-cash person like me, this was a rude awakening.

A drug habit would have been less expensive—only kidding (sort of).

Standard shoes would be so uncomfortable.

How to calm my nerves before going out on the floor. Now I have a plan for doing so, but it would have been so much more helpful if I had known what to expect.

You need a thick skin if you want to get better. If you ask judges or coaches for feedback on how to improve, they will be honest with you.

If you stand next to the water dispenser at the competition, and it leaks water on the floor, your shoes may get wet, which will make the soles stick to the dance floor. This can be a real issue when you are dancing Standard!

As much as someone tried to explain what to expect, the real deal was so much more than I could have imagined. It can be a bit overwhelming at first.

Listen and learn from the judges' comments, but do not allow their opinions to take away from the joy you feel when dancing.

Being me is perfect. While it's helpful to watch other dancers to see technique and understand musical interpretations, I strive to never copy. Instead I seek my own unique expression.

How important communicating well with my instructor would be. I tape a note with my dance goals inside my dance bag to remind myself to share them with him often.

The prize money you receive when you win a scholarship is no more than $300 for first place at most competitions. I thought that winning would pay back my investment for the competition. Over the years, I have tracked my expenses and winnings, and I get back about five-to-10 percent of what I invest."

While some of these are funny in retrospect, others are more serious in nature. I hope they help you avoid the mistakes many of us made because we didn't have resources like this book to learn from. Before we wrap up this chapter, let's look at some ballroom dancing "dos and don'ts" that you should know before you compete.

The Dos and Don'ts of Ballroom Dancing: What You Must Know Before Competing

❝ Do the right thing. It will gratify some people and astonish the rest."

- MARK TWAIN

Being new in the ballroom world can be a bit overwhelming. It is like entering a parallel universe with different rules and customs. These top-ten dos are meant to help you maneuver like a pro from day-one of your ballroom journey.

1. **Mind your posture on and off the dance floor.** Remember that all judges are former dancers. Good posture is one of the most important aspects of this sport and art. Patrice Tanaka, author of *Becoming Ginger Rogers*, shares in her book that her instructor reminded her to straighten up as she walked off the dance floor, because judges are watching you all the time. They want to see that you are embracing this sport on and off the dance floor. You can learn more about Patrice's journey in her interview insight on page 33.

2. **Practice random acts of kindness and avoid gossip.** It is never too early to offer positive and sincere feedback to other dancers. I still remember a woman who came up to me during my very first competition to compliment my dress. It was an understated, rented dress, and she said it was so appropriate for my dancing level (Pre-Bronze). At that point I had no idea what that meant, but I knew she was sincere, and I was so surprised by her random act of kindness. I decided then and there that I was going to do the same as I progressed on my competing journey. Remember to offer only honest positive feedback. You don't want to say something insincere just to appear nice. If you see someone who exudes happiness on the dance floor, but may not be a technically correct dancer, offer feedback on the positive energy. What makes this sport so unique is the camaraderie that is shared among dancers, instructors, judges, and audience members. Avoid gossiping or making negative remarks about other dancers. It only makes you look bad, and it isn't helpful. If you have something valuable to say about how someone could improve her look or appearance, do so directly and tactfully.

3. **Be generous and pay it forward.** Offer to help someone who may be in need. One of the young girls on our team wants to be a professional ballroom dancer after college. Because her finances are a bit tight, I offered to buy her a pair of shoes. My friend Laura Benton decided to offer one of our other students a dressmaker's credit, so the young girl could rent a dress for a large competition. If you see someone who is new and may not have the right jewelry, offer to lend yours. These generous acts often create a powerful wave of kindness that continues to flow long after your initial gesture.

4. **Greet everyone with a smile (including judges).** Remember to share your passion with others and have fun while you compete. Everyone in the ballroom loves to dance, and smiling is contagious. Judges appreciate it when you exude joy for dancing. Remember, this is their passion, profession, and life.

5. **Wish other dancers "good luck" by saying "dance well."** This is the standard greeting in the ballroom world, and it is a great reminder to focus on what matters: the dancing. Where you place is not the most important aspect of competing, even if it sometimes feels this way.

6. **Accept compliments gracefully.** This is my instructor's pet peeve, and I had to learn how to do it well. I was so humbled by compliments when I started to dance that I wasn't able to gracefully accept them. It really isn't very hard. When someone offers you positive feedback, say "thank you" or "that is so kind of you to say." Then stop talking. There is no need to go into details about how badly you feel or how nervous you are or how many mistakes you just made. You don't have to explain how much your dress costs or how uncomfortable you are out on the floor. Enjoy the feedback and breathe it in.

7. **Always congratulate other competitors.** Sometimes you win and sometimes you don't. Be gracious. Always say congratulations to the persons higher and lower on the podium. It's easy to get swept up in the excitement if you are lucky enough to win, but try to make it a habit to seek out the person who got second and say congrats. Good sportsmanship goes a long way. As Forrest Vance states in his interview insight on page 184, "It's an elegant and friendly sport, and I expect my students to act accordingly."

8. **Never argue in public (including in the ballroom, practice room, hotel, restaurant, or hallways).** Remember, judges see you everywhere. If you have a disagreement with your instructor, pause the conversation until you can speak in private. The best place to do so is in a separate room or outside the hotel. Competing can send you on an emotional roller coaster, but it is never a good idea to let others know that you are succumbing to the pressure.

This chapter was designed to help you prepare to compete like a pro. By following as many of these guidelines as possible, you will compete with greater joy and success. Before heading to Chapter 6 and learning how to compete on a budget, let's summarize this chapter.

Chapter Summary

- A major key to success in ballroom competing is excellent preparation. The more you know and can plan for, the less stress you will experience.

- Judges start to judge you as soon as you leave your house or enter the competition venue. Remember to show up as a true competitor and display the respect due to the elegant world of ballroom.

- It's important to become familiar with the competition venue. Locate the ballroom and practice rooms, restrooms, food vendors, and shops to buy emergency products.

- Become familiar with your heat sheets and program, so you know where you need to be, when. Use your heat sheets as guidelines, but don't over-rely on them. Make it a habit to be in the ballroom 45 minutes to an hour prior to your heats, in case the event runs early.

- Order your competition video the night before, or as early as possible before your first heat. If the videographer doesn't know you want to be recorded, he won't be able to produce a video for you.

- Give yourself several breaks throughout the competition. It's important to recharge and avoid becoming overwhelmed.

- Follow "Your Competition Checklist" well in advance of your first competition to make sure you have taken care of every detail needed to compete like a pro.

- Be a graceful competitor and offer positive feedback to others. Don't gossip or make unkind comments about others. You never know. The person you think of as flawed may become one of your best ballroom buddies in the future.

- Say "dance well" to encourage others as they get ready to compete.

- Accept compliments gracefully by saying "thank you." This is an extremely supportive sport, and you'll find others love to share honest and helpful compliments about your dancing and attire.

Chapter Takeaways

Take a moment to summarize your takeaways from this chapter. These notes will come in handy as you prepare for your next competition.

After reading this chapter I realized that:

_____

My most valuable takeaway is:

_____

I have added the following action steps to my preparation "to-do" list:

_____

_____

_____

_____

_____

At my next competition, I will make sure I do the following (List several commitments you have made in order to increase your level of preparedness, professionalism, grace, or sportsmanship):

_____

_____

_____

Interview Insight: Yolanda Vargas

ON-DECK CAPTAIN, CERTIFIED DANCE INSTRUCTOR BY THE IMPERIAL SOCIETY OF TEACHERS OF DANCING (ISTD), PRO-AM COMPETITOR, AND STUDIO OWNER OF INFINITY DANCE SPORT CENTER LOCATED IN SAN DIEGO, CA.

Jessika Ferm: *What are some of the most important tips you would like to share for new competitors about how to make their competition experience the best possible?*

Yolanda Vargas: Attend a competition as a spectator first. Not everyone is cut out for competing. Some just like to dance or perform, and that's okay. There are so many local one-day events now, that the probability of finding one close by is very good. When you go, focus on the Newcomer, Pre-Bronze, and Bronze categories, as well as the people who appear to be about your age. These are the people you would be up against if you were competing that day.

It can be sensory overload. The sport has its own nomenclature, which can make it next to impossible to understand what is going on. Purchase a program and do your best to follow along. Everyone is stunning, the dresses are gorgeous, and the dancing is magical. Avoid comparing yourself to other dancers at this point. Instead, imagine yourself on the dance floor and enjoy the process. This is where the dream begins.

Jessika Ferm: *That is a great tip—to attend a competition as a spectator first. Can you talk a little about the different people who will play a role at the competition?*

Yolanda Vargas: There are several people who make a competition a great experience, starting with the event organizer. The organizer will hire a crew of people to ensure that everything runs smoothly. You will also notice several judges. Their boss that weekend is the chairman, who oversees the entire event and ensures that everything happens according to set rules and guidelines. There is also an emcee, who will always call out the "heat number," and at times will tell you what you're watching on the floor. There are many others working on the stage: the DJ, a scrutineer (score tabulator), and an invigilator (a judge who ensures dancers are dancing/staying within the proper categories). The ticket-takers at the door can also be helpful to you as you learn about the event. They can point you to the dressing rooms, bathrooms, vendor area, restaurants, and the on-deck area.

The on-deck area is where all competitors must go to properly enter and exit the dance floor. This area is usually adjacent to the stage, but opposite of where the judges sit or stand. This is where I can be found many, many weekends throughout the year. I love it when competitors ask me questions in the on-deck area. That's the place to double-check where we are in the program, when you are scheduled to go on the floor, if there are any changes to the program (and often times there are), how long it will be before you go on, when the next awards ceremony will be held, and most importantly—if you have time to go to the bathroom!

Jessika Ferm: *What are some of the common mistakes new competitors make?*

Yolanda Vargas: The biggest one is "assuming." Dancers will think they have time to run to the coffee shop to grab a quick cup of coffee, only to come back and find out they have missed their event. I always tell people this is the non-thinking portion of the weekend. If you have questions, ASK the on-deck captain. Oftentimes people will tell me they don't want to bother me. It is not a bother at all. That is what we are there for.

Another big mistake for many first-timers is the lack of preparation. Not only is dance training imperative, but grooming is essential. I overheard a judge state that if dancers don't put much thought into their hair, makeup, and dress, then how much time do they put into their dancing? It is a complete package. I'm not saying you need to spend $3,500 on your first gown. Sleek hair, appropriate makeup, and a practice dress or skirt with light accessories will do fine. I have seen women in tears because they are so under-prepared in costuming and grooming. When you're standing next to someone on deck, and you know you're competing against that dancer, it is just natural to start comparing. How you respond at that moment can have an impact that will affect the rest of your competition and weekend.

Jessika Ferm: *What dos and don'ts would you offer a first-time competitor to help him or her compete with grace and joy?*

Yolanda Vargas: As a first-timer, don't worry so much about the outcome or score. You cannot predict how you are going to respond to a whole new situation (sleeping in a hotel, traveling, new clothes/costume, makeup, lights, judges, etc.). And you have absolutely no control over how well-trained your competition is. You may be up against someone who is in the studio four days a week versus your two days. Freaking out or stressing about all the "what ifs" can detract from the whole experience. You are supposed to be having fun, after all! Remember, dance is an art form, and each judge will view your dancing differently. One judge may like your hands in the air, and another may like them close to your body. You have no idea what they are looking for, so just do your best and enjoy.

Do gracefully accept the outcome and overall experience. The important part is the journey. From the moment you set the goal to compete, you set a standard for yourself. Ask yourself if you got better during the journey. If your answer is yes, then you won. The joy and happiness that I see on so many faces comes from doing the best they could at that moment, getting better, attaining new levels of success, enjoying the exhilaration of the competition, meeting new people from so many walks of life, hearing their stories, and traveling to new and exciting cities. If you didn't get the score you were hoping for, learn from that and keep moving forward.

Lastly, always be sure to get a DVD and/or purchase the many photos taken of your dancing. I like my students to see all of their bad photos as well as the good. These visual aids are impartial and very instructive. Once you're over the horror of a bad foot position, you can fix it for the next time.

Interview Insight: Andrea Ringgold

ON-DECK CAPTAIN. ANDREA IS CO-OWNER OF THE MARYLAND DANCESPORT CHAMPIONSHIPS COMPETITION. SHE RESIDES IN CENTREVILLE, MD.

Jessika Ferm: *What are some of the most important tips you would like to share for new competitors about how to make their competition experience the best possible?*

Andrea Ringgold: It can be stressful to attend your first competition. One of the best strategies for reducing your stress level and calming the nerves is to familiarize yourself with the competition as soon as possible.

When you arrive, find out where the ballroom is. If it is open, go inside and get a feel for it. If the floor is up, dance on it. Check to see if the bathrooms are inside or outside the ballroom. Any details you can cover prior to the day of the competition will help you feel more prepared and confident.

On the morning of your first heat, go down early (at least one hour prior to starting), and have your dress, hair, and makeup done. Again, dance on the floor in your dance shoes to feel the floor. Is it more tacky than you are used to? Or is it a bit slippery or fast? These insights will help you adjust effortlessly and build your confidence.

Introduce yourself to the on-deck captain as soon as possible. If it is your first competition, share your name and who you dance with. This way, we can find you if we need you and assist you every step of the way to make sure you have a fabulous competition. We want to help you remove any unnecessary stress, so you will have a more enjoyable competition. I like to think of myself in the on-deck captain role as Lucy from the Peanuts cartoon, sitting behind my little information desk. It's my job to help you and make sure you have a great experience. I take pride in my job and want to exceed your expectations.

Some teachers are wonderful and hold their students' hands the first time, but in general you want to remember that you are responsible for your own experience. Don't expect or rely on your teacher to take care of you. The more variables you can control yourself, the better.

Jessika Ferm: *What are some of the common mistakes new competitors make?*

Andrea Ringgold: Thinking that your heat sheet is set in stone. I've had so many students show up at 9:20 A.M. for a 9:30 A.M. heat, only to find that the competition is running early, and they have missed their heats. Remember, the heat sheet is only a general guideline of when you are dancing. The heat sheet you print on Thursday may change by Friday. It is best to rely on the heat sheet that is given to you at the competition, and then double-check as you go through the event. It is a good practice to be in the ballroom at least one hour prior to your listed heats. Again, being early just eliminates unnecessary stressors.

Another mistake for newer students is that they don't know how to read their marks or score sheets. Take the time to learn how to read your marks. Look for themes from the judges about your strong and weak dances. They can really help you get the most from your dancing. Be sure to review them with your instructor once you are back in the studio.

Jessika Ferm: *What "Dos and Don'ts" would you offer a first-time competitor eager to compete with grace and joy?*

Andrea Ringgold: Do introduce yourself to the other dancers in the on-deck area or ballroom. The ballroom world is one big family, and almost all the people you meet are exceptionally nice. Reach out. You may be surprised to find that your most fierce competitor becomes a lifelong friend.

Don't expect that a judge you are friendly with or a coach you have worked with will mark you well at the competition. Judges will mark what they see and will compare you to the other dancers on the floor at that time. Luckily, judges take their neutrality seriously, and they will give you scores that reflect what they see at that moment. It's important to know that it isn't personal. They may very much like you as a person but see areas for growth in your dancing, which will be reflected in their scores.

Interview Insight: Forrest Vance

FORMER UNDEFEATED U.S. RHYTHM CHAMPION, THREE-TIME WORLD AND U.S. PRO-AM CHAMPION, AND FIFTEEN-TIME U.S. TOP TEACHER. HE RESIDES IN SCOTTSDALE, AZ.

Jessika Ferm: *You are one of ballroom's most accomplished Pro/Am instructors. What are some of your philosophies or strategies that help your students and you be so successful?*

Forrest Vance: All my students welcome technique. Whether they are social dancers or competitors, they have a desire to use proper movement and technique to dance well. They are also disciplined and know that a good foundation will help them be successful in the long run. I'm not a big believer in what I call "flash and trash," as it relates to dancing. What good is it if students use what appears to be fancy arm styling, if it is artificially produced and throws them off balance?

At the beginning of the season, I sit down with all my students and ask them about their goals. Then we develop a game plan to get them there. My students have to embrace the "whole package," including impeccable hairstyling, make-up, dress, and attitude. I also expect all my students to carry themselves gracefully on and off the dance floor. For example, I encourage them to congratulate other competitors when they win, because at the next competition, they may beat that person. This is an elegant and friendly sport, and I expect my students to act accordingly.

The joy of this sport is that you get to know people from all over the country who have the same passion for dance that you do. It's easy to strike up a conversation. If you are an amateur competitor, take advantage of the opportunity to make new friends. People who dance are into looking good, being in shape, and striving to be their personal best.

I think that my personal success is rooted in my passion for teaching. While I have earned several key professional titles, the ones I am most proud of are those I earned while competing with my students. I love to judge and coach, but the secret to my accomplishments has been my unwavering commitment to my students and their success.

Jessika Ferm: *What are your non-negotiables when it comes to your competing ladies?*

Forrest Vance: All my students must have a desire to learn and be open to criticism. As a teacher, it is my job to correct my students, so they can reach the goals they set for themselves. While it is sometimes hard, I ask all my students to be willing to hear factual and honest feedback, so they can improve and grow. I honor the fact that they work hard to earn money to invest in their dancing, and I see it as my responsibly to help them protect that investment. If all I do is inflate their egos, I am doing them a disservice.

I also don't accept negativity on my team. If one student is negatively affecting the rest, I will sit that person down and have a frank conversation. If the situation continues without improvement, I will let that student go. I don't want one bad apple to ruin the bunch.

Jessika Ferm: *What common characteristics do your students have that you most enjoy?*

Forrest Vance: The cool thing about my students is that they are all successful in their lives. I've found it tremendously educational and inspirational to learn from them throughout my career. I grew up poor in a small rural town and had limited training in how to interact with wealthy and successful people. My students early on in my career took me under their wings and taught me the skills and tools that helped me create the life I enjoy today.

Jessika Ferm: *Do you have any pet peeves that you think students and professionals could benefit from avoiding?*

Forrest Vance: Our world has become overly familiar, and there is a casual approach to almost everything we do. I'm old school and value etiquette and professionalism. I think we have lost some glamour in exchange for comfort. I would encourage any amateur or professional dancer to dress the part and use more formality. You can never go wrong by addressing someone as "sir" or "ma'am" and being clean-shaven and well put-together. At my competition, The People's Choice, I have a dress code for the evening events. I want everyone to dress up and enjoy the way they feel when wearing ball gowns and tuxedos or suits. Everything at my competition is about glamour and having a first-class experience. I'm trying to keep the joy of old-world ballroom alive.

6

Competing On a Budget

Dig within. Within is the wellspring of Good; and it is always ready to bubble up, if you just dig.

- MARCUS AURELIUS

If you are working your way through this book one chapter at a time, you will have already:

- Decided if you want to compete (Chapter 1).

- Identified the type of competitor you are, set SMART competition goals, and figured out where you want to go (Chapter 2).

- Discovered how to deal with some of the challenging emotions that ballroom competing can trigger (Chapter 3).

- Made sure you can check off all of the "Top-Ten Appearance Musts" or have a plan for doing so before your next competition (Chapter 4).

- Created your own personal checklist to get competition-ready (Chapter 5).

Specifically designed for the intermediate-to-advanced competitor, the next two chapters share tips and tools for competing on a budget and competing like a pro, every time.

This doesn't mean that soon-to-be or newer competitors won't gain invaluable information from these chapters. You will! I highly encourage you to read them carefully and absorb as much as possible. They will be invaluable chapters to return to after you have completed your first competition or are ready to take your dancing to the next level.

How to Maximize Your Competing Dollars

" *Don't tell me what you value, show me your budget, and I'll tell you what you value."*

- JOE BIDEN

A few of my ballroom dancing friends are able to compete in over 200 heats per competition, month after month for the whole year. They are able to purchase exquisite, one-of-a-kind custom-made gowns. They often work alone with an instructor whose other students compete less frequently. They travel to amazing places in the U.S. and abroad to explore their dancing. And they work with the best coaches in the business on a regular basis. Ah, what bliss! I wish this were true for me, but unfortunately it is not. Nor is it true for most competitive ballroom dancers.

As you start to compete, you want to avoid comparing yourself to others. Some of my dear friends have unlimited resources, and if I try to keep up with them and their unique circumstances, I will fail. Remember, your ballroom journey is uniquely yours. You work with the resources that are available to you, including your time commitment, physical ability, and financial resources.

In this section we will explore how you can compete for years to come on a budget or with a spending plan that works for you. It is important to remember, however, that if your budget is limited, your progress may take longer, and your goals may not be reached as quickly as you would like. On the other hand, just because you throw money at this sport doesn't mean you will be a great dancer. Remembering the concept of the Balanced Ballroom Dancer (BBD) becomes important as we discuss strategies for cutting costs and maximizing results. We will review tips for staying balanced and centered in more detail in Chapter 7. The key to competing successfully on a budget is to carefully prioritize how you spend your money. While a gorgeous new gown would be fun, you may need to spend those funds on lessons to improve your dancing instead.

Let's start by reviewing the major cost categories associated with ballroom competing:

- Dance lessons
- Coaching lessons
- Entry fees/competition selection
- Travel
- Hotel rooms
- Food
- Costuming
- Hair/makeup
- Videos/pictures

DANCE LESSONS

Often when you compete, the number of dance lessons you take increases. To keep your lessons within your budget, maximize how you take them and what you do in-between lessons.

Pro/Am World Open Latin B Champion Rhonda Lee has found a great way to maximize her dance lessons without stretching too far outside her financial comfort-zone. In her interview insight on page 201, she shares her formula. She stacks her lessons (taking two in one day), prepares a plan that spells out for her instructor the specific and tactical things she wants to work on at each lesson, and commits to solo practice on a consistent basis between lessons. That strategy allows Rhonda to be a champion AND compete within her budget.

Studio Owner and Prominent Competition Emcee John DePalma encourages students to take group lessons at the studio to help manage their budgets. In his interview insight on page 83 he states:

> "Group lessons teach you how to dance from the waist down. They give you the mechanics: patterns, footwork, timing, and rhythm. Group lessons alone will not teach you how to dance or prepare you for competition, though. Private lessons will teach you everything you need to know, but private lessons alone will take longer to accomplish the same goal as group and private lessons combined."

Experienced Pro/Am and Am/Am Champion-Level Competitor Gene Brockert balances the lessons he takes with his professional partner with individual practice with his amateur partners. As an amateur, he pushes himself to learn as much as he can by himself and with his Am/Am partner, and then he uses his lessons with his coach to help him resolve specific issues or technical challenges. You can learn more about Gene's tips for competing in both Pro/Am and Am/Am on page 204.

Strategic Budget Tips:

- Stack your lessons (two or three lessons in a row), so you can get more out of each session.

- Come prepared to your lessons with a "wish list" of items you want to improve. Please remember that your instructor may have a plan for you, and it's important to make sure your wants and needs are aligned.

- Take charge of your dancing. Set aside at least three-to-four hours a week to work on improving the parts of your dancing that you control.

- Buy lessons in bulk if your studio offers a discount.

- Sign up for group classes that focus on the "mechanics."

- If you rent floor space, ask the studio owner if you can get a discount by buying floor space in bulk.

- Consider getting an Am/Am or practice partner to take personal ownership of your dancing. Learn to be a more well-rounded dancer.

COACHING LESSONS

When you are in the "competing season," it's extremely helpful to work with a coach to make significant shifts and changes in your dancing. It's also tempting to fall into the trap of working with every coach who shows up at the studio, hoping that doing so will propel your dancing. The truth is that too much coaching, too close to a competition, can have the reverse effect.

The following tips will help you maximize your coaching budget and get the results you desire:

Strategic Budget Tips:

- Plan your coaching budget at the beginning of the competing season and stick to the plan. Account for:

  ○ Regular coaching sessions (weekly or monthly).

  ○ Traveling coaches who come to your studio quarterly or once a year.

  ○ "Gotta-Have Coaching," which includes unplanned-for opportunities. For example, when my partner and I were working with our bi-annual coach, Professional Smooth Champion, Coach, and Judge Jonathan Roberts had an unexpected opening. I grabbed the opportunity because I always wanted to work with him. The good news was that I had money allocated for "Gotta-Have Coaching," so it didn't jeopardize my coaching budget.

- Share your coaching spending plan with your instructor, and don't deviate from it. Once, when we added a new coach to our plan, I told my instructor that we'd have to delete something from the budget to make room for the amazing coach we really wanted to work with. Together we decided to drop one competition, so I could stay within my budget. Remember your non-negotiable standards (if you need a refresher, refer back to page 22). They become especially valuable during planning and budgeting. If you are in an Am/Am relationship, I encourage you to develop a plan together and stick with it.

ENTRY FEES/COMPETITION SELECTION

Different competitions have different entry fees. If you are competing on a budget, you must determine how much each competition will cost you. Depending on your teacher's fee structure, he may charge per-entry, per-day, per-style, per-package, or a mix of everything. Refer to Chapter 1 for a review of the ways instructors and studios charge for their competing services. Your goal is to avoid being bamboozled by unexpected fees too close to a competition. As a general rule, one-day competitions are less expensive per-entry than larger national competitions.

For Am/Am couples, entry fees are less of a financial concern. But you still want to manage and plan for how many competitions you are going to do throughout the year, in order to stay within budget. For example, if you are competing in Am/Am at the champion level, it may actually be less expensive to do an NDCA event rather than an "all inclusive" USADance event, because of the limited entries for which you can sign up. If you are competing on a budget and need to manage your finances, the following tips will help you find your sweet spot:

Strategic Budget Tips:

- Create a "wish list" of entries for a particular competition. Next, draft a "bare minimum" version of the list, including the heats you absolutely want to do. Calculate the difference, or ask your instructor to share two proposals with you. You may opt to take one of the multi-dances out, or you might dance in only one age category. Sometimes I'll drop a style at one competition and instead do it at the next competition in order to manage my cash flow. Remember, you have a lot of options when it comes to entries.

- Select a mix of one-day and multi-day competitions to get more for your money. One-day competitions also save you money on hotel and travel expenses, since all the dances take place on one day.

- When opting to do a competition where the entries are more expensive, limit your levels and age groups. These competitions often have quarter- and semi- finals, and you may actually dance more than you thought you would when considering the entry form. Please note that some instructors charge for callbacks, and you'll want to know in advance how much you will be paying. It's important to ask your instructor for a breakdown of services, so you can plan accordingly.

- Some competitions offer a discount if you get your entries in before the "early bird" deadline. Check each competition website for special deals.

- Get your entries in on time to avoid late fees. While it is your instructor's responsibility to get the entry forms in on time, it's a good idea to double check the deadline and ensure all forms and payments are submitted on time. Remember to give your instructor the check well in advance of the deadline, so that it can be cashed to pay entry fees.

- Tickets to the ballroom are sometimes cheaper if you buy them using the entry form vs. buying them at the door. Check the form and verify with your instructor. Each small saving adds up!

- Some competitions may charge the industry average per- entry, but the hotel might be more expensive. Keep these expenses in mind as you select the competition that is best for you.

- If you only dance one style or on one day, you don't have to stay at the competition after you are finished dancing. Save money by dancing one day and traveling home the next. You will save money on the entries, hotel, and food expenses.

TRAVEL

There are competitions in almost every major city in American, and you can compete every week should you choose to. When you decide to travel to a competition with your instructor, you will incur travel expenses. It's important to remember that you pay for your instructor's travel expenses, as well as your own. Depending on how many students are competing, travel costs will be shared evenly among the group. So it may be a good idea to attend competitions with a team of students, if you are competing on a budget. Airfare varies greatly. Oddly enough, it is sometimes cheaper to travel from the East Coast to the West Coast than from the East Coast to the Midwest. If you design a competition plan for the year, you may find that buying all your tickets in advance will save you money.

For Am/Am couples, make sure you include your travel expenses in your plan. Consider whether local competitions within driving distance are better options, versus those requiring airfare and a hotel stay.

Strategic Budget Tips:

- Plan your competitions as far in advance as you can to take advantage of air travel deals.

- Set up a flight alert on a websites like Kayak.com to check for deals on flights to your competition cities.

- Pick an airline and use it as much as possible. Sign up for their loyalty programs to earn flight miles.

- Use your miles to pay for flights.

- Drive to competitions that are within a four- to seven- hour radius (if your instructor is willing), or carpool with other competitors. If you have established a solid dance community, you may ask dancers at other studios which competitions they are doing, and drive together if no one from your studio is going.

- To get the best rates, buy airplane tickets in bulk, if you know which competitions you are attending.

HOTEL ROOM

You will also pay for your instructor's hotel room, along with your own, while competing. Hotel chains range from the Embassy Suites to the Ritz Carlton. Competition organizers negotiate room rates that are often more advantageous than the ones you get online or by calling the hotel directly. Sometimes, I find that, by visiting sites like Hotels.com, I can get a better rate than the one negotiated by the organizers. Plus I collect points per-stay, which I can apply to fee nights in the future. It's all about timing. The more detailed your competition plan, the easier it is to get good deals.

Most hotel rooms have two double beds. When competing on a budget, it's a great idea to bunk with another competitor. Several of my experienced friends also request a cot in the room, so it can be shared three ways. Again, having a solid ballroom community helps you find people to split expenses with. Sharing a room with your instructor is not encouraged. They are professionals who need space and time away from you during the competition. The good news: if your instructor competes with several students at the same competition, travel expenses are divided evenly among all the students.

Strategic Budget Tips:

- Research online before booking your hotel. See if there are any special rates that are better than the ones negotiated by the organizer. Get a roommate or two! Ask around to see who is competing and would like share a room. Offer a special deal to anyone willing to sleep on a cot.

- If your instructor is competing with a professional partner who is also doing Pro/Am, you may be able to split the hotel cost with other students, if the pro couple shares a room.

FOOD

Competition and hotel food can be expensive and often lacking in quality. If you are driving to the competition, pack a cooler with food. If you are flying, seek out a local grocery store and stock up on bottled water, snacks, breakfast foods, etc. When breakfast is not included in a hotel stay, I find that I can save at least $20 a day by packing my own breakfast food. Some students pay for their instructor's meals, and some don't. Make sure you have discussed these details with your instructor prior to committing to a competition. Some instructors charge a day rate that includes food, in order to avoid any confusion. It may be a great idea to discuss what types of food expenses you are willing to absorb.

For example, you may opt to pay for breakfast and lunch, since most of the time you will be competing during the morning and day. If you are on package, dinner is usually included. If not, you may opt to let your instructor mange his own dinner expenses. That way you can avoid any awkward discussions about paying for potentially elaborate dinners or drinks.

If you are on package, make sure you know when the dinners are offered and if you will be able to attend them. You may be dancing heats that prevent you from eating the dinners included in your package. In that case, you need to decide whether or not it is beneficial to be on package. Being on package often saves you money on entries, so do your math before deciding to be on or off package. Please note that if you are dancing during dinner service, it is perfectly acceptable to ask for a take-out container to enjoy your dinner after you finish dancing.

Strategic Budget Tips:

- Pack as much food as you can bring. If you drive, stock up on bottled water, snacks, and breakfast items. If you fly, find the nearest grocery store and stock up right away. Buying bottled water at the competition can add up quickly and is an unnecessary expense. I often bring my Magic Bullet mixer, so I can make smoothies for breakfast and mid-day snacks.

- Locate restaurants outside the hotel. You may find a good local restaurant just around the corner with a reasonably priced menu.

COSTUMING

For most female competitors, costuming can be a significant expense. I remember thinking that there was one zero too many at the end of price tags when I first started competing. I couldn't believe that I would need to spend several thousand dollars on my costume in order to compete. The truth is, you don't have to. But you certainly can if you choose to do so. If you are competing on a budget, you have several options.

You can start by competing in a nice practice dress. These dresses range from $150-to-$300, and with the appropriate jewelry, they can look quite stunning. A great resource for practice wear is Dance America (dance-america.com), but you can also find great options from many competition vendors.

Another option is to rent dresses. That's what I did the entire first year I competed. At the end of my first year, I bought a beautiful used dress from a professional competitor who had gained a dressmaker- sponsor and didn't need her dress anymore. It was still a big investment, but it was almost half the cost of a brand-new gown. At the beginning of my second year, I invested in my first "big" dress, which I later sold back to the dressmaker for a significant credit that was applied to my next dress. While there is an initial investment required, trading in your dresses is much like leasing a car. You make an initial down payment and then trade it in every few years for a new model. In the long run, you end up paying the same amount, but you get to dance in a new dress every year.

One budget option I have exercised successfully is that I will approach a competitor with a dress I really like and offer my name and number, in case she wants to sell the dress in the future. If you do this, be respectful and tactful without being pushy. Whenever I get a sincere compliment on my dress, I tell the person it is for sale. Remember, if you have a dress that you have used for a year or so, you may be close to changing it for a new one. Selling your dress for cash to another competitor is a great way to recover some of your initial investment and have the cash to select a new dress from a dressmaker or individual.

Another option is to buy an inexpensive dress from Asia, but please be careful. You get what you pay for. Sometimes the dress that's delivered does not resemble the online picture. As a rule, spend your money on lessons instead of dresses, if you have limited financial resources. Once your dancing skill improves, go ahead and invest in a high-quality dress.

Dresses with removable skirts can be used for both American Rhythm and American Smooth. You also can use an American Smooth dress for International Standard by adding floats (the signature difference between a Smooth and a Standard dress). When you are on a budget, the key is to be creative and prioritize how you spend your competing dollars.

Strategic Budget Tips:

- Invest in a well-tailored practice dress and use ballroom jewelry to add extra sparkle.

- Rent dresses from reputable dress-rental companies as you get started or when you begin dancing a new style. You may not continue dancing that style and over-investing in an expensive gown is not prudent. I highly recommend Rhythmic Rentals. To learn about their gowns and rental process, visit rhythmicrentals.com.

- Borrow or rent a dress from a friend. While some competitors are protective of their dresses (understandable as they are a major investment), some are willing to rent or lend you a dress as you start to compete. You may also want to check the consignment rack at most costume vendors for dresses that are priced within your budget.

HAIR/MAKEUP

As discussed in several chapters, you don't want to skimp on hair and makeup. You can, however, save a bit of money by learning to style your own hair and apply tasteful makeup. For the newer competitor, I still recommend working with a professional stylist for both hair and makeup. Should you wish to save money, the following strategies will guide you to a successful look.

Strategic Budget Tips:

- Practice, practice, practice. Creating a gorgeous ballroom hairstyle is much more complicated than you might think. At smaller competitions where there is no professional stylist, I have learned to shape my hair into a tight bun in the back with a nicely slick front and sides. It took me several tries to get it right, so don't assume you will be able to figure it out the day of your competition. Prepare your hair before a lesson and practice in it. You'd be surprised how much your hair moves during a sharp Tango head tilt.

- Purchase the right hairspray, hairpins, and elastics. Lisa Bentley DeBevec shares her preferred brands in her interview insight on page 148.

- Watch YouTube videos that demonstrate how to apply stage makeup, and practice putting it on. Again, stage makeup is much different from the everyday look you wear for work or a night out. Learn to skillfully attach false eyelashes.

VIDEO/PICTURES

In the beginning, videos and pictures are essential to learning your strengths and weaknesses as a dancer. I highly recommend that you get a video of your first competition and the next five after that. This way, you create a library of your journey and can see your progress. As you become more experienced, you can pick a few competitions throughout the year to tape. I always order videos from competitions in which I launch a new style of dance, have a new routine, or wear a new dress. That way, I can see what I need to improve and develop.

If you are competing on a budget, order videos of the heats you most want to learn from (instead of all of them). I always record our scholarship dances and not my multi-dances. But you may want to record your multi-dances and get the video before you start your scholarship dances in the evening to make last-minute changes to improve your dancing. There are no right or wrong answers. Consider what you want to spend, and allocate your available cash accordingly. The key to competing on a budget is to save money in as many ways as possible.

While pictures are fun and can be great learning tools, you don't need to buy all of them. Sit down at the photographer's booth and look at all your pictures. You can learn a great deal from viewing them, including your posture, stage presence, confidence, dress fit, etc. If you are on a budget, I recommend visiting the photographer's website and creating an account. That way you can save and order the pictures you like the most. I prefer to do so after the competition, when I'm less emotional and can be objective about my dancing and the pictures I select. Please note that most photographers offer a discount if you buy pictures at the competition. If you know for sure that you want to order a few specific pictures, by all means do so at the competition, and save the others for later.

Strategic Budget Tips:

- Pick the heats that will give you the most bang for your buck.

- Set aside time after you return from the competition to purchase photos. Waiting until you get home may prevent you from making expensive emotional or impulsive purchases.

While there are many other ways to compete on a budget, these strategies will help you plan—and spend—effectively. Ask other competitors how they save money. The best tips come from competitors who have already tried and solidified their systems—and are experts at maximizing their return on investment.

Chapter Summary

- Most competing ballroom dancers have a spending cap or a budget they must adhere to. By carefully planning for expenses such as instructor and coaching lessons, competition fees, travel, hotel, food, costuming, and miscellaneous expenses, you can stretch your competing dollars to get more bang for your buck.

- Stacking your lessons is a great strategy for getting a bigger return on investment. It puts more ownership on you to get the same results that someone with twice as many lessons may get.

- Mix your one-on-one lessons with technical group classes to stretch your available cash.

- Avoid getting emotionally attached to famous visiting coaches. Instead, create a budget item titled, "Dream Coaches," and decide in advance how many sessions you will do each year. That way, when celebrities come to town, you can objectively decide if they fit your category.

- Manage your entries and strategically pick competitions that are less expensive. Don't forget to consider all the expenses associated with the competition to avoid unexpected charges.

- Share a room with a competing buddy (or two) to save money.

- Bring your own food whenever possible. Hotels often charge a significant mark-up on water and other necessities.

- Consider renting or borrowing costumes if you are on a budget, at least until you are sure you want to invest in a "big dress."

- When you order your video, carefully consider how many heats you want to view. To manage a budget, pick the heats that will give you the most valuable information.

Chapter Takeaways

Take a moment to summarize your takeaways from this chapter. These notes will come in handy as you prepare for your next competition.

After reading this chapter I realized that:

_____

My most valuable takeaway is:

_____

To manage my competing budget, I will:

_____

_____

_____

_____

Interview Insight:
Rhonda Lee

Photo by: Vera Lee

STARTED AS A PRO/AM INTERNATIONAL LATIN DANCER IN 2005. SHE HAS WON THREE WORLD PRO-AM LATIN B OPEN CHAMPIONSHIP TITLES AT OHIO STAR BALL AND TWO OPEN TO THE WORLD NATIONAL TITLES AT USDC.

Outside of ballroom she is a financial consultant and resides in San Mateo, CA.

Jessika Ferm: *You have competed for over eight years and have accomplished several important milestones during your dancing journey. What do you consider some of your secrets to success?*

Rhonda Lee: I can attribute my success to careful attention in three areas: practicing solo, having the right pro, and committing to effective goals.

Solo practice: To be successful as a top Pro/Am competitor, you must be willing to practice on your own. Some dancers have the financial ability to practice while taking copious lessons, but many of us don't. Because most Pro/Am students start learning as adults, we may be playing catch-up to the many years of work the pros or experienced dancers have already put in. On top of that, you may also be working to counteract the effects of age and years of bad habits, to boot.

To be successful, you must be willing to do the work. There are no short cuts in this sport. If you aren't willing to put in the hours in the studio, you will not succeed as a high-level competitor. Depending on how well you practice, you could either amaze your teachers with your prowess or move along at a frustrating snail's pace.

Solo practice is rewarding. I love to learn and explore what my body can do. That's not to say there aren't stretches of time when it can be incredibly frustrating, lonely, boring, and tedious. But those are the times when you have to call upon your commitment to your goals (and your dance friends) to get you through.

Having the right instructor: The second success factor for me has been teaming up with the right instructor. I chose my pro, Daniele Gozzi, not only for his pro finalist dance accomplishments, but also for his depth of knowledge and potential to guide me through the learning process as unerringly as possible. It was also important that he is professional, disciplined, has a good work ethic, and is emotionally intelligent. Not having the right teacher can add years to a dancer's journey.

I can't emphasize enough how having the right teacher has helped me pursue and achieve my goals. If you don't have a teacher who has the right information and can communicate it effectively, it won't matter how much practice you put in. As with any good professional, I look for a pro with a skill level that surpasses mine and who has an active interest in continuing to improve his own skills. I know that if my pro doesn't stagnate, I won't either.

Setting goals and understanding the commitments attached to them: I've seen many dancers wander through their dancing with an ultimate goal in mind, but without an actual plan of how to get there. Some dancers think that if they simply follow whatever their pro is teaching them in their lessons, they'll become the dancers they want to be.

But, as in life, "fortune comes to he who seeks her." I take it as my responsibility to let my pros and coaches know what my goals are by word AND action. If they know that I am serious about dance and willing to commit my time and resources to meet my goals, they usually are quite happy to come up with a pathway for me to get there.

Unless your teacher is very sure of what your goals are, he or she will simply go about the job of teaching at whatever pace the teacher or you seem comfortable with. Give your teacher specific goals within a specific time frame, and normally he or she will work to help you get there. If teachers are capable and professional, they will do their part.

One last note, I recommend creating attainable short-term goals that are realistic in scope. If you speak to any of the finalists in my division, all of us work many hours in the studio. We make dancing a high priority in our lives. It is a huge commitment of time and resources, and we make sacrifices to pursue it. If you cannot make this type of commitment, you need to look at your goals and adjust them to the reality of your situation. Not all of us can put in the time and effort required to reach the level danced at the world or national finals. We have other commitments in life, and that is okay. You can still pursue your passion and be quite happy with it. Set realistic or slightly stretched goals in line with your level of commitment, and see where it takes you.

Jessika Ferm: *These are excellent tips, Rhonda. I know that you also compete with limited financial resources. What strategies would you share with dancers who may need to compete on a budget?*

Rhonda Lee: Make the most of your lesson time. I have a rather amusing and telling story on lessons from the first year I started competing on a national level. One of the finalists in my division and I had lunch in order to get to know one another a bit and talk dance. She asked me how many lessons I took with my pro. I replied "two." She said, "Oh, two a day?" My shocked reply was, "No, two a week!"

Lessons are the path to improving in your dance skills. They are also very expensive, so early on I learned to make the most of them. Taking my two lessons in a single block during the week gives me the opportunity to work out with my pro what I should be working on in my solo practice for the rest of the week.

I would receive a new area to work on—in line with my short-term goals—at the beginning of a cycle. My pro would give me an understanding of the subject, and how I might tell if I was accomplishing the work when I practiced by myself. The rest of the week, I would explore in my body my understanding of the work.

The following week in my lessons, I would come back with questions that arose from my solo practice; in turn, it would spur further discussion that strengthened and confirmed my understanding of the subject. This would continue through the weeks until I showed significant progress in the area and started doing repetitions for muscle memory. A new cycle would begin as I finished up with repetitions to cement the previous improvements.

If you switch subjects too early in the cycle, you run the risk that nothing gets in permanently. You need time to teach your body and commit the changes to muscle memory.

Jessika Ferm: *What else did you learn from this approach?*

Rhonda Lee: I learned that working on fundamentals and concepts of dancing was a much more efficient way to improve my dancing than individual movement corrections. If given a correction, I would immediately ask: Is this something I do across all dances or all movements in one of the dances? If the answer was yes, I knew to practice and understand it in a larger context. In this way, "one" correction makes a large impact across all of your dancing.

Jessika Ferm: *Do you have any advice for the new dancer who is interested in beginning to compete?*

Rhonda Lee: Make a thoughtful decision as to when to start competing nationally. I did not do any comps outside of my local area until my skill level was such that I had a chance at making it to the finals at the larger, national- level comps. Traveling outside of your local area for a comp is expensive. You are not only responsible for your expenses, but those of your pro. If you are on a budget, I would seriously consider doing more dancing at local comps to gain experience and skill before paying more to travel to a larger competition.

Photo by: Bonita Brockert

Interview Insight: Gene Brockert

OPEN GOLD DANCER PRO/AM AND CHAMPION-LEVEL AM/AM COMPETITOR.

Gene's accomplishments in Pro/Am and Am/Am include Senior 2 Championship Standard Finalist at the National DanceSport Championships, U.S. Gentlemen's Standard Pro/Am Finalist, and Am/Am Senior Standard Champion at the Ohio Star Ball. Outside the ballroom world, Gene is a project manager for a custom testing company. He resides in Cincinnati, Ohio.

Jessika Ferm: *You began dancing Pro/Am with your teacher and wife, Bonita Brockert. How did you end up dancing Am/Am?*

Gene Brockert: Bonita is a popular Pro/Am competitive teacher and coach, and she strongly believes the amateur experience creates a more well- rounded dancer. One-on-one lessons are powerful, but she recommended that I work with an amateur partner in order to become a more advanced dancer. Few pros have time to give all their competitive students adequate practice time, so having another strong partner to practice with is invaluable and necessary to acquire partnering skills you cannot develop by solo practice. The amateur relationship forces you to take more responsibility and learn on your own. It pushes you to figure things out by yourself or as a team, instead of over-relying on your teacher to compensate for your weaknesses. As the gentleman, I had to learn how to be clear in my movements and lead steps without being "back lead." Bonita encourages all her Pro/Am students to dance in Am/Am relationships if they want to become skilled dancers. There is also more "floor time" for dancers doing both Pro/Am & amateur, especially for men. Amateur regionals and nationals always have quarterfinals and often first rounds, which is rarely the case at Pro/Am events.

Jessika Ferm: *What do you enjoy most about dancing Am/Am?*

Gene Brockert: The difference I enjoy the most is that at Am/Am competitions I compete against my peers. My dance partner and I are judged against other amateur couples who have reached the same proficiency level. In Pro/Am, Bonita and I are judged as a couple, but I mostly compete against other female dancers. There certainly are events when I compete against other gentlemen, but at the higher levels there just aren't many gentleman competitors in my age category. At the Bronze and Silver levels in amateur, there is a tremendous amount of competition. It's not uncommon at larger USADance events to have 30-to-50 couples competing together.

Jessika Ferm: *How often do you compete in each type of competition, and what is your practice schedule like?*

Gene Brockert: My job has been demanding the last couple of years, and I haven't been able to compete or practice as much as I used to. Today, I do about four amateur and five Pro/Am (NDCA) competitions a year. I often do both categories at NDCA events if my partner is available for the same events. When I had two amateur partners (Smooth and Standard or Latin and Standard), I practiced two evenings a week and took lessons two days per week with my partners. I currently dance with one partner other than Bonita, and I take multiple lessons on one evening and practice on another evening.

Jessika Ferm: *How did you find your Am/Am partners, and what are some of the key success factors you have learned in establishing a powerful partnership?*

Gene Brockert: My first partner was recommended to me by Bonita, and my second partner was someone I knew through competing. To be a successful amateur partnership, it's important to have the same goals for your dancing and mutual respect for one another. Discussion is very important, arguing is nonproductive, and you must know when to move on in your practice in order to make your time productive. Begin by trying to implement your own dance responsibility as individuals, and then try again as a couple. Work with those approaches for a reasonable time before moving on. If you've tried that approach without much success, then ask your teacher. My Am/Am partner, Jill [insert last name], and I always make a list of our problems for Bonita to address at our next session. You will hit roadblocks and need your coach's intervention. That's why it's so important to have your "peg" coach set you right on a regular and consistent schedule.

Jessika Ferm: *If you had to pick one type of competing, which would you pick, Pro/Am or Am/Am?*

Gene Brockert: I'd pick Pro/Am because it allows me to dance with my wife. I love spending time with her. I actually have more success placement-wise as an amateur competitor, but when it comes down to it, nothing is as good as being with my wife.

Jessika Ferm: *How do you balance your dancing, work, and life?*

Gene Brockert: It's not always easy to find a sense of balance. Outside of work, dancing is my main activity, but I also love spending time in our garden and with our animals and friends.

7

Competing Like a Pro, Every Time

It's not what we do once in a while that shapes our lives. It's what we do consistently.

- ANTHONY ROBBINS

Photo by: Stephen Marino Photography

Competing on a budget is an art in itself and requires planning, preparation, and discipline. In this chapter, we will explore how to use those same skills in order to develop "competition mastery" and consistently compete like a pro.

In the book *Mastery: The Keys to Success and Long-Term Fulfillment*, Author George Leonard shares a fictional example to answer a question many of us ask when we begin to dance (New York: Plume, 1992). While his example uses tennis as an analogy, it works perfectly well for ballroom students.

"How long…will it take [me] to master this thing?

[The] instructor responds, Do you mean how long would it take for you to automatically get into position and hit a forehand effectively to a target?

Yes. She pauses. It's a question she always dreads.

Well for someone like you, who starts tennis as an adult, if you practice an hour three times a week, it would take, on average, five years.

Five years!

Ideally, about half of that would be instruction. Of course, if you're particularly motivated, it could be less than that.

The student decides to try another question. How long will it be before I can play competitively?

Competitively? That's a loaded term. I would say you could probably start playing after about six months. But you shouldn't start playing with winning as a major consideration until you have reasonable control of forehand, backhand, and serve. And that would be about a year or a year and a half" (p.9).

As you embark on this next chapter, just remember that you must practice competing in order to compete like a pro. Each competition has a unique flair and you learn new and different things from each. My ballroom competing friend Candace Riley said to me recently, "I wish I had known when I started that competing is a totally different skill from dancing," and she is right.

Top teacher and former U.S. and World Professional Smooth Champion Shalene Archer mentions in her insight on page 98 that the unique atmosphere that is generated on the competition floor can't be reproduced back at the studio, so the more you compete, the better you will become. Sometimes, dancers who are successful and celebrated at the studio, falter under the pressures of competing simply because they haven't learned the skill of competing yet.

In this chapter, we begin by look at debriefing strategies and tips for getting ready for your next competition. If you don't stop to take in what you can do better, differently, or more/less the next time, you have wasted the opportunity to hone your craft. Next we will discuss how to take personal ownership of your ballroom dancing and learn how to build powerful relationships with your instructor/dance partner. We will also review communication strategies that help strengthen your dance partnership while competing, and take a closer look at the telltale signs that it may be time to let go and find another instructor/dance partner. We will also discuss the powerful concept called "embracing grace," where you will learn strategies for producing positive vibrational energy that inspires others to be their personal best. To wrap up this chapter and the book, we take a deep dive into the concept of balance and ballroom dancing and competing.

Debriefing Strategies That Propel Your Dancing

 Character—the willingness to accept responsibility for one's own life—is the source from which self-respect spring."

- JOAN DIDION

Once you return from a competition, you may go through a variety of emotions. In Chapter 3, we discussed the concept of the "competition blues," a stage most dancers go through, in which, even if you won everything, you come back feeling a bit blue or sad.

I have found that getting back to a comprehensive plan is the best way to beat the blues and tap into the energy you experienced while at the competition (assuming you had a good one). The following tips will help you maximize your competing experience and propel you forward in no time:

SPEND ONE LESSON JUST TALKING

Yes, I said it. No dancing, just talking. If you are on a budget and are concerned that this may be "wasting your precious dancing dollars," trust me, it won't. In fact, it is likely to pay you back tenfold. If you don't stop and debrief, you'll miss the opportunity to learn what to improve, how to change, and what to do differently next time. Below are some powerful questions to answer prior to your session:

- What were you most proud of accomplishing?

- What top-two mistakes did you make overall at this competition that you don't want to make again?

- If you could do one thing differently about your dancing what would it be?

- If you could improve one thing about your dance partnership what would it be?

- If you could develop one competition-skill before your next competition, what would it be?

- In what areas do you believe you can "self-medicate," and where do you need your instructor's/dance partner's/coach's help to resolve or improve?

When debriefing your session, make sure to take personal ownership of the things you can improve or change, and seek help from your instructor/dance partner/coach with the things you can't.

The debriefing meeting helps both you and your instructor make any necessary adjustment to your competing plan to make sure you get closer to meeting your goals.

CREATE SMART ACTION STEPS

Once you've had your meeting, and you know what you want to change, improve, or modify to compete better next time, create SMART action steps that are short and sweet. We discussed the SMART concept in detail in Chapter 2, but as a quick reminder, SMART stands for specific, measurable, attainable, relevant and timed. Examples include:

- I will spend 30 minutes of personal practice time this week doing X, Y, and Z exercises to strengthen Q.

- I will spend no more than two hours online searching for a new competing dress that fits me better than the one I have now.

- I will call today to make an appointment with X for hair and makeup in preparation for my next competition.

- For our next coaching session with X, we will work on Y for at least one lesson.

IMPLEMENT YOUR ACTION STEPS

At first this may seem like an obvious statement, but I've fallen victim to missing it more than once. I come back from a competition, and I'm excited to do my debriefing meeting and map out my goals. Then life happens, and I get sucked back into work and life. While I had every intention of implementing my action steps, I just didn't get to it. What a waste of time and information! If you wait more than two weeks to act on the things you know you need to change, you are missing a tremendous opportunity for development. To avoid falling into this trap, do the following as soon as your action steps have been established:

- Put your commitments on your calendar or day planner. Make each an appointment and keep it like you would a business or personal meeting. This is a date with your future ballroom self, and you don't want to miss your own awesomeness!

- Share your action step with a friend or accountability partner, someone who will check in with you about what you say you are going to do. If she does the same with you, you can have some fun together and share experiences and celebrate accomplishments.

- Make a promise to your instructor/dance partner that you will implement one of your action steps by a certain time (preferably your next lesson) and ask to be held accountable for it.

Nothing will be different if you don't DO something differently. Sometimes when you have competitions too close together, there isn't enough time to make adjustments or changes. It may not be a bad idea to take a scheduled competing break at some time during the year, so that you have time and energy to work on the things you want to develop between competitions. Top Amateurs like Beverly Moore and Giovanni Fortezza have established a system and process for competing over 20 times a year, while leaving time to work on their mental, physical, emotional, and dancing game between competitions. To learn more about how they do it, see their insights on pages 122 and 45.

Getting Ready for the Next "Go-Round"

> " Do the one thing you think you cannot do. Fail at it. Try again. Do better the second time. The only people who never tumble are those who never mount the high wire. This is your moment. Own it."

- OPRAH WINFREY

Once you have debriefed your last competition and designed and executed your action steps, it's usually time for the next go-round. The following section will help you get back on the horse again and enjoy the ride. Remember, the more you compete, the better you will become. Competing is a skill just like dance technique. My competing dance friend Janet Simsic has used a spreadsheet since she started dancing to track all her placements and accomplishments over years of dancing. She uses it to record her progress and review results at various competitions. It is a great way to notice improvements or patterns over your competing journey.

Review your competition goals: Take a moment to reflect on your competition goals. Are they clear and concise? Are you in complete control of accomplishing them, avoiding placements as your key indicator of success? Are you and your instructor/dance partner in alignment with your goals? Have you decided what you will do by yourself and as a couple to celebrate your accomplishments or disappointments?

Check your communication plan: Remember to review your communication standards and agreed-upon plan for interacting during the competition with your instructor/dance partner. Clear up any possible confusion and commit to work hard to follow the plan. For more tips on how to establish and follow a communication plan, return to Chapter 6.

Confirm appointments: Make sure that you have confirmed all appointments for hair, makeup, or coaching sessions at the competition. Once you enter the event doors, it's easy to get wrapped up in the excitement.

Pack like a pro: Have you reviewed your competition checklist in Chapter 5 to make sure you have packed and prepared everything from food to dresses and jewelry?

Your continuous competition success depends on your ability to stay committed to your goals and plans. It is also imperative that, as you become more experienced, you take increased personal ownership of your dancing and practice. In the next section we will review strategies to help you sharpen your skills by going for what you want and developing powerful communication strategies with your instructor/dance partner.

Your Dancing, Your Responsibility

❝ Every man is guilty of all the good he did not do."

- VOLTAIRE

For the first one or two competitions, it is normal to lean on your instructor to guide you along the way. As you become experienced in competing, the responsibility shifts more to you.

Your success in dancing is your responsibility. You must take charge of your time, practice, finances, organization, preparation, and success. This section will dive into several strategies that you can use to ensure that you do everything you can to get the most from your dancing—and compete like a pro every time.

Continue to work on the basics: All judges, professionals, and top amateurs interviewed for this book emphasize the importance of working on the basics. In experienced Coach and Judge Glenis Dee Creger's interview insight (page 43), she describes a professional couple who sought her out for coaching. As they began working together, they made it clear that they didn't want to work on Bronze figures, as they considered it beneath them. Glenis, in turn, decided they weren't the right fit for her and stopped coaching them. When it comes down to it, it's all about the basics. As amateur students, we can take complete ownership of working on our basics.

I have a space in my basement where I practice many of my Rhythm basics. You'd be surprised how little space you actually need, even for basic Smooth and Standard moves. Work with your instructor or coach to come up with a foundational practice plan that you can do at home or on the road if you travel for work.

Self-medicate as much as possible: Take ownership of your dancing by watching your own videos and pictures. Identify what you know isn't correct and try to fix the most glaring issues. When you have tried everything you can think of, seek help from your instructor or coach. If you wait to get feedback on what you can improve, you are wasting valuable time that could be spent developing your own dancing. For great tips on how to self-medicate, see Toni Redpath's interview insight on page 86. Top Am/Am and Pro/Am Competitor Gene Brockert encourages Am/Am couples to try to resolve things by themselves first and then as a couple. If that doesn't work, reach out to the coach. You can learn more about Gene's tips for powerful partnering on page 204.

Go for what you want: Don't sit around waiting or hoping that your teacher will map out your plan for you. When World and U.S. Pro/Am Open Gold Champion Beverly Moore decided she wanted to dance with her new teacher, Alain Doucet, she mapped out a plan that included flying several hours each way, renting a car, and getting an apartment in a different city to be able to work with him. Consider what you are willing to do to get where you want to go.

Warm up before practice and competition: While this tip may seem obvious, many dancers forget or over-rely on their teachers to help them get ready. They come to their lessons waiting to be "taught" and haven't taken time to adequately prepare their bodies. It is not your teacher's responsibility to warm up with you, and it is a waste of a time using any part of a lesson doing what you could have done in advance. As World and U.S. Professional 9-Dance Champion Alexandra Perzhu shares in her interview insight (page 248), listen to your favorite music as you warm up. It's important to make sure your body is adequately is adequately stretched to avoid injuries. Her husband and professional partner, Peter Perzhu, is extremely flexible as a dancer. Alexandra encourages all of Peter's students to make sure they are warmed up appropriately in order to follow his lead.

Create a ritual and follow it without flaw: When excellence becomes the norm, you know you are acting and thinking like a champion. I love New York City Ballet Choreographer Twyla Tharp's book *The Creative Habit: Learn It and Use It for Life* (New York: Simon and Schuster, 2003). In it, she describes her commitment to her daily ritual:

> "I begin each day of my life with a ritual: I wake up at 5:30 A.M., put on my workout clothes, my leg warmers, my sweatshirts, and my hat. I walk outside my Manhattan home, hail a taxi, and tell the driver to take me to the Pumping Iron gym at 91st Street and First Avenue, where I work out for two hours. The ritual isn't the stretching and weight training I put my body though each morning at the gym; the ritual is the cab. The moment I tell the driver where to go I have completed the ritual" (p.14).

Consider what daily rituals you have that help you compete like a pro, each time.

The more you take personal ownership, the faster you will reach your goals. Let's take a deeper look into how you can apply the concept of personal accountability as you develop your communication skills with your instructor/dance partner.

Communication Strategies That Strengthen Your Dance Partnership While Competing

> " Knowing how to have a successful relationship is a lifelong study in itself! Dancers are just people who bring their 'stuff' to the dance floor—so if people struggle in general, chances are they will struggle in their dance partnerships."
>
> - DIANE JARMOLOW

Few things can strain a relationship like ballroom competing. It's not uncommon to see Am/Am, Pro/Am, and husband/wife teams fall apart under the emotional pressures of practicing and dancing together. When we add the competition factor to the mix, we complicate it even more. Whatever issues or disagreements you have brewing inside are sure to come up once you add the heat of competition. The good news is that the opposite is also true.

Competing offers you an opportunity to be your best self and work on your emotional intelligence, communication, and partnership skills. Outside the ballroom world, I am a master-level executive coach and certified behavioral analyst. My job is to help others assess their behaviors and actions and assist them in maximizing their interactions with others. You'd think it would be easy for me to apply those same strategies to myself as I'm dancing, but no such luck for me. Instead, I struggle just like all the dancers I know to be a good partner and not act emotionally or let my frustrations affect my dance relationship.

In this section, I will share some of the most powerful communication strategies I use with corporate clients. I have translated them into strategies for building sustainable dance partnerships. We will also review strategies offered by ballroom experts like Diane Jarmolow, Peter and Alexandra Perzhu, Michael Mead, Toni Redpath, Slawek Sochacki, and Marzena Stachura. Another great book for ballroom partnership strategies is *Ballroom Dancing is Not for Sissies: An R-Rated Guide to Partnerships* by Arthur and Elizabeth Seagull. You can find it on amazon.com.

Let's review the five steps to being an outstanding competition partner.

STEP 1: START WITH YOU

As the famous Chinese philosopher Lao-tzu said, "He who knows others is wise. He who knows himself is enlightened." Until you truly know yourself, you can't be effective with others. When we lack self-awareness or the willingness to look at ourselves first, we look to the other person as the problem. We may end up blaming him for our lack of results or progress, and we may have difficulty being empathetic or compassionate.

If we always look to the other person to change or improve in order for the partnership to work, we set ourselves up to fail. We can't change other people, but we have 100 percent control over ourselves. Another famous saying goes, "Wherever you go, there you are." It reminds us that we take anything that isn't working internally to the next partnership. Switching instructors or partners may not resolve the issues you are having unless you work on changing what isn't working within you first.

When Author, Judge and Former Pro/Am and Professional Competitor Diane Jarmolow competed, she realized that no matter how much help she was getting from her coaches and instructor/dance partner, she wasn't progressing like she wanted. Instead of blaming the coaches and her partner, she decided to seek alternative modalities like ballet, Pilates, and Feldenkrais to gain different perspectives. All those were helpful, but it wasn't until her yoga teacher taught her about the skeleton that her life and dance career changed forever. Once she gained new information about how the body was put together, she was able to translate it into her own movements and had a dance breakthrough. Her dance partner didn't "make" her do it. She took it upon herself to get the information that would make her a better partner. You can learn more about Diane's tips for personal introspection and partnership strategies on page 251.

When asked what his students have in common, World and U.S. Professional 9-Dance Champion Peter Perzhu says that they are all driven to be their own personal best and are open to feedback to help them improve in order to reach their goals. Peter currently has a waiting list for amateur students who want to work with him, and he is particularly picky about the students he chooses to work with. He and his wife, Alexandra Perzhu, want to work with students who have the right attitude. Dancing skills they can teach, but they can't change attitudes. You can read more about their tips in their interview insight on page 248.

The following strategies and questions will help you dig deeper within yourself to increase your self-awareness and personal accountability while in a competitive dance partnership:

Strategy:

- Make a list of the personal attributes or characteristics that you are proud of, that help make you an outstanding partner. Make another list of the attributes or characteristics that may prevent you from being your best self as a partner. Pick one strength and list ways to maximize it when interacting with others. List one "flaw" that you want to work on to help the partnership blossom. You don't need to share this list with your instructor/dance partner, but you certainly can if you think it will be helpful. Remember, your personal development is no one else's responsibility. Sometimes working on things in silence helps you "own" them. Your reward may come when your partner realizes that you have changed or are trying to change to improve the relationship.

- Ask a personal friend or dance buddy to offer you honest and direct feedback on your strengths and weaknesses as a friend. As your relationship with your instructor/dance partner progresses, it often takes the shape of a friendship. You may as well learn from your current circle of friends how to maximize your partner-relationship proactively.

- Ask your instructor/dance partner for one thing that you can improve to make your relationship even better. Don't ask for two, three, or a long list. Just one thing. Avoid asking her to share one with you. If she does, great, but this exercise is all about you. Remember, you have no control over how/if/when your partner chooses to change. When we focus on working on one thing, we typically stick with it. A list of things becomes a chore.

- Seek activities outside ballroom dancing and competing to gain a fresh perspective on how you can grow and develop. I find that I'm the most creative and inspired after I take a dancing break or when I've watched someone execute a touching musical performance on stage. If you'd like to learn more about how to improve your dancing by understanding the skeleton, for example, look up the *Move Like a Champion* book and DVD by Diane Jarmolow and Kasia Kosak. I highly recommend them for any level and style of dancer. See Chapter 8 for ordering details.

STEP 2: ESTABLISH UPFRONT AGREEMENTS FOR COMPETITION PRACTICE AND PERFORMANCE

As with any business partnership or personal relationship, it's important to have crystal-clear standards and expectations. To avoid miscommunications or emotionally triggered conversations, establish "upfront agreements" before you start practicing or preparing for competitions.

The concept of "upfront agreements" is that you establish a plan for how to handle things that are likely to happen or go wrong *in advance*, so when they occur, you have a plan already in place. Here are some categories that ballroom competitors often struggle with, for which you may want to establish upfront agreements:

Categories:

- **How to handle disagreements during practice:** Consider how you want to interact with one another in front of other students, instructors, studio owners, or coaches. Establish communication rules for how to interact or respectfully disagree when other people are present.

- **How to handle disagreements or frustrations during competitions:** Establish agreements or rules for interacting in the ballroom, practice room, and in front of judges and other students.

- **How to manage frustrations in the on-deck area, on the floor, and in-between heats:** Too often you see gorgeous competitors dance, and then between heats you watch them argue or share crude remarks while coming off the floor. Judges notice. Some of the judges interviewed in this book mentioned that arguing between instructors and dance partners, between heats, is a pet peeve. It shows a lack of professionalism from both the instructor and the student. Include in your agreement how to manage frustrations while on the floor.

- **How to handle disappointments over placements, dancing performance, and callbacks:** Every student will experience disappointments at some point on the competitive journey. Decide as a partnership how you will handle these challenging emotions to prevent them from casting you in a poor light.

- **How to address sensitive issues:** At some point in all partnerships, you will come up against a sensitive issue that needs to be discussed. It could involve hurt feelings, money issues, tardiness, lack of stamina, you name it. Decide in advance how you will address sensitive issues and honor those agreements flawlessly.

- **How (and when) to give critical feedback:** Critical feedback helps us grow in the long run, but there are appropriate times and places for critical conversations. Agree in advance how and when to have these conversations to avoid pushing one another's triggers.

- **How to address "non-negotiable scope creep:"** If you worked through Chapter 2 and began establishing your non-negotiable ballroom standards, you know what would have to take place for you to walk away from a competition, instructor, or dance partner. Make sure your non-negotiables are crystal clear, and your instructor/dance partner knows exactly where the boundaries are. If we aren't clear, or we begin to flip-flop on our non-negotiables, they tend to expand in scope (I call that scope creep). And after a while, they become negotiable. This can happen in a blink, so be especially careful to establish agreements and make sure this doesn't happen.

STEP 3: ADDRESS MISCOMMUNICATIONS OR DISAGREEMENTS "LIKE A PRO"

You may not be a certified professional coach or expert listener, but you can learn the strategies that the pros use to avoid unnecessary miscommunications and disagreements. Here is a basic yet powerful process that works really well when sharpening your partnership communication skills.

Acknowledge: It's important to acknowledge the miscommunication or disagreement. Always take ownership of your part of the conversation; if you perceive that you are not at fault, acknowledge that the conversation made you unhappy, uncomfortable, sad, etc. You may start by saying something like, "I'm upset that we had a disagreement," or "I realize I wasn't clear the last time we spoke," or "I think I made a mistake."

Invite: Next, you want to invite the person to have a new and different conversation. You may say something like, "Would you be willing to have that conversation again and this time I will…." Or, "Could we revisit the conversation we had earlier? I'm not sure it came across the way I wanted it to." Or "I recognize that we had a miscommunication. Is this a good time to clear it up?"

State: Take ownership of what you brought to the conversation. State what you consider to be the facts and contributing circumstances. Ask your instructor/dance partner to state how he sees the facts or details. You may want to start this part of the conversation with something like, "I believe that the following three reasons contributed to our disagreement." Or "When you said X, I thought you meant Y, which confused me." Or "I've been bothered by this for a while, and I realize that my stored-up emotions got in the way."

Recommit: Once all the facts and details have been sorted out, recommit to a new way of interacting or resolving the issue. You may say something like, "Let's review the steps we both agree with." Or "Since we are starting over, what are the most important points to you?" Or "What do we do as a team to make sure these issues don't reappear?"

Strategy:

- Share this Acknowledge, Invite, State, Recommit (AISR) process with your instructor/dance partner and agree to use it if you have to address miscommunications or disagreements.

- Practice using it with people outside the ballroom world as well. It works with any important relationship in your life.

STEP 4: STAY IN YOUR "LOVE PLACE"

Several years ago, I observed the young niece of a friend standing silently in the living room with her eyes closed. When I asked her what she was doing, she looked straight at me and said, 'I'm in my love place." Out of the mouths of babes! I have used "the love place" analogy with clients for years, and I regularly share it with my executive coaching clients, including take-charge, high-profile CEOs. Sometimes when we struggle to "be present" with an individual we are angry or upset with, it's hard to think of anything we actually like about that person. Consistently reminding yourself of all the things you like, love, or appreciate about your instructor/dance partner will greatly help you maximize your interactions.

Strategy:

- Make a list of all the things you value/like/love about your instructor/dance partner. Read it during times of stress or increased pressure to remind you of that person's unique strengths.

- Make a habit of sharing one thing you like about your partner after each lesson or practice. Verbal affirmations will help your partner and you reconnect.

- If you are struggling with anger, frustration, impatience, or any other intense emotion, try viewing your instructor/dance partner from "your love place." Remind yourself what you like about this person when you aren't feeling negative. Take a a quick one-minute break to grab some water and re-center.

- Create a ritual that gets the two of you into the right mental and emotional space for practice and competition. Every now and then, when we go through a stressful time, my instructor and I start our practice by dancing a Bachatta for one minute to put us in the right state of mind. Since we don't compete in this dance, it helps me reconnect and remember why I love to dance in the first place.

- Find your "love language" by taking the free quiz on the site 5lovelanguages.com. It will reveal your preferred approach to receiving love or appreciation. Don't assume that your instructor is motivated that same way you are. If you want to show your appreciation for another, it may be helpful to know the preferred language. For example, if your language is "words of affirmation," you may want to tell your instructor/dance partner that you value positive verbal feedback. If your instructor/dance partner responds to "acts of service," then offering a favorite snack or a clean towel during competition may best communicate your appreciation.

STEP 5: CREATE A PARTNERSHIP GUIDELINE DOCUMENT

Having established your upfront agreements in step 2, you are now ready to create partnership guidelines to facilitate greater communicate. Toni Redpath and Michael Mead have developed a program called "The Elite Competitor" for professional and amateur clients. It requires you to list several guidelines for interacting on and off the competitive floor. I suggest you create a similar list with your instructor/dance partner. It can outline anything from how to interact with each other to how to approach (or avoid) judges and other students. When you create this document as a partnership, both parties take ownership and are clear about expectations. I have had great success with this exercise; it works.

Strategy:

Create a short and easy-to-read guidelines document that addresses all or some of the following (please add your own categories as well):

- Timeliness (for lessons and competitions).

- Language (list language that is encouraged and words that are unacceptable).

- Personal accountability (expectations for interactions, practice, and competing).

- Interactions with coaches (how to speak with them and what to wear during lessons).

- Results (how to view or discuss results).

- Interactions with judges (who to approach and what to say).

- Debriefing competitions (when to discuss what you've learned from the competition and decide what adjustments or modifications to make).

- Time together and time alone (when to get together for team dinners and when to spend time alone). World and U.S. 9-Dance Champion Peter Perzhu expects his competing ladies to participate in group dinner and lunches. He states on his interview insight on page 248, "It builds team sprit and camaraderie, which is really important when you compete often and are spending a lot of time together."

The five steps to building powerful relationships for competitive duos help you minimize miscommunications and maximize your dancing mojo. Intentional planning is the key!

When You Know It's Time To Let Go

> **"** If you are brave enough to say goodbye, life will reward you with a new hello."

PAULO COELHO

If you have tried *really, really* hard to make your dancing relationship work, but you've come to realize that it's just not the right fit for you, then it's probably time to part ways. As the famous business author Jim Collins wrote in his book *Good to Great: Why Some Companies Make the Leap…and Others Don't* "When you know you need to make a people change, act" (New York: Harper Collins Publishers, Inc., 2001, p.56). This saying goes for any relationship. Most of us stay too long in situations that aren't serving us, because we are afraid to let go or to disappoint our partners. The decision to leave is never easy and often comes with a series of challenging emotions including sadness, guilt, anger, fear, anxiety, and disappointment. Once we've accepted our decision to part ways, we tend to feel positive emotions including relief, happiness, and excitement for new beginnings.

LETTING GO OF THE "FIRST"

For many, changing instructors/dance partners the first time is the hardest. We usually form a special and unique bond with the first person who introduces us to the wonderful world of ballroom dancing. It can almost feel like a crush or an intense obsession. A competing friend of mine calls it his "dance heart"; when he dances with a partner (Pro or Am), he gives her his dance heart. You can imagine how hard it is for him to let go and move on!

The tricky part, I believe, is that we are actually falling in love with dance and with the feelings and emotions it creates within us. At first, we may inadvertently transfer those emotions to our instructor/dance partner (this can happen in the reverse when an instructor becomes enamored of a student). It's important to remember that your first instructor/dance partner may not be your "forever partner." That person will most likely always hold a very special place in your heart. That doesn't mean, however, that he or she is the right person to help you meet your dancing goals for life.

It's not unlike what happens in the animal kingdom when a new offspring is born. It is said that the first person or animal a duckling sees when it emerges from the egg is assumed to be its mother. In the ballroom world, you are like a newborn duckling, emerging from the egg the moment you first walk into the studio. You assume your first instructor is a nurturing person who will guide and protect you. Sometimes this is the case, but sometimes it's not.

The challenging part is that dance relationships are complex by nature. They often start out as formal student/teacher relationships. The more we compete and take lessons, the more time we spend together as a team. It naturally fosters a more relaxed relationship, and it can become difficult to separate close feelings from the business relationship that is Pro/Am dancing. You also experience many emotional highs and lows together, which you rarely do with people other than close friends and significant others. As a result, the relationship is not always clear-cut.

As in life, some partnerships last for life, and others don't. Sometimes the beauty of certain relationships is that they are meant to start us on one part of the journey, so we then can let go, spread our wings, and move on. I love the saying "When the student is ready, the Master will appear." When you are truly ready to move on, you must be willing to let go. No reputable, professional, experienced instructor wants to dance with a student who has not yet let go of a current partner. If you are ready to go, have faith. Know that the next person who is meant to take you on your journey will appear.

MANAGING YOUR EMOTIONS WHILE LETTING GO

Even after we've let go, challenging emotions may reappear. For example, a dear ballroom friend of mine, who left her first instructor after dancing together for several years, called me crying. She couldn't understand why she was still feeling sad and angry about the split several months earlier, even though she was now dancing with a wonderful new instructor.

As we sorted out her feelings, she recognized that she was sad that the person she had started her dancing journey with simply wasn't meant to continue growing with her. Another powerful feeling— anger—also emerged during our conversation. The more she processed the situation, the more angry she became at her former instructor. She said, "He failed in helping me establish goals. He didn't share resources to improve (such as inviting coaches or providing tools for personal dancing development) and he kept pushing me down emotionally."

After listening intently, I offered a different take on where her anger was coming from. I wondered if she wasn't actually angry with herself for allowing him to treat her unprofessionally and for putting up with the relationship for so long. While he may not have been a particularly good teacher, the onus was on her to clearly identify what she needed and wanted.

After considering my challenge, she agreed. She was angry with herself for staying too long in a relationship that she knew wasn't a fit for her. We did a couple of clearing exercises, and she felt like a stone had been lifted off her shoulders. Today she can look back at her first instructor-relationship and bless it. She learned several key lessons and is a better dancer today because of it.

The truth is that she didn't possess the tools and experience she has today, when she first started dancing. Her instructor lead her to experience the amazing emotional depths of ballroom dancing, and she did what many of us do at first–she just went along with it. She realized that she was really sad and angry with herself for not seeing what was happening and stopping it sooner. The second time around, she picked an instructor who is much better suited for her. He is helping her reconnect with her dance passion, while caring for her as a person along the way.

If you are going through a split with your instructor/dance partner, take the time to grieve. It may seem odd to people outside the ballroom world that you are so attached to your instructor/dance partner and that it bothers you to such an extent. I can see how confusing it would be to people on the outside looking in. Ballroom dancing is emotional, AND it lets us connect to our deepest selves. It can be a confusing experience, but with time you will come to know how to be more objective in selecting an instructor/dance partner.

Thanks to the lessons in this book, you will approach your next instructor/dance partner candidate already having established your dancing goals, being clear about the type of dancer you are, having your non-negotiables clearly defined, and sharing a list of the characteristics you need and want in a future dance partnership. As you can imagine, picking your next partner will look a lot different from the day you first walked into the studio, trusting and naïve.

If you are a soon-to-be or newer competitor, you are getting this information early. Good for you. Use it to avoid many of the pitfalls listed in this book. If you are an intermediate to advanced competitor, and you are at the point where you know you need to make a move, use these tools to select your next fit with preparation, intention, and clarity.

GRACEFULLY LETTING GO—YOUR INSTRUCTOR'S RESPONSIBILITY

Truly self-aware instructors/dance partners will know when the time has come to part ways and will initiate the conversation. In my professional career as an executive coach, I have learned to see the signs when it's time to let a client go. I always tell them when we first start to work together (upfront agreement) that when they or I feel that the time is right to part, we begin our exit plan. I encourage them to own their feelings and trust that they'll know when the time is right. Sometimes, it's my job as a coach to let them know that they are ready, even when they don't feel it yet. If I'm overly attached to them financially or emotionally, my decision to keep them working with me beyond what is right for them may be fueled by my fears or ego. At that point, the relationship shifts from being about the clients to being about me. This is not a healthy working relationship, and these are good indicators that it's time to part ways.

I know that I am part of my clients' journeys for as long as it's meant to be. Sometimes in the ballroom world, instructors/dance partners become overly attached to their students for emotional and financial reasons and may not be able to stay neutral about the student's needs (which should ALWAYS come first).

THE COMPLEXITIES THAT MAKE UP BALLROOM RELATIONSHIPS

I don't believe instructors/dance partner enter into relationships with malicious intent. I do know, however, that many instructors/dance partners are not taught how to be powerful guides.

Ballroom dancing has a unique component to it, which bears discussing at this point. Most students who are able to afford ballroom dancing are at a stage in their lives when they have extra time and financial resources. This usually indicates that they have been successful in their lives and careers and have developed skills and experiences that have matured them. Many younger dance instructors, on the other hand, begin to teach and dance fresh out of high school or college, choosing ballroom dancing as their first profession. They come to the relationship with less life and business and experiences, and they may have cultural backgrounds in which the rules of communication and the interaction between student and teacher is more dominant or structured.

Put this together, and we usually see an interesting divide. The younger, less experienced ballroom instructor (life student) is now the expert. The student, who is more experienced in life, is the beginner. Self-aware instructors are able to tap into this discrepancy and learn from the student about life and business, while the student blossoms and grows as a dancer.

Unfortunately, this is not always the case. Sometimes, less-experienced or less-self-aware instructors feel challenged by a student's life experience or business savvy. The instructor responds by trying to control the relationship. In my role as a mental-game dance coach, I've seen too many students financially and emotionally manipulated by their instructors—to the point that it borders on abuse. Remember, you should never be treated in a way that is unprofessional or disrespectful, particularly when you are a client paying for a service.

Consider how Top-Teacher Forrest Vance approached his lack of life and business experience early in his career, as he noted in his interview insight, page 184:

> "The cool thing about my students is that they are all successful in their lives. I've found it tremendously educational and inspirational to learn from them throughout my career. I grew up poor in a small rural town and had limited training in how to interact with wealthy and successful people. My students early on in my career took me under their wings and taught me the skills and tools that helped me create the life I enjoy today."

Please note that I'm making a generalization here. There are many extremely experienced and professional instructors who do not fit this mold. My intention in addressing this issue is to help solve a unique, but not uncommon, challenge that some instructors and students struggle with.

If you are a professional dancer or instructor who would like help building your business by creating powerful student/teacher relationships, please don't hesitate to contact me for a confidential and complimentary chat. I can be reached at Jessika@nextleveldancing.com. You may also find Diane Jarmolow's SalesFree Sales Training Program a great resource. Learn more about her programs by visiting teachballroomdancing.com

If you are a dancer and would like help working through the process of letting an instructor/dance partner go, or if you need help selecting the next "right" fit, you may want to consider my ballroom coaching program. Through my company Next Level Dancing, I offer group coaching programs and one-on-one coaching. For more information, please visit nextleveldancing.com or email info@ nextleveldancing.com

As your coach, I will help you see your priorities, goals, and challenges clearly, so solutions flow more easily to you. I will never advise you to leave (or stay with) your current partner or instructor, nor will I recommend a particular instructor to dance with. Those are your decisions to make, once we have focused you and put a strategic plan in place.

TELL-TALE SIGNS THAT AN EXIT PLAN MAY BE IN ORDER

While this list isn't complete, it may help you sort out where you are with your current instructor, and determine your next step. It may be time to leave if:

- You have applied the strategies detailed in this book, yet there is no measurable change in your relationship. Remember, most of these tools are self-focused. Once you have tried everything you possibly can, consider if the relationship is better, worse, or the same. Then decide if you can live with what you've got, or if you need to move on.

- You have had numerous conversations or attempts to communicate with your instructor/ dance partner about the changes you would like made, but he isn't open to change or interested in working on improvements.

- Your instructor/dance partner is unwilling to change or seek outside coaching or other professional help in order to improve your relationship and dancing.

- Your competing scores consistently show a lack of progress, despite your commitment and dedication to improving your skills. And, instead of looking inward to help change your results, your instructor/dance partner blames you, the judges, the competition organizers—I could go on, but you get the point.

- You engage in unhealthy communications including blaming, foul language, inappropriate displays of anger, a lack of empathy toward one another, and obvious detachment or avoidance while practicing or competing.

- Your instructor/dance partner makes inappropriate advances toward or comments about you; when confronted and asked to stop, he continues to do so.

Remember, if your instructor/dance partner consistently violates your non-negotiables or refuses to act in a professional manner, it's time to go. No questions asked. People with boundary issues have difficulty accepting other people's feelings, emotions, and standards, which you need to guard fiercely.

So far we have discussed both how to build relationships, and how to let go of relationships. Now let's take a look at how you can share your light through dancing and embrace grace, on and off the dance floor.

Embracing Grace On and Off the Dance Floor

> " The winds of God's grace are always blowing, it is for us to raise our sails."

— RAMAKRISHNA

When I founded Next Level Dancing, LLC, I was looking for a memorable slogan and wanted something that defines the business and me at our core. I kept noodling on the words "grace" and "embrace" in a variety of formations. One day, my associate Laura Benton looked over my shoulder and she said "Embrace Grace; keep it short and sweet." She was right. This "slogan" has since become our company mantra. It's the name of our dress rental/consignment division, and it's interwoven into everything we do.

Embrace Grace has a double meaning for me. One of my dance and life mentors is Grace Kelly. To me, she embodies class, elegance, and grace, which I strive to emulate. Another meaning of the word "grace" involves divine or higher powers. Grace reminds me to treat others with respect and kindness and display my highest self in all situations.

As we explore this concept, consider what "embracing grace" means to you. How can you bring your highest self to the ballroom and all interactions with others? What would make your loved ones proud of you? What would it take for you to be an even more amazing version of yourself? What character flaws do you need to overcome and what strengths do you need to amplify in order to be your best self?

Embracing grace doesn't mean striving for perfection. It simply means that you will hold yourself to your highest standard and bring as much goodness to the world as possible. Diane Jarmolow, DVIDA© national examiner, author, and co-founder of *Move Like a Champion,* sums it up in her interview insight on page 251, "Your dancing is a reflection of your inner being, so stay conscious of your thoughts and make your inner being a beautiful one." My dear friend and fellow Pro/Am competitor Christina Diaz exemplifies grace in her interview insight, page 254, stating:

> "Several people in the audience compliment us on our 'glow' during our dancing…. There is something about ballroom, and especially Smooth, that gives me a positive energy that I want to share with the world….It allows my love for dance to permeate my body and it makes me and others feel happy. Isn't that beautiful?"

Let's look at a few ways that you can embody this concept and become a positive vibrational force, on and off the dance floor.

Say please, thank you, and I'm sorry: I know. Your mom or dad probably discussed this with you many years ago, but it's time to put these powerful words to use. When we are grateful, courteous, and attentive to others, we share our best selves with them. If someone offers you a compliment, say "thank you." If you bump into someone on the dance floor, check in with them after the heat to see if she is okay. Good manners never go out of style, and they spread a sense of goodness to all you meet. I love the book *A Simple Act of Gratitude: How Learning to Say Thank You Changed My Life*, by John Kralik. At one point in his life, he experienced the proverbial "rock bottom." Inspired by a thank you note from his girlfriend, he set out to write 365 thank you notes, one a day, for a year. As you can imagine, this small, unassuming exercise in gratitude changed his life—and the lives of those his notes touched. Never underestimate the power of gratitude!

Practice "random acts of kindness": If you notice that someone is in need, share what you can. At one competition, a woman I was just getting to know mentioned that she was feeling a bit lightheaded and hadn't eaten recently. I had an extra power bar in my bag and shared it with her. She was thrilled. In fact, I recently heard that she now shares bars with everyone who needs them. Good people "pay it forward," and the cycle of goodness expands.

Many years ago, when I first started my business, I heard the saying, "givers gain," and it stuck with me. While you don't want to focus on what you will gain by doing something nice, givers always receive more because it taps into positive vibrational energy. Say nice things to others. Offer honest compliments freely. Make someone's day by doing something unexpected. Help someone who is struggling. If you know of someone who can't afford to buy a dress or a pair of competing shoes, and you can, consider sending an anonymous credit for a shoe or dress vendor. Shortly, I will be starting a non-profit division of Next Level Dancing, LLC, called "Dancing Dreams." The division will enable us to introduce ballroom dancing and competing to those who otherwise can't afford it. We will collect and share used dresses and shoes in good condition, at no cost, to those who need them. We will be accepting donations for entry fees, competition fees, instructor fees, etc. If you are interested in learning more, please send an email to info@nextleveldancing.com and write "Dancing Dreams" in the subject line.

Exude only positive energy: This can be tough, especially as we compete. I certainly know from experience that many of my thoughts and words while competing don't fit in the "positive energy" bucket. For those of us who are still struggling with human failings, this may take some getting used to. One initial strategy is to stop gossiping or thinking negative thoughts about others (even when their costumes, hair, or makeup warrants a second look). What you think manifests into beliefs and actions. Practice thinking good thoughts and avoid beating yourself up. If you are struggling with the challenging emotions that often are experienced in "Stage 2" of dancing, remember to honor these feelings without wallowing in them. For more information about "The Stages of Learning," see my first book *The Ballroom Dance Coach: Expert Strategies to Take Your Dancing to the Next Level.*

Smile! It's the fastest and easiest way to tap into positive energy. It's really hard for the head and heart to think negative thoughts when we are smiling. Actually, the muscles used to smile send triggers to the brain, releasing "feel good chemicals" that make you feel happy. The other alternative is to frown, which actually requires more muscles than smiling and produces negative energy. A great way to practice smiling is on the dance floor. If you make a mistake in your routine, smile. If you unexpectedly bump into someone, continue smiling. Don't let the judges know by looking at your face that something bad, incorrect, or unexpected has happened. What they don't see, they can't mark.

Want good for yourself and others: Most competitors want to win or place well, and that is what makes competition so special. It's okay to be disappointed when we don't win, at least for a little while.

Practice being a gracious competitor by congratulating those who win or place better than you do. Remember, it may be your turn next. I believe there is infinite goodness in the universe. When you want or acquire something, you don't use up all the available resources, so everyone else misses out. It just may not be their time. Send goodness to others, and it will return to you tenfold.

Assume that people are good and well-intentioned. When we make negative assumptions about others, we miss the opportunity to build powerful relationships with them.

Some competitors become so consumed with winning that they may transform from warm and friendly to cold and distant, seemingly overnight. The only suggestion I have is to leave them alone. Remove yourself from their presence and energy. Trust that they are exactly where they need to be on their journey. A friend in the ballroom competing world recently told me that she used to be a highly driven and sometimes harsh competitor. All she cared about was winning. If someone stood in her way, she didn't care if she ran him over. One day she woke up and realized that she didn't want to be that person anymore. Thus began her journey of humility, gratitude, and graciousness. Today, she can see her old self in some of the people on the scene, and each time she thanks herself for turning a corner all those years ago. Remember, it's not necessarily your "job" to help others see the light. Just be the light and wish them well. Maybe you will inspire them to change.

Give grace and assume others mean well: One of my business clients uses the term "give grace" with her leadership team. She expects everyone on her team to see the best in others and assume they are coming from a good place. This strategy avoids a lot of unnecessary miscommunications and sets the stage for powerful long-term relationships. In the ballroom world, assume that people are good and well-intentioned. When we make negative assumptions about others, we miss the opportunity to build powerful relationships with them.

For example, one of the girls who used to compete with me never acknowledged me or said hello while we were on the floor or on-deck area. This seemed a bit odd to me, as we spend a lot of together, and most competitors become friends or are encouraging and vocal in cheering one another on. One day, I asked a mutual friend if the girl in question was upset with me or didn't like me. She said, "No, that is just how she competes. She is an extremely friendly and outgoing person, but when she competes, she focuses and doesn't interact with others. After the competition, you will find that she is extremely engaging and caring." I was so glad I asked! I had incorrectly assumed her standoffishness was a reflection of how she felt about me. By giving others grace and assuming only the positive, we avoid getting stuck in confusing or negative thinking.

Be there for your instructor/dance partner: Remember, you are a team while competing. Whenever possible, treat your partner like you would a good friend or loved one. Bring him a towel or a cup of water if he is dancing hard or managing a lot of students. Ask him what you can do for him to make his experience even better. I know. We have talked about your being the client in the Pro/Am relationship, and while this is still true, your Pro is still a person who is probably working hard for you while competing. Show your appreciation by being thankful, generous, and kind.

Being a positive force in the ballroom community means you will enjoy a more rewarding experience, and those around you will benefit from your contagious energy. It doesn't mean you have to be perfect or a "Ms. Goody Two-Shoes." Practice implementing just a few of these strategies and see what happens. Focus on being the highest version of yourself, and note how you feel and how others interact with you. I love the saying, "I will hold myself to a standard of grace, not perfection."

The Balanced Ballroom Dancer: Strategies for Continuing Your Personal Development On and Off the Dance Floor

> " Your hand opens and closes, opens and closes. If it were always a fist or always stretched open, you would be paralyzed. Your deepest presence is in every small contracting and expanding, the two as beautifully balanced and coordinated as birds' wings."

> - RUMI

It may seem at first that "balanced" and "ballroom" are an impossible combination and that the words don't belong in the same sentence. After all, isn't ballroom dancing and competing all about intensity, unwavering commitment, and a "go big or go home" mentality? Sure, it can be! But if it becomes all that, we are sure to burn out or make unbalanced decisions that end up hurting us or our loved ones, in the long run.

Most amateurs have full-time jobs outside the ballroom world. That is why our designation is Amateur instead of Professional. While you may be a Professional Amateur at heart, it's important not to let dancing or competing become your "end all and be all." As my ballroom competing friend Janet Simsic, a pediatric cardiologist outside of dancing, said:

> "My regular job is about life and death. I don't want my ballroom dancing or competing to feel that way also. I dance to get away from the difficult decisions I sometimes have to make at work and just enjoy dancing because it makes me feel great. While I love to dance, it is still just a hobby."

When I first began, I became enthralled with dancing and competing and made some decisions emotionally, financially, and physically that I wouldn't do again. Through those decisions and experiences, I learned to become a balanced ballroom dancer. I'm now able to dance, compete, and explore for years to come without rocking my foundation.

Most of the serious ballroom dancers I know have fallen into the same hole I did (to various degrees). Depending on how far they fell, it took some dedicated time and commitment to dig their way out.

Ideally, you are reading this book before you have fallen too deeply. If so, you will find that the tips in this chapter can transform your life and dancing experience into something that will fuel you for years to come.

The trick to becoming a BBD is to identify where you are out of balance, and then design strategies to take you back to center. It's especially important to recognize that your lack of balance has less to do with your dancing and more to do with how you live your life.

For example, let's say that you felt out of balance in the number of competitions you have signed up for, and you began to feel overwhelmed. It may seem logical to just take a few competitions out. Simply cutting down on competitions, however, without considering what made you commit to so many in the first place, won't fix the problem. Instead you are more likely to substitute the reduction in competitions with more lessons or coaching, which will move you back to the place you started from. The hunger and drive to achieve, move forward, or win, is still fueling your actions. They will simply manifest differently.

The information in this section is shared and adapted with permission from my dear friend and mentor Annette Franks. She is a counselor and consultant, motivational speaker, and addiction specialist located in Columbus, Ohio. She is also the founder of the Balancing Body, Mind & Spirit Life Enrichment Retreat in Costa Rica, which I attend each year. To learn more, visit Annette's website at annettefranks.com. You can also download several of Annette's free articles and checklists on holistic self-care, integrating mind-body-health practices, from her website. Annette's written materials and retreats emphasize and explore the importance of holistic life balance and grounding in all areas of our lives.

While each person is unique, and the best plan would be one that is highly individualized, in this section we will look at four major "layers" that provide balance:

1. **Physical**

2. **Emotional**

3. **Intellectual**

4. **Spiritual**

Each layer becomes a foundational step in a pyramid, with "joy" sitting at the top of the pyramid and serving as the outcome of the work we do in each layer.

Grounding Pyramid

Integration Authenticity Freedom Empowerment

Joy

Spiritual Grounding
"Feeding Our Soul"

Intellectual Grounding
"Stimulating Our Minds & Opening Our Hearts"

Emotional Grounding
"Honoring and Embracing Our Emotions & Building Healthy Relationships"

Physical Grounding
"Creating Safe Space & Maintaining Healthy Self-Care"

Let's start by looking at the most foundational layer, the physical.

PHYSICAL GROUNDING: CREATING SAFE SPACE AND MAINTAINING HEALTHY SELF-CARE.

If we don't take care of our bodies, we will immediately create cracks in the foundation that will eventually make our houses fall over.

At one point in my life, I needed help handling an emotional situation and went to see a therapist. She listened to my circumstances and said, "Your homework before our next session is to cook all your meals at home." I looked at her a bit perplexed and said, "Are you sure that I will feel emotionally better if I cook and eat at home for two weeks." She said, "Just do it and we'll debrief next time I see you." Since what I was doing on my own wasn't working, I took her advice to heart.

Two weeks later, I returned with a smile. When she asked me what I learned, I told her that the act of preparing healthy, tasty, and nourishing foods for myself was a form of self-healing, and I was feeling better each day I cooked. To me, it was like magic. I had no idea that eating out three times a day, every day was depleting me physically, emotionally, and financially. I used eating out as an escape from dealing with underlying issues. Today, several years later, I'm still eating most of my meals at home, and I go out for dinner as a treat.

Remember, taking care of yourself physically isn't just diet and exercise. It is also staying present in the moment, taking in sounds, smells, tastes, feelings, and sight.

Taking care of ourselves physically is imperative. Take a moment to complete the checklist on the following page to see how balanced you are physically.

Please read each statement and carefully check the response that most often describes your lifestyle. This worksheet is for your own self-reflection. No one will see your responses unless you freely choose to share them.

	Usually	Sometimes	Not Usually
I eat five to six small meals a day.			
I always eat breakfast.			
I eat a balanced diet.			
I drink at least six to seven 10-ounce glasses of water daily.			
I breathe deeply versus shallowly.			
I work out at least three times a week for at least 30 minutes each time.			
I sleep seven to eight hours a day.			
I have a consistent bedtime and wake-up time.			
I feel rested when I wake up in the morning.			
While I'm still lying in bed I'm aware of my physical body.			
I spend a few moments or more every morning savoring how I feel emotionally and physically, as I lay in bed.			
I'm aware of my feet touching the floor when I get out of bed in the morning.			
I walk slowly when I walk from one place to another.			
When I'm in the shower, I notice the water temperature and how the water feels on my skin.			
I notice birds, trees, and flowers when I'm outside.			
I take at least four to six short work breaks throughout my day.			
I listen to music that relaxes or soothes me daily.			
I feel financially secure.			
I feel I have vibrant health.			
I have energy and enthusiasm for my hobbies and interests (including dancing).			
I have quiet time for myself each day.			

	Usually	Sometimes	Not Usually
I am comfortable with silence and being alone.			
I spend time enjoying the outdoors/nature on a daily basis.			
I avoid alcohol or drink it only in moderation (fewer than two glasses a week).			
I don't eat at fast food chains.			
I eat organic foods each day.			
I avoid sodas and energy drinks.			
I avoid caffeine or drink only one cup of caffeinated coffee/tea a day.			
My weight remains fairly stable and consistent.			
I avoid foods with white flour and refined sugar.			
I get a physical exam by a qualified health professional each year.			
I see a chiropractor, massage therapist, or body worker on a regular basis.			
I eat food considered to be "super foods" such as aloe vera, bee products, blue-green algae, cacao, coconuts, goji berries, hemp seed, maca, spirulina and marine phytoplankton.			

Take a look at your list and identify areas where you may be physically out of balance. For example, you may not be getting enough sleep or have enough quality quiet time. Or your diet may not be aligned, and you aren't feeding your body enough nutrients to sustain your dancing and work life. You may be moving so quickly that you don't take the time to notice the world around you and inadvertently increase your stress and tax your nervous system. You may be eating just to feel full, but forget to savor every bite.

For the areas you checked "sometimes" or "not usually," consider how they affect your physical balance. Design an action step for the one checkbox that you truly wish to change in order to have more balance on and off the floor. You may want to turn to page 246 to record your answers.

Undefeated World and U.S. Smooth Champion Slawek Sochacki underscores the importance of balance in his interview insight on page 256:

> "Eating well and taking care of your body is essential. If you commit to dancing and competing, you want to make sure your body is nurtured, so it can sustain the increased physical and mental work that is associated with it."

Annette also recommends practicing the following strategies daily:

- **Do more conscious breathing.** Our breath connects our minds and thoughts to our body. Pay attention to your breathing patterns, taking deep full breaths versus shallow breaths.

- **Consciously feel your feet touch the earth as you walk.**

- **Drink plenty of water.**

- **Pay attention to your five major senses throughout each day:**

  1. Sight

  2. Hearing

  3. Smell

  4. Touch

  5. Taste

- **Pay close attention to your thoughts, voice, tone, words, body movements, and gestures.** As you heighten your awareness of all your contact functions (the five major sense plus thinking, talking, and movements) you will begin to notice more readily what areas you may need to address.

- **Consider if you:**

  ○ Notice the beauty around you.

  ○ Notice both the obvious and subtle sounds embedded in nature all around you.

  ○ Notice the subtle smells around you.

  ○ Are consciously feeling each footstep touching the ground when you are walking.

  ○ Fully savor each bite of food you put in your mouth.

  ○ Immediate thoughts are positive and optimistic or negative and pessimistic.

  ○ Body posture and facial gestures radiate confidence and joy.

The next layer is called "emotional grounding," and it builds on our physical grounding. It's almost impossible to be emotionally stable and build healthy personal and professional relationships when our physical foundation is cracking.

EMOTIONAL GROUNDING: HONORING AND EMBRACING OUR EMOTIONS AND BUILDING HEALTHY RELATIONSHIPS

When we feel off-balance emotionally, we may act in ways or say things that hurt other people. As we discussed in Chapter 3, dancing tends to bring out emotions that we aren't always prepared to handle. The more grounded you are emotionally, the less the increased pressure or stress will affect you in your dancing. You will be able to resolve conflict, build powerful relationships, communicate more effectively, and dance with greater joy.

Take a moment to check the boxes that correlate to your truth. Remember that there are no right or wrong answers. Just more personal awareness.

	Usually	Sometimes	Not Usually
I have energy and enthusiasm for my hobbies and outside interests (outside of ballroom).			
After a long workday, I greet my spouse/significant other with the same enthusiasm and respect I give my favorite colleague, ballroom buddy, or friends.			
I have at least three close people in my life whom I can trust and confide in.			
I'm able to ask for help and support in dealing with difficult personal issues.			
I have satisfying and meaningful relationships in my life.			
I have quiet time for myself every day.			
I'm comfortable with silence and being alone.			
I actively invest in people and events that enhance and support my well-being.			
I maintain active involvement and open and honest communication with emotionally safe and trustworthy people.			
I am comfortable experiencing and embracing a wide range of feelings deeply.			
I manage my emotions in healthy ways.			
I have released unresolved hurts and trauma.			
I maintain (or reclaim) a positive sense of self-worth.			

	Usually	Sometimes	Not Usually
I believe I'm lovable.			
I'm mindful of how much I use technology (email, texting, TV, social media, web, etc.) and have strategies for limiting its use.			
I am mindful of how much I'm talking versus listening when interacting with others.			
I stay present when communicating with others and avoid letting my mind wander.			
I don't over-schedule or break commitments for meetings or appointments with others.			
I graciously accept compliments.			
I'm relaxed in social settings.			
I'm approachable and inviting.			

When you reflect on your answers, what is becoming clear? Do you notice that you may have built strong personal relationships, but are still holding on the past stories or hurts? Or do you feel comfortable receiving compliments, but may not offer as many as you could? Do you over-commit at times and end up cancelling on people or situations you really would love to attend to?

Whatever your "aha's" may be, take a moment to reflect on an action step you would like to take in order to provide more emotional balance. Use page 247 to record your answers. Maybe it is time to have a conversation with a friend, colleague, peer, or boss to redefine your relationship. Or you may be ready to listen more and talk less when in a group setting.

Remember that emotional balancing is about giving, taking, and building powerful relationships with others. If you are competing too much, and your significant other or friends no longer get to spend any time with you, you may be sacrificing more than you bargained for. Or you may be so internally driven to practice and take lessons that you don't set aside enough time to just be present. There is a fine line between enjoying and thriving in your dancing, versus having it become an addiction that takes over in an unhealthy way. The best thing you can do for your dancing is to balance your life, and let all aspects of your life be nurtured.

Slawek also mentions in his interview insight on page 256:

> "One of our success factors has been to find balance between our passion and commitment to dance and the rest of our lives. It helps that we have a young son, which forces us to prioritize. We have to be efficient and manage our time well in order to pick him up at daycare. It's important as a committed dancer to have balance and avoid burning out."

If we get stuck trying to make everyone happy or achieve more and greater results, it may be helpful to keep the words of actor Michael York in mind. He said, "Success is the outward manifestation of inward fulfillment."

The next layer is our intellectual grounding. Let's take a closer look at how we can remain BBDs by incorporating and nourishing our minds.

INTELLECTUAL GROUNDING: STIMULATING OUR MINDS AND OPENING OUR HEARTS

I happen to be a person who loves intellectual stimulation. As a dancer, I can get stuck in the theory of doing things the "correct" way. In order to get out of my own head, I sometimes pick a coach who is more "heart" driven to remind me to balance my need for information by listening to my own dance heart. Out of the four layers, this is the one that I personally tend to become out of balance with.

Take a moment to check the boxes that correlate to your inner need and practice for intellectual stimulation.

	Usually	Sometimes	Not Usually
I attend seminars and conferences at least twice a year to stimulate and expand my knowledge outside of ballroom.			
I attend workshops or dance camps to gain more knowledge and enhance my dancing.			
I read and listen to materials at least twice a week that stimulate and enhance my knowledge base outside of ballroom.			
I read and listen to materials at least twice a week that stimulate and enhance my knowledge base for my dancing.			
I have a comprehensive understanding of how the body and brain work together.			

	Usually	Sometimes	Not Usually
I read things that help me understand myself better.			
I seek to understand and gather information before approaching others about sensitive situations.			
I have learned the importance of saying "yes" and "no," and am clear with others about what I am willing and not willing to do.			
I have clarity about how my past may or may not affect my current actions, attitudes, or behaviors.			
I trust my intuition and have an "inner knowing."			
I'm open to different ways of looking at an issue.			
I keep up with current events and world affairs.			
I know what I want and what is important to me.			
When I speak about my needs with others, I keep their needs in mind as well.			

If all the new information we add is about ballroom dancing, we may become drained or overly consumed in a short while. To be a BBD, remember to open your mind to different types of information. Most professional dancers find inspiration in things outside of ballroom. If you don't set aside time to explore things that interest you, dancing may begin to feel like a chore.

For me, going to Annette's weeklong retreat in Costa Rica each year, has helped me look at my dancing differently. I also love cooking and find that throwing a dinner party and learning how to cook a new dish, inspires my creativity. I now use a more comprehensive lens to view my dancing, and it has made me a much better dancer and competitor.

Let's look at the most powerful layer next, our spiritual grounding.

SPIRITUAL GROUNDING: FEEDING OUR SOUL

The final layer of our house is the most powerful; it's our spiritual connection. While we are not necessarily talking about religion or God, it certainly can be. For our purposes, think of it as anything that feeds your soul at a deep and profound level. The spiritual grounding layer includes seeing the best in all living things and being able to give and love unconditionally. This is what I spoke about earlier, when discussing the concept of "embracing grace." When I go to Costa Rica, I feed my brain, body, and soul, as it has become a deeply spiritual journey for me.

Take a moment to check the boxes that correlate to your spiritual awareness and practice.

	Usually	Sometimes	Not Usually
I do volunteer work within or outside my dancing commitments.			
I am able to give and receive lovingly and unconditionally.			
I believe my life has purpose and meaning.			
I engage in random acts of kindness without expecting anything in return.			
I actively attend or support spiritual groups.			
I have developed a deep spiritual connection to God or my higher power as I understand it.			
I pray and/or meditate daily.			
I radiate love and passion for life.			
I believe something bigger is guiding me.			
I spend time alone each day.			
I feel divine energy flow on a daily basis.			
I believe we are all one.			
I have a gentle and compassionate nature.			
I am not overly attached to material things.			
I honor the earth and natural resources.			
I'm free from anxiety and worry.			
I live from a place of gratitude.			

If you haven't yet begun your spiritual journey and don't know where to start, I recommend being silent and still for 15-to-30 minutes each day. Just let your thoughts flow. Often times we are too busy to take time to enjoy life and hear, see, smell, touch, or feel the divine that is in all things. In the summer, my morning ritual is to sit quietly in the sunshine for a few minutes, just to listen to the birds, feel the sun on my skin, and smell the flowers in my back yard. Sometimes I watch my beloved dog take a snooze on the back porch. When we slow down to take in all that is around us, it's hard not to experience deep feelings of joy and gratitude.

Another great tip is to have a notepad by your bed, write down five things you are grateful for each day, and thank God or the Universe for all that you have. It may be that you are healthy enough to dance, or have people in your life who care about and love you. It doesn't matter what it is, the simple act of acknowledging what you are grateful for connects you with the divine.

The beauty about connecting to the divine is that you have to do a lot less to gain a lot more. You don't have to "work hard" to be in touch with the spirit. All you have to do is be present more often. You are already loved, perfect, and whole.

When we realize that it's not about placements or performing, we are able to free ourselves to dance from a place of pure joy.

If you've seen me dance or compete, you may notice that I often touch my necklace right before going onto the floor. It is small ritual I do to remind me that I dance to honor my spirit and the divine. It also helps me center and remember why I dance and how it makes me feel. We are so blessed to be able to do this sport. When we realize that it's not about placements or performing, we are able to free ourselves to dance from a place of pure joy.

Committing to practicing these BBD tips will ensure that you enjoy competing for years to come and assist you in blending and merging your two worlds (ballroom and non-ballroom). You may actually find that being more attentive to balancing yourself on a daily basis will have an immediate effect on your dancing.

MANAGING THE ADDICTIVE ASPECTS OF BALLROOM DANCING

Some joke about ballroom being an addictive sport, and the truth is that it can be. Of course, addictions can have serious consequences. In her book, *The Energy of Money: A Spiritual Guide to Financial and Personal Fulfillment*, author Maria Nemeth, Ph.D shares, "Addictive behavior, like driven behavior, can be measured by the extent to which it interferes with our lives, and leads us further from our authentic choices and goals." She also states, "The first sign of an addiction is that you get withdrawal symptoms when you try to stop using the substance or engaging the behavior in question" (New York: The Ballantine Publishing Company, 1997, p.117).

I remember the painful moment when I realized that I had become addicted to ballroom dancing. I hope that by sharing this personal story, you take a moment to reflect on your dancing to make sure it hasn't taken over your life.

At one point on my dancing journey, I decided to leave my marriage. When my then-husband and I were in counseling together, he looked over at the therapist and said with utter desperation in his voice, "Tell her to get a hold of her dancing addiction!" I remember looking straight at him and the therapist and declaring that quitting dance was not an option. I reacted like an alcoholic who had been confronted with an intervention and was told that she couldn't touch alcohol again. I remember the intense feelings of fear that came over me when faced with the choice to stop dancing, even for a short while, as we figured out our marriage situation. The sad truth is that I couldn't give it up, and I realize now that I had developed a deeply unhealthy relationship to my dancing. It's clear to me now that I used dancing to avoid dealing with issues in my marriage, but hindsight is, as they say, 20-20. In short, I had become addicted, and it took several months of deep personal work to find the place in which dancing and competing can reside together in harmony.

I slow down and cuddle up. I don't practice, dance, or expand my mental dancing game. I focus on just being, instead of pushing forward or sharpening my skills.

I know I'm not the only one who has gone through this process, as several of my dear ballroom friends have shared similar stories. One of my ballroom friends sarcastically said, "It's only slightly less addictive than cocaine."

One of the biggest lessons I have learned, in an effort to remain a BBD, is to take "mini-breaks" from dancing to make sure I'm not developing an unhealthy addiction or obsession to it. Each year, I take one to two months off dancing to focus on my personal development and just enjoy life. I go to Costa Rica, travel, see friends, buy something nice for my house, read books, and hang out with my non-dancing friends. I slow down and cuddle up. I don't practice, dance, or expand my mental dancing game. I focus on just being, instead of pushing forward or sharpening my skills. I have been doing so consistently for several years now, and I actually find that when I get back from my mini-breaks, I'm rejuvenated and ALWAYS dance as if I've had world-class coaching while away. It's amazing what your mind and body will do if you let it rest for a while. If you decide to take a mini-break, be courteous and let your instructor/dance partner know well in advance. Remember, your instructor depends on your lessons for income, and your dance partners count on you for practice time. It's only fair to give them a time frame and return date in order to minimize confusion or drama.

If you find that ballroom dancing or competing has taken over your life, finances, or emotional well-being, my recommendation is to seek out a qualified addiction specialist, counselor, or 12-step program to learn more about addictions. Annette Franks is one of the country's leading experts on addiction, and she does seminars and keynotes on the brain disease of addiction. To learn more or to download free resources, visit Annette's website at annettefranks.com.

Former ballroom professional Juliet McMains wrote an interesting book titled *Glamour Addiction: Inside the American Ballroom Dance Industry*. While I wouldn't consider this book a "weekend read," as it is written in a more academic tone, it does offer some entertaining fictional stories that shed light on both the positive and challenging sides of ballroom dancing.

Before we leave this chapter and move to Chapter 8 to review the resources you may want to check out, take a moment to fill out the "Chapter Takeaway" section on page 246. Remember, nothing will happen or be different if you don't move into action.

A great quotation to end this chapter is by Joseph Campbell. He said, *"Your sacred space is where you can find yourself over and over again."* Remember, your answers are within you, and a wonderful way to access them is to slow down and breathe.

Chapter Summary

- It's important to debrief your competition as soon as you return home. Focus on what you can do to improve for the next competition and what you need to keep working on.

- Create SMART action steps based on your debriefing session to stay focused on your commitments.

- Move into action. Nothing will be different if you don't act differently.

- In getting ready for your next competition, remember to review your competing goals, check your communication plan with your instructor/dance partner to make sure you are aligned, confirm appointments, and make sure you have packed everything you need.

- Take responsibility for your own dancing. Work on the basics, self-medicate, and make a habit to always warm-up prior to practice.

- Invest in your dance relationship as you would any other important partnership. Develop communication strategies and upfront agreements, address miscommunications, focus on the positives, and create a partnership guideline agreement.

- Sometimes, in spite of your hard work, a relationship just isn't a fit, and it's time to let go. Not all relationships are meant to last forever.

- Embrace grace on and off the dance floor. Be a positive force, spreading goodness and light.

- Being a BBD involves developing the four layers—physical, emotional, intellectual, and spiritual grounding—resulting in pure joy.

Chapter Takeaways

Take a moment to summarize your takeaways from this chapter. These notes will come in handy as you prepare for your next competition.

After reading this chapter I realized that I:

_____

My most valuable takeaway was:

_____

In preparation for my next competition debriefing meeting, I will:

_____

For my next competition, I will make sure I don't forget to:

_____

I will take personal ownership of my dancing and competing by:

_____

I will sit down with my instructor/dance partner this week and introduce him/her to the following step from the "communication strategies" section of this chapter:

Step 1: Start with you
Step 2: Establish upfront agreements
Step 3: Address miscommunications or disagreements
Step 4: Stay in your "love place"
Step 5: Prepare a partnership guideline document

I will talk to my instructor about what an exit plan would look like should I need one.

YES I will by: _____   NO I won't because: _____

If you picked no, consider why you wouldn't and list your hesitation and fears below. If you aren't comfortable doing so, consider what conversations or communication strategies you need to engage in to feel comfortable checking "yes."

I'm going to practice the following "embrace grace" strategies this week/month on and off the dance floor:

_____

To become a BBD, I will work on the following to improve my:

physical grounding: _____

emotional grounding: _____

intellectual grounding: _____

spiritual grounding: _____

Photo by: Ryan Kenner Photography

Interview Insight: Peter and Alexandra Perzhu

UNITED STATES AND WORLD CHAMPION 9-DANCERS, COACHES, AND OWNERS OF ARTHUR MURRAY ST. AUGUSTINE BALLROOM STUDIO IN ST. AUGUSTINE, FLORIDA.

Jessika Ferm: *Peter, not only are you a U.S. and World Champion professional dancer, but you also are a top teacher competing almost every weekend with your students. What type of student do you attract, and what are some of their common characteristics?*

Peter Perzhu: All my current ladies came to me ready to compete. They knew who Alexandra and I were, and I believe they sought us out because of our professional reputation and success with Pro/Am students. None of my ladies live in St. Augustine, so they travel to dance with me, which means they are motivated and focused. I would say that all of them are driven to be their personal best, and they are open to feedback that helps them improve and reach their goals. They are also disciplined and hard-working and are serious about competing.

Jessika Ferm: *In your opinion as a teacher, what are some of the benefits of competing?*

Peter Perzhu: There are a lot of benefits to competing, and each student gains something special from the experiences. For example, some students benefit from expanding their social networks, and others gain increased self-confidence through competing. Competing gives students measurable milestones for reaching their goals faster, which is a great motivator for almost all our students.

Jessika Ferm: *What are some of your expectations for your competing ladies when they attend competitions?*

Peter Perzhu: All my ladies are seasoned competitors, and they support and treat each other with respect. We work as a team when we compete, and I encourage my students to sit together at the same table during competitions and participate in group dinners or lunches. It builds team spirit and camaraderie, which is really important when you compete often and are spending a lot of time together.

Alexandra Perzhu: All of our students are sophisticated and have impeccable style. We do expect them to be dressed and groomed appropriately, and we offer suggestions and advice to make sure they look their personal best. If there is anything we don't like or approve of, we tell them right away. Because all of our students want to be and look their best, they are always open to feedback. When you move up to a new level of dancing, we may need to review how these changes need to be reflected in your dancing persona, and we offer feedback that helps you embrace a new style or approach. We expect all our students to listen to our feedback and take it to heart in order to help them reach their goals.

Jessika Ferm: *Your students are very lucky to have both of you on their competing team. What are some other benefits your students receive from having both of you attend competitions?*

Alexandra Perzhu: Because I don't have as many competing gentlemen right now, I am able to set aside time for Peter's students during competitions to help them maximize their success. As a lady competitor myself, I understand the importance of being well prepared. I ensure that all our competitive ladies are groomed and dressed for success. I do all their hair and makeup, and I spend 90 minutes with each of them to help them prepare mentally and emotionally to compete at their best. If they are looking for a new dress, I take them to the dress vendors with Peter to discuss options. I love working with Dawn Smart at Doré Designs because she does all my dresses, and I trust her taste and experience. Most of our students end up working with Dawn because they know that she will make them look and feel beautiful, but we work with other vendors as well if a student finds the right dress somewhere else.

I often serve as a good sounding board to Peter's students to help them manage the emotional roller coaster that sometimes take place while competing. It isn't always a good idea for students to address their frustrations with their teachers, and I'm often able to help a student refocus or redirect challenging emotions in the moment. That way, it doesn't affect their dancing, and Peter and his students can focus on dancing with joy and ease instead.

Peter Perzhu: I love it when Alexandra is in the ballroom watching my students and me dance, because she can offer us invaluable feedback about how we look on the floor and how we can improve. I can't see it because I'm dancing with them. I trust her judgment implicitly, and so do my ladies. Alexandra is my co-pilot, and we work as a team for the benefit of our students.

Jessika Ferm: *What are some strategies that you encourage students to use to get ready to compete?*

Alexandra Perzhu: I tell students to listen to their favorite music as they warm up. Play something that makes you feel good, and avoid listening to songs that make you overly emotional or sad. You need to prepare yourself to compete, not snuggle up in bed to cry. You want to get in tune with the right "competing emotions" and feel inspired and energized.

It is also imperative for students to warm up their bodies before coming down to the ballroom. Peter is one of those dancers and teachers who has an amazing amount of flexibly, and it's important for his ladies to be as flexible and fluid as possible in order to feed back the energy to his frame. Another tip is to arrive in the ballroom early, and try not to talk to a lot of people when you are getting ready to compete. If you do, you may lose some of the energy you created while warming up in your room, and you may not have the right mindset needed to project power and grace to the audience and the judges.

Finally, watch other people dance in order to get inspired. Sometimes just watching others will help you get motivated and energized.

Peter Perzhu: Practice is key. When you get to the competition floor, you can't think of your frame or footwork. When you are competing, you need to dance from the heart and be in the moment. Remember how lucky you are to be able to do this.

Interview Insight:
Diane Jarmolow

Photo by: Sophie Maher

FOUNDER OF THE BALLROOM DANCE TEACHERS COLLEGE. DIANE IS A DVIDA® NATIONAL EXAMINER, AUTHOR OF *TEACH LIKE A PRO*, AND COFOUNDER OF *MOVE LIKE A CHAMPION*. SHE RESIDES IN OAKLAND, CA.

Jessika Ferm: *You are one of ballroom's most unassuming key players, having authored many DVIDA manuals and owned the largest ballroom studio in the US, the Metronome Ballroom, for many years. What tips would you give amateur competitors to help them compete successfully?*

Diane Jarmolow: I would encourage amateur competitors to define their purpose for competing. If their goals are solely for their own gain, the experience will be shallow and short-lived. If, for example, a dancer is driven to achieve status or beat other people, then competing will never be satisfying. On the other hand, if the goals are self-improvement, personal challenge, or sharing the love of dance with others, then competition will be satisfying, regardless of the official results.

I would also tell them to be open to the transformation that is possible through working with a partner and coaches. Embrace the experience, and never forget the amazing adventure that is partner dancing.

And I'd advise competitors to learn to "do it right." Fundamentals are so important, and too often dancers are in an enormous rush to do the "fancy" stuff. Slow and steady wins the race, and *all great dancers* work on developing technique.

Jessika Ferm: *In your role as an adjudicator, what are some of the biggest mistakes you see newer dancers or competitors making in practice or on the floor?*

Diane Jarmolow: New dancers have a lot to learn and retain for competition. Often dancers seem to forget everything they've learned. They get off time, look down, forget their choreography, move faster than the music, etc. All of these mistakes clear up with time, repetition, and experience. With time, they also begin to remember that dancing is supposed to be fun, and they begin to lighten up.

The bigger mistake, the one the causes the most grief, is the way in which dance partners relate to one another. Dance partnerships are just like any other relationships. Knowing how to have a successful relationship is a lifelong study in itself! Dancers are just people who bring their "stuff" to the dance floor. If people struggle in relationships in general, chances are they will struggle in their dance partnerships. Examples of relationship frustrations:

- Failing to listen to one another.

- Interrupting while the other is talking.

- Sulking or holding a grudge.

- Getting upset at mistakes.

- Blaming the other person.

All of these unproductive relationship habits can be helped by these relationship tools:

- Practice "active listening." Repeat back to your partner what he/she has just said, so your partner feels "heard."

- Be accountable and professional.

- Don't take things personally or be overly sensitive. Know that your partner is doing his or her best to communicate feelings.

- Practice appreciation. After each session, list three-to-five things that you appreciate about your partner.

- Be open to getting help from coaches when you reach a deadlock.

Jessika Ferm: *Kasia Kozak and you are the creators and authors of the acclaimed Move Like a Champion book and DVD program. Why did you design this program, and how can it assist new-to-advanced competitors in their dancing?*

Diane Jarmolow: I had many personal frustrations as a professional dancer. My coaches would use their hands to place my head in the correct position, or they would tell me to relax my shoulders, but I had no way of recalling these positions on my own. I did not know that what was going on *inside* my body would produce the aesthetic on the *outside*. I became acutely aware that I wasn't progressing, and my coaches were getting frustrated, having to repeat the same corrections over and over.

I realized that I had to do something outside of ballroom training to find answers. I sought out ballet, Pilates, Feldenkrais, and yoga. Little by little, I got a sense of how the body works, and I started to improve. But my epiphany came one day in yoga.

My yoga teacher had brought a full-size skeleton to class to demonstrate how the shoulders work. She pointed out the two inverted triangular bones, the shoulder blades, and showed how they float in all directions—they are not connected to the ribcage in the back. The only connection the shoulder blades have to the rest of the skeleton is through the clavicles (collar bones), which then connect to the scapula (breast bone). She led us through exercises, allowing us to feel our shoulder blades move in different positions. Then she showed us the placement that creates the beautiful upper carriage and lifted sternum that we see in the dancers we most admire. Voila! *Once I knew how things worked*, I could direct my body into the position I wanted.

In the meantime, Kasia was independently studying all kinds of movement modalities. She knew that teaching steps and choreography was far from sufficient to transform regular people into beautiful dancers. We recognized that our common passion was to develop a language and system to teach ballroom dancers what we had discovered. We spent 18 months studying anatomy and analyzing which bones *went where* in order to create the movement we use in our ballroom and Latin dancing.

For example, we figured out the relationship between the pelvis and femur bones that creates hip action (we call these *Inside Out Eights* and *Rock the Boat*), and how we create outside and inside of turns (*Bottle Bush*). We analyzed how the head turns (between the 1st and 2nd cervical vertebrae), so that it can turn precisely without dragging the shoulder with it, as we see so often in Promenade Position (*Just Say No*). We learned how the bones in the feet work to create heel leads, pointed toes, and inside edges (*Feet with Attitude*).

We realized that most people who come to a dance studio for their wedding dance, social reasons, fitness, and exercise don't want to spend time in "science" class. So we created *Move Like a Champion*, so anyone can learn to improve body movement with one exercise in just a few minutes.

Our mission is twofold: *(1) help all students learn about their bodies, so they can move the way top dancers move;* and *(2) give dance teachers a powerful system for teaching students and reducing frustration.* Wouldn't it be great if a student never had to hear "relax your shoulders" ever again!

Jessika Ferm: *What one tip would you give competition newcomers to help them dance with greater joy and grace?*

Diane Jarmolow: Have a ritual before every practice, performance, and competition that centers you, connects you with your partner, and inspires you. For example, breathe deeply and send both calm and energy into each part of your body; hold your partner's hands and look into his or her eyes; and say words of appreciation like "thank you for the opportunity to dance." Then remind yourself of the dancer you want to be—present, joyful, graceful. Your dancing is a reflection of your inner being, so stay conscious of your thoughts, and make your inner being a beautiful one!

Photo by: Stephen Marino

Interview Insight: Christina Diaz

PRO-AM SILVER DANCER AND HOLDER OF PRESTIGIOUS TITLES INCLUDING BRONZE WORLD RHYTHM, SMOOTH, STANDARD, AND 10-DANCE CHAMPION AT USDC 2012.

Outside the ballroom world, Christina is a captain in the United States Air Force and resides in Huntington Beach, CA.

Jessika Ferm: *You dance and compete in all four styles. What is your secret to success?*

Christina Diaz: I would say that it is consistency. When I go through the process of learning new choreography, styling, or technique, I take lessons or coaching first, and then I set aside time before my next lesson to work on it by myself. I combine the physical and mental process to deepen my learning. I do not rely solely on my lessons with Matt Gregory; instead, I work to process the new information on my own in order to maximize my growth.

Other dancers who seem to be stuck at a certain place or level often ask me what I do to get the results I experience, and I try to remind them that I spend a considerable amount of time in the studio practicing on my own. I didn't just wake up accomplished. I work every day to get better.

Jessika Ferm: *Whom do you coach with?*

Christina Diaz: I coach with Heather Smith for Smooth and Standard. She is also my mental and attitude coach and the number-one person I look to for guidance. I also work regularly with Ray Rivers for all styles and Tony Meredith for Latin. When I first started, I didn't do a lot of coaching. I had my hands full learning steps and styles. I think it would have overwhelmed me if I had received too much information early on. Now I probably take a coaching session every two to three weeks.

Jessika Ferm: *What is the most valuable information you have learned from your coaches?*

Christina Diaz: My coaches help me set goals and work toward them slowly and consistently. When I first started to work with Heather Smith, she gave me small tangible goals. Once I accomplished them, she gave me new ones. I let my coaches guide my progress and challenge me to do more when they feel I'm ready. Heather gives me very practical changes—styling options, head shaping choices—that I understand in that moment. It takes lots of practice to make them part of my routines, but immediate and executable things like that make a big difference for me. Other coaches may be more theoretical, but I have found that what works best for me is when I am able to implement and work on pieces one at a time.

Jessika Ferm: *You are moving from Bronze to Silver. How is the transition going?*

Christina Diaz: At first I was a bit nervous, but now I'm fired up and ready to tackle the challenge. I danced my first Silver competition in the Smooth style. While I struggled a bit because of the new choreography, I walked away from it feeling very successful. Matt and I had several people in the audience compliment us on our "glow" during our dancing. This reminded me why I dance. There is something about ballroom, and especially Smooth, that gives me a positive energy I want to share with the world. I think that style, in particular, allows my love for dance to permeate my body, and it makes me and others feel happy.

Jessika Ferm: *What is the one thing in your dance partnership that is most challenging?*

Christina Diaz: The most challenging aspect of our partnership is communication during practice. I am a perfectionist and often will get "stuck" trying to master a certain movement. Matt works with me to get it right but will often make the call that we need to move on. I must trust Matt as the professional to guide me in my progress.

Jessika Ferm: *What do you think makes your dance relationship so unique?*

Christina Diaz: Matt and I have a very genuine connection, and we radiate a certain energy that comes from our common love of dance and music. For us, it's not all about winning or accomplishing goals. It's about our journey together, doing what we love to do.

Interview Insight: Slawek Sochacki and Marzena Stachura

Photo by: Mary Tweeddale

UNDEFEATED WORLD AND U.S. SMOOTH CHAMPIONS, WINNING PRO/AM TEACHERS AND COACHES. THEY RESIDE IN ALISO VIEJO, CA.

Jessika Ferm: *You are the undefeated World and U.S. Smooth Champions. What tips would you share with new-to-intermediate competitors to help them stand out on the floor?*

Marzena Stachura: The first part is how you present yourself. It is always important to make a good first impression. Even as a beginner, make sure you have a look that is presentable and shows that you take competing seriously. You don't have to have an expensive gown, but you need to do your hair and look clean and well put-together. You want to look as much like a professional as you can, even if you are a beginner. I liken it to going shopping in a store. The first thing you look at when you buy a new product is the packaging. It attracts you. Then the product, or your dancing, has to be good, or you won't get a second chance. Your job is to sell your dancing to the judges in order to get their attention.

The second part is dancing as well as you can technically. Spend time working on your foundation. Many new dancers want to rush through the steps and reach what they think is a higher level of dancing. This is often a mistake. Judges appreciate quality over quantity, and we encourage our students to think of their dancing as they did their education. In most countries, elementary school lasts six to eight years, so you learn the foundation. Think of this as your Bronze level. Then high school is shorter, to teach you the next set of skills to advance your foundation. This would be your Silver dancing, which is often shorter than Bronze because it is meant to prepare you for your final stage, which is Gold or the College/University level. We usually say that Gold or Open is your lifetime dancing level, because you can work in this level and master your craft for as many years as you would like.

Slawek Sochacki: I start by helping my students articulate their goals and identify their reasons for dancing. Each student is different, so their dancing or competing plan must be customized for them. In the end, it always comes back to having a good foundation and doing the correct technique. My tip for new competitors is to invest in your Bronze level if you want to be successful in the long run.

Jessika Ferm: *What advice did you receive on your dancing journey that stayed with you and helped you be successful? What tips do you want to share to help students get the most from their dancing?*

Marzena Stachura: Dedicated practice, practice, practice. Have a goal for every practice and stick to your plan. Sometimes Slawek and I even set a timer for each area we are working on, so we don't use too much time trying to work on one specific aspect of our dancing.

The other thing our coaches taught us when we started was to invest in our foundation. When you have a strong foundation, you can weather any storm.

Slawek Sochacki: One of our success factors has been finding balance between our passion and commitment to dance and the rest of our lives. It helps that we have a young son, who forces us to prioritize. We have to be efficient and manage our time well in order to pick him up at daycare. It's important for a committed dancer to have balance to avoid burning out.

It's also important to have time to be inspired by others and to find exciting new things to incorporate into your dancing. Eating well and taking care of your body are essential. If you commit to dancing and competing, you want to make sure your body is nurtured, so it can sustain the increased physical and mental work that is associated with it.

Another tip I learned from one of my coaches is that for every one-hour lesson I receive, I needed to practice by myself for two hours. For students who really want to compete well, it is imperative to practice, so when they come to their lessons, they are prepared to advance more quickly. Remember that practice has to be quality. If you practice incorrectly, it can actually hurt your dancing instead of help it. Work with your instructor to ensure that you have a good practice plan.

Jessika Ferm: *What pitfalls or mistakes do you see students making on or off the dance floor that may prevent them from reaching their goals or full potential?*

Marzena Stachura: Showing their mistakes on their faces when they compete. It's important to try to make the dancing as believable as possible. Everyone makes mistakes, but the key is to move on after a mistake, so it doesn't affect the rest of the routine. It is not uncommon for my students to make a mistake, and if they can't brush it off, it creates two or three additional mistakes. When you make a mistake, try to make it look like it was part of the routine. Remember that not all judges are looking at you at the same time, but if you show your mistake on your face, they will know immediately that something is off, and it may affect their scores. The key to being a successful competitor is to convince the majority of the judges of your skill and talent. You can't impress all judges. In ballroom competing, the key is getting as many judges to favor your dancing as possible. The winner will not necessarily have all first placements. He or she will have the highest average placements.

Slawek Sochacki: One major pitfall is trying to be perfect. Marzena and I know that we are far from perfect, but we strive to be as good as we can be. Dancing should be a joy. Students invest a lot of money and time into competing, and I remind them to focus on why they dance in the first place and not over-focus on their mistakes or try to be perfect. When we began competing in the U.S., after spending 15 years representing Poland in 10-Dance, we wanted to dance for the joy of it. We have experienced tremendous success in our dancing since then, and we believe it is because we don't try to be perfect. We try to share with the audience our love for dance.

Jessika Ferm: *What else do you want to share that you think would be helpful?*

Marzena Stachura: Believe in your teacher. If you find someone you love to dance with, then trust his or her process. Many students are impatient and don't realize that it takes hours and hours to become a great dancer. Most teachers have their students' best interests at heart, because their dancing is a reflection of the teacher's brand. They want the student to be successful. We recommend the book *Bounce: Mozart, Federer, Picasso, Beckham, and the Science of Success* by Matthew Syed, and we share it with all of our students. In the book, Matthew talks about the "10,000 Rule," which debunks the myth that it is all about talent. Amazing results actually come from 10,000 repetitions. Dedicated practice makes you a master of your craft.

Slawek Sochacki: Be yourself. Most judges want to see *your* version of the dances you do, not for you to try to look like someone else. While ballroom dancing is an athletic sport, it also is a beautiful form of art, which you have the chance to express.

8

Your Dancing and Competing Resources

The greatest achievement of the human spirit is to live up to one's opportunities and make the most of one's resources.

- LUC DE CLAPIERS

Photo by: Tom Wehrung

I'm pleased to provide the following list of highly recommended dancing resources. These books, websites, products, and services will help round out your "ballroom dancing and competing library." Most of the books listed are available at the public library. Of course, you may opt to buy some of these resources and share them with your dancing community. You might even consider starting a lending library of dance resources with your ballroom friends.

Books

- *10-Minute Toughness: The Mental-Training Program for Winning Before the Game Begins*, by Jason Selk
- *The 5 Love Languages: The Secret to Love That Lasts*, by Gary D. Chapman
- *A Simple Act of Gratitude: How Learning to Say Thank You Changed My Life*, by John Kralik
- *The Anatomy of Change: A Way to Move Through Life's Transitions*, by Richard Strozzi-Heckler
- *Answering Your Call: A Guide for Living Your Deepest Purpose*, by John P. Schuster
- *Ask and It Is Given: Learning to Manifest Your Desires*, by Esther Hicks, Jerry Hicks and Wayne W. Dyer
- *Ballroom: Culture and Costumes in Competitive Dance*, by Jonathan S. Marion
- *The Ballroom Dance Coach: Expert Strategies to Take Your Dancing to the Next Level*, by Jessika Ferm
- *Ballroom Dancing is Not for Sissies: An R-Rated Guide for Partnership*, by Elizabeth A. Seagull and Arthur A. Seagull
- *Ballroom! Obsession and Passion Inside the World of Competitive Dance*, by Sharon Savoy
- *Becoming Ginger Rogers: How Ballroom Dancing Made Me a Happier Woman, Better Partner, and Smarter CEO*, by Patrice Tanaka
- *Body Mind, Mastery: Training for Sport and Life*, by Dan Millman
- *Bounce: Mozart, Federer, Picasso, Beckham, and the Science of Success*, by Matthew Syed
- *The Creative Habit: Learn It and Use It for Life*, by Twyla Tharp
- *Crucial Conversations: Tools for Talking When Stakes are High*, by Kerry Patterson, Joseph Grenny, Ron McMIllan, and Al Switzler
- *Dance to Your Maximum: The Competitive Ballroom Dancer's Workbook*, by Maximiliaan Winkelhuis
- *Destructive Emotions: How Can We Overcome Them*, by Dalai Lama and Daniel Goleman
- *The Energy of Money: A Spiritual Guide to Financial and Personal Fulfillment*, by Maria Nemeth, Ph.D.
- *Feel the Fear and Do it Anyway*, by Susan Jeffers, Ph.D
- *Find Your Courage! 12 Acts for Becoming Fearless at Work and in Life*, by Margie Warrell
- *Glamour Addiction: Inside the American Ballroom Dance Industry*, by Juliet McMains
- *Good to Great: Why Some Companies Make the Leap… and Others Don't*, by Jim Collins
- *How We Choose to Be Happy: The 9 Choices of Extremely Happy People–Their Secrets, Their Stories*, by Rick Foster and Greg Hicks

- *The Inner Athlete: Realizing Your Fullest Potential*, by Dan Millman
- *The Intuitive Body: Discovering the Wisdom of Conscious Embodiment and Aikido*, by Wendy Palmer
- *Latin: Thinking, Sensing, and Doing in Latin American Dancing*, by Ruud Vermey
- *Learned Optimism: How to Change Your Mind and Your Life*, by Martin E.P. Seligman
- *Mastery: The Keys to Success and Long-Term Fulfillment*, by George Leonard
- *Mind Gym: An Athlete's Guide to Inner Excellence*, by Gary Mack and David Casstevens
- *Move Like a Champion Book and DVD*, by Diane Jarmolow and Kasia Kozak
- *The Passion Plan: A Step-by-Step Guide to Discovering, Developing, and Living Your Passion*, by Richard Chang
- *Poised for Success: Mastering the Four Qualities That Distinguish Outstanding Professionals*, by Jacqueline Whitmore
- *The Power of Full Engagement: Managing Energy, Not Time, Is the Key to High Performance and Personal Renewal*, by Jim Loehr and Tony Schwartz
- *The Power of Habit: Why We Do What We Do In Business and Life*, by Charles Duhigg
- *The Power of Intention: Learning to Co-Create Your World Your Way*, by Wayne W. Dyer
- *Presence: An Exploration of Profound Change in People, Organizations, and Society*, by Peter Senge, C.Otto Scharmer, Joseph Jaworski, and Betty Sue Flowers
- *The Road Less Traveled: A New Psychology of Love, Traditional Values, and Spiritual Growth*, by M. Scott Peck
- *Smart Women Finish Rich*, by David Bach
- *The Speed of Trust: The One Thing That Changes Everything*, by Stephen M.R. Covey and Rebecca R. Merrill
- *Stop Playing Safe: Rethink Risk. Unlock the Power of Courage. Achieve Outstanding Success*, by Margie Warrell
- *The Talent Code: Greatness Isn't Born. It's Grown, Here's How*, by Daniel Coyle
- *Talent is Overrated: What Really Separates World-Class Performers from Everybody Else*, by Geoff Colvin
- *Teach Like a Pro: The Ultimate Guide for Ballroom Dance Instructors*, by Diane Jarmolow and Brandee Selck
- *The Way of the Champion: Lessons from Sun Tzu's The Art of War and Other Tao Wisdom for Sprits & Life*, by Jerry Lynch, Ph.D. and Chungliang Al Huang
- *The Year of Dancing Dangerously: One Women's Journey from Beginner to Winner*, by Lydia Raurell

Online Resources

Life and Business Resource Websites:

- 5LoveLanguages.com
- AnnetteFranks.com
- DeepakChopra.com
- JimCollins.com
- Marcandangel.com

Great Online Articles (Sports Psychology):

- psychologytoday.com/blog/greaseless/201107/what-let-down
- coachdeanhebert.wordpress.com/2009/10/22/post-race-depression/
- blogs.hbr.org/schwartz/2012/08/our-unhealthy-obsession-with-winning.html

Ballroom News and Discussion Groups:

- DanceBeat.com
- Dance-Forums.com
- Facebook dance groups. Search for Education Department WDC&AL on Facebook and request to join. You may also want to ask to join the group USA Dance, Inc.

Rules and Regulations Websites:

- NDCA.org
- USADance.org

Shopping: Books, Practice Videos, DVDs and Music:

- BallroomDancers.com (shopping, The Learning Center, and classifieds)
- BallroomPlaylist.com
- DanceVision.com (shopping and dance camps)
- DSI-London.com: The book, *Dance to Your Maximum* by Maximiliaan Winkelhuis is published in the United Kingdom and can be ordered and shipped to you in the United States by visiting the DSI London website. You can also ordered it directly from us at Next Level Dancing by going to nextleveldancing.com/shop.html.
- MoveLikeaChampion.com
- NextLevelDancing.com (shopping, workshops, and newsletter)

Workshops and Dance Camps:

- DanceVision.com (shopping and dance camps)
- NextLevelDancing.com (shopping, workshops, and newsletter)
- LaBlastFitness.com (exercise program specifically designed for ballroom dancers)
- TeachBallroomDancing.com (teacher training resources)

Costumes, Accessories, Shoes, and Competition Prep

The following list includes many popular competition vendors. Please note this is not an all-inclusive list. There are many talented individuals and companies that can provide your competition necessities. You should always refer to competition websites to see which vendors will be attending your upcoming competitions.

Ballroom Costumes:

- BallroomDancers.com
- Dance America: Dance-America.com
- Designs To Shine: DesignsToShine.com
- Deirdre of London: DeirdreOfLondon.com
- Donna, Inc.: DonnaInc.net
- Doré Designs: DoreDesigns.com
- Elle Dance Studio, Inc.: ElleDanceStudio.com
- Encore Ballroom Couture: EncoreBallroomCouture.com
- Jordy International: JordyInternational.com
- Randall Designs: RandallDesigns.net
- Rhinestone Dress Rentals: RhinestoneDressRentals.com
- Rhythmic Rentals: RhythmicRentals.com
- Star Dance Shop: stardanceshop.com

Accessories and Shoe Vendors:

- Capezio: Capezio.com
- Dance America: Dance-America.com
- DanzAnn: danzann2011@hotmail.com
- DanzWorld: DanceShopper.com
- Showtime: ShowtimeDanceShoes.com
- Supadance: SupadanceUSA.com

Hair and Makeup Specialists:

- Boyko: Boyko.co
- Lisa De Bevec: Glamrpuss.com
- Linda Doyle: brushesbylinda@sbcglobal.net
- Margaret Burns: PurpleTigerDance.com

Product Recommendations:

- LipSense by SeneGence: Senegence.com. (our preferred vendor is Sandra Helinski, distributor #26392)

Onsite Photography and Videography:

- Alliance Video and Photography: alliance-consulting.photoreflect.com
- Front Row Productions: frontrowproductions.net
- Park West Photography: parkwestphoto.photoreflect.com
- Ryan Kenner Photography: ryankennerphotography.com
- Stephen Marino Photography: stephenmarino.com

Ballroom Dancing Exercise Plan by Michelle Ladd, Co-Owner of The Human Form Fitness

As with all exercise, if you experience joint pain or discomfort while performing any of these, stop and consult with a qualified professional. If you have any injuries or physical restrictions that keep these exercises from being a good fit for you, avoid them and/or consult with a qualified professional.

At The Human Form, all of our ballroom dancers engage in strength training of some kind. We use a wide variety of exercises depending on their strength, flexibility, muscle imbalances, and level of athleticism. Though our programs are very individualized in this way, almost everyone can benefit from strengthening their upper back, deep abdominal muscles, glutes, and balance. These muscles are integral in proper posture and the movement patterns required in both social and competitive ballroom dancing.

We've chosen a sampling of exercises that we use regularly at The Human Form to get you started*. They can be done without equipment in a gym, at home, or in a hotel room. Start slowly and conservatively. If you complete them successfully, without a great amount of soreness or pain, then gradually increase the number of reps (or amount of time spent performing the exercise) each week. Exercise should never be stagnant; you should always be improving in some way. Your body adapts relatively quickly to activities, so what was effective in the beginning of a program will be less and less effective the longer you do it, unless you change it or make it harder in some way.

So, let's get started! We'll begin by alternating two exercises, targeting your glutes and abdominals:

LUNGES
2-3 sets of 8-12 reps on each leg.

Start in a split stance position (shown below) with your back knee on the floor, using a pad under your knee if necessary. Your front and back knees should be at 90-degree angles. Be sure the front knee is directly over the ankle or shoelaces of your front foot. The opposite knee should remain under the hip or slightly behind it during the exercise. Gently draw the navel toward the spine and press into the floor the heel of your front foot to raise yourself up until both legs are relatively straight. Reverse the procedure to lower yourself to the floor, but do not allow the knee to touch the floor. Throughout the entire exercise, the glute (aka butt muscle) of your front leg should be contracted. Driving up through the front heel will help with this. Pay special attention to this muscle as this is the key to a proper lunge, as well as to avoiding knee pain. If you are able and have access to them, you can add a dumbbell in each hand for added difficulty. Repeat for the desired number of reps and then switch legs.

SIDE PLANKS

2-3 sets of 30-60 seconds on each side.

Lay on one hip with both knees at 90 degrees (as shown in 1st photo), propping your upper body up with your elbow. Be sure your elbow is directly underneath your shoulder. Do not "slouch" into your shoulder. Keep your hips and shoulders stacked on top of each other; brace your core muscles, and lift your hip off ground. Hold as long as you can without sacrificing good form. Repeat on the other side. When you can perform two sets of 60 seconds on each side, move to the advanced position, shown in the second photo. Perform this with both legs straight, one foot in front of the other. Once you can hold this for two sets of 60 seconds on each side, you can stack your feet, one on top of the other, for an even more advanced position.

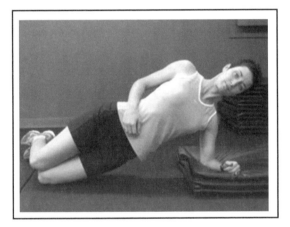

Complete the above exercises in a "circuit" fashion. Perform one set of lunges (right leg as well as left leg) and then perform one set of planks (right side as well as left side). Take a 60-second break and go through the circuit one or two more times, depending on your athletic ability and time frame.

After completing two-to-three sets total of each of the above exercises, then do the prone cobra.

PRONE COBRA

180 seconds total, broken up in increments appropriate for you, resting as needed.

Begin by lying on your stomach, with your hands at sides, palms **down**. Lift only the upper half of your torso (shoulder blade area only) off ground. Lift your hands off ground, turning your palms **out** and pointing your thumbs up, with your nose toward the floor. The key to this exercise is focusing on pinching your shoulder

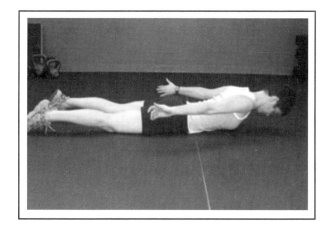

blades together, while externally rotating the hands (thumbs point to ceiling). Keep your head in a neutral position. Avoid lifting your upper body too high off the ground with your lower back. This is for the upper portion of your torso only. If you feel low-back pain, lower your chest toward the floor and be sure you are tightly contracting your abdominal muscles as well. This is an "isometric hold" exercise, so you stay in this position as long as you can. The goal is three minutes total, but you will likely need to break this up into 30-, 45- or 60- second increments in the beginning. Hold it longer each week, resting in-between, until you can do three minutes without resting.

Once you have completed three minutes total of your prone cobra, finish up with some balance work.

SINGLE LEG BALANCE

2 sets of 30 seconds on each leg.

Though balancing on one leg may seem simple, we have a few instructions that may make it more of a challenge than you'd expect. Stand near a wall or railing, so you have something to steady yourself against when necessary. Lift one foot off the ground (only a little if you are unsteady, higher if you feel more stable). Be sure you have even pressure on the front and back pads of your foot. Also, do not let your arch collapse toward the floor. Avoid collapsing into your hip. Stand tall throughout your entire body, as if a string is pulling your head up toward the ceiling. Keep your eyes focused straight ahead, while keeping your chest up high. For an added challenge, close your eyes!

If you have time, desire, and a qualified person to guide you, you can certainly benefit from a longer or more detailed exercise program, but this is a great place to start for beginners or those who are short on time.

Annual Goal-Planning Worksheet

For additional help on how to use these forms, please refer to the Next Level Dancing article "How to Create Powerful Annual Dancing Goals That Get Results," available at nextleveldancing.com/resources/html

STEP 1: CONDUCT AN AUDIT OF YOUR PREVIOUS YEAR'S DANCING SUCCESSES AND DISAPPOINTMENTS

Successes:	Disappointments:

What I'm most proud of:	What I'm most disappointed in:

STEP 2: MAKE A LIST OF WHAT YOU REALLY WANT AND BELIEVE YOU CAN DO—AND DREAM OF ACCOMPLISHING

What I really want and believe I can do:	What I dream of accomplishing:

One of my REALLY BIG goals, which I may not accomplish this year, but may in the future is:

STEP 3: CREATE YOUR ANNUAL DANCING GOALS

This year, my overall goal is:

My sub-goals are (could be by-month or competition):

STEP 4: REVIEW YOUR GOALS WITH YOUR PARTNER (PROFESSIONAL, AMATEUR, OR SIGNIFICANT OTHER)

I learned that I need to do or take the following into consideration in order to be a balanced dancer:

About the Author

Photo by: Tom Wehrung

A master-level, award-winning executive coach, Jessika Ferm took her first ballroom dance lesson in 2009, at the insistence of a business coach who felt she was working too much and needed a hobby. Little did Jessika know that this seemingly small step would permanently change her life. After just a few lessons, Jessika fell in love with ballroom dancing. In four short years, she earned several distinguished awards in the Pro/Am arena, including the World Pro/Am Bronze Rhythm Championship at the Ohio Star Ball and United States Bronze Rhythm and 9-Dance Championships at USDC. Today, Jessika is an active competitor on the national stage competing in all four styles of ballroom dance.

As her passion for ballroom grew, Jessika founded Columbus, Ohio-based Next Level Dancing, LLC, a business dedicated to promoting high-quality dancing resources—books, workshops, dresses, and advice—to help competing and social ballroom dancers sharpen their mental games, reach their dancing goals, and embrace their dancing joy.

Committed to helping amateur dancers manage the emotional highs and lows of competition, Jessika uses her expertise as a certified professional business and executive leadership coach to help ballroom dancers take ownership of their dancing journeys and create successful outcomes. To that end, Next Level Dancing offers a variety of coaching programs—from one-on-one coaching to group training programs—that incorporate tips, tools, secrets, and strategies from the worlds of ballroom dancing, sports psychology, personal development, and business management. Jessika arms her coaching clients with the skills necessary to maximize the joy of ballroom dancing—while minimizing the stress of competitions.

Jessika wrote *Competing Like a Pro* as a follow-up to her internationally acclaimed book *The Ballroom Dance Coach: Expert Strategies to Take Your Dancing to the Next Level.* Featuring interviews with dozens of top judges, competition organizers, professional dancers, amateur dancers, costume designers, hair stylists, and make-up artists, Jessika's books give amateur dancers unprecedented access to the world of professional dancing. Ballroom dancers seeking to evolve from hobbyists to champions rely on Jessika's books for hands-on advice, hard-won strategies, and reliable resources.

Jessika holds a master's degree in teaching and instructional design, as well as a bachelor's degree in business management and leadership, from Johnson & Wales University in Providence, Rhode Island. Recognized for her business acumen and coaching expertise, she has been named a "Forty Under Forty" by *Columbus Business First* and a "Top Ten Business Coach" by the *Boston Women's Business Journal.*

A native of Gothenburg, Sweden, Jessika now calls Columbus, Ohio home.
For more information, email info@nextleveldancing.com or visit nextleveldancing.com.

Mastering JavaScript Functional Programming

Second Edition

Write clean, robust, and maintainable web and server code using functional JavaScript

Federico Kereki

BIRMINGHAM - MUMBAI

Mastering JavaScript Functional Programming
Second Edition

Commissioning Editor: Wilson D'souza
Acquisition Editor: Shweta Bairoliya
Content Development Editor: Aamir Ahmed
Senior Editor: Hayden Edwards
Technical Editor: Jane Dsouza
Copy Editor: Safis Editing
Project Coordinator: Manthan Patel
Proofreader: Safis Editing
Indexer: Manju Arasan
Production Designer: Joshua Misquitta

First published: November 2017
Second edition: January 2020

Production reference: 1240120

Published by Packt Publishing Ltd.
Livery Place
35 Livery Street
Birmingham
B3 2PB, UK.

ISBN 978-1-83921-306-9

www.packt.com

Writing a book involves many people, and even if I cannot mention and name all of them, there are some who really deserve to be highlighted.

At Packt Publishing, I want to thank Larissa Pinto, Senior Acquisition Editor, for proposing the theme for this book and helping me get started with it. Thanks must also go to Mohammed Yusuf Imaratwale, Content Development Editor, and Ralph Rosario, Technical Editor, for their help in giving shape to the book and making it clearer and better structured. I also want to send my appreciation to the reviewers, Gerónimo García Sgritta and Steve Perkins, who went through the initial draft, enhancing it with their comments.

There are some other people who deserve extra consideration. This book was written under unusual circumstances, around 10,000 miles away from home! I had gone from Uruguay, where I live, to work on a project in India, and that's where I wrote every single page of the text. This would not have been possible if I hadn't had complete support from my family, who stayed in Montevideo, but who were constantly nearby, thanks to the internet and modern communications. In particular, I must single out my wife, Sylvia Tosar, not only for supporting and aiding me both with the project and the book, but also for dealing with everything, and the rest of the family on her own in Uruguay—this book wouldn't have been possible otherwise, and she is the greatest reason the book could be written!

For the second edition

Revisiting and expanding a book for a second edition is a challenging, interesting task. I had great support from Packt, and I must now thank Aamir Ahmed, Content Development Editor; Jane D'souza, Technical Editor; and Crystian Bietti and (again, for double merit!) Steve Perkins, reviewers—both of whom helped produce a much better text.

– Federico Kereki

Packt.com

Subscribe to our online digital library for full access to over 7,000 books and videos, as well as industry leading tools to help you plan your personal development and advance your career. For more information, please visit our website.

Why subscribe?

- Spend less time learning and more time coding with practical eBooks and Videos from over 4,000 industry professionals

- Improve your learning with Skill Plans built especially for you

- Get a free eBook or video every month

- Fully searchable for easy access to vital information

- Copy and paste, print, and bookmark content

Did you know that Packt offers eBook versions of every book published, with PDF and ePub files available? You can upgrade to the eBook version at www.packt.com and as a print book customer, you are entitled to a discount on the eBook copy. Get in touch with us at customercare@packtpub.com for more details.

At www.packt.com, you can also read a collection of free technical articles, sign up for a range of free newsletters, and receive exclusive discounts and offers on Packt books and eBooks.

Contributors

About the author

Federico Kereki is an Uruguayan systems engineer, with a master's degree in education, and more than 30 years of experience as a consultant, system developer, university professor, and writer.

He is currently a subject matter expert at Globant, where he gets to use a good mixture of development frameworks, programming tools, and operating systems, such as JavaScript, Node.js, React and Redux, SOA, Containers, and PHP, with both Windows and Linux.

He has taught several computer science courses at Universidad de la República, Universidad ORT Uruguay, and Universidad de la Empresa. He has also written texts for these courses.

He has written several articles—on JavaScript, web development, and open source topics—for magazines such as *Linux Journal* and *LinuxPro Magazine* in the United States, *Linux+* and *Mundo Linux* in Europe, and for websites such as Linux.com and IBM Developer Works. He has also written booklets on computer security (*Linux in the Time of Malware* and *SSH: A Modern Lock for Your Server*), a book on GWT programming (*Essential GWT: Building for the Web with Google Web Toolkit*), and another one on JavaScript development (*Modern JavaScript Web Development Cookbook*).

Federico has given talks on functional programming with JavaScript at public conferences (such as JSCONF 2016 and Development Week Santiago 2019) and has used these techniques to develop internet systems for businesses in Uruguay and abroad.

His current interests tend toward software quality and software engineering—with agile methodologies topmost—while on the practical side, he works with diverse languages, tools, and frameworks, and open source software (FLOSS) wherever possible!

He usually resides, works, and teaches in Uruguay, but this book was fully written while on a project in India, and the revisions for the second edition were finished during a sojourn in Mexico.

About the reviewers

Steve Perkins is the author of *Hibernate Search by Example*. He has been working with Java and JavaScript since the late-1990's, with forays into Scala, Groovy, and Go. Steve lives in Atlanta, GA, with his wife and two children, and is currently a software architect at Banyan Hills Technologies, where he works on a platform for IoT device management and analytics.

When he is not writing code or spending time with family, Steve plays guitar and loses games at bridge and backgammon. You can visit his technical blog at steveperkins.com, and follow him on Twitter at @stevedperkins.

Cristian "Pusher" Bietti is an entrepreneur who is proactive and has a creative attitude to facing challenges in new technologies, with a great hunger to learn more! A senior developer with more than 18 years of experience in software development and software design and trained in a wide variety of technologies, he has participated in big banking projects and small applications for mobile and social networks, including video games.

He has focused on frontend and user experience (UI/UX). He is a subject matter expert at Globant, and he works in the Fintech industry as a technical leader and developer because he loves coding.

Packt is searching for authors like you

If you're interested in becoming an author for Packt, please visit authors.packtpub.com and apply today. We have worked with thousands of developers and tech professionals, just like you, to help them share their insight with the global tech community. You can make a general application, apply for a specific hot topic that we are recruiting an author for, or submit your own idea.

Table of Contents

Preface 1

Technical Requirements 7

Chapter 1: Becoming Functional - Several Questions 9
  What is functional programming? 9
    Theory versus practice 10
    A different way of thinking 11
    What FP is not 11
  Why use FP? 12
    What we need 12
    What we get 13
    Not all is gold 14
  Is JavaScript functional? 14
    JavaScript as a tool 15
    Going functional with JavaScript 16
    Key features of JavaScript 17
      Functions as first-class objects 17
      Recursion 18
      Closures 19
      Arrow functions 20
      Spread 21
  How do we work with JavaScript? 23
    Using transpilers 24
    Working online 26
    Testing 27
  Summary 28
  Questions 28

Chapter 2: Thinking Functionally - A First Example 31
  Our problem – doing something only once 31
    Solution 1 – hoping for the best! 32
    Solution 2 – using a global flag 33
    Solution 3 – removing the handler 34
    Solution 4 – changing the handler 35
    Solution 5 – disabling the button 35
    Solution 6 – redefining the handler 36
    Solution 7 – using a local flag 36
  A functional solution to our problem 37
    A higher-order solution 38
    Testing the solution manually 39

Testing the solution automatically   41
Producing an even better solution   43
Summary   44
Questions   45
Chapter 3: Starting Out with Functions - A Core Concept   47
  All about functions   47
Of lambdas and functions   48
Arrow functions – the modern way   51
    Returning values   52
    Handling the this value   52
    Working with arguments   54
    One argument or many?   56
Functions as objects   57
    A React-Redux reducer   58
    An unnecessary mistake   60
    Working with methods   61
  Using functions in FP ways   62
Injection – sorting it out   62
Callbacks, promises, and continuations   65
Continuation passing style   65
Polyfills   67
    Detecting Ajax   67
    Adding missing functions   69
Stubbing   70
Immediate invocation   71
Summary   74
Questions   74
Chapter 4: Behaving Properly - Pure Functions   77
  Pure functions   77
Referential transparency   78
Side effects   80
    Usual side effects   80
    Global state   81
    Inner state   82
    Argument mutation   84
    Troublesome functions   85
Advantages of pure functions   87
    Order of execution   87
    Memoization   88
    Self-documentation   92
    Testing   92
  Impure functions   93
Avoiding impure functions   93
    Avoiding the usage of state   93
    Injecting impure functions   95
Is your function pure?   97

Testing – pure versus impure   98
Testing pure functions   99
Testing purified functions   100
Testing impure functions   103
Summary   106
Questions   106

Chapter 5: Programming Declaratively - A Better Style   109
Transformations   110
Reducing an array to a value   110
Summing an array   112
Calculating an average   113
Calculating several values at once   115
Folding left and right   116
Applying an operation – map   118
Extracting data from objects   120
Parsing numbers tacitly   121
Working with ranges   122
Emulating map() with reduce()   124
Dealing with arrays of arrays   125
Flattening an array   125
Mapping and flattening – flatMap()   128
Emulating flat() and flatMap()   130
More general looping   132
Logical higher-order functions   134
Filtering an array   135
A reduce() example   136
Emulating filter() with reduce()   137
Searching an array   138
A special search case   139
Emulating find() and findIndex() with reduce()   139
Higher-level predicates – some, every   140
Checking negatives – none   141
Working with async functions   142
Some strange behaviors   143
Async-ready looping   145
Looping over async calls   145
Mapping async calls   146
Filtering with async calls   147
Reducing async calls   148
Summary   149
Questions   149

Chapter 6: Producing Functions - Higher-Order Functions   153
Wrapping functions – keeping behavior   154
Logging   155
Logging in a functional way   155
Taking exceptions into account   157

Working in a purer way	158
Timing functions	161
Memoizing functions	163
Simple memoization	164
More complex memoization	166
Memoization testing	168
Altering a function's behavior	**171**
Doing things once, revisited	171
Logically negating a function	174
Inverting the results	175
Arity changing	177
Changing functions in other ways	**178**
Turning operations into functions	178
Implementing operations	179
A handier implementation	180
Turning functions into promises	181
Getting a property from an object	182
Demethodizing – turning methods into functions	184
Finding the optimum	186
Summary	**188**
Questions	**188**
Chapter 7: Transforming Functions - Currying and Partial Application	191
A bit of theory	**192**
Currying	**193**
Dealing with many parameters	193
Currying by hand	196
Currying with bind()	198
Currying with eval()	201
Partial application	**203**
Partial application with arrow functions	204
Partial application with eval()	205
Partial application with closures	209
Partial currying	**212**
Partial currying with bind()	213
Partial currying with closures	216
Final thoughts	**217**
Parameter order	217
Being functional	219
Summary	**220**
Questions	**221**
Chapter 8: Connecting Functions - Pipelining and Composition	223
Pipelining	**224**
Piping in Unix/Linux	224
Revisiting an example	226

Creating pipelines 227
  Building pipelines by hand 227
  Using other constructs 229
Debugging pipelines 231
  Using tee 231
  Tapping into a flow 233
  Using a logging wrapper 234
Pointfree style 235
  Defining pointfree functions 235
  Converting to pointfree style 236
Chaining and fluent interfaces 238
An example of fluent APIs 238
Chaining method calls 239
Composing 242
Some examples of composition 242
  Unary operators 243
  Counting files 244
  Finding unique words 244
Composing with higher-order functions 246
Testing composed functions 250
Transducing 255
Composing reducers 258
Generalizing for all reducers 259
Summary 260
Questions 261

Chapter 9: Designing Functions - Recursion 263
Using recursion 264
Thinking recursively 265
  Decrease and conquer – searching 266
  Decrease and conquer – doing powers 267
  Divide and conquer – the Towers of Hanoi 268
  Divide and conquer – sorting 271
  Dynamic programming – making change 272
Higher-order functions revisited 274
  Mapping and filtering 275
  Other higher-order functions 278
Searching and backtracking 281
  The eight queens puzzle 281
  Traversing a tree structure 285
Recursion techniques 288
Tail call optimization 289
Continuation passing style 292
Trampolines and thunks 296
Recursion elimination 299
Summary 299
Questions 300

Chapter 10: Ensuring Purity - Immutability   303
Going the straightforward JavaScript way   304
    Mutator functions   304
    Constants   305
    Freezing   306
    Cloning and mutating   308
    Getters and setters   312
       Getting a property   312
       Setting a property by path   313
    Lenses   315
       Working with lenses   315
       Implementing lenses with objects   318
       Implementing lenses with functions   321
    Prisms   324
       Working with prisms   324
       Implementing prisms   327
Creating persistent data structures   327
    Working with lists   328
    Updating objects   330
    A final caveat   335
Summary   335
Questions   336

Chapter 11: Implementing Design Patterns - The Functional Way   339
Understanding design patterns   340
    Design pattern categories   341
    Do we need design patterns?   342
Object-oriented design patterns   343
    Facade and adapter   344
    Decorator or wrapper   346
    Strategy, Template, and Command   352
    Observer and reactive programming   354
       Basic concepts and terms   355
       Operators for observables   357
       Detecting multi-clicks   360
       Providing typeahead searches   362
    Other patterns   366
Functional design patterns   367
Summary   369
Questions   369

Chapter 12: Building Better Containers - Functional Data Types   373
Specifying data types   373
    Signatures for functions   374
    Other data type options   376
Building containers   378

Extending current data types   379
Containers and functors   381
    Wrapping a value – a basic container   381
    Enhancing our container – functors   383
    Dealing with missing values with Maybe   385
        Dealing with varying API results   387
        Implementing Prisms   391
Monads   393
    Adding operations   394
    Handling alternatives – the Either monad   397
    Calling a function – the Try monad   400
    Unexpected monads – promises   401
Functions as data structures   402
    Binary trees in Haskell   402
    Functions as binary trees   404
Summary   410
Questions   410

Bibliography   413

Answers to Questions   415

Other Books You May Enjoy   443

Index   447

Preface

In computer programming, paradigms abound. Some examples include imperative programming, structured (*goto-less*) programming, **object-oriented programming** (OOP), aspect-oriented programming, and declarative programming. Lately, there has been renewed interest in a particular paradigm that can arguably be considered to be older than most (if not all) of the cited ones—**Functional Programming** (FP). FP emphasizes writing functions and connecting them in simple ways to produce a more understandable and more easily tested code. Thus, given the increased complexity of today's web applications, it's logical that a safer, cleaner way of programming would be of interest.

This interest in FP comes hand in hand with the evolution of JavaScript. Despite its somewhat hasty creation (reportedly managed in only 10 days, in 1995, by Brendan Eich at Netscape), today it's a standardized and quickly growing language, with features more advanced than most other similarly popular languages. The ubiquity of the language, which can now be found in browsers, servers, mobile phones, and whatnot, has also impelled interest in better development strategies. Also, even if JavaScript wasn't conceived as a functional language by itself, the fact is that it provides all the features you'd require to work in that fashion, which is another plus.

It must also be said that FP hasn't been generally applied in industry, possibly because it has a certain aura of difficulty, and it is thought to be *theoretical* rather than *practical*, even *mathematical*, and possibly uses vocabulary and concepts that are foreign to developers—for example, functors? Monads? Folding? Category theory? While learning all this theory will certainly be of help, it can also be argued that even with zero knowledge of the previous terms, you can understand the tenets of FP, and see how to apply it in your own programming.

FP is not something that you have to do on your own, without any help. There are many libraries and frameworks that incorporate, in greater or lesser degrees, the concepts of FP. Starting with jQuery (which does include some FP concepts), passing through Underscore and its close relative, Lodash, or other libraries such as Ramda, and getting to more complete web development tools such as React and Redux, Angular, or Elm (a 100% functional language, which compiles into JavaScript), the list of functional aids for your coding is ever growing.

Learning how to use FP can be a worthwhile investment, and even though you may not get to use all of its methods and techniques, just starting to apply some of them will pay dividends in better code. You need not try to apply all of FP from the start, and you need not try to abandon every non-functional feature in the language either. JavaScript assuredly has some bad features, but it also has several very good and powerful ones. The idea is not to throw away everything you've learned and use and adopt a 100% functional way; rather, the guiding idea is *evolution, not revolution*. In that sense, it can be said that what we'll be doing is not FP, but rather **Sorta Functional Programming** (SFP), aiming for a fusion of paradigms.

A final comment about the style of the code in this book—it is quite true that there are several very good libraries that provide you with FP tools: Underscore, Lodash, Ramda, and more are counted among them. However, I preferred to eschew their usage, because I wanted to show how things really work. It's easy to apply a given function from some package or other, but by coding everything out (a *vanilla FP*, if you wish), it's my belief that you get to understand things more deeply. Also, as I will comment in some places, because of the power and clarity of arrow functions and other features, the *pure JavaScript* versions can be even simpler to understand!

Who this book is for

This book is geared toward programmers with a good working knowledge of JavaScript, working either on the client side (browsers) or the server side (Node.js), who are interested in applying techniques to be able to write better, testable, understandable, and maintainable code. Some background in computer science (including, for example, data structures) and good programming practices will also come in handy.

What this book covers

In this book, we'll cover FP in a practical way; though, at times, we will mention some theoretical points:

Chapter 1, *Becoming Functional – Several Questions*, discusses FP, gives reasons for its usage, and lists the tools that you'll need to take advantage of the rest of the book.

Chapter 2, *Thinking Functionally – A First Example*, will provide the first example of FP by considering a common web-related problem and going over several solutions, to finally center on a functional solution.

Chapter 3, *Starting Out with Functions – A Core Concept*, will go over the central concept of FP, that is, functions, and the different options available in JavaScript.

Chapter 4, *Behaving Properly – Pure Functions*, will consider the concept of purity and pure functions, and demonstrate how it leads to simpler coding and easier testing.

Chapter 5, *Programming Declaratively – A Better Style*, will use simple data structures to show how to produce results that work not in an imperative way, but in a declarative fashion.

Chapter 6, *Producing Functions – Higher-Order Functions*, will deal with higher-order functions, which receive other functions as parameters and produce new functions as results.

Chapter 7, *Transforming Functions – Currying and Partial Application*, will explore some methods for producing new and specialized functions from earlier ones.

Chapter 8, *Connecting Functions – Pipelining and Composition*, will show the key concepts regarding how to build new functions by joining previously defined ones.

Chapter 9, *Designing Functions – Recursion*, will look at how a key concept in FP, recursion, can be applied to designing algorithms and functions.

Chapter 10, *Ensuring Purity – Immutability*, will present some tools that can help you to work in a pure fashion by providing immutable objects and data structures.

Chapter 11, *Implementing Design Patterns – The Functional Way*, will show how several popular OOP design patterns are implemented (or not needed!) when you program in FP ways.

Chapter 12, *Building Better Containers – Functional Data Types*, will explore some more high-level functional patterns, introducing types, containers, functors, monads, and several other more advanced FP concepts.

I have tried to keep the examples in this book simple and down to earth because I want to focus on the functional aspects and not on the intricacies of this or that problem. Some programming texts are geared toward learning, say, a given framework, and then work on a given problem, showing how to fully work it out with the chosen tools. (In fact, at the very beginning of planning for this book, I entertained the idea of developing an application that would use all the FP things I had in mind, but there was no way to fit all of that within a single project. Exaggerating a bit, I felt like an MD trying to find a patient on whom to apply all of his medical knowledge and treatments!) So, I have opted to show plenty of individual techniques, which can be used in multiple situations. Rather than building a house, I want to show you how to put the bricks together, how to wire things up, and so on, so that you will be able to apply whatever you need, as you see fit.

To get the most out of this book

To understand the concepts and code in this book, you don't need much more than a JavaScript environment and a text editor. To be honest, I even developed some of the examples working fully online, with tools such as JSFiddle (at `https://jsfiddle.net/`) and the like, and absolutely nothing else.

In this book, we'll be using ES2019, Node 13, and the code will run on any OS such as Linux, Mac OSX, or Windows; please do check the *Technical Requirements* section, for some other tools we'll also work with.

Finally, you will need some experience with the latest version of JavaScript, because it includes several features that can help you write more concise and compact code. We will frequently include pointers to online documentation, such as the documentation available on the **Mozilla Development Network (MDM)** at `https://developer.mozilla.org/`, to help you get more in-depth knowledge.

Download the example code files

You can download the example code files for this book from your account at `www.packt.com`. If you purchased this book elsewhere, you can visit `www.packtpub.com/support` and register to have the files emailed directly to you.

You can download the code files by following these steps:

1. Log in or register at `www.packt.com`.
2. Select the **Support** tab.
3. Click on **Code Downloads**.
4. Enter the name of the book in the **Search** box and follow the onscreen instructions.

Once the file is downloaded, please make sure that you unzip or extract the folder using the latest version of:

- WinRAR/7-Zip for Windows
- Zipeg/iZip/UnRarX for Mac
- 7-Zip/PeaZip for Linux

The code bundle for the book is also hosted on GitHub at `https://github.com/PacktPublishing/Mastering-JavaScript-Functional-Programming-2nd-Edition-`. In case there's an update to the code, it will be updated on the existing GitHub repository.

We also have other code bundles from our rich catalog of books and videos available at https://github.com/PacktPublishing/. Check them out!

Conventions used

There are a number of text conventions used throughout this book.

`CodeInText`: Indicates code words in text, database table names, folder names, filenames, file extensions, pathnames, dummy URLs, user input, and Twitter handles. Here is an example: "Let's review our `once()` function."

A block of code is set as follows:

```
function newCounter() {
  let count = 0;
  return function() {
    count++;
    return count;
  };
}

const nc = newCounter();
console.log(nc()); // 1
console.log(nc()); // 2
console.log(nc()); // 3
```

When we wish to draw your attention to a particular part of a code block, the relevant lines or items are set in bold:

```
function fact(n) {
  if (n === 0) {
    return 1;

  } else {
    return n * fact(n - 1);
  }
}

console.log(fact(5)); // 120
```

Bold: Indicates a new term, an important word, or words that you see on screen. For example, words in menus or dialog boxes appear in the text like this. Here is an example: "Select the **EXPERIMENTAL** option to fully enable ES10 support."

Warnings or important notes appear like this.

 Tips and tricks appear like this.

Get in touch

Feedback from our readers is always welcome.

General feedback: If you have questions about any aspect of this book, mention the book title in the subject of your message and email us at customercare@packtpub.com.

Errata: Although we have taken every care to ensure the accuracy of our content, mistakes do happen. If you have found a mistake in this book, we would be grateful if you would report this to us. Please visit www.packtpub.com/support/errata, selecting your book, clicking on the Errata Submission Form link, and entering the details.

Piracy: If you come across any illegal copies of our works in any form on the internet, we would be grateful if you would provide us with the location address or website name. Please contact us at copyright@packt.com with a link to the material.

If you are interested in becoming an author: If there is a topic that you have expertise in and you are interested in either writing or contributing to a book, please visit authors.packtpub.com.

Reviews

Please leave a review. Once you have read and used this book, why not leave a review on the site that you purchased it from? Potential readers can then see and use your unbiased opinion to make purchase decisions, we at Packt can understand what you think about our products, and our authors can see your feedback on their book. Thank you!

For more information about Packt, please visit packt.com.

Technical Requirements

To develop and test the code in this book, I used several versions of commonly available software, including browsers and Node.js, as well as some other packages.

For this second edition, my main machine runs the *Tumbleweed* rolling release of OpenSUSE Linux, from `https://www.opensuse.org/#Tumbleweed`, currently including kernel 5.3.5. (The *rolling* term implies that the software is updated on a continuous basis, to keep getting the latest versions of all packages.) I've also tested portions of the code of this book on different Windows 7 and Windows 10 machines.

As to browsers, I usually work with Chrome, from `https://www.google.com/chrome/browser/`, and at the current time, I'm up to version 78. I also use Firefox, from `https://www.mozilla.org/en-US/firefox/`, and I got version 72 in my machine. I have also run code using the online JSFiddle environment, at `https://jsfiddle.net/`.

On the server side, I use Node.js, from `https://nodejs.org/`, currently at version 13.6.

For transpilation, I used Babel, from `https://babeljs.io/`: the current version of the `babel-cli` package is 7.7.7.

For testing, I went with Jasmine, from `https://jasmine.github.io/`, and the latest version in my machine is 3.5.0.

Finally, for code formatting, I used Prettier, from `https://prettier.io/`. You can either install it locally, or run it online at `https://prettier.io/playground/`; the version I have is 1.19.1.

The JavaScript world is quite dynamic, and it's a safe bet that by the time you get to read this book, all the software listed above will have been updated several times. Every single piece of software I used when I wrote the 1st edition of this book, received several updates over time. However, given the standardization of JavaScript, and the high importance of back compatibility, you shouldn't have problems with other versions.

Becoming Functional - Several Questions **1**

Functional programming (or **FP**) has been around since the earliest days of computing, and is going through a sort of revival because of its increased use with several frameworks and libraries, most particularly in **JavaScript** (**JS**). In this chapter, we shall do the following:

- Introduce some concepts of FP to give a small taste of what it means.
- Show the benefits (and problems) implied by the usage of FP and why we should use it.
- Start thinking about why JavaScript can be considered an appropriate language for FP.
- Go over the language features and tools that you should be aware of in order to fully take advantage of everything in this book.

By the end of this chapter, you'll have the basic tools that we'll be using in the rest of the book, so let's get started by learning about functional programming.

What is functional programming?

If you go back in computer history, you'll find that the second oldest programming language still in use, Lisp, is based on FP. Since then, there have been many more functional languages, and FP has been applied more widely. But even so, if you ask people what FP is, you'll probably get two widely dissimilar answers.

For trivia or history buffs, the oldest language still in use is Fortran, which appeared in 1957, a year before Lisp. Quite shortly after Lisp came another long-lived language, COBOL, for business-oriented programming.

Depending on whom you ask, you'll either learn that it's a modern, advanced, enlightened approach to programming that leaves every other paradigm behind or that it's mainly a theoretical thing, with more complications than benefits, practically impossible to implement in the real world. And, as usual, the real answer is not in the extremes, but somewhere in between. Let's start by looking at the theory versus practice and see how we plan to use FP.

Theory versus practice

In this book, we won't be going about FP in a theoretical way. Instead, our point is to show you how some of its techniques and tenets can be successfully applied for common, everyday JavaScript programming. But—and this is important—we won't be going about this in a dogmatic fashion, but in a very practical way. We won't dismiss useful JavaScript constructs simply because they don't happen to fulfill the academic expectations of FP. Similarly, we won't avoid practical JavaScript features just to fit the FP paradigm. In fact, we could almost say that we'll be doing **Sorta Functional Programming (SFP)** because our code will be a mixture of FP features, more classical imperative ones, and **object-oriented programming (OOP)**.

Be careful, though: what we just said doesn't mean that we'll be leaving all the theory by the side. We'll be picky, and just touch the main theoretical points, learn some vocabulary and definitions, and explain core FP concepts, but we'll always be keeping in sight the idea of producing actual, useful JavaScript code, rather than trying to meet some mystical, dogmatic FP criteria.

OOP has been a way to solve the inherent complexity of writing large programs and systems, and developing clean, extensible, scalable application architectures; however, because of the scale of today's web applications, the complexity of all codebases is continuously growing. Also, the newer features of JavaScript make it possible to develop applications that wouldn't even have been possible just a few years ago; think of mobile (hybrid) apps that are made with Ionic, Apache Cordova, or React Native or desktop apps that are made with Electron or NW.js, for example. JavaScript has also migrated to the backend with Node.js, so today, the scope of usage for the language has grown in a serious way that deals with all the added complexity of modern designs.

A different way of thinking

FP is a different way of writing programs, and can sometimes be difficult to learn. In most languages, programming is done in an imperative fashion: a program is a sequence of statements, executed in a prescribed fashion, and the desired result is achieved by creating objects and manipulating them, which usually means modifying the objects themselves. FP is based on producing the desired result by evaluating expressions built out of functions that are composed together. In FP, it's common to pass functions around (such as passing parameters to other functions or returning functions as the result of a calculation), to not use loops (opting for recursion instead), and to skip side effects (such as modifying objects or global variables).

In other words, FP focuses on *what* should be done, rather than on *how*. Instead of worrying about loops or arrays, you work at a higher level, considering what you need to be done. After becoming accustomed to this style, you'll find that your code becomes simpler, shorter, and more elegant, and can be easily tested and debugged. However, don't fall into the trap of considering FP as the goal! Think of FP only as a means to an end, as with all software tools. Functional code isn't good just for being functional, and writing bad code is just as possible with FP as with any other technique!

What FP is not

Since we have been saying some things about what FP is, let's also clear up some common misconceptions, and look at what FP is *not*:

- **FP isn't just an academic ivory tower thing**: It is true that the **lambda calculus** upon which it is based was developed by Alonzo Church in 1936 as a tool to prove an important result in theoretical computer science (which preceded modern computer languages by more than 20 years!); however, FP languages are being used today for all kinds of systems.
- **FP isn't the opposite of object-oriented programming (OOP)**: It isn't a case of choosing declarative or imperative ways of programming. You can mix and match as best suits you, and we'll be doing this throughout this book, bringing together the best of all worlds.
- **FP isn't overly complex to learn**: Some of the FP languages are rather different from JavaScript, but the differences are mostly syntactic. Once you learn the basic concepts, you'll see that you can get the same results in JavaScript as with FP languages.

It may also be relevant to mention that several modern frameworks, such as the React and Redux combination, include FP ideas.

For example, in React, it's said that the **view** (whatever the user gets to see at a given moment) is a function of the current **state**. You use a function to compute what HTML and CSS must be produced at each moment, thinking in a **black-box** fashion.

Similarly, in Redux you have the concept of **actions** that are processed by **reducers**. An action provides some data, and a reducer is a function that produces the new state for the application in a functional way out of the current state and the provided data.

So, both because of the theoretical advantages (we'll be getting to those in the following section) and the practical ones (such as getting to use the latest frameworks and libraries), it makes sense to consider FP coding. Let's get on with it.

Why use FP?

Throughout the years, there have been many programming styles and fads. However, FP has proven quite resilient and is of great interest today. Why would you want to use FP? The question should rather first be, *what do you want to get?* and only then, *does FP get you that?* Let's answer these important questions in the following sections.

What we need

We can certainly agree that the following list of concerns is universal. Our code should have the following qualities:

- **Modular**: The functionality of your program should be divided into independent modules, each of which contains what it needs to perform one aspect of the program's functionality. Changes in a module or function shouldn't affect the rest of the code.
- **Understandable**: A reader of your program should be able to discern its components, their functions, and their relationships without undue effort. This is closely linked with the **maintainability** of the code; your code will have to be maintained at some time in the future, whether to be changed or to have new functionality added.
- **Testable**: **Unit tests** try out small parts of your program, verifying their behavior independently of the rest of the code. Your programming style should favor writing code that simplifies the job of writing unit tests. Unit tests are also like documentation in that they can help readers understand what the code is supposed to do.

- **Extensible**: It's a fact that your program will someday require maintenance, possibly to add new functionality. Those changes should impact the structure and data flow of the original code only minimally (if at all). Small changes shouldn't imply large, serious refactoring of your code.
- **Reusable**: **Code reuse** has the goal of saving resources, time, and money, and reducing redundancy by taking advantage of previously written code. There are some characteristics that help this goal, such as **modularity** (which we already mentioned), **high cohesion** (all the pieces in a module belong together), **low coupling** (modules are independent of each other), **separation of concerns** (the parts of a program should overlap in functionality as little as possible), and **information hiding** (internal changes in a module shouldn't affect the rest of the system).

What we get

So does FP give you the five characteristics we just listed in the previous section?

- In FP, the goal is to write separate independent functions that are joined together to produce the final results.
- Programs that are written in a functional style usually tend to be cleaner, shorter, and easier to understand.
- Functions can be tested on their own, and FP code has advantages in achieving this.
- You can reuse functions in other programs because they stand on their own, not depending on the rest of the system. Most functional programs share common functions, several of which we'll be considering in this book.
- Functional code is free from side effects, which means you can understand the objective of a function by studying it without having to consider the rest of the program.

Finally, once you get used to the FP style of programming, code becomes more understandable and easier to extend. So it seems that all five characteristics can be achieved with FP!

 For a well-balanced look at the reasons to use FP, I'd suggest reading *Why Functional Programming Matters*, by John Hughes; it's available online at `www.cs.kent.ac.uk/people/staff/dat/miranda/whyfp90.pdf`. It's not geared towards JavaScript, but the arguments are easily understandable, anyway.

Not all is gold

However, let's strive for a bit of balance. Using FP isn't a silver bullet that will automagically make your code better. Some FP solutions are actually tricky, and there are developers who greatly enjoy writing code and then asking, *what does this do?* If you aren't careful, your code may become *write-only* and practically impossible to maintain; there goes understandable, extensible, and reusable out the door!

Another disadvantage is that you may find it harder to find FP-savvy developers. (Quick question: how many *functional programmers sought* job ads have you ever seen?) The vast majority of today's web code is written in imperative, non-functional ways, and most coders are used to that way of working. For some, having to switch gears and start writing programs in a different way may prove an unpassable barrier.

Finally, if you try to go fully functional, you may find yourself at odds with JavaScript, and simple tasks may become hard to do. As we said at the beginning, we'll opt for *sorta FP*, so we won't be drastically rejecting any language features that aren't 100% functional. After all, we want to use FP to simplify our coding, not to make it more complex!

So, while I'll strive to show you the advantages of going functional in your code, as with any change, there will always be some difficulties. However, I'm fully convinced that you'll be able to surmount them and that your organization will develop better code by applying FP. Dare to change! So, given that you accept that FP may apply to your own problems, let's now consider the other question, can we use JavaScript in a functional way and is it appropriate?

Is JavaScript functional?

At about this time, there is another important question that you should be asking: *Is JavaScript a functional language?* Usually, when thinking about FP, the list of languages that are mentioned does not include JavaScript, but does include less common options, such as Clojure, Erlang, Haskell, and Scala; however, there is no precise definition for FP languages or a precise set of features that such languages should include. The main point is that you can consider a language to be functional if it supports the common programming style associated with FP. Let's start by learning about why we would want to use JavaScript at all and how the language has evolved to its current version, and then see some of the key features that we'll be using to work in a functional way.

JavaScript as a tool

What is JavaScript? If you consider **popularity indices**, such as the ones at `www.tiobe.com/tiobe-index/` or `http://pypl.github.io/PYPL.html`, you'll find that JavaScript is consistently in the top ten most popular languages. From a more academic point of view, the language is sort of a mixture, borrowing features from several different languages. Several libraries helped the growth of the language by providing features that weren't so easily available, such as classes and inheritance (today's version of the language does support classes, but that was not the case not too long ago), that otherwise had to be achieved by doing some **prototype** tricks.

 The name *JavaScript* was chosen to take advantage of the popularity of Java—just as a marketing ploy! Its first name was *Mocha*, then, *LiveScript*, and only then, *JavaScript*.

JavaScript has grown to be incredibly powerful. But, as with all power tools, it gives you a way to not only produce great solutions, but also to do great harm. FP could be considered as a way to reduce or leave aside some of the worst parts of the language and focus on working in a safer, better way; however, due to the immense amount of existing JavaScript code, you cannot expect it to facilitate large reworkings of the language that would cause most sites to fail. You must learn to live with the good and the bad, and simply avoid the latter parts.

In addition, the language has a broad variety of available libraries that complete or extend the language in many ways. In this book, we'll be focusing on using JavaScript on its own, but we will make references to existing, available code.

If we ask whether JavaScript is actually functional, the answer will be, once again, *sorta*. It can be seen as functional because of several features, such as first-class functions, anonymous functions, recursion, and closures—we'll get back to this later. On the other hand, it also has plenty of *non-FP* aspects, such as side effects (**impurity**), mutable objects, and practical limits to recursion. So, when programming in a functional way, we'll be taking advantage of all the relevant, appropriate language features, and we'll try to minimize the problems caused by the more conventional parts of the language. In this sense, JavaScript will or won't be functional, depending on *your* programming style!

If you want to use FP, you should decide which language to use; however, opting for fully functional languages may not be so wise. Today, developing code isn't as simple as just using a language; you will surely require frameworks, libraries, and other sundry tools. If we can take advantage of all the provided tools but at the same time introduce FP ways of working in our code, we'll be getting the best of both worlds, never mind whether JavaScript is functional!

Going functional with JavaScript

JavaScript has evolved through the years, and the version we'll be using is (informally) called JS10, and (formally) ECMAScript 2019, usually shortened to ES2019 or ES10; this version was finalized in June 2019. The previous versions were as follows:

- ECMAScript 1, June 1997
- ECMAScript 2, June 1998, which was basically the same as the previous version
- ECMAScript 3, December 1999, with several new functionalities
- ECMAScript 5, December 2009 (and no, there never was an ECMAScript 4, because it was abandoned)
- ECMAScript 5.1, June 2011
- ECMAScript 6 (or ES6; later renamed ES2015), June 2015
- ECMAScript 7 (also ES7, or ES2016), June 2016
- ECMAScript 8 (ES8 or ES2017), June 2017
- ECMAScript 9 (ES9 or ES2018), June 2018

 ECMA originally stood for **European Computer Manufacturers Association**, but nowadays the name isn't considered an acronym anymore. The organization is responsible for more standards other than JavaScript, including JSON, C#, Dart, and others. For more details, go to its site at www.ecma-international.org/.

You can read the standard language specification at www.ecma-international.org/ecma-262/7.0/. Whenever we refer to JavaScript in the text without further specification, ES10 (ES2019) is what is being referred to; however, in terms of the language features that are used in the book, if you were just to use ES2015, then you'd mostly have no problems with this book.

No browsers fully implement ES10; most provide an older version, JavaScript 5 (from 2009), with an (always growing) smattering of features from ES6 up to ES10. This will prove to be a problem, but fortunately, a solvable one; we'll get to this shortly. We'll be using ES10 throughout the book.

In fact, there are only a few differences between ES2016 and ES2015, such as the `Array.prototype.includes` method and the exponentiation operator, `**`. There are more differences between ES2017 and ES2016—such as `async` and `await`, some string padding functions, and more—but they won't impact our code. We will also be looking at alternatives for even more modern additions, such as `flatMap()`, in later chapters.

As we are going to work with JavaScript, let's start by considering its most important features that pertain to our FP goals.

Key features of JavaScript

JavaScript isn't a purely functional language, but it has all the features that we need for it to work as if it were. The main features of the language that we will be using are as follows:

- Functions as first-class objects
- Recursion
- Arrow functions
- Closures
- Spread

Let's see some examples of each one and find out why they will be useful to us. Keep in mind, though, that there are more features of JavaScript that we will be using; the upcoming sections just highlight the most important features in terms of what we will be using for FP.

Functions as first-class objects

Saying that functions are **first-class objects** (also called **first-class citizens**) means that you can do everything with functions that you can do with other objects. For example, you can store a function in a variable, you can pass it to a function, you can print it out, and so on. This is really the key to doing FP; we will often be passing functions as parameters (to other functions) or returning a function as the result of a function call.

If you have been doing async Ajax calls, then you have already been using this feature: a **callback** is a function that will be called after the Ajax call finishes and is passed as a parameter. Using jQuery, you could write something like the following:

```
$.get("some/url", someData, function(result, status) {
    // check status, and do something
    // with the result
});
```

The `$.get()` function receives a callback function as a parameter and calls it after the result is obtained.

This is better solved, in a more modern way, by using promises or `async/await`, but for the sake of our example, the older way is enough. We'll be getting back to promises, though, in the section called *Building better containers* in Chapter 12, *Building Better Containers – Functional Data Types*, when we discuss monads; in particular, see the section called *Unexpected Monads - Promises*.

Since functions can be stored in variables, you could also write something like the following. Pay attention to how we use the doSomething variable in the $.get(...) call:

```
var doSomething = function(result, status) {
    // check status, and do something
    // with the result
};

$.get("some/url", someData, doSomething);
```

We'll be seeing more examples of this in Chapter 6, *Producing Functions – Higher-Order Functions*.

Recursion

Recursion is the most potent tool for developing algorithms and a great aid for solving large classes of problems. The idea is that a function can at a certain point call itself, and when *that* call is done, continue working with whatever result it has received. This is usually quite helpful for certain classes of problems or definitions. The most often quoted example is the factorial function (the factorial of *n* is written as *n!*) as defined for nonnegative integer values:

- If *n* is 0, then *n!=1*
- If *n* is greater than 0, then $n! = n * (n-1)!$

The value of *n!* is the number of ways that you can order *n* different elements in a row. For example, if you want to place five books in line, you can pick any of the five for the first place, and then order the other four in every possible way, so *5! = 5*4!*. If you continue to work this example, you'll get *5! = 5*4*3*2*1=120*, so *n!* is the product of all numbers up to *n*.

This can be immediately turned into code:

```
function fact(n) {
 if (n === 0) {
 return 1;

 } else {
 return n * fact(n - 1);
 }
}

console.log(fact(5)); // 120
```

Recursion will be a great aid for the design of algorithms. By using recursion, you could do without any `while` or `for` loops—not that we *want* to do that, but it's interesting that we *can*! We'll be devoting the entirety of `Chapter 9`, *Designing Functions – Recursion*, to designing algorithms and writing functions recursively.

Closures

Closures are a way to implement data hiding (with private variables), which leads to modules and other nice features. The key concept of closures is that when you define a function, it can refer to not only its own local variables but also to everything outside of the context of the function. We can write a counting function that will keep its own count by means of a closure:

```
function newCounter() {
 let count = 0;
 return function() {
 count++;
 return count;
 };
}

const nc = newCounter();
console.log(nc()); // 1
console.log(nc()); // 2
console.log(nc()); // 3
```

Even after `newCounter()` exits, the inner function still has access to `count`, but that variable is not accessible to any other parts of your code.

 This isn't a very good example of FP— a function (`nc()`, in this case) isn't expected to return different results when called with the same parameters!

We'll find several uses for closures, such as **memoization** (see Chapter 4, *Behaving Properly – Pure Functions*, and Chapter 6, *Producing Functions – Higher-Order Functions*) and the **module** pattern (see Chapter 3, *Starting out with Functions – A Core Concept*, and Chapter 11, *Implementing Design Patterns – The Functional Way*), among others.

Arrow functions

Arrow functions are just a shorter, more succinct way of creating an (unnamed) function. Arrow functions can be used almost everywhere a classical function can be used, except that they cannot be used as constructors. The syntax is either `(parameter, anotherparameter, ...etc) => { statements }` or `(parameter, anotherparameter, ...etc) => expression`. The first allows you to write as much code as you want, and the second is short for `{ return expression }`. We could rewrite our earlier Ajax example as follows:

```
$.get("some/url", data, (result, status) => {
  // check status, and do something
  // with the result
});
```

A new version of the factorial code could be like the following code:

```
const fact2 = n => {
  if (n === 0) {
    return 1;

  } else {
    return n * fact2(n - 1);
  }
};
console.log(fact2(5)); // also 120
```

Arrow functions are usually called **anonymous** functions because of their lack of a name. If you need to refer to an arrow function, you'll have to assign it to a variable or object attribute, as we did here; otherwise, you won't be able to use it. We'll learn more about this in the section called *Arrow functions* in `Chapter 3`, *Starting out with Functions - A Core Concept*.

You would probably write the latter as a one-liner—can you see the equivalence to our earlier code? Using a ternary operator in lieu of an `if` is quite common:

```
const fact3 = n => (n === 0 ? 1 : n * fact3(n - 1));

console.log(fact3(5)); // again 120
```

With this shorter form, you don't have to write `return`—it's implied.

In lambda calculus, a function such as `x => 2*x` would be represented as $\lambda x.2^*x$. Although there are syntactical differences, the definitions are analogous. Functions with more parameters are a bit more complicated; *(x,y)=>x+y* would be expressed as $\lambda x.\lambda y.x+y$. We'll learn more about this in the section called *Lambdas and functions*, in `Chapter 3`, *Starting out with Functions - A Core Concept*, and in the section called *Currying*, in `Chapter 7`, *Transforming Functions - Currying and Partial Application*.

There's one other small thing to bear in mind: when the arrow function has a single parameter, you can omit the parentheses around it. I usually prefer leaving them, but I've applied a JS beautifier, *Prettier*, to the code, which removes them. It's really up to you whether to include them or not! (For more on this tool, check out `https://github.com/prettier/prettier`.) By the way, my options for formatting were `--print-width 75 --tab-width 2 --no-bracket-spacing`.

Spread

The spread operator (see `https://developer.mozilla.org/en/docs/Web/JavaScript/Reference/Operators/Spread_operator`) lets you expand an expression in places where you would otherwise require multiple arguments, elements, or variables. For example, you can replace arguments in a function call, as shown in the following code:

```
const x = [1, 2, 3];

function sum3(a, b, c) {
  return a + b + c;
```

```
    }

    const y = sum3(...x); // equivalent to sum3(1,2,3)
    console.log(y); // 6
```

You can also create or join arrays, as shown in the following code:

```
    const f = [1, 2, 3];

    const g = [4, ...f, 5]; // [4,1,2,3,5]

    const h = [...f, ...g]; // [1,2,3,4,1,2,3,5]
```

It works with objects too:

```
    const p = { some: 3, data: 5 };

    const q = { more: 8, ...p }; // { more:8, some:3, data:5 }
```

You can also use it to work with functions that expect separate parameters instead of an array. Common examples of this would be `Math.min()` and `Math.max()`:

```
    const numbers = [2, 2, 9, 6, 0, 1, 2, 4, 5, 6];
    const minA = Math.min(...numbers); // 0

    const maxArray = arr => Math.max(...arr);
    const maxA = maxArray(numbers); // 9
```

You can also write the following equality since the `.apply()` method requires an array of arguments, but `.call()` expects individual arguments:

```
    someFn.apply(thisArg, someArray) === someFn.call(thisArg, ...someArray);
```

If you have problems remembering what arguments are required by `.apply()` and `.call()`, this mnemonic may help: *A is for an array, and C is for a comma.* See `https://developer.mozilla.org/en-US/docs/Web/ JavaScript/Reference/Global_Objects/Function/apply` and `https:// developer.mozilla.org/en-US/docs/Web/JavaScript/Reference/ Global_Objects/Function/call` for more information.

Using the spread operator helps write a shorter, more concise code, and we will be taking advantage of it. We have seen all of the most important JavaScript features that we will be using. Let's round off the chapter by looking at some tools that we'll be working with.

How do we work with JavaScript?

This is all well and good, but as we mentioned before, it so happens that the JavaScript version available almost everywhere isn't ES10, but rather the earlier JS5. An exception to this is Node.js. It is based on Chrome's v8 high-performance JavaScript engine, which already has several ES10 features available. Nonetheless, as of today, ES10 coverage isn't 100% complete, and there are features that you will miss. (Check out `https://nodejs.org/en/docs/es6/` for more on Node.js and v8.) This will surely change in the future, as Internet Explorer will fade away, and the newest Microsoft's browser will share Chrome's engine, but for the time being, we must still deal with older, less powerful engines.

So what can you do if you want to code using the latest version, but the available one is an earlier, poorer one? Or what happens if most of your users are using older browsers, which don't support the fancy features you're keen on using? Let's see some solutions for this.

 If you want to be sure of your choices before using any given new feature, check out the compatibility table at `https://kangax.github.io/compat-table/es6/` (see *Figure 1.1*). For Node.js specifically, check out `http://node.green/`.

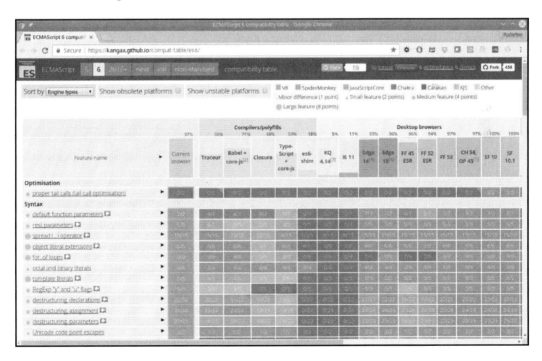

Figure 1.1. - The latest JavaScript features may not be widely and fully supported, so you'll have to check before using them.

Using transpilers

In order to get out of this availability and compatibility problem, there are a couple of **transpilers** that you can use. Transpilers take your original ES10 code, which might use the most modern JavaScript features, and transforms it into equivalent JS5 code. It's a source-to-source transformation, instead of a source-to-object code that would be used in compilation. You can code using advanced ES10 features, but the user's browsers will receive JS5 code. A transpiler will also let you keep up with upcoming versions of the language, despite the time needed by browsers to adopt new standards across desktop and mobile devices.

If you wonder where the word transpiler came from, it is a portmanteau of *translate* and *compiler*. There are many such combinations in technological speak: *email* (*electronic* and *mail*), *emoticon* (*emotion* and *icon*), *malware* (*malicious* and *software*), or *alphanumeric* (*alphabetic* and *numeric*), and many more.

The most common transpilers for JavaScript are Babel (at `https://babeljs.io/`) and Traceur (at `https://github.com/google/traceur-compiler`). With tools such as npm or webpack, it's fairly easy to configure things so that your code will get automatically transpiled and provided to end-users. You can also carry out transpilation online; see *Figure 1.2* for an example of this using Babel's online environment:

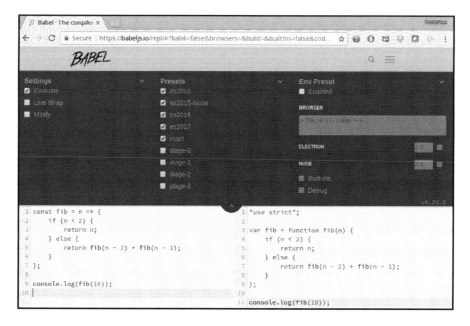

Figure 1.2 - The Babel transpiler converts ES10 code into compatible JS5 code

If you prefer Traceur, you can use its tool at `https://google.github.io/traceur-compiler/demo/repl.html#` instead, but you'll have to open a developer console to see the results of your running code (see *Figure 1.3* for an example of transpiled code). Select the **EXPERIMENTAL** option to fully enable ES10 support:

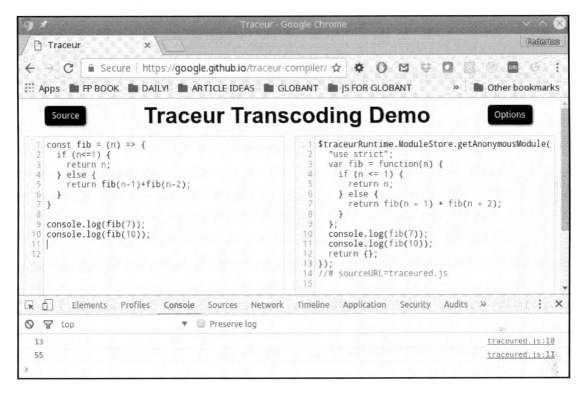

Figure 1.3 - The Traceur transpiler is an equally valid alternative for ES10-to-JS5 translation

Using transpilers is also a great way to learn new language features. Just type in some code on the left and see the equivalent code on the right. Alternatively, you can use the **command-line interface** (**CLI**) tools to transpile a source file and then inspect the produced output.

There's a final possibility that you may want to consider: instead of JavaScript, opt for Microsoft's TypeScript (at `http://www.typescriptlang.org/`), a superset of the language that is itself compiled to JS5. The main advantage of TypeScript is the ability to add (optional) static type checks to JavaScript, which helps detect certain programming errors at compile time. But beware: as with Babel or Traceur, not all of ES10 will be available.

You can also perform type checks without using TypeScript by using Facebook's Flow (see `https://flow.org/`).

If you opt to go with TypeScript, you can also test it online at their **playground** (see `http://www.typescriptlang.org/play/`). You can set options to be more or less strict with data type checks, and you can also run your code on the spot (see *Figure 1.4* for more details):

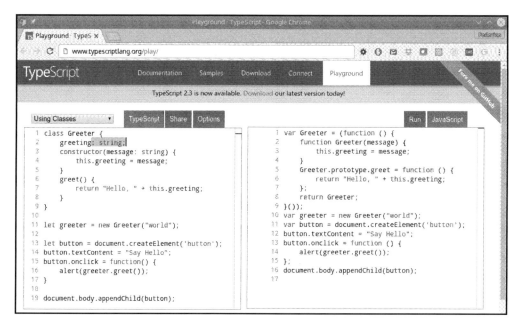

Figure 1.4 - TypeScript adds type-checking features for safer programming

By using TypeScript, you will be able to avoid common type-related mistakes. A positive trend is that most tools (frameworks, libraries, and so on) are slowly going in this direction, so work will be easier.

Working online

There are some more online tools that you can use to test out your JavaScript code. Check out JSFiddle (at `https://jsfiddle.net/`), CodePen (at `https://codepen.io/`), and JSBin (at `http://jsbin.com/`), among others. You may have to specify whether to use Babel or Traceur; otherwise, newer language features will be rejected. You can see an example of JSFiddle in *Figure 1.5*:

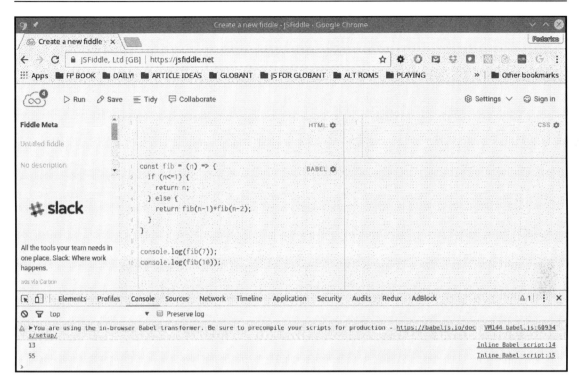

Figure 1.5 - JSFiddle lets you try out modern JavaScript code (plus HTML and CSS) without requiring any other tools

Using these tools provides a very quick way to try out code or do small experiments—and I can truly vouch for this since I've tested much of the code in the book in this way!

Testing

We will also touch on testing, which is, after all, one of FP's main advantages. For this, we will be using Jasmine (`https://jasmine.github.io/`), though we could also opt for Mocha (`http://mochajs.org/`).

You can run Jasmine test suites with a runner, such as Karma (`https://karma-runner.github.io`), but I opted for standalone tests; see `https://github.com/jasmine/jasmine#installation` for details.

Summary

In this chapter, we have seen the basics of FP, a bit of its history, its advantages (and also some possible disadvantages, to be fair), why we can apply it in JavaScript (which isn't usually considered a functional language), and what tools we'll need in order to go through the rest of this book.

In Chapter 2, *Thinking Functionally - A First Example*, we'll go over an example of a simple problem, look at it in *common* ways, and end by solving it in a functional manner and analyzing the advantages of our method.

Questions

1.1. **Classes as first-class objects**: We learned that functions are first-class objects, but did you know that *classes* also are? (Though, of course, speaking of classes as *objects* does sound weird.) Look at the following example and see what makes it tick! Be careful: there's some purposefully weird code in it:

```
const makeSaluteClass = term =>
  class {
    constructor(x) {
      this.x = x;
    }

    salute(y) {
      console.log(`${this.x} says "${term}" to ${y}`);
    }
  };

const Spanish = makeSaluteClass("HOLA");
new Spanish("ALFA").salute("BETA");
// ALFA says "HOLA" to BETA

new (makeSaluteClass("HELLO"))("GAMMA").salute("DELTA");
// GAMMA says "HELLO" to DELTA

const fullSalute = (c, x, y) => new c(x).salute(y);
const French = makeSaluteClass("BON JOUR");
fullSalute(French, "EPSILON", "ZETA");
// EPSILON says "BON JOUR" to ZETA
```

1.2. **Factorial errors**: Factorials, as we defined them, should only be calculated for non-negative integers; however, the function that we wrote in the *Recursion* section doesn't verify whether its argument is valid. Can you add the necessary checks? Try to avoid repeated, redundant tests!

1.3. **Climbing factorial:** Our implementation of a factorial starts by multiplying by *n*, then by *n-1*, then *n-2*, and so on in what we could call a *downward fashion*. Can you write a new version of the factorial function that will loop *upwards*?

1.4. **Code squeezing**: Not that it's a goal in itself, but by using arrow functions and some other JavaScript features, you can shorten `newCounter()` to half its length. Can you see how?

Thinking Functionally - A First Example **2**

In `Chapter 1`, *Becoming Functional – Several Questions*, we went over what FP is, mentioned some advantages of applying it, and listed some tools we'd be needing in JavaScript, but let's now leave theory behind, and start by considering a simple problem and how to solve it in a functional way.

In this chapter, we will do the following:

- Look at a simple, common, e-commerce related problem
- Consider several usual ways to solve it, with their associated defects
- Find a way to solve the problem by looking at it functionally
- Devise a higher-order solution that can be applied to other problems
- Work out how to carry out unit testing for functional solutions

In future chapters, we'll be coming back to some of the topics listed here, so we won't be going into too much detail. We'll just show how FP can give a different outlook for our problem and leave further details for later. After working through this chapter, you will have had a first look at a common problem and at a way of solving it by thinking functionally, as a prelude for the rest of this book.

Our problem – doing something only once

Let's consider a simple but common situation. You have developed an e-commerce site; the user can fill their shopping cart, and in the end, they must click on a **Bill me** button so their credit card will be charged. However, the user shouldn't click twice (or more) or they will be billed several times.

The HTML part of your application might have something like this somewhere:

```
<button id="billButton" onclick="billTheUser(some, sales, data)">Bill
me</button>
```

And, among the scripts, you'd have something similar to the following code:

```
function billTheUser(some, sales, data) {
  window.alert("Billing the user...");
  // actually bill the user
}
```

 Assigning the events handler directly in HTML, the way I did it, isn't recommended. Rather, unobtrusively, you should assign the handler through code. So, *do as I say, not as I do!*

This is a very bare-bones explanation of the problem and your web page, but it's enough for our purposes. Let's now get to thinking about ways of avoiding repeated clicks on that button. *How can we manage to avoid the user clicking more than once?* That's an interesting problem, with several possible solutions—let's get started by looking at bad ones!

How many ways can you think of to solve our problem? Let's go over several solutions and analyze their quality.

Solution 1 – hoping for the best!

How can we solve the problem? The first *solution* may seem like a joke: do nothing, tell the user *not* to click twice, and hope for the best! Your page might look like *Figure 2.1*:

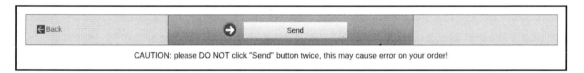

Figure 2.1: An actual screenshot of a page, just warning you against clicking more than once

This is a way to weasel out of the problem; I've seen several websites that just warn the user about the risks of clicking more than once (see *Figure 2.1*) and actually do nothing to prevent the situation: *The user got billed twice? We warned them... it's their fault!*

Your solution might simply look like the following code:

```
<button id="billButton" onclick="billTheUser(some, sales, data)">Bill
me</button>
<b>WARNING: PRESS ONLY ONCE, DO NOT PRESS AGAIN!!</b>
```

Okay, so this isn't actually a solution; let's move on to more serious proposals.

Solution 2 – using a global flag

The solution most people would probably think of first is using some global variable to record whether the user has already clicked on the button. You'd define a flag named something like `clicked`, initialized with `false`. When the user clicks on the button, if `clicked` was `false`, you'd change it to `true` and execute the function; otherwise, you wouldn't do anything at all. See all of this in the following code:

```
let clicked = false;
.
.
.
function billTheUser(some, sales, data) {
  if (!clicked) {
    clicked = true;
    window.alert("Billing the user...");
    // actually bill the user
  }
}
```

 For more good reasons *not* to use global variables, read `http://wiki.c2.com/?GlobalVariablesAreBad`.

This obviously works, but it has several problems that must be addressed:

- You are using a global variable, and you could change its value by accident. Global variables aren't a good idea, neither in JavaScript nor in other languages.
- You must also remember to re-initialize it to `false` when the user starts buying again. If you don't, the user won't be able to make a second purchase because paying will have become impossible.
- You will have difficulties testing this code because it depends on external things (that is, the `clicked` variable).

So, this isn't a very good solution. Let's keep thinking!

Solution 3 – removing the handler

We may go for a lateral kind of solution, and instead of having the function avoid repeated clicks, we might just remove the possibility of clicking altogether. The following code does just that; the first thing that `billTheUser()` does is remove the `onclick` handler from the button, so no further calls will be possible:

```
function billTheUser(some, sales, data) {
  document.getElementById("billButton").onclick = null;
  window.alert("Billing the user...");
  // actually bill the user
}
```

This solution also has some problems:

- The code is tightly coupled to the button, so you won't be able to reuse it elsewhere.
- You must remember to reset the handler, otherwise, the user won't be able to make a second buy.
- Testing will also be harder because you'll have to provide some DOM elements.

We can enhance this solution a bit and avoid coupling the function to the button by providing the latter's ID as an extra argument in the call. (This idea can also be applied to some of the following solutions.) The HTML part would be as follows, and note the extra argument to `billTheUser()`:

```
<button
  id="billButton"
  onclick="billTheUser('billButton', some, sales, data)"
>
  Bill me
</button>;
```

We also have to change the called function, so it will use the received `buttonId` value to access the corresponding button:

```
function billTheUser(buttonId, some, sales, data) {
  document.getElementById(buttonId).onclick = null;
  window.alert("Billing the user...");
  // actually bill the user
}
```

This solution is somewhat better. But, in essence, we are still using a global element—not a variable, but the `onclick` value. So, despite the enhancement, this isn't a very good solution either. Let's move on.

Solution 4 – changing the handler

A variant to the previous solution would be not to remove the click function, but rather assign a new one instead. We are using functions as first-class objects here when we assign the `alreadyBilled()` function to the click event. The function warning the user that they have already clicked could be something as follows:

```
function alreadyBilled() {
  window.alert("Your billing process is running; don't click, please.");
}
```

Our `billTheUser()` function would then be like the following code—and note how instead of assigning `null` to the `onclick` handler as in the previous section, now the `alreadyBilled()` function is assigned:

```
function billTheUser(some, sales, data) {
  document.getElementById("billButton").onclick = alreadyBilled;
  window.alert("Billing the user...");
  // actually bill the user
}
```

There's a good point to this solution; if the user clicks a second time, they'll get a warning not to do that, but they won't be billed again. (From the point of view of the user experience, it's better.) However, this solution still has the very same objections as the previous one (code coupled to the button, needing to reset the handler, and harder testing), so we won't consider it quite good anyway.

Solution 5 – disabling the button

A similar idea here is instead of removing the event handler, we can disable the button so the user won't be able to click. You might have a function like the following code, which does exactly that by setting the `disabled` attribute of the button:

```
function billTheUser(some, sales, data) {
  document.getElementById("billButton").setAttribute("disabled", "true");
  window.alert("Billing the user...");
  // actually bill the user
}
```

This also works, but we still have objections as with the previous solutions (coupling the code to the button, needing to re-enable the button, and harder testing), so we don't like this solution either.

Solution 6 – redefining the handler

Another idea: instead of changing anything in the button, let's have the event handler change itself. The trick is in the second line; by assigning a new value to the `billTheUser` variable, we are actually dynamically changing what the function does! The first time you call the function, it will do its thing, but it will also change itself out of existence, by giving its name to a new function:

```
function billTheUser(some, sales, data) {
  billTheUser = function() {};
  window.alert("Billing the user...");
  // actually bill the user
}
```

There's a special trick in the solution. Functions are global, so the `billTheUser=...` line actually changes the function's inner workings. From that point on, `billTheUser` will be the new (null) function. This solution is still hard to test. Even worse, how would you restore the functionality of `billTheUser`, setting it back to its original objective?

Solution 7 – using a local flag

We can go back to the idea of using a flag, but instead of making it global (which was our main objection), we can use an **Immediately Invoked Function Expression (IIFE)**, which we'll see more on in Chapter 3, *Starting Out with Functions – A Core Concept*, and Chapter 11, *Implementing Design Patterns – The Functional Way*. With this, we can use a closure, so `clicked` will be local to the function, and not visible anywhere else:

```
var billTheUser = (clicked => {
  return (some, sales, data) => {
    if (!clicked) {
      clicked = true;
      window.alert("Billing the user...");
      // actually bill the user
    }
  };
})(false);
```

See how `clicked` gets its initial `false` value from the call at the end.

This solution is along the lines of the global variable solution but using a private, local variable is an enhancement. About the only drawback we could find is that you'll have to rework every function that needs to be called only once to work in this fashion (and, as we'll see in the following section, our FP solution is similar to it in some ways). Okay, it's not too hard to do, but don't forget the **Don't Repeat Yourself (DRY)** advice!

We have now gone through multiple ways of solving our *do something only once* problem—but as we've seen, they were not very good! Let's think about the problem in a functional way, and we'll get a more general solution.

A functional solution to our problem

Let's try to be more general; after all, requiring that some function or other be executed only once isn't that outlandish, and may be required elsewhere! Let's lay down some principles:

- The original function (the one that may be called only once) should do whatever it is expected to do and nothing else.
- We don't want to modify the original function in any way.
- We need to have a new function that will call the original one only once.
- We want a general solution that we can apply to any number of original functions.

 The first principle listed previously is the *single responsibility principle* (the *S* in S.O.L.I.D.), which states that every function should be responsible for a single functionality. For more on S.O.L.I.D., check the article by *Uncle Bob* (Robert C. Martin, who wrote the five principles) at http://butunclebob.com/ArticleS.UncleBob.PrinciplesOfOod.

Can we do it? Yes, and we'll write a *higher-order function*, which we'll be able to apply to any function, to produce a new function that will work only once. Let's see how! We will introduce higher-order functions (to which we'll later dedicate Chapter 6, *Producing Functions – Higher-Order Functions*) and then we'll go about testing our functional solution, as well as providing some enhancements to it.

A higher-order solution

If we don't want to modify the original function, we'll create a higher-order function, which we'll (inspiredly!) name once(). This function will receive a function as a parameter and will return a new function, which will work only a single time. (As we mentioned before, we'll be seeing more of higher-order functions in Chapter 6, *Producing Functions – Higher-Order Functions*; in particular, see the *Doing things once, revisited* section.)

 Underscore and Lodash already have a similar function, invoked as _.once(). Ramda also provides R.once(), and most FP libraries include similar functionality, so you wouldn't have to program it on your own.

Our once() function may seem imposing at first, but as you get accustomed to working in FP fashion, you'll get used to this sort of code and find it to be quite understandable:

```
const once = fn => {
  let done = false;
  return (...args) => {
    if (!done) {
      done = true;
      fn(...args);
    }
  };
};
```

Let's go over some of the finer points of this function:

- The first line shows that once() receives a function (fn) as its parameter.
- We are defining an internal, private done variable, by taking advantage of closure, as in *Solution 7*, previously. We opted *not* to call it clicked, as previously, because you don't necessarily need to click on a button to call the function, so we went for a more general term. Each time you apply once() to some function, a new, distinct done variable will be created and will be accessible only from the returned function.
- The return (...args) => ... line says that once() will return a function, with some (one or more, or possibly zero) parameters. Note that we are using the spread syntax we saw in Chapter 1, *Becoming Functional – Several Questions*. With older versions of JavaScript, you'd have to work with the arguments object; see https://developer.mozilla.org/en/docs/Web/JavaScript/Reference/Functions/arguments for more on that. The modern JavaScript way is simpler and shorter!

- We assign `done = true` before calling `fn()`, just in case that function throws an exception. Of course, if you don't want to disable the function unless it has successfully ended, then you could move the assignment just below the `fn()` call.
- After the setting is done, we finally call the original function. Note the use of the spread operator to pass along whatever parameters the original `fn()` had.

So, how would we use it? We don't even need to store the newly generated function in any place. We can simply write the `onclick` method, shown as follows:

```
<button id="billButton" onclick="once(billTheUser)(some, sales, data)">
   Bill me
</button>;
```

Pay close attention to the syntax! When the user clicks on the button, the function that gets called with the `(some, sales, data)` argument isn't `billTheUser()`, but rather the result of having called `once()` with `billTheUser` as a parameter. That result is the one that can be called only a single time.

 Note that our `once()` function uses functions as first-class objects, arrow functions, closures, and the spread operator; back in Chapter 1, *Becoming Functional – Several Questions*, we said we'd be needing those, so we're keeping our word! All we are missing here from that chapter is recursion, but as the Rolling Stones sang, *You Can't Always Get What You Want!*

We now have a functional way of getting a function to do its thing only once; how would we test it? Let's get into that topic now.

Testing the solution manually

We can run a simple test. Let's write a `squeak()` function that will, appropriately, squeak when called! The code is simple:

```
const squeak = a => console.log(a, " squeak!!");

squeak("original"); // "original squeak!!"
squeak("original"); // "original squeak!!"
squeak("original"); // "original squeak!!"
```

If we apply `once()` to it, we get a new function that will squeak only once. See the highlighted line in the following code:

```
const squeakOnce = once(squeak);

squeakOnce("only once"); // "only once squeak!!"
squeakOnce("only once"); // no output
squeakOnce("only once"); // no output
```

Check out the results at CodePen or see *Figure 2.2*:

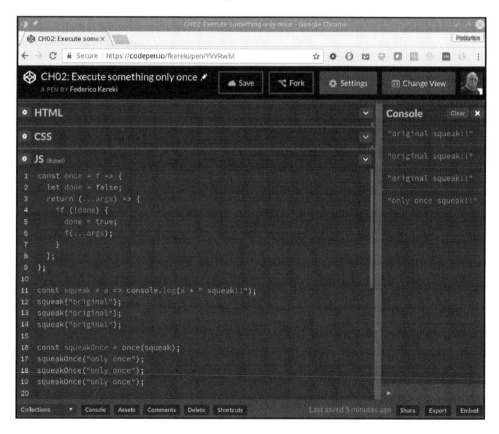

Figure 2.2: Testing our once() higher-order function

The previous steps showed us how we could test our `once()` function by hand, but the method we used is not exactly ideal. Let's see why, and how to do better, in the next section.

Testing the solution automatically

Running tests by hand is no good: it gets tiresome and boring and that leads, after a while, to not running the tests any longer. Let's do better and write some automatic tests with Jasmine. Following the instructions over at `https://jasmine.github.io/pages/getting_started.html`, I set up a standalone runner; the required HTML code, using Jasmine Spec Runner 2.6.1, is as follows:

```html
<!DOCTYPE html>
<html>
<head>
  <meta charset="utf-8">
  <title>Jasmine Spec Runner v2.6.1</title>

  <link rel="shortcut icon" type="image/png"
        href="lib/jasmine-2.6.1/jasmine_favicon.png">
  <link rel="stylesheet" href="lib/jasmine-2.6.1/jasmine.css">

  <script src="lib/jasmine-2.6.1/jasmine.js"></script>
  <script src="lib/jasmine-2.6.1/jasmine-html.js"></script>
  <script src="lib/jasmine-2.6.1/boot.js"></script>

  <script src="src/once.js"></script>
  <script src="tests/once.test.1.js"></script>
</head>
<body>
</body>
</html>
```

The `src/once.js` file has the `once()` definition that we just saw, and `tests/once.test.js` has the actual suite of tests. The code for our tests is the following:

```js
describe("once", () => {
  beforeEach(() => {
    window.myFn = () => {};
    spyOn(window, "myFn");
  });

  it("without 'once', a function always runs", () => {
    myFn();
    myFn();
    myFn();
    expect(myFn).toHaveBeenCalledTimes(3);
  });

  it("with 'once', a function runs one time", () => {
    window.onceFn = once(window.myFn);
```

```
        spyOn(window, "onceFn").and.callThrough();
        onceFn();
        onceFn();
        onceFn();
        expect(onceFn).toHaveBeenCalledTimes(3);
        expect(myFn).toHaveBeenCalledTimes(1);
    });
});
```

There are several points to note here:

- To spy on a function, it must be associated with an object. (Alternatively, you can also directly create a spy using Jasmine's `createSpy()` method.) Global functions are associated with the window object, so `window.fn` is a way of saying that `fn` is actually global.

- When you spy on a function, Jasmine intercepts your calls and registers that the function was called, with which arguments, and how many times it was called. So, for all we care, `window.fn` could simply be `null` because it will never be executed.

- The first test only checks that if we call the function several times, it gets called that number of times. This is trivial, but if that didn't happen, we'd be doing something really wrong!

- In the second group of tests, we want to see that the `once()` function (`window.onceFn()`) gets called, but only once. So, we tell Jasmine to spy on `onceFn` but let calls pass through. Any calls to `fn()` will also get counted. In our case, as expected, despite calling `onceFn()` three times, `fn()` gets called only once.

We can see the results in *Figure 2.3*:

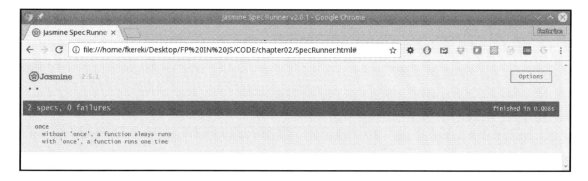

Figure 2.3: Running automatic tests on our function with Jasmine

Now we have seen not only how to test our functional solution by hand but also in an automatic way, so we are done with testing. Let's just finish by considering an even better solution, also achieved in a functional way.

Producing an even better solution

In one of the previous solutions, we mentioned that it would be a good idea to do something every time after the first click, and not silently ignore the user's clicks. We'll write a new higher-order function that takes a second parameter—a function to be called every time from the second call onward. Our new function will be called onceAndAfter() and can be written as follows:

```
const onceAndAfter = (f, g) => {
  let done = false;
  return (...args) => {
    if (!done) {
      done = true;
      f(...args);
    } else {
      g(...args);
    }
  };
};
```

We have ventured further in higher-order functions; onceAndAfter() takes *two* functions as parameters and produces a third one, which includes the other two within.

You could make onceAndAfter() more powerful by giving a default value for g, along the lines of const onceAndAfter = (f, g = () => {}), so if you didn't want to specify the second function, it would still work fine because it would call a *do-nothing* function, instead of causing an error.

We can do a quick-and-dirty test, along the same lines as we did earlier. Let's add a creak() creaking function to our previous squeak() one, and check out what happens if we apply onceAndAfter() to them. We can then get a makeSound() function that should squeak() once and creak() afterward:

```
const squeak = (x) => console.log(x, "squeak!!");
const creak = (x) => console.log(x, "creak!!");
const makeSound = onceAndAfter(squeak, creak);

makeSound("door"); // "door squeak!!"
makeSound("door"); // "door creak!!"
```

```
makeSound("door"); // "door creak!!"
makeSound("door"); // "door creak!!"
```

Writing a test for this new function isn't hard, only a bit longer. We have to check which function was called and how many times:

```
describe("onceAndAfter", () => {
  it("should call the first function once, and the other after", () => {
    func1 = () => {};
    spyOn(window, "func1");
    func2 = () => {};
    spyOn(window, "func2");
    onceFn = onceAndAfter(func1, func2);

    onceFn();
    expect(func1).toHaveBeenCalledTimes(1);
    expect(func2).toHaveBeenCalledTimes(0);

    onceFn();
    expect(func1).toHaveBeenCalledTimes(1);
    expect(func2).toHaveBeenCalledTimes(1);

    onceFn();
    expect(func1).toHaveBeenCalledTimes(1);
    expect(func2).toHaveBeenCalledTimes(2);

    onceFn();
    expect(func1).toHaveBeenCalledTimes(1);
    expect(func2).toHaveBeenCalledTimes(3);
  });
});
```

Notice that we always check that `func1()` is called only once. Similarly, we check `func2()`; the count of calls starts at zero (the time that `func1()` is called), and from then on, it goes up by one on each call.

Summary

In this chapter, we've seen a common, simple problem, based on a real-life situation, and after analyzing several typical ways of solving that, we went for a *functional thinking* solution. We saw how to apply FP to our problem, and we found a more general higher-order solution that we could apply to similar problems with no further code changes. We saw how to write unit tests for our code to round out the development job.

Finally, we produced an even better solution (from the point of view of the user experience) and saw how to code it and how to unit test it. Now, you've started to get a grip on how to solve a problem functionally; next, in `Chapter 3`, *Starting Out with Functions – a Core Concept*, we'll be delving more deeply into functions, which are at the core of all FP.

Questions

2.1. **No extra variables**: Our functional implementation required using an extra variable, `done`, to mark whether the function had already been called. Not that it matters, but could you make do without using any extra variables? Note that we aren't telling you *not* to use any variables, it's just a matter of not adding any new ones, such as `done`, and only as an exercise!

2.2. **Alternating functions**: In the spirit of our `onceAndAfter()` function, could you write an `alternator()` higher-order function that gets two functions as arguments and on each call, alternatively calls one and another? The expected behavior should be as in the following example:

```
let sayA = () => console.log("A");
let sayB = () => console.log("B");
let alt = alternator(sayA, sayB);

alt(); // A
alt(); // B
alt(); // A
alt(); // B
alt(); // A
alt(); // B
```

2.3. **Everything has a limit!** As an extension of `once()`, could you write a higher-order function, `thisManyTimes(fn,n)`, that would let you call the `fn()` function up to n times, but would afterward do nothing? To give an example, `once(fn)` and `thisManyTimes(fn,1)` would produce functions that behave in exactly the same way.

Starting Out with Functions - A Core Concept

3

In Chapter 2, *Thinking Functionally – A First Example*, we went over an example of **Functional Programming (FP)** thinking, but let's now look at the basics and review functions. In Chapter 1, *Becoming Functional – Several Questions*, we mentioned that two important JavaScript features were functions: first-class objects and closures.

In this chapter, we'll cover several important topics:

- Functions in JavaScript, including how to define them, with a particular focus on arrow functions
- Currying and functions as first-class objects
- Several ways of using functions in an FP way

After all this content, you'll be up to date as to the generic and specific concepts relating to functions, which are, after all, at the core of FP!

All about functions

Let's get started with a short review of functions in JavaScript and their relationship to FP concepts. We can start something that we mainly mentioned in the *Functions as first-class objects* section in Chapter 1, *Becoming Functional - Several Questions*, and in a couple of places in Chapter 2, *Thinking Functionally - A First Example*, about functions as first-class objects, and then go on to several considerations about their usage in actual coding.

In particular, we'll be looking at the following:

- Some basic and very important concepts about lambda calculus, which is the theoretical basis for FP
- Arrow functions, which are the most direct translation of lambda calculus into JavaScript
- Using functions as first-class objects, a key concept in FP

Of lambdas and functions

In lambda calculus terms, a function can look like λx.2*x. The understanding is that the variable after the λ character is the parameter for the function, and the expression after the dot is where you would replace whatever value is passed as an argument. Later in this chapter, we will see that this particular example could be written as x => 2*x in JavaScript in arrow function form, which, as you can see, is very similar in form.

 If you sometimes wonder about the difference between arguments and parameters, a mnemonic with some alliteration may help: *Parameters are Potential, Arguments are Actual.* Parameters are placeholders for potential values that will be passed, and arguments are the actual values passed to the function. In other words, when you define the function, you list its parameters, and when you call it, you provide arguments.

Applying a function means that you provide an actual argument to it, which is written in the usual way, by using parentheses. For example, (λx.2*x)(3) would be calculated as 6. What's the equivalent of these lambda functions in JavaScript? That's an interesting question! There are several ways of defining functions, and not all have the same meaning.

 A good article that shows the many ways of defining functions, methods, and more is *The Many Faces of Functions in JavaScript* by Leo Balter and Rick Waldron, at `https://bocoup.com/blog/the-many-faces-of-functions-in-javascript`—give it a look!

In how many ways can you define a function in JavaScript? The answer is probably in more ways than you thought! At the very least, you could write the following:

- A named function declaration: `function first(...) {...};`
- An anonymous function expression: `var second = function(...) {...};`
- A named function expression: `var third = function someName(...) {...};`

- An immediately-invoked expression: `var fourth = (function() { ...; return function(...) {...}; })();`
- A function constructor: `var fifth = new Function(...);`
- An arrow function: `var sixth = (...) => {...};`

And, if you wanted, you could add object method declarations, since they actually imply functions as well, but the preceding list should be enough.

JavaScript also allows us to define generator functions (as in `function*(...) {...}`) that actually return a `Generator` object, and `async` functions that are really a mix of generators and promises. We won't be using these kinds of functions, but you can read more about them at `https://developer.mozilla.org/en/docs/Web/JavaScript/Reference/Statements/function*` and `https://developer.mozilla.org/en-US/docs/Web/JavaScript/Reference/Statements/async_function`—they can be useful in other contexts.

What's the difference between all these ways of defining functions, and why should we care? Let's go over them, one by one:

- The first definition, a standalone declaration starting with the `function` keyword, is probably the most used definition in JavaScript, and defines a function named `first` (that is, `first.name=="first"`). Because of *hoisting*, this function will be accessible everywhere in the scope where it's defined.

You can read more about hoisting at `https://developer.mozilla.org/en-US/docs/Glossary/Hoisting`. Keep in mind that it applies only to declarations and not to initializations.

- The second definition, which assigns a function to a variable, also produces a function, but an *anonymous* (that is, not named) one; however, many JavaScript engines are capable of deducing what the name should be, and will then set `second.name === "second"`. (Look at the following code, which shows a case where the anonymous function has no name assigned.) Since the assignment isn't hoisted, the function will only be accessible after the assignment has been executed. Also, you'd probably prefer defining the variable with `const` rather than `var`, because you wouldn't (*shouldn't*) be changing the function:

```
var second = function() {};
console.log(second.name);
// "second"
```

```
var myArray = new Array(3);
myArray[1] = function() {};
console.log(myArray[1].name);
// ""
```

- The third definition is the same as the second, except that the function now has its own name: `third.name === "someName"`.

The name of a function is relevant when you want to call it, and also if you plan to perform recursive calls; we'll come back to this in Chapter 9, *Designing Functions – Recursion*. If you just want a function for, say, a callback, you can use one without a name; however, note that named functions are more easily recognized in an error traceback, the kind of listing you get to use when you are trying to understand what happened, and which function called what.

- The fourth definition, with an immediately invoked expression, lets you use a closure. An inner function can use variables or other functions, defined in its outer function, in a totally private, encapsulated, way. Going back to the counter-making function that we saw in the *Closures* section of Chapter 1, *Becoming Functional – Several Questions*, we could write something like the following:

```
var myCounter = (function(initialValue = 0) {
  let count = initialValue;
  return function() {
    count++;
    return count;
  };
})(77);

myCounter(); // 78
myCounter(); // 79
myCounter(); // 80
```

Study the code carefully: the outer function receives an argument (77, in this case) that is used as the initial value of `count` (if no initial value is provided, we start at 0). The inner function can access `count` (because of the closure), but the variable cannot be accessed anywhere else. In all aspects, the returned function is a common function—the only difference is its access to private elements. This is also the basis of the *module* pattern.

- The fifth definition isn't safe, and you shouldn't use it! You pass the names of the arguments first, then the actual function body as a string, and the equivalent of `eval()` is used to create the function, which could allow many dangerous hacks, so don't do this! Just to whet your curiosity, let's look at an example of rewriting the very simple `sum3()` function we saw back in the *Spread* section of `Chapter 1`, *Becoming Functional - Several Questions*:

```
var sum3 = new Function("x", "y", "z", "var t = x+y+z; return
t;");
sum3(4, 6, 7); // 17
```

 This sort of definition is not only unsafe, but has some other quirks—they don't create closures with their creation contexts, and so they are always global. See `https://developer.mozilla.org/en-US/docs/Web/JavaScript/Reference/Global_Objects/Function` for more on this, but remember that using this way of creating functions isn't a good idea!

- Finally, the last definition, which uses an arrow `=>` definition, is the most compact way to define a function, and the one we'll try to use whenever possible.

At this point, we have seen several ways of defining a function, but let's now focus on arrow functions, a style we'll be favoring in our coding for this book.

Arrow functions – the modern way

Even if the arrow functions work pretty much in the same way as the other functions, there are some important differences between them and the usual functions. Arrow functions can implicitly return a value even with no `return` statement present, the value of `this` is not bound, and there is no `arguments` object. Let's go over these three points.

 There are some extra differences: arrow functions cannot be used as constructors, they do not have a `prototype` property, and they cannot be used as generators because they don't allow the `yield` keyword. For more details on these points, see `https://developer.mozilla.org/en-US/docs/Web/JavaScript/Reference/Functions/Arrow_functions#No_binding_of_this`.

In this section, we'll go into several JavaScript function-related topics, including:

- How to return different values
- How to handle problems with the value of `this`

- How to work with varying numbers of arguments
- An important concept, *currying*, for which we'll find many usages in the rest of the book

Returning values

In the lambda coding style, functions only consist of a result. For the sake of brevity, the new arrow functions provide a syntax for this. When you write something like (x, y, z) => followed by an expression, a return is implied. For instance, the following two functions actually do the same as the sum3() function that we showed previously:

```
const f1 = (x, y, z) => x + y + z;

const f2 = (x, y, z) => {
  return x + y + z;
};
```

If you want to return an object, then you must use parentheses; otherwise, JavaScript will assume that code follows.

A matter of style: when you define an arrow function with only one parameter, you can omit the parentheses around it. For consistency, I prefer to always include them. However, *Prettier*, the formatting tool I use (we mentioned it in Chapter 1, *Becoming Functional - Several Questions*) doesn't approve. Feel free to choose your style!

And a final note: lest you think this is a wildly improbable case, check out the *Questions* section later in this chapter for a very common scenario!

Handling the this value

A classic problem with JavaScript is the handling of this, whose value isn't always what you expect it to be. ES2015 solved this with arrow functions, which inherit the proper this value so that problems are avoided. Look at the following code for an example of the possible problems: by the time the timeout function is called, this will point to the global (window) variable instead of the new object, so you'll get undefined in the console:

```
function ShowItself1(identity) {
  this.identity = identity;
  setTimeout(function() {
    console.log(this.identity);
  }, 1000);
```

```
}

var x = new ShowItself1("Functional");
// after one second, undefined is displayed
```

There are two classic ways of solving this with old-fashioned JavaScript and the arrow way of working:

- One solution uses a closure and defines a local variable (usually named `that` or sometimes `self`), which will get the original value of `this`, so it won't be undefined.
- The second way uses `bind()`, so the timeout function will be bound to the correct value of `this`.
- The third, more modern way just uses an arrow function, so `this` gets the correct value (pointing to the object) without further ado.

 We will also be using `bind()`. See the *Of lambdas and functions* section.

Let's see the three solutions in actual code. We use a closure for the first timeout, binding for the second, and an arrow function for the third:

```
function ShowItself2(identity) {
  this.identity = identity;
  let that = this;
  setTimeout(function() {
    console.log(that.identity);
  }, 1000);

  setTimeout(
    function() {
      console.log(this.identity);
    }.bind(this),
    2000
  );

  setTimeout(() => {
    console.log(this.identity);
  }, 3000);
}

var x = new ShowItself2("JavaScript");
// after one second, "JavaScript"
```

```
// after another second, the same
// after yet another second, once again
```

If you run this code, you'll get `JavaScript` after one second, then again after another second, and yet a third time after another second; all three methods worked correctly, so whichever you pick really depends on which you like better.

Working with arguments

In `Chapter 1`, *Becoming Functional - Several Questions*, and `Chapter 2`, *Thinking Functionally - A First Example*, we saw some uses of the spread (. . .) operator. However, the most practical usage we'll be making of it has to do with working with arguments; we'll see some cases of this in `Chapter 6`, *Producing Functions – Higher-Order Functions*. Let's review our `once()` function:

```
const once = func => {
  let done = false;
  return (...args) => {
    if (!done) {
      done = true;
      func(...args);
    }
  };
};
```

Why are we writing `return (...args) =>` and then afterwards `func(...args)`? The answer has to do with the more modern way of handling a variable number (possibly zero) of arguments. How did you manage such kinds of code in older versions of JavaScript? The answer has to do with the `arguments` object (*not* an array!) that lets you access the actual arguments passed to the function.

 For more on this, read `https://developer.mozilla.org/en/docs/Web/JavaScript/Reference/Functions/arguments`.

In JavaScript 5 and earlier, if we wanted a function to be able to process any number of arguments, we had to write code as follows:

```
function somethingElse() {
  // get arguments and do something
}

function listArguments() {
```

```
  console.log(arguments);
  var myArray = Array.prototype.slice.call(arguments);
  console.log(myArray);
  somethingElse.apply(null, myArray);
}

listArguments(22, 9, 60);
// (3) [22, 9, 60, callee: function, Symbol(Symbol.iterator): function]
// (3) [22, 9, 60]
```

The first log shows that `arguments` is actually an object; the second log corresponds to a simple array. Also, note the complicated way that is needed to call `somethingElse()`, which requires using `apply()`.

What would be the equivalent code in the latest JavaScript version? It is much shorter, and that's why we'll be seeing several examples of the usage of the spread operator in the book:

```
function listArguments2(...args) {
  console.log(args);
  somethingElse(...args);
}

listArguments2(12, 4, 56);
// (3) [12, 4, 56]
```

You should bear in mind the following points when looking at this code:

- By writing `listArguments2(...args)`, we immediately and clearly express that our new function receives several (possibly zero) arguments.
- You need not do anything to get an array. The console log shows that `args` is really an array.
- Writing `somethingElse(...args)` is much clearer than the alternative way that we had to use earlier (using `apply()`).

By the way, the `arguments` object is still available in the current version of JavaScript. If you want to create an array from it, you have two alternative ways of doing so, without having to resort to the `Array.prototype.slice.call` trick:

- Use the `from()` method and write `var myArray=Array.from(arguments)`.
- Write `let myArray=[...arguments]`, which shows yet another type of usage of the spread operator.

When we get to the topic of higher-order functions, writing functions that deal with other functions, with a possibly unknown number of parameters, will be commonplace.

JavaScript provides a much shorter way of doing this, and that's why you'll have to get accustomed to this usage. It's worth it!

One argument or many?

It's also possible to write functions that return functions, and in Chapter 6, *Producing Functions - Higher-Order Functions*, we will be seeing more of this. For instance, in lambda calculus, you don't write functions with several parameters, but only one; you do this by using a technique called **currying** (why would you do this? Hold that thought; we'll come to this later).

 Currying gets its name from Haskell Curry, who developed the concept. Note that there is an FP language that is named after him—*Haskell*; double recognition!

For instance, the function that we saw previously that sums three numbers would be written as follows:

```
const altSum3 = x => y => z => x + y + z;
```

Why did I change the function's name? Simply put, because this is *not* the same function as the one we saw previously. As is, though, it can be used to produce the very same results as our earlier function. That said, it differs in an important way. Let's look at how you would use it, say, to sum the numbers 1, 2, and 3:

```
altSum3(1)(2)(3); // 6
```

 Test yourself before reading on, and think on this: what would have been returned if you had written altSum3(1,2,3) instead? Tip: it would not be a number! For the full answer, keep reading.

How does this work? Separating it into many calls can help; this would be the way the previous expression is actually calculated by the JavaScript interpreter:

```
let fn1 = altSum3(1);
let fn2 = fn1(2);
let fn3 = fn2(3);
```

Think functionally! The result of calling altSum3(1) is, according to the definition, a function, which, in virtue of a closure, resolves to be equivalent to the following:

```
let fn1 = y => z => 1 + y + z;
```

Our `altSum3()` function is meant to receive a single argument, not three! The result of this call, `fn1`, is also a single-argument function. When you use `fn1(2)`, the result is again a function, also with a single parameter, which is equivalent to the following:

```
let fn2 = z => 1 + 2 + z;
```

And when you calculate `fn2(3)`, a value is finally returned—great! As we said, the function performs the same kind of calculations as we saw earlier, but in an intrinsically different way.

You might think that currying is just a peculiar trick: who would want to only use single-argument functions? You'll see the reasons for this when we consider how to join functions together in `Chapter 8`, *Connecting Functions – Pipelining and Composition*, and `Chapter 12`, *Building Better Containers – Functional Data Types*, where it won't be feasible to pass more than one parameter from one step to the next.

Functions as objects

The concept of first-class objects means that functions can be created, assigned, changed, passed as parameters, and returned as a result of yet other functions in the very same way that you can with, say, numbers or strings. Let's start with its definition. Let's look at how you usually define a function:

```
function xyzzy(...) { ... }
```

This is (almost) equivalent to writing the following:

```
var xyzzy = function(...) { ... }
```

However, this is not true for **hoisting**. In this case, JavaScript moves all definitions to the top of the current scope, but does not move the assignments; so, with the first definition you can invoke `xyzzy(...)` from any place in your code, but with the second, you cannot invoke the function until the assignment has been executed.

 See the parallel with the Colossal Cave Adventure game? Invoking `xyzzy(...)` anywhere won't always work! And, if you have never played that famous interactive fiction game, try it online—for example, at `http://www.web-adventures.org/cgi-bin/webfrotz?s=Adventure` or `http://www.amc.com/shows/halt-and-catch-fire/colossal-cave-adventure/landing`.

The point that we want to make is that a function can be assigned to a variable and can also be reassigned if desired. In a similar vein, we can define functions on the spot, when they are needed. We can even do this without naming them: as with common expressions, if they are used only once, then you don't need to name them or store them in a variable.

A React-Redux reducer

We can see another example that involves assigning functions. As we mentioned earlier in this chapter, React-Redux works by dispatching actions that are processed by a reducer. Usually, the reducer includes code with a switch:

```
function doAction(state = initialState, action) {
  let newState = {};
  switch (action.type) {
    case "CREATE":
      // update state, generating newState,
      // depending on the action data
      // to create a new item
      return newState;

    case "DELETE":
      // update state, generating newState,
      // after deleting an item
      return newState;

    case "UPDATE":
      // update an item,
      // and generate an updated state
      return newState;

    default:
      return state;
  }
}
```

 Providing `initialState` as a default value for `state` is a simple way of initializing the global state the first time around. Pay no attention to that default; it's not relevant for our example, but I included it just for the sake of completeness.

By taking advantage of the possibility of storing functions, we can build a **dispatch table** and simplify the preceding code. First, we initialize an object with the code for the functions for each action type.

Basically, we are just taking the preceding code and creating separate functions:

```
const dispatchTable = {
  CREATE: (state, action) => {
    // update state, generating newState;
    // depending on the action data
    // to create a new item
    return newState;
  },

  DELETE: (state, action) => {
    // update state, generating newState,
    // after deleting an item
    return newState;
  },

  UPDATE: (state, action) => {
    // update an item,
    // and generate an updated state
    return newState;
  }
};
```

We store the different functions that process each type of action as attributes in an object that will work as a dispatcher table. This object is created only once and is constant during the execution of the application. With it, we can now rewrite the action-processing code in a single line of code:

```
function doAction2(state = initialState, action) {
  return dispatchTable[action.type]
    ? dispatchTable[action.type](state, action)
    : state;
}
```

Let's analyze it: given the action, if action.type matches an attribute in the dispatching object, we execute the corresponding function taken from the object where it was stored. If there isn't a match, we just return the current state as Redux requires. This kind of code wouldn't be possible if we couldn't handle functions (storing and recalling them) as first-class objects.

An unnecessary mistake

There is, however, a common (though in fact, harmless) mistake that is usually made. You often see code like this:

```
fetch("some/remote/url").then(function(data) {
  processResult(data);
});
```

What does this code do? The idea is that a remote URL is fetched, and when the data arrives, a function is called—and this function itself calls `processResult` with `data` as an argument. That is to say, in the `then()` part, we want a function that, given `data`, calculates `processResult(data)`. But don't we already have such a function?

 A small bit of theory: in lambda calculus terms, we are replacing *λx.func x* with simply *func*—this is called an **eta conversion**, or more specifically, an **eta reduction**. (If you were to do it the other way round, it would be an **eta abstraction**.) In our case, it could be considered a (very, very small!) optimization, but its main advantage is shorter, more compact code.

Basically, there is a rule that you can apply whenever you see something like the following:

```
function someFunction(someData) {
  return someOtherFunction(someData);
}
```

This rule states that you can replace code resembling the preceding code with just `someOtherFunction`. So, in our example, we can directly write what follows:

```
fetch("some/remote/url").then(processResult);
```

This code is exactly equivalent to the previous method that we looked at (although it is infinitesimally quicker, since you avoid one function call), but it is simpler to understand?

This programming style is called **pointfree** style or **tacit** style, and its main characteristic is that you never specify the arguments for each function application. An advantage of this way of coding is that it helps the writer (and the future readers of the code) think about the functions themselves and their meanings instead of working at a low level, passing data around and working with it. In the shorter version of the code, there are no extraneous or irrelevant details: if you understand what the called function does, then you understand the meaning of the complete piece of code. In our text, we'll often (but not necessarily always) work in this way.

Unix/Linux users may already be accustomed to this style, because they work in a similar way when they use pipes to pass the result of a command as an input to another. When you write something as `ls|grep doc|sort`, the output of `ls` is the input to `grep`, and the latter's output is the input to `sort`—but input arguments aren't written out anywhere; they are implied. We'll come back to this in the *Pointfree style* section of `Chapter 8, Connecting Functions - Pipelining and Composition`.

Working with methods

There is, however, a case that you should be aware of: what happens if you are calling an object's method? Look at the following code:

```
fetch("some/remote/url").then(function(data) {
  myObject.store(data);
});
```

If your original code had been something along the lines of the preceding code, then the seemingly obvious transformed code would fail:

```
fetch("some/remote/url").then(myObject.store);
```

Why? The reason is that in the original code, the called method is bound to an object (`myObject`), but in the modified code, it isn't bound and is just a `free` function. We can then fix it in a simple way by using `bind()`, as follows:

```
fetch("some/remote/url").then(myObject.store.bind(myObject));
```

This is a general solution. When dealing with a method, you cannot just assign it; you must use `bind()` so that the correct context will be available. Look at the following code:

```
function doSomeMethod(someData) {
  return someObject.someMethod(someData);
}
```

Following this rule, code like the preceding code should be converted to the following:

```
const doSomeMethod = someObject.someMethod.bind(someObject);
```

Read more on `bind()` at `https://developer.mozilla.org/en/docs/Web/JavaScript/Reference/Global_objects/Function/bind`.

This looks rather awkward, and not too elegant, but it's required so that the method will be associated with the correct object. We will see one application of this when we *promisify* functions in `Chapter 6`, *Producing Functions - Higher-Order Functions*. Even if this code isn't so nice to look at, whenever you have to work with objects (and remember, we didn't say that we would be trying to aim for fully FP code, and did say that we would accept other constructs if they made things easier), you'll have to remember to bind methods before passing them as first-class objects in pointfree style.

Using functions in FP ways

There are several common coding patterns that actually take advantage of FP style, even if you weren't aware of it. In this section, we will go through them and look at the functional aspects of the code so that you can get more accustomed to this coding style.

Then, we'll look in detail at using functions in an FP way by considering several FP techniques, such as the following:

- Injection, which is needed for sorting different strategies, as well as other uses
- Callbacks and promises, introducing the continuation-passing style
- Polyfilling and stubbing
- Immediate invocation schemes

Injection – sorting it out

The first example of passing functions as parameters is provided by the `Array.prototype.sort()` method. If you have an array of strings and you want to sort it, you can just use the `sort()` method. For example, to alphabetically sort an array with the colors of the rainbow, we would write something like the following:

```
var colors = [
  "violet",
  "indigo",
  "blue",
  "green",
  "yellow",
  "orange",
  "red"
];
colors.sort();
console.log(colors);
// ["blue", "green", "indigo", "orange", "red", "violet", "yellow"]
```

Note that we didn't have to provide any parameters to the `sort()` call, but the array got sorted perfectly well. By default, this method sorts strings according to their ASCII internal representation. So, if you use this method to sort an array of numbers, it will fail, since it will decide that 20 must be between 100 and 3, because 100 precedes 20 (taken as strings!) and the latter precedes 3, so this needs fixing! The following code shows the problem:

```
var someNumbers = [3, 20, 100];
someNumbers.sort();

console.log(someNumbers);
// [100, 20, 3]
```

But let's forget numbers for a while and stick to sorting strings. We want to ask ourselves what would happen if we wanted to sort some Spanish words (`palabras`) but following the appropriate locale rules? We would be sorting strings, but the results wouldn't be correct:

```
var palabras = ["ñandú", "oasis", "mano", "natural", "mítico", "musical"];
palabras.sort();

console.log(palabras);
// ["mano", "musical", "mítico", "natural", "oasis", "ñandú"] --=wrong
result!
```

 For language or biology buffs, "ñandú" in English is *rhea*, a running bird somewhat similar to ostriches. There aren't many Spanish words beginning with *ñ*, and we happen to have these birds in my country, Uruguay, so that's the reason for the odd word!

Oops! In Spanish, *ñ* comes between *n* and *o*, but "ñandú" got sorted at the end. Also, "mítico" (in English, *mythical*; note the accented *í*) should appear between "mano" and "musical" because the tilde should be ignored. The appropriate way of solving this is by providing a comparison function to `sort()`. In this case, we can use the `localeCompare()` method as follows:

```
palabras.sort((a, b) => a.localeCompare(b, "es"));

console.log(palabras);
// ["mano", "mítico", "musical", "natural", "ñandú",
   "oasis"]
```

The `a.localeCompare(b, "es")` call compares the a and b strings and returns a negative value should a precede b, a positive value should a follow b, and 0 if a and b are the same—but according to Spanish ("es") ordering rules.

Now things are right! And the code could be made clearer by introducing a new function, `spanishComparison()`, to perform the required strings comparison:

```
const spanishComparison = (a, b) => a.localeCompare(b, "es");

palabras.sort(spanishComparison);
// sorts the palabras array according to Spanish rules:
// ["mano", "mítico", "musical", "natural", "ñandú",
"oasis"]
```

In upcoming chapters, we will be discussing how FP lets you write code in a more declarative fashion, producing more understandable code, and this sort of small change helps: when readers of the code get to the `sort`, they will immediately deduce what is being done, even if the comment wasn't present.

This way of changing the way that the `sort()` function works by injecting different comparison functions is actually a case of the strategy design pattern. We'll be learning more about this in `Chapter 11`, *Implementing Design Patterns – the Functional Way*.

Providing a `sort` function as a parameter (in a very FP way!) can also help with several other problems, such as the following:

- `sort()` only works with strings. If you want to sort numbers (as we tried to do previously), you have to provide a function that will compare numerically. For example, you would write something like `myNumbers.sort((a,b) => a-b)`.
- If you want to sort objects by a given attribute, you will use a function that compares to it. For example, you could sort people by age with something along the lines of `myPeople.sort((a,b) => a.age - b.age)`.

For more on the `localeCompare()` possibilities, see `https://developer. mozilla.org/en/docs/Web/JavaScript/Reference/Global_Objects/ String/localeCompare`. You can specify which locale rules to apply, in which order to place upper/lowercase letters, whether to ignore punctuation, and much more. But be careful: not all browsers may support the required extra parameters.

This is a simple example that you have probably used before, but it's an FP pattern, after all. Let's move on to an even more common usage of functions as parameters when you perform Ajax calls.

Callbacks, promises, and continuations

Probably the most used example of functions passed as first-class objects has to do with callbacks and promises. In Node, reading a file is accomplished asynchronously with something like the following code:

```
const fs = require("fs");

fs.readFile("someFile.txt", (err, data) => {
  if (err) {
    console.error(err); // or throw an error, or otherwise handle the
problem
  } else {
    console.log(data.toString()); // do something with the data
  }
});
```

The `readFile()` function requires a callback—in this example an anonymous function—that will get called when the file reading operation is finished.

A better way is using promises; read more at `https://developer.mozilla.org/en-US/docs/Web/JavaScript/Reference/Global_Objects/Promise`. With this, when performing an Ajax web service call using the more modern `fetch()` function, you could write something along the lines of the following code:

```
fetch("some/remote/url")
  .then(data => {
    // Do some work with the returned data
  })
  .catch(error => {
    // Process all errors here
  });
```

Note that if you had defined appropriate `processData(data)` and `processError(error)` functions, the code could have been shortened to `fetch("some/remote/url").then(processData).catch(processError)` along the lines that we saw previously.

Finally, you should also look into using `async/await`; read more about it at `https://developer.mozilla.org/en-US/docs/Web/JavaScript/Reference/Statements/async_function` and `https://developer.mozilla.org/en-US/docs/Web/JavaScript/Reference/Operators/await`.

Continuation passing style

The preceding code, in which you call a function but also pass another function that is to be executed when the input/output operation is finished, can be considered a case of **continuation passing style (CPS)**. What is this technique of coding? One way of looking at it is by thinking about the question: *how would you program if using the* return *statement was forbidden?*

At first glance, this may appear to be an impossible situation. We can get out of our fix, however, by passing a callback to the called function, so that when that procedure is ready to return to the caller, instead of actually returning, it invokes the passed callback. By doing this, the callback provides the called function with the way to continue the process, hence the word *continuation*. We won't get into this now, but in Chapter 9, *Designing Functions - Recursion*, we will study it in depth. In particular, CPS will help us to avoid an important recursion restriction, as we'll see.

Working out how to use continuations is sometimes challenging, but always possible. An interesting advantage of this way of coding is that by specifying yourself how the process is going to continue, you can go beyond all the usual structures (if, while, return, and so on) and implement whatever mechanisms you want. This can be very useful in some kinds of problems where the process isn't necessarily linear. Of course, this can also lead to you inventing a kind of control structure that is far worse than the possible usage of GOTO statements that you might imagine! *Figure 3.1* shows the dangers of that practice!

Figure 3.1: What's the worse that could happen if you start messing with the program flow?

 This XKCD comic is available online at https://xkcd.com/292/

You are not limited to passing a single continuation. As with promises, you can provide two or more alternative callbacks. And this, by the way, can provide a solution to the problem of how you would work with exceptions. If we simply allowed a function to throw an error, it would be an implied return to the caller, and we don't want this. The way out of this is to provide an alternative callback (that is, a different continuation) to be used whenever an exception is thrown (in Chapter 12, *Building Better Containers - Functional Data Types*, we'll find another solution using monads):

```
function doSomething(a, b, c, normalContinuation, errorContinuation) {
    let r = 0;
    // ... do some calculations involving a, b, and c,
    // and store the result in r
    // if an error happens, invoke:
    // errorContinuation("description of the error")
    // otherwise, invoke:
    // normalContinuation(r)
}
```

Using CPS can even allow you to go beyond the control structures that JavaScript provides, but that would be beyond the objectives of this book, so I'll let you research that on your own!

Polyfills

Being able to assign functions dynamically (in the same way that you can assign different values to a variable) also allows you to work more efficiently when defining polyfills.

Detecting Ajax

Let's go back a bit in time to when Ajax started to appear. Given that different browsers implemented Ajax calls in distinct fashions, you would always have to code around these differences. The following code shows how you would go about implementing an Ajax call by testing several different conditions:

```
function getAjax() {
    let ajax = null;
    if (window.XMLHttpRequest) {
        // modern browser? use XMLHttpRequest
        ajax = new XMLHttpRequest();
    } else if (window.ActiveXObject) {
        // otherwise, use ActiveX for IE5 and IE6
        ajax = new ActiveXObject("Microsoft.XMLHTTP");
    } else {
```

```
      throw new Error("No Ajax support!");
   }
   return ajax;
}
```

This worked, but implied that you would redo the Ajax check for each and every call, even though the results of the test wouldn't ever change. There's a more efficient way to do this, and it has to do with using functions as first-class objects. We could define *two* different functions, test for the condition only once, and then assign the correct function to be used later; study the following code for such an alternative:

```
(function initializeGetAjax() {
  let myAjax = null;

  if (window.XMLHttpRequest) {
    // modern browsers? use XMLHttpRequest
    myAjax = function() {
      return new XMLHttpRequest();
    };
  } else if (window.ActiveXObject) {
    // it's ActiveX for IE5 and IE6
    myAjax = function() {
      new ActiveXObject("Microsoft.XMLHTTP");
    };
  } else {
    myAjax = function() {
      throw new Error("No Ajax support!");
    };
  }
  window.getAjax = myAjax;
})();
```

This piece of code shows two important concepts. First, we can dynamically assign a function: when this code runs, window.getAjax (that is, the global getAjax variable) will get one of three possible values according to the current browser. When you later call getAjax() in your code, the right function will execute without you needing to do any further browser-detection tests.

The second interesting idea is that we define the initializeGetAjax function, and immediately run it—this pattern is called the **immediately invoked function expression (IIFE)**. The function runs, but *cleans up after itself*, because all its variables are local and won't even exist after the function runs. We'll learn more about this later.

Adding missing functions

This idea of defining a function on the run also allows us to write *polyfills* that provide otherwise missing functions. For example, let's say that we had some code such as the following:

```
if (currentName.indexOf("Mr.") !== -1) {
  // it's a man
  ...
}
```

Instead of this, you might very much prefer using the newer, clearer way of, and just write the following:

```
if (currentName.includes("Mr.")) {
  // it's a man
  ...
}
```

What happens if your browser doesn't provide `.includes()`? Once again, we can define the appropriate function on the fly, but only if needed. If `.includes()` is available, you need to do nothing, but if it is missing, you need to define a polyfill that will provide the very same workings. The following code shows an example of such a polyfill:

 You can find polyfills for many modern JavaScript features at Mozilla's developer site. For example, the polyfill we used for `includes` was taken directly from `https://developer.mozilla.org/en/docs/Web/ JavaScript/Reference/Global_Objects/String/includes`.

```
if (!String.prototype.includes) {
  String.prototype.includes = function(search, start) {
    "use strict";
    if (typeof start !== "number") {
      start = 0;
    }

    if (start + search.length > this.length) {
      return false;
    } else {
      return this.indexOf(search, start) !== -1;
    }
  };
}
```

When this code runs, it checks whether the String prototype already has the includes method. If not, it assigns a function to it that does the same job, so from that point onward, you'll be able to use .includes() without further worries. By the way, there are other ways of defining a polyfill: check the answer to question *3.5* for an alternative.

 Directly modifying a standard type's prototype object is usually frowned upon, because in essence, it's equivalent to using a global variable, and thus it's prone to errors; however, this case (writing a polyfill for a well established and known function) is quite unlikely to provoke any conflicts.

Finally, if you happened to think that the Ajax example shown previously was old hat, consider this: if you want to use the more modern fetch() way of calling services, you will also find that not all modern browsers support it (check http://caniuse.com/#search=fetch to verify this), and so you'll have to use a polyfill, such as the one at https://github.com/github/fetch. Study the code and you'll see that it basically uses the same method as described previously to see whether a polyfill is needed and to create it.

Stubbing

Here, we will look at a use case that is similar in some aspects to using a polyfill: having a function do different work depending on the environment. The idea is to perform **stubbing**, an idea that comes from testing that involves replacing a function with another that does a simpler job, instead of doing the actual work.

Stubbing is commonly used with logging functions. You may want the application to perform detailed logging when in development, but not to say a peep when in production. A common solution would be to write something along the lines of the following:

```
let myLog = someText => {
  if (DEVELOPMENT) {
    console.log(someText); // or some other way of logging
  } else {
    // do nothing
  }
}
```

This works, but as in the example of Ajax detection, it does more work than it needs to because it checks whether the application is in development every time.

We could simplify the code (and get a really, really tiny performance gain!) if we stub out the logging function so that it won't actually log anything; an easy implementation is as follows:

```
let myLog;
if (DEVELOPMENT) {
  myLog = someText => console.log(someText);
} else {
  myLog = someText => {};
}
```

We can even do better with the ternary operator:

```
const myLog = DEVELOPMENT
  ? someText => console.log(someText)
  : someText => {};
```

This is a bit more cryptic, but I prefer it because it uses a `const`, which cannot be modified.

 Given that JavaScript allows us to call functions with more parameters than arguments, and given that we aren't doing anything in `myLog()` when we are not in development, we could also have written `() => {}` and it would have worked fine. However, I do prefer keeping the same signature, and that's why I specified the `someText` argument, even if it wouldn't be used. It's your call!

You'll notice that we are using the concept of functions as first-class objects over and over again; look through all the code samples and you'll see!

Immediate invocation

There's yet another common usage of functions, usually seen in popular libraries and frameworks, that lets you bring some modularity advantages from other languages into JavaScript (even the older versions!). The usual way of writing this is something like the following:

```
(function() {
  // do something...
})();
```

 Another equivalent style is `(function(){ ... }())`—note the different placement of the parentheses for the function call. Both styles have their fans; pick whichever suits you, but just follow it consistently.

You can also have the same style, but pass some arguments to the function that will be used as the initial values for its parameters:

```
(function(a, b) {
  // do something, using the
  // received arguments for a and b...
})(some, values);
```

Finally, you could also return something from the function:

```
let x = (function(a, b) {
  // ...return an object or function
})(some, values);
```

As we mentioned previously, the pattern itself is called the IIFE (pronounced *iffy*). The name is easy to understand: you are defining a function and calling it right away, so it gets executed on the spot. Why would you do this, instead of simply writing the code inline? The reason has to do with scopes.

 Note the parentheses around the function. These help the parser understand that we are writing an expression. If you were to omit the first set of parentheses, JavaScript would think you were writing a function declaration instead of an invocation. The parentheses also serve as a visual note, so readers of your code will immediately recognize the IIFE.

If you define any variables or functions within the IIFE, then because of how JavaScript defines the scope of functions, those definitions will be internal, and no other part of your code will be able to access them. Imagine that you wanted to write some complicated initialization, like the following:

```
function ready() { ... }

function set() { ... }

function go() { ... }

// initialize things calling ready(),
// set() and go() appropriately
```

What could go wrong? The problem hinges on the fact that you could (by accident) have a function with the same name of any of the three here, and hoisting would imply that the *last* function would be called:

```
function ready() {
  console.log("ready");
}
```

```
function set() {
  console.log("set");
}

function go() {
  console.log("go");
}

ready();
set();
go();

function set() {
  console.log("UNEXPECTED...");
}
// "ready"
// "UNEXPECTED"
// "go"
```

Oops! If you had used an IIFE, the problem wouldn't have happened. Also, the three inner functions wouldn't even be visible to the rest of the code, which helps to keep the global namespace less polluted. The following code shows a very common pattern for this:

```
(function() {
  function ready() {
    console.log("ready");
  }

  function set() {
    console.log("set");
  }

  function go() {
    console.log("go");
  }

  ready();
  set();
  go();
})();

function set() {
  console.log("UNEXPECTED...");
}
// "ready"
// "set"
// "go"
```

To see an example involving returned values, we could revisit the example from Chapter 1, *Becoming Functional - Several Questions*, and write the following, which would create a single counter:

```
const myCounter = (function() {
  let count = 0;
  return function() {
    count++;
    return count;
  };
})();
```

Then, every call to myCounter() would return an incremented count, but there is no chance that any other part of your code will overwrite the inner count variable because it's only accessible within the returned function.

Summary

In this chapter, we went over several ways of defining functions in JavaScript, focusing mainly on arrow functions, which have several advantages over standard functions, including being terser. We learned about the concept of currying (which we'll be revisiting later), considered some aspects of functions as first-class objects, and lastly, we considered several techniques that happen to be fully FP in concept. Rest assured that we'll be using everything in this chapter as the building blocks for more advanced techniques in the rest of the book; just wait and see!

In Chapter 4, *Behaving Properly – Pure Functions*, we will delve even more deeply into functions and learn about the concept of *pure functions*, which will lead us to an even better style of programming.

Questions

3.1 **Uninitialized object?** React-Redux programmers usually code **action creators** to simplify the creation of actions that will later be processed by a reducer. Actions are objects, which must include a type attribute that is used to determine what kind of action you are dispatching. The following code supposedly does this, but can you explain the unexpected results?

```
const simpleAction = t => {
  type: t;
};
```

```
console.log(simpleAction("INITIALIZE"));
// undefined
```

3.2. **Are arrows allowed?** Would everything be the same if you
defined listArguments() and listArguments2() from the *Working with arguments*
section by using arrow functions instead of the way we did, with the function keyword?

3.3. **One liner**: Some programmer, particularly thrifty with lines of code, suggested
rewriting doAction2() as a one-liner, even though you can't tell this from the formatting!
What do you think: is it correct or isn't it?

```
const doAction3 = (state = initialState, action) =>
  (dispatchTable[action.type] &&
    dispatchTable[action.type](state, action)) ||
  state;
```

3.4. **Spot the bug!** A programmer, working with a global store for state (similar in concept
to those of Redux, Mobx, Vuex, and others used by different web frameworks) wanted to
log (for debugging purposes) all calls to the store's set() method. After creating the new
store object, he wrote the following so that the arguments to store.set() would be
logged before actually being processed. Unfortunately, the code didn't work as expected.
What's the problem? Can you spot the mistake?

```
window.store = new Store();
const oldSet = window.store.set;
window.store.set = (...data) => (console.log(...data), oldSet(...data));
```

3.5. **Bindless binding**: Suppose that bind() was not available; how could you do a polyfill
for it?

4
Behaving Properly - Pure Functions

In `Chapter 3`, *Starting Out with Functions – A Core Concept*, we considered functions as the key elements in **Functional Programming (FP)**, went into detail about arrow functions, and introduced some concepts, such as injection, callbacks, polyfilling, and stubbing. In this chapter, we'll have the opportunity to revisit or apply some of those ideas. We will also do the following:

- Consider the notion of *purity*, and why we should care about *pure functions*—and *impure* functions as well!
- Examine the concept of *referential transparency*.
- Recognize the problems implied by side effects.
- Show some advantages of pure functions.
- Describe the main reasons behind impure functions.
- Find ways to minimize the number of impure functions.
- Focus on ways of testing both pure and impure functions.

Pure functions

Pure functions behave in the same way as mathematical functions and provide diverse benefits. A function is pure if it satisfies two conditions:

- **Given the same arguments, the function always calculates and returns the same result**: This should be true no matter how many times it's invoked or under which conditions you call it. This result cannot depend on any *outside* information or state, which could change during the program execution and cause it to return a different value. Nor can the function result depend on I/O results, random numbers, some other external variable, or a value that is not directly controllable.

- **When calculating its result, the function doesn't cause any observable** *side effects*: This includes output to I/O devices, the mutation of objects, changes to a program's state outside of the function, and so on.

If you want, you can simply say that pure functions don't depend on (and don't modify) anything outside their scope and always return the same result for the same input arguments.

Another word used in this context is **idempotency**, but it's not exactly the same. An idempotent function can be called as many times as desired, and will always produce the same result; however, this doesn't imply that the function is free from side effects. Idempotency is usually mentioned in the context of RESTful services. Let's look at a simple example showing the difference between purity and idempotency. A PUT call would cause a database record to be updated (a side effect), but if you repeat the call, the element will not be further modified, so the global state of the database won't change any further.

We might also invoke a software design principle and remind ourselves that a function should *do one thing, only one thing, and nothing but that thing*. If a function does anything else and has some hidden functionality, then that dependency on the state will mean that we won't be able to predict the function's output and make things harder for us as developers.

Let's look into these conditions in more detail.

Referential transparency

In mathematics, **referential transparency** is the property that lets you replace an expression with its value without changing the results of whatever you were doing.

 The counterpart of referential transparency is, appropriately enough, **referential opacity**. A referentially opaque function cannot guarantee that it will always produce the same result, even when called with the same arguments.

To give a simple example, let's consider what happens with an optimizing compiler that performs *constant folding*. Suppose you have a sentence like this:

```
const x = 1 + 2 * 3;
```

The compiler might optimize the code to the following by noting that 2 * 3 is a constant value:

```
const x = 1 + 6;
```

Even better, a new round of optimization could avoid the sum altogether:

```
const x = 7;
```

To save execution time, the compiler is taking advantage of the fact that all mathematical expressions and functions are (by definition) referentially transparent. On the other hand, if the compiler cannot predict the output of a given expression, it won't be able to optimize the code in any fashion, and the calculation will have to be done at runtime.

 In lambda calculus, if you replace the value of an expression involving a function with the calculated value for the function, then that operation is called a **β (beta) reduction**. Note that you can only do this safely with referentially transparent functions.

All arithmetical expressions (involving both mathematical operators and functions) are referentially transparent: 22*9 can always be replaced by 198. Expressions involving I/O are not transparent, given that their results cannot be known until they are executed. For the same reason, expressions involving date- and time-related functions or random numbers are also not transparent.

With regard to JavaScript functions that you can produce yourself, it's quite easy to write some that won't fulfill the *referential transparency* condition. In fact, a function is not even required to return a value, though the JavaScript interpreter will return an undefined value in that situation.

 Some languages distinguish between functions, which are expected to return a value, and procedures, which do not return anything, but that's not the case with JavaScript. There are also some languages that provide the means to ensure that functions are referentially transparent.

If you wanted to, you could classify functions as the following:

- **Pure functions**: These return a value that depends only on its arguments and have no side effects whatsoever.
- **Side effects**: These don't return anything (actually, in JavaScript, these functions return an `undefined` value, but that's not relevant here), but do produce some kind of side effects.
- **Functions with side effects**: This means that they return a value that may not only depend on the function arguments, but also involve side effects.

In FP, much emphasis is put on the first group, referentially transparent pure functions. Not only can a compiler reason about the program behavior (and thus be able to optimize the generated code), but also the programmer can more easily reason about the program and the relationship between its components. This in turn can help prove the correctness of an algorithm or optimize the code by replacing a function with an equivalent one.

Side effects

What are **side effects**? We can define these as a change in state or an interaction with outside elements (the user, a web service, another computer, whatever) that occurs during the execution of some calculations or a process.

There's a possible misunderstanding as to the scope of this meaning. In common daily speech, when you speak of side effects, it's a bit like talking about *collateral damage*—some unintended consequences for a given action; however, in computing, we include every possible effect or change outside the function. If you write a function that is meant to perform a `console.log()` call to display a result, then that would be considered a side effect, even if it's exactly what you intended the function to do in the first place!

In this section, we will look at the following:

- Common side effects in JavaScript programming
- The problems that global and inner states cause
- The possibility of functions mutating their arguments
- Some functions that are always troublesome

Usual side effects

In programming, there are (too many!) things that are considered side effects. In JavaScript programming, including both frontend and backend coding, the more common ones you may find include the following:

- Changing global variables.
- Mutating objects received as arguments.
- Performing any kind of I/O, such as showing an alert message or logging some text.
- Working with, and changing, the filesystem.
- Updating a database.
- Calling a web service.

- Querying or modifying the DOM.
- Triggering any external process.
- Just calling another function that happens to produce a side effect of its own. You could say that impurity is contagious: a function that calls an impure function automatically becomes impure on its own!

With this definition, let's start looking at what can cause functional impurity (or *referential opaqueness*).

Global state

Of all the preceding points, the most common reason for side effects is the usage of nonlocal variables that share a global state with other parts of the program. Since pure functions, by definition, always return the same output value given the same input arguments, if a function refers to anything outside its internal state, it automatically becomes impure. Furthermore, and this is a hindrance to debugging, to understand what a function has done, you must understand how the state got its current values, and that means understanding all of the past history from your program: not easy!

Let's write a function to detect whether a person is a legal adult by checking whether they were born at least 18 years ago. (Okay, that's not precise enough, because we are not considering the day and month of birth, but bear with me; the problem is elsewhere.) A version of an `isOldEnough()` function could be as follows:

```
let limitYear = 1999;

const isOldEnough = birthYear => birthYear <= limitYear;

console.log(isOldEnough(1960)); // true
console.log(isOldEnough(2001)); // false
```

The `isOldEnough()` function correctly detects whether a person is at least 18 years old, but it depends on an external variable for that (the variable is good for 2017 only). You cannot tell what the function does unless you know about the external variable and how it got its value. Testing would also be hard; you'd have to remember creating the global `limitYear` variable or all your tests would fail to run. Even though the function works, the implementation isn't the best that it could possibly be.

There is an exception to this rule. Check out the following case: is the following `circleArea()` function, which calculates the area of a circle given its radius, pure or not?

```
const PI = 3.14159265358979;
const circleArea = r => PI * Math.pow(r, 2); // or PI * r ** 2
```

Even though the function is accessing an external state, the fact that `PI` is a constant (and thus cannot be modified) would allow us to substitute it inside `circleArea` with no functional change, and so we should accept that the function is pure. The function will always return the same value for the same argument, and thus fulfills our purity requirements.

 Even if you were to use `Math.PI` instead of a constant as we defined in the code (a better idea, by the way), the argument would still be the same; the constant cannot be changed, so the function remains pure.

Here, we have dealt with problems caused by the global state; let's now move on to the inner state.

Inner state

The notion is also extended to internal variables, in which a local state is stored and then used for future calls. In this case, the external state is unchanged, but there are side effects that imply future differences as to the returned values from the function. Let's imagine a `roundFix()` rounding function that takes into account whether it has been rounding up or down too much so that the next time, it will round the other way, bringing the accumulated difference closer to zero. Our function will have to accumulate the effects of previous roundings to decide how to proceed next. The implementation could be as follows:

```
const roundFix = (function() {
  let accum = 0;
  return n => {
    // reals get rounded up or down
    // depending on the sign of accum
    let nRounded = accum > 0 ? Math.ceil(n) : Math.floor(n);
    console.log("accum", accum.toFixed(5), " result", nRounded);
    accum += n - nRounded;
    return nRounded;
  };
})();
```

Some comments regarding this function:

- The `console.log()` line is just for the sake of this example; it wouldn't be included in the real-world function. It lists the accumulated difference up to the point and the result it will return: the given number rounded up or down.
- We are using the IIFE pattern that we saw in the `myCounter()` example in the *Immediate Invocation* section of `Chapter 3`, *Starting Out with Functions – A Core Concept*, in order to get a hidden internal variable.
- The nRounded calculation could also be written as `Math[accum > 0 ? "ceil": "floor"](n)`—we test `accum` to see what method to invoke (`"ceil"` or `"floor"`) and then use the `Object["method"]` notation to indirectly invoke `Object.method()`. The way we used it, I think, is more clear, but I just wanted to give you a heads up in case you happen to find this other coding style.

Running this function with just two values (recognize them?) shows that results are not always the same for a given input. The `result` part of the console log shows how the value got rounded, up or down:

```
roundFix(3.14159); // accum  0.00000    result 3
roundFix(2.71828); // accum  0.14159    result 3
roundFix(2.71828); // accum -0.14013    result 2
roundFix(3.14159); // accum  0.57815    result 4
roundFix(2.71828); // accum -0.28026    result 2
roundFix(2.71828); // accum  0.43802    result 3
roundFix(2.71828); // accum  0.15630    result 3
```

The first time around, `accum` is zero, so `3.14159` gets rounded down and `accum` becomes `0.14159` in our favor. The second time, since `accum` is positive (meaning that we have been rounding in our favor), then `2.71828` gets rounded up to 3, and now `accum` becomes negative. The third time, the same `2.71828` value gets rounded down to 2, because then the accumulated difference was negative—we got different values for the same input! The rest of the example is similar; you can get the same value rounded up or down, depending on the accumulated differences, because the function's result depends on its inner state.

This usage of the internal state is the reason why many FP programmers think that using objects is potentially bad. In OOP, we developers are used to storing information (attributes) and using them for future calculations; however, this usage is considered impure, insofar as repeated method calls may return different values, despite the fact that the same arguments are being passed.

We have now dealt with the problems caused by both global and inner states, but there are still more possible side effects. For example, what happens if a function changes the values of its arguments? Let's consider this next.

Argument mutation

You also need to be aware of the possibility that an impure function will modify its arguments. In JavaScript, arguments are passed by value, except in the case of arrays and objects, which are passed by reference. This implies that any modification to the parameters of the function will affect an actual modification of the original object or array. This can be further obscured by the fact that there are several **mutator** methods, that change the underlying objects by definition. For example, say you wanted a function that would find the maximum element of an array of strings (of course, if it were an array of numbers, you could simply use `Math.max()` with no further ado). A short implementation could be as follows:

```
const maxStrings = a => a.sort().pop();

let countries = ["Argentina", "Uruguay", "Brasil", "Paraguay"];
console.log(maxStrings(countries)); // "Uruguay"
```

The function does provide the correct result (and if you worry about foreign languages, we already saw a way around that in the *Injection - sorting it out* section of Chapter 3, *Starting Out with Functions – A Core Concept*), but it has a defect. Let's see what happened with the original array:

```
console.log(countries); // ["Argentina", "Brasil", "Paraguay"]
```

Oops—the original array was modified; this is a side effect by definition! If you were to call `maxStrings(countries)` again, then instead of returning the same result as before, it would produce another value; clearly, this is not a pure function. In this case, a quick solution is to work on a copy of the array (and we can use the spread operator to help), but we'll be dealing with more ways of avoiding these sorts of problems in Chapter 10, *Ensuring Purity – Immutability*:

```
const maxStrings2 = a => [...a].sort().pop();

let countries = ["Argentina", "Uruguay", "Brasil", "Paraguay"];
console.log(maxStrings2(countries)); // "Uruguay"
console.log(countries); // ["Argentina", "Uruguay", "Brasil", "Paraguay"]
```

So now we have found yet another cause for side effects: functions that modify their own arguments. There's a final case to consider: functions that just have to be impure!

Troublesome functions

Finally, some functions also cause problems. For instance, `Math.random()` is impure: it doesn't always return the same value, and it would certainly defeat its purpose if it did! Furthermore, each call to the function modifies a global *seed* value, from which the next *random* value will be calculated.

 The fact that random numbers are actually calculated by an internal function, and are therefore not random at all (if you know the formula that's used and the initial value of the seed), implies that *pseudorandom* would be a better name for them.

For instance, consider the following function that generates random letters (`"A"` to `"Z"`):

```
const getRandomLetter = () => {
  const min = "A".charCodeAt();
  const max = "Z".charCodeAt();
  return String.fromCharCode(
    Math.floor(Math.random() * (1 + max - min)) + min
  );
};
```

The fact that it receives no arguments, but is expected to produce *different* results upon each call, clearly points out that this function is impure.

 Go to `https://developer.mozilla.org/en-US/docs/Web/JavaScript/Reference/Global_Objects/Math/random` for the explanation for the `getRandomLetter()` function I wrote and `https://developer.mozilla.org/en-US/docs/Web/JavaScript/Reference/Global_Objects/String` for the `.charCodeAt()` method.

Impurity can be inherited by calling functions. If a function uses an impure function, it immediately becomes impure itself. We might want to use `getRandomLetter()` in order to generate random filenames, with an optional given extension; our `getRandomFileName()` function could then be as follows:

```
const getRandomFileName = (fileExtension = "") => {
  const NAME_LENGTH = 12;
  let namePart = new Array(NAME_LENGTH);
  for (let i = 0; i < NAME_LENGTH; i++) {
    namePart[i] = getRandomLetter();
  }
  return namePart.join("") + fileExtension;
};
```

In `Chapter 5`, *Programming Declaratively – A Better Style*, we will see a more functional way of initializing a `namePart` array, by using `map()`.

Because of its usage of `getRandomLetter()`, `getRandomFileName()` is also impure, though it performs as expected, correctly producing totally random file names:

```
console.log(getRandomFileName(".pdf"));   // "SVHSSKHXPQKG.pdf"
console.log(getRandomFileName(".pdf"));   // "DCHKTMNWFHYZ.pdf"
console.log(getRandomFileName(".pdf"));   // "GBTEFTVVHADO.pdf"
console.log(getRandomFileName(".pdf"));   // "ATCBVUOSXLXW.pdf"
console.log(getRandomFileName(".pdf"));   // "OIFADZKKNVAH.pdf"
```

Keep this function in mind; we'll see some ways around the unit testing problem later in this chapter, and we'll rewrite it a bit to help out with that.

The concern about impurity also extends to functions that access the current time or date, because their results will depend on an outside condition (namely the time of day) that is part of the *global state* of the application. We could rewrite our `isOldEnough()` function to remove the dependency upon a global variable, but it wouldn't help much. An attempt could be as follows:

```
const isOldEnough2 = birthYear =>
  birthYear <= new Date().getFullYear() - 18;

console.log(isOldEnough2(1960)); // true
console.log(isOldEnough2(2001)); // false
```

A problem has been removed—the new `isOldEnough2()` function is now *safer*. Also, as long as you don't use it near midnight just before new year's day, it will consistently return the same results, so you could say, paraphrasing the Ivory Soap slogan from the nineteenth century, that it's *about 99.44% pure*; however, an inconvenience remains: how would you test it? If you were to write some tests that worked fine today, then next year they'd start to fail. We'll have to work a bit to solve this, and we'll see how later on.

Several other functions that are also impure are those that cause I/O. If a function gets input from a source (a web service, the user himself, a file, or some other source), then obviously the returned result may vary. You should also consider the possibility of an I/O error, so the very same function, calling the same service or reading the same file, might at some point fail for reasons outside its control (you should assume that your filesystem, database, socket, and so on could be unavailable, and thus a given function call might produce an error instead of the expected constant, unvarying, answer).

Even a pure output and a generally safe statement (such as a `console.log()`) that doesn't change anything internally (at least in a visible way) causes some side effects because the user does see a change: the produced output.

Does this imply that we won't ever be able to write a program that requires random numbers, handles dates, or performs I/O, and also uses pure functions? Not at all—but it does mean that some functions won't be pure, and they will have some disadvantages that we will have to consider; we'll return to this in a bit.

Advantages of pure functions

The main advantage of using pure functions comes from the fact that they don't have any side effects. When you call a pure function, you don't need to worry about anything other than which arguments you are passing to it. Also, more to the point, you can be sure that you cannot cause any problems or break anything else because the function will only work with whatever you give it, and not with outside sources. But this is not their only advantage. Let's learn more in the following sections.

Order of execution

Another way of looking at what we have been saying in this chapter is to see pure functions as **robust**. You know that their execution—in whichever order—won't ever have any sort of impact on the system. This idea can be extended further: you could evaluate pure functions in parallel, resting assured that results wouldn't vary from what you would get in a single-threaded execution.

 Unfortunately, JavaScript greatly restricts us in our parallel programming. We can make do, in very restricted ways, with web workers, but that's about as far as it goes. For Node developers, the `cluster` module may help out, though it isn't actually an alternative to threads, and only lets you spawn multiple processes, letting you use all available CPU cores. To sum it up, you don't get facilities such as Java's threads, for example, so parallelization isn't really an FP advantage in JavaScript terms.

When you work with pure functions, another consideration to keep in mind is that there's no explicit need to specify the order in which they should be called. If you work with mathematics, an expression such as `f(2) + f(5)` is always the same as `f(5) + f(2)`; this is called the **commutative property**.

However, when you deal with impure functions, that can be `false`, as shown in the following purposefully written tricky function:

```
var mult = 1;
const f = x => {
 mult = -mult;
   return x * mult;
};

console.log(f(2) + f(5)); //  3
console.log(f(5) + f(2)); // -3
```

With impure functions such as the previous one, you cannot assume that calculating `f(3)+f(3)` would produce the same result as `2*f(3)`, or that `f(4)-f(4)` would actually be 0; check it out for yourself! More common mathematical properties down the drain.

Why should you care? When you are writing code, willingly or not, you are always keeping in mind those properties you learned about, such as the commutative property. So while you might think that both expressions should produce the same result and code accordingly, you may be in for a surprise when using impure functions, with hard-to-find bugs that are difficult to fix.

Memoization

Since the output of a pure function for a given input is always the same, you can cache the function results and avoid a possibly costly recalculation. This process, which implies evaluating an expression only the first time and caching the result for later calls, is called **memoization**.

We will come back to this idea in Chapter 6, *Producing Functions – Higher-Order Functions*, but let's look at an example done by hand. The Fibonacci sequence is always used for this example because of its simplicity and its hidden calculation costs. This sequence is defined as follows:

- For $n=0$, *fib*$(n)=0$
- For $n=1$, *fib*$(n)=1$
- For $n>1$, *fib*$(n)=$*fib*$(n-2)+$*fib*$(n-1)$

Fibonacci's name actually comes from *filius Bonacci*, or *son of Bonacci*. He is best known for having introduced the usage of digits 0-9 as we know them today, instead of the cumbersome Roman numbers. He derived the sequence named after him as the answer to a puzzle involving rabbits!

You can read more about it, and Fibonacci's life in general, at `https://en.` `wikipedia.org/wiki/Fibonacci_number#History` or `https://plus.` `maths.org/content/life-and-numbers-fibonacci`.

If you run the numbers, the sequence starts with 0, then 1, and from that point onwards, each term is the sum of the two previous ones: 1 again, then 2, 3, 5, 8, 13, 21, and so on. Programming this series by using recursion is simple; we'll revisit this example in `Chapter` `9`, *Designing Functions – Recursion*. The following code, a direct translation of the definition, will do:

```
const fib = (n) => {
  if (n == 0) {
    return 0;

  } else if (n == 1) {
    return 1;

  } else {
    return fib(n - 2) + fib(n - 1);
  }
}
//
console.log(fib(10)); // 55, a bit slowly
```

If you really go for one-liners, you could also write `const fib = (n)` `=> (n<=1) ? n : fib(n-2)+fib(n-1)`—do you see why? And more importantly, is it worth the loss of clarity?

If you try out this function for growing values of n, you'll soon realize that there is a problem, and computation starts taking too much time. For example, on my machine, I took some timings, measured in milliseconds and plotted them on the following graph (of course, your mileage may vary). Since the function is quite speedy, I had to run calculations 100 times for values of n between 0 and 40. Even then, the times for small values of n were really tiny; it was only from 25 onwards that I got interesting numbers.

The chart (see *Figure 4.1*) shows an exponential growth, which bodes ill:

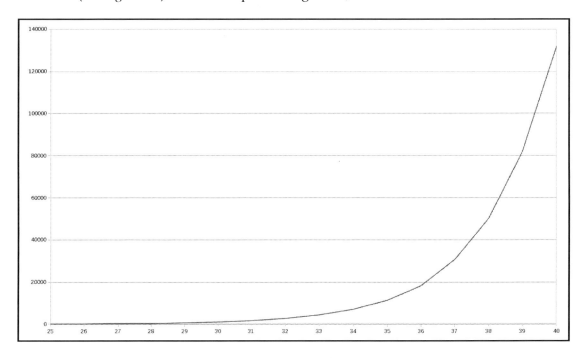

Figure 4.1: Calculation times for the fib() recursive function go up exponentially

If we draw a diagram of all the calls required to calculate fib(6), you'll notice the problem. Each node represents a call to calculate fib(n): we just note the value of n in the node. Every call, except those for *n=0* or *1*, requires further calls, as you can see in *Figure 4.2*:

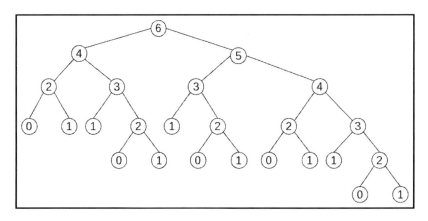

Figure 4.2: All the required calculations for fib(6) show lots of duplication

The reason for the increasing delays becomes obvious: for example, the calculation for fib(2) was repeated on four different occasions and fib(3) was itself calculated three times. Given that our function is pure, we could have stored the calculated values to avoid running the numbers over and over again. A possible version, using a cache array for previously calculated values, would be as follows:

```
let cache = [];
const fib2 = (n) => {
  if (cache[n] === undefined) {
    if (n === 0) {
      cache[0] = 0;

    } else if (n === 1) {
      cache[1] = 1;

    } else {
      cache[n] = fib2(n - 2) + fib2(n - 1);
    }
  }

  return cache[n];
}

console.log(fib2(10)); // 55, as before, but more quickly!
```

Initially, the cache array is empty. Whenever we need to calculate the value of fib2(n), we check whether it was already calculated beforehand. If that's not true, we do the calculation, but with a twist: instead of immediately returning the value, first we store it in the cache and then we return it. This means that no calculation will be done twice: after we have calculated fib2(n) for a certain n, future calls will not repeat the procedure, and will simply return the value that was already evaluated before.

A few short notes:

- We memoized the function by hand, but we can do it with a higher-order function. We'll see this later in Chapter 6, *Producing Functions – Higher-Order Functions*. It is perfectly possible to memoize a function without having to change or rewrite it.
- Using a global variable for the cache isn't a very good practice; we could have used an IIFE and a closure to hide the cache from sight—do you see how? See the myCounter() example in the *Immediate invocation* section of Chapter 3, *Starting Out with Functions – A Core Concept*, to review how we'd do this.

- Of course, you will be constrained by the available cache space, and it's possible you could eventually crash your application by eating up all available RAM. Resorting to external memory (a database, a file, or a cloud solution) would probably eat up all the performance advantages of caching. There are some standard solutions (involving eventually deleting items from the cache) but they are beyond the scope of this book.

Of course, you don't need to do this for every pure function in your program. You'd do this sort of optimization only for frequently called functions that take a certain important amount of time—if it were otherwise, then the added cache management time would end up costing more than whatever you expected to save!

Self-documentation

Pure functions have another advantage. Since everything the function needs to work with is given to it through its parameters, with no kind of hidden dependency whatsoever, when you read its source code, you have all you need to understand the function's objective.

An extra advantage: knowing that a function doesn't access anything beyond its parameters makes you more confident in using it, since you won't be accidentally producing a side effect; the only thing the function will accomplish is what you already learned through its documentation.

Unit tests (which we'll be covering in the next section) also work as documentation, because they provide examples of what the function returns when given certain arguments. Most programmers will agree that the best kind of documentation is full of examples, and each unit test can be considered such a sample case.

Testing

Yet another advantage of pure functions—and one of the most important ones—has to do with unit testing. Pure functions have a single responsibility: producing their output in terms of their input. So when you write tests for pure functions, your work is greatly simplified because there is no context to consider and no state to simulate.

You can simply focus on providing inputs and checking outputs because all function calls can be reproduced in isolation, independently from the *rest of the world*.

We have seen several aspects of pure functions. Let's move on and learn about impure functions a bit, and finish by testing both pure and impure functions.

Impure functions

If you decided to completely forego all kinds of side effects, then your programs would only be able to work with hardcoded inputs, and wouldn't be able to show you the calculated results! Similarly, most web pages would be useless: you wouldn't be able to make any web services calls or update the DOM; you'd have static pages only. And your Node code would be really useless for server-side work, as it wouldn't be able to perform any I/O.

Reducing side effects is a good goal in FP, but we shouldn't go overboard with it! So let's think of how to avoid using impure functions, if possible, and how to deal with them if not, looking for the best possible way to contain or limit their scope.

Avoiding impure functions

Earlier in this chapter, we saw the more common reasons for using impure functions. Let's now consider how we can reduce the number of impure functions, even if doing away with all of them isn't really feasible. Basically, we'll have two methods for this:

- Avoiding the usage of state
- Using a common pattern, *injection*, to have impurity in a controlled fashion

Avoiding the usage of state

With regard to the usage of the global state—both getting and setting it—the solution is well known. The key points to this are as follows:

- Provide whatever is needed of the global state to the function as arguments.
- If the function needs to update the state, it shouldn't do it directly, but rather produce a new version of the state and return it.
- It should be the responsibility of the caller to take the returned state, if any, and update the global state.

This is the technique that Redux uses for its reducers. The signature for a reducer is `(previousState, action) => newState`, meaning that it takes a state and an action as parameters and returns a new state as the result. Most specifically, the reducer is not supposed to simply change the `previousState` argument, which must remain untouched (we'll learn more about this in `Chapter 10`, *Ensuring Purity – Immutability*).

With regard to our first version of the `isOldEnough()` function, which used a global `limitYear` variable, the change is simple enough: we just have to provide `limitYear` as a parameter for the function. With this change, it will become pure, since it will produce its result by only using its parameters. Even better, we should provide the current year and let the function do the math instead of forcing the caller to do so. Our newer version of the adult age test could then be as follows:

```
const isOldEnough3 = (currentYear, birthYear) => birthYear <=
currentYear-18;
```

Obviously, we'll have to change all the calls to provide the required `limitYear` argument (we could also use currying, as we will see in Chapter 7, *Transforming Functions – Currying and Partial Application*). The responsibility of initializing the value of `limitYear` still remains outside of the function, as before, but we have managed to avoid a defect.

We can also apply this solution to our peculiar `roundFix()` function. As you will recall, the function worked by accumulating the differences caused by rounding, and deciding whether to round up or down depending on the sign of that accumulator. We cannot avoid using that state, but we can split off the rounding part from the accumulating part. Our original code (with fewer comments and logging) looked as follows:

```
const roundFix1 = (function() {
  let accum = 0;
  return n => {
    let nRounded = accum > 0 ? Math.ceil(n) : Math.floor(n);
    accum += n - nRounded;
    return nRounded;
  };
})();
```

The newer version would have two parameters:

```
const roundFix2 = (a, n) => {
  let r = a > 0 ? Math.ceil(n) : Math.floor(n);
  a += n - r;
  return {a, r};
};
```

How would you use this function? Initializing the accumulator, passing it to the function, and updating it afterward are now the responsibility of the caller code. You would have something like the following:

```
let accum = 0;

// ...some other code...
```

```
let {a, r} = roundFix2(accum, 3.1415);
accum = a;
console.log(accum, r); // 0.1415 3
```

Note the following:

- The `accum` phrase is now part of the global state of the application.
- Since `roundFix2()` needs it, the current accumulator value is provided in each call.
- The caller is responsible for updating the global state, not `roundFix2()`.

 Note the usage of the destructuring assignment in order to allow a function to return more than a value and easily store each one in a different variable. For more on this, go to `https://developer.mozilla.org/en/docs/Web/JavaScript/Reference/Operators/Destructuring_assignment`.

This new `roundFix2()` function is totally pure and can be easily tested. If you want to hide the accumulator from the rest of the application, you could still use a closure, as we have seen in other examples, but that would again introduce impurity in your code—your call!

Injecting impure functions

If a function becomes impure because it needs to call another function that is itself impure, a way around this problem is to inject the required function in the call. This technique actually provides more flexibility in your code and allows for easier future changes, as well as less complex unit testing.

Let's consider the random filename generator function that we saw earlier. The problematic part of this function is its usage of `getRandomLetter()` to produce the filename:

```
const getRandomFileName = (fileExtension = "") => {
  ...
  for (let i = 0; i < NAME_LENGTH; i++) {
    namePart[i] = getRandomLetter();
  }
  ...
};
```

A way to solve this is to replace the impure function with an injected external one; we must now provide a `randomLetterFunc()` argument for our random filename function to use:

```
const getRandomFileName2 = (fileExtension = "", randomLetterFunc) => {
  const NAME_LENGTH = 12;
```

```
    let namePart = new Array(NAME_LENGTH);
    for (let i = 0; i < NAME_LENGTH; i++) {
      namePart[i] = randomLetterFunc();
    }
    return namePart.join("") + fileExtension;
};
```

Now, we have removed the inherent impurity from this function. If we want to provide a predefined pseudorandom function that actually returns fixed, known, values, we will be able to easily unit test this function; we'll be seeing how to do this in the following examples. The usage of the function will change, and we would have to write the following:

```
    let fn = getRandomFileName2(".pdf", getRandomLetter);
```

If this bothers you, you may want to provide a default value for the randomLetterFunc **parameter**, as follows:

```
const getRandomFileName2 = (
  fileExtension = "",
  randomLetterFunc = getRandomLetter
) => {
  ...
};
```

You can also solve this using partial application, as we'll be seeing in Chapter 7, *Transforming Functions – Currying and Partial Application*.

This hasn't actually avoided the usage of impure functions. Normally, you'll call getRandomFileName() by providing it with the random letter generator we wrote, so it will behave as an impure function; however, for testing purposes, if you provide a function that returns predefined (that is, not random) letters, you'll be able to test it as if it was pure much more easily.

But what about the original problem function, getRandomLetter()? We can apply the same trick and write a new version, like the following, which will have an argument that will produce random numbers:

```
const getRandomLetter = (getRandomInt = Math.random) => {
  const min = "A".charCodeAt();
  const max = "Z".charCodeAt();
  return String.fromCharCode(
    Math.floor(getRandomInt() * (1 + max - min)) + min
  );
};
```

For normal usage, `getRandomFileName()` would call `getRandomLetter()` without providing any parameters, which would imply that the called function would behave in its expected random ways. But if we want to test whether the function does what we wanted, we can run it with an injected function that will return whatever we decide, letting us test it thoroughly.

This idea is actually very important and has a wide spectrum of applications to other problems. For example, instead of having a function directly access the DOM, we can provide it with injected functions that would do this. For testing purposes, it would be simple to verify that the tested function actually does what it needs to do without really interacting with the DOM (of course, we'd have to find some other way to test those DOM-related functions). This can also apply to functions that need to update the DOM, generate new elements, and do all sorts of manipulations—you just use some intermediary functions.

Is your function pure?

Let's end this section by considering an important question: can you ensure that a function is actually pure? To show the difficulties of this task, we'll go back to the simple `sum3()` function that we saw in the *Spread* section of `Chapter 1`, *Becoming Functional – Several Questions*, just rewritten to use arrow functions for brevity. Would you say that this function is pure? It certainly looks like it!

```
const sum3 = (x, y, z) => x + y + z;
```

Let's see: the function doesn't access anything but its parameters, doesn't even try to modify them (not that it could (or could it?)), doesn't perform any I/O, or work with any of the impure functions or methods that we mentioned earlier. What could go wrong?

The answer has to do with checking your assumptions. For example, who says the arguments for this function should be numbers? You might say to yourself *Okay, they could be strings, but the function would still be pure, wouldn't it?*, but for an (assuredly evil!) answer to that, see the following code:

```
let x = {};
x.valueOf = Math.random;

let y = 1;
let z = 2;

console.log(sum3(x, y, z)); // 3.2034400919849431
console.log(sum3(x, y, z)); // 3.8537045249277906
console.log(sum3(x, y, z)); // 3.0833258308458734
```

Note the way that we assigned a new function to the `x.valueOf` method. We are taking full advantage of the fact that functions are first-class objects. See the *An unnecessary mistake* section in `Chapter 3`, *Starting Out with Functions – A Core Concept*, for more on this.

Well, `sum3()` ought to be pure, but it actually depends on whatever parameters you pass to it; in JavaScript, you can make a pure function behave in an impure way! You might console yourself by thinking that surely no one would pass such arguments, but edge cases are usually where bugs reside. But you need not resign yourself to abandoning the idea of pure functions. By adding some type checking (TypeScript might come in handy, as mentioned in the *Using transpilers* section of `Chapter 1`, *Becoming Functional – Several Questions*), you could at least prevent some cases, though JavaScript won't ever let you be totally sure that your code is *always* pure!

Over the course of these sections, we have gone through the characteristics of both pure and impure functions. Let's finish the chapter by looking at how we can test all these sorts of functions.

Testing – pure versus impure

We have seen how pure functions are conceptually better than impure ones, but we cannot set out on a crusade to vanquish all impurity from our code. First, no one can deny that side effects can be useful, or at least unavoidable: you will need to interact with the DOM or call a web service, and there are no ways to do this in a pure way. So, rather than bemoaning the fact that you have to allow for impurity, try to structure your code so that you can isolate the impure functions and let the rest of your code be the best it can possibly be.

With this in mind, you'll have to be able to write unit tests for all kinds of functions, pure or impure. Writing unit tests for functions is different, in terms of both their difficulty and complexity than dealing with pure or impure functions. While coding tests for the former is usually quite simple and follows a basic pattern, the latter usually requires scaffolding and complex setups. So let's finish this chapter by seeing how to go about testing both types of function.

Testing pure functions

Given the characteristics of pure functions that we have already described, most of your unit tests could simply be the following:

- Call the function with a given set of arguments.
- Verify that the results match what you expected.

Let's start with a couple of simple examples. Testing the isOldEnough() function would have been more complex than we needed for the version that required access to a global variable. On the other hand, the last version, isOldEnough3(), which didn't require anything because it received two parameters, is simple to test:

```
describe("isOldEnough", function() {
  it("is false for people younger than 18", () => {
    expect(isOldEnough3(1978, 1963)).toBe(false);
  });
  it("is true for people older than 18", () => {
    expect(isOldEnough3(1988, 1965)).toBe(true);
  });
  it("is true for people exactly 18", () => {
    expect(isOldEnough3(1998, 1980)).toBe(true);
  });
});
```

Testing another of the pure functions that we wrote is equally simple, but we must be careful because of precision considerations. If we test the circleArea function, we must use the Jasmine toBeCloseTo() matcher, which allows for approximate equality when dealing with floating-point numbers. Other than this, the tests are just about the same—call the function with known arguments and check the expected results:

```
describe("circle area", function() {
  it("is zero for radius 0", () => {
    let area = circleArea(0);
    expect(area).toBe(0);
  });
  it("is PI for radius 1", () => {
    let area = circleArea(1);
    expect(area).toBeCloseTo(Math.PI);
  });
  it("is approximately 12.5664 for radius 2", () => {
    let area = circleArea(2);
    expect(area).toBeCloseTo(12.5664);
  });
});
```

No difficulty whatsoever! The test run reports success for both suites (see *Figure 4.3*):

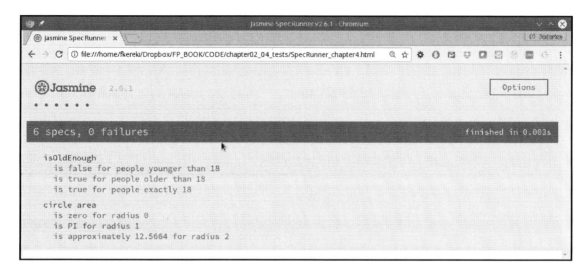

Figure 4.3: A successful test run for a pair of simple pure functions

Now that we don't have to worry about pure functions, let's move on to the impure ones that we dealt with by transforming them into pure equivalents.

Testing purified functions

When we considered the following `roundFix` special function, which required us to use the state to accumulate the differences due to rounding, we produced a new version by providing the current state as an added parameter and by having the function return two values—the rounded one and the updated state:

```
const roundFix2 = (a, n) => {
  let r = a > 0 ? Math.ceil(n) : Math.floor(n);
  a += n - r;
  return {a, r};
};
```

This function is now pure, but testing it requires validating not only the returned values but also the updated states. We can base our tests on the experiments we did previously. Once again, we have to use `toBeCloseTo()` for dealing with floating-point numbers, but we can use `toBe()` with integers, which produces no rounding errors. We could write our tests as follows:

```
describe("roundFix2", function() {
  it("should round 3.14159 to 3 if differences are 0", () => {
    const {a, r} = roundFix2(0.0, 3.14159);
    expect(a).toBeCloseTo(0.14159);
    expect(r).toBe(3);
  });
  it("should round 2.71828 to 3 if differences are 0.14159", () => {
    const {a, r} = roundFix2(0.14159, 2.71828);
    expect(a).toBeCloseTo(-0.14013);
    expect(r).toBe(3);
  });
  it("should round 2.71828 to 2 if differences are -0.14013", () => {
    const {a, r} = roundFix2(-0.14013, 2.71828);
    expect(a).toBeCloseTo(0.57815);
    expect(r).toBe(2);
  });
  it("should round 3.14159 to 4 if differences are 0.57815", () => {
    const {a, r} = roundFix2(0.57815, 3.14159);
    expect(a).toBeCloseTo(-0.28026);
    expect(r).toBe(4);
  });
});
```

We took care to include several cases, with positive, zero, or negative accumulated differences, and checking whether it rounded up or down on each occasion. We could certainly go further by rounding negative numbers, but the idea is clear: if your function takes the current state as a parameter and updates it, the only difference with the pure functions tests are that you will also have to test whether the returned state matches your expectations.

Let's now consider the alternative way of testing for our pure `getRandomLetter()` variant; let's call it `getRandomLetter2()`. This is simple: you just have to provide a function that will itself produce *random* numbers. (This kind of function, in testing parlance, is called a **stub**). There's no limit to the complexity of a stub, but you'll want to keep it simple.

We can then do some tests, based on our knowledge of the workings of the function, to verify that low values produce an A and values close to 1 produce a Z, so we can have a little confidence that no extra values are produced. We should also test that a middle value (around 0.5) should produce a letter around the middle of the alphabet; however, keep in mind that this kind of test is not very good—if we substituted an equally valid getRandomLetter() variant, it might be the case that the new function could work perfectly well, but not pass this test, because of a different internal implementation! Our tests could be written as follows:

```
describe("getRandomLetter2", function() {
  it("returns A for values close to 0", () => {
    const letterSmall = getRandomLetter2(() => 0.0001);
    expect(letterSmall).toBe("A");
  });
  it("returns Z for values close to 1", () => {
    const letterBig = getRandomLetter2(() => 0.99999);
    expect(letterBig).toBe("Z");
  });
  it("returns a middle letter for values around 0.5", () => {
    const letterMiddle = getRandomLetter2(() => 0.49384712);
    expect(letterMiddle).toBeGreaterThan("G");
    expect(letterMiddle).toBeLessThan("S");
  });
  it("returns an ascending sequence of letters for ascending values", () =>
{
    const a = [0.09, 0.22, 0.6];
    const f = () => a.shift(); // impure!!
    const letter1 = getRandomLetter2(f);
    const letter2 = getRandomLetter2(f);
    const letter3 = getRandomLetter2(f);
    expect(letter1).toBeLessThan(letter2);
    expect(letter2).toBeLessThan(letter3);
  });
});
```

Testing our filename generator can be done in a similar way, by using stubs. We can provide a simple stub that will return the letters of "SORTOFRANDOM" in sequence (this function is quite impure; can you see why?). So we can verify that the returned filename matches the expected name and a couple more properties of the returned filename, such as its length and its extension. Our test could then be written as follows:

```
describe("getRandomFileName", function() {
  let a = [];
  const f = () => a.shift();
  beforeEach(() => {
    a = "SORTOFRANDOM".split("");
```

```
  });
  it("uses the given letters for the file name", () => {
    const fileName = getRandomFileName("", f);
    expect(fileName.startsWith("SORTOFRANDOM")).toBe(true);
  });
  it("includes the right extension, and has the right length", () => {
    const fileName = getRandomFileName(".pdf", f);
    expect(fileName.endsWith(".pdf")).toBe(true);
    expect(fileName.length).toBe(16);
  });
});
```

Testing *purified* impure functions is very much the same as testing originally pure functions. Now we need to consider some cases of truly impure functions, because, as we said, it's quite certain that at some time or another you'll have to use such functions.

Testing impure functions

For starters, we'll go back to our `getRandomLetter()` function. With insider knowledge about its implementation (this is called **white-box testing**, as opposed to **black-box testing**, where we know nothing about the function code itself), we can *spy* (a Jasmine term) on the `Math.random()` method and set a *mock* function that will return whatever values we desire.

We can revisit some of the test cases that we went through in the previous section. In the first case, we set `Math.random()` to return `0.0001` (and test that it was actually called) and we also test that the final return was A. In the second case, just for variety, we set things up so that `Math.random()` can be called twice, returning two different values. We also verify that there were two calls to the function and that both results were Z. The third case shows yet another way of checking how many times `Math.random()` (or rather, our mocked function) was called. Our revisited tests could look as follows:

```
describe("getRandomLetter", function() {
  it("returns A for values close to 0", () => {
    spyOn(Math, "random").and.returnValue(0.0001);
    const letterSmall = getRandomLetter();
    expect(Math.random).toHaveBeenCalled();
    expect(letterSmall).toBe("A");
  });
  it("returns Z for values close to 1", () => {
    spyOn(Math, "random").and.returnValues(0.98, 0.999);
    const letterBig1 = getRandomLetter();
    const letterBig2 = getRandomLetter();
    expect(Math.random).toHaveBeenCalledTimes(2);
```

```
      expect(letterBig1).toBe("Z");
      expect(letterBig2).toBe("Z");
    });
    it("returns a middle letter for values around 0.5", () => {
      spyOn(Math, "random").and.returnValue(0.49384712);
      const letterMiddle = getRandomLetter();
      expect(Math.random.calls.count()).toEqual(1);
      expect(letterMiddle).toBeGreaterThan("G");
      expect(letterMiddle).toBeLessThan("S");
    });
  });
```

 Of course, you wouldn't go around inventing whatever tests came into your head. In all likelihood, you'll work from the description of the desired `getRandomLetter()` function, which was written before you started to code or test it. In our case, I'm making do as if that specification did exist, and it pointedly said, for example, that values close to 0 should produce an A, values close to 1 should return Z, and the function should return ascending letters for ascending `random` values.

Now, how would you test the original `getRandomFileName()` function, the one that called the impure `getRandomLetter()` function? That's a much more complicated problem. What kind of expectations do you have? You cannot know the results it will give, so you won't be able to write any `.toBe()` type of tests. What you can do is to test for some properties of the expected results, and also, if your function implies randomness of some kind, you can repeat the tests as many times as you want so that you have a bigger chance of catching a bug. We could do some tests along the lines of the following code:

```
describe("getRandomFileName, with an impure getRandomLetter function",
function() {
  it("generates 12 letter long names", () => {
    for (let i = 0; i < 100; i++) {
      expect(getRandomFileName().length).toBe(12);
    }
  });
  it("generates names with letters A to Z, only", () => {
    for (let i = 0; i < 100; i++) {
      let n = getRandomFileName();
      for (j = 0; j < n.length; n++) {
        expect(n[j] >= "A" && n[j] <= "Z").toBe(true);
      }
    }
  });
  it("includes the right extension if provided", () => {
    const fileName1 = getRandomFileName(".pdf");
    expect(fileName1.length).toBe(16);
```

```
    expect(fileName1.endsWith(".pdf")).toBe(true);
  });
  it("doesn't include any extension if not provided", () => {
    const fileName2 = getRandomFileName();
    expect(fileName2.length).toBe(12);
    expect(fileName2.includes(".")).toBe(false);
  });
});
```

We are not passing any random letter generator function to `getFileName()`, so it will use the original, impure one. We ran some of the tests a hundred times, as extra insurance.

 When testing code, always remember that *absence of evidence* isn't *evidence of absence*. Even if our repeated tests succeed, there is no guarantee that, with some other random input, they won't produce an unexpected, and hitherto undetected, error.

Let's do another *property* test. Suppose we want to test a shuffling algorithm; we might decide to implement the Fisher-Yates version along the lines of the following code. As implemented, the algorithm is doubly impure: it doesn't always produce the same result (obviously!) and it modifies its input parameter:

```
const shuffle = arr => {
  const len = arr.length;
  for (let i = 0; i < len - 1; i++) {
    let r = Math.floor(Math.random() * (len - i));
    [arr[i], arr[i + r]] = [arr[i + r], arr[i]];
  }
  return arr;
};

var xxx = [11, 22, 33, 44, 55, 66, 77, 88];
console.log(shuffle(xxx));
// [55, 77, 88, 44, 33, 11, 66, 22]
```

 For more on this algorithm—including some pitfalls for the unwary programmer—see `https://en.wikipedia.org/wiki/Fisher-Yates_shuffle`.

How could you test this algorithm? Given that the result won't be predictable, we can check for the properties of its output. We can call it with a known array and then test some properties of it:

```
describe("shuffleTest", function() {
  it("shouldn't change the array length", () => {
```

```
        let a = [22, 9, 60, 12, 4, 56];
        shuffle(a);
        expect(a.length).toBe(6);
    });
    it("shouldn't change the values", () => {
        let a = [22, 9, 60, 12, 4, 56];
        shuffle(a);
        expect(a.includes(22)).toBe(true);
        expect(a.includes(9)).toBe(true);
        expect(a.includes(60)).toBe(true);
        expect(a.includes(12)).toBe(true);
        expect(a.includes(4)).toBe(true);
        expect(a.includes(56)).toBe(true);
    });
});
```

We had to write the second part of the unit tests in that way because, as we saw, `shuffle()` modifies the input parameter.

Summary

In this chapter, we introduced the concept of *pure functions* and studied why they matter. We also saw the problems caused by *side effects*, one of the causes of impure functions, looked at some ways of *purifying* such impure functions, and finally, we saw several ways of performing unit tests, for both pure and impure functions. With these techniques, you'll be able to favor using pure functions in your programming, and when impure functions are needed, you'll have some ways of using them in a controlled way.

In Chapter 5, *Programming Declaratively – A Better Style*, we'll show other advantages of FP: how you can program in a declarative fashion at a higher level for simpler and more powerful code.

Questions

4.1. **Minimalistic function**: Functional programmers sometimes tend to write code in a minimalistic way. Can you examine the following version of the Fibonacci function and explain whether it works, and if so, how?

```
const fib2 = n => (n < 2 ? n : fib2(n - 2) + fib2(n - 1));
```

4.2. A cheap way: The following version of the Fibonacci function is quite efficient and doesn't do any unnecessary or repeated computations. Can you see how? Here's a suggestion: try to calculate `fib4(6)` by hand and compare it with the example given earlier in the book:

```
const fib4 = (n, a = 0, b = 1) => (n === 0 ? a : fib4(n - 1, b, a + b));
```

4.3. A shuffle test: How would you write unit tests for `shuffle()` to test whether it works correctly with arrays with *repeated* values?

4.4. Breaking laws: Using `toBeCloseTo()` is very practical, but it can cause some problems. Some basic mathematics properties are as follows:

- A number should equal itself: for any number *a*, *a* should equal *a*.
- If a number *a* equals number *b*, then *b* should equal *a*.
- If *a* equals *b*, and *b* equals *c*, then *a* should equal *c*.
- If *a* equals *b*, and *c* equals *d*, then *a+c* should equal *b+d*.
- If *a* equals *b*, and *c* equals *d*, then *a-c* should equal *b-d*.
- If *a* equals *b*, and *c* equals *d*, then *a*c* should equal *b*d*.
- If *a* equals *b*, and *c* equals *d*, then *a/c* should equal *b/d*.

Does `toBeCloseTo()` also satisfy all these properties?

4.5. Must return? A simple, almost philosophical question: must pure functions always `return` something? Could you have a pure function that didn't include a `return`?

4.6. JavaScript does math? In the *Testing purified functions* section, we mentioned the need for `toBeCloseTo()` because of precision problems. A related question, often asked in job interviews, is: *what will the following code output, and why?*

```
const a = 0.1;
const b = 0.2;
const c = 0.3;

if (a + b === c) {
  console.log("Math works!");
} else {
  console.log("Math failure?");
}
```

Programming Declaratively - A Better Style

5

Up to now, we haven't really been able to appreciate the possibilities of **Functional Programming (FP)** as it pertains to working in a higher-level, declarative fashion. In this chapter, we will correct this, and start getting shorter, more concise, and easier to understand code, by using some **higher-order functions (HOF)**; that is, functions that take functions as parameters, such as the following:

- `reduce()` and `reduceRight()` to apply an operation to a whole array, reducing it to a single result
- `map()` to transform one array into another by applying a function to each of its elements
- `flat()` to make a single array out of an array of arrays
- `flatMap()` to mix together mapping and flattening
- `forEach()` to simplify writing loops by abstracting the necessary looping code

We'll also be able to perform searches and selections with the following:

- `filter()` to pick some elements from an array
- `find()` and `findIndex()` to search for elements that satisfy a condition
- A pair of predicates, `every()` and `some()`, to check an array for a Boolean test

Using these functions lets you work more declaratively, and you'll see that your focus will shift to what you need to do and not so much how it's going to be done; the dirty details are hidden inside our functions. Instead of writing a series of possibly nested `for` loops, we'll focus on using functions as building blocks to specify our desired result.

We will also be using these functions to work with events in a declarative style, as we'll see in `Chapter 11`, *Implementing Design Patterns – The Functional Way*, when we use the *observer* pattern.

We will also be able to work in a *fluent* fashion, in which the output of a function becomes the input of the next one, a style we will look at later.

Transformations

The first set of operations that we are going to consider work on an array and process it in the base of a function to produce some results. There are several possible results: a single value with the `reduce()` operation; a new array with `map()`; or just about any kind of result with `forEach()`.

If you Google around, you will find some articles that declare that these functions are not efficient because a loop done by hand can be faster. This, while possibly true, is practically irrelevant. Unless your code really suffers from speed problems and you are able to measure that the slowness derives from the use of these higher-order functions, trying to avoid them using longer code, with a higher probability of bugs, simply doesn't make much sense.

Let's start by considering the preceding list of functions in order, starting with the most general of all, which, as we'll see, can even be used to emulate the rest of the transformations in this chapter!

Reducing an array to a value

Answer this question: how many times have you had to loop through an array, performing an operation (say, summing) to produce a single value (maybe the sum of all the array values) as a result? Probably many, many, many times. This kind of operation can usually be implemented functionally by applying `reduce()` and `reduceRight()`. Let's start with the former!

Time for some terminology! In usual FP parlance, we speak of **folding** operations: `reduce()` is **foldl** (for *fold left*) or just plain **fold**, and `reduceRight()` is correspondingly known as **foldr**. In category theory terms, both operations are **catamorphisms**: the reduction of all the values in a *container* down to a single result.

The inner workings of the `reduce()` function are illustrated in *Figure 5.1*. See how it traverses the array, applying a reducing function to each element and to the accumulated value:

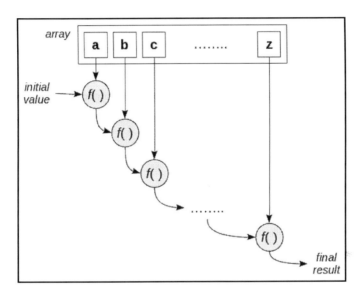

Figure 5.1: The workings of the reduce operation

Why should you always try to use `reduce()` or `reduceRight()` instead of hand-coded loops? The following points might answer this question:

- All the aspects of loop control are automatically taken care of, so you don't even have the possibility of, say, an *off-by-one* mistake.
- The initialization and handling of the result values are also done implicitly.
- Unless you work really hard at being impure and modifying the original array, your code will be side effect free.

Now that we can `reduce()` an array, let's see some of its practical use cases.

Summing an array

The most common example of the application of reduce(), usually seen in all textbooks and on all web pages, is the summing of all of the elements of an array. So, in order to keep with tradition, let's start with precisely this example!

Basically, to reduce an array, you must provide a **dyadic** function (that is, a function with two parameters; **binary** would be another name for that) and an initial value. In our case, the function will sum its two arguments. Initially, the function will be applied to the provided initial value and the first element of the array, so for us, the first result we have to provide is a zero, and the first result will be the first element itself. Then, the function will be applied again, this time to the result of the previous operation, and the second element of the array, and so the second result will be the sum of the first two elements of the array. Progressing in this fashion along the whole array, the final result will be the sum of all its elements:

```
const myArray = [22, 9, 60, 12, 4, 56];
const sum = (x, y) => x + y;
const mySum = myArray.reduce(sum, 0); // 163
```

You don't actually need the sum definition—you could have just written myArray.reduce((x,y) => x+y, 0)—however, when written in this fashion, the meaning of the code is clearer: you want to reduce the array to a single value by sum-ming all its elements. Instead of having to write out the loop, initializing a variable to hold the result of the calculations, and going through the array doing the sums, you just declare what operation should be performed. This is what I meant when I said that programming with functions such as those that we'll see in this chapter allows you to work more declaratively, focusing on *what* rather than *how*.

You can also even do this without providing the initial value: if you skip it, the first value of the array will be used, and the internal loop will start with the second element of the array; however, be careful if the array is empty, and if you skipped providing an initial value, as you'll get a runtime error! See https://developer.mozilla.org/en-US/docs/Web/JavaScript/Reference/Global_Objects/Array/Reduce for more details.

We can change the reducing function to see how it progresses through its calculations by just including a little bit of impurity!

```
const sumAndLog = (x, y) => {
 console.log(`${x}+${y}=${x + y}`);
  return x + y;
};

myArray.reduce(sumAndLog, 0);
```

The output would be as follows:

```
0+22=22
22+9=31
31+60=91
91+12=103
103+4=107
107+56=163
```

You can see how the first sum was done by adding the initial value (0) and the first element of the array, how that result was used in the second addition, and so on.

 Part of the reason for the *foldl* name seen previously (at least, its ending l) should now be clear: the reducing operation proceeds from left to right, from the first element to the last. You may wonder, however, how it would have been named if it had been defined by a right-to-left language (such as Arabic, Hebrew, Farsi, or Urdu) speaker!

This example is common and well-known; let's now do something a bit more complicated. As we'll find out, reduce() will be quite useful for many different objectives!

Calculating an average

Let's work a bit more. How do you calculate the average of a list of numbers? If you were explaining this to someone, your answer would surely be something like *sum all the elements in the list and divide that by the number of elements*. This, in programming terms, is not a **procedural** description (you don't explain how to sum elements, or how to traverse the array), but rather a **declarative** one, since you say what to do, not how to do it.

We can transform that description of the calculation into an almost self-explanatory function:

```
const average = arr => arr.reduce(sum, 0) / arr.length;

console.log(average(myArray)); // 27.166667
```

The definition of `average()` follows what would be a verbal explanation: sum the elements of the array, starting from 0, and divide by the array's length—simpler: impossible!

As we mentioned in the previous section, you could also have written `arr.reduce(sum)` without specifying the initial value (0) for the reduction; it's even shorter and closer to the verbal description of the required calculation. This, however, is less safe, because it would fail (producing a runtime error) should the array be empty. So it's better to always provide the starting value.

This isn't, however, the only way of calculating the average. The reducing function also gets passed the index of the current position of the array as well as the array itself, so you could do something different than last time:

```
const average2 = (sum, val, ind, arr) => {
  sum += val;
  return ind === arr.length - 1 ? sum / arr.length : sum;
};

console.log(myArray.reduce(average2, 0)); // 27.166667
```

Given the current index (and, obviously, having access to the array's length), we can do some trickery: in this case, we always sum values, but if we are at the end of the array, we also throw in a division so that the average value of the array will be returned. This is slick, but from the point of view of legibility, I'm certain we can agree that the first version we saw was more declarative and closer to the mathematical definition than this second version.

Getting the array and the index means that you could also turn the function into an impure one. Avoid this! Everybody who sees a `reduce()` call will automatically assume it's a pure function, and will surely introduce bugs when using it.

It would also be possible to modify `Array.prototype` to add the new function. Modifying prototypes is usually frowned upon because of the possibility of clashes with different libraries, at the very least. However, if you accept this idea, you could then write the following code:

```
Array.prototype.average = function() {
  return this.reduce((x, y) => x + y, 0) / this.length;
};

let myAvg = [22, 9, 60, 12, 4, 56].average(); // 27.166667
```

Do take note of the need for the outer `function()` (instead of an arrow function) because of the implicit handling of `this`, which wouldn't be bound otherwise. We have now extended the `Array.prototype` so that `average()` becomes globally available as a method.

Both this example and the previous one required calculating a single result, but it's possible to go beyond this and calculate several values in a single pass. Let's see how.

Calculating several values at once

What would you do if, instead of a single value, you needed to calculate two or more results? This would seem to be a case for providing a clear advantage for common loops, but there's a trick that you can use. Let's yet again revisit the average calculation. We might want to do it the old-fashioned way, by looping and at the same time summing and counting all numbers. Well, `reduce()` only lets you produce a single result, but there's no reason you can't return an object with as many fields as desired:

```
const average3 = arr => {
  const sumCount = arr.reduce(
    (accum, value) => ({sum: value + accum.sum, count: accum.count + 1}),
    {sum: 0, count: 0}
  );

  return sumCount.sum / sumCount.count;
};

console.log(average3(myArray)); // 27.166667
```

Examine the code carefully. We need two variables: one for the sum and one for the count of all numbers. We provide an object as the initial value for the accumulator, with two properties set to `0`, and our reducing function updates those two properties.

By the way, using an object isn't the only option. You could also produce any other data structure; let's see an example with an array. The resemblance is pretty obvious:

```
const average4 = arr => {
  const sumCount = arr.reduce(
    (accum, value) => [accum[0] + value, accum[1] + 1],
    [0, 0]
  );
  return sumCount[0] / sumCount[1];
};

console.log(average4(myArray)); // 27.166667
```

To be frank, I think it's way more obscure than the solution with the object. Just consider this an alternative (not very recommendable) way of calculating many values at once!

We have now seen several examples of the use of reduce(), so it's high time to meet a variant of it, reduceRight(), which works in a very similar fashion.

Folding left and right

The complementary reduceRight() method works just as reduce() does, only starting at the end and looping until the beginning of the array. For many operations (such as the calculation of averages that we saw previously), this makes no difference, but there are some cases in which it will.

We shall be seeing a clear case of this in Chapter 8, *Connecting Functions – Pipelining and Composition*, when we compare pipelining and composition: let's go with a simpler example here:

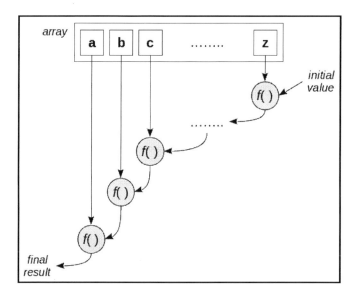

Figure 5.2: The reduceRight() operation works the same way as reduce(), but in reverse order

You can read more about reduceRight() at https://developer.mozilla.org/en-US/docs/Web/JavaScript/Reference/Global_Objects/Array/ReduceRight.

Suppose that we want to implement a function to reverse a string. A solution could be to transform the string into an array by using `split()`, then reversing that array, and finally using `join()` to make it whole again:

```
const reverseString = str => {
  let arr = str.split("");
  arr.reverse();
  return arr.join("");
};

console.log(reverseString("MONTEVIDEO"));   // OEDIVETNOM
```

This solution works (and yes, it can be shortened, but that's not the point here), but let's do it in another way, just to experiment with `reduceRight()`:

```
const reverseString2 = str =>
  str.split("").reduceRight((x, y) => x + y, "");

console.log(reverseString2("OEDIVETNOM"));   // MONTEVIDEO
```

Given that the addition operator also works with strings, we could also have written `reduceRight(sum, "")`. And, if instead of the function we used, we had written `(x,y) => y+x`, the result would have been our original string; can you see why?

From the previous examples, you can also get an idea: if you first apply `reverse()` to an array and then use `reduce()`, the effect will be the same as if you had just applied `reduceRight()` to the original array. There is only one point to take into account: `reverse()` alters the given array, so you would be causing an unintended side effect by reversing the original array! The only way out would be first generating a copy of the array and only then doing the rest. Too much work; best to keep using `reduceRight()`!

However, we can draw another conclusion, showing a result we had foretold: it is possible, albeit more cumbersome, to use `reduce()` to simulate the same result as `reduceRight()`—and in later sections, we'll also use it to emulate the other functions in the chapter. Let's now move on to another common and powerful operation: mapping.

Applying an operation – map

Processing lists of elements and applying some kind of operation to each of them is a quite common pattern in computer programming. Writing loops that systematically go through all the elements of an array or collection, starting at the first and looping until finishing with the last, and performing some kind of process on each of them is a basic coding exercise, usually learned in the first days of all programming courses. We already saw one such kind of operation in the previous section with `reduce()` and `reduceRight()`; let's now turn to a new one, called `map()`.

In mathematics, a **map** is a transformation of elements from a **domain** into elements of a **codomain**. For example, you might transform numbers into strings or strings into numbers, but also numbers to numbers, or strings to strings: the important point is that you have a way to transform an element of the first **kind** or **domain** (think **type**, if it helps) into an element of the second kind, or **codomain**. In our case, this will mean taking the elements of an array and applying a function to each of them to produce a new array. In more computer-like terms, the map function transforms an array of inputs into an array of outputs.

Some more terminology: We would say that an array is a **functor** because it provides a mapping operation with some prespecified properties, which we shall see later. And, in category theory, which we'll talk about a little in `Chapter 12`, *Building Better Containers – Functional Data Types*, the mapping operation itself would be called a **morphism**.

The inner workings of the `map()` operation can be seen in *Figure 5.3*:

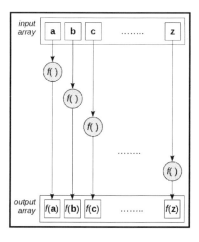

Figure 5.3: The map() operation transforms each element of the input array by applying a mapping function

The jQuery library provides a function, `$.map(array, callback)`, that is similar to the `map()` method. Be careful, though, for there are important differences. The jQuery function processes the undefined values of the array, while `map()` skips them. Also, if the applied function produces an array as its result, jQuery *flattens* it and adds each of its individual elements separately, while `map()` just includes those arrays in the result.

What are the advantages of using `map()` over using a straightforward loop?

- First, you don't have to write any loops, so that's one less possible source of bugs.
- Second, you don't even have to access the original array or the index position, even though they are there for you to use if you really need them.
- Lastly, a new array is produced, so your code is pure (though, of course, if you really want to produce side effects, you can!).

In JavaScript, `map()` is basically available only for arrays (you can read more about this at `https://developer.mozilla.org/en-US/docs/Web/JavaScript/Reference/Global_Objects/Array/map`); however, in the *Extending current data types* section in `Chapter 12`, *Building Better Containers – Functional Data Types*, we will learn how to make it available for other basic types, such as numbers, Booleans, strings, and even functions. Also, libraries, such as LoDash, Underscore, and Ramda, provide similar functionalities.

There are only two caveats when using this:

- Always return something from your mapping function. If you forget this, then you'll just produce an `undefined`-filled array, because JavaScript always provides a default `return undefined` for all functions.
- If the input array elements are objects or arrays, and you include them in the output array, then JavaScript will still allow the original elements to be accessed.

There's an alternative way of doing `map()`: check the `Array.from()` method at `https://developer.mozilla.org/en-US/docs/Web/JavaScript/Reference/Global_Objects/Array/from` and pay special attention to its second argument!

As we did earlier with `reduce()`, let's now look at some examples of the use of `map()` for common processes so that you'll better appreciate its power and convenience.

Extracting data from objects

Let's start with a simple example. Suppose that we have some geographic data (as shown in the following snippet) related to some South American countries and the coordinates (latitude and longitude) of their capitals. Let's say that we want to calculate the average position of those cities. (No, I don't have a clue why we'd want to do that.) How would we go about it?

```
const markers = [
  {name: "AR", lat: -34.6, lon: -58.4},
  {name: "BO", lat: -16.5, lon: -68.1},
  {name: "BR", lat: -15.8, lon: -47.9},
  {name: "CL", lat: -33.4, lon: -70.7},
  {name: "CO", lat:   4.6, lon: -74.0},
  {name: "EC", lat:  -0.3, lon: -78.6},
  {name: "PE", lat: -12.0, lon: -77.0},
  {name: "PY", lat: -25.2, lon: -57.5},
  {name: "UY", lat: -34.9, lon: -56.2},
  {name: "VE", lat:  10.5, lon: -66.9},
];
```

 In case you are wondering if and why all the data are negative, it's just because the countries shown here are all south of the Equator and west of the Greenwich Meridian; however, there are some South American countries with positive latitudes, such as Colombia or Venezuela, so not all have negative data. We'll come back to this question a little later when we study the `some()` and `every()` methods.

We would want to use our `average()` function (which we developed earlier in this chapter), but there is a problem: that function can only be applied to an array of *numbers*, and what we have here is an array of *objects*. We can, however, do a trick: we can focus on calculating the average latitude (we can deal with the longitude later, in a similar fashion). We can map each element of the array to just its latitude, and we would then have an appropriate input for `average()`. The solution would be something like the following:

```
let averageLat = average(markers.map(x => x.lat)); // -15.76
let averageLon = average(markers.map(x => x.lon)); // -65.53
```

If you had extended `Array.prototype`, you could then have written an equivalent version, in a different style, using `average()` as a method instead of a function:

```
let averageLat2 = markers.map(x => x.lat).average();
let averageLon2 = markers.map(x => x.lon).average();
```

We will be learning more about these styles in `Chapter 8`, *Connecting Functions – Pipelining and Composition.*

Mapping an array to extract data is powerful, but you must be careful. Let's now look at a case that *seems* right, but produces incorrect results!

Parsing numbers tacitly

Working with the map is usually far safer and simpler than looping by hand, but some edge cases may trip you up. Say you received an array of strings representing numeric values, and you wanted to parse them into actual numbers. Can you explain the following results?

```
["123.45", "67.8", "90"].map(parseFloat);
// [123.45, 67.8, 90]

["123.45", "-67.8", "90"].map(parseInt);
// [123, NaN, NaN]
```

Let's analyze the results. When we used `parseFloat()` to get floating-point results, everything was okay; however, when we wanted to truncate the results to integer values, then the output was really awry, and weird NaN values appeared. What happened?

The answer lies in a problem with tacit programming. (We have already seen some uses of tacit programming in the *An unnecessary mistake* section of `Chapter 3`, *Starting Out with Functions – A Core Concept,* and we'll be seeing more in `Chapter 8`, *Connecting Functions – Pipelining and Composition.*) When you don't explicitly show the parameters to a function, it's easy to have some oversights. Look at the following code, which will lead us to the solution:

```
["123.45", "-67.8", "90"].map(x => parseFloat(x));
// [123.45, -67.8, 90]

["123.45", "-67.8", "90"].map(x => parseInt(x));
// [123, -67, 90]
```

The reason for the unexpected behavior with `parseInt()` is that this function can also receive a second parameter—namely, the radix to be used when converting the string to a number. For instance, a call such as `parseInt("100010100001", 2)` will convert the binary number 100010100001 to decimal.

You can read more about `parseInt()` at `https://developer.mozilla.org/en/docs/Web/JavaScript/Reference/Global_Objects/parseInt`, where the radix parameter is explained in detail. You should always provide it because some browsers might interpret strings with a leading zero to be octal, which would once again produce unwanted results.

So what happens when we provide `parseInt()` to `map()`? Remember that `map()` calls your mapping function with three parameters: the array element value, its index, and the array itself. When `parseInt` receives these values, it ignores the array, but assumes that the provided index is actually a radix and `NaN` values are produced, since the original strings are not valid numbers in the given radix.

Okay, we saw that some functions can lead you astray when doing mapping, and you now know what to look out for. Let's keep enhancing the way we that we work, by using ranges to help you write code that would usually require a hand-written loop.

Working with ranges

Let's now turn to a helper function, which will come in handy for many uses. We want a `range(start, stop)` function that generates an array of numbers, with values ranging from `start` (inclusive) to `stop` (exclusive):

```
const range = (start, stop) =>
  new Array(stop - start).fill(0).map((v, i) => start + i);

let from2To6 = range(2, 7); // [2, 3, 4, 5, 6]
```

Why `fill(0)`? All undefined array elements are skipped by `map()`, so we need to fill them with something or our code will have no effect.

Libraries such as Underscore and Lodash provide a more powerful version of our `range` function, letting you go in ascending or descending order and also specifying the step to use—as in `_.range(0, -8, -2)`, which produces `[0, -2, -4, -6]`—but for our needs, the version we wrote is enough. Read the *Questions* section at the end of this chapter.

How can we use it? In the following section, we'll see some uses for controlled looping with `forEach()`, but we can redo our factorial function by applying `range()` and then `reduce()`. The idea of this is to simply generate all the numbers from 1 to *n* and then multiply them together:

```
const factorialByRange = n => range(1, n + 1).reduce((x, y) => x * y, 1);

factorialByRange(5); // 120
factorialByRange(3); // 6
```

It's important to check the border cases, but the function also works for zero; can you see why? The reason for this is that the produced range is empty (the call is `range(1,1)`, which returns an empty array) and then `reduce()` doesn't do any calculations, and simply returns the initial value (one), which is correct.

 In `Chapter 7`, *Transforming Functions - Currying and Partial Application*, we'll have the opportunity to use `range()` to generate source code; check out the *Currying with eval()* and *Partial application with eval()* sections.

You could use these numeric ranges to produce other kinds of ranges. For example, should you need an array with the alphabet, you could certainly (and tediously) write `["A", "B", "C"`... up to ...`"X", "Y", "Z"]`. A simpler solution would be to generate a range with the ASCII codes for the alphabet and map those into letters:

```
const ALPHABET = range("A".charCodeAt(), "Z".charCodeAt() + 1).map(x =>
  String.fromCharCode(x)
);

// ["A", "B", "C", ... "X", "Y", "Z"]
```

Note the use of `charCodeAt()` to get the ASCII codes for the letters and `String.fromCharCode(x)` to transform the ASCII code back into a character.

Mapping is very important and quite often used, so let's now analyze how you could implement it on your own, which could help you develop code of your own for more complex cases.

Emulating map() with reduce()

Earlier in this chapter, we saw how `reduce()` could be used to implement `reduceRight()`. Now let's see how `reduce()` can also be used to provide a polyfill for `map()` (not that you will need it, because browsers usually provide both methods, but just to get more of an idea of what you can achieve with these tools).

Our own `myMap()` is a one-liner, but it can be hard to understand. The idea is that we apply the function to each element of the array and we `concat()` the result to (an initially empty) result array. When the loop finishes working with the input array, the result array will have the desired output values:

```
const myMap = (arr, fn) => arr.reduce((x, y) => x.concat(fn(y)), []);
```

Let's test this with an array and a simple function. We will use both the original `map()` method and our `myMap()`, and obviously the results should match!

```
const myArray = [22, 9, 60, 12, 4, 56];
const dup = x => 2 * x;

console.log(myArray.map(dup));      // [44, 18, 120, 24, 8, 112]
console.log(myMap(myArray, dup));   // [44, 18, 120, 24, 8, 112]
console.log(myArray);               // [22, 9, 60, 12, 4, 56]
```

The first log shows the expected result, produced by `map()`. The second output gives the same result, so it seems that `myMap()` works! And the final output is just to check that the original input array wasn't modified in any way; mapping operations should always produce a new array.

All the previous examples in the chapter focused on simple arrays. But what happens if things get more complicated, say if you had to deal with an array whose elements were arrays themselves? Fortunately, there's a way out for that. Let's move on.

Dealing with arrays of arrays

So far, we have worked with an array of (single) values as an input, but what would happen if your input happened to be an array of arrays? If you consider this to be a farfetched case, there are many possible scenarios where this could apply:

- For some applications, you could have a table of distances, which in JavaScript would actually be an array of arrays: `distance[i][j]` would be the distance between points `i` and `j`. How could you find the maximum distance between any two points? With a common array, finding a maximum would be simple, but how do you deal with an array of arrays?
- A more complex example, also in a geographical vein: you could query a geographical API for cities matching a string and the response could be an array of countries, each with an array of states, each itself with an array of matching cities: an array of arrays of arrays!

In the first case, you could want to have a single array with all distances, and in the second, an array with all cities; how can you manage this? A new operation, **flattening**, is required; let's take a look.

Flattening an array

In ES2019, two operations were added to JavaScript: `flat()`, which we'll look at now, and `flatMap()`, which we'll look at a bit later. It's easier to show what they do than to explain—bear with me!

 As often happens, not all browsers have been updated to include these new methods, and Microsoft's Internet Explorer and Edge (among others) are both deficient in this regard, so for web programming, you'll probably have to include a polyfill, or use some kind of implementation, which we'll be learning about soon. As usual, for updated compatibility data, check out the **Can I use?** site, in this case, at `https://caniuse.com/#feat=array-flat`.

The `flat()` method creates a new array, concatenating all elements of its subarrays to the desired level, which is, by default, `1`:

```
const a = [[1, 2], [3, 4, [5, 6, 7]], 8, [[[9, 10]]]];

console.log(a.flat()); // or a.flat(1)
// [ 1, 2, 3, 4, [ 5, 6, 7 ], 8, [ 9, 10 ] ]

console.log(a.flat(2));
// [ 1, 2, 3, 4, 5, 6, 7, 8, [ 9, 10 ] ]

console.log(a.flat(Infinity));
// [ 1, 2, 3, 4, 5, 6, 7, 8, 9, 10 ]
```

So how could we use this function to solve our problems? Using `flat()`, spreading, and `Math.max()` answers the first question (in a way that we saw back in Chapter 1, *Becoming Functional – Several Questions*, in the section called *Spread*; we could use the `maxArray()` function we wrote back then), and we can also use `reduce()` for variety. Suppose we have the following table of distances:

```
const distances = [
    [0, 20, 35, 40],
    [20, 0, 10, 50],
    [35, 10, 0, 30],
    [40, 50, 30, 0],
];
```

Then, we can find our maximum distance in a couple of ways: we either flatten the array, spread it, and use `Math.max()`, or flatten the array and use reducing to explicitly find the maximum:

```
const maxDist1 = Math.max(...distances.flat());
// 50

const maxDist2 = distances.flat().reduce((p, d) => Math.max(p, d), 0);
// also 50
```

Let's go back to the second question. Suppose we queried a geographical API for cities that have `"LINCOLN"` in their names and we got the following answer:

```
const apiAnswer = [
  {
    country: "AR",
    name: "Argentine",
    states: [
      {
        state: "1",
```

```
        name: "Buenos Aires",
        cities: [{city: 3846864, name: "Lincoln"}],
      },
    ],
  },
  {
    country: "GB",
    name: "Great Britain",
    states: [
      {
        state: "ENG",
        name: "England",
        cities: [{city: 2644487, name: "Lincoln"}],
      },
    ],
  },
  {
    country: "US",
    name: "United States of America",
    states: [
      {
        state: "CA",
        name: "California",
        cities: [{city: 5072006, name: "Lincoln"}],
      },

      .
      . several lines clipped out
      .

      {
        state: "IL",
        name: "Illinois",
        cities: [
          {city: 4899911, name: "Lincoln Park"},
          {city: 4899966, name: "Lincoln Square"},
        ],
      },
    ],
  },
];
```

Extracting the list of cities can be done by applying `flatMap()` twice:

```
console.log(
  apiAnswer
    .map(x => x.states)
    .flat()
    .map(y => y.cities)
    .flat()
```

```
);

/*
[ { city: 3846864, name: 'Lincoln' },
  { city: 2644487, name: 'Lincoln' },
  { city: 5072006, name: 'Lincoln' },
  { city: 8531960, name: 'Lincoln' },
  { city: 4769608, name: 'Lincolnia' },
  { city: 4999311, name: 'Lincoln Park' },
  { city: 5072006, name: 'Lincoln' },
  { city: 4899911, name: 'Lincoln Park' },
  { city: 4899966, name: 'Lincoln Square' } ]
*/
```

We have seen how to use `flat()` to flatten an array; let's now see how to use `flatMap()`, an interesting mixture of `flat()` and `map()`, to further streamline our coding, and even further shorten our preceding second solution!

 Think this exercise wasn't hard enough and that its output was sort of lame? Try out exercise 5.8 for a more challenging version!

Mapping and flattening – flatMap()

Basically, what `flatMap()` does is first apply a `map()` function and then apply `flat()` to the result of the mapping operation. This is an interesting combination because it lets you produce a new array with a different number of elements. (With the usual `map()` operation, the output array will be exactly the same length as the input array). If your mapping operation produces an array with two or more elements, then the output array will include many output values, and if you produce an empty array, the output array will include fewer values.

Let's look at a (somehow nonsensical) example. Assume that we have a list of names, such as `"Winston Spencer Churchill"`, `"Abraham Lincoln"`, and `"Socrates"`. Our rule is that if a name has several words, exclude the initial one (the first name, we assume) and separate the rest (last names), but if a name is a single word, just drop it (assuming the person had no last name):

```
const names = [
  "Winston Spencer Churchill",
  "Plato",
  "Abraham Lincoln",
  "Socrates",
```

```
    "Charles Darwin",
];

const lastNames = names.flatMap(x => {
  const s = x.split(" ");
  return s.length === 1 ? [] : s.splice(1);
}); // [ 'Spencer', 'Churchill', 'Lincoln', 'Darwin' ]
```

As we can see, the output array has a different number of elements than the input one: just because of this, we could consider flatMap() to be an upgraded version of map(), even including some aspects of filter(), like when we excluded single names.

Let's now move on to a simple example. Keeping with the Lincolnian theme from the last section, let's count how many words are in Lincoln's Gettysburg address, given as an array of sentences.

 Usually, this address is considered to be 272 words long, but the version I found doesn't produce that number! This may be because there are five manuscript copies of the address written by Lincoln himself, plus another version transcribed from shorthand notes taken at the event. In any case, I will leave the discrepancy to historians and stick to coding!

We can use flatMap() to split each sentence into an array of words and then just see the length of the flattened array:

```
const gettysburg = [
  "Four score and seven years ago our fathers brought forth, ",
  "on this continent, a new nation, conceived in liberty, and ",
  "dedicated to the proposition that all men are created equal.",
  "Now we are engaged in a great civil war, testing whether that ",
  "nation, or any nation so conceived and so dedicated, can long ",
  "endure.",
  "We are met on a great battle field of that war.",
  "We have come to dedicate a portion of that field, as a final ",
  "resting place for those who here gave their lives, that that ",
  "nation might live.",
  "It is altogether fitting and proper that we should do this.",
  "But, in a larger sense, we cannot dedicate, we cannot consecrate, ",
  "we cannot hallow, this ground.",
  "The brave men, living and dead, who struggled here, have ",
  "consecrated it far above our poor power to add or detract.",
  "The world will little note nor long remember what we say here, ",
  "but it can never forget what they did here.",
  "It is for us the living, rather, to be dedicated here to the ",
  "unfinished work which they who fought here have thus far so nobly ",
  "advanced.",
  "It is rather for us to be here dedicated to the great task ",
```

```
    "remaining before us— that from these honored dead we take increased ",
    "devotion to that cause for which they here gave the last full ",
    "measure of devotion— that we here highly resolve that these dead ",
    "shall not have died in vain— that this nation, under God, shall have ",
    "a new birth of freedom- and that government of the people, by the ",
    "people, for the people, shall not perish from the earth.",
];

console.log(gettysburg.flatMap(s => s.split(" ")).length);
```

Let's go back to the problem with the cities. If we notice that each map() was followed by a flat(), an alternative solution is immediately obvious. Compare this solution with the one we wrote in the *Flattening an array* section; it's essentially the same, but conflates each map() with its following flat():

```
console.log(apiAnswer.flatMap(x => x.states).flatMap(y => y.cities));
/*
[ { city: 3846864, name: 'Lincoln' },
  { city: 2644487, name: 'Lincoln' },
  { city: 5072006, name: 'Lincoln' },
  { city: 8531960, name: 'Lincoln' },
  { city: 4769608, name: 'Lincolnia' },
  { city: 4999311, name: 'Lincoln Park' },
  { city: 5072006, name: 'Lincoln' },
  { city: 4899911, name: 'Lincoln Park' },
  { city: 4899966, name: 'Lincoln Square' } ]
*/
```

We have now seen the new operations. Let's now learn how to emulate them, should you not have them readily available.

 It's perfectly possible to solve the problems in this section without using any sort of mapping, but that wouldn't do as a proper example for this section! See exercise 5.9 for an alternative to the word counting problem.

Emulating flat() and flatMap()

We have already seen how reduce() could be used to emulate map(). Let's now see how to work out equivalents for flat() and flatMap() to get more practice. We'll also throw in a recursive version, a topic we'll come back to in Chapter 9, *Designing Functions – Recursion*. As was mentioned earlier, we are not aiming for the fastest or smallest or any particular version of the code; rather, we want to focus on using the concepts we've been looking at in this book.

Totally flattening an array can be done with a recursive call. We use `reduce()` to process the array element by element, and if an element happens to be an array, we recursively flatten it:

```
const flatAll = arr =>
   arr.reduce((f, v) => f.concat(Array.isArray(v) ? flatAll(v) : v), []);
```

Flattening an array to a given level (not infinity; let's leave that for later) is easy if you can first flatten an array one level. We can do this either by using spreading or with `reduce`. Let's write a `flatOne()` function that flattens just a single level of an array. There are two versions of this; pick whichever you prefer:

```
const flatOne1 = arr => [].concat(...arr);
```

```
const flatOne2 = arr => arr.reduce((f, v) => f.concat(v), []);
```

Using either of these two functions, we can manage to flatten an array of several levels, and we can do this in two different ways. Our two versions of a `flat()` function use our previous `flatOne()` and `flatAll()` functions, but the first one only uses common looping, while the second one works in a fully recursive way. Which one do you prefer?

```
const flat1 = (arr, n = 1) => {
   if (n === Infinity) {
      return flatAll(arr);

   } else {
      let result = arr;
      range(0, n).forEach(() => {
         result = flatOne(result);
      });
      return result;
   }
};

const flat2 = (arr, n = 1) =>
   n === Infinity
      ? flatAll(arr)
      : n === 1
      ? flatOne(arr)
      : flat2(flatOne(arr), n - 1);
```

Personally, I think the recursive one is nicer, and more aligned with the theme of this book, but it's up to you, really (though if you don't feel comfortable with the ternary operator, then the recursive version is definitely not for you!).

If you wish to polyfill these functions (despite our suggestions not to), it's not complex, and is similar to what we did some pages back with the `average()` method. I took care not to create any extra methods:

```
if (!Array.prototype.flat) {
  Array.prototype.flat = function(n = 1) {
    this.flatAllX = () =>
      this.reduce(
        (f, v) => f.concat(Array.isArray(v) ? v.flat(Infinity) : v),
        []
      );

    this.flatOneX = () => this.reduce((f, v) => f.concat(v), []);

    return n === Infinity
      ? this.flatAllX()
      : n === 1
      ? this.flatOneX()
      : this.flatOneX().flat(n - 1);
  };
}
```

Our `flatOneX()` and `flatAllX()` methods are just copies of what we developed before, and you'll recognize the code of our previous `flat2()` function at the end of our implementation.

Finally, emulating `flatMap()` is simplicity itself, and we can just skip it because it's just a matter of applying `map()` first, and then `flat()`; no big deal!

We have seen how to work with arrays in several ways, but sometimes what you need isn't really well served by any of the functions we have seen. Let's move on to more general ways of doing loops, for greater power.

More general looping

The preceding examples that we've seen simply loop through arrays, doing some work. However, sometimes you need to do a loop, but the required process doesn't really fit `map()` or `reduce()`. So what can be done in such cases? There is a `forEach()` method that can help.

Read more about the specification of the `forEach()` method at `https://developer.mozilla.org/en-US/docs/Web/JavaScript/Reference/Global_Objects/Array/forEach`.

You must provide a callback that will receive the value, the index, and the array on which you are operating. (The last two arguments are optional.) JavaScript will take care of the loop control, and you can do whatever you want at each step. For instance, we can program an object copy method by using some `Object` methods to copy the source object attributes one at a time and generate a new object:

```javascript
const objCopy = obj => {
  let copy = Object.create(Object.getPrototypeOf(obj));
  Object.getOwnPropertyNames(obj).forEach(prop =>
    Object.defineProperty(
      copy,
      prop,
      Object.getOwnPropertyDescriptor(obj, prop)
    )
  );
  return copy;
};

const myObj = {fk: 22, st: 12, desc: "couple"};
const myCopy = objCopy(myObj);
console.log(myObj, myCopy); // {fk: 22, st: 12, desc: "couple"}, twice
```

Yes, of course we could have written `myCopy={...myObj}`, but where's the fun in that? Okay, it would be better, but I needed a nice example to use `forEach()` with. Sorry about that! Also, there are some hidden inconveniences in that code, which we'll explain in Chapter 10, *Ensuring Purity – Immutability*, when we try to get really frozen, unmodifiable objects. Just a hint: the new object may share values with the old one because we have a *shallow* copy, not a *deep* one. We'll learn more about this later in the book.

If you use the `range()` function that we defined previously, you can also perform common loops of the `for(i=0; i<10; i++)` variety. We might write yet another version of factorial (!) using that:

```
const factorial4 = n => {
  let result = 1;
  range(1, n + 1).forEach(v => (result *= v));
  return result;
};

console.log(factorial4(5)); // 120
```

This definition of factorial really matches the usual description: it generates all the numbers from 1 to *n* inclusive and multiplies them—simple!

 For greater generality, you might want to expand `range()` so it can generate ascending and descending ranges of values, possibly also stepping by a number other than 1. This would practically allow you to replace all the loops in your code with `forEach()` loops.

At this point, we have seen many ways of processing arrays to generate results, but there are other objectives that might interest you, so let's now move on to logical functions, which will also simplify your coding needs.

Logical higher-order functions

Up to now, we have been using higher-order functions to produce new results, but there are also some other functions that produce logical results by applying a predicate to all the elements of an array. (By the way, we'll be seeing much more about higher-order functions in the next chapter.)

 A bit of terminology: the word **predicate** can be used in several senses (as in *predicate logic*), but for us, in computer science, it has the meaning of *a function that returns true or false*. Okay, this isn't a very formal definition, but it's enough for our needs. For example, saying that we will filter an array depending on a predicate just means that we get to decide which elements are included or excluded depending on the result of the predicate.

Using these functions implies that your code will become shorter: you can, with a single line of code, get the results corresponding to the whole set of values.

Filtering an array

A common need that we will encounter is to filter the elements of an array according to a certain condition. The `filter()` method lets you inspect each element of an array in the same fashion as `map()`. The difference is that instead of producing a new element, the result of your function determines whether the input value will be kept in the output (if the function returned `true`) or if it will be skipped (if the function returned `false`). Also similar to `map()`, `filter()` doesn't alter the original array, but rather returns a new array with the chosen items.

See *Figure 5.4* for a diagram showing the input and output:

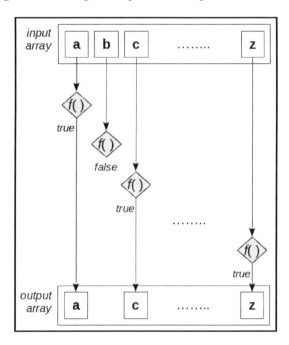

Figure 5.4: The filter() method picks the elements of an array that satisfy a given predicate

Read more on the `filter()` function at https://developer.mozilla.org/en/docs/Web/JavaScript/Reference/Global_Objects/Array/filter.

There are a couple of things to remember when filtering an array:

- **Always return something from your predicate**: If you forget to include a `return`, the function will implicitly return `undefined`, and since that's a *falsy* value, the output will be an empty array.
- **The copy that is made is shallow**: If the input array elements are objects or arrays, then the original elements will still be accessible.

Let's get into more detail by first seeing a practical example of `filter()` and then moving on to look at how you could implement that functionality on your own by using `reduce()`.

A reduce() example

Let's look at a practical example. Suppose a service has returned a JSON object, which itself has an array of objects containing an account `id` and the account `balance`. How can we get the list of IDs that are *in the red*, with a negative balance? The input data could be as follows:

```
const serviceResult = {
  accountsData: [
    {
      id: "F220960K",
      balance: 1024,
    },
    {
      id: "S120456T",
      balance: 2260,
    },
    {
      id: "J140793A",
      balance: -38,
    },
    {
      id: "M120396V",
      balance: -114,
    },
    {
      id: "A120289L",
      balance: 55000,
    },
  ],
};
```

We could get the delinquent accounts with something like the following. You can check that the value of the `delinquent` variable correctly includes the two IDs of accounts with a negative balance:

```
const delinquent = serviceResult.accountsData.filter(v => v.balance < 0);

console.log(delinquent); // two objects, with id's J140793A and M120396V
```

By the way, given that the filtering operation produced yet another array, if you just wanted the accounts IDs, you could get them by mapping the output to just get the ID field:

```
const delinquentIds = delinquent.map(v => v.id);
```

And if you didn't care for the intermediate result, a one-liner would have done as well:

```
const delinquentIds2 = serviceResult.accountsData
    .filter(v => v.balance < 0)
    .map(v => v.id);
```

Filtering is a very useful function, so now, to get a better handle on it, let's see how you could emulate it, which you could even use as a basis for more sophisticated, powerful functions of your own.

Emulating filter() with reduce()

As we did before with `map()`, we can also create our own version of `filter()` by using `reduce()`. The idea is similar: loop through all the elements of the input array, apply the predicate to it, and if the result is `true`, add the original element to the output array. When the loop is done, the output array will only have those elements for which the predicate was `true`:

```
const myFilter = (arr, fn) =>
  arr.reduce((x, y) => (fn(y) ? x.concat(y) : x), []);
```

We can quickly see that our function works as expected:

```
console.log(myFilter(serviceResult.accountsData, v => v.balance < 0));
// two objects, with id's J140793A and M120396V
```

The output is the same pair of accounts that we saw earlier in this section.

Searching an array

Sometimes, instead of filtering all the elements of an array, you want to find an element that satisfies a given predicate. There are a couple of functions that can be used for this, depending on your specific needs:

- `find()` searches through the array and returns the value of the first element that satisfies a given condition, or `undefined` if no such element is found
- `findIndex()` performs a similar task, but instead of returning an element, it returns the index of the first element in the array that satisfies the condition, or -1 if none were found

The similarity to `includes()` and `indexOf()` is clear; these functions search for a specific value instead of an element that satisfies a more general condition. We can easily write equivalent one-liners:

```
arr.includes(value); // arr.find(v => v === value)
arr.indexOf(value);  // arr.findIndex(v => v === value)
```

Going back to the geographic data we used earlier, we could easily find a given country by using the `find()` method. For instance, let's get data for Brazil (`"BR"`); it just takes a single line of code:

```
markers = [
  {name: "UY", lat: -34.9, lon: -56.2},
  {name: "AR", lat: -34.6, lon: -58.4},
  {name: "BR", lat: -15.8, lon: -47.9},
  //...
  {name: "BO", lat: -16.5, lon: -68.1}
];

let brazilData = markers.find(v => v.name === "BR");
// {name:"BR", lat:-15.8, lon:-47.9}
```

We couldn't use the simpler `includes()` method because we have to delve into the object to get the field we want. If we wanted the position of the country in the array, we would have used `findIndex()`:

```
let brazilIndex = markers.findIndex(v => v.name === "BR"); // 2

let mexicoIndex = markers.findIndex(v => v.name === "MX"); // -1
```

Okay, this was simple! What about a special case, which could even be a trick interview question? Read on!

A special search case

Now, for variety, a little quiz. Suppose you had an array of numbers and wanted to run a sanity check, studying whether any of them was NaN. How would you do this? A tip: don't try checking the types of the array elements—even though NaN stands for **not a number**, typeof NaN === "number". You'll get a surprising result if you try to do the search in an *obvious way*:

```
[1, 2, NaN, 4].findIndex(x => x === NaN); // -1
```

What's going on here? It's a bit of interesting JavaScript trivia: NaN is the only value that isn't equal to itself. Should you need to look for NaN, you'll have to use the new isNaN() function, as follows:

```
[1, 2, NaN, 4].findIndex(x => isNaN(x)); // 2
```

This was a particular case, but worth knowing about; I actually had to deal with this case once! Now, let's continue as we have done previously, by emulating the searching methods with reduce() so that we can see more examples of the power of that function.

Emulating find() and findIndex() with reduce()

As with the other methods, let's finish this section by studying how to implement the methods we showed by using the omnipotent reduce(). This is a good exercise to get accustomed to working with higher-order functions, even if you are never going to actually use these polyfills!

The find() function requires a bit of work. We start the search with an undefined value, and if we find an array element so that the predicate is true, we change the accumulated value to that of the array:

```
arr.find(fn);
// arr.reduce((x, y) => (x === undefined && fn(y) ? y : x), undefined);
```

For findIndex(), we must remember that the callback function receives the accumulated value, the array's current element, and the index of the current element, but other than that, the equivalent expression is quite similar to the one for find(); comparing them is worth the time:

```
arr.findIndex(fn);
// arr.reduce((x, y, i) => (x == -1 && fn(y) ? i : x), -1);
```

The initial accumulated value is −1 here, which will be the returned value if no element fulfills the predicate. Whenever the accumulated value is still −1, but we find an element that satisfies the predicate, we change the accumulated value to the array index.

Okay, we are now done with searches: let's move on to consider higher-level predicates that will simplify testing arrays for a condition, but always in the declarative style we've been using so far.

Higher-level predicates – some, every

The last functions we are going to consider greatly simplify going through arrays to test for conditions. These functions are as follows:

- `every()`, which is `true` if and only if *every* element in the array satisfies a given predicate
- `some()`, which is `true` if at least *one* element in the array satisfies the predicate

For example, we could easily check our hypothesis about all the countries having negative coordinates:

```
markers.every(v => v.lat < 0 && v.lon < 0); // false

markers.some(v => v.lat < 0 && v.lon < 0);  // true
```

If we want to find equivalents to these two functions in terms of `reduce()`, the two alternatives show nice symmetry:

```
arr.every(fn);
// arr.reduce((x, y) => x && fn(y), true);

arr.some(fn);
// arr.reduce((x, y) => x || fn(y), false);
```

The first folding operation evaluates `fn(y)`, and ANDs the result with the previous tests; the only way the final result will be `true` is if every test comes out `true`. The second folding operation is similar, but ORs the result with the previous results, and will produce `true`, unless every test comes out `false`.

In terms of Boolean algebra, we would say that the alternative formulations for `every()` and `some()` exhibit duality. This duality is the same kind that appears in the expressions `x === x && true` and `x === x || false`; if x is a Boolean value, and we exchange `&&` and `||`, and also `true` and `false`, then we transform one expression into the other, and both are valid.

In this section, we saw how to check for a given Boolean condition. Let's finish by seeing how to check a negative condition by inventing a method of our own.

Checking negatives – none

If you wanted, you could also define `none()` as the complement of `every()`. This new function would be `true` only if none of the elements of the array satisfied the given predicate. The simplest way of coding this would be by noting that if no elements satisfy the condition, then all elements satisfy the negation of the condition:

```
const none = (arr, fn) => arr.every(v => !fn(v));
```

If you want, you can turn it into a method by modifying the array prototype, as we saw earlier; it's still a bad practice, but it's what we have until we start looking into better methods for composing and chaining functions, as we will see in Chapter 8, *Connecting Functions – Pipelining and Composition*:

```
Array.prototype.none = function(fn) {
  return this.every(v => !fn(v));
};
```

We had to use `function()` instead of an arrow function for the same reasons we saw earlier; in this sort of case, we need `this` to be correctly assigned. Other than that, it's simple coding, and we now have a `none()` method available for all arrays.

In Chapter 6, *Producing Functions – Higher-Order Functions*, we will see other ways of negating a function by writing an appropriate higher-order function of our own.

In this and the preceding section, we worked with everyday problems, and we saw how to solve them in a declarative way. However, things change a bit when you start working with `async` functions. New solutions will be needed, as we will see in the following section.

Working with async functions

All the examples and code that we studied in the previous sections were meant to be used with common functions, specifically meaning not async ones. When you want to do mapping, filtering, reducing, and so on, but the function you use is an async one, the results may surprise you. In order to simplify our work and not have to deal with actual API calls, let's create a `fakeAPI(delay, value)` function that will just delay a while and then return the given value:

```
const fakeAPI = (delay, value) =>
  new Promise(resolve => setTimeout(() => resolve(value), delay));
```

Let's also have a function to display what `fakeAPI()` returns, so we can see that things are working as expected:

```
const useResult = x => console.log(new Date(), x);
```

We are using the modern `async/await` features to simplify our code:

```
(async () => {
  console.log("START");
  console.log(new Date());
  const result = await fakeAPI(1000, 229);
  useResult(result);
  console.log("END");
})();
/*
START
2019-10-13T19:11:56.209Z
2019-10-13T19:11:57.214Z 229
END
*/
```

The results are previsible: we get the START text, then about 1 second (1000 milliseconds) later, we get the result of the fake API call (229), and finally the END text. What could go wrong?

Why are we using the *immediate invocation* pattern that we saw in `Chapter 3, Starting Out with Functions – A Core Concept`? The reason is that you can only use `await` within an `async` function. There is a proposal that will allow the use of `await` with top-level modules (see `https://v8.dev/features/top-level-await` for more on this), but it hasn't made its way into JavaScript yet, and it applies to modules only, not general scripts.

The key problem is that all the functions we saw earlier in this chapter are not `async` *aware*, so they won't really work as you'd expect. Let's start looking at this.

Some strange behaviors

Let's start with a simple quiz: are the results what you expected? Let's look at a couple of examples of code involving `async` calls and maybe we'll see some unexpected results. First, let's look at a common straightforward sequence of `async` calls:

```
(async () => {
  console.log("START SEQUENCE");

  const x1 = await fakeAPI(1000, 1);
  useResult(x1);
  const x2 = await fakeAPI(2000, 2);
  useResult(x2);
  const x3 = await fakeAPI(3000, 3);
  useResult(x3);
  const x4 = await fakeAPI(4000, 4);
  useResult(x4);

  console.log("END SEQUENCE");
})();
```

If you run this code, you'll get the following results, which are surely what you would expect—a START SEQUENCE text, four individual lines with the results of the fake API calls, and a final END SEQUENCE text. Nothing special here—everything is fine!

```
START SEQUENCE
2019-10-12T13:38:42.367Z 1
2019-10-12T13:38:43.375Z 2
2019-10-12T13:38:44.878Z 3
2019-10-12T13:38:46.880Z 4
END SEQUENCE
```

Now let's go for an alternative second version, which you'd probably expect to be equivalent to the first one. The only difference here is that here we are using looping to do the four API calls; it should be the same, shouldn't it? (We could also have used a `forEach` loop with the `range()` function that we saw earlier, but that makes no difference.) I kept using an IIFE, though in this particular case it wasn't needed; can you see why?

```
(() => {
  console.log("START FOREACH");

  [1, 2, 3, 4].forEach(async n => {
    const x = await fakeAPI(n * 1000, n);
    useResult(x);
  });

  console.log("END FOREACH");
})();
```

This piece of code certainly looks equivalent to the first one, but it produces something quite different!

```
START FOREACH
END FOREACH
2019-10-12T13:34:57.876Z 1
2019-10-12T13:34:58.383Z 2
2019-10-12T13:34:58.874Z 3
2019-10-12T13:34:59.374Z 4
```

The `END FOREACH` text appears before the results of the API calls. What's happening? The answer is what we mentioned before: methods similar to `forEach` and the like are meant to be used with common, sync function calls, and behave strangely with `async` function calls. The key concept is that `async` functions always return promises, so that after getting the `START FOREACH` text, the loop is actually creating four promises (which will get resolved at some time), but without waiting for them, and our code goes on to print the `END FOREACH` text.

 You can verify this yourself by looking at the polyfill for `reduce()` at `https://developer.mozilla.org/en-US/docs/Web/JavaScript/Reference/Global_Objects/Array/Reduce#Polyfill`.

The problem is not only with `forEach()`, but rather affects all similar methods as well. Let's see how we can work around this situation and write `async`-aware functions to let us keep working in a declarative fashion, as we did earlier in the chapter.

Async-ready looping

If we cannot directly use methods such as `forEach()`, `map()`, and the like, we'll have to develop new versions of our own. Let's see how to achieve this.

Looping over async calls

Since `async` calls return promises, we can emulate `forEach()` with `reduce()` by starting with a resolved promise and chaining to it the promises for each value in the array. The `then()` methods will be called in the right order, so the results will be correct. The following piece of code manages to get the right, expected results:

```
const forEachAsync = (arr, fn) =>
  arr.reduce(
    (promise, value) => promise.then(() => fn(value)),
    Promise.resolve()
  );

(async () => {
  console.log("START FOREACH VIA REDUCE");
  await forEachAsync([1, 2, 3, 4], async n => {
    const x = await fakeAPI(n * 1000, n);
    useResult(x);
  });
  console.log("END FOREACH VIA REDUCE");
})();

/*
START FOREACH VIA REDUCE
2019-10-13T20:02:23.437Z 1
2019-10-13T20:02:24.446Z 2
2019-10-13T20:02:25.949Z 3
2019-10-13T20:02:27.952Z 4
END FOREACH VIA REDUCE
*/
```

As `forEachAsync()` returns a promise, we mustn't forget to `await` it before showing the final text message. Other than not forgetting all the `await` statements, the code is pretty much similar to what we build using `forEach()`, with the crucial difference that this does work as expected!

Mapping async calls

Can we use the other functions? Writing `mapAsync()`, a version of `map` that can work with an `async` mapping function, is simple because you can take advantage of `Promise.all()` to create a promise out of an array of promises:

```
const mapAsync = (arr, fn) => Promise.all(arr.map(fn));

(async () => {
  console.log("START MAP");

  const mapped = await mapAsync([1, 2, 3, 4], async n => {
    const x = await fakeAPI(n * 1000, n);
    return x;
  });

  useResult(mapped);
  console.log("END MAP");
})();

/*
START MAP
2019-10-13T20:06:21.149Z [ 1, 2, 3, 4 ]
END MAP
*/
```

The structure of the solution is similar to the `forEachAsync()` code. As before, we must remember to await the result of `mapAsync()` before continuing the process. Other than that, the logic is straightforward, and the results are as expected.

Filtering with async calls

Filtering with an `async` function is a tad more complicated. We will have to use `mapAsync()` to produce an array of `true`/`false` values, and then use the standard `filter()` method to pick values out of the original array depending on what the `async` filtering function returned. Let's try out a simple example, calling the API and accepting only even results by means of a `fakeFilter()` function, which, for our example, accepts even numbers and rejects odd ones:

```
const filterAsync = (arr, fn) =>
  mapAsync(arr, fn).then(arr2 => arr.filter((v, i) => Boolean(arr2[i])));

const fakeFilter = (value) =>
  new Promise(resolve =>
    setTimeout(() => resolve(value % 2 === 0), 1000)
  );

(async () => {
  console.log("START FILTER");

  const filtered = await filterAsync([1, 2, 3, 4], async n => {
    const x = await fakeFilter(n);
    return x;
  });

  useResult(filtered);
  console.log("END FILTER");
})();
/*
START FILTER
2019-10-13T21:24:36.478Z [ 2, 4 ]
END FILTER
*/
```

Note that the result of the mapping of `async` calls is a Boolean array (`arr2`), which we then use with `filter()` to select elements from the original array of values (`arr`); this can be tricky to understand!

Reducing async calls

Finally, finding an equivalent for `reduce()` is a bit more complex, but after the other functions that we've seen, not so much. The key idea is the same as in `forEachAsync`: each function call will return a promise, which must be awaited in order to update the accumulator in an upcoming `then()`. To do the reducing, let's have a `fakeSum()` async function that will just sum the API-returned values:

```
const reduceAsync = (arr, fn, init) =>
  Promise.resolve(init).then(accum =>
    forEachAsync(arr, async (v, i) => {
      accum = await fn(accum, v, i);
    }).then(() => accum)
  );

const fakeSum = (value1, value2) =>
  new Promise(resolve => setTimeout(() => resolve(value1 + value2), 1000));

(async () => {
  console.log("START REDUCE");

  const summed = await reduceAsync(
    [1, 2, 3, 4],
    async (_accum, n) => {
      const accum = await _accum;
      const x = await fakeSum(accum, n);
      useResult(`accumulator=${accum} value=${x} `);
      return x;
    },
    0
  );

  useResult(summed);
  console.log("END REDUCE");
})();
/*
START REDUCE
2019-10-13T21:29:01.841Z 'accumulator=0 value=1 '
2019-10-13T21:29:02.846Z 'accumulator=1 value=3 '
2019-10-13T21:29:03.847Z 'accumulator=3 value=6 '
2019-10-13T21:29:04.849Z 'accumulator=6 value=10 '
2019-10-13T21:29:04.849Z 10
END REDUCE
*/
```

Note the important detail: in our reducing function, we must `await` the value of the accumulator, and only afterward `await` the result of our `async` function. This is an important point, which you must not miss: since we are reducing in async fashion, getting the accumulator is also an async matter, so we get to `await` both the accumulator and the new API call.

By looking at these equivalents, we have seen that `async` functions, despite producing problems with the usual declarative methods that we studied at the beginning of the chapter, may also be handled by similar new functions of our own, so we can keep the new style even for these cases. Even if we have to use a somewhat different set of functions, your code will still be declarative, tighter, and clearer; an all-round win!

Summary

In this chapter, we started working with higher-order functions in order to show a more declarative way of working, with shorter, more expressive code. We went over several operations: we used `.reduce()` and `.reduceRight()` to get a single result from an array, `.map()` to apply a function to each element of an array, `.forEach()` to simplify looping, `flat()` and `flatMap()` to work with arrays of arrays, `.filter()` to pick elements from an array, `.find()` and `.findIndex()` to search in the arrays, and `.every()` and `.some()` to verify general logic conditions. Furthermore, we considered some unexpected situations that happen when you deal with `async` functions and we wrote special functions for those cases.

In `Chapter 6`, *Producing Functions – Higher-Order Functions*, we will continue working with higher-order functions, but we will then turn to writing our own ones to gain more expressive power for our coding.

Questions

5.1. **Filtering... but what?** Suppose you have an array, called `someArray`, and you apply the following `.filter()` to it, which at first sight doesn't even look like valid JavaScript code. What will be in the new array and why?

```
let newArray = someArray.filter(Boolean);
```

5.2. Generating HTML code, with restrictions: Using the `filter()`...`map()`...`reduce()` sequence is quite common (even allowing that sometimes you won't use all three), and we'll come back to this in the *Functional design patterns* section in `Chapter 11`, *Implementing Design Patterns – The Functional Way*. The problem here is how to use those functions (and no others!) to produce an unordered list of elements (`<ul>`...`</ul>`) that can later be used onscreen. Your input is an array of objects like the following (does the list of characters date me?) and you must produce a list of each name that corresponds to chess or checkers players:

```
var characters = [
    {name: "Fred", plays: "bowling"},
    {name: "Barney", plays: "chess"},
    {name: "Wilma", plays: "bridge"},
    {name: "Betty", plays: "checkers"},
    .
    .
    .
    {name: "Pebbles", plays: "chess"}
];
```

The output would be something like the following (though it doesn't matter if you don't generate spaces and indentation). It would be easier if you could use, say, `.join()`, but in this case, it won't be allowed; only the three mentioned functions can be used:

```
<div>
    <ul>
        <li>Barney</li>
        <li>Betty</li>
        .
        .
        .
        <li>Pebbles</li>
    </ul>
</div>;
```

5.3. More formal testing: In some of the preceding examples, such as those in the *Emulating map() with reduce()* section, we didn't write actual unit tests, but instead were satisfied with doing some console logging. Can you write appropriate unit tests instead?

5.4. Ranging far and wide: The `range()` function that we saw here can have many uses, but lacks a bit in generality. Can you expand it to allow for, say, descending ranges, as in `range(10,1)`? (What should the last number in the range be?) And could you also allow for a step size to be included to specify the difference between successive numbers in the range? With this, `range(1,10,2)` would produce `[1, 3, 5, 7, 9]`.

5.5. Doing the alphabet: What would have happened in the *Working with ranges* section if instead of writing `map(x => String.fromCharCode(x))`, you had simply written `map(String.fromCharCode)`? Can you explain the different behavior? Hint: we already saw a similar problem elsewhere in this chapter.

5.6. Producing a CSV: In a certain application, you want to enable the user to download a set of data as a **comma-separated value (CSV)** file by using a data URI. (You can read more about this at `https://developer.mozilla.org/en-US/docs/Web/HTTP/Basics_of_HTTP/Data_URIs/`.) Of course, the first problem is producing the CSV itself! Assume that you have an array of arrays of numeric values, as shown in the following snippet, and write a function that will transform that structure into a CSV string that you will then be able to plug into the URI. As usual, \n stands for the newline character:

```
let myData = [[1, 2, 3, 4], [5, 6, 7, 8], [9, 10, 11, 12]];
let myCSV = dataToCsv(myData); // "1,2,3,4\n5,6,7,8\n9,10,11,12\n"
```

5.7. An empty question: Check that `flat1()` and `flat2()` properly work if applied to arrays with empty places, such as `[22, , 9, , , 60, , ]`. Why do they work?

5.8. Producing better output: Modify the cities query to produce a list of strings that includes not only the name of the city, but the state and country as well.

5.9. Old-style code only! Can you rewrite the word-counting solution without using any mapping or reducing at all? This is more of a JavaScript problem than a functional programming one, but why not?

5.10. Async chaining: Our `...Async()` functions are not methods; can you modify them and add them to `Array.prototype` so that we can write, for example, `[1,2,3,4].mapAsync(...)`? And by the way, will chaining work with your solution?

5.11. Missing equivalents: We wrote `forEach()`, `map()`, `filter()`, and `reduce()` async equivalents, but we didn't do the same for `find()`, `findIndex()`, `some()`, and `every()`; can you do that?

6
Producing Functions - Higher-Order Functions

In Chapter 5, *Programming Declaratively – A Better Style*, we worked with some predefined higher-order functions and were able to see how their usage lets us write declarative code so that we can gain in understandability as well as in compactness. In this chapter, we are going to go further in the direction of higher-order functions and develop our own. We can roughly classify the kinds of results that we are going to get into three groups:

- **Wrapped functions**: These keep their original functionality while adding some kind of new feature. In this group, we can consider *logging* (adding log production capacity to any function), *timing* (producing time and performance data for a given function), and *memoization* (this caches results to avoid future rework).

- **Altered functions**: These differ in some key points from their original versions. Here, we can include the once() function (we wrote it in Chapter 2, *Thinking Functionally – A First Example*), which changes the original function so that it only runs once, functions such as not() or invert(), which alter what the function returns, and arity-related conversions, which produce a new function with a fixed number of parameters.

- **Other productions**: These provide new operations, turn functions into promises, allow enhanced search functions, or decouple methods from objects so that we can use them in other contexts as if they were common functions. We shall leave a special case – transducers – for Chapter 8, *Connecting Functions – Pipelining and Composition*.

Wrapping functions – keeping behavior

In this section, we'll consider some higher-order functions that provide a *wrapper* around other functions to enhance them in some way but without altering their original objective. In terms of d*esign patterns* (which we'll be revisiting in Chapter 11, *Implementing Design Patterns – The Functional Way*), we can also speak of *decorators*. This pattern is based on the concept of adding some behavior to an object (in our case, a function) without affecting other objects. The term *decorator* is also popular because of its usage in frameworks such as Angular or (in an experimental mode) for general programming in JavaScript.

 Decorators are being considered for general adoption in JavaScript, but are currently (December 2019) still at Stage 2, *Draft* level, and it may be a while until they get to Stage 3 (*Candidate*) and finally Stage 4 (*Finished*, meaning officially adopted). You can read more about the proposal for decorators at https://tc39.github.io/proposal-decorators/ and about the JavaScript adoption process itself, called TC39, at https://tc39.github.io/process-document/. See the *Questions* section in Chapter 11, *Implementing Design Patterns – The Functional Way*, for more information.

As for the term *wrapper*, it's more important and pervasive than you might have thought; in fact, JavaScript uses it widely. Where? You already know that object properties and methods are accessed through dot notation. However, you also know that you can write code such as myString.length or 22.9.toPrecision(5)—where are those properties and methods coming from, given that neither strings nor numbers are objects? JavaScript actually creates a *wrapper object* around your primitive value. This object inherits all the methods that are appropriate to the wrapped value. As soon as the needed evaluation has been done, JavaScript throws away the just-created wrapper. We cannot do anything about these transient wrappers, but there is a concept we will come back to regarding a wrapper that allows methods to be called on things that are not of the appropriate type. This is an interesting idea; see Chapter 12, *Building Better Containers – Functional Data Types*, for more applications of that!

In this section, we'll look at three examples:

- Adding logging to a function
- Getting timing information from functions
- Using caching (*memoizing*) to improve the performance of functions

Let's get to work!

Logging

Let's start with a common problem. When debugging code, you usually need to add some kind of logging information to see if a function was called, with what arguments, what it returned, and so on. (Yes, of course, you can simply use a debugger and set breakpoints, but bear with me for this example!) Working normally, this means that you'll have to modify the code of the function itself, both at entry and on exit, to produce some logging output. For example, your original code could be something like the following:

```
function someFunction(param1, param2, param3) {
  // do something
  // do something else
  // and a bit more,
  // and finally
  return some expression;
}
```

In this case, you would have to modify so that it looks something like the following. Here, we need to add an `auxValue` variable to store the value that we want to log and return:

```
function someFunction(param1, param2, param3) {
  console.log("entering someFunction: ", param1, param2, param3);
  // do something
  // do something else
  // and a bit more,
  // and finally
  const auxValue = some expression;
  console.log("exiting someFunction: ", auxValue);
  return auxValue;
}
```

If the function can return at several places, you'll have to modify all the `return` statements to log the values that are to be returned. And if you are just calculating the return expression on the fly, you'll need an auxiliary variable to capture that value.

In the next section, we'll learn about logging and some special cases of it, such as functions that throw exceptions, as well as working in a purer way.

Logging in a functional way

Doing logging by modifying your functions as we showed isn't difficult, but modifying code is always dangerous and prone to *accidents*. So, let's put our FP hats on and think of a new way of doing this. We have a function that performs some kind of work and we want to know the arguments it receives and the value it returns.

Here, we can write a higher-order function that will have a single parameter – the original function – and return a new function that will do the following, in sequence:

1. Log the received arguments
2. Call the original function, catching its returned value
3. Log that value
4. Return it to the caller

A possible solution would be as follows:

```
const addLogging = fn => (...args) => {
  console.log(`entering ${fn.name}: ${args})`);
  const valueToReturn = fn(...args);
  console.log(`exiting ${fn.name}: ${valueToReturn}`);
  return valueToReturn;
};
```

The function returned by `addLogging()` behaves as follows:

- The first `console.log(...)` line shows the original function's name and its list of arguments.
- Then, the original function, `fn()`, is called and the returned value is stored.
- The second `console.log(...)` line shows the function name (again) and its returned value.
- Finally, the value that `fn()` calculated is returned.

If you were doing this for a Node application, you would probably opt for a better way of logging by using libraries such as Winston, Morgan, or Bunyan, depending on what you wanted to log. However, our focus is on showing you how to wrap the original function, and the needed changes for using those libraries would be small.

For example, we can use it with the upcoming functions—which are written, I agree, in an overly complicated way, just to have an appropriate example! We'll have a function that accomplishes subtraction by changing the sign of the second number and then adding it to the first. The following code does this:

```
function subtract(a, b) {
  b = changeSign(b);
  return a + b;
}

function changeSign(c) {
  return -c;
```

```
}

subtract = addLogging(subtract);

changeSign = addLogging(changeSign);

let x = subtract(7, 5);
```

The result of executing the previous line would be the following lines of logging:

```
entering subtract: 7, 5
entering changeSign: 5
exiting changeSign: -5
exiting subtract: 2
```

All the changes we had to do in our code were the reassignments of subtract() and changeSign(), which essentially replaced them everywhere with their new log-producing wrapped versions. Any call to those two functions will produce this output.

 We'll see a possible error because we're not reassigning the wrapped logging function while memoizing in the following section.

This works fine for most functions, but what would happen if the wrapped function threw an exception? Let's take a look.

Taking exceptions into account

Let's enhance our logging function a bit by considering an adjustment. What happens to your log if the function throws an error? Fortunately, this is easy to solve. We just have to add a try/catch structure, as shown in the following code:

```
const addLogging2 = fn => (...args) => {
  console.log(`entering ${fn.name}: ${args}`);
  try {
    const valueToReturn = fn(...args);
    console.log(`exiting ${fn.name}: ${valueToReturn}`);
    return valueToReturn;
  } catch (thrownError) {
    console.log(`exiting ${fn.name}: threw ${thrownError}`);
    throw thrownError;
  }
};
```

With this change, if the function threw an error, you'd also get an appropriate logging message, and the exception would be rethrown for processing.

Other changes to get an even better logging output would be up to you – adding date and time data, enhancing the way parameters are listed, and so on. However, our implementation still has an important defect; let's make it better and purer.

Working in a purer way

When we wrote the addLogging() function, we looked at some precepts we saw in Chapter 4, *Behaving Properly – Pure Functions*, because we included an impure element (console.log()) in our code. With this, not only did we lose flexibility (would you be able to select an alternate way of logging?) but we also complicated our testing. We could manage to test it by spying on the console.log() method, but that isn't very clean: we depend on knowing the internals of the function we want to test, instead of doing a purely black-box test. Take a look at the following example for a clearer understanding of this:

```
describe("a logging function", function() {
  it("should log twice with well behaved functions", () => {
    let something = (a, b) => `result=${a}:${b}`;
    something = addLogging(something);

    spyOn(window.console, "log");
    something(22, 9);
    expect(window.console.log).toHaveBeenCalledTimes(2);
    expect(window.console.log).toHaveBeenCalledWith(
      "entering something: 22,9"
    );
    expect(window.console.log).toHaveBeenCalledWith(
      "exiting something: result=22:9"
    );
  });

  it("should report a thrown exception", () => {
    let thrower = (a, b, c) => {
      throw "CRASH!";
    };
    spyOn(window.console, "log");
    expect(thrower).toThrow();

    thrower = addLogging(thrower);
    try {
      thrower(1, 2, 3);
    } catch (e) {
      expect(window.console.log).toHaveBeenCalledTimes(2);
```

```
      expect(window.console.log).toHaveBeenCalledWith(
        "entering thrower: 1,2,3"
      );
      expect(window.console.log).toHaveBeenCalledWith(
        "exiting thrower: threw CRASH!"
      );
    }
  });
});
```

Running this test shows that `addLogging()` behaves as expected, so this is a solution. Our first test just does a simple subtraction and verifies that logging was called with appropriate data, while the second test checks an error-throwing function to also verify that the correct logs were produced.

Even so, being able to test our function in this way doesn't solve the lack of flexibility we mentioned. We should pay attention to what we wrote in the *Injecting impure functions* section – the logging function should be passed as an argument to the wrapper function so that we can change it if we need to:

```
const addLogging3 = (fn, logger = console.log) => (...args) => {
  logger(`entering ${fn.name}: ${args}`);
  try {
    const valueToReturn = fn(...args);
    logger(`exiting ${fn.name}: ${valueToReturn}`);
    return valueToReturn;
  } catch (thrownError) {
    logger(`exiting ${fn.name}: threw ${thrownError}`);
    throw thrownError;
  }
};
```

If we don't do anything, the logging wrapper will obviously produce the same results as in the previous section. However, we could provide a different logger – for example, with Node, we could use *winston*, a common logging tool, and the results would vary accordingly:

See `https://github.com/winstonjs/winston` for more on *winston*.

```
const winston = require("winston");
const myLogger = t => winston.log("debug", "Logging by winston: %s", t);
winston.level = "debug";
```

```
subtract = addLogging3(subtract, myLogger);
changeSign = addLogging3(changeSign, myLogger);
let x = subtract(7, 5);

// debug: Logging by winston: entering subtract: 7,5
// debug: Logging by winston: entering changeSign: 5
// debug: Logging by winston: exiting changeSign: -5
// debug: Logging by winston: exiting subtract: 2
```

Now that we have followed our own advice, we can take advantage of stubs. The code for testing is practically the same as before; however, we are using a stub, dummy.logger(), with no provided functionality or side effects, so it's safer all around. In this case, the real function that was being invoked originally, console.log(), can't do any harm, but that's not always the case, so using a stub is recommended:

```
describe("after addLogging3()", function() {
  let dummy;

  beforeEach(() => {
    dummy = { logger() {} };
    spyOn(dummy, "logger");
  });

  it("should call the provided logger", () => {
    let something = (a, b) => `result=${a}:${b}`;
    something = addLogging3(something, dummy.logger);

    something(22, 9);
    expect(dummy.logger).toHaveBeenCalledTimes(2);
    expect(dummy.logger).toHaveBeenCalledWith("entering something: 22,9");
    expect(dummy.logger).toHaveBeenCalledWith(
      "exiting something: result=22:9"
    );
  });

  it("a throwing function should be reported", () => {
    let thrower = (a, b, c) => {
      throw "CRASH!";
    };
    thrower = addLogging3(thrower, dummy.logger);

    try {
      thrower(1, 2, 3);
    } catch (e) {
      expect(dummy.logger).toHaveBeenCalledTimes(2);
      expect(dummy.logger).toHaveBeenCalledWith("entering thrower: 1,2,3");
      expect(dummy.logger).toHaveBeenCalledWith(
```

```
            "exiting thrower: threw CRASH!"
        );
    }
  });
});
```

The preceding tests work exactly like the previous ones we wrote earlier, but use and inspect the dummy logger instead of dealing with the original `console.log()` calls. Writing the test in this way avoids all possible problems due to side effects, so it's much cleaner and safer.

When applying FP techniques, always keep in mind that if you are somehow complicating your own job – for example, making it difficult to test any of your functions – then you must be doing something wrong. In our case, the mere fact that the output of `addLogging()` was an impure function should have raised an alarm. Of course, given the simplicity of the code, in this particular case, you might decide that it's not worth a fix, that you can do without testing, and that you don't need to be able to change the way logging is produced. However, long experience in software development suggests that, sooner or later, you'll come to regret that sort of decision, so try to go with the cleaner solution instead.

Now that we have dealt with logging, we'll look at another need: timing functions for performance reasons.

Timing functions

Another possible application for wrapped functions is to record and log the timing of each function invocation in a fully transparent way. Simply put, we want to be able to tell how long a function call takes, most likely for performance studies. However, in the same way we dealt with logging, we don't want to have to modify the original function and will use a higher-order function instead.

 If you plan to optimize your code, remember the following three rules: *Don't do it, Don't do it yet,* and *Don't do it without measuring.* It has been mentioned that much bad code arises from early attempts at optimization, so don't start by trying to write optimal code, don't try to optimize until you recognize the need for it, and don't do it haphazardly, without trying to determine the reasons for the slowdown by measuring all the parts of your application.

Along the lines of the preceding example, we can write an `addTiming()` function that, given any function, will produce a wrapped version that will write out timing data on the console but will otherwise work in exactly the same way:

```
const myPut = (text, name, tStart, tEnd) =>
  console.log(`${name} - ${text} ${tEnd - tStart} ms`);

const myGet = () => performance.now();

const addTiming = (fn, getTime = myGet, output = myPut) => (...args) => {
  let tStart = getTime();

  try {
    const valueToReturn = fn(...args);
    output("normal exit", fn.name, tStart, getTime());
    return valueToReturn;

  } catch (thrownError) {
    output("exception thrown", fn.name, tStart, getTime());
    throw thrownError;
  }
};
```

Note that, along the lines of the enhancement we applied in the previous section to the logging function, we are providing separate logger and time access functions. Writing tests for our `addTiming()` function should prove easy, given that we can inject both impure functions.

Using `performance.now()` provides the highest accuracy. If you don't need such precision as what's provided by that function (and it's arguable that it is overkill), you could simply substitute `Date.now()`. For more on these alternatives, see https://developer.mozilla.org/en-US/docs/Web/API/Performance/now and https://developer.mozilla.org/en/docs/Web/JavaScript/Reference/Global_Objects/Date/now. You could also consider using `console.time()` and `console.timeEnd()`; see https://developer.mozilla.org/en-US/docs/Web/API/Console/time for more information.

To be able to try out the logging functionality, I've modified the `subtract()` function so that it throws an error if you attempt to subtract 0. (Yes, of course, you can subtract 0 from another number, but I wanted to have some kind error-throwing situation, at any cost!)

You could also list the input parameters, if desired, for more information:

```
subtract = addTiming(subtract);

let x = subtract(7, 5);   // subtract - normal exit 0.10500000000001819 ms

let y = subtract(4, 0);   // subtract - exception thrown 0.0949999999999136
                          // ms
```

The preceding code is quite similar to the previous `addLogging()` function, and that's reasonable—in both cases, we are adding some code before the actual function call, and then some new code after the function returns. You might even consider writing a *higher-higher-order function*, which would receive three functions and produce a new higher-order function as output (such as `addLogging()` or `addTiming()`) that would call the first function at the beginning, and then the second function if the wrapped function returned a value, or the third function if an error had been thrown! What about that?

Memoizing functions

In `Chapter 4`, *Behaving Properly – Pure Functions*, we considered the case of the Fibonacci function and learned how we could transform it, by hand, into a much more efficient version by means of *memoization*: caching calculated values to avoid recalculations. A *memoized* function is one that will avoid redoing a process if the result was found earlier. We want to be able to turn any function into a memoized one so that we can get a more optimized version.

A real-life memoizing solution should also take into account the available RAM and have some ways of avoiding filling it up; however, this is beyond the scope of this book. Also, we won't be looking into performance issues; those optimizations are also beyond the scope of this book.

For simplicity, let's only consider functions with a single, non-structured parameter and leave functions with more complex parameters (objects, arrays) or more than one parameter for later.

The kind of values we can handle with ease are JavaScript's primitive values: data that aren't objects and have no methods. JavaScript has six of these: `boolean`, `null`, `number`, `string`, `symbol`, and `undefined`. Usually, we only see the first four as actual arguments. You can find out more by going to `https://developer.mozilla.org/en-US/docs/Glossary/Primitive`.

We won't be aiming to produce the best-ever memoizing solution, but let's study the subject a bit and produce several variants of a memoizing higher-order function. First, we'll deal with functions with a single parameter and then consider functions with several parameters.

Simple memoization

We will work with the Fibonacci function we mentioned previously, which is a simple case: it receives a single numeric parameter. This function is as follows:

```
function fib(n) {
  if (n == 0) {
    return 0;
  } else if (n == 1) {
    return 1;
  } else {
    return fib(n - 2) + fib(n - 1);
  }
}
```

The solution we created previously was general in concept, but particularly in its implementation: we had to directly modify the code of the function in order to take advantage of said memoization. Now, we should look into a way of doing this automatically, in the same fashion as we do it with other wrapped functions. The solution would be a `memoize()` function that wraps any other function in order to apply memoization:

```
const memoize = fn => {
  let cache = {};
  return x => (x in cache ? cache[x] : (cache[x] = fn(x)));
};
```

How does this work? The returned function, for any given argument, checks whether the argument was already received, that is, whether it can be found as a key in the cache object. If so, there's no need for calculation, and the cached value is returned. Otherwise, we calculate the missing value and store it in the cache. (We are using a closure to hide the cache from external access.) Here, we are assuming that the memoized function receives only one argument (x) and that it is a primitive value, which can then be directly used as a key value for the cache object; we'll consider other cases later.

Is this working? We'll have to time it – and we happen to have a useful `addTiming()` function for that! First, we take some timings for the original `fib()` function. We want to time the complete calculation and not each individual recursive call, so we write an auxiliar `testFib()` function and that's the one we'll time.

We should repeat the timing operations and do an average but, since we just want to confirm that memoizing works, we'll tolerate differences:

```
const testFib = n => fib(n);

addTiming(testFib)(45); // 15,382.255 ms
addTiming(testFib)(40); //  1,600.600 ms
addTiming(testFib)(35); //    146.900 ms
```

Your own times will vary, of course, depending on your specific CPU, RAM, and so on. However, the results seem logical: the exponential growth we mentioned in Chapter 4, *Behaving Properly – Pure Functions*, appears to be present, and times grow quickly. Now, let's memoize fib(). We should get shorter times... shouldn't we?

```
const testMemoFib = memoize(n => fib(n));

addTiming(testMemoFib)(45); // 15,537.575 ms
addTiming(testMemoFib)(45); //      0.005 ms... good!
addTiming(testMemoFib)(40); //  1,368.880 ms... recalculating?
addTiming(testMemoFib)(35); //    123.970 ms... here too?
```

Something's wrong! The times should have gone down, but they are just about the same. This is because of a common error, which I've even seen in some articles and on some web pages. We are timing testMemoFib(), but nobody calls that function, except for timing, and that only happens once! Internally, all recursive calls are to fib(), which isn't memoized. If we called testMemoFib(45) again, *that* call would be cached, and it would return almost immediately, but that optimization doesn't apply to the internal fib() calls. This is the reason why the calls for testMemoFib(40) and testMemoFib(35) weren't optimized – when we did the calculation for testMemoFib(45), that was the only value that got cached.

The correct solution is as follows:

```
fib = memoize(fib);

addTiming(fib)(45); // 0.080 ms
addTiming(fib)(40); // 0.025 ms
addTiming(fib)(35); // 0.009 ms
```

Now, when calculating fib(45), all the intermediate Fibonacci values (from fib(0) to fib(45) itself) are stored, so the forthcoming calls have practically no work to do.

Now that we know how to memoize single-argument functions, let's look at functions with more arguments.

More complex memoization

What can we do if we have to work with a function that receives two or more arguments, or that can receive arrays or objects as arguments? Of course, like in the problem that we looked at in Chapter 2, *Thinking Functionally – A First Example*, about having a function do its job only once, we could simply ignore the question: if the function to be memoized is unary, we go through the memoization process; otherwise, if the function has a different arity, we just don't do anything!

 The number of parameters of a function is called the *arity* of the function, or its *valence*. You may speak in three different ways: you can say a function has arity 1, 2, 3, and so on; you can say that a function is unary, binary, ternary, and so on; or you can say it's monadic, dyadic, triadic, and so on. Take your pick!

Our first attempt could be just memoizing unary functions, and leave the rest alone, as in the following code:

```
const memoize2 = fn => {
  if (fn.length === 1) {
    let cache = {};
    return x => (x in cache ? cache[x] : (cache[x] = fn(x)));
  } else {
    return fn;
  }
};
```

Working more seriously, if we want to be able to memoize any function, we must find a way to generate cache keys. To do this, we have to find a way to convert any kind of argument into a string. We cannot use a non-primitive as a cache key directly. We could attempt to convert the value into a string with something like strX = String(x), but we'll have problems. With arrays, it seems this could work. However, take a look at the following three cases, involving different arrays but with a twist:

```
var a = [1, 5, 3, 8, 7, 4, 6];
String(a); // "1,5,3,8,7,4,6"

var b = [[1, 5], [3, 8, 7, 4, 6]];
String(b); // "1,5,3,8,7,4,6"

var c = [[1, 5, 3], [8, 7, 4, 6]];
String(c); // "1,5,3,8,7,4,6"
```

These three cases produce the same result. If we were only considering a single array argument, we'd probably be able to make do, but when different arrays produce the same key, that's a problem. Things become worse if we have to receive objects as arguments, because the String() representation of any object is, invariably, "[object Object]":

```
var d = {a: "fk"};
String(d); // "[object Object]"

var e = [{p: 1, q: 3}, {p: 2, q: 6}];
String(e); // "[object Object],[object Object]"
```

The simplest solution is to use JSON.stringify() to convert whatever arguments we have received into a useful, distinct string:

```
var a = [1, 5, 3, 8, 7, 4, 6];
JSON.stringify(a); // "[1,5,3,8,7,4,6]"

var b = [[1, 5], [3, 8, 7, 4, 6]];
JSON.stringify(b); // "[[1,5],[3,8,7,4,6]]"

var c = [[1, 5, 3], [8, 7, 4, 6]];
JSON.stringify(c); // "[[1,5,3],[8,7,4,6]]"

var d = {a: "fk"};
JSON.stringify(d); // "{"a":"fk"}"

var e = [{p: 1, q: 3}, {p: 2, q: 6}];
JSON.stringify(e); // "[{"p":1,"q":3},{"p":2,"q":6}]"
```

For performance, our logic should be as follows: if the function that we are memoizing receives a single argument that's a primitive value, we can use that argument directly as a cache key. In other cases, we would use the result of JSON.stringify() that's applied to the array of arguments. Our enhanced memoizing higher-order function could be as follows:

```
const memoize3 = fn => {
  let cache = {};
  const PRIMITIVES = ["number", "string", "boolean"];
  return (...args) => {
    let strX =
      args.length === 1 && PRIMITIVES.includes(typeof args[0])
        ? args[0]
        : JSON.stringify(args);
    return strX in cache ? cache[strX] : (cache[strX] = fn(...args));
  };
};
```

In terms of universality, this is the safest version. If you are sure about the type of parameters in the function you are going to process, it's arguable that our first version was faster. On the other hand, if you want to have easier-to-understand code, even at the cost of some wasted CPU cycles, you could go with a simpler version:

```
const memoize4 = fn => {
  let cache = {};
  return (...args) => {
    let strX = JSON.stringify(args);
    return strX in cache ? cache[strX] : (cache[strX] = fn(...args));
  };
};
```

 If you want to learn about the development of a top-performance memoizing function, read Caio Gondim's *How I wrote the world's fastest JavaScript memoization library* article, available online at https://community.risingstack.com/the-worlds-fastest-javascript-memoization-library/.

So far, we have achieved several interesting memoizing functions, but how will we manage to write tests for them? Let's analyze this problem now.

Memoization testing

Testing the memoization higher-order function poses an interesting problem – just how would you go about it? The first idea would be to look into the cache – but that's private and not visible. Of course, we could change `memoize()` so that it uses a global cache or somehow allows external access to the cache, but doing that sort of internal exam is frowned upon: you should try to do your tests based on external properties only.

Accepting that we shouldn't try to examine the cache, we could go for a time control: calling a function such as `fib()`, for a large value of n, should take longer if the function isn't memoized. This is certainly possible, but it's also prone to possible failures: something external to your tests could run at just the wrong time and it could be possible that your memoized run would take longer than the original one. Okay, it's possible, but not probable – but your test isn't fully reliable.

So, let's go for a more direct analysis of the number of actual calls to the memoized function. Working with a non-memoized, original `fib()`, we could test whether the function works normally and check how many calls it makes:

```
var fib = null;
beforeEach(() => {
```

```
fib = n => {
  if (n == 0) {
    return 0;
  } else if (n == 1) {
    return 1;
  } else {
    return fib(n - 2) + fib(n - 1);
  }
};
});

describe("the original fib", function() {
  it("should produce correct results", () => {
    expect(fib(0)).toBe(0);
    expect(fib(1)).toBe(1);
    expect(fib(5)).toBe(5);
    expect(fib(8)).toBe(21);
    expect(fib(10)).toBe(55);
  });

  it("should repeat calculations", () => {
    spyOn(window,"fib").and.callThrough();
    expect(fib(6)).toBe(8);
    expect(fib).toHaveBeenCalledTimes(25);
  });
});
```

The preceding code is fairly straightforward: we are using the Fibonacci function we developed earlier and testing that it produces correct values. For instance, the fact that `fib(6)` equals 8 is easy to verify, but where do you find out that the function is called 25 times? For the answer to this, let's revisit the diagram we looked at in Chapter 4, *Behaving Properly – Pure Functions*:

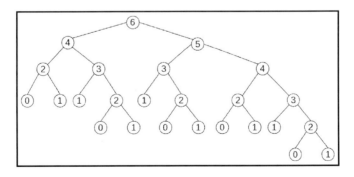

Figure 6.1: All the recursive calls needed for calculating fib(6)

Each node is a call; just by counting, we can see that in order to calculate `fib(6)`, 25 calls are actually made to `fib()`. Now, let's turn to the memoized version of the function. Testing that it still produces the same results is easy:

```
describe("the memoized fib", function() {
  beforeEach(() => {
    fib = memoize(fib);
  });

  it("should produce same results", () => {
    expect(fib(0)).toBe(0);
    expect(fib(1)).toBe(1);
    expect(fib(5)).toBe(5);
    expect(fib(8)).toBe(21);
    expect(fib(10)).toBe(55);
  });

  it("shouldn't repeat calculations", () => {
    spyOn(window, "fib").and.callThrough();

    expect(fib(6)).toBe(8); // 11 calls
    expect(fib).toHaveBeenCalledTimes(11);

    expect(fib(5)).toBe(5); // 1 call
    expect(fib(4)).toBe(3); // 1 call
    expect(fib(3)).toBe(2); // 1 call
    expect(fib).toHaveBeenCalledTimes(14);
  });
});
```

But why is it called 11 times for calculating `fib(6)`, and then three times more after calculating `fib(5)`, `fib(4)`, and `fib(3)`? To answer the first part of this question, let's analyze the diagram we looked at earlier:

- First, we call `fib(6)`, which calls `fib(4)` and `fib(5)`. This is three calls.
- When calculating `fib(4)`, `fib(2)` and `fib(3)` are called; the count is up to five.
- When calculating `fib(5)`, `fib(3)` and `fib(4)` are called; the count climbs to 11.
- Finally, `fib(6)` is calculated and cached.
- `fib(3)` and `fib(4)` are both cached, so no more calls are made.
- `fib(5)` is calculated and cached.
- When calculating `fib(2)`, `fib(0)` and `fib(1)` are called; now, we have seven calls.
- When calculating `fib(3)`, `fib(1)` and `fib(2)` are called; the count is up to nine.

- `fib(4)` is calculated and cached.
- `fib(1)` and `fib(2)` are both already cached, so no further calls are made.
- `fib(3)` is calculated and cached.
- When calculating `fib(0)` and `fib(1)`, no extra calls are made and both are cached.
- `fib(2)` is calculated and cached.

Whew! So, the count of calls for `fib(6)` is 11. Given that all the values of `fib(n)` have been cached, for n from 0 to 6, it's easy to see why calculating `fib(5)`, `fib(4)`, and `fib(3)` only adds three calls: all the other required values are already cached.

In this section, we've dealt with several examples that implied wrapping functions so that they keep working, but with some kind of extra feature added in. Now, let's look at a different case where we want to change the way a function actually works.

Altering a function's behavior

In the previous section, we considered some ways of wrapping functions so that they maintain their original functionality, even though they've been enhanced in some way. Now, we'll turn to modify what the functions do so that the new results will differ from the original function's ones.

We'll be covering the following topics:

- Revisiting the problem of having a function work, but just once
- Negating or inverting a function's result
- Changing the arity of a function

Let's get started!

Doing things once, revisited

Back in `Chapter 2`, *Thinking Functionally – A First Example*, we went through an example of developing an FP-style solution for a simple problem: fixing things so that a given function works only once. The following code is what we wrote back then:

```
const once = func => {
  let done = false;
  return (...args) => {
    if (!done) {
```

```
            done = true;
            func(...args);
        }
    };
};
```

This is a perfectly fine solution; it works well and we have nothing to object to. We can, however, think of a variation. We could observe that the given function gets called once, but its return value gets lost. This is easy to fix: all we need to do is add a `return` statement. However, that wouldn't be enough; what would the function return if it's called more? We can take a page out of the memoizing solution and store the function's return value for future calls.

Let's store the function's value in a variable (`result`) so that we can return it later:

```
const once2 = func => {
    let done = false;
    let result;
    return (...args) => {
        if (!done) {
            done = true;
            result = func(...args);
        }
        return result;
    };
};
```

The first time the function gets called, its value is stored in `result`; further calls just return that value with no further process. You could also think of making the function work only once, but for each set of arguments. You wouldn't have to do any work for that – `memoize()` would be enough!

Back in `Chapter 2`, *Thinking Functionally – A First Example*, in the *An even better solution* section, we considered a possible alternative to `once()`: another higher-order function that took two functions as parameters and allowed the first function to be called only once, calling the second function from that point on. Adding a `return` statement to the code from before, it would have been as follows:

```
const onceAndAfter = (f, g) => {
    let done = false;
    return (...args) => {
        if (!done) {
            done = true;
            return f(...args);
        } else {
            return g(...args);
```

```
      }
    };
  };
```

We can rewrite this if we remember that functions are first-order objects. Instead of using a flag to remember which function to call, we can use a variable (toCall) to directly store whichever function needs to be called. Logically, that variable will be initialized to the first function, but will then change to the second one. The following code implements that change:

```
const onceAndAfter2 = (f, g) => {
  let toCall = f;
  return (...args) => {
    let result = toCall(...args);
    toCall = g;
    return result;
  };
};
```

The toCall variable is initialized with f, so f() will get called the first time, but then toCall gets the g value, implying that all future calls will execute g() instead. The very same example we looked at earlier in this book would still work:

```
const squeak = (x) => console.log(x, "squeak!!");

const creak = (x) => console.log(x, "creak!!");

const makeSound = onceAndAfter2(squeak, creak);

makeSound("door"); // "door squeak!!"
makeSound("door"); // "door creak!!"
makeSound("door"); // "door creak!!"
makeSound("door"); // "door creak!!"
```

In terms of performance, the difference may be negligible. The reason for showing this further variation is to show that you should keep in mind that, by storing functions, you can often produce results in a simpler way. Using flags to store state is a common technique that's used everywhere in procedural programming. However, here, we manage to skip that usage and produce the same result. Now, let's look at some new examples of wrapping functions to change their behaviors.

Logically negating a function

Let's consider the `filter()` method from Chapter 5, *Programming Declaratively – A Better Style*. Given a predicate, we can filter the array to only include those elements for which the predicate is true. But how would you do a reverse filter and *exclude* the elements for which the predicate is true?

The first solution should be pretty obvious: rework the predicate so that it returns the opposite of whatever it originally returned. In Chapter 5, *Programming Declaratively – A Better Style*, we looked at the following example:

```
const delinquent = serviceResult.accountsData.filter(v => v.balance < 0);
```

So, we could just write it the other way round, in either of these two equivalent fashions. Note the different ways of writing the same predicate to test for non-negative values:

```
const notDelinquent = serviceResult.accountsData.filter(
  v => v.balance >= 0
);

const notDelinquent2 = serviceResult.accountsData.filter(
  v => !(v.balance < 0)
);
```

That's perfectly fine, but we could also have had something like the following in our code:

```
const isNegativeBalance = v => v.balance < 0;

// ...many lines later...

const delinquent2 = serviceResult.accountsData.filter(isNegativeBalance);
```

In this case, rewriting the original function isn't possible. However, working in a functional way, we can just write a higher-order function that will take any predicate, evaluate it, and then negate its result. A possible implementation would be quite simple, thanks to modern JavaScript syntax:

```
const not = fn => (...args) => !fn(...args);
```

Working in this way, we could have rewritten the preceding filter as follows; to test for non-negative balances, we use the original `isNegativeBalance()` function, which is negated via our `not()` higher-order function:

```
const isNegativeBalance = v => v.balance < 0;

// ...many lines later...
```

```
const notDelinquent3 = serviceResult.accountsData.filter(
  not(isNegativeBalance)
);
```

There is an additional solution we might want to try out – instead of reversing the condition (as we did), we could write a new filtering method (possibly `filterNot()`?) that would work in the opposite way to `filter()`. The following code shows how this new function would be written:

```
const filterNot = arr => fn => arr.filter(not(fn));
```

This solution doesn't fully match `filter()` since you cannot use it as a method, but we could either add it to `Array.prototype` or apply some methods. We'll look at these methods in Chapter 8, *Connecting Functions – Pipelining and Composition*. However, it's more interesting to note that we used the negated function, so `not()` is actually necessary for both solutions to the reverse filtering problem. In the upcoming *Demethodizing – turning methods into functions* section, we will see that we have yet another solution since we will be able to decouple methods such as `filter()` from the objects they apply to, thereby changing them into common functions.

As for negating the function *versus* using a new `filterNot()`, even though both possibilities are equally valid, I think using `not()` is clearer; if you already understand how filtering works, then you can practically read it aloud and it will be understandable: we want those that don't have a negative balance, right? Now, let's consider a related problem: inverting the results of a function.

Inverting the results

In the same vein as the preceding filtering problem, let's revisit the sorting problem from the *Injection – sorting it out* section of Chapter 3, *Starting Out with Functions – A Core Concept*. Here, we wanted to sort an array with a specific method. Therefore, we used `.sort()`, providing it with a comparison function that basically pointed out which of the two strings should go first. To refresh your memory, given two strings, the function should do the following:

- Return a negative number if the first string should precede the second one
- Return 0 if the strings are the same
- Return a positive number if the first string should follow the second one

Let's go back to the code we looked at for sorting in Spanish. We had to write a special comparison function so that sorting would take into account the special character order rules from Spanish, such as including the letter *ñ* between *n* and *o*, and more. The code for this was as follows:

```
const spanishComparison = (a, b) => a.localeCompare(b, "es");

palabras.sort(spanishComparison); // sorts the palabras array according to
Spanish rules
```

We are facing a similar problem: how can we manage to sort in *descending* order? Given what we saw in the previous section, two alternatives should immediately come to mind:

- Write a function that will invert the result from the comparing function. This will invert the result of all the decisions as to which string should precede, and the final result will be an array sorted in exactly the opposite way.
- Write a `sortDescending()` function or method that does its work in the opposite fashion to `sort()`.

Let's write an `invert()` function that will change the result of a comparison. The code itself is quite similar to that of `not()`:

```
const invert = fn => (...args) => -fn(...args);
```

Given this higher-order function, we can sort in descending order by providing a suitably inverted comparison function. Take a look at the last few lines, where we use `invert()` to change the result of the sorting comparison:

```
const spanishComparison = (a, b) => a.localeCompare(b, "es");

var palabras = ["ñandú", "oasis", "mano", "natural", "mítico", "musical"];

palabras.sort(spanishComparison);
// ["mano", "mítico", "musical", "natural", "ñandú",
"oasis"]
palabras.sort(invert(spanishComparison));
// ["oasis", "ñandú", "natural", "musical", "mítico",
"mano"]
```

The output is as expected: when we `invert()` the comparison function, the results are in the opposite order. Writing unit tests would be quite easy, given that we already have some test cases with their expected results, wouldn't it?

Arity changing

Back in the *Parsing numbers tacitly* section of `Chapter 5`, *Programming Declaratively – A Better Style*, we saw that using `parseInt()` with `reduce()` would produce problems because of the unexpected arity of that function, which took more than one argument—remember the example from earlier?

```
["123.45", "-67.8", "90"].map(parseInt); // problem: parseInt isn't
                                          // monadic!
                                          // [123, NaN, NaN]
```

We have more than one way to solve this. In `Chapter 5`, *Programming Declaratively – A Better Style*, we went with an arrow function. This was a simple solution, with the added advantage of being clear to understand. In `Chapter 7`, *Transforming Functions – Currying and Partial Application*, we will look at yet another, based on partial application. For now, let's go with a higher-order function. What we need is a function that will take another function as a parameter and turn it into a unary function. Using JavaScript's spread operator and an arrow function, this is easy to manage:

```
const unary = fn => (...args) => fn(args[0]);
```

Using this function, our number parsing problem goes away:

```
["123.45", "-67.8", "90"].map(unary(parseInt));   // [123, -67, 90]
```

It goes without saying that it would be equally simple to define further `binary()`, `ternary()`, and other functions that would turn any function into an equivalent, restricted-arity, version. Let's not go overboard and just look at a couple of all the possible functions:

```
const binary = fn => (...args) => fn(args[0], args[1]);
const ternary = fn => (...args) => fn(args[0], args[1], args[2]);
```

This works, but spelling out all the parameters can become tiresome. We can even go one better by using array operations and spreading and make a generic function to deal with all of these cases, as follows:

```
const arity = (fn, n) => (...args) => fn(...args.slice(0, n));
```

With this generic `arity()` function, we can give alternative definitions for `unary()`, `binary()`, and so on. We could even rewrite the earlier functions as follows:

```
const unary = fn => arity(fn, 1);
const binary = fn => arity(fn, 2);
const ternary = fn => arity(fn, 3);
```

You may be thinking that there aren't many cases in which you would want to apply this kind of solution, but in fact, there are many more than you would expect. Going through all of JavaScript's functions and methods, you can easily produce a list starting with `apply()`, `assign()`, `bind()`, `concat()`, `copyWithin()`, and many more! If you wanted to use any of those in a tacit way, you would probably need to fix its arity so that it would work with a fixed, non-variable number of parameters.

 If you want a nice list of JavaScript functions and methods, check out `https://developer.mozilla.org/en/docs/Web/JavaScript/Guide/Functions` and `https://developer.mozilla.org/en-US/docs/Web/JavaScript/Reference/Methods_Index`. As for tacit programming (or pointfree style), we'll be coming back to it in `Chapter 8`, *Connecting Functions – Pipelining and Composition*.

So far, we have learned how to wrap functions while keeping their original behavior or by changing it in some fashion. Now, let's consider some other ways of modifying functions.

Changing functions in other ways

Let's end this chapter by considering some other sundry functions that provide results such as new finders, decoupling methods from objects, and more. Our examples will include the following:

- Turning operations (such as adding with the + operator) into functions
- Turning functions into promises
- Accessing objects to get the value of a property
- Turning methods into functions
- A better way of finding optimum values

Turning operations into functions

We have already seen several cases in which we needed to write a function just to add or multiply a pair of numbers. For example, in the *Summing an array* section of `Chapter 5`, *Programming Declaratively – A Better Style*, we had to write code equivalent to the following:

```
const mySum = myArray.reduce((x, y) => x + y, 0);
```

In the *Working with ranges* section of `Chapter 5`, *Programming Declaratively – A Better Style*, to calculate a factorial, we wrote this:

```
const factorialByRange = n => range(1, n + 1).reduce((x, y) => x * y, 1);
```

It would have been easier if we could just turn a binary operator into a function that calculates the same result. The preceding two examples could have been written more succinctly, as follows. Can you understand the change we made?

```
const mySum = myArray.reduce(binaryOp("+"), 0);
```

```
const factorialByRange = n => range(1, n + 1).reduce(binaryOp("*"), 1);
```

We haven't looked at how `binaryOp()` is implemented yet, but the key notion is that instead of an infix operator (like we use when we write 22+9), we now have a function (as if we could write our sum like +(22,9), which certainly isn't valid JavaScript). Let's see how we can make this work.

Implementing operations

How would we write this `binaryOp()` function? There are at least two ways of doing so: a safe but long one and a riskier and shorter alternative. The first would require listing each possible operator. The following code does this by using a longish `switch`:

```
const binaryOp1 = op => {
  switch (op) {
     case "+":
        return (x, y) => x + y;
     case "-":
        return (x, y) => x - y;
     case "*":
        return (x, y) => x * y;
     //
     // etc.
     //
  }
};
```

This solution is perfectly fine but requires too much work. The second is more dangerous, but shorter. Please consider this just as an example, for learning purposes; using `eval()` isn't recommended, for security reasons! Our second version would simply use `Function()` to create a new function that uses the desired operator, as follows:

```
const binaryOp2 = op => new Function("x", "y", `return x ${op} y;`);
```

If you follow this trail of thought, you may also define a `unaryOp()` function, even though there are fewer applications for it. (I leave this implementation to you; it's quite similar to what we already wrote.) In `Chapter 7`, *Transforming Functions – Currying and Partial Application*, we will look at an alternative way of creating this unary function by using partial application.

A handier implementation

Let's get ahead of ourselves. Doing FP doesn't mean always getting down to the very basic, simplest possible functions. For example, in an upcoming section of this book, we will need a function to check whether a number is negative, and we'll consider (see the *Converting into pointfree style* section of `Chapter 8`, *Connecting Functions – Pipelining and Composition*) using `binaryOp2()` to write it:

```
const isNegative = curry(binaryOp2(">"))(0);
```

Don't worry about the `curry()` function now (we'll get to it soon, in `Chapter 7`, *Transforming Functions – Currying and Partial Application*) – the idea is that it fixes the first argument to 0 so that our function will check for a given number, n, if $0>n$. The point here is that the function we just wrote isn't very clear. We could do better if we defined a binary operation function that also lets us specify one of its parameters – the left one or the right one – in addition to the operator to be used. Here, we can write the following couple of functions, which define the functions where the left or right operators are missing:

```
const binaryLeftOp = (x, op) => y => binaryOp2(op)(x,y);
```

```
const binaryOpRight = (op, y) => x => binaryOp2(op)(x,y);
```

With these new functions, we could simply write either of the following two definitions, though I think the second is clearer. I'd rather test whether a number is less than 0 than whether 0 is greater than the number:

```
const isNegative1 = binaryLeftOp(0, ">");
```

```
const isNegative2 = binaryOpRight("<", 0);
```

What is the point of this? Don't strive for some kind of *basic simplicity* or *going down to basics* code. We can transform an operator into a function, but if you can do better and simplify your coding by also specifying one of the two parameters for the operation, just do it! The idea of FP is to help write better code, and creating artificial limitations won't help anybody.

Of course, for a simple function such as checking whether a number is negative, I would never want to complicate things with currying, binary operators, pointfree style, or anything else, and I'd just write the following with no further ado:

```
const isNegative3 = x => x < 0;
```

So far, we have seen several ways of solving the same problem. Keep in mind that FP doesn't force you to pick one single way of doing things; instead, it allows you a lot of freedom in deciding on which way to go!

Turning functions into promises

In Node, most asynchronous functions require a callback such as `(err,data)=>{...}`: if `err` is `null`, the function was successful and `data` is its result, while if `err` has some value, the function failed and `err` gives the cause. (See `https://nodejs.org/api/errors.html#errors_node_js_style_callbacks` for more on this.)

However, you might prefer to work with promises instead. So, we can think of writing a higher-order function that will transform a function that requires a callback into a promise that lets you use the `.then()` and `.catch()` methods. (In `Chapter 12`, *Building Better Containers – Functional Data Types*, we will see that promises are actually monads, so this transformation is interesting in yet another way.)

 Node, since version 8, already provides the `util.promisify()` function, which turns an async function into a promise. See `https://nodejs.org/dist/latest-v8.x/docs/api/util.html#util_util_promisify_original` for more on that.

How can we manage this? The transformation is rather simple. Given a function, we produce a new one: this will return a promise that, upon calling the original function with some parameters, will either `reject()` or `resolve()` the promise appropriately. The `promisify()` function does exactly that:

```
const promisify = fn => (...args) =>
  new Promise((resolve, reject) =>
    fn(...args, (err, data) => (err ? reject(err) : resolve(data)))
  );
```

When working in Node, the following style is fairly common:

```
const fs = require("fs");

const cb = (err, data) =>
```

```
        err ? console.log("ERROR", err) : console.log("SUCCESS", data);

    fs.readFile("./exists.txt", cb); // success, list the data
    fs.readFile("./doesnt_exist.txt", cb); // failure, show exception
```

However, you can use promises instead by using the promisify() function. However, in current versions of Node, you would use util.promisify():

```
    const fspromise = promisify(fs.readFile.bind(fs));

    const goodRead = data => console.log("SUCCESSFUL PROMISE", data);
    const badRead = err => console.log("UNSUCCESSFUL PROMISE", err);

    fspromise("./readme.txt") // success
      .then(goodRead)
      .catch(badRead);

    fspromise("./readmenot.txt") // failure
      .then(goodRead)
      .catch(badRead);
```

Now, you can use fspromise() instead of the original method. To do so, we had to bind fs.readFile, as we mentioned in the *An unnecessary mistake* section of Chapter 3, *Starting Out with Functions – A Core Concept*.

Getting a property from an object

There is a simple function that we could also produce. Extracting an attribute from an object is a commonly required operation. For example, in Chapter 5, *Programming Declaratively – A Better Style*, we had to get latitudes and longitudes to be able to calculate an average. The code for this was as follows:

```
    markers = [
      {name: "UY", lat: -34.9, lon: -56.2},
      {name: "AR", lat: -34.6, lon: -58.4},
      {name: "BR", lat: -15.8, lon: -47.9},
      ...
      {name: "BO", lat: -16.5, lon: -68.1}
    ];

    let averageLat = average(markers.map(x => x.lat));
    let averageLon = average(markers.map(x => x.lon));
```

We saw another example of this when we learned how to filter an array; in our example, we wanted to get the IDs for all the accounts with a negative balance. After filtering out all other accounts, we still needed to extract the ID field:

```
const delinquent = serviceResult.accountsData.filter(v => v.balance < 0);
const delinquentIds = delinquent.map(v => v.id);
```

 We could have joined those two lines and produced the desired result with a one-liner, but that's not relevant here. In fact, unless the `delinquent` intermediate result was needed for some reason, most FP programmers would go for the one-line solution.

What do we need? We need a higher-order function that will receive the name of an attribute and produce a new function that will be able to extract an attribute from an object. Using the arrow function syntax, this function is easy to write:

```
const getField = attr => obj => obj[attr];
```

 In the *Getters and setters* section of Chapter 10, *Ensuring Purity – Immutability*, we'll write an even more general version of this function that's able to "go deep" into an object to get an attribute of it, regardless of its location within the object.

With this function, the coordinates extraction process could have been written as follows:

```
let averageLat = average(markers.map(getField("lat")));
let averageLon = average(markers.map(getField("lon")));
```

For variety, we could have used an auxiliary variable to get the delinquent IDs, as follows:

```
const getId = getField("id");
const delinquent = serviceResult.accountsData.filter(v => v.balance < 0);
const delinquentIds = delinquent.map(getId);
```

Make sure that you fully understand what's going on here. The result of the `getField()` call is a function, which will be used in further expressions. The `map()` method requires a mapping function and is what `getField()` produces.

Demethodizing – turning methods into functions

Methods such as `filter()` and `map()` are only available for arrays; however, you may want to apply them to, say, a `NodeList` or a `String`, and you'd be out of luck. Also, we are focusing on strings, so having to use these functions as methods is not exactly what we had in mind. Finally, whenever we create a new function (such as `none()`, which we saw in the *Checking negatives* section of `Chapter 5`, *Programming Declaratively – A Better Style*), it cannot be applied in the same way as its peers (`some()` and `every()`, in this case) unless you do some prototype trickery. This is rightly frowned upon and not recommended.

Read the *Extending current data types* section of `Chapter 12`, *Building Better Containers – Functional Data Types*, where we will make `map()` available for most basic types.

So... what can we do? We can apply the old saying *If the mountain won't come to Muhammad, then Muhammad must go to the mountain* and, instead of worrying about not being able to create new methods, we will turn the existing methods into functions. We can do this if we convert each method into a function that will receive, as its first parameter, the object it will work on.

Decoupling methods from objects can help you because once you achieve this separation, everything turns out to be a function and your code will be simpler. (Remember what we wrote in the *Logically negating a function* section, regarding a possible `filterNot()` function in comparison to the `filter()` method?) A decoupled method works similarly to how *generic* functions do in other languages since they can be applied to diverse data types.

Take a look at `https://developer.mozilla.org/en-US/docs/Web/ JavaScript/Reference/Global_Objects/Function` for explanations on `apply()`, `call()`, and `bind()`. We are going to use these for our implementation. Back in `Chapter 1`, *Becoming Functional – Several Questions*, we saw the equivalence between `apply()` and `call()` when we used the spread operator.

There are three distinct, but similar, ways to implement this in JavaScript. The first argument in the list (`arg0`) will correspond to the object, the other arguments (`args`) to the actual ones for the called method. The three equivalent versions would be as follows. Note that any of them could be used as a `demethodize()` function; pick whichever you prefer!

```
const demethodize1 = fn => (arg0, ...args) => fn.apply(arg0, args);
const demethodize2 = fn => (arg0, ...args) => fn.call(arg0, ...args);
const demethodize3 = fn => (...args) => fn.bind(...args)();
```

There's yet another way of doing this: `const demethodize = Function.prototype.bind.bind(Function.prototype.call)`. If you want to understand how this works, read Leland Richardson's *Clever Way to Demethodize Native JS Methods*, at `http://www.intelligiblebabble.com/clever-way-to-demethodize-native-js-methods`.

Let's look at some applications of these! Starting with a simple example, we can use `map()` to loop over a string without converting it into an array of characters first. Say you wanted to separate a string into individual letters and make them uppercase; we could this by using `split()` and `toUpperCase()`:

```
const name = "FUNCTIONAL";
const result = name.split("").map(x => x.toUpperCase());
/*
 ["F", "U", "N", "C", "T", "I", "O", "N", "A", "L"]
*/
```

However, if we demethodize `map()` and `toUpperCase()`, we can simply write the following:

```
const map = demethodize(Array.prototype.map);
const toUpperCase = demethodize(String.prototype.toUpperCase);

const result2 = map(name, toUpperCase);
/*
 ["F", "U", "N", "C", "T", "I", "O", "N", "A", "L"]
*/
```

 For this particular case, we could have turned the string into uppercase and then split it into separate letters, as in `name.toUpperCase().split("")`, but it wouldn't have been such a nice example, with two usages of demethodizing being used.

In a similar way, we could convert an array of decimal amounts into properly formatted strings, with thousands of separators and decimal points:

```
const toLocaleString = demethodize(Number.prototype.toLocaleString);

const numbers = [2209.6, 124.56, 1048576];
const strings = numbers.map(toLocaleString);
/*
 ["2,209.6", "124.56", "1,048,576"]
*/
```

Alternatively, given the preceding demethodized `map()` function, this would have also worked:

```
const strings2 = map(numbers, toLocaleString);
```

The idea of demethodizing a method to turn it into a function will prove to be quite useful in diverse situations. We have already seen some examples where we could have applied it, and there will be more such cases in the rest of this book.

Finding the optimum

Let's end this section by creating an extension of the `find()` method. Suppose we want to find the optimum value—let's suppose it's the maximum—of an array of numbers. We could make do with this:

```
const findOptimum = arr => Math.max(...arr);

const myArray = [22, 9, 60, 12, 4, 56];
findOptimum(myArray); // 60
```

Now, is this sufficiently general? There are at least a pair of problems with this approach. First, are you sure that the optimum of a set will always be the maximum? If you were considering several mortgages, the one with the *lowest* interest rate could be the best, couldn't it? That is, assuming that always wanting the *maximum* of a set is too constrictive.

 You could do a roundabout trick: if you change the signs of all the numbers in an array, find its maximum, and change its sign, then you actually get the minimum of the array. In our case, `-findOptimum(myArray.map((x) => -x))` would correctly produce 4—but it's not easily understandable code, is it?

Second, this way of finding the maximum depends on each option having a numeric value. But how would you find the optimum if such a value didn't exist? The usual way depends on comparing elements with each another and picking the one that comes on top of the comparison: compare the first element with the second and keep the best of those two; then, compare that value with the third element and keep the best; and then keep at it until you have finished going through all the elements.

The way to solve this problem with more generality is to assume the existence of a `comparator()` function, which takes two elements as arguments and returns the best of those. If you could associate a numeric value with each element, then the comparator function could simply compare those values. In other cases, it could do whatever logic is needed in order to decide what element comes out on top.

Let's try to create an appropriate higher-order function; our newer version will use
`reduce()`, as follows:

```
const findOptimum2 = fn => arr => arr.reduce(fn);
```

With this, we can easily replicate the maximum- and minimum-finding functions – we just
have to provide the appropriate reducing functions:

```
const findMaximum = findOptimum2((x, y) => (x > y ? x : y));
const findMinimum = findOptimum2((x, y) => (x < y ? x : y));

findMaximum(myArray); // 60
findMinimum(myArray); // 4
```

Let's go one better and compare non-numeric values. Let's imagine a superhero card game:
each card represents a hero and has several numeric attributes, such as Strength, Powers,
and Tech. When two heroes fight each other, the one with more categories with higher
values than the other is the winner. Let's implement a comparator for this; a suitable
`compareHeroes()` function could be as follows:

```
const compareHeroes = (card1, card2) => {
  const oneIfBigger = (x, y) => (x > y ? 1 : 0);
  const wins1 =
    oneIfBigger(card1.strength, card2.strength) +
    oneIfBigger(card1.powers, card2.powers) +
    oneIfBigger(card1.tech, card2.tech);
  const wins2 =
    oneIfBigger(card2.strength, card1.strength) +
    oneIfBigger(card2.powers, card1.powers) +
    oneIfBigger(card2.tech, card1.tech);
    return wins1 > wins2 ? card1 : card2;
};
```

Then, we can apply this to our *tournament* of heroes. Let's create a constructor to build the
heroes:

```
function Hero(n, s, p, t) {
  this.name = n;
  this.strength = s;
  this.powers = p;
  this.tech = t;
}
```

Now, let's create our own league of heroes:

```
const codingLeagueOfAmerica = [
  new Hero("Forceful", 20, 15, 2),
```

```
    new Hero("Electrico", 12, 21, 8),
    new Hero("Speediest", 8, 11, 4),
    new Hero("TechWiz", 6, 16, 30)
];
```

With these definitions, we can write a `findBestHero()` function to get the top hero:

```
const findBestHero = findOptimum2(compareHeroes);

findBestHero(codingLeagueOfAmerica); // Electrico is the top hero!
```

 When you rank elements according to one-to-one comparisons, unexpected results may be produced. For instance, with our superheroes comparison rules, you could find three heroes where the results show that the first beats the second, the second beats the third, but the third beats the first! In mathematical terms, this means that the comparison function is not transitive and that you don't have a *total ordering* for the set.

With this, we have seen several ways of modifying functions in order to produce newer variants with enhanced processing; think of particular cases you might be facing and consider whether a higher-order function might help you out.

Summary

In this chapter, we learned how to write higher-order functions of our own that can either wrap another function to provide some new feature, alter a function's objective so that it does something else, or even provide totally new features, such as decoupling methods from objects or creating better finders. The main takeaway from this chapter is that you have a way of modifying the behavior of a function without actually having to modify its own code; higher-order functions can manage this in an orderly way.

In Chapter 7, *Transforming Functions – Currying and Partial Application*, we'll keep working with higher-order functions and learn how to produce specialized versions of existing functions with predefined arguments by using currying and partial application.

Questions

6.1. **A border case**: What happens with our `getField()` function if we apply it to a null object? What should its behavior be? If necessary, modify the function.

6.2. How many? How many calls would be needed to calculate `fib(50)` without memoizing? For example, to calculate `fib(0)` or `fib(1)`, one call is enough with no further recursion needed, and for `fib(6)`, we saw that 25 calls were required. Can you find a formula to do this calculation?

6.3. A randomizing balancer: Write a higher-order function, that is, `randomizer(fn1, fn2, ...)`, that will receive a variable number of functions as arguments and return a new function that will, on each call, randomly call one of `fn1`, `fn2`, and so on. You could possibly use this to balance calls to different services on a server if each function was able to do an Ajax call. For bonus points, ensure that no function will be called twice in a row.

6.4. Just say no! In this chapter, we wrote a `not()` function that worked with Boolean functions and a `negate()` function that worked with numerical ones. Can you go one better and write a single `opposite()` function that will behave as `not()` or `negate()` as needed?

6.5. Missing companion: If we have a `getField()` function, we should also have a `setField()` one, so can you define it? We'll be needing both `getField()` and `setField()` in *Chapter 10, Ensuring Purity – Immutability,* when we work with getters, setters, and lenses. Note that `setField()` shouldn't directly modify an object; instead, it should return a new object with a changed value – it should be a pure function!

6.6. Wrong function length: Our `arity()` function works well, but the produced functions don't have the correct `length` attribute. Can you write a different arity-changing function without this defect?

```
const f1 = arity(parseInt,1);
const f2 = arity(parseInt,2);
/*
   f1.length === 0
   f2.length === 0
*/
```

6.7. Not reinventing the wheel: When we wrote `findMaximum()` and `findMinimum()`, we wrote our own functions to compare two values – but JavaScript already provides appropriate functions for that! Can you figure out alternative versions of our code based on that hint?

7
Transforming Functions - Currying and Partial Application

In Chapter 6, *Producing Functions – Higher-Order Functions*, we saw several ways of manipulating functions, to get new versions with some change in their functionality. In this chapter, we will go into a particular kind of transformation, a sort of *factory* method, that lets you produce new versions of any given function, with some fixed arguments.

We will be considering the following:

- **Currying**: A classic FP theoretical function that transforms a function with many parameters into a sequence of unary functions.
- **Partial application**: Another time-honored FP transformation, which produces new versions of functions by fixing some of their arguments.
- **Partial currying (a name of my own)**: Can be seen as a mixture of the two previous transformations.

To be fair, we'll also see that some of these techniques can be emulated, possibly with greater clarity, by simple arrow functions. However, since you are quite liable to find currying and partial application in all sorts of texts and web pages on FP, it is quite important that you are aware of their meaning and usage, even if you opt for a simpler way out. Using the techniques in this chapter will provide you with a different way of producing functions out of other functions, and we'll look at several applications of the ideas in the following sections.

A bit of theory

The concepts that we are going to discuss in this chapter are in some ways very similar, and in other ways quite different. It's common to find some confusion as to their real meanings and there are plenty of web pages that misuse terms. You could even say that all the transformations in this chapter are roughly equivalent since they let you transform a function into another one that fixes some parameters, leaving others free and eventually leading to the same result. Okay, I agree, this isn't very clear! So, let's start by clearing the air, and providing some short definitions, which we will expand on later. (If you feel that your eyes are glazing over, please just skip this section and come back to it later!) Yes, you may find the following descriptions a bit perplexing, but bear with us—we'll go into more detail in just a bit:

- *Currying* is the process of transforming an *m*-ary function (that is, a function of arity *m*) into a sequence of *m* unary functions, each of which receives one argument of the original function, from left to right. (The first function receives the first argument of the original function, and returns a second function that receives the second argument, and returns a third function that receives the third argument, and so on.) Upon being called with an argument, each function produces the next one in the sequence, and the last one does the actual calculations.

- *Partial application* is the idea of providing *n* arguments to an *m*-ary function, being *n* less than or equal to *m*, to transform it into a function with (*m-n*) parameters. Each time you provide some arguments, a new function is produced, with smaller arity. When you provide the last arguments, the actual calculations are performed.

- *Partial currying* is a mixture of both of the preceding ideas: you provide *n* arguments (from left to right) to an *m*-ary function and you produce a new function of arity (*m-n*). When this new function receives some other arguments, also from left to right, it will produce yet another function. When the last parameters are provided, the function produces the correct calculations.

In this chapter, we are going to see these three transformations, what they require, and ways of implementing them. With respect to this, we will go into more than one way of coding each higher-order function and that will give us several insights into interesting ways of coding JavaScript, which you might find interesting for other applications.

Currying

We already mentioned currying back in the *Arrow functions* section of `Chapter 1`, *Becoming Functional – Several Questions*, and in the *One argument or many?* section of `Chapter 3`, *Starting Out with Functions – A Core Concept*, but let's be more thorough here. Currying is a technique that enables you to only work with single-variable functions, even if you need a multiple-variable one.

 The idea of converting a multi-variable function into a series of single-variable functions (or, more rigorously, reducing operators with several operands, to a sequence of applications of a single operand operator) was worked on by Moses Schönfinkel, and there have been some authors who suggest, not necessarily tongue-in-cheek, that currying would be more correctly named *Schönfinkeling*!

In the next sections, we will first see how to deal with functions that have many parameters, and then we'll move on to see how to do currying by hand, or by using `bind()` or `eval()`.

Dealing with many parameters

The idea of currying, by itself, is simple. If you need a function with, say, three parameters, you could write something like the following by using arrow functions:

```
const make3 = (a, b, c) => String(100 * a + 10 * b + c);
```

Alternatively, you can have a sequence of functions, each with a single parameter, as shown here:

```
const make3curried = a => b => c => String(100 * a + 10 * b + c);
```

Alternatively, you might want to consider them as nested functions, like the following code snippet:

```
const make3curried2 = function(a) {
  return function(b) {
    return function(c) {
      return String(100 * a + 10 * b + c);
    };
  };
};
```

In terms of usage, there's an important difference in how you'd use each function. While you would call the first in the usual fashion, such as `make3(1,2,4)`, that wouldn't work with the second definition. Let's work out why: `make3curried()` is a *unary* (single parameter), so we should write `make3curried(1)`. But what does this return? According to the preceding definition, this also returns a unary function—and *that* function also returns a unary function! So, the correct call to get the same result as with the ternary function would be `make3curried(1)(2)(4)`! See *Figure 7.1*:

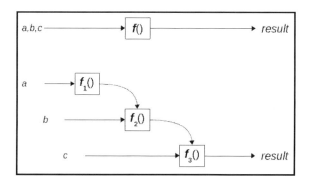

Figure 7.1: The difference between a common function and a curried equivalent.

Study this carefully—we have the first function, and when we apply an argument to it, we get a second function. Applying an argument to it produces a third function and a final application produces the desired result. This can be seen as a needless exercise in theoretical computing, but it actually brings some advantages, because you can then always work with unary functions, even if you need functions with more parameters.

 Since there is a currying transformation, there is also an uncurrying one! In our case, we would write `make3uncurried = (a, b, c) => make3curried(a)(b)(c)` to revert the currying process and make it usable, once again, to provide all parameters in one sitting.

In some languages, such as Haskell, functions are only allowed to take a single parameter—but then again, the syntax of the language allows you to invoke functions as if multiple parameters were permitted. For our example, in Haskell, writing `make3curried 1 2 4` would have produced the result `124`, without anybody even needing to be aware that it involved *three* function calls, each with one of our arguments. Since you don't write parentheses around parameters, and you don't separate them with commas, you cannot tell that you are not providing a triplet of values instead of three singular ones.

Currying is basic in Scala or Haskell, which are fully functional languages, but JavaScript has enough features to allow us to define and use currying in our work. It won't be as easy since, after all, it's not built-in—but we'll be able to manage.

So, to review the basic concepts, the key differences between our original make3() and make3curried() are as follows:

- make3() is a ternary function, but make3curried() is unary.
- make3() returns a string; make3curried() returns another function—which, itself, returns a *second* function, which returns yet a *third* function, which finally does return a string!
- You can produce a string by writing something like make3(1,2,4), which returns 124, but you'll have to write make3curried(1)(2)(4) to get the same result.

Why would you go to all this bother? Let's just look at a simple example, and further on we will look at more examples. Suppose you had a function that calculated the **Value-added Tax (VAT)** for an amount, as shown here:

```
const addVAT = (rate, amount) => amount * (1 + rate / 100);

addVAT(20, 500); // 600 -- that is, 500 + 20%
addVAT(15, 200); // 230 -- 200 +15%
```

If you had to apply a single, constant rate, you could then curry the addVAT() function, to produce a more specialized version that is always applied your given rate. For example, if your national rate was 6%, you could then have something like the following:

```
const addVATcurried = rate => amount => amount * (1 + rate / 100);

const addNationalVAT = addVATcurried(6);

addNationalVAT(1500); // 1590 -- 1500 + 6%
```

The first line defines a curried version of our VAT-calculating function. Given a tax rate, addVATcurried() returns a new function, which when given an amount of money, finally adds the original tax rate to it. So, if the national tax rate were 6%, then addNationalVAT() would be a function that added 6% to any amount given to it. For example, if we were to calculate addNationalVAT(1500), as in the preceding code, the result would be 1590: $1500, plus 6% tax.

Of course, you would probably be justified in saying that this currying thing is a bit too much just to add 6% tax, but the simplification is what counts. Let's look at one more example. In your application, you may want to include some logging, with a function such as the following:

```
let myLog = (severity, logText) => {
  // display logText in an appropriate way,
  // according to its severity ("NORMAL", "WARNING", or "ERROR")
};
```

However, with this approach, every time you wanted to display a normal log message, you would write myLog("NORMAL", some normal text), and for warnings, you'd write myLog("WARNING", some warning)—but you could simplify this a bit with currying, by fixing the first parameter of myLog() as follows, with a curry() function that we'll look at later. Our code could then be as follows:

```
myLog = curry(myLog);
// replace myLog by a curried version of itself

const myNormalLog = myLog("NORMAL");
const myWarningLog = myLog("WARNING");
const myErrorLog = myLog("ERROR");
```

What do you gain? Now you can just write myNormalLog("some normal text") or myWarningLog("some warning"), because you have curried myLog() and then fixed its argument—this makes for simpler, easier-to-read code!

By the way, if you prefer, you could have also achieved the same result in a single step, with the original uncurried myLog() function, by currying it case by case:

```
const myNormalLog2 = curry(myLog)("NORMAL");
const myWarningLog2 = curry(myLog)("WARNING");
const myErrorLog2 = curry(myLog)("ERROR");
```

So, having a curry() function lets you fix some arguments while leaving others still open; let's see how to do this in three different ways.

Currying by hand

Before trying more complex things, we could curry a function by hand, without any special auxiliary functions or anything else. And, in fact, if we just want to implement currying for a special case, there's no need to do anything complex, because we can manage with simple arrow functions: we saw that for both make3curried() and addVATcurried(), so there's no need to revisit that idea.

Instead, let's look into some ways of doing that automatically, so we will be able to produce an equivalent curried version of any function, even without knowing its arity beforehand. Going further, we might want to code a more intelligent version of a function that could work differently depending on the number of received arguments. For example, we could have a `sum(x,y)` function that behaved as in the following examples:

```
sum(3, 5); // 8; did you expect otherwise?

const add3 = sum(3);

add3(5);    // 8

sum(3)(5); // 8 -- as if it were curried
```

We can achieve that behavior by hand. Our function would be something like the following:

```
const sum = (x, y) => {
  if (x !== undefined && y !== undefined) {
    return x + y;

  } else if (x !== undefined && y == undefined) {
    return z => sum(x, z);

  } else {
    return sum;
  }
};
```

Let's recap what we did here. Our curried-by-hand function has this behavior:

- If we call it with two arguments, it adds them, and returns the sum; this provides our first use case, as in `sum(3,5)==8`.
- If only one argument is provided, it returns a new function. This new function expects a single argument, and will return the sum of that argument and the original one: this behavior is what we expected in the other two use cases, such as `add2(3)==5` or `sum(2)(7)==9`.
- Finally, if no arguments are provided, it returns itself. This means that we would be able to write `sum()(1)(2)` if we desired. (No, I cannot think of a reason for wanting to write that.)

So, if we want, we can incorporate currying in the definition itself of a function. However, you'll have to agree that having to deal with all the special cases in each function could easily become troublesome, as well as error-prone. So, let's try to work out some more generic ways of accomplishing the same result, without any kind of particular coding.

Currying with bind()

We can find a solution to currying by using the `bind()` method. This allows us to fix one argument (or more, if need be; we won't be needing to do that here, but later on we will use it) and provide a function with that fixed argument. Of course, many libraries (such as Lodash, Underscore, Ramda, and others) provide this functionality, but we want to see how to implement that by ourselves.

 Read more on `.bind()` at `https://developer.mozilla.org/en/docs/Web/JavaScript/Reference/Global_objects/Function/bind`—it will be useful since we'll take advantage of this method at other points in this chapter.

Our implementation is quite short but will require some explanation:

```
const curryByBind = fn =>
  fn.length === 0 ? fn() : p => curryByBind(fn.bind(null, p));
```

Start by noticing that `curryByBind()` always returns a new function, which depends on the `fn` function given as its parameter. If the function has no (more) parameters left (when `fn.length===0`) because all parameters have already been fixed, we can simply evaluate it by using `fn()`. Otherwise, the result of currying the function will be a new function that receives a single argument, and itself produces a newly curried function, with another fixed argument. Let's see this in action, with a detailed example, using the `make3()` function we saw at the beginning of this chapter once again:

```
const make3 = (a, b, c) => String(100 * a + 10 * b + c);

// f1 is a function that will fix make3's 1st parameter
const f1 = curryByBind(make3);

 // f2 is a function that will fix make3's 2nd parameter
const f2 = f1(6);

// f3 is a function that will fix make3's last parameter
const f3 = f2(5);

// "658" will be now calculated, since there are
// no more parameters to fix
const f4 = f3(8);
```

The explanation of this code is as follows:

- The first function, f1(), has not received any arguments yet. Its result is a function of a single parameter, which will itself produce a curried version of make3(), with its first argument fixed to whatever it's given.
- Calling f1(6) produces a new unary function, f2(), which will itself produce a curried version of make3()—but with its first argument set to 6, so actually the new function will end up fixing the second parameter of make3().
- Similarly, calling f2(5) produces yet a third unary function, f3(), which will produce a version of make3(), but fixing its third argument, since the first two have already been fixed.
- Finally, when we calculate f3(8), this fixes the last parameter of make3() to 8, and since there are no more arguments left, the thrice-bound make3() function is called and the result "658" is produced.

If you wanted to curry the function by hand, you could use JavaScript's .bind() method. The sequence would be as follows:

```
const step1 = make3.bind(null, 6);
const step2 = step1.bind(null, 5);
const step3 = step2.bind(null, 8);

step3(); // "658"
```

In each step, we provide a further parameter. (The null value is required, to provide context. If it were a method attached to an object, we would provide that object as the first parameter to .bind(). Since that's not the case, null is expected.) This is equivalent to what our code does, with the exception that the last time, curryByBind() does the actual calculation, instead of making you do it, as in step3().

Testing this transformation is rather simple—because there are not many possible ways of currying:

```
const make3 = (a, b, c) => String(100 * a + 10 * b + c);

describe("with curryByBind", function() {
  it("you fix arguments one by one", () => {
    const make3a = curryByBind(make3);
    const make3b = make3a(1)(2);
    const make3c = make3b(3);
    expect(make3c).toBe(make3(1, 2, 3));
  });
});
```

What else could you test? Maybe functions with just one parameter could be added, but there are no more to try.

If we wanted to curry a function with a variable number of parameters, then using `fn.length` wouldn't work; it only has a value for functions with a fixed number of parameters. We can solve this simply, by providing the desired number of arguments:

```
const curryByBind2 = (fn, len = fn.length) =>
  len === 0 ? fn() : p => curryByBind2(fn.bind(null, p), len - 1);

const sum2 = (...args) => args.reduce((x, y) => x + y, 0);
sum2.length; // 0; curryByBind() wouldn't work

sum2(1, 5, 3); // 9
sum2(1, 5, 3, 7); // 16
sum2(1, 5, 3, 7, 4); // 20

curriedSum5 = curryByBind2(sum2, 5); // curriedSum5 will expect 5
parameters
curriedSum5(1)(5)(3)(7)(4); // 20
```

The new `curryByBind2()` function works as before, but instead of depending on `fn.length`, it works with the `len` parameter, which defaults to `fn.length`, for standard functions with a constant number of parameters. Notice that when `len` isn't 0, the returned function calls `curryByBind2()` with `len-1` as its last argument—this makes sense, because if one argument has just been fixed, then there is one fewer parameter left to fix.

In our example, the `sum()` function can work with any number of parameters, and JavaScript informs us that `sum.length` is zero. However, when currying the function, if we set `len` to 5, currying will be done as if `sum()` was a five-parameter function—and the last line in the preceding code shows that this is really the case.

As before, testing is rather simple, given that we have no variants to try:

```
const sum2 = (...args) => args.reduce((x, y) => x + y, 0);

describe("with curryByBind2", function() {
  it("you fix arguments one by one", () => {
    const suma = curryByBind2(sum2, 5);
    const sumb = suma(1)(2)(3)(4)(5);
    expect(sumb).toBe(sum2(1, 2, 3, 4, 5));
  });
  it("you can also work with arity 1", () => {
    const suma = curryByBind2(sum2, 1);
    const sumb = suma(111);
    expect(sumb).toBe(sum2(111));
```

```
    });
  });
```

We tested setting the arity of the curried function to 1, as a border case, but there are no more possibilities.

Currying with eval()

There's another interesting way of currying a function—by creating a new one by means of `eval()`. Yes—that unsafe, dangerous `eval()`! (Remember what we said earlier: this is for learning purposes, but you'll be better off avoiding the potential security headaches that `eval()` can bring!) We will also be using the `range()` function that we wrote in the *Working with ranges* section of Chapter 5, *Programming Declaratively – A Better Style*.

 Languages such as LISP have always had the possibility of generating and executing LISP code. JavaScript shares that functionality, but it's not often used—mainly because of the dangers it may entail! However, in our case, since we want to generate new functions, it seems logical to take advantage of this neglected capability.

The idea is simple: in the *A bit of theory* section (earlier in this chapter), we saw that we could easily curry a function by using arrow functions, as shown here:

```
const make3 = (a, b, c) => String(100 * a + 10 * b + c);

const make3curried = a => b => c => String(100 * a + 10 * b + c);
```

Let's apply a couple of changes to the second version, to rewrite it in a way that will help us, as you'll see. First, we can just change the names of the parameters, and directly call the original `make3()` function:

```
const make3curried = x1 => x2 => x3 => make3(x1, x2, x3);
```

Why are we doing this? The answer is short: to help generate the required code automatically. We will be using the `range()` function we wrote back in the *Working with ranges* section of Chapter 5, *Programming Declaratively – A Better Style*, to avoid needing to write an explicit loop:

```
const range = (start, stop) =>
  new Array(stop - start).fill(0).map((v, i) => start + i);

const curryByEval = (fn, len = fn.length) =>
  eval(`${range(0, len).map(i => `x${i}`).join("=>")} =>
    ${fn.name}(${range(0, len).map(i => `x${i}`).join(",")})`);
```

This is quite a chunk of code to digest and, in fact, it should instead be coded in several separate lines to make it more understandable. Let's see how this works when applied to the make3() function as input:

1. The range() function produces an array with the values [0,1,2]. If we don't provide a len argument, make3.length (that is, 3) will be used.
2. We use map() to generate a new array with the values ["x0","x1","x2"].
3. We join() the values in that array to produce x0=>x1=>x2, which will be the beginning of the code that we will eval().
4. We then add an arrow, the name of the function, and an opening parenthesis, to make the middle part of our newly generated code: => make3(.
5. We use range(), map(), and join() again, but this time to generate a list of arguments: x0,x1,x2.
6. We finally add a closing parenthesis, and after applying eval(), we get the curried version of make3().

After following all these steps, in our case, the resulting function would be as follows:

```
curryByEval(make3); // x0=>x1=>x2=> make3(x0,x1,x2)
```

There's only one problem: if the original function didn't have a name, the transformation wouldn't work. (For more about that, check out the *Of lambdas and functions* section of Chapter 3, *Starting Out with Functions – A Core Concept*.) We could work around the function name problem by including the actual code of the function to be curried:

```
const curryByEval2 = (fn, len = fn.length) =>
  eval(`${range(0, len).map(i => `x${i}`).join("=>")} =>
  (${fn.toString()})(${range(0, len).map(i => `x${i}`).join(",")})`);
```

The only change is that instead of including the original function name, we substitute its actual code:

```
curryByEval2(make3); // x0=>x1=>x2=> ((a,b,c) => 100*a+10*b+c)(x0,x1,x2)
```

The produced function is surprising, having a full function followed by its parameters—but that's actually valid JavaScript! In fact, instead of the add() function, as follows, you could also write the function definition followed by its arguments, as in the last line in the following code:

```
const add = (x, y) => x + y;
add(2, 5); // 7

((x, y) => x + y)(2, 5); // 7
```

When you want to call a function, you write it, and follow with its arguments within parentheses—so that's all we are doing, even if it looks weird! We are now done with currying, possibly the best known FP technique, so let's move on to partial application, so you'll have even more flexibility for your own coding.

Partial application

The second transformation that we will be considering lets you fix some of the parameters of the function, creating a new function that will receive the rest of them. Let's make this clear with a nonsense example. Imagine you have a function with five parameters. You might want to fix the second and fifth parameters, and partial application would then produce a new version of the function that fixed those two parameters but left the other three open for new calls. If you called the resulting function with the three required arguments, it would produce the correct answer, by using the original two fixed parameters plus the newly provided three.

The idea of specifying only some of the parameters in function application, producing a function of the remaining parameters, is called **projection**: you are said to be *projecting* the function onto the remaining arguments. We will not use this term, but I wanted to cite it, just in case you happen to find it somewhere else.

Let's consider an example, using the `fetch()` API, which is widely considered to be the modern way to go for Ajax calls. You might want to fetch several resources, always specifying the same parameters for the call (for example, request headers) and only changing the URL to search. So, by using partial application, you could create a new `myFetch()` function that would always provide fixed parameters.

You can read more on `fetch()` at https://developer.mozilla.org/en-US/docs/Web/API/Fetch_API/Using_Fetch. According to http://caniuse.com/#search=fetch, you can use it in most browsers, except for (oh, surprise!) Internet Explorer, but you can get around this limitation with a polyfill, such as the one found at https://github.com/github/fetch.

Let's assume we have a `partial()` function that implements this kind of application and see how we'd use that to produce our new version of `fetch()`:

```
const myParameters = {
  method: "GET",
  headers: new Headers(),
  cache: "default"
```

```
};

const myFetch = partial(fetch, undefined, myParameters);
// undefined means the first argument for fetch is not yet defined
// the second argument for fetch() is set to myParameters

myFetch("a/first/url")
  .then(/* do something */)
  .catch(/* on error */);

myFetch("a/second/url")
  .then(/* do something else */)
  .catch(/* on error */);
```

If the request parameters had been the first argument for fetch(), currying would have worked. (We'll have more to say about the order of parameters later.) With partial application, you can replace any arguments, no matter which, so in this case, myFetch() ends up as a unary function. This new function will get data from any URL you wish, always passing the same set of parameters for the GET operation.

Partial application with arrow functions

Trying to do partial application by hand, as we did with currying, is too complicated. For instance, for a function with five parameters, you would have to write code that would allow the user to provide any of the 32 possible combinations of fixed and unfixed parameters, 32 being equal to 2 raised to the fifth power. And, even if you could simplify the problem, it would still remain hard to write and maintain. See *Figure 7.2* for one of many possible combinations:

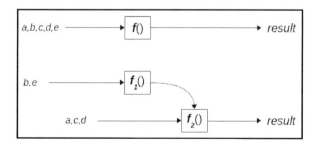

Figure 7.2: Partial application may let you first provide some parameters, and then provide the rest, to finally get the result.

Doing partial application with arrow functions, however, is much simpler. With the example we mentioned previously, we would have something like the following code. In this case, we will assume we want to fix the second parameter to 22, and the fifth parameter to 1960:

```
const nonsense = (a, b, c, d, e) => `${a}/${b}/${c}/${d}/${e}`;

const fix2and5 = (a, c, d) => nonsense(a, 22, c, d, 1960);
```

Doing partial application in this way is quite simple, though we may want to find a more general solution. You can set any number of parameters, by creating a new function out of the previous one but fixing some more parameters. (Wrappers as in the previous Chapter 6, *Producing Functions - Higher Order Functions*, could be used.) For instance, you might now want to also fix the last parameter of the new fix2and5() function to 9, as shown in the following code; there's nothing easier:

```
const fixLast = (a, c) => fix2and5(a, c, 9);
```

You might also have written nonsense(a, 22, c, 9, 1960), if you wished to, but the fact remains that fixing parameters by using arrow functions is simple. Let's now consider, as we said, a more general solution.

Partial application with eval()

If we want to be able to do partial application fixing of any combination of parameters, we must have a way to specify which arguments are to be left free and which will be fixed from that point on. Some libraries, such as Underscore or Lodash, use a special object, _, to signify an omitted parameter. In this fashion, still using the same nonsense() function, we would write the following:

```
const fix2and5 = _.partial(nonsense, _, 22, _, _, 1960);
```

We could do the same sort of thing by having a global variable that would represent a pending, not yet fixed argument, but let's make it simpler, and just write undefined to represent a missing parameter.

When checking for undefined, remember to always use the === operator; with ==, it happens that null==undefined, and you don't want that. See https://developer.mozilla.org/en/docs/Web/JavaScript/Reference/Global_Objects/undefined for more on this.

We want to write a function that will partially apply some arguments and leave the rest open for the future. We want to write code similar to the following and produce a new function in the same fashion as we earlier did with arrow functions:

```
const nonsense = (a, b, c, d, e) => `${a}/${b}/${c}/${d}/${e}`;

const fix2and5 = partialByEval(
  nonsense,
  undefined,
  22,
  undefined,
  undefined,
  1960
);
// fix2and5 would become (X0, X2, X3) => nonsense(X0, 22, X2, X3, 1960);
```

We can go back to using `eval()` and work out something like the following:

```
const range = (start, stop) =>
  new Array(stop - start).fill(0).map((v, i) => start + i);

const partialByEval = (fn, ...args) => {
  const rangeArgs = range(0, fn.length);

  const leftList = rangeArgs
    .map(v => (args[v] === undefined ? `x${v}` : null))
    .filter(v => !!v)
    .join(",");

  const rightList = rangeArgs
    .map(v => (args[v] === undefined ? `x${v}` : args[v]))
    .join(",");

  return eval(`(${leftList}) => ${fn.name}(${rightList})`);
};
```

Let's break down this function step by step. Once again, we are using our `range()` function:

- `rangeArgs` is an array with numbers from zero up to (but not including) the number of parameters in the input function.
- `leftList` is a string, representing the list of variables that haven't been applied. In our example, it would be `"X0,X2,X3"`, since we did provide values for the second and fifth arguments. This string will be used to generate the left part of the arrow function.

- `rightList` is a string, representing the list of the parameters for the call to the provided function. In our case, it would be `"X0,'Z',X2,X3,1960"`. We will use this string to generate the right part of the arrow function.

After having generated both lists, the remaining part of the code consists of just producing the appropriate string and giving it to `eval()` to get back a function.

> If we were doing partial application on a function with a variable number of arguments, we could have substituted `args.length` for `fn.length`, or provided an extra (optional) parameter with the number to use, as we did in the *Currying* section of this chapter.

By the way, I deliberately expressed this function in this long way, to make it more clear. (We already saw somewhat similar—though shorter—code, when we did currying using `eval()`.) However, be aware that you might also find a shorter, more intense and obscure version, and that's the kind of code that gives FP a bad name! Our new version of the code could be:

```
const partialByEval2 = (fn, ...args) =>
  eval(
    `(${range(0, fn.length)
      .map(v => (args[v] === undefined ? `x${v}` : null))
      .filter(v => !!v)
      .join(",")}) => ${fn.name}(${range(0, fn.length)
      .map(v => (args[v] == undefined ? `x${v}` : args[v]))
      .join(",")})`
  );
```

Let's finish this section by writing some tests. Here are some things we should consider:

- When we do partial application, the arity of the produced function should decrease.
- The original function should be called when arguments are in the correct order.

We could write something like the following, allowing the fixing of arguments in different places. Instead of using a spy or mock, we can directly work with the `nonsense()` function we had because it's quite efficient:

```
const nonsense = (a, b, c, d, e) => `${a}/${b}/${c}/${d}/${e}`;

describe("with partialByEval()", function() {
  it("you could fix no arguments", () => {
    const nonsensePC0 = partialByEval(nonsense);
    expect(nonsensePC0.length).toBe(5);
    expect(nonsensePC0(0, 1, 2, 3, 4)).toBe(nonsense(0, 1, 2, 3, 4));
```

```
  });
  it("you could fix only some initial arguments", () => {
    const nonsensePC1 = partialByEval(nonsense, 1, 2, 3);
    expect(nonsensePC1.length).toBe(2);
    expect(nonsensePC1(4, 5)).toBe(nonsense(1, 2, 3, 4, 5));
  });
  it("you could skip some arguments", () => {
    const nonsensePC2 = partialByEval(
      nonsense,
      undefined,
      22,
      undefined,
      44
    );
    expect(nonsensePC2.length).toBe(3);
    expect(nonsensePC2(11, 33, 55)).toBe(nonsense(11, 22, 33, 44, 55));
  });
  it("you could fix only some last arguments", () => {
    const nonsensePC3 = partialByEval(
      nonsense,
      undefined,
      undefined,
      undefined,
      444,
      555
    );
    expect(nonsensePC3.length).toBe(3);
    expect(nonsensePC3(111, 222, 333)).toBe(
      nonsense(111, 222, 333, 444, 555)
    );
  });
  it("you could fix ALL the arguments", () => {
    const nonsensePC4 = partialByEval(nonsense, 6, 7, 8, 9, 0);
    expect(nonsensePC4.length).toBe(0);
    expect(nonsensePC4()).toBe(nonsense(6, 7, 8, 9, 0));
  });
});
```

We wrote a partial application higher-order function, but it's not as flexible as we would like. For instance, we can fix a few arguments in the first instance, but then we have to provide all the rest of the arguments in the next call. It would be better if, after calling partialByEval(), we got a new function, and if we didn't provide all required arguments, we would get yet another function, and another, and so on, until all parameters had been provided—somewhat along the lines of what happens with currying. So, let's change the way we're doing partial application and consider another solution.

Partial application with closures

Let's examine yet another way of doing partial application, by using closures. (You may want to go over that topic in Chapter 1, *Becoming Functional – Several Questions*.) This way of doing partial application will behave in a fashion somewhat reminiscent of the curry() functions we wrote earlier in this chapter, and solve the lack of flexibility that we mentioned at the end of the previous section. Our new implementation would be as follows:

```
const partialByClosure = (fn, ...args) => {
  const partialize = (...args1) => (...args2) => {
    for (let i = 0; i < args1.length && args2.length; i++) {
      if (args1[i] === undefined) {
        args1[i] = args2.shift();
      }
    }

    const allParams = [...args1, ...args2];
    return (allParams.includes(undefined) || allParams.length < fn.length
      ? partialize
      : fn)(...allParams);
  };

  return partialize(...args);
};
```

Wow—a longish bit of code! The key is the inner partialize() function. Given a list of parameters (args1), it produces a function that receives a second list of parameters (args2):

- First, it replaces all possible undefined values in args1 with values from args2.
- Then, if any parameters are left in args2, it also appends them to those of args1, producing allParams.
- Finally, if that list of arguments does not include any more undefined values, and it is sufficiently long, it calls the original function.
- Otherwise, it partializes itself, to wait for more parameters.

An example will make it more clear. Let's go back to our trusty make3() function and construct a partial version of it:

```
const make3 = (a, b, c) => String(100 * a + 10 * b + c);
const f1 = partialByClosure(make3, undefined, 4);
```

Now let's write a second function:

```
const f2 = f1(7);
```

What happens? The original list of parameters ([undefined, 4]) gets merged with the new list (a single element—in this case, [7]), producing a function that now receives 7 and 4 as its first two arguments. However, this isn't yet ready, because the original function requires three arguments. We could write the following:

```
const f3 = f2(9);
```

Then, the current list of arguments would be merged with the new argument, producing [7,4,9]. Since the list is now complete, the original function will be evaluated, producing 749 as the final result.

There are important similarities between the structure of this code and the other higher-order function we wrote earlier, in the *Currying with bind()* section:

- If all the arguments have been provided, the original function is called.

- Otherwise, if some arguments are still required (when currying, it's just a matter of counting arguments; when doing partial application, you must also consider the possibility of having some undefined parameters), the higher-order function calls itself to produce a new version of the function that will *wait* for the missing arguments.

Let's finish by writing some tests that will show the enhancements in our new way of doing partial application. Basically, all the tests we did earlier would work, but we must also try applying arguments in sequence, so we should get the final result after two or more application steps. However, since we can now call our intermediate functions with any number of parameters, we cannot test arities: for all those intermediate functions, we get that function.length===0. Our tests could be as follows:

```
describe("with partialByClosure()", function() {
  it("you could fix no arguments", () => {
    const nonsensePC0 = partialByClosure(nonsense);
    expect(nonsensePC0(0, 1, 2, 3, 4)).toBe(nonsense(0, 1, 2, 3, 4));
  });

  it("you could fix only some initial arguments, and then some more", () =>
{
    const nonsensePC1 = partialByClosure(nonsense, 1, 2, 3);
    const nonsensePC1b = nonsensePC1(undefined, 5);
    expect(nonsensePC1b(4)).toBe(nonsense(1, 2, 3, 4, 5));
```

```
  });

  it("you could skip some arguments", () => {
    const nonsensePC2 = partialByClosure(
      nonsense,
      undefined,
      22,
      undefined,
      44
    );
    expect(nonsensePC2(11, 33, 55)).toBe(nonsense(11, 22, 33, 44, 55));
  });

  it("you could fix only some last arguments", () => {
    const nonsensePC3 = partialByClosure(
      nonsense,
      undefined,
      undefined,
      undefined,
      444,
      555
    );
    expect(nonsensePC3(111)(222, 333)).toBe(
      nonsense(111, 222, 333, 444, 555)
    );
  });

  it("you could simulate currying", () => {
    const nonsensePC4 = partialByClosure(nonsense);
    expect(nonsensePC4(6)(7)(8)(9)(0)).toBe(nonsense(6, 7, 8, 9, 0));
  });

  it("you could fix ALL the arguments", () => {
    const nonsensePC5 = partialByClosure(nonsense, 16, 17, 18, 19, 20);
    expect(nonsensePC5()).toBe(nonsense(16, 17, 18, 19, 20));
  });
});
```

The code is longer than before, but the tests themselves are easy to understand. The next-to-last test should remind you of currying, by the way! We have now seen how to do currying and partial application. Let's finish the chapter with a hybrid method, partial currying, which includes aspects of both techniques.

Partial currying

The last transformation we will look at is a sort of mixture of currying and partial application. If you google it, in some places you will find it called *currying*, and in others, *partial application*, but as it happens, it fits neither, so I'm sitting on the fence and calling it *partial currying*!

The idea of this is, given a function, to fix its first few arguments and produce a new function that will receive the rest of them. However, if that new function is given fewer arguments, it will fix whatever it was given and produce a newer function, to receive the rest of them, until all the arguments are given and the final result can be calculated. See *Figure 7.3*:

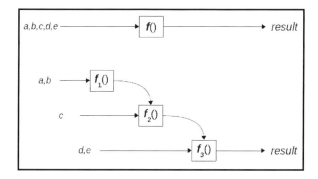

Figure 7.3: Partial currying is a mixture of currying and partial application. You may provide arguments from the left, in any quantity, until all have been provided, and then the result is calculated.

To look at an example, let's go back to the `nonsense()` function we have been using in previous sections, as follows. Assume we already have a `partialCurry()` function:

```
const nonsense = (a, b, c, d, e) => `${a}/${b}/${c}/${d}/${e}`;

const pcNonsense = partialCurry(nonsense);
const fix1And2 = pcNonsense(9, 22); // fix1And2 is now a ternary function
const fix3 = fix1And2(60); // fix3 is a binary function
const fix4and5 = fix3(12, 4); // fix4and5 === nonsense(9,22,60,12,4),
"9/22/60/12/4"
```

The original function had an arity of 5. When we *partial curry* that function, and give it arguments 9 and 22, it becomes a ternary function, because out of the original five parameters, two have become fixed. If we take that ternary function and give it a single argument (60), the result is yet another function: in this case, a binary one, because now we have fixed the first three of the original five parameters. The final call, providing the last two arguments, then does the job of actually calculating the desired result.

There are some points in common with currying and partial application, but also some differences, as follows:

- The original function is transformed into a series of functions, each of which produces the next one until the last in the series actually carries out its calculations.
- You always provide parameters starting from the first one (the leftmost one), as in currying, but you can provide more than one, as in partial application.
- When currying a function, all the intermediate functions are unary, but with partial currying that need not be so. However, if in each instance we were to provide a single argument, then the result would require as many steps as plain currying.

So, we have our definition—let's now see how we can implement our new higher-order function; we'll probably be reusing a few concepts from the previous sections in this chapter.

Partial currying with bind()

Similar to what we did with currying, there's a simple way to do partial currying. We will take advantage of the fact that bind() can actually fix many arguments at once:

```
const partialCurryingByBind = fn =>
  fn.length === 0
    ? fn()
    : (...pp) => partialCurryingByBind(fn.bind(null, ...pp));
```

Compare the code to the previous curryByBind() function and you'll see the very small differences:

```
const curryByBind = fn =>
  fn.length === 0
    ? fn()
    : p => curryByBind(fn.bind(null, p));
```

The mechanism is exactly the same. The only difference is that in our new function, we can bind many arguments at the same time, while in curryByBind() we always bind just one. We can revisit our earlier example—and the only difference is that we can get the final result in fewer steps:

```
const make3 = (a, b, c) => String(100 * a + 10 * b + c);

const f1 = partialCurryingByBind(make3);
```

```
const f2 = f1(6, 5); // f2 is a function, that fixes make3's first two
arguments
const f3 = f2(8); // "658" is calculated, since there are no more
parameters to fix
```

By the way, and just to be aware of the existing possibilities, you can fix some parameters when currying as shown here:

```
const g1 = partialCurryingByBind(make3)(8, 7);
const g2 = g1(6); // "876"
```

Testing this function is easy and the examples we provided are a very good starting point. Note, however, that since we allow the fixing of any number of arguments, we cannot test the arity of the intermediate functions. Our tests could be as follows, then:

```
const make3 = (a, b, c) => String(100 * a + 10 * b + c);

describe("with partialCurryingByBind", function() {
  it("you could fix arguments in several steps", () => {
    const make3a = partialCurryingByBind(make3);
    const make3b = make3a(1, 2);
    const make3c = make3b(3);
    expect(make3c).toBe(make3(1, 2, 3));
  });

  it("you could fix arguments in a single step", () => {
    const make3a = partialCurryingByBind(make3);
    const make3b = make3a(10, 11, 12);
    expect(make3b).toBe(make3(10, 11, 12));
  });

  it("you could fix ALL the arguments", () => {
    const make3all = partialCurryingByBind(make3);
    expect(make3all(20, 21, 22)).toBe(make3(20, 21, 22));
  });

  it("you could fix one argument at a time", () => {
    const make3one = partialCurryingByBind(make3)(30)(31)(32);
    expect(make3one).toBe(make3(30, 31, 32));
  });
});
```

Now, let's consider functions with a variable number of parameters. As before, we'll have to provide an extra value, and we'll get the following implementation:

```
const partialCurryingByBind2 = (fn, len = fn.length) =>
  len === 0
    ? fn()
    : (...pp) =>
        partialCurryingByBind2(
          fn.bind(null, ...pp),
          len - pp.length
        );
```

We can try this out in a simple way, revisiting our currying example from earlier in the chapter, but now using partial currying, as shown here:

```
const sum = (...args) => args.reduce((x, y) => x + y, 0);

pcSum5 = partialCurryingByBind2(sum2, 5);
// curriedSum5 will expect 5 parameters

pcSum5(1, 5)(3)(7, 4); // 20
```

When we called the new pcSum5() function with arguments (1,5), it produced a new function that expected three more. Providing it with one single parameter (3), a third function was created, to wait for the last two. Finally, when we provided the last two values (7,4) to that last function, the original function was called, to calculate the result (20).

We can also add some tests for this alternate way of doing partial currying:

```
const sum2 = (...args) => args.reduce((x, y) => x + y, 0);

describe("with partialCurryingByBind2", function() {
  it("you could fix arguments in several steps", () => {
    const suma = partialCurryingByBind2(sum2, 3);
    const sumb = suma(1, 2);
    const sumc = sumb(3);
    expect(sumc).toBe(sum2(1, 2, 3));
  });

  it("you could fix arguments in a single step", () => {
    const suma = partialCurryingByBind2(sum2, 4);
    const sumb = suma(10, 11, 12, 13);
    expect(sumb).toBe(sum(10, 11, 12, 13));
  });

  it("you could fix ALL the arguments", () => {
    const sumall = partialCurryingByBind2(sum2, 5);
```

```
        expect(sumall(20, 21, 22, 23, 24)).toBe(sum2(20, 21, 22, 23, 24));
    });

    it("you could fix one argument at a time", () => {
        const sumone = partialCurryingByBind2(sum2, 6)(30)(31)(32)(33)(34)(35);
        expect(sumone).toBe(sum2(30, 31, 32, 33, 34, 35));
    });
});
```

Trying out different arities is better than sticking to just one, so we did that for variety.

Partial currying with closures

As with partial application, there's a solution that works with closures. Since we have gone over many of the required details, let's jump directly into the code:

```
const partialCurryByClosure = fn => {
    const curryize = (...args1) => (...args2) => {
        const allParams = [...args1, ...args2];
        return (allParams.length < func.length ? curryize : fn)(
            ...allParams
        );
    };

    return curryize();
};
```

If you compare `partialCurryByClosure()` and `partialByClosure()`, the main difference is that with partial currying, since we are always providing arguments from the left, and there is no way to skip some, you concatenate whatever arguments you had with the new ones, and check whether you got enough. If the new list of arguments has reached the expected arity of the original function, you can call it and get the final result. In other cases, you just use `curryize()` to get a new intermediate function, which will wait for more arguments.

As earlier, if you have to deal with functions with a varying number of parameters, you can provide an extra argument to the partial currying function:

```
const partialCurryByClosure2 = (fn, len = fn.length) => {
    const curryize = (...args1) => (...args2) => {
        const allParams = [...args1, ...args2];
        return (allParams.length < len ? curryize : fn)(...allParams);
    };
    return curryize();
};
```

The results are exactly the same as in the previous section, *Partial currying with bind()*, so it's not worth repeating them. You could also easily change the tests we wrote to use `partialCurryByClosure()` instead of `partialCurryByBind()` and they would work.

Final thoughts

Let's finish this chapter with two more philosophical considerations regarding currying and partial application, which may cause a bit of a discussion:

- First, many libraries are just wrong as to the order of their parameters, making them harder to use.
- Second, I don't usually even use the higher-order functions in this chapter, going for simpler JavaScript code!

That's probably not what you were expecting at this time, so let's go over those two points in more detail, so you'll see it's not a matter of *do as I say, not as I do...* or *as the libraries do*!

Parameter order

There's a problem that's common to not only functions such as Underscore's or LoDash's `_.map(list, mappingFunction)` or `_.reduce(list, reducingFunction, initialValue)`, but also to some that we have produced in this book, such as the result of `demethodize()`, for example. (See the *Demethodizing - turning methods into functions* section of `Chapter 6`, *Producing Functions – Higher-Order Functions*, to review that higher-order function.) The problem is that the *order* of their parameters doesn't really help with currying.

When currying a function, you will probably want to store intermediate results. When we do something like in the code that follows, we assume that you are going to reuse the curried function with the fixed argument and that means that the first argument to the original function is the least likely to change. Let's now consider a specific case. Answer this question: what's more likely—that you'll use `map()` to apply the same function to several different arrays, or that you'll apply several different functions to the same array? With validations or transformations, the former is more likely, but that's not what we get!

We can write a simple function to flip the parameters for a binary function, as shown here:

```
const flipTwo = fn => (p1, p2) => fn(p2, p1);
```

Note that even if the original `fn()` function could receive more or fewer arguments, after applying `flipTwo()` to it, the arity of the resulting function will be fixed to 2. We will be taking advantage of this fact in the following section.

With this, you could then write code as follows:

```
const myMap = curry(flipTwo(demethodize(map)));
const makeString = v => String(v);

const stringify = myMap(makeString);
let x = stringify(anArray);
let y = stringify(anotherArray);
let z = stringify(yetAnotherArray);
```

The most common use case is that you'll want to apply the function to several different lists, and neither the library functions nor our own *demethodized* ones provide for that. However, by using `flipTwo()`, we can work in a fashion we would prefer.

In this particular case, we might have solved our problem by using partial application instead of currying, because with that we could fix the second argument to `map()` without any further bother. However, flipping arguments to produce new functions that have a different order of parameters is also an often-used technique, and it's important that you're aware of it.

For situations such as with `reduce()`, which usually receives three arguments (the list, the function, and the initial value), we may opt for this:

```
const flip3 = fn => (p1, p2, p3) => fn(p2, p3, p1);

const myReduce = partialCurry(flip3(demethodize(Array.prototype.reduce)));

const sum = (x, y) => x + y;
const sumAll = myReduce(sum, 0);
sumAll(anArray);
sumAll(anotherArray);
```

Here, we used partial currying to simplify the expression for `sumAll()`. The alternative would have been using common currying, and then we would have defined `sumAll = myReduce(sum)(0)`.

If you want, you can also go for more esoteric parameter rearranging functions, but you usually won't need more than these two. For really complex situations, you may instead opt for using arrow functions (as we did when defining `flipTwo()` and `flip3()`) and make it clear what kind of reordering you need.

Being functional

Now that we are nearing the end of this chapter, a confession is in order: I do not always use currying and partial application as shown above! Don't misunderstand me, I *do* apply those techniques—but sometimes it makes for longer, less clear, not necessarily better code. Let me show you what I'm talking about.

If I'm writing my own function and then I want to curry it in order to fix the first parameter, currying (or partial application, or partial currying) doesn't really make a difference, in comparison to arrow functions. I'd have to write the following:

```
const myFunction = (a, b, c) => { ... };
const myCurriedFunction = curry(myFunction)(fixed_first_argument);

// and later in the code...
myCurriedFunction(second_argument)(third_argument);
```

Currying the function, and giving it a first parameter, all in the same line, may be considered not so clear; the alternative calls for an added variable and one more line of code. Later, the future call isn't so good either; however, partial currying makes it simpler: `myPartiallyCurriedFunction(second_argument, third_argument)`. In any case, when I compare the final code with the use of arrow functions, I think the other solutions aren't really any better; make your own evaluation of the sample that follows:

```
const myFunction = (a, b, c) => { ... };
const myFixedFirst = (b, c) => myFunction(fixed_first_argument, b, c);

// and later...
myFixedFirst(second_argument, third_argument);
```

Where I do think that currying and partial application is quite good is in my small library of demethodized, pre-curried, basic higher-order functions. I have my own set of functions, such as the following:

```
const _plainMap = demethodize(Array.prototype.map);
const myMap = curry(_plainMap, 2);
const myMapX = curry(flipTwo(_plainMap));

const _plainReduce = demethodize(Array.prototype.reduce);
```

```
const myReduce = curry(_plainReduce, 3);
const myReduceX = curry(flip3(_plainReduce));

const _plainFilter = demethodize(Array.prototype.filter);
const myFilter = curry(_plainFilter, 2);
const myFilterX = curry(flipTwo(_plainFilter));

// ...and more functions in the same vein
```

Here are some points to note about the code:

- I have these functions in a separate module, and I only export the myXXX() named ones.
- The other functions are private, and I use the leading underscore to remind me of that.
- I use the my... prefix to remember that these are *my* functions and not the normal JavaScript ones. Some people would rather keep the standard names such as map() or filter(), but I prefer distinct names.
- Since most of the JavaScript methods have a variable arity, I had to specify it when currying.
- I always provide the third argument (the initial value for reducing) to reduce(), so the arity I chose for that function is three.
- When currying flipped functions, you don't need to specify the number of parameters, because flipping already does that for you.

In the end, it all comes down to a personal decision; experiment with the techniques that we've looked at in this chapter and see which ones you prefer!

Summary

In this chapter, we have considered a new way of producing functions, by fixing arguments to an existing function in several different ways: currying—which originally came from computer theory; partial application—which is more flexible; and partial currying, which combines good aspects from both of the previous methods. Using these transformations, you can simplify your coding, because you can generate more specialized versions of general functions, without any hassle.

In Chapter 8, *Connecting Functions – Pipelining and Composition*, we will turn back to some concepts we looked at in the chapter on pure functions, and we will consider ways of ensuring that functions cannot become *impure by accident*, by seeking ways to make their arguments immutable, making them impossible to mutate.

Questions

7.1. **Sum as you will**: The following exercise will help you understand some of the concepts we dealt with in this chapter, even if you solve it without using any of the functions we looked at. Write a summany() function that lets you sum an indeterminate quantity of numbers, in the following fashion. Note that when the function is called with no arguments, the sum is returned:

```
let result = sumMany((9)(2)(3)(1)(4)(3)());
 // 22
```

7.2. **Working stylishly**: Write an applyStyle() function that will let you apply basic styling to strings, in the following way. Use either currying or partial application:

```
const makeBold = applyStyle("b");
document.getElementById("myCity").innerHTML =
makeBold("Montevideo");
// <b>Montevideo</b>, to produce Montevideo

const makeUnderline = applyStyle("u");
document.getElementById("myCountry").innerHTML =
makeUnderline("Uruguay");
// <u>Uruguay</u>, to produce Uruguay
```

7.3. **Currying by prototype**: Modify Function.prototype to provide a curry() method that will work like the curry() function we saw in the chapter. Completing the following code should produce the following results:

```
Function.prototype.curry = function() {
    // ...your code goes here...
};

const sum3 = (a, b, c) => 100 * a + 10 * b + c;
sum3.curry()(1)(2)(4); // 124

const sum3C = sum3.curry()(2)(2);
sum3C(9); // 229
```

7.4. Uncurrying the curried: Write an `unCurry(fn, arity)` function that receives as arguments a (curried) function and its expected arity, and returns an uncurried version of `fn()`; that is, a function that will receive *n* arguments and produce a result (providing the expected arity is needed because you have no way of determining it on your own):

```
const make3 = (a, b, c) => String(100 * a + 10 * b + c);

const make3c = curry(make3);
console.log(make3c(1)(2)(3)); // 123

const remake3 = uncurry(make3c, 3);
console.log(remake3(1, 2, 3)); // 123
```

7.5. Mystery questions function: What does the following function, purposefully written in an unhelpful way, actually do?

```
const what = who => (...why) =>
  who.length <= why.length
    ? who(...why)
    : (...when) => what(who)(...why, ...when);
```

7.6. Yet more curry! Here is another proposal for a `curry()` function: can you see why it works? A hint: the code is related to something we saw in the chapter:

```
const curry = fn => (...args) =>
 args.length >= fn.length ? fn(...args) : curry(fn.bind(null, ...args));
```

8
Connecting Functions - Pipelining and Composition

In Chapter 7, *Transforming Functions – Currying and Partial Application*, we looked at several ways we can build new functions by applying higher-order functions. In this chapter, we will go to the core of FP and learn how to create sequences of function calls and how to combine them to produce a more complex result out of several simpler components. To do this, we will cover the following topics:

- **Pipelining**: A way to join functions together in a similar way to Unix/Linux pipes.
- **Chaining**: This may be considered a variant of pipelining, but is restricted to objects.
- **Composing**: This is a classic operation with its origins in basic computer theory.
- **Transducing**: An optimized way to compose map/filter/reduce operations.

Along the way, we will be touching on related concepts, such as the following:

- **Pointfree style**, which is often used with pipelining and composition
- **Debugging** composed or piped functions, for which we'll whip up some auxiliary tools
- **Testing** composed or piped functions, which won't prove to be of high complexity

Armed with these techniques, you'll be able to combine small functions to create larger ones, which is a characteristic of functional programming and will help you develop better code.

Pipelining

Pipelining and composition are techniques that are used to set up functions so that they work in sequence so that the output from a function becomes the input for the next function. There are two ways of looking at this: from a computer point of view, and from a mathematical point of view. We'll look at both in this section. Most FP texts start with the latter, but since I assume that most of you will prefer computers over math, let's start with the former instead.

Piping in Unix/Linux

In Unix/Linux, executing a command and passing its output as input to a second command, whose output will yield the input of a third command, and so on, is called a *pipeline*. This is quite a common application of the philosophy of Unix, as explained in a Bell Laboratories article, written by the creator of the pipelining concept himself, Doug McIlroy:

- Make each program do one thing well. To do a new job, build afresh rather than complicate old programs by adding new *features*.
- Expect the output of every program to become the input to another, so far unknown, program.

 Given the historical importance of Unix, I'd recommend reading some of the seminal articles describing the (then new) operating system, in the *Bell System Technical Journal*, July 1978, at http://emulator.pdp-11.org.ru/misc/1978.07_-_Bell_System_Technical_Journal.pdf. The two quoted rules are in the *Style* section, in the *Foreword* article.

Let's consider a simple example to get started. Suppose I want to know how many LibreOffice text documents there are in a directory. There are many ways to do this, but this will do. We will execute three commands, piping (that's the meaning of the | character) each command's output as input to the next one. Suppose we go to cd /home/fkereki/Documents and then do the following (please ignore the dollar sign, which is just the console prompt):

```
$ ls -1 | grep "odt$" | wc -l
4
```

What does this mean? How does it work? We have to analyze this process step by step:

- The first part of the pipeline, `ls -1`, lists all the files in the directory (`/home/fkereki/Documents`, as per our `cd` command), in a single column, one filename per line.
- The output from the first command is provided as input to `grep "odt$"`, which filters (lets pass) only those lines that finish with `"odt"`, the standard file extension for LibreOffice Writer.
- The filtered output is provided to the counting command, `wc -1`, which counts how many lines there are in its input.

 You can find out more about pipelines in Section 6.2, *Filters*, of the *UNIX Time-Sharing System* article by Dennis Ritchie and Ken Thompson, also in the issue of the Bell Laboratories journal that I mentioned previously.

From the point of view of FP, this is a key concept. We want to build more complex operations out of simple, single-purpose, shorter functions. Pipelining is what the Unix shell uses to apply that concept, which it does by simplifying the job of executing a command, taking its output, and providing it as input to yet another command. We will be applying similar concepts in our own functional style in JavaScript later:

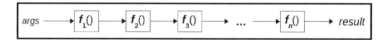

Figure 8.1: Pipelines in JavaScript are similar to Unix/Linux pipelines. The output of each function becomes the input for the next

By the way (and no—rest assured, this isn't turning into a shell tutorial!), you can also make pipelines accept parameters. For example, if I happened to want to count how many files I had with this or that extension, I could create a function such as `cfe`, standing for *count for extension*:

```
$ function cfe() {
    ls -1 | grep "$1\$"| wc -1
}
```

Then, I could use `cfe` as a command, giving it the desired extension as an argument:

```
$ cfe odt
4
$ cfe pdf
6
```

cfe executes my pipeline and tells me I have 4 odt files (LibreOffice) and 6 pdf ones; nice! We will also want to write similar parametric pipelines: we are not constrained to only have fixed functions in our flow; we have full liberty as to what we want to include. Having worked in Linux, we can now go back to coding. Let's see how.

Revisiting an example

We can start tying ends together by revisiting a problem from a previous chapter. Remember when we had to calculate the average latitude and longitude for some geographic data that we looked at in the *Extracting data from objects* section of Chapter 5, *Programming Declaratively – A Better Style*? Basically, we started with some data such as the following and the problem was to calculate the average latitude and longitude of the given points:

```
const markers = [
    {name: "AR", lat: -34.6, lon: -58.4},
    {name: "BO", lat: -16.5, lon: -68.1},
    {name: "BR", lat: -15.8, lon: -47.9},
    {name: "CL", lat: -33.4, lon: -70.7},
    {name: "CO", lat:   4.6, lon: -74.0},
    {name: "EC", lat:  -0.3, lon: -78.6},
    {name: "PE", lat: -12.0, lon: -77.0},
    {name: "PY", lat: -25.2, lon: -57.5},
    {name: "UY", lat: -34.9, lon: -56.2},
    {name: "VE", lat:  10.5, lon: -66.9},
];
```

With what we know, we can write a solution in terms of the following:

- Being able to extract the latitude (and, afterward, the longitude) from each point
- Using that function to create an array of latitudes
- Pipelining the resulting array to the average function we wrote in *Calculating an average* section of the aforementioned chapter

To do the first task, we can use the myMap() function from the *Parameters order* section of Chapter 7, *Transforming Functions – Currying and Partial Application*. For the second task, we can make do with the getField() function from the *Getting a property from an object* section of Chapter 6, *Producing Functions – Higher-Order Functions*, plus a bit of currying to fix some values. Finally, for the third task, we'll just use the (yet unwritten!) pipelining function we'll be developing soon! In full, our solution could look like this:

```
const average = arr => arr.reduce(sum, 0) / arr.length;
const getField = attr => obj => obj[attr];
```

```
const myMap = curry(flipTwo(demethodize(array.prototype.map)));

const getLat = curry(getField)("lat");
const getAllLats = curry(myMap)(getLat);

let averageLat = pipeline(getAllLats, average);
// and similar code to average longitudes
```

Of course, you can always yield to the temptation of going for a couple of *one-liners*, but would it be much clearer or better?

```
let averageLat2 = pipeline(curry(myMap)(curry(getField)("lat")), average);
let averageLon2 = pipeline(curry(myMap)(curry(getField)("lon")), average);
```

Whether this makes sense to you will depend on your experience with FP. In any case, no matter which solution you take, the fact remains that adding pipelining (and later on, composition) to your set of tools can help you write tighter, declarative, simpler-to-understand code.

Now, let's learn how to pipeline functions in the right way.

Creating pipelines

We want to be able to generate a pipeline of several functions. We can do this in two different ways: by building the pipeline by hand, in a problem-specific way, or by seeking to use more generic constructs that can be applied with generality. Let's look at both.

Building pipelines by hand

Let's go with a Node example, similar to the command-line pipeline we built earlier in this chapter. Here, we'll build the pipeline we need by hand. We need a function to read all the files in a directory. We can do that (this isn't recommended because of the synchronous call, which is normally not good in a server environment) with something like this:

```
function getDir(path) {
  const fs = require("fs");
  const files = fs.readdirSync(path);
  return files;
}
```

Filtering the odt files is quite simple. We start with the following function:

```
const filterByText = (text, arr) => arr.filter(v => v.endsWith(text));
```

This function takes an array and filters out any elements that do not end with the given text. So, we can now write the following:

```
const filterOdt = arr => filterByText(".odt", arr);
```

Better still, we can apply currying and go for pointfree style, as shown in the *An unnecessary mistake* section of Chapter 3, *Starting Out with Functions – A Core Concept*:

```
const filterOdt2 = curry(filterByText)(".odt");
```

Both versions of the filtering function are equivalent; which one you use comes down to your tastes. Finally, to count elements in an array, we can simply write the following. Since length is not a function, we cannot apply our demethodizing trick:

```
const count = arr => arr.length;
```

With these functions, we could write something like this:

```
const countOdtFiles = path => {
  const files = getDir(path);
  const filteredFiles = filterOdt(files);
  const countOfFiles = count(filteredFiles);
  return countOfFiles;
};

countOdtFiles("/home/fkereki/Documents"); // 4, as with the command line
solution
```

We are essentially doing the same process as in Linux: getting the files, keeping only the odt ones, and counting how many files result from this. If you wanted to get rid of all the intermediate variables, you could also go for a *one-liner* definition that does exactly the same job in the very same way, albeit with fewer lines:

```
const countOdtFiles2 = path => count(filterOdt(getDir(path)));

countOdtFiles2("/home/fkereki/Documents"); // 4, as before
```

This gets to the crux of the matter: both implementations of our file-counting function have disadvantages. The first definition uses several intermediate variables to hold the results and makes a multiline function out of what was a single line of code in the Linux shell. The second, much shorter, definition, on the other hand, is quite harder to understand, insofar as we are writing the steps of the computation in seemingly reverse order! Our pipeline has to read files first, then filter them, and finally count them, but those functions appear *the other way round* in our definition!

We can certainly implement pipelining by hand, as we have seen, but it would be better if we could go for a more declarative style.

Let's move on and try to build a better pipeline in a more clear and understandable way by trying to apply some of the concepts we've already seen.

Using other constructs

If we think in functional terms, what we have is a list of functions and we want to apply them sequentially, starting with the first, then applying the second to whatever the first function produced as its result, and then applying the third to the second function's results, and so on. If we were just fixing a pipeline of two functions, you could use the following code:

```
const pipeTwo = (f, g) => (...args) => g(f(...args));
```

This is the basic definition we provided earlier in this chapter: we evaluate the first function, and its output becomes the input for the second function; quite straightforward! You might object, though, that this pipeline, of only two functions, is a bit too limited! This is not as useless as it may seem because we can compose longer pipelines—though I'll admit that it requires too much writing! Suppose we wanted to write our three-function pipeline (from the previous section); we could do so in two different, equivalent ways:

```
const countOdtFiles3 = path =>
  pipeTwo(pipeTwo(getDir, filterOdt), count)(path);

const countOdtFiles4 = path =>
  pipeTwo(getDir, pipeTwo(filterOdt, count))(path);
```

 We are taking advantage of the fact that piping is an associative operation. In mathematics, the associative property is the one that says that we can compute *1+2+3* either by adding *1+2* first and then adding that result to 3, or by adding 1 to the result of adding *2+3*: in other terms, *1+2+3* is the same as *(1+2)+3* or *1+(2+3)*.

How do they work? How is it that they are equivalent? Following the execution of a given call will be useful; it's quite easy to get confused with so many calls! The first implementation can be followed step by step until the final result, which matches what we already know:

```
countOdtFiles3("/home/fkereki/Documents") ===
  pipeTwo(pipeTwo(getDir, filterOdt), count)("/home/fkereki/Documents") ===
    count(pipeTwo(getDir, filterOdt)("/home/fkereki/Documents")) ===
      count(filterOdt(getDir("/home/fkereki/Documents"))) // 4
```

The second implementation also comes to the same final result:

```
countOdtFiles4("/home/fkereki/Documents") ===
  pipeTwo(getDir, pipeTwo(filterOdt, count))("/home/fkereki/Documents") ===
    pipeTwo(filterOdt, count)(getDir("/home/fkereki/Documents")) ===
      count(filterOdt(getDir("/home/fkereki/Documents"))) // 4
```

Both derivations arrived at the same final expression—the same we had written by hand earlier, in fact—so we now know that we can make do with just a basic *pipe of two* higher-order functions, but we'd really like to be able to work in a shorter, more compact way. A first implementation could be along the lines of the following:

```
const pipeline = (...fns) => (...args) => {
  let result = fns[0](...args);
  for (let i = 1; i < fns.length; i++) {
    result = fns[i](result);
  }
  return result;
};

pipeline(getDir, filterOdt, count)("/home/fkereki/Documents"); // still 4
```

This does work—and the way of specifying our file-counting pipeline is much clearer since the functions are given in their proper order. However, the implementation of the `pipeline()` function is not very functional and goes back to old, imperative, loop by hand methods. We can do better using `reduce()`, as we did in Chapter 5, *Programming Declaratively – A Better Style*.

 If you check out some FP libraries, the function that we are calling `pipeline()` here may also be known as `flow()`—because data flows from left to right – or `sequence()`—alluding to the fact that operations are performed in ascending sequence—but the semantics are the same.

The idea is to start the evaluation with the first function, pass the result to the second, then that result to the third, and so on. By doing this, we can pipeline with shorter code:

```
const pipeline2 = (...fns) =>
  fns.reduce((result, f) => (...args) => f(result(...args)));

pipeline2(getDir, filterOdt, count)("/home/fkereki/Documents"); // 4
```

This code is more declarative. However, you could have gone one better by writing it using our `pipeTwo()` function, which does the same thing but in a more concise manner:

```
const pipeline3 = (...fns) => fns.reduce(pipeTwo);

pipeline3(getDir, filterOdt, count)("/home/fkereki/Documents"); // again 4
```

You can understand this code by realizing that it uses the associative property that we mentioned previously and pipes the first function to the second; then, it pipes the result of this to the third function, and so on.

Which version is better? I would say that the version that refers to the `pipeTwo()` function is clearer: if you know how `reduce()` works, you can readily understand that our pipeline goes through the functions two at a time, starting from the first—and that matches what you know about how pipes work. The other versions that we wrote are more or less declarative, but not as simple to understand.

Before we look at other ways in which we can compose functions, let's consider how we would go about debugging our pipelines.

Debugging pipelines

Now, let's turn to a practical question: how do you debug your code? With pipelining, you can't really see what's passing on from function to function, so how do you do it? We have two answers for that: one (also) comes from the Unix/Linux world, and the other (the most appropriate for this book) uses wrappers to provide some logs.

Using tee

The first solution we'll use implies adding a function to the pipeline, which will just log its input. We want to implement something similar to the `tee` Linux command, which can intercept the standard data flow in a pipeline and send a copy to an alternate file or device. Remembering that `/dev/tty` is the usual console, we could execute something similar to the following and get an onscreen copy of everything that passes through the `tee` command:

```
$ ls -1 | grep "odt$" | tee /dev/tty | wc -l

...the list of files with names ending in odt...
4
```

We could write a similar function with ease:

```
const tee = arg => {
  console.log(arg);
  return arg;
};
```

> If you are aware of the uses of the comma operator, you can be more concise and just write `const tee = (arg) => (console.log(arg), arg)`—do you see why? Check out `https://developer.mozilla.org/en-US/docs/Web/JavaScript/Reference/Operators/Comma_Operator` for the answer!

Our logging function is short and to the point: it will receive a single argument, list it, and pass it on to the next function in the pipe. We can see it working in the following code:

```
console.log(
  pipeline2(getDir, tee, filterOdt, tee, count)(
    "/home/fkereki/Documents"
  )
);

[...the list of all the files in the directory...]
[...the list of files with names ending in odt...]
4
```

We could do even better if our `tee()` function could receive a logger function as a parameter, as we did in the *Logging in a functional way* section of `Chapter 6`, *Producing Functions – Higher-Order Functions*; it's just a matter of making the same kind of change we managed there. The same good design concepts are applied again!

```
const tee2 = (arg, logger = console.log) => {
  logger(arg);
  return args;
};
```

> Be aware that there might be a binding problem when passing `console.log` in that way. It would be safer to write `console.log.bind(console)` just as a precaution.

This function works exactly in the same way as the previous `tee()`, though it will allow us to be flexible when it comes to applying and testing. However, in our case, this would just be a particular enhancement.

Now, let's consider an even more generic tapping function, with more possibilities than just doing a bit of logging.

Tapping into a flow

If you wish, you could write an enhanced `tee()` function that could produce more debugging information, possibly send the reported data to a file or remote service, and so on—there are many possibilities you can explore. You could also explore a more general solution, of which `tee()` would just be a particular case and which would also allow us to create personalized tapping functions. This can be seen in the following diagram:

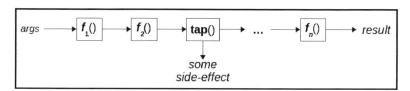

Figure 8.2: Tapping allows you to apply a function so that you can inspect data as it flows through the pipeline

When working with pipelines, you might want to put a logging function in the middle of it, or you might want some other kind of *snooping* function—possibly for storing data somewhere, calling a service, or some other kind of side effect. We could have a generic `tap()` function, which would allow us to inspect data as it moves along our pipeline, that would behave in the following way:

```
const tap = curry((fn, x) => (fn(x), x));
```

This is probably a candidate for the *trickiest-looking-code-in-the-book* award, so let's explain it. We want to produce a function that, given a function, `fn()`, and an argument, `x`, will evaluate `fn(x)` (to produce whatever sort of side effect we may be interested in) but return `x` (so the pipeline goes on without interference). The comma operator has exactly that behavior: if you write something similar to `(a, b, c)`, JavaScript will evaluate the three expressions in order and use the last value as the expression's value.

 The comma has several uses in JavaScript and you can read more about its usage as an operator at `https://developer.mozilla.org/en-US/docs/Web/JavaScript/Reference/Operators/Comma_Operator`.

Now, we can take advantage of currying to produce several different tapping functions. The one we wrote in the previous section, `tee()`, could also be written in the following fashion:

```
const tee3 = tap(console.log);
```

By the way, you could have also written `tap()` without currying, but you'll have to admit it loses some of its mystery! This is demonstrated here:

```
const tap2 = fn => x => (fn(x), x);
```

This does exactly the same job, and you'll recognize this way of currying as what we looked at in the *Currying by hand* section of `Chapter 7`, *Transforming Functions – Currying and Partial Application*. Now that we have learned how to tap into a pipeline, let's move on to a different way of doing logging by revisiting some concepts we looked at in previous chapters.

Using a logging wrapper

The second idea we mentioned is based on the `addLogging()` function that we wrote in the *Logging* section of `Chapter 6`, *Producing Functions – Higher-Order Functions*. The idea was to wrap a function with some logging functionality so that, on entry, the arguments would be printed and, on exit, the result of the function would be shown:

```
pipeline2(
  addLogging(getDir),
  addLogging(filterOdt),
  addLogging(count))("/home/fkereki/Documents"));

entering getDir: /home/fkereki/Documents
exiting getDir: ...the list of all the files in the directory...
entering filterOdt: ...the same list of files...
exiting filterOdt: ...the list of files with names ending in odt...
entering count: ...the list of files with names ending in odt...
exiting count: 4
```

We can trivially verify that the `pipeline()` function is doing its thing correctly—whatever a function produces, as a result, is given as input to the next function in the line and we can also understand what's happening with each call. Of course, you don't need to add logging to *every* function in the pipeline: you would probably do so in the places where you suspected an error was occurring.

Now that we've looked at how to join functions, let's take a look at a very common way of defining functions in FP, *pointfree style*, which you may encounter.

Pointfree style

When you join functions together, either in pipeline fashion or with composition, as we'll see later in this chapter, you don't need any intermediate variables to hold the results that will become arguments to the next function in line: they are implicit. Similarly, you can write functions without mentioning their parameters; this is called the pointfree style.

 Pointfree style is also called *tacit* programming and *pointless* programming by detractors! The term *point* itself means a function parameter, while pointfree refers to not naming those parameters.

Defining pointfree functions

You can easily recognize a pointfree function definition because it doesn't need the `function` keyword or the `=>` symbol. Let's revisit some of the previous functions we wrote in this chapter and check them out. For example, the definition of our original file-counting functions is as follows:

```
const countOdtFiles3 = path =>
  pipeTwo(pipeTwo(getDir, filterOdt), count)(path);

const countOdtFiles4 = path =>
  pipeTwo(getDir, pipeTwo(filterOdt, count))(path);
```

The preceding code could be rewritten as follows:

```
const countOdtFiles3b = pipeTwo(pipeTwo(getDir, filterOdt), count);

const countOdtFiles4b = pipeTwo(getDir, pipeTwo(filterOdt, count));
```

The new definitions don't make reference to the parameter for the newly defined functions. You can deduce this by examining the first function in the pipeline (`getDir()`, in this case) and seeing what it receives as arguments. (Using type signatures, as we'll see in Chapter 12, *Building Better Containers – Functional Data Types*, would be of great help in terms of documentation.) Similarly, the definition for `getLat()` is pointfree:

```
const getLat = curry(getField)("lat");
```

What should be the equivalent full style definition? You'd have to examine the `getField()` function (we looked at this in the *Revisiting an example* section) to decide that it expects an object as an argument. However, making that need explicit by writing the following wouldn't make much sense:

```
const getLat = obj => curry(getField)("lat")(obj);
```

If you were willing to write all this, you may wish to stick with the following:

```
const getLat = obj => obj.lat;
```

Then, you could simply not care about currying!

Converting to pointfree style

On the other hand, you had better pause for a minute and try not to write *everything* in pointfree code, whatever it might cost. For example, consider the `isNegativeBalance()` function we wrote back in Chapter 6, *Producing Functions – Higher-Order Functions*:

```
const isNegativeBalance = v => v.balance < 0;
```

Can we write this in a pointfree style? Yes, we can, and we'll see how—but I'm not sure we'd want to code this way! We can consider building a pipeline of two functions: one will extract the balance from the given object, while the other will check whether it's negative. Due to this, we will write our alternative version of the balance-checking function like so:

```
const isNegativeBalance2 = pipeline(getBalance, isNegative);
```

To extract the balance attribute from a given object, we can use `getField()` and a bit of currying, and then write the following:

```
const getBalance = curry(getField)("balance");
```

For the second function, we could write the following code:

```
const isNegative = x => x < 0;
```

There goes our pointfree goal! Instead, we can use the `binaryOp()` function, also from the same chapter we mentioned earlier, plus some more currying, to write the following:

```
const isNegative = curry(binaryOp(">"))(0);
```

I wrote the test the other way around (0>x instead of x<0) just for ease of coding. An alternative would have been to use the enhanced functions I mentioned in the *A handier implementation* section of `Chapter 6`, *Producing Functions – Higher-Order Functions*, which is a bit less complex, as follows:

```
const isNegative = binaryOpRight("<", 0);
```

So, finally, we could write the following:

```
const isNegativeBalance2 = pipeline(
  curry(getField)("balance"),
  curry(binaryOp(">"))(0)
);
```

Alternatively, we could write the following:

```
const isNegativeBalance3 = pipeline(
  curry(getField)("balance"),
  binaryOpRight("<", 0)
);
```

Do you really think that's an improvement? Our new versions of `isNegativeBalance()` don't make a reference to their argument and are fully pointfree, but the idea of using pointfree style should be to help improve the clarity and readability of your code, and not to produce obfuscation and opaqueness! I doubt anybody would look at our new versions of the function and consider them to be an advantage over the original, for any possible reason.

If you find that your code is becoming harder to understand, and that's only due to your intent on using pointfree programming, stop and roll back your changes. Remember our doctrine for this book: we want to do FP, but we don't want to go overboard with it—and using the pointfree style is not a requirement!

In this section, we've learned how to build pipelines of functions—this is a powerful technique. For objects and arrays, however, we have another special technique that you may have used already: chaining. Let's take a look at this now.

Chaining and fluent interfaces

When you work with objects or arrays, there is another way of linking the execution of several calls together: by applying *chaining*. For example, when you work with arrays, if you apply a map() or filter() method, the result is a new array, which you can then apply a new further map() or filter() to, and so forth. We used such methods when we defined the range() function back in the *Working with ranges* section of Chapter 5, *Programming Declaratively – A Better Style*:

```
const range = (start, stop) =>
  new Array(stop - start).fill(0).map((v, i) => start + i);
```

First, we created a new array; then, we applied the fill() method to it, which updated the array in place (side effect) and returned the updated array, to which we finally applied a map() method. The latter method generated a new array, to which we could have applied further mappings, filtering, or any other available method.

Let's take a look at a common example of fluent, chained APIs, and then consider how we can do this on our own.

An example of fluent APIs

This style of continuous chained operation is also used in fluent APIs or interfaces. To give just one example, the graphic D3.js library (see https://d3js.org/ for more on it) frequently uses this style. The following example, taken from https://bl.ocks.org/mbostock/4063269, shows it in action:

```
var node = svg
  .selectAll(".node")
  .data(pack(root).leaves())
  .enter()
  .append("g")
  .attr("class", "node")
  .attr("transform", function(d) {
    return "translate(" + d.x + "," + d.y + ")";
  });
```

Each method works on the previous object and provides access to a new object that future method calls will be applied to (such as the selectAll() or append() methods) or updates the current one (like the attr() attribute setting calls do). This style is not unique and several other well-known libraries (jQuery comes to mind) also apply it.

Can we automate this? In this case, the answer is *possibly, but I'd rather not*. In my opinion, using `pipeline()` or `compose()` works just as well, and manages the same result. With object chaining, you are limited to returning new objects or arrays or something that methods can be applied to. (Remember, if you are working with standard types, such as strings or numbers, you can't add methods to them unless you mess with their prototype, which isn't recommended!). With composition, however, you can return any kind of value; the only restriction is that the next function in line must be expecting the data type that you are providing.

On the other hand, if you are writing your own API, then you can provide a fluent interface by just having each method return this—unless, of course, it needs to return something else! If you were working with someone else's API, you could also do some trickery by using a proxy, but be aware there could be cases in which your proxied code might fail: maybe another proxy is being used, or there are some getters or setters that somehow cause problems, and so on.

You may want to read up on proxy objects at `https://developer.mozilla.org/en/docs/Web/JavaScript/Reference/Global_Objects/Proxy` – they are very powerful and allow for interesting metaprogramming functionalities, but they can also trap you with technicalities and will also cause an (albeit slight) slowdown in your proxied code.

Let's now take a look at how to chain calls so that we can apply them to any class.

Chaining method calls

Let's go for a basic example. We could have a `City` class with `name`, latitude (`lat`), and longitude (`long`) attributes:

```
class City {
  constructor(name, lat, long) {
    this.name = name;
    this.lat = lat;
    this.long = long;
  }

  getName() {
    return this.name;
  }

  setName(newName) {
    this.name = newName;
```

```
  }

  setLat(newLat) {
    this.lat = newLat;
  }

  setLong(newLong) {
    this.long = newLong;
  }

  getCoords() {
    return [this.lat, this.long];
  }
}
```

This is a common class with a few methods; everything's quite normal. We could use this class as follows and provide details about my native city, Montevideo, Uruguay:

```
let myCity = new City("Montevideo, Uruguay", -34.9011, -56.1645);
console.log(myCity.getCoords(), myCity.getName());
// [ -34.9011, -56.1645 ] 'Montevideo, Uruguay'
```

If we wanted to allow the setters to be handled in a fluent manner, we could set up a proxy to detect such calls and provide the missing return this. How can we do that? If the original method doesn't return anything, JavaScript will include a return undefined statement by default so that we can detect whether that's what the method is returning and substitute return this instead. Of course, this is a problem: what would we do if we had a method that could legally return an undefined value on its own because of its semantics? We could have some kind of *exceptions list* to tell our proxy not to add anything in those cases, but let's not get into that.

The code for our handler is as follows. Whenever the method of an object is invoked, a get is implicitly called and we catch it. If we are getting a function, then we wrap it with some code of our own that will call the original method and then decide whether to return its value or a reference to the proxied object instead. If we weren't getting a function, then we would return the requested property's value. Our chainify() function will take care of assigning the handler to an object and creating the needed proxy:

```
const getHandler = {
  get(target, property, receiver) {
    if (typeof target[property] === "function") {
      // requesting a method? return a wrapped version
      return (...args) => {
        const result = target[property](...args);
        return result === undefined ? receiver : result;
      };
```

```
      } else {
        // an attribute was requested - just return it
        return target[property];
      }
    },
  };
  const chainify = obj => new Proxy(obj, getHandler);
```

We need to check whether the invoked `get()` was for a function or for an attribute. In the first case, we wrap the method with extra code so that it will execute it and then return its results (if any) or a reference to the object itself. In the second case, we just return the attribute, which is the expected behavior.

With this, we can *chainify* any object, so we'll get a chance to inspect any called methods. As I'm writing this, I'm currently living in Pune, India, so let's reflect that change:

```
  myCity = chainify(myCity);

  console.log(myCity
    .setName("Pune, India")
    .setLat(18.5626)
    .setLong(73.8087)
    .getCoords(),
    myCity.getName());

  // [ 18.5626, 73.8087 ] 'Pune, India'
```

Notice the following:

- We changed `myCity` to be a proxified version of itself.
- We are calling several setters in a fluent fashion and they are working fine since our proxy is taking care of providing the value for the following call.
- The calls to `getCoords()` and `getName()` are intercepted, but nothing special is done because they already return a value.

Is working in a chained way worth it? That's up to you—but remember that there may be cases in which this approach fails, so be wary! Now, let's move on to composing, the other most common way of joining functions together.

Composing

Composing is quite similar to pipelining, but has its roots in mathematical theory. The concept of composition is simply—a sequence of function calls, in which the output of one function is the input for the next one—but the order is reversed from the one in pipelining. So, if you have a series of functions, from left to right, when pipelining, the first function of the series to be applied is the leftmost one, but when you use composition, you start with the rightmost one.

Let's investigate this a bit more. When you define the composition of, say, three functions as ($f \circ g \circ h$), and apply this composition to x, this is equivalent to writing $f(g(h(x)))$. It's important to note that, as with pipelining, the arity of the first function to be applied (actually the last one in the list) can be anything, but all the other functions must be unary. Also, apart from the difference as to the sequence of function evaluations, composing is an important tool in FP because it also abstracts implementation details (putting your focus on what you need to accomplish, rather than on the specific details for achieving that), thereby letting you work in a more declarative fashion.

 If it helps, you can read ($f \circ g \circ h$) as *f after g after h*, so that it becomes clear that h is the first function to be applied, while f is the last.

Given its similarity to pipelining, it will be no surprise that implementing composition won't be very hard. However, there will still be some important and interesting details to go over. Let's take a look at some examples of composition before moving on to using higher-order functions and finishing with some considerations about testing composed functions.

Some examples of composition

It may not be a surprise to you, but we have already seen several examples of composition—or, at the very least, cases in which the solutions we achieved were functionally equivalent to using composition. Let's review some of these and work with some new examples too.

Unary operators

In the *Logically negating a function* section of `Chapter 6`, *Producing Functions – Higher-Order Functions*, we wrote a `not()` function that, given another function, would logically invert its result. We used that function to negate a check for negative balances; the sample code for this could be as follows:

```
const not = fn => (...args) => !fn(...args);

const positiveBalance = not(isNegativeBalance);
```

In another section of that very same chapter, *Turning operations into functions*, I left you with the challenge of writing a `unaryOp()` function that would provide unary functions equivalent to common JavaScript operators. If you met that challenge, you should be able to write something like the following:

```
const logicalNot = unaryOp("!");
```

Assuming the existence of a `compose()` function, you could have also written the following:

```
const positiveBalance = compose(logicalNot, isNegativeBalance);
```

Which one do you prefer? It's a matter of taste, really—but I think the second version makes it clearer what we are trying to do. With the `not()` function, you have to check what it does in order to understand the general code. With composition, you still need to know what `logicalNot()` is, but the global construct is open to see.

To look at just one more example in the same vein, you could have managed to get the same results that we got in the *Inverting results* section, in the same chapter. Recall that we had a function that could compare strings according to the Spanish language rules, but we wanted to invert the sense of the comparison so that it was sorted in descending order:

```
const changeSign = unaryOp("-");

palabras.sort(compose(changeSign, spanishComparison));
```

This code produces the same result that our previous sorting problem did, but the logic is expressed more clearly and with less code: a typical FP result! Let's look at some more examples of composing functions by reviewing another task we went over earlier.

Counting files

We can also go back to our pipeline. We had written a single-line function to count the `odt` files in a given path:

```
const countOdtFiles2 = path => count(filterOdt(getDir(path)));
```

Disregarding (at least for the moment) the observation that this code is not as clear as the pipeline version that we got to develop later, we could have also written this function with composition:

```
const countOdtFiles2b = path => compose(count, filterOdt, getDir)(path);

countOdtFiles2b("/home/fkereki/Documents"); // 4, no change here
```

 We could have also written the function in pointfree fashion, without specifying the `path` parameter, with `const countOdtFiles2 = compose(count, filterOdt, getDir)`, but I wanted to parallel the previous definition.

It would also be possible to see this written in *one-liner* fashion:

```
compose(count, filterOdt, getDir)("/home/fkereki/Documents");
```

Even if it's not as clear as the pipeline version (and that's just my opinion, which may be biased by my liking of Linux!), this declarative implementation makes it clear that we depend on combining three distinct functions to get our result—this is easy to see and applies the idea of building large solutions out of simpler pieces of code.

Let's take a look at another example that's designed to compose as many functions as possible.

Finding unique words

Finally, let's go for another example, which, I agree, could have also been used for pipelining. Suppose you have some text and want to extract all the unique words from it: how would you go about doing this? If you think about it in steps (instead of trying to create a full solution in a single bit step), you would probably come up with a solution similar to this:

1. Ignore all non-alphabetic characters
2. Put everything in uppercase

3. Split the text into words
4. Create a set of words

Why a set? Because it automatically discards repeated values; check out `https://developer.mozilla.org/en/docs/Web/JavaScript/Reference/Global_Objects/Set` for more on this. By the way, we will be using the `Array.from()` method to produce an array out of our set; see `https://developer.mozilla.org/en-US/docs/Web/JavaScript/Reference/Global_Objects/Array/from` for more information.

Now, using FP, let's solve each problem:

```
const removeNonAlpha = str => str.replace(/[^a-z]/gi, " ");
const toUpperCase = demethodize(String.prototype.toUpperCase);
const splitInWords = str => str.trim().split(/\s+/);
const arrayToSet = arr => new Set(arr);
const setToList = set => Array.from(set).sort();
```

With these functions, the result can be written as follows:

```
const getUniqueWords = compose(
  setToList,
  arrayToSet,
  splitInWords,
  toUpperCase,
  removeNonAlpha
);
```

Since you don't get to see the arguments of any of the composed functions, you really don't need to show the parameter for `getUniqueWords()` either, so the pointfree style is natural to use in this case.

Now, let's test our function. To do this, let's apply this function to the first two sentences of Abraham Lincoln's address at Gettysburg (which we already used in an example back in the *Mapping and flattening – flatMap* section of `Chapter 5`, *Programming Declaratively – A Better Style*) and print out the 43 different words (trust me, I counted them!) they comprised:

```
const GETTYSBURG_1_2 = `Four score and seven years ago
our fathers brought forth on this continent, a new nation,
conceived in liberty, and dedicated to the proposition
that all men are created equal. Now we are engaged in a
great civil war, testing whether that nation, or any
nation so conceived and so dedicated, can long
endure.`;
```

```
console.log(getUniqueWords(GETTYSBURG_1_2));
[ 'A',
'AGO',
'ALL',
'AND',
'ANY',
'ARE',
'BROUGHT',
'CAN',
'CIVIL',
.
.
.
'TESTING',|
'THAT',
'THE',
'THIS',
'TO',
'WAR',
'WE',
'WHETHER',
'YEARS' ]
```

Of course, you could have written `getUniqueWords()` in a shorter way, but the point I'm making is that by composing your solution out of several shorter steps, your code is clearer and easier to grasp. However, if you wish to say that a pipelined solution seems better, then it's just a matter of opinion!

At this point, we have looked at many examples of function composition, but there's another way to manage this—by using higher-order functions.

Composing with higher-order functions

It's pretty obvious that composing by hand could easily be done in a similar fashion to pipelining. For example, the unique word counting function that we wrote previously could be written in simple JavaScript style:

```
const getUniqueWords1 = str => {
  const str1 = removeNonAlpha(str);
  const str2 = toUpperCase(str1);
  const arr1 = splitInWords(str2);
  const set1 = arrayToSet(arr1);
  const arr2 = setToList(set1);
  return arr2;
};
```

Alternatively, it could be written more concisely (and more obscurely!) in *one-liner* style:

```
const getUniqueWords2 = str =>
  setToList(arrayToSet(splitInWords(toUpperCase(removeNonAlpha(str)))));

console.log(getUniqueWords2(GETTYSBURG_1_2));
// [ 'A', 'AGO', 'ALL', 'AND', ... 'WAR', 'WE', 'WHETHER', 'YEARS' ]
```

This works fine, but like we did when we studied pipelining, let's go and look for a more general solution that won't require writing a special function each time we want to compose some other functions.

Composing two functions is quite easy and requires making a small change with regard to our pipeTwo() function, which we looked at earlier in this chapter:

```
const pipeTwo = (f, g) => (...args) => g(f(...args));
const composeTwo = (f, g) => (...args) => f(g(...args));
```

The only difference is that, with piping, you apply the leftmost function first, while with composing, you start with the rightmost function first. This variation suggests that we could have used the flipTwo() higher-order function from the *Parameters order* section of Chapter 7, *Transforming Functions – Currying and Partial Application*. Is it clearer? Here is the code:

```
const composeTwoByFlipping = flipTwo(pipeTwo);
```

In any case, if we wanted to compose more than two functions, we could have also taken advantage of the associative property in order to write something like the following:

```
const getUniqueWords3 = composeTwo(
  setToList,
  composeTwo(
    arrayToSet,
    composeTwo(splitInWords, composeTwo(toUpperCase, removeNonAlpha))
  )
);

console.log(getUniqueWords3(GETTYSBURG_1_2));
// [ 'A', 'AGO', 'ALL', 'AND', ... 'WAR', 'WE', 'WHETHER', 'YEARS' ] OK
again
```

Even though this works, let's go for a better solution—we can provide at least two. The first way has to do with the fact that pipelining and composing work *in reverse* of each other. We apply functions from left to right when pipelining, and from right to left when composing. Thus, we can achieve the same result that we achieved with a composition by reversing the order of the functions and doing pipelining instead; a very functional solution, which I really like! This is as follows:

```
const compose = (...fns) => pipeline(...(fns.reverse()));

console.log(
  compose(
    setToList,
    arrayToSet,
    splitInWords,
    toUpperCase,
    removeNonAlpha
  ) (GETTYSBURG_1_2)
);

/*
 [ 'A', 'AGO', 'ALL', 'AND', ... 'WAR', 'WE', 'WHETHER', 'YEARS' ]
 OK once more
*/
```

The only tricky part is the usage of the spread operator before calling `pipeline()`. After reversing the `fns` array, we must spread its elements in order to call `pipeline()` correctly.

The other solution, which is less declarative, is to use `reduceRight()` so that instead of reversing the list of functions, we reverse the order of processing them:

```
const compose2 = (...fns) => fns.reduceRight(pipeTwo);

console.log(
  compose2(
    setToList,
    arrayToSet,
    splitInWords,
    toUpperCase,
    removeNonAlpha
  ) (GETTYSBURG_1_2)
);

/*
 [ 'A', 'AGO', 'ALL', 'AND', ... 'WAR', 'WE', 'WHETHER', 'YEARS' ]
 still OK
*/
```

Why/how does this work? Let's follow the inner workings of this call. To make this clearer, we can replace `pipeTwo()` with its definition:

```
const compose2b = (...fns) =>
  fns.reduceRight((f,g) => (...args) => g(f(...args)));
```

Let's take a closer look:

- Since no initial value is provided, `f()` is `removeNonAlpha()` and `g()` is `toUpperCase()`, so the first intermediate result is a function, `(...args) => toUpperCase(removeNonAlpha(...args))`; let's call it `step1()`.
- The second time, `f()` is `step1()` from the previous step, while `g()` is `splitInWords()`, so the new result is a function, `(...args) => splitInWords(step1(...args)))`, which we can call `step2()`.
- The third time around, in the same fashion, we get `(...args) => arrayToSet(step2(...args))))`, which we call `step3()`.
- Finally, the result is `(...args) => setToList(step3(...args))`, a function; let's call it `step4()`.

The final result turns out to be a function that receives `(...args)` and starts by applying `removeNonAlpha()` to it, then `toUpperCase()`, and so on, before finishing by applying `setToList()`.

It may come as a surprise that we can also make this work with `reduce()`—can you see why? The reasoning is similar to what we did previously, so we'll leave this as an exercise to you:

```
const compose3 = (...fns) => fns.reduce(composeTwo);
```

After working out how `compose3()` works, you might want to write a version of `pipeline()` that uses `reduceRight()`, just for symmetry, to round things out!

We will end this section by mentioning that, in terms of testing and debugging, we can apply the same ideas that we applied to pipelining; however, remember that composition *goes the other way*! We won't gain anything by providing yet more examples of the same kind, so let's consider a common way of chaining operations when using objects and see whether it's advantageous or not, given our growing FP knowledge and experience.

Testing composed functions

Let's finish this chapter by giving some consideration to testing for pipelined or composed functions. Given that the mechanism for both operations is similar, we will look at examples of both. They won't differ, other than their logical differences due to the left-to-right or right-to-left order of function evaluation.

When it comes to pipelining, we can start by looking at how to test the `pipeTwo()` function since the setup will be similar to `pipeline()`. We need to create some spies and check whether they were called the correct number of times and whether they received the correct arguments each time. We will set the spies so that they provide a known answer to a call. By doing this, we can check whether the output of a function becomes the input of the next in the pipeline:

```
var fn1, fn2;

describe("pipeTwo", function() {
  beforeEach(() => {
    fn1 = () => {};
    fn2 = () => {};
  });

  it("works with single arguments", () => {
    spyOn(window, "fn1").and.returnValue(1);
    spyOn(window, "fn2").and.returnValue(2);

    const pipe = pipeTwo(fn1, fn2);
    const result = pipe(22);

    expect(fn1).toHaveBeenCalledTimes(1);
    expect(fn2).toHaveBeenCalledTimes(1);
    expect(fn1).toHaveBeenCalledWith(22);
    expect(fn2).toHaveBeenCalledWith(1);
    expect(result).toBe(2);
  });

  it("works with multiple arguments", () => {
    spyOn(window, "fn1").and.returnValue(11);
    spyOn(window, "fn2").and.returnValue(22);

    const pipe = pipeTwo(fn1, fn2);
    const result = pipe(12, 4, 56);

    expect(fn1).toHaveBeenCalledTimes(1);
    expect(fn2).toHaveBeenCalledTimes(1);
    expect(fn1).toHaveBeenCalledWith(12, 4, 56);
```

```
    expect(fn2).toHaveBeenCalledWith(11);
    expect(result).toBe(22);
  });
});
```

There isn't much to test, given that our function always receives two functions as parameters. The only difference between the tests is that one shows a pipeline that's been applied to a single argument, while the other shows it being applied to several arguments.

Moving on to `pipeline()`, the tests would be quite similar. However, we can add a test for a single-function pipeline (border case!) and another with four functions:

```
describe("pipeline", function() {
  beforeEach(() => {
    fn1 = () => {};
    fn2 = () => {};
    fn3 = () => {};
    fn4 = () => {};
  });

  it("works with a single function", () => {
    spyOn(window, "fn1").and.returnValue(11);

    const pipe = pipeline(fn1);
    const result = pipe(60);

    expect(fn1).toHaveBeenCalledTimes(1);
    expect(fn1).toHaveBeenCalledWith(60);
    expect(result).toBe(11);
  });

  // we omit here tests for 2 functions,
  // which are similar to those for pipeTwo()

  it("works with 4 functions, multiple arguments", () => {
    spyOn(window, "fn1").and.returnValue(111);
    spyOn(window, "fn2").and.returnValue(222);
    spyOn(window, "fn3").and.returnValue(333);
    spyOn(window, "fn4").and.returnValue(444);

    const pipe = pipeline(fn1, fn2, fn3, fn4);
    const result = pipe(24, 11, 63);

    expect(fn1).toHaveBeenCalledTimes(1);
    expect(fn2).toHaveBeenCalledTimes(1);
    expect(fn3).toHaveBeenCalledTimes(1);
    expect(fn4).toHaveBeenCalledTimes(1);
    expect(fn1).toHaveBeenCalledWith(24, 11, 63);
```

```
        expect(fn2).toHaveBeenCalledWith(111);
        expect(fn3).toHaveBeenCalledWith(222);
        expect(fn4).toHaveBeenCalledWith(333);
        expect(result).toBe(444);
    });
});
```

Finally, for composition, the style is the same (except that the order of function evaluation is reversed), so let's take a look at a single test—here, I simply changed the order of the functions in the preceding test:

```
describe("compose", function() {
    beforeEach(() => {
        fn1 = () => {};
        fn2 = () => {};
        fn3 = () => {};
        fn4 = () => {};
    });

    // other tests omitted...

    it("works with 4 functions, multiple arguments", () => {
        spyOn(window, "fn1").and.returnValue(111);
        spyOn(window, "fn2").and.returnValue(222);
        spyOn(window, "fn3").and.returnValue(333);
        spyOn(window, "fn4").and.returnValue(444);

        const pipe = compose(fn4, fn3, fn2, fn1);
        const result = pipe(24, 11, 63);

        expect(fn1).toHaveBeenCalledTimes(1);
        expect(fn2).toHaveBeenCalledTimes(1);
        expect(fn3).toHaveBeenCalledTimes(1);
        expect(fn4).toHaveBeenCalledTimes(1);

        expect(fn1).toHaveBeenCalledWith(24, 11, 63);
        expect(fn2).toHaveBeenCalledWith(111);
        expect(fn3).toHaveBeenCalledWith(222);
        expect(fn4).toHaveBeenCalledWith(333);
        expect(result).toBe(444);
    });
});
```

Finally, to test the `chainify()` function, I opted to use the preceding `City` object I created—I didn't want to mess with mocks, stubs, spies, and the like; I wanted to ensure that the code worked under normal conditions:

```
class City {
    // as above
}

var myCity;

describe("chainify", function() {
  beforeEach(() => {
    myCity = new City("Montevideo, Uruguay", -34.9011, -56.1645);
    myCity = chainify(myCity);
  });

  it("doesn't affect get functions", () => {
    expect(myCity.getName()).toBe("Montevideo, Uruguay");
    expect(myCity.getCoords()[0]).toBe(-34.9011);
    expect(myCity.getCoords()[1]).toBe(-56.1645);
  });

  it("doesn't affect getting attributes", () => {
    expect(myCity.name).toBe("Montevideo, Uruguay");
    expect(myCity.lat).toBe(-34.9011);
    expect(myCity.long).toBe(-56.1645);
  });

  it("returns itself from setting functions", () => {
    expect(myCity.setName("Other name")).toBe(myCity);
    expect(myCity.setLat(11)).toBe(myCity);
    expect(myCity.setLong(22)).toBe(myCity);
  });

  it("allows chaining", () => {
    const newCoords = myCity
      .setName("Pune, India")
      .setLat(18.5626)
      .setLong(73.8087)
      .getCoords();

    expect(myCity.name).toBe("Pune, India");
    expect(newCoords[0]).toBe(18.5626);
    expect(newCoords[1]).toBe(73.8087);
  });
});
```

The final result of all of these tests can be seen in the following screenshot:

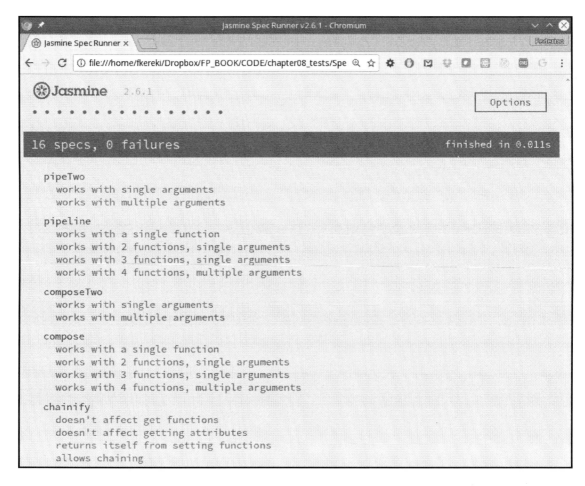

Figure 8.3: A successful run of testing for composed functions

As we can see, all our tests passed successfully; good!

Here, we have looked at the important methods we can use to build functions by using pipelining, chaining, and composition. This works very well, but we'll see that there's a particular case in which the performance of your code could be affected and that we'll need a new way to handle composition: *transducing*.

Transducing

Now, let's consider a performance problem in JavaScript that happens when we're dealing with large arrays and applying several map/filter/reduce operations. If you start with an array and apply such operations (via chaining, as we saw earlier in this chapter), you get the desired result, but many intermediate arrays are created, processed, and discarded—and that causes delays. If you are dealing with short arrays, the extra time won't make an impact, but if you are processing larger arrays (as in a big data process, maybe in Node, where you're working with the results of a large database query), then you will have cause to look for some optimization. We'll do this by learning about a new tool for composing functions: *transducing*.

First, let's create some functions and data. We'll make do with a basically nonsensical example since we aren't focusing on the actual operations but on the general process. We'll start with some filtering functions and some mappings:

```
const testOdd = x => x % 2 === 1;
const testUnderFifty = x => x < 50;
const duplicate = x => x + x;
const addThree = x => x + 3;
```

Now, let's apply those maps and filters to an array. First, we drop the even numbers, duplicate the kept odd numbers, drop results over 50, and end by adding three to all the results:

```
const myArray = [22, 9, 60, 24, 11, 63];

const a0 = myArray
  .filter(testOdd)
  .map(duplicate)
  .filter(testUnderFifty)
  .map(addThree);

/*
[ 21, 25 ]
*/
```

The following diagram shows how this sequence of operations works:

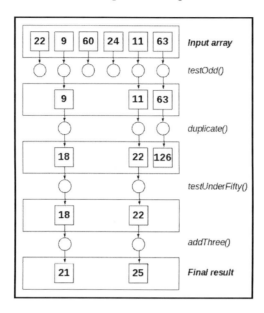

Figure 8.4: Chaining map/filter/reduce operations causes intermediate arrays to be created and later discarded

Here, we can see that chaining together several map/filter/reduce operations causes intermediate arrays (three, in this case) to be created and later discarded—and for large arrays, that can become cumbersome.

How can we optimize this? The problem here is that processing applies the first transformation to the input array; then, the second transformation is applied to the resulting array; then the third, and so on. The alternative solution would be to take the first element of the input array and apply all the transformations in sequence to it. Then, you would need to take the second element of the input array and apply all the transformations to it, then take the third, and so on. In a sort of pseudocode, the difference is between the following schemes:

```
for each transformation to be applied:
    for each element in the input list:
        apply the transformation to the element
```

With this logic, we go transformation by transformation, applying it to each list and generating a new one. This will require several intermediate lists to be produced. The alternative is as follows:

```
for each element in the input list:
    for each transformation to be applied:
        apply the transformation to the element
```

In this variant, we go element by element and apply all the transformations to it in sequence so that we arrive at the final output list without any intermediate ones.

Now, the problem is being able to transpose the transformations; how can we do this? We saw this key concept in Chapter 5, *Programming Declaratively – A Better Style*, and that we can define map() and filter() in terms of reduce(). By using those definitions, instead of a sequence of different functions, we will be applying the same operation (reduce) at each step, and here is the secret! As shown in the following diagram, we change the order of evaluation by composing all the transformations so that they can be applied in a single pass, with no intermediate arrays whatsoever:

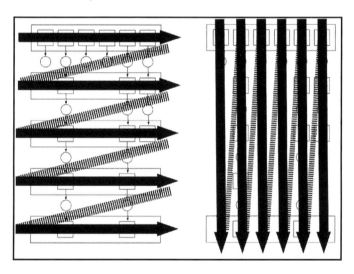

Figure 8.5: By applying transducers, we will change the order of evaluation but get the same result

Instead of applying a first reduce operation, passing its result to a second, its result to a third, and so on, we will compose all the reducing functions into a single one! Let's analyze this.

Composing reducers

Essentially, what we want is to transform each function (testOdd(), duplicate(), and so on) into a reducing operation that will call the following reducer. A couple of higher-order functions will help; one for mapping functions and an other for filtering ones. With this idea, the result of an operation will be passed to the next one, avoiding intermediate arrays:

```
const mapTR = fn => reducer => (accum, value) => reducer(accum, fn(value));

const filterTR = fn => reducer => (accum, value) =>
  fn(value) ? reducer(accum, value) : accum;
```

These two transforming functions are transducers: functions that accept a reducing function and return a new reducing function.

The word *transduce* comes from Latin, meaning *transform, transport, convert, change over*, and is applied in many different fields, including biology, psychology, machine learning, physics, electronics, and more.

How do we use these transducers? We can write code such as the following, though we'll want a more abstract, generic version later:

```
const testOddR = filterTR(testOdd);
const testUnderFiftyR = filterTR(testUnderFifty);
const duplicateR = mapTR(duplicate);
const addThreeR = mapTR(addThree);
```

Each of our original four functions is transformed, so they will calculate their result and call a reducer to deal with this further. As an example, addThreeR() will add three to its input and pass the incremented value to the next reducer, which in this case is addToArray(). This will build up the final resulting array. Now, we can write our whole transformation in a single step:

```
const addToArray = (a, v) => {
  a.push(v);
  return a;
};

const a1 = myArray.reduce(
```

```
        testOddR(duplicateR(testUnderFiftyR(addThreeR(addToArray)))),
        []
);

/*
[ 21, 25 ]
*/
```

This is quite a mouthful, but it works! However, we can simplify our code by using the `compose()` function:

```
const makeReducer1 = (arr, fns) =>
    arr.reduce(compose(...fns)(addToArray), []);

const a2 = makeReducer1(myArray, [
    testOddR,
    duplicateR,
    testUnderFiftyR,
    addThreeR,
]);

/*
[ 21, 25 ]
*/
```

The code is the same, but pay particular attention to the `compose(...fns)(addToArray)` expression: we compose all the mapping and filtering functions—with the last one being `addToArray`—to build up the output. However, this is not as general as we may want it to be: why do we have to create an array? Why can't we have a different final reducing function? We can go one better by generalizing a bit more.

Generalizing for all reducers

To be able to work with all kinds of reducers and produce whatever kind of result they build, we'll need to make a small change. The idea is simple: let's modify our `makeReducer()` function so that it will accept a final reducer and a starting value for the accumulator:

```
const makeReducer2 = (arr, fns, reducer = addToArray, initial = []) =>
    arr.reduce(compose(...fns)(reducer), initial);

const a3 = makeReducer2(myArray, [
    testOddR,
    duplicateR,
    testUnderFiftyR,
```

```
        addThreeR,
]);

/*
[ 21, 25 ]
*/
```

To make this function more usable, we specified our array-building function (and `[]` as a starting accumulator value) so that if you skip those two parameters, you'll get a reducer that produces an array. Now, let's look at the other option: instead of an array, let's calculate the sum of the resulting numbers after all the mapping and filtering:

```
const sum = makeReducer2(
  myArray,
  [testOddR, duplicateR, testUnderFiftyR, addThreeR],
  (acc, value) => acc + value,
  0
);

/*
46
*/
```

By using transducers, we have been able to optimize a sequence of map/filter/reduce operations so that the input array is processed once and directly produces the output result (whether that be an array or a single value) without creating any intermediate arrays; a good gain!

Summary

In this chapter, we have learned how to create new functions by joining several other functions in different ways through pipelining and composition. We also looked at fluent interfaces, which apply chaining, and transducing, a way to compose reducers in order to get higher speed sequences of transformations. With these methods, you'll be able to create new functions out of existing ones and keep programming in the declarative way we've been favoring.

In Chapter 9, *Designing Functions – Recursion*, we will move on to function design and study the usage of recursion, which is a basic tool in functional programming and allows for very clean algorithm designs.

Questions

8.1. Headline capitalization: Let's define *headline-style capitalization,* so ensure that a sentence is all written in lowercase, except the first letter of each word. (The real definition of this style is more complicated, so let's simplify it for this question.) Write a `headline(sentence)` function that will receive a string as an argument and return an appropriately capitalized version. Spaces separate words. Build this function by composing smaller functions:

```
console.log(headline("Alice's ADVENTURES in WoNdErLaNd"));
    // Alice's Adventures In Wonderland
```

8.2. Pending tasks: A web service returns a result such as the following, showing, person by person, all their assigned tasks. Tasks may be finished (`done===true`) or pending (`done===false`). Your goal is to produce an array with the IDs of the pending tasks for a given person, identified by name, which should match the `responsible` field. Solve this by using composition or pipelining:

```
const allTasks = {
        date: "2017-09-22",
        byPerson: [
            {
                responsible: "EG",
                tasks: [
                    {id: 111, desc: "task 111", done: false},
                    {id: 222, desc: "task 222", done: false}
                ]
            },
            {
                responsible: "FK",
                tasks: [
                    {id: 555, desc: "task 555", done: false},
                    {id: 777, desc: "task 777", done: true},
                    {id: 999, desc: "task 999", done: false}
                ]
            },
            {
                responsible: "ST",
                tasks: [{id: 444, desc: "task 444", done: true}]
            }
        ]
    };
```

Make sure your code doesn't throw an exception if, for example, the person you are looking for doesn't appear in the web service result!

In the last chapter of this book, Chapter 12, *Building Better Containers – Functional Data Types*, we will look at a different way of solving this by using Maybe monads. This greatly simplifies the problem of dealing with possibly missing data.

8.3. **Thinking in abstract terms**: Suppose you are looking through somewhat old code and you find a function that looks like the following one. (I'm keeping the names vague and abstract so that you can focus on the structure and not on the actual functionality). Can you transform this into pointfree style?

```
function getSomeResults(things) {
    return sort(group(filter(select(things))));
};
```

8.4. **Undetected impurity?** Did you notice that the addToArray() function we wrote is actually impure? (Check out the *Argument mutation* section of Chapter 4, *Behaving Properly – Pure Functions*, if you aren't convinced!) Would it be better if we wrote it as follows? Should we go for it?

```
const addToArray = (a, v) => [...a, v];
```

8.5. **Needless transducing?** We used transducers to simplify any sequence of mapping and filtering operations. Would you have needed this if you only had map() operations? What if you only had filter() operations?

9
Designing Functions - Recursion

In Chapter 8, *Connecting Functions – Pipelining and Composition*, we considered yet more ways to create new functions out of combining previous existing ones. Here, we are going to get into a different theme: how to actually design and write functions, in a typically functional way, by applying recursive techniques.

We will be covering the following topics:

- Understanding what recursion is and how to think in order to produce recursive solutions
- Applying recursion to some well-known problems, such as making a change or the Tower of Hanoi
- Using recursion instead of iteration to re-implement some higher-order functions from earlier chapters
- Writing search and backtrack algorithms with ease
- Traversing data structures, such as trees, to work with file system directories or with the browser DOM
- Getting around some limitations caused by browser JavaScript engine considerations

Using recursion

Recursion is a key technique in FP, to the degree that there are some languages that do not provide for any kind of iteration or loops and work exclusively with recursion (Haskell, which we already mentioned, is a prime example of that). A basic fact of computer science is that whatever you can do with recursion, you can also do with iteration (loops), and vice versa. The key concept is that there are many algorithms whose definition is far easier if you work recursively. On the other hand, recursion is not always taught, or many programmers, even knowing about it, prefer not to use it. Therefore, in this section, we shall see several examples of recursive thinking, so that you can adapt it for your functional coding.

A typical, oft-quoted, and very old computer joke!

Dictionary definition:
recursion: *(n) see* **recursion**

But what is recursion? There are many ways to define what recursion is, but the simplest one I've seen runs along the lines of *a function calls itself again and again, until it doesn't.* Recursion is a natural technique for several kinds of problems, such as the following:

- Mathematical definitions, such as the Fibonacci sequence or the factorial of a number.
- Data-structure-related algorithms, with recursively defined structures, such as **lists** (a list is either empty or consists of a head node followed by a list of nodes) or **trees** (a tree might be defined as a special node, called the root, linked to zero or more trees).
- Syntax analysis for compilers, based on grammar rules, which themselves depend on other rules, which also depend on other rules, and so on.
- And many more! It even appears in art and humor, as shown in the following screenshot:

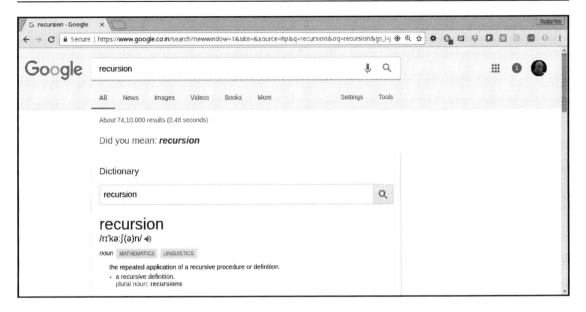

Google itself jokes about it: if you ask about recursion, it answers "Did you mean: recursion!"

In any case, a recursive function, apart from some easy, base cases, in which no further computation is required, always needs to call itself one or more times in order to perform part of the required calculations. This concept may be not very clear at the moment, so, in the following sections, we will see how we can think in a recursive fashion and then solve several common problems by applying this technique.

Thinking recursively

The key to solving problems recursively is assuming that you already have a function that does whatever you need and just calling it normally. (Doesn't this sound weird? Actually, it is quite appropriate: if you want to solve a problem by using recursion, you must first have solved it before...) On the other hand, if you try to work out in your head how the recursive calls work and attempt to follow the flow in your mind, you'll probably just get lost. So what you need to do is the following:

1. Assume you already have an appropriate function to solve your problem.
2. See how the big problem can be solved by solving one (or more) smaller problems.
3. Solve those problems by using the imagined function from step 1.
4. Decide what your base cases are. Make sure that they are simple enough that they are solved directly, without requiring any more calls.

With these points in mind, you can solve problems by recursion because you'll have the basic structure for your recursive solution.

There are three usual methods for solving problems by applying recursion:

- **Decrease and conquer** is the simplest case, in which solving a problem directly depends on solving a single, simpler case of itself.
- **Divide and conquer** is a more general approach. The idea is to try to divide your problem into two or more smaller versions, solve them recursively, and use these solutions to solve the original problem. The only difference between this technique and decrease and conquer is that, here, you have to solve two or more other problems, instead of only one.
- **Dynamic programming** can be seen as a variant of divide and conquer: basically, you solve a complex problem by breaking it into a set of somewhat simpler versions of the same problem and solving each in order; however, a key idea in this strategy is to store previously found solutions, so that whenever you find yourself needing the solution to a simpler case again you won't directly apply recursion, but rather use the stored result and avoid unnecessary repeated calculations.

In this section, we shall look at a few problems and solve them by thinking in a recursive way. Of course, we shall see more applications of recursion in the rest of the chapter; here, we'll focus on the key decisions and questions that are needed to create such an algorithm.

Decrease and conquer – searching

The most usual case of recursion involves just a single, simple case. We have already seen some examples of this, such as the ubiquitous factorial calculation: to calculate the factorial of *n*, you previously needed to calculate the factorial of *n*-1. (See Chapter 1, *Becoming Functional – Several Questions*.) Let's turn now to a nonmathematical example.

To search for an element in an array, you would also use this decrease and conquer strategy. If the array is empty, then obviously the searched-for value isn't there; otherwise, the result is in the array if and only if it's the first element in it, or if it's in the rest of the array. The following code does just that:

```
const search = (arr, key) => {
  if (arr.length === 0) {
    return false;

  } else if (arr[0] === key) {
    return true;
```

```
    } else {
      return search(arr.slice(1), key);
    }
  };
```

This implementation directly mirrors our explanation, and it's easy to verify its correctness.

By the way, just as a precaution, let's look at two further implementations of the same concept. You can shorten the search function a bit—is it still clear? We are using a ternary operator to detect whether the array is empty, and a Boolean || operator to return true if the first element is the sought one or else return the result of the recursive search:

```
const search2 = (arr, key) =>
  arr.length === 0 ? false : arr[0] === key || search2(arr.slice(1), key);
```

Sparseness can go even further! Using && as a shortcut is a common idiom:

```
const search3 = (arr, key) =>
  arr.length && (arr[0] === key || search3(arr.slice(1), key));
```

I'm not really suggesting that you code the function in this way—rather, consider it a warning against the tendency that some FP developers have to try to go for the tightest, shortest possible solution and never mind clarity!

Decrease and conquer – doing powers

Another classic example has to do with calculating the powers of numbers in an efficient way. If you want to calculate, say, 2 to the 13th power (2^{13}), then you can do this with 12 multiplications; however, you can do much better by writing 2^{13} as the following:

$= 2$ times 2^{12}
$= 2$ times 4^{6}
$= 2$ times 16^{3}
$= 2$ times 16 times 16^{2}
$= 2$ times 16 times 256^{1}
$= 8192$

This reduction in the total number of multiplications may not look very impressive, but, in terms of algorithmic complexity, it allows us to bring down the order of the calculations from $O(n)$ to $O(lg\ n)$. In some cryptographic-related methods, which have to raise numbers to really high exponents, this makes a very important difference. We can implement this recursive algorithm in a few lines of code, as shown in the following code:

```
const powerN = (base, power) => {
  if (power === 0) {
    return 1;

  } else if (power % 2) { // odd power?
    return base * powerN(base, power - 1);

  } else { // even power?
    return powerN(base * base, power / 2);
  }
};
```

When implemented for production, bit operations are used, instead of modulus and divisions. Checking whether a number is odd can be written as `power & 1`, and division by 2 is achieved with `power >> 1`. These alternative calculations are way faster than the replaced operations.

Calculating a power is simple when the base case is reached (raising something to the zeroth power), or is based upon previously calculating a power for a smaller exponent. (If you wanted to, you could add another base case for raising something to the power of one.) These observations show that we are seeing a textbook case for the decrease and conquer recursive strategy.

Finally, some of our higher-order functions, such as `map()`, `reduce()`, and `filter()`, also apply this technique; we'll look into this later on in this chapter.

Divide and conquer – the Towers of Hanoi

With the divide and conquer strategy, solving a problem requires two or more recursive solutions. For starters, let's consider a classic puzzle, invented by a French mathematician, Édouard Lucas, in the nineteenth century. The puzzle involves a temple in India, with 3 posts a 64 golden disks of decreasing diameter. The priests have to move the disks from the first post to the last one following two rules: only one disk can be moved at a time, and a larger disk can never be placed on top of a smaller disk. According to the legend, when the 64 disks are moved, the world will end. This puzzle is usually marketed under the name *Towers of Hanoi* (yes, they changed countries!) with fewer than 10 disks. See *Figure 9.1*:

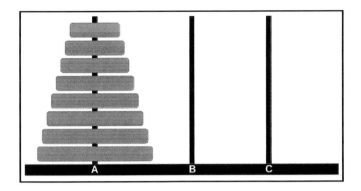

Figure 9.1: The classic Towers of Hanoi puzzle has a simple recursive solution.

 The solution for n disks requires 2^n-1 movements. The original puzzle, requiring $2^{64}-1$ movements, at one movement per second, would take more than 584 billion years to finish, a very long time, considering that the universe's age is evaluated to only be 13.8 billion years!

Suppose that we already had a function that was able to solve the problem of moving any number of disks from a source post to a destination post using the remaining post as an extra aid. Think about solving the general problem if you already had a function to solve that problem: `hanoi(disks, from, to, extra)`. If you wanted to move several disks from one post to another, then you could solve it easily using this (still unwritten!) function by carrying out the following steps:

1. Moving all of the disks but the last one to the extra post.
2. Moving the last disk to the destination post.
3. Moving all the disks from the extra post (where you had placed them earlier) to the destination.

But what about our base cases? We could decide that, to move a single disk, you needn't use the function; you just go ahead and move it. When coded, it becomes the following:

```
const hanoi = (disks, from, to, extra) => {
  if (disks === 1) {
    console.log(`Move disk 1 from post ${from} to post ${to}`);

  } else {
    hanoi(disks - 1, from, extra, to);
    console.log(`Move disk ${disks} from post ${from} to post ${to}`);
    hanoi(disks - 1, extra, to, from);
  }
};
```

We can quickly verify that this code works:

```
hanoi (4, "A", "B", "C"); // we want to move all disks from A to B
Move disk 1 from post A to post C
Move disk 2 from post A to post B
Move disk 1 from post C to post B
Move disk 3 from post A to post C
Move disk 1 from post B to post A
Move disk 2 from post B to post C
Move disk 1 from post A to post C
Move disk 4 from post A to post B
Move disk 1 from post C to post B
Move disk 2 from post C to post A
Move disk 1 from post B to post A
Move disk 3 from post C to post B
Move disk 1 from post A to post C
Move disk 2 from post A to post B
Move disk 1 from post C to post B
```

There's only a small detail to consider, which can simplify the function even further. In this code, our base case (the one that needs no further recursion) is when `disks` equals one. You could also solve this in a different way by letting the disks go down to zero and simply not doing anything—after all, moving zero disks from one post to another is achieved by doing nothing at all! The revised code would be as follows:

```
const hanoi2 = (disks, from, to, extra) => {
  if (disks > 0) {
    hanoi(disks - 1, from, extra, to);
    console.log(`Move disk ${disks} from post ${from} to post ${to}`);
    hanoi(disks - 1, extra, to, from);
  }
};
```

Instead of checking whether there are any disks to move before doing the recursive call, we can just skip the check and have the function test, at the next level, whether there's something to be done.

 If you are doing the puzzle by hand, there's a simple solution for that: on odd turns, always move the smaller disk to the next post (if the total number of disks is odd) or to the previous post (if the total number of disks is even). On even turns, do the only possible move that doesn't imply the smaller disk.

So, the principle for recursive algorithm design works: assume you already have your desired function and use it to build it!

Divide and conquer – sorting

We can see another example of the divide and conquer strategy with sorting. A way to sort arrays, called *quicksort*, is based upon the following steps:

1. If your array has 0 or 1 elements, do nothing; it's already sorted (this is the base case).
2. Pick an element of the array (called the **pivot**) and split the rest of the array into two subarrays: the elements smaller than your chosen element and the elements greater than or equal to your chosen element.
3. Recursively sort each subarray.
4. Concatenate both sorted results, with the pivot in-between, to produce the sorted version of the original array.

Let's see a simple version of this (there are some better-optimized implementations, but we are interested in the recursive logic now). Usually, picking a random element of the array is suggested to avoid some bad performance border cases, but for our example, let's just take the first one:

```
const quicksort = arr => {
  if (arr.length < 2) {
    return arr;

  } else {
    const pivot = arr[0];
    const smaller = arr.slice(1).filter(x => x < pivot);
    const greaterEqual = arr.slice(1).filter(x => x >= pivot);
    return [...quicksort(smaller), pivot, ...quicksort(greaterEqual)];
  }
};

console.log(quicksort([22, 9, 60, 12, 4, 56]));
// [4, 9, 12, 22, 56, 60]
```

We can see how this works in *Figure 9.2*: the pivot for each array and subarray is underlined. Splitting is shown with dotted arrows and is joined with full lines:

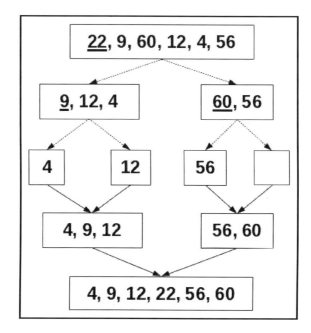

Figure 9.2: Quicksort sorts an array recursively, applying the divide and conquer strategy, to reduce the original problem to smaller ones

Writing Quicksort correctly is not trivial; see question 9.8 at the end of this chapter for an alternative version that happens to be *almost* right, but not totally correct!

We have already seen the basic strategies to reduce a problem to simpler versions of itself. Let's now look at an important optimization that is key for many algorithms.

Dynamic programming – making change

The third general strategy, dynamic programming, assumes that you will have to solve many smaller problems, but, instead of using recursion each and every time, it depends on you having stored the previously found solutions... memoization, in other words! In Chapter 4, *Behaving Properly – Pure Functions*, and later in a better fashion in Chapter 6, *Producing Functions – Higher-Order Functions*, we already saw how to optimize the calculations of the usual Fibonacci series, avoiding unnecessary repeated calls. Let's now consider another problem.

Given a certain number of dollars and the list of existing bill values, calculate in how many different ways we can pay that amount of dollars with different combinations of bills. It is assumed that you have access to an unlimited number of each bill. How can we go about solving this? Let's start by considering the base cases, where no further computation is needed. They are as follows:

- Paying negative values is not possible, so in such cases, we should return zero
- Paying zero dollars is only possible in a single way (by giving no bills), so in this case, we should return 1
- Paying any positive amount of dollars isn't possible if no bills are provided, so in this case, also return 0

Finally, we can answer the question: in how many ways can we pay N dollars with a given set of bills? We can consider two cases: we do not use the larger bill at all and pay the amount using only smaller denomination bills, or we can take one bill of the larger amount and reconsider the question. (Let's forget the avoidance of repeated calculations for now):

- In the first case, we should invoke our supposedly existing function with the same value of N, but prune the largest bill denomination from the list of available bills.
- In the second case, we should invoke our function with N minus the largest bill denomination, keeping the list of bills the same, as shown in the following code:

```
const makeChange = (n, bills) => {
  if (n < 0) {
    return 0; // no way of paying negative amounts

  } else if (n == 0) {
    return 1; // one single way of paying $0: with no bills

  } else if (bills.length == 0) {
    // here, n>0
    return 0; // no bills? no way of paying

  } else {
    return makeChange(n, bills.slice(1)) + makeChange(n - bills[0],
bills);
  }
};

console.log(makeChange(64, [100, 50, 20, 10, 5, 2, 1]));
// 969 ways of paying $64
```

Now let's do some optimizing. This algorithm often needs to recalculate the same values over and over. (To verify this, add `console.log(n, bills.length)` as the first line in `makeChange()`—but be ready for plenty of output!) However, we already have a solution for this: memoization! Since we are applying this technique to a binary function, we'll need a version of the memoization algorithm that deals with more than one parameter. The memoizing function and its application would be as follows:

```
const memoize3 = fn => {
  let cache = {};
  return (...args) => {
    let strX = JSON.stringify(args);
    return strX in cache ? cache[strX] : (cache[strX] = fn(...args));
  };
};

const makeChange = memoize3((n, bills) => {
  // ...same as above
});
```

The memoized version of `makeChange()` is far more efficient, and you can verify it with logging. While it is certainly possible to deal with the repetitions by yourself (for example, by keeping an array of already computed values), the memoization solution is, in my opinion, better, because it composes two functions to produce a better solution for the given problem.

Higher-order functions revisited

Classic FP techniques do not use iteration at all, but work exclusively with recursion as the only way to do some looping. Let's revisit some of the functions that we have already seen in Chapter 5, *Programming Declaratively – A Better Style*, such as map(), reduce(), find(), and filter(), to see how we can make do with just recursion.

We are not planning to exchange the basic JavaScript functions for ours, though: it's highly likely that performance will be worse for our recursive polyfills and we won't derive any advantages just from having the functions use recursion. Rather, we want to study how iterations are performed in a recursive way so that our efforts are more pedagogical than practical, OK?

Mapping and filtering

Mapping and filtering are quite similar insofar as both imply going through all the elements in an array and applying a callback to each to produce output. Let's first work out the mapping logic, which will have several points to solve, and then we should see that filtering has become almost trivially easy, requiring just small changes.

For mapping, given how we are developing recursive functions, we need a base case. Fortunately, that's easy: mapping an empty array just produces a new empty array. Mapping a nonempty array can be done by first applying the mapping function to the first element of the array, then recursively mapping the rest of the array, and finally producing a single array accumulating both results.

Based on this idea, we can work out a simple initial version: let's call it mapR(), just to remember that we are dealing with our own, recursive version of map(); however, be careful: our polyfill has some bugs! We'll deal with them one at a time. Here's our first attempt at writing our own mapping code:

```
const mapR = (arr, cb) =>
    arr.length === 0 ? [] : [cb(arr[0])].concat(mapR(arr.slice(1), cb));
```

Let's test it out:

```
let aaa = [ 1, 2, 4, 5, 7];
const timesTen = x => x * 10;

console.log(aaa.map(timesTen));    // [10, 20, 40, 50, 70]
console.log(mapR(aaa, timesTen)); // [10, 20, 40, 50, 70]
```

Great! Our mapR() function seemingly produces the same results as map(). However, shouldn't our callback function receive a couple more parameters, specifically the index at the array and the original array itself?

Check out the definition for the callback function for map() at https://developer.mozilla.org/en/docs/Web/JavaScript/Reference/Global_Objects/Array/map.

Our implementation isn't quite ready yet. Let's first see how it fails by using a simple example:

```
const timesTenPlusI = (v, i) => 10 * v + i;

console.log(aaa.map(timesTenPlusI));     // [10, 21, 42, 53, 74]
console.log(mapR2(aaa, timesTenPlusI)); // [NaN, NaN, NaN, NaN, NaN]
```

Generating the appropriate index position will require an extra parameter for the recursion, but it is basically simple: when we start out, we have index=0, and when we call our function recursively, it's starting at position index+1. Accessing the original array requires yet another parameter, which will never change, and now we have a better mapping function:

```
const mapR2 = (arr, cb, i = 0, orig = arr) =>
  arr.length == 0
    ? []
    : [cb(arr[0], i, orig)].concat(
        mapR2(arr.slice(1), cb, i + 1, orig)
      );

let aaa = [1, 2, 4, 5, 7];
const senseless = (x, i, a) => x * 10 + i + a[i] / 10;
console.log(aaa.map(senseless));      // [10.1, 21.2, 42.4, 53.5, 74.7]
console.log(mapR2(aaa, senseless));   // [10.1, 21.2, 42.4, 53.5, 74.7]
```

Great! When you do recursion instead of iteration, you don't have access to an index, so, if you need it (as in our case), you'll have to generate it on your own. This is an often-used technique, so working out our map() substitute was a good idea.

However, having extra arguments in the function is not so good; a developer might accidentally provide them and then the results would be unpredictable. So, using another usual technique, let's define an inner function, mapLoop(), to handle looping. This is, in fact, the usual way in which looping is achieved when you only use recursion; look at the following code, in which the extra function just isn't accessible from outside:

```
const mapR3 = (orig, cb) => {
  const mapLoop = (arr, i) =>
    arr.length == 0
      ? []
      : [cb(arr[0], i, orig)].concat(
          mapR3(arr.slice(1), cb, i + 1, orig)
        );
  return mapLoop(orig, 0);
};
```

There's only one pending issue: if the original array has some missing elements, they should be skipped during the loop. Let's look at an example:

```
[1, 2, , , 5].map(tenTimes)
// [10, 20, undefined x 2, 50]
```

Fortunately, fixing this is simple—and be glad that all the experience gained here will help us write the other functions in this section! Can you understand the fix in the following code?

```
const mapR4 = (orig, cb) => {
  const mapLoop = (arr, i) => {
    if (arr.length == 0) {
      return [];

    } else {
      const mapRest = mapR4(arr.slice(1), cb, i + 1, orig);
      if (!(0 in arr)) {
        return [,].concat(mapRest);

      } else {
        return [cb(arr[0], i, orig)].concat(mapRest);
      }
    }
  };

  return mapLoop(orig, 0);
};

console.log(mapR4(aaa, timesTen)); // [10, 20, undefined × 2, 50]
```

Wow! This was more than we bargained for, but we saw several techniques: how to replace iteration with recursion, how to accumulate a result across iterations, and how to generate and provide the index value—good tips! Furthermore, writing filtering code will prove much easier, since we'll be able to apply very much the same logic as we did for mapping. The main difference is that we use the callback function to decide whether an element goes into the output array, so the inner loop function is a tad longer:

```
const filterR = (orig, cb) => {
  const filterLoop = (arr, i) => {
    if (arr.length == 0) {
      return [];

    } else {
      const filterRest = filterR(arr.slice(1), cb, i + 1, orig);
      if (!(0 in arr)) {
        return filterRest;

      } else if (cb(arr[0], i, orig)) {
        return [arr[0]].concat(filterRest);

      } else {
        return filterRest;
```

```
            }
          }
      };

      return filterLoop(orig, 0);
  };


  let aaa = [1, 12, , , 5, 22, 9, 60];
  const isOdd = x => x % 2;
  console.log(aaa.filter(isOdd));    // [1, 5, 9]
  console.log(filterR(aaa, isOdd)); // [1, 5, 9]
```

Okay, we managed to implement two of our basic higher-order functions with pretty similar recursive functions. What about the others?

Other higher-order functions

Programming reduce() is, from the outset, a bit trickier, since you can decide to omit the initial value for the accumulator. Since we mentioned earlier that providing that value is generally better, let's work here under the assumption that it will be given; dealing with the other possibility won't be too hard.

The base case is simple: if the array is empty, the result is the accumulator; otherwise, we must apply the reduce function to the current element and the accumulator, update the latter, and then continue working with the rest of the array. This can be a bit confusing because of the ternary operators, but, after all we've seen, it should be clear enough. Look at the following code for the details:

```
  const reduceR = (orig, cb, accum) => {
    const reduceLoop = (arr, i) => {
      return arr.length == 0
        ? accum
        : reduceR(
          arr.slice(1),
          cb,
          !(0 in arr) ? accum : cb(accum, arr[0], i, orig),
          i + 1,
          orig
        );
    };

    return reduceLoop(orig, 0);
  };
```

```
let bbb = [1, 2, , 5, 7, 8, 10, 21, 40];
console.log(bbb.reduce((x, y) => x + y, 0));    // 94
console.log(reduce2(bbb, (x, y) => x + y, 0)); // 94
```

On the other hand, `find()` is particularly apt for recursive logic, since the very definition of how you (attempt to) find something, is recursive in itself:

- You look at the first place you think of, and, if you find what you were seeking, you are done.
- Alternatively, you look at the other places to see if what you seek is there.

We are only missing the base case, but that's simple, and we already saw this earlier in the chapter: if you have no places left to search, then you know you won't be successful in your search:

```
const findR = (arr, cb) => {
  if (arr.length === 0) {
    return undefined;

  } else {
    return cb(arr[0]) ? arr[0] : findR(arr.slice(1), cb);
  }
};
```

If you want to shorten the code a bit, you can do this by using the ternary operator a couple of times:

```
const findR2 = (arr, cb) =>
  arr.length === 0
    ? undefined
    : cb(arr[0])
    ? arr[0]
    : findR(arr.slice(1), cb);
```

We can quickly verify whether this works:

```
let aaa = [1, 12, , , 5, 22, 9, 60];

const isTwentySomething = x => 20 <= x && x <= 29;
console.log(findR(aaa, isTwentySomething)); // 22

const isThirtySomething = x => 30 <= x && x <= 39;
console.log(findR(aaa, isThirtySomething)); // undefined
```

Let's finish with our pipelining function. The definition of a pipeline lends itself to quick implementation:

- If we want to pipeline a single function, then that's the result of the pipeline.
- If we want to pipeline several functions, then we must first apply the initial function, and then pass that result as input to the pipeline of the other functions.

We can directly turn this into code:

```
const pipelineR = (first, ...rest) =>
    rest.length == 0
        ? first
        : (...args) => pipelineR(...rest)(first(...args));
```

We can verify its correctness with a simple example. Let's pipeline several calls to a couple of functions, one of which just adds one to its argument and the other of which multiplies by ten:

```
const plus1 = x => x + 1;
const by10 = x => x * 10;

pipelineR(
    by10,
    plus1,
    plus1,
    plus1,
    by10,
    plus1,
    by10,
    by10,
    plus1,
    plus1,
    plus1
)(2);
// 23103
```

If you follow the math, you'll be able to check that the pipelining is working fine. Doing the same for composition is easy, except that you cannot use the spread operator to simplify the function definition, and you'll have to work with array indices—work it out!

Searching and backtracking

Searching for solutions to problems, especially when there is no direct algorithm and you must resort to trial and error, is particularly appropriate for recursion. Many of these algorithms fall into a scheme such as the following:

- Out of many choices available, pick one.
- If no options are available, you've failed.
- If you could pick one, apply the same algorithm, but find a solution to the rest.
- If you succeed, you are done.
- Otherwise, try another choice.

With small variations, you can also apply similar logic to find a good—or possibly, optimum—solution to a given problem. Each time you find a possible solution, you match it with previous ones that you might have found and decide which to keep. This may go on until all possible solutions have been evaluated, or until a good enough solution has been found.

There are many problems to which this logic applies. They are as follows:

- Finding a way out of mazes—pick any path, mark it as already followed, and try to find a way out of the maze that won't reuse that path: if you succeed, you are done, and if you do not, go back to pick a different path.
- Filling out sudoku puzzles—if an empty cell can contain only a single number, then assign it; otherwise, run through all of the possible assignments and, for each one, recursively try to see if the rest of the puzzle can be filled out.
- Playing chess—where you aren't likely to be able to follow through all possible move sequences and so instead you opt for the best-estimated position.

Let's apply these techniques to two problems: solving the eight queens puzzle and traversing a complete file directory.

The eight queens puzzle

The eight queens puzzle was invented in the nineteenth century and involves placing eight chess queens on a standard chessboard. The special condition is that no queen should be able to attack another—implying that no pair of queens may share a row, column, or diagonal line. The puzzle may ask for any solution or for the total number of distinct solutions, which is what we will attempt to find.

The puzzle may also be generalized to *n* queens, by working on an *n* x *n* square board. It is known that there are solutions for all values of *n*, except *n*=2 (pretty simple to see why: after placing one queen, all of the board is threatened) and *n*=3 (if you place a queen in the center, all of the board is threatened, and if you place a queen on a side, only two squares are not threatened, but they threaten each other, making it impossible to place queens on them).

Let's start our solution with the top-level logic. Because of the given rules, there will be a single queen in each column, so we use a `places()` array to take note of each queen's row within the given column. The `SIZE` constant could be modified to solve a more general problem. We'll count each found distribution of queens in the `solutions` variable. Finally, the `finder()` function will perform the recursive search for solutions. The basic skeleton for the code would be as follows:

```
const SIZE = 8;
let places = Array(SIZE);
let solutions = 0;

finder();

console.log(`Solutions found: ${solutions}`);
```

Let's get into the required logic. When we want to place a queen in a given row within a certain column, we must check whether any of the previously placed queens were already placed on the same row or in a diagonal leading from the row. See *Figure 9.3*:

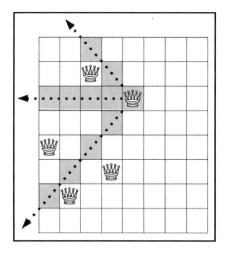

Figure 9.3: Before placing a queen in a column, we must check the previously placed queens' positions

Let's write a `checkPlace(column, row)` function to verify whether a queen can be safely placed in the given square. The most straightforward way is by using `.every()`, as shown in the following code:

```
const checkPlace = (column, row) =>
  places
    .slice(0, column)
    .every((v, i) => v !== row && Math.abs(v - row) !== column - i);
```

This declarative fashion seems best: when we place a queen in a position, we want to make sure that every other previously placed queen is in a different row and diagonal. A recursive solution would have been possible too, so let's see that. How do we know that a square is safe?

- A base case is that, when there are no more columns to check, the square is safe.
- If the square is in the same row or diagonal as any other queen, it's not safe.
- If we have checked a column and found no problem, we can now recursively check the following one.

The required code to check whether a position in a column can be occupied by a queen is therefore as follows:

```
const checkPlace2 = (column, row) => {
 const checkColumn = i => {
    if (i == column) {
      return true;

    } else if (
      places[i] == row ||
      Math.abs(places[i] - row) == column - i
    ) {
      return false;

    } else {
      return checkColumn(i + 1);
    }
  };

  return checkColumn(0);
};
```

The code works, but I wouldn't be using it since the declarative version is clearer. Anyway, having worked out this check, we can pay attention to the main `finder()` logic, which will do the recursive search. The process proceeds as we described at the beginning: trying out a possible placement for a queen, and if that is acceptable, using the same search procedure to try and place the remaining queens. We start at column 0, and our base case is when we reach the last column, meaning that all queens have been successfully placed: we can print out the solution, count it, and go back to search for a new configuration.

Check out how we use `map()` and a simple arrow function to print the rows of the queens, column by column, as numbers between 1 and 8, instead of 0 and 7. In chess, rows are numbered from 1 to 8 (and columns from a to h, but that doesn't matter here).

Check out the following code, which applies the logic that we described previously:

```
const finder = (column = 0) => {
  if (column === SIZE) {
    // all columns tried out?
    console.log(places.map(x => x + 1)); // print out solution
    solutions++; // count it

  } else {
    const testRowsInColumn = j => {
      if (j < SIZE) {
        if (checkPlace(column, j)) {
          places[column] = j;
          finder(column + 1);
        }
        testRowsInColumn(j + 1);
      }
    };

    testRowsInColumn(0);
  }
};
```

The inner `testRowsInColumn()` function also fulfills an iterative role, but recursively. The idea is to attempt placing a queen in every possible row, starting at zero: if the square is safe, `finder()` is called to start searching from the next column onward. No matter whether a solution was or wasn't found, all rows in the column are tried out, since we are interested in the total number of solutions; in other search problems, you might be content with finding just any solution, and you would stop your search right there.

We have come this far, so let's find the answer to our problem!

```
[1, 5, 8, 6, 3, 7, 2, 4]
[1, 6, 8, 3, 7, 4, 2, 5]
[1, 7, 4, 6, 8, 2, 5, 3]
[1, 7, 5, 8, 2, 4, 6, 3]
...
... 84 lines snipped out ...
...
[8, 2, 4, 1, 7, 5, 3, 6]
[8, 2, 5, 3, 1, 7, 4, 6]
[8, 3, 1, 6, 2, 5, 7, 4]
[8, 4, 1, 3, 6, 2, 7, 5]
Solutions found: 92
```

Each solution is given as the row positions for the queens, column by column, and there are 92 solutions in all.

Traversing a tree structure

Data structures, which include recursion in their definition, are naturally appropriate for recursive techniques. Let's consider, for example, how to traverse a complete filesystem directory, listing all of its contents. Where's the recursion? The answer is clear if you consider that each directory can do either of the following:

- Be empty—a base case, in which there's nothing to do
- Include one or more entries, each of which is either a file or a directory itself

Let's work out a full recursive directory listing—meaning that when we encounter a directory, we also list its contents, and if those include more directories, we also list them, and so on. We'll be using the same node functions as in getDir() (from the *Building pipelines by hand* section in Chapter 8, *Connecting Functions – Pipelining and Composition*), plus a few more in order to test whether a directory entry is a symbolic link (which we won't follow to avoid possible infinite loops), a directory (which will require a recursive listing), or a common file:

```
const fs = require("fs");

const recursiveDir = path => {
  console.log(path);
  fs.readdirSync(path).forEach(entry => {
    if (entry.startsWith(".")) {
      // skip it!

    } else {
```

```
          const full = path + "/" + entry;
          const stats = fs.lstatSync(full);

          if (stats.isSymbolicLink()) {
            console.log("L ", full); // symlink, don't follow

          } else if (stats.isDirectory()) {
            console.log("D ", full);
            recursiveDir(full);

          } else {
            console.log(" ", full);
          }
        }
      });
    };
```

The listing is long but correct. I opted to list the /boot directory in my own OpenSUSE Linux laptop, and this was produced:

```
  recursiveDir("/boot");
  /boot
      /boot/System.map-4.11.8-1-default
      /boot/boot.readme
      /boot/config-4.11.8-1-default
  D   /boot/efi
  D   /boot/efi/EFI
  D   /boot/efi/EFI/boot
      /boot/efi/EFI/boot/bootx64.efi
      /boot/efi/EFI/boot/fallback.efi
      ...
      ... many omitted lines
      ...
  L   /boot/initrd
      /boot/initrd-4.11.8-1-default
      /boot/message
      /boot/symtypes-4.11.8-1-default.gz
      /boot/symvers-4.11.8-1-default.gz
      /boot/sysctl.conf-4.11.8-1-default
      /boot/vmlinux-4.11.8-1-default.gz
  L   /boot/vmlinuz
      /boot/vmlinuz-4.11.8-1-default
```

By the way, we can apply the same structure to a similar problem: traversing a DOM structure. We could list all of the tags, starting from a given element, by using essentially the same approach: we list a node and (by applying the same algorithm) all of its children. The base case is also the same as before: when a node has no children, no more recursive calls are done. You can see this in the following code:

```
const traverseDom = (node, depth = 0) => {
  console.log(`${"| ".repeat(depth)}<${node.nodeName.toLowerCase()}>`);
  for (let i = 0; i < node.children.length; i++) {
    traverseDom(node.children[i], depth + 1);
  }
};
```

We are using the depth variable to know how many levels below the original element we are. We could also use it to make the traversing logic stop at a certain level, of course; in our case, we are using it only to add some bars and spaces to appropriately indent each element according to its place in the DOM hierarchy. The result of this function is shown in the following code. It would be easy to list more information and not just the element tag, but I wanted to focus on the recursive process:

```
traverseDom(document.body);
<body>
| <script>
| <div>
| | <div>
| | | <a>
| | | <div>
| | | | <ul>
| | | | | <li>
| | | | | | <a>
| | | | | | | <div>
| | | | | | | | <div>
| | | | | | | <div>
| | | | | | | | <br>
| | | | | | | <div>
| | | | | | <ul>
| | | | | | | <li>
| | | | | | | | <a>
| | | | | | | <li>
...etc!
```

However, there's an ugly point there: why are we doing a loop to go through all of the children? We should know better! The problem is that the structure we get from the DOM isn't really an array; however, there's a way out: we can use `Array.from()` to create a real array out of it and then write a more declarative solution. The following code solves the problem in a better way:

```
const traverseDom2 = (node, depth = 0) => {
  console.log(`${"| ".repeat(depth)}<${node.nodeName.toLowerCase()}>`);
  Array.from(node.children).forEach(child =>
    traverseDom2(child, depth + 1)
  );
};
```

Writing `[...node.children].forEach()` would have worked as well, but I think using `Array.from()` makes it clearer to any reader that we are trying to make an array out of something that looks like one, but really isn't.

We have now seen many ideas about the usage of recursion, and we've seen many applications of it; however, there are some cases in which you may run into problems, so let's now consider some tweaks that may come in handy for specific problems.

Recursion techniques

While recursion is a very good technique, it may face some problems because of the details the way it is actually implemented. Each function call, recursive or not, requires an entry in the internal JavaScript stack. When you are working with recursion, each recursive call itself counts as another call, and you might find that there are some situations in which your code will crash and throw an error because it ran out of memory, just because of multiple calls. On the other hand, with most current JavaScript engines, you can probably have several thousand pending recursive calls without a problem (but with earlier browsers and smaller machines, the number could drop into the hundreds and could feasibly go even lower), so it could be argued that at present, you are not likely to suffer from any particular memory problems.

In any case, let's review the problem and go over some possible solutions in the following sections, because even if you don't get to actually apply them, they represent valid FP ideas for which you may find a place in yet other problems. We will be looking at the following solutions:

- **Tail call optimization**, a technique that speeds up recursion
- **Continuation passing style**, an important FP technique that can help with recursion
- A couple of interestingly named techniques, **trampolines** and **thunks**, which are also common FP tools
- **Recursion elimination**, a technique that is rather beyond the scope of this book, but which still may be applied.

Tail call optimization

When is a recursive call not a recursive call? Put this way, the question may make little sense, but there's a common optimization—for other languages, alas, but not JavaScript!—that explains the answer. If the recursive call is the very last thing a function will do, then the call could be transformed to a simple jump to the start of the function without needing to create a new stack entry. (Why? The stack entry wouldn't be required: after the recursive call is done, the function would have nothing else to do, so there is no need to further save any of the elements that have been pushed into the stack upon entering the function.) The original stack entry would then no longer be needed and could simply be replaced by a new one, corresponding to the recent call.

The fact that a recursive call, a quintessential FP technique, is being implemented by a base imperative GO TO statement can be considered an ultimate irony!

These calls are known as **tail calls** (for obvious reasons) and have higher efficiency, not only because of the saved stack space, but also because a jump is quite a bit faster than any alternative. If the browser implements this enhancement, then it is using a **tail call optimization (TCO)**; however, a glance at the compatibility tables at `http://kangax.github.io/compat-table/es6/` shows that at the time of writing (at the end of 2019), the only browser that provides TCO is Safari.

Figure 9.4: To understand this joke, you must have previously understood it!

 This XKCD comic is available online at `https://xkcd.com/1270/`

There's a simple (though nonstandard) test that lets you verify whether your browser provides TCO (I found this snippet of code in several places on the web, but I'm sorry to say I cannot attest to the original author (although I believe it is Csaba Hellinger, from Hungary)). Calling `detectTCO()` lets you know whether your browser does or does not use TCO:

```
"use strict";

function detectTCO() {
  const outerStackLen = new Error().stack.length;
  return (function inner() {
    const innerStackLen = new Error().stack.length;
    return innerStackLen <= outerStackLen;
  })();
}
```

The `Error().stack` result is not a JavaScript standard, but modern browsers support it, albeit in somewhat different ways. In any case, the idea is that, when a function with a long name calls another function with a shorter name, the stack trace should do the following:

- It should get shorter if the browser implements TCO, since the old entry for the longer-named function would be replaced with the entry for the shorter-named one.
- It should get longer without TCO, since a completely new stack entry would be created without doing away with the original one.

I'm using Chrome on my Linux laptop, and I added a `console.log()` statement to show `Error().stack`. You can see that both stack entries (for `inner()` and `detectTCO()`) are *live*, so there's no TCO:

```
Error
  at inner (<anonymous>:6:13)
  at detectTCO (<anonymous>:9:6)
  at <anonymous>:1:1
```

Of course, there's also another way of learning whether your environment includes TCO: just try out the following function, which does nothing, with large enough numbers. If you manage to run it with numbers like, say, 100,000 or 1,000,000, you can be fairly sure that your JavaScript engine is doing TCO! A possible such function could be the following:

```
function justLoop(n) {
   n && justLoop(n - 1); // until n is zero
}
```

Let's finish this section with a very short quiz to be sure that we understand what tail calls are. Is the recursive call in the factorial function that we saw in Chapter 1, *Becoming Functional – Several Questions*, a tail call?

```
function fact(n) {
  if (n === 0) {
    return 1;

  } else {
    return n * fact(n - 1);
  }
}
```

Think about it, because the answer is important! You might be tempted to answer in the affirmative, but the correct answer is a *no*. There's good reason for this, and it's a key point: after the recursive call is done, and the value for `fact(n-1)` has been calculated, the function *still* has work to do. (So doing the recursive call wasn't actually the last thing the function would do.) You can see it more clearly if you write the function in this equivalent way:

```
function fact2(n) {
  if (n === 0) {
    return 1;

  } else {
    const aux = fact2(n - 1);
    return n * aux;
  }
}
```

So there should be two takeaways from this section: TCO isn't usually offered by browsers, and, even if it were, you cannot take advantage of it if your calls aren't actual tail calls. Now that we know what the problem is, let's see some FP ways of working around it!

Continuation passing style

If we have recursive calls stacked too high, we already know that our logic will fail. On the other hand, we know that tail calls should alleviate that problem, but don't, because of browser implementations! However, there's a way out of this. Let's first consider how we can transform recursive calls into tail calls by using a well-known FP concept—**continuations**—and we'll leave the problem of solving TCO limitations for the next section. (We mentioned continuations in the *Callbacks, promises, and continuations* section of `Chapter 3`, *Starting Out with Functions – A Core Concept*, but we didn't go into detail.)

In FP parlance, a continuation is something that represents the state of a process and allows processing to continue. This may be too abstract, so let's get down to earth for our needs. The key idea is that, when you call a function, you also provide it with a continuation (in reality, a simple function) that will be called at return time.

Let's look at a trivial example. Suppose you have a function that returns the time of the day and you want to show this on the console. The usual way to do this could be as follows:

```
function getTime() {
  return new Date().toTimeString();
}

console.log(getTime()); // "21:00:24 GMT+0530 (IST)"
```

If you were doing **continuation passing style (CPS)**, you would pass a continuation to the getTime() function. Instead of returning a calculated value, the function would invoke the continuation, giving it the value as a parameter:

```
function getTime2(cont) {
  return cont(new Date().toTimeString());
}

getTime2(console.log); // similar result as above
```

What's the difference? The key is that we can apply this mechanism to make a recursive call into a tail call because all of the code that comes after will be provided in the recursive call itself. To make this clear, let's revisit the factorial function in the version that made it explicit that we weren't doing tail calls. The following code is fully equivalent to the previous one:

```
function fact2(n) {
  if (n === 0) {
    return 1;

  } else {
    const aux = fact2(n - 1);
    return n * aux;
  }
}
```

We will add a new parameter to the function for the continuation. What do we do with the result of the `fact(n-1)` call? We multiply it by n, so let's provide a continuation that will do just that. I'll rename the factorial function as `factC()` to make it clear that we are working with continuations, as shown in the following code:

```
function factC(n, cont) {
  if (n === 0) {
    return cont(1);

  } else {
    return factC(n - 1, x => cont(n * x));
  }
}
```

How would we get the final result? Easy: we can call `factC()` with a continuation that will just return whatever it's given:

```
factC(7, x => x); // 5040, correctly
```

In FP, a function that returns its argument as a result is usually called `identity()` for obvious reasons. In combinatory logic (which we won't be using), we would speak of the *I* combinator.

Can you understand how it worked? Then let's try out a more complex case with the Fibonacci function, which has two recursive calls in it, as shown in the following highlighted code:

```
const fibC = (n, cont) => {
  if (n <= 1) {
    return cont(n);

  } else {
    return fibC(n - 2, p => fibC(n - 1, q => cont(p + q)));
  }
};
```

This is trickier: we call `fibC()` with n−2 and a continuation that says that whatever that call returned, call `fibC()` with n−1, and when *that* call returns, sum the results of both calls and pass that result to the original continuation.

Let's see just one more example, one that involves a loop with an undefined number of recursive calls. By then, you should have some idea about how to apply CPS to your code—though I'll readily admit, it can become really complex!

We saw this function in the *Traversing a tree structure* section earlier in this chapter. The idea was to print out the DOM structure, like this:

```
<body>
| <script>
| <div>
| | <div>
| | | <a>
| | | <div>
| | | | <ul>
| | | | | <li>
| | | | | | <a>
| | | | | | | <div>
| | | | | | | | <div>
| | | | | | | <div>
| | | | | | | | | <br>
| | | | | | | <div>
| | | | | | <ul>
| | | | | | | <li>
| | | | | | | | <a>
| | | | | | | <li>
...etc!
```

The function we ended up designing back then was the following:

```
const traverseDom2 = (node, depth = 0) => {
  console.log(`${"| ".repeat(depth)}<${node.nodeName.toLowerCase()}>`);
  Array.from(node.children).forEach(child =>
    traverseDom2(child, depth + 1)
  );
};
```

Let's start by making this fully recursive, getting rid of the `forEach()` loop. We have seen this technique before, so we can just move on to the following result; note how the following code forms its loops by using recursion:

```
var traverseDom3 = (node, depth = 0) => {
  console.log(`${"| ".repeat(depth)}<${node.nodeName.toLowerCase()}>`);
  const traverseChildren = (children, i = 0) => {
    if (i < children.length) {
      traverseDom3(children[i], depth + 1);
      return traverseChildren(children, i + 1); // loop
    }
    return;
  };
  return traverseChildren(Array.from(node.children));
};
```

Now, we have to add a continuation to `traverseDom3()`. The only difference from the previous cases is that the function doesn't return anything, so we won't be passing any arguments to the continuation. It's also important to remember the implicit `return` at the end of the `traverseChildren()` loop: we must call the continuation:

```
var traverseDom3C = (node, depth = 0, cont = () => {}) => {
  console.log(`${"| ".repeat(depth)}<${node.nodeName.toLowerCase()}>`);
  const traverseChildren = (children, i = 0) => {
    if (i < children.length) {
      return traverseDom3C(children[i], depth + 1, () =>
        traverseChildren(children, i + 1)
      );
    }
    return cont();
  };
  return traverseChildren(Array.from(node.children));
};
```

We opted to give a default value to `cont`, so we can simply call `traverseDom3C(document.body)` as before. If we try out this logic, it works—but the problem of the potentially high number of pending calls hasn't been solved; let's look for a solution to this in the following section.

Trampolines and thunks

For the last solution to our problem, we shall have to think about the cause of the problem. Each pending recursive call creates a new entry stack. Whenever the stack gets too empty, the program crashes and our algorithm is history. So, if we can work out a way to avoid the stack growth, we should be free. The solution, in this case, is quite imposing and requires thunks and a trampoline—let's see what these are!

First, a **thunk** is really quite simple: it's just a nullary function (so, with no parameters) that helps delay a computation, providing a form of **lazy evaluation**. If you have a thunk, then, unless you call it, you won't get its value. For example, if you want to get the current date and time in ISO format, you could get it with `new Date().toISOString()`; however, if you provide a thunk that calculates that, you won't get the value until you actually invoke it:

```
const getIsoDateAndTime = () => new Date().toISOString(); // a thunk

const isoDateAndTime = getIsoDateAndTime(); // getting the thunk's value
```

What's the use of this? The problem with recursion is that a function calls itself, and calls itself, and calls itself, and so on until the stack blows over. Instead of directly calling itself, we are going to have the function return a thunk, which, when executed, will actually recursively call the function. So, instead of having the stack grow more and more, it will actually be quite flat, since the function will never get to actually call itself; the stack will grow by one position, when you call the function, and then get back to its size, as soon as the function returns its thunk.

But who gets to do the recursion? That's where the concept of a **trampoline** comes in. A trampoline is just a loop that calls a function, gets its return, and, if it is a thunk, then it calls it so that recursion will proceed, but in a flat, linear, way! The loop is exited when the thunk evaluation returns an actual value instead of a new function. Look at the following code:

```
const trampoline = (fn) => {
  while (typeof fn === 'function') {
    fn = fn();
  }
  return fn;
};
```

How can we apply this to an actual function? Let's start with a simple one that just sums all numbers from 1 to *n*, but in a recursive, guaranteed-to-cause-stack-crash fashion. Our simple sumAll() function could just be the following:

```
const sumAll = n => (n == 0 ? 0 : n + sumAll(n - 1));
```

However, if we start trying this function out, we'll eventually stumble and get a crash, as you can see in the following examples:

```
sumAll(10); // 55
sumAll(100); // 5050
sumAll(1000); // 500500
sumAll(10000); // Uncaught RangeError: Maximum call stack size exceeded
```

The stack problem will come up sooner or later depending on your machine, your memory size, and so on, but it will come, no doubt about that. Let's rewrite the function in continuation-passing style so that it will become tail recursive. We will just apply the same technique that we saw earlier, as shown in the following code:

```
const sumAllC = (n, cont) =>
  n === 0 ? cont(0) : sumAllC(n - 1, v => cont(v + n));

sumAllC(10000, console.log); // crash as earlier
```

Now, let's apply a simple rule: whenever you are going to return from a call, instead return a thunk that will, when executed, do the call that you actually wanted to do. The following code implements that change:

```
const sumAllT = (n, cont) =>
  n === 0 ? () => cont(0) : () => sumAllT(n - 1, v => () => cont(v + n));
```

Whenever there would have been a call to a function, we now return a thunk. How do we get to run this function? This is the missing detail. You need an initial call that will invoke sumAllT() the first time and (unless the function was called with a zero argument) a thunk will be immediately returned. The trampoline function will call the thunk, and that will cause a new call, and so on, until we eventually get a thunk that simply returns a value, and then the calculation will be ended:

```
const sumAll2 = n => trampoline(sumAllT(n, x => x));
```

In fact, you probably wouldn't want a separate sumAllT() function, so you'd go for something like this:

```
const sumAll3 = n => {
  const sumAllT = (n, cont) =>
    n === 0 ? () => cont(0) : () => sumAllT(n - 1, v => () => cont(v + n));

  return trampoline(sumAllT(n, x => x));
};
```

There's only one problem left: what would we do if the result of our recursive function wasn't a value, but rather a function? The problem there would be on the trampoline() code that, as long as the result of the thunk evaluation is a function, goes back again and again to evaluate it. The simplest solution would be to return a thunk, but wrapped in an object, as shown in the following code:

```
function Thunk(fn) {
  this.fn = fn;
}

var trampoline2 = thk => {
  while (typeof thk === "object" && thk.constructor.name === "Thunk") {
    thk = thk.fn();
  }
  return thk;
};
```

The difference now would be that, instead of returning a thunk, you'd write something as `return (v) => new Thunk(() => cont(v+n))`, so our new trampolining function can now distinguish an actual thunk (which is meant to be invoked and executed) from any other kind of result (which is meant to be returned).

So if you happen to have a recursive algorithm, but it won't run because of stack limits, you can fix it in a reasonable way by going through the following steps:

1. Changing all recursive calls to tail recursion using continuations
2. Replacing all `return` statements so that they'll return thunks
3. Replacing the call to the original function with a trampoline call to start the calculations

Of course, this doesn't come free. You'll notice that, when using this mechanism, there's extra work involving returning thunks, evaluating them, and so on, so you can expect the total time to go up. Nonetheless, this is a cheap price to pay if the alternative is having a nonworking solution to a problem!

Recursion elimination

There's yet one other possibility that you might want to explore, but that falls beyond the realm of FP and into algorithm design. It's a computer science fact that any algorithm that is implemented using recursion has an equivalent version that doesn't use recursion at all and instead depends on a stack. There are ways to systematically transform recursive algorithms into iterative ones, so, if you run out of all options (that is, if not even continuations or thunks can help you), then you'd have a final opportunity to achieve your goals by replacing all recursion with iteration. We won't be getting into this—as I said, this elimination has little to do with FP—but it's important to know that the tool exists and that you might be able to use it.

Summary

In this chapter, we saw how we can use recursion, a basic tool in FP, as a powerful technique to create algorithms for problems that would probably require far more complex solutions otherwise. We started by considering what recursion is and how to think recursively in order to solve problems, then moved on to see some recursive solutions to several problems in different areas, and ended by analyzing potential problems with deep recursion and how to solve them.

In Chapter 10, *Ensuring Purity – Immutability*, we shall get back to a concept we saw earlier in the book, function purity, and see some techniques that will help us guarantee that a function won't have any side effects by ensuring the immutability of arguments and data structures.

Questions

9.1. **Into reverse**: Can you program a reverse() function, but implement it in a recursive fashion? Obviously, the best way to go about this would be using the standard string reverse() method, as detailed in https://developer.mozilla.org/en-US/docs/Web/JavaScript/Reference/Global_Objects/Array/reverse, but that wouldn't do for a question on recursion, would it?

9.2. **Climbing steps**: Suppose you want to climb up a ladder with *n* steps. At each time you raise your foot, you may opt to climb up one or two rungs. In how many different ways can you climb up that ladder? For example, you can climb a four-rung ladder in five different ways:

- Always taking one step at a time
- Always taking two steps at a time
- Taking two steps first, then one, and then one
- Taking one step first, then two, and then one
- Taking one step first, then another one, and finishing with two

9.3. **Longest common subsequence**: A classic dynamic programming problem is as follows: given two strings, find the length of the longest subsequence present in both of them. Be careful: we define a subsequence as a sequence of characters that appear in the same relative order, but not necessarily next to each other. For example, the longest common subsequence of INTERNATIONAL and CONTRACTOR is N...T...R...A...T...O. Try it out with or without memoizing and see the difference!

9.4. **Symmetrical queens**: In the eight queens puzzle that we previously solved, there is only one solution that shows symmetry in the placement of the queens. Can you modify your algorithm to find it?

9.5. Sorting recursively: There are many sorting algorithms that can be described with recursion; can you implement them?

- **Selection sort**: Find the maximum element of the array, remove it, recursively sort the rest, and then push the maximum element to the end of the sorted rest.
- **Insertion sort**: Take the first element of the array, sort the rest, and finish by inserting the removed element into its correct place in the sorted rest.
- **Merge sort**: Divide the array into two parts, sort each one, and finish by merging the two sorted parts into a sorted list.

9.6. Completing callbacks: In our `findR()` function, we did not provide all possible parameters to the `cb()` callback. Can you fix that? Your solution should be along the lines of what we did for `map()` and other functions.

9.7. Recursive logic: We didn't get to code `every()` and `some()` using recursion: can you do that?

9.8 What could go wrong? A developer decided that he could write a somewhat shorter version of Quicksort. He reasoned that the pivot didn't need any special handling since it would be set into its correct place anyway when sorting `greaterEqual`. Can you foresee any possible problems with this? The following code highlights the changes that the developer made with regard to the original version we saw earlier:

```
const quicksort = arr => {
  if (arr.length < 2) {
    return arr;

  } else {
    const pivot = arr[0];
    const smaller = arr.filter(x => x < pivot);
    const greaterEqual = arr.filter(x => x >= pivot);
    return [...quicksort(smaller), ...quicksort(greaterEqual)];
  }
};
```

9.9. More efficiency: Let's try to make `quicksort()` a bit more efficient by avoiding having to call `filter()` twice. Along the lines of what we saw in the *Calculating several values at once* section in Chapter 5, *Programming Declaratively – A Better Style*, write a `partition(arr, pr)` function that ,given an array `arr` and a predicate `fn`, will return two arrays: the values of `arr` for which `fn` is `true` in the first one, and the rest of the values of `arr` in the second one:

```
const quicksort = arr => {
  if (arr.length < 2) {
    return arr;

  } else {
    const pivot = arr[0];
    const [smaller, greaterEqual] = partition(arr.slice(1), x => x <
pivot);
    return [...quicksort(smaller), pivot, ...quicksort(greaterEqual)];
  }
};
```

Ensuring Purity - Immutability

10

In Chapter 4, *Behaving Properly – Pure Functions*, when we considered pure functions and their advantages, we saw that side effects such as modifying a received argument or a global variable were frequent causes of impurity. Now, after several chapters dealing with many aspects and tools of FP, let's talk about the concept of *immutability*: how to work with objects in such a way that accidentally modifying them will become harder or, even better, impossible.

We cannot force developers to work in a safe, guarded way, but if we find some way to make data structures immutable (meaning that they cannot be directly changed, except through some interface that never allows us to modify the original data and produces new objects instead), then we'll have an enforceable solution. In this chapter, we will look at two distinct approaches to working with such immutable objects and data structures:

- **Basic JavaScript ways**, such as freezing objects, plus cloning to create new ones instead of modifying existing objects
- **Persistent data structures**, with methods that allow us to update them without changing the original and without the need to clone everything either, for higher performance

A warning: the code in this chapter isn't production-ready; I wanted to focus on the main points and not on all the myriad details having to do with properties, getters, setters, lenses, prototypes, and more that you should take into account for a full, bulletproof, solution. For actual development, I'd very much recommend going with a third-party library, but only after checking that it really applies to your situation. We'll be recommending several such libraries, but of course, there are many more that you could use.

Going the straightforward JavaScript way

One of the biggest causes of side effects was the possibility of a function modifying global objects or its arguments. All non-primitive objects are passed as references, so if/when you modify them, the original objects will be changed. If we want to stop this (without just depending on the goodwill and clean coding of our developers), we may want to consider some straightforward JavaScript techniques to disallow those side effects:

- Avoiding mutator functions that directly modify the object that they are applied to
- Using `const` declarations to prevent variables from being changed
- Freezing objects so that they can't be modified in any way
- Creating (changed) clones of objects to avoid modifying the original
- Using getters and setters to control what is changed and how
- Using a functional concept—lenses—to access and set attributes

Let's take a look at each technique in more detail.

Mutator functions

A common source of unexpected problems comes from the fact that several JavaScript methods are actually mutators that modify the underlying object. In this case, by merely using them, you will be causing a side effect, which you may not even recognize. Arrays are the most basic sources of problems and the list of troublesome methods isn't short:

- `copyWithin()` lets you copy elements within the array.
- `fill()` fills an array with a given value.
- `push()` and `pop()` let you add or delete elements at the end of an array.
- `shift()` and `unshift()` work in the same way as `push()` and `pop()`, but at the beginning of the array.
- `splice()` lets you add or delete elements anywhere within the array.
- `reverse()` and `sort()` modify the array in place, reversing its elements or ordering them.

 Refer to `https://developer.mozilla.org/en-US/docs/Web/JavaScript/ Reference/Global_Objects/Array#Mutator_methods` for more on each method.

Let's take a look at an example we saw in the *Argument mutation* section of `Chapter` 4, *Behaving Properly – Pure Functions*:

```
const maxStrings = a => a.sort().pop();

let countries = ["Argentina", "Uruguay", "Brasil", "Paraguay"];

console.log(maxStrings(countries)); // "Uruguay"
console.log(countries); // ["Argentina", "Brasil", "Paraguay"]
```

Our `maxStrings()` function returns the highest value in the array, but also modifies the original array; this is a side effect of the `sort()` and `pop()` mutator functions. In this case and others, you might generate a copy of the array and then work with that: both the spread operator and `.slice()` are useful:

```
const maxStrings2 = a => [...a].sort().pop();

const maxStrings3 = a => a.slice().sort().pop();

let countries = ["Argentina", "Uruguay", "Brasil", "Paraguay"];

console.log(maxStrings2(countries)); // "Uruguay"
console.log(maxStrings3(countries)); // "Uruguay"

console.log(countries); // ["Argentina", "Uruguay", "Brasil", "Paraguay"] –
unchanged
```

Both new versions of our `maxStrings()` functions are now functional, without side effects, because the mutator methods have been applied to copies of the original argument.

Of course, setter methods are also mutators and will logically produce side effects because they can do just about anything. If this is the case, you'll have to go for some of the other solutions that will be described later in this chapter.

Constants

If the mutations don't happen because of using some JavaScript methods, then we might want to attempt to use `const` definitions, but that just won't work. In JavaScript, a `const` definition means that the *reference* to the object or array cannot change (you cannot assign a different object to it) but you can still modify the properties of the object itself. We can see this in the following code:

```
const myObj = {d: 22, m: 9};
console.log(myObj);
```

```
// {d: 22, m: 9}

myObj = {d: 12, m: 4};
// Uncaught TypeError: Assignment to constant variable.

myObj.d = 12; // but this is fine!
myObj.m = 4;
console.log(myObj);
// {d: 12, m: 4}
```

You cannot modify the value of myObj by assigning it a new value, but you can modify the current value of myObj so that only the reference to an object is constant, and not the object's values themselves. (By the way, this would have also happened with arrays.) So, if you decide to use const everywhere, you will only be safe against direct assignments to objects and arrays. More modest side effects, such as changing an attribute or an array element, will still be possible, so this is not a solution.

There are two methods that can work: using *freezing* to provide unmodifiable structures, and *cloning* to produce modified new ones. These are probably not the best ways to go about forbidding objects from being changed but can be used as a makeshift solution. Let's take a look at them in more detail, starting with freezing.

Freezing

If we want to avoid the possibility of a programmer accidentally or willingly modifying an object, freezing it is a valid solution. After an object has been frozen, any attempts at modifying it will silently fail—JavaScript won't report an error or throw an exception, but it won't alter the object either. In the following example, if we attempt to make the same changes we made in the previous section, they just won't have any effect, and myObj will be unchanged:

```
const myObj = { d: 22, m: 9 };
Object.freeze(myObj);

myObj.d = 12; // won't have effect...
myObj.m = 4;

console.log(myObj);
// Object {d: 22, m: 9}
```

Don't confuse freezing with sealing: `Object.seal()`, when applied to an object, prohibits adding or deleting properties to it. This means that the structure of the object is immutable, but the attributes themselves can be changed. `Object.freeze()` includes not only sealing properties but also making them unchangeable. See `https://developer.mozilla.org/en/docs/Web/JavaScript/Reference/Global_Objects/Object/seal` and `https://developer.mozilla.org/en/docs/Web/JavaScript/Reference/Global_Objects/Object/freeze` for more on this.

There is only one problem with this solution: freezing an object is a *shallow* operation that freezes the attributes themselves, similar to what a `const` declaration does. If any of the attributes are objects or arrays themselves, with further objects or arrays as properties, and so on, they can still be modified. We will only be considering data here; you may also want to freeze, say, functions, but for most use cases, it's data you want to protect:

```
let myObj3 = {
  d: 22,
  m: 9,
  o: {c: "MVD", i: "UY", f: {a: 56}}
};

Object.freeze(myObj3);
console.log(myObj3);   // {d:22, m:9, o:{c:"MVD", i:"UY", f:{ a:56}}}
```

This is only partially successful, as we can see when we try changing some attributes:

```
myObj3.d = 8888;        // wont' work, as earlier
myObj3.o.f.a = 9999;    // oops, does work!!
console.log(myObj3);    // {d:22, m:9, o:{c:"MVD", i:"UY", f:{ a:9999 }}}
```

Modifying `myObj3.d` didn't work because the object is frozen, but that doesn't extend to objects within `myObj3`, so changing `myObj3.o.f.a` did work.

If we want to achieve real immutability for our object, we need to write a routine that will freeze all the levels of an object. Fortunately, it's easy to achieve this by applying recursion. (We saw similar applications of recursion in the *Traversing a tree structure* section of the previous `Chapter 9`, *Designing Functions - Recursion*.) Mainly, the idea is to freeze the object itself and then recursively freeze each of its properties. We must ensure that we only freeze the object's own properties; we shouldn't mess with the prototype of the object, for example:

```
const deepFreeze = obj => {
  if (obj && typeof obj === "object" && !Object.isFrozen(obj)) {
    Object.freeze(obj);
    Object.getOwnPropertyNames(obj).forEach(prop => deepFreeze(obj[prop]));
```

```
    }

  return obj;
};
```

Note that, in the same way as `Object.freeze()` works, `deepFreeze()` also freezes the object *in place*. I wanted to keep the original semantics of the operation so that the returned object will always be the original one. If we wanted to work in a purer fashion, we should make a copy of the original object first (we'll learn how to do this in the next section) and then freeze that.

A small possible problem remains, but with a very bad result: what would happen if an object included a reference to itself? We can avoid this if we skip freezing already frozen objects: backward circular references would be ignored since the objects they refer to would already be frozen. So, the logic we wrote took care of that problem and there's nothing more to be done!

If we apply `deepFreeze()` to an object, we can safely pass it to any function, knowing that there simply is no way in which it can be modified. You can also use this property to test whether a function modifies its arguments: deep freeze them, call the function, and if the function depends on modifying its arguments, it won't work because the changes will be silently ignored. So, how can we return a result from a function if it involves a received object? This can be solved in many ways. A simple one uses cloning, as we'll see.

 Check the *Questions* section at the end of this chapter for another way of freezing an object by means of proxies.

In this section, we dealt with one of the methods we can use to avoid changes in objects. Now, let's look at an alternative involving cloning.

Cloning and mutating

If mutating an object isn't allowed, then you must create a new object. For example, if you use Redux, a reducer is a function that receives the current state and an action (essentially, an object with new data) and produces the new state. Modifying the current state is totally forbidden and we could avoid this error by always working with frozen objects, as we saw in the previous section. To fulfill the reducer's requirements, we have to be able to clone the original state, as well as mutate it according to the received action. The resulting object will become the new state.

You may want to revisit the *More general looping* section of Chapter 5, *Programming Declaratively – A Better Style,* where we wrote a basic objCopy() function that provides a different approach from the one shown here.

To round things off, we should also freeze the returned object, just like we did with the original state. But let's start at the beginning: how do we clone an object? Of course, you can always do this by hand, but that's not something you'd really want to consider when working with large, complex objects. For example, if you wanted to clone oldObject to produce newObject, doing it by hand would imply a lot of code:

```
let oldObject = {
  d: 22,
  m: 9,
  o: {c: "MVD", i: "UY", f: {a: 56}}
};

let newObject = {
  d: oldObject.d,
  m: oldObject.m,
  o: {c: oldObject.o.c, i: oldObject.o.i, f: {a: oldObject.o.f.a}}
};
```

This manual solution is obviously a lot of work, and error-prone as well; you could easily forget an attribute! Going for more automatic solutions, there are a couple of straightforward ways of copying arrays or objects in JavaScript, but they have the same *shallowness* problem. You can make a (shallow) copy of an object with Object.assign() or by using spreading:

```
let newObject1 = Object.assign({}, myObj);
let newObject2 = {...myObj};
```

To create a (again, shallow) copy of an array, you can either use slice() or spreading, as we saw in the *Mutator functions* section earlier in this chapter:

```
let myArray = [1, 2, 3, 4];
let newArray1 = myArray.slice();
let newArray2 = [...myArray];
```

What's the problem with these solutions? If an object or array includes objects (which may themselves include objects), we get the same problem that we had when freezing: objects are copied by reference, which means that a change in the new object will also imply changing the old object:

```
let oldObject = {
  d: 22,
```

```
    m: 9,
    o: { c: "MVD", i: "UY", f: { a: 56 } }
};
let newObject = Object.assign({}, oldObject);

newObject.d = 8888;
newObject.o.f.a = 9999;

console.log(newObject);
// {d:8888, m:9, o: {c:"MVD", i:"UY", f: {a:9999}}} -- ok

console.log(oldObject);
// {d:22, m:9, o: {c:"MVD", i:"UY", f: {a:9999}}} -- oops!!
```

In this case, notice what happened when we changed some properties of `newObject`. Changing `newObject.d` worked fine, but changing `newObject.o.f.a` also impacted `oldObject` since `newObject.o` and `oldObject.o` are actually references to the very same object.

There is a simple solution to this based on JSON. If we `stringify()` the original object and then `parse()` the result, we'll get a new object that's totally separate from the old one:

```
const jsonCopy = obj => JSON.parse(JSON.stringify(obj));
```

By using `JSON.stringify()`, we can convert our object into an string.
Then, `JSON.parse()` creates a (new) object out of that string; simple! This works with both arrays and objects, but there's a problem. If any of the properties of the object have a constructor, they won't be invoked: the result will always be composed of plain JavaScript objects. We can see this very simply with a `Date()`:

```
let myDate = new Date();
let newDate = jsonCopy(myDate);
console.log(typeof myDate, typeof newDate); // object string
```

While `myDate` is an object, `newDate` turns out to be a string with a value, `"2019-11-08T01:32:56.365Z"`, which is the current date and time at the moment we did the conversion.

We could do a recursive solution, just like we did with deep freezing, and the logic is quite similar. Whenever we find a property that is really an object, we invoke the appropriate constructor:

```
const deepCopy = obj => {
  let aux = obj;
  if (obj && typeof obj === "object") {
    aux = new obj.constructor();
```

```
    Object.getOwnPropertyNames(obj).forEach(
      prop => (aux[prop] = deepCopy(obj[prop]))
    );
  }

  return aux;
};
```

Whenever we find that a property of an object is actually another object, we invoke its constructor before continuing. This solves the problem we found with dates or, in fact, with any object! If we run the preceding code, but using deepCopy() instead of jsonCopy(), we'll get object object as output, as it should be. If we check the types and constructors, everything will match. Furthermore, the data changing experiment will also work fine now:

```
let oldObject = {
  d: 22,
  m: 9,
  o: { c: "MVD", i: "UY", f: { a: 56 } }
};

let newObject = deepCopy(oldObject);
newObject.d = 8888;
newObject.o.f.a = 9999;

console.log(newObject);
// {d:8888, m:9, o:{c:"MVD", i:"UY", f:{a:9999}}}

console.log(oldObject);
// {d:22, m:9, o:{c:"MVD", i:"UY", f:{a:56}}} -- unchanged!
```

Let's check out the last few lines. Modifying newObject had absolutely no impact on oldObject, so both objects are completely separate.

Now that we know how to copy an object, we can follow these steps:

1. Receive a (frozen) object as an argument
2. Make a copy of it, which won't be frozen
3. Take values from that copy that we can use in our code
4. Modify the copy at will
5. Freeze it
6. Return it as the result of the function

All of this is viable, though a bit cumbersome. So, let's add a couple of functions that will help bring everything together.

Getters and setters

When following the steps provided at the end of the previous section, you'll notice that every time you want to update a field, things become troublesome and prone to errors. Let's use a common technique to add a pair of functions, getters, and setters. These are as follows:

- *getters* can be used to get values from a frozen object by unfreezing them so that they can be used.
- *setters* allow you to modify any property of an object. You can do this by creating a new and updated version of it, leaving the original untouched.

Let's build our getters and setters.

Getting a property

Back in the *Getting a property from an object* section of Chapter 6, *Producing Functions – Higher-Order Functions*, we wrote a simple getField() function that could handle getting a single attribute out of an object. (See question 6.5 in that chapter for the missing companion setField() function.) Let's take a look at how we can code this. We can have a straightforward version, as follows:

```
const getField = attr => obj => obj[attr];
```

We can even go one better by applying currying so that we have a more general version:

```
const getField = curry((attr, obj) => obj[attr]);
```

We could get a deep attribute out of an object by composing a series of applications of getField() calls, but that would be rather cumbersome. Instead, let's create a function that will receive a *path*—an array of field names—and return the corresponding part of the object or be undefined if the path doesn't exist. Using recursion is appropriate here and simplifies coding! Observe the following code:

```
const getByPath = (arr, obj) => {
  if (arr[0] in obj) {
    return arr.length > 1
      ? getByPath(arr.slice(1), obj[arr[0]])
      : deepCopy(obj[arr[0]]);
  } else {
    return undefined;
  }
};
```

Basically, we look for the first string in the path to see whether it exists in the object. If it doesn't, the operation fails, so we return `undefined`. If successful, and we have still more strings in the path, we use recursion to keep digging into the object; otherwise, we return a deep copy of the value of the attribute.

Once an object has been frozen, you cannot *defrost* it, so we must resort to making a new copy of it; `deepCopy()` is appropriate for doing this. Let's try out our new function:

```
let myObj3 = {
  d: 22,
  m: 9,
  o: {c: "MVD", i: "UY", f: {a: 56}}
};
deepFreeze(myObj3);

console.log(getByPath(["d"], myObj3)); // 22
console.log(getByPath(["o"], myObj3)); // {c: "MVD", i: "UY", f: {a: 56}}
console.log(getByPath(["o", "c"], myObj3)); // "MVD"
console.log(getByPath(["o", "f", "a"], myObj3)); // 56
```

We can also check that returned objects are not frozen:

```
let fObj = getByPath(["o", "f"], myObj3);
console.log(fObj); // {a: 56}

fObj.a = 9999;
console.log(fObj); // {a: 9999} -- it's not frozen
```

Here, you can see that we could directly update the `fObj` object, so that means it wasn't frozen. Now that we've written our getter, we can move on to creating a setter.

Setting a property by path

Now, we can code a similar `setByPath()` function that will take a path, a value, and an object and update an object. This is *not* a pure function, but we'll use it to write a pure one; wait and see! Here is the code:

```
const setByPath = (arr, value, obj) => {
  if (!(arr[0] in obj)) {
    obj[arr[0]] =
      arr.length === 1 ? null : Number.isInteger(arr[1]) ? [] : {};
  }

  if (arr.length > 1) {
    return setByPath(arr.slice(1), value, obj[arr[0]]);
```

```
  } else {
    obj[arr[0]] = value;
    return obj;
  }
};
```

Here, we are using recursion to get into the object, creating new attributes if needed, until we have traveled the full length of the path. One important detail when creating attributes is whether we need an array or an object. We can determine that by checking the next element in the path: if it's a number, then we need an array; otherwise, an object will do. When we get to the end of the path, we simply assign the new given value.

 If you like this way of doing things, you should check out the *seamless-immutable* library, which works in this fashion. The *seamless* part of the name alludes to the fact that you still work with normal objects—albeit frozen—which means you can use map(), reduce(), and so on. You can read more about this at https://github.com/rtfeldman/seamless-immutable.

Now, you can write a function that will be able to take a frozen object and update an attribute within it, returning a new, also frozen, object:

```
const updateObject = (arr, obj, value) => {
  let newObj = deepCopy(obj);
  setByPath(arr, value, newObj);
  return deepFreeze(newObj);
};
```

Let's check out how it works. To do this, we'll run several updates on the myObj3 object we have been using:

```
let new1 = updateObject(["m"], myObj3, "sep");
// {d: 22, m: "sep", o: {c: "MVD", i: "UY", f: {a: 56}}};

let new2 =updateObject(["b"], myObj3, 220960);
// {d: 22, m: 9, o: {c: "MVD", i: "UY", f: {a: 56}}, b: 220960};

let new3 =updateObject(["o", "f", "a"], myObj3, 9999);
// {d: 22, m: 9, o: {c: "MVD", i: "UY", f: {a: 9999}}};

let new4 =updateObject(["o", "f", "j", "k", "l"], myObj3, "deep");
// {d: 22, m: 9, o: {c: "MVD", i: "UY", f: {a: 56, j: {k: "deep"}}}};
```

Given this pair of functions, we have finally gotten ourselves a way to keep immutability:

- Objects must be frozen from the beginning
- Getting data from objects is done with `getByPath()`
- Setting data is done with `updateObject()`, which internally uses `setByPath()`

In this section, we learned how to get and set values from an object in a way that keeps objects immutable. Let's now take a look at a variation of this concept—*lenses*—that will allow us to not only get and set values but also apply a function to the data.

Lenses

There's another way to get and set values, which goes by the name of *optics*, including *lenses* and *prisms* (which we'll look at later in this chapter). What are lenses? They are functional ways of *focusing* (another optical term!) on a given spot in an object so that we can access or modify its value in a non-mutating way. In this section, we'll look at some examples of usage of lenses and consider two implementations: first, a simple one based on objects, and then a more complete one that's interesting because of some of the techniques we will be using.

 Several libraries provide full implementations of lenses that are production-ready and more complete than what we saw in this chapter; for example, check out Ramda: `http://ramdajs.com/docs/#lens`

Working with lenses

Both implementations will share basic functionality, so let's start by skipping what lenses are or how they are built and look at some examples of their usage instead. First, let's create a sample object that we will work with: some data about a writer (his name sounds familiar) and his books:

```
const author = {
  user: "fkereki",
  name: {
    first: "Federico",
    middle: "",
    last: "Kereki",
  },
  books: [
    {name: "Google Web Toolkit", year: 2010},
```

```
        {name: "Functional Programming", year: 2017},
        {name: "Javascript Cookbook", year: 2018},
    ],
};
```

We shall assume that several functions exist; we'll see how they are implemented in upcoming sections. A lens depends on having a getter and a setter for a given attribute, and we can build one by directly using `lens()` or by means of `lensProp()` for briefer coding. Let's create a lens for the `user` attribute:

```
const lens1 = lens(getField("user"), setField("user"));
```

This defines a lens that focuses on the user attribute. Since this is a common operation, it can also be written more compactly:

```
const lens1 = lensProp("user");
```

Both of these lenses allow us to focus on the `user` attribute of whatever object we use them with. With lenses, there are three basic operations, and we'll follow tradition by using the names that most (if not all) libraries follow:

- `view()`: Used to access the value of an attribute
- `set()`: Used to modify the value of an attribute
- `over()`: Used to apply a function to an attribute and change its value

These functions are curried (as we saw in the previous chapter). So, to access the `user` attribute, we can write something similar to the following:

```
console.log(view(lens1, author));
console.log(view(lens1)(author));
/*
   fkereki, in both cases
*/
```

The `view()` function takes a lens as its first parameter. When this is applied to an object, it produces the value of whatever the lens focuses on—in our case, the `user` attribute. Of course, you could apply sequences of `view()` functions to get to deeper parts of the object:

```
console.log(view(lensProp("last"), view(lensProp("name"), author)));
/*
   Kereki
*/
```

Instead of writing such a series of `view()` calls, we'll compose lenses so that we can focus more deeply on an object. Let's take a look at one final example, which shows how we access an array:

```
const lensBooks = lensProp("books");
console.log(
  "The author wrote " + view(lensBooks, author).length + " book(s)"
);
/*

    The author wrote 3 book(s)

*/
```

In the future, should there be any change in the `author` structure, a simple change in the `lensBooks` definition would be enough to keep the rest of the code unchanged.

> You can also use lenses to access other structures: refer to question *10.5* for a way to use lenses with arrays, and question *10.6* for how to use lenses so that they work with maps.

Moving on, the `set()` function allows us to set the value of the focus of the lens:

```
console.log(set(lens1, "FEFK", author));
/*
  user: "FEFK",
  name: {first: "Federico", middle: "", last: "Kereki"},
  books: [
    {name: "Google Web Toolkit", year: 2010},
    {name: "Functional Programming", year: 2017},
    {name: "Javascript Cookbook", year: 2018},
  ],
}
*/
```

The result of `set()` is a new object with a changed value. Using `over()` is similar in that a new object is returned, but in this case, the value is changed by applying a mapping function to it:

```
const newAuthor = over(lens1, x => x + x + x, author);
console.log(newAuthor);
/*
  user: "fkerekifkerekifkereki",
  name: {first: "Federico", middle: "", last: "Kereki"},
  books: [
    {name: "GWT", year: 2010},
    {name: "FP", year: 2017},
    {name: "CB", year: 2018},
```

```
    ],
  }
 */
```

There are more functions you can do with lenses, but we'll just go with these three for now.

 Take a look at question *10.4* for an interesting idea on how to use lenses to access *virtual attributes* that don't actually exist in an object.

To finish this section, I'd recommend looking at some third-party optics libraries to get a glimpse into all the functionality that's available. Now that we have an idea of what to expect when using lenses, let's learn how to implement them.

Implementing lenses with objects

The simplest way to implement a lens is by representing it with an object with just two properties: a getter and a setter. In this case, we'd have something like this:

```
const lens = (getter, setter) => ({getter, setter});
```

This is easy to understand: given a getter and a setter, `lens()` just creates an object with those two attributes. With this definition, `lensProp()` would be as follows:

```
const lensProp = attr => lens(getField(attr), setField(attr));
```

The first function, `lensProp()`, creates a getter/setter pair by using `getField()` and `setField()`; very straightforward. Now that we have our lens, how do we implement the three basic functions that we saw in the previous section? Viewing an attribute just requires applying the getter:

```
const view = curry((lens, obj) => lens.getter(obj));
```

To be consistent with the rest of the functions we've been using, we are going to apply currying. Similarly, setting an attribute is a matter of applying the setter:

```
const set = curry((lens, newVal, obj) => lens.setter(newVal, obj));
```

Finally, applying a mapping function to an attribute is sort of a *two-for-one* operation: we use the getter to get the current value of the attribute, we apply the function to it, and we use the setter to store the calculated result:

```
const over = curry((lens, mapfn, obj) =>
  lens.setter(mapfn(lens.getter(obj)), obj)
);
```

Now that we can do all three operations, we have working lenses! What about composition? Lenses have a peculiar characteristic: they're composed backward, or left-to-right, so you start with the most generic and end with the most specific. That certainly goes against intuition: we'll learn about this in more detail in the next section, but for now, we'll keep with tradition:

```
const composeTwoLenses = (lens1, lens2) => ({
  getter: obj => lens2.getter(lens1.getter(obj)),
  setter: curry((newVal, obj) =>
    lens1.setter(lens2.setter(newVal, lens1.getter(obj)), obj)
  ),
});
```

The code is sort of impressive, but not too hard to understand. The getter for the composition of two lenses is the result of using the first lens' getter and then applying the second lens' getter to that result. The setter for the composition is just a tad more complex, but follows along the same lines; can you see how it works? Now, we can compose lenses easily; let's start with an invented nonsensical object:

```
const deepObject = {
  a: 1,
  b: 2,
  c: {
    d: 3,
    e: {
      f: 6,
      g: {i: 9, j: {k: 11}},
      h: 8,
    },
  },
};
```

Now, we can define a few lenses:

```
const lC = lensProp("c");
const lE = lensProp("e");
const lG = lensProp("g");
const lJ = lensProp("j");
```

We can try composing our new lens in a couple of ways, just for variety, and to check that everything works:

```
const lJK = composeTwoLenses(lJ, lK);
const lGJK = composeTwoLenses(lG, lJK);
const lEGJK = composeTwoLenses(lE, lGJK);
const lCEGJK1 = composeTwoLenses(lC, lEGJK);
console.log(view(lCEGJK1)(deepObject));

const lCE = composeTwoLenses(lC, lE);
const lCEG = composeTwoLenses(lCE, lG);
const lCEGJ = composeTwoLenses(lCEG, lJ);
const lCEGJK2 = composeTwoLenses(lCEGJ, lK);
console.log(view(lCEGJK2)(deepObject));

/*
    11 both times
*/
```

With `lCEGJ1`, we composed some lenses, starting with the latter ones. With `lCEGJ2`, we started with the lenses at the beginning, but the results are the same. Now, let's try setting some values. We want to get down to the k attribute and set it to 60. We can do this by using the same lens we just applied:

```
const setTo60 = set(lCEGJ1, 60, deepObject);
/*
  {a: 1, b: 2, c: {d: 3, e: {f: 6, g: {i: 9, j: { k: 60 }}, h: 8}}}
*/
```

The composed lens worked perfectly, and the value was changed. (Also, a new object was returned; the original is unmodified, as we wanted.) To finish, let's also verify that we can do `over()` with our lens and try to duplicate the k value so that it becomes 22. Just for variety, let's use the other composed lens, even though we know that it works in the same way:

```
const setToDouble = over(lCEGJK2, x => x * 2, deepObject);
/*
  {a: 1, b: 2, c: {d: 3, e: {f: 6, g: {i: 9, j: { k: 22 }}, h: 8}}}
*/
```

Now, we have learned how to implement lenses in a simple fashion. However, let's consider a different way of achieving the same objective by using actual functions to represent a lens. This will allow us to do composition in the standard way, without the need for any special lens function.

Implementing lenses with functions

The previous implementation of lenses with objects works well, but we want to look at a different way of doing things that will let us work with more advanced functional ideas. This will involve some concepts we'll be analyzing in more detail in Chapter 12, *Building Better Containers – Functional Data Types*, but here, we'll use just what we need so that you don't have to go and read that chapter now! Our lenses will work in the same way that the preceding ones did, except that since they will be functions, we'll be able to compose them with no special composing code.

What's the key concept here? A lens will be a function, based on a getter and a setter pair, that will construct a *container* (actually an object, but let's go with the container name) with a value attribute and a map method (in Chapter 12, *Building Better Containers – Functional Data Types*, we'll see that this is a *functor*, but you don't need to know that now). By having specific mapping methods, we'll implement our view(), set(), and over() functions. Our lens() function is as follows. We'll explain the details of this later:

```
const lens = (getter, setter) => fn => obj =>
  fn(getter(obj)).map(value => setter(value, obj));
```

Let's consider its parameters:

- The getter and setter parameters are the same as before; we can even use the very same lensProp() function that we used earlier in this chapter.
- The fn function is the magic sauce that makes everything work: depending on what we want to do with the lens, we'll provide a specific function—more on this later!
- The obj parameter is the object that we want to apply the lens to.

Let's code our view() function. For this, we'll need an auxiliary class, Constant, that, given a value, v, produces a container with that value, and a map function that returns the very same container:

```
class Constant {
  constructor(v) {
    this.value = v;
    this.map = () => this;
  }
}
```

With this, we can now code view():

```
const view = curry(
  (lensAttr, obj) => lensAttr(x => new Constant(x))(obj).value
```

```
);
const user = view(lensProp("user"), author);
/*
    fkereki
*/
```

What happens here? Let's follow this step by step; it's a bit tricky!

1. We use `lensProp()` to create a lens focusing on the user attribute.
2. Our `view()` function passes the constant-building function to `lens()`.
3. Our `lens()` function uses the getter to access the user attribute in the author object.
4. Then, the value that we received is used to create a constant container.
5. The `map()` method is invoked—that method returns the very same container.
6. The value attribute of the container is accessed, and that's the value that the getter retrieved in *step 3*; wow!

With that under our belt, let's move on to `set()` and `over()`, which will require a different auxiliary function, to create a container whose value may vary:

```
class Variable {
  constructor(v) {
    this.value = v;
    this.map = fn => new Variable(fn(v));
  }
}
```

In this case (as opposed to `Constant` objects), the `map()` method really does something: when provided with a function, it applies it to the value of the container and returns a new `Variable` object with the resulting value. The `set()` function can be implemented easily:

```
const set = curry(
  (lensAttr, newVal, obj) =>
    lensAttr(() => new Variable(newVal))(obj).value
);

const changedUser = set(lensProp("user"), "FEFK", author);
/*
{
  user: "FEFK",
  name: {first: "Federico", middle: "", last: "Kereki"},
  books: [
    {name: "GWT", year: 2010},
    {name: "FP", year: 2017},
```

```
      {name: "CB", year: 2018},
    ],
  };
  */
```

In this case, when the lens invokes the container's `map()` method, it will produce a new container with a new value, and that makes all the difference. To understand how this works, follow the same six steps we saw for `get()`—the only difference will be in *step 5*, where a new, different container is produced.

Now that we've survived this (tricky indeed!) code, the `over()` function is simple, and the only difference is that instead of mapping to a given value, you use the mapping `mapfn` function provided to compute the new value for the container:

```
const over = curry(
  (lensAttr, mapfn, obj) =>
    lensAttr(x => new Variable(mapfn(x)))(obj).value
);

const newAuthor = over(lensProp("user"), x => x + x + x, author);
/*
  user: "fkerekifkerekifkereki",
  name: {first: "Federico", middle: "", last: "Kereki"},
  books: [
    {name: "GWT", year: 2010},
    {name: "FP", year: 2017},
    {name: "CB", year: 2018},
  ],
}
*/
```

As you can see, the difference between `set()` and `over()` is that, in the former case, you provide the value to replace the original one, while in the latter case, you provide a function to calculate the new value. Other than that, both are similar.

To finish, let's verify that `compose()` can be applied to our functor-based lenses:

```
const lastName = view(
  compose(
    lensProp("name"),
    lensProp("last")
  )
)(author);
/*
    Kereki
*/
```

Here, we created two individual lenses for `name` and `last`, and we composed them with the very same `compose()` function that we developed back in `Chapter 8`, *Connecting Functions – Pipelining and Composition*. Using this composite lens, we focused on the last name of the author without any problem, so everything worked as expected.

 It seems to go against logic that lenses should be composed from left to right; this appears to be backward. This is something that troubles developers, and if you Google for an explanation, you'll find many. To combat this question on your own, I suggest spelling out how `compose()` works in full—two functions will be enough—and then substitute the definitions of lenses; you'll see why and how everything works out.

Now that we've looked at lenses, we can move on and look at prisms, another optics tool.

Prisms

Lenses, as we saw in the previous section, are useful for working with *product* types. However, prisms are useful for working with *sum* types. But what are they? (We'll look at products and unions in more detail in the *Data types* section of the next chapter.) The idea is that a product type is always built out of the same options, such as an object from a class, while a sum type will likely have different structures—extra or missing attributes, for example. When you use a lens, you assume that the object that you'll be applying it to has a known structure with no variations, but what do you use if the object may have different structures? The answer is prisms. Let's take a look at how they are used first; then, we'll look at their implementation.

Working with prisms

Working with prisms is similar to using lenses, except for what happens when an attribute is not present. Let's take a look at an example from the previous section:

```
const author = {
  user: "fkereki",
  name: {
    first: "Federico",
    middle: "",
    last: "Kereki"
  },
  books: [
    { name: "GWT", year: 2010 },
    { name: "FP", year: 2017 },
    { name: "CB", year: 2018 }
```

```
    ]
};
```

If we wanted to access the user attribute using prisms, we would write something like the following—don't worry about the details; we'll look at the actual implementation later:

```
const pUser = prismProp("user");

console.log(review(pUser, author).toString());

/*
    fkereki
*/
```

Here, we define a prism using a prismProp() function, which parallels our previous lensProp() one. Then, we use the prism with the preview() function, which is analog to get() with lenses, and the result is the same as if we had used lenses; no surprises there. What would have happened if we asked for a non-existing pseudonym attribute? Let's see:

```
const pPseudonym = prismProp("pseudonym");

console.log(preview(pPseudonym, author).toString());
/*
    undefined
*/
```

So far, we may not be able to see any differences, but let's see what happens if we try to compose lenses or prisms with several missing attributes. Say you wanted to access a (missing!) pseudonym.usedSince attribute with lenses, without taking precautions and checking that the attributes exist. Here, you would get the following output:

```
const lPseudonym = lensProp("pseudonym");
const lUsedSince = lensProp("usedSince");

console.log(
  "PSEUDONYM, USED SINCE",
  view(compose(lPseudonym, lUsedSince))(author)
);
/*
    TypeError: Cannot read property 'usedSince' of undefined
    .
    . many more error lines, snipped out
    .
*/
```

On the other hand, since prisms already take missing values into account, this would cause no problems, and we'd simply get an `undefined` result:

```
const pUsedSince = prismProp("usedSince");

console.log(
  "PSEUDONYM, USED SINCE",
  review(compose(pPseudonym, pUsedSince))(author).toString()
);
/*
    undefined
*/
```

What happens if we want to set a value? The analog function to `set()` is `review()`; let's take a look at how it would work. The idea is that whatever attribute we specify will be set, if, and only if, the attribute already exists. So, if we attempt to change the `user.name` attribute, this will work:

```
const fullAuthor2 = review(
  compose(prismProp("name"), prismProp("first")),
  "FREDERICK",
  author
);

/*
{ user: 'fkereki',
  name: { first: 'FREDERICK', middle: '', last: 'Kereki' },
  books:
   [ { name: 'GWT', year: 2010 },
     { name: 'FP', year: 2017 },
     { name: 'CB', year: 2018 } ] }
*/
```

However, if we try to modify the (non-existent) `pseudonym` attribute, the original, unchanged object will be returned:

```
const fullAuthor3 = review(pPseudonym, "NEW ALIAS", author);

/*
{ user: 'fkereki',
  name: { first: 'Federico', middle: '', last: 'Kereki' },
  books:
   [ { name: 'GWT', year: 2010 },
     { name: 'FP', year: 2017 },
     { name: 'CB', year: 2018 } ] }
*/
```

So, using prisms takes care of all possible missing or optional fields. How do we implement this new optic? Let's take a look.

Implementing prisms

How do we implement prisms? We will take our cue from our lenses implementation and make a few changes. When getting an attribute, we must check whether the object we are processing is not `null` or `undefined` and whether the attribute we want is in the object. We can make do by making small changes to our original `getField()` function:

```
const getFieldP = curry((attr, obj) =>
  obj && attr in obj ? obj[attr] : undefined
);
```

Here, we're checking for the existence of the object and the attribute: if everything's fine, we return `obj[attr]`; otherwise, we return undefined otherwise. The changes for `setField()` are very similar:

```
const setFieldP = curry((attr, value, obj) =>
  obj && attr in obj ? { ...obj, [attr]: value } : { ...obj }
);
```

If the object and the attribute both exist, we return a new object by changing the attribute's value; otherwise, we return a copy of the object. That's all there is to it!

Now that we've learned how to access objects in functional ways; let's analyze persistent data structures that can be modified in very efficient ways, without the need for a full copy of the original object.

Creating persistent data structures

If you want to change something in a data structure and you just go and change it, your code will be full of side effects. On the other hand, copying complete structures every time is a waste of time and space. There's a middle ground to this that has to do with persistent data structures, which, if handled correctly, let you apply changes while creating new structures in an efficient way.

Given that there are many possible data structures you could work with, let's just take a look at a few examples:

- Working with lists, one of the simplest data structures
- Working with objects, a very common necessity in JavaScript programs
- Dealing with arrays, which will prove to be harder to work with

Let's get started!

Working with lists

Let's consider a simple procedure: suppose you have a list and you want to add a new element to it. How would you do this? Here, we can assume that each node is a `NodeList` object:

```
class ListNode {
  constructor(value, next = null) {
    this.value = value;
    this.next = next;
  }
}
```

A possible list would be as follows, where a `list` variable would point to the first element. Take a look at the following diagram; can you tell what is missing in the list and where?

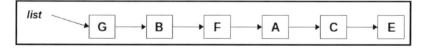

Figure 10.1: The initial list

If you wanted to add **D** between **B** and **F** (the sample list is something musicians will understand: the *Circle of Thirds*, a musical concept, but missing the **D** note), the simplest solution would be to add a new node and change an existing one. This would result in the following:

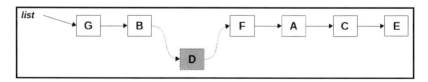

Figure 10.2: The list now has a new element – we had to modify an existing one to perform the addition

However, working in this way is obviously non-functional and it's clear we are modifying data. There is a different way of working, and that's by creating a persistent data structure, in which all the alterations (insertions, deletions, and modifications) are done separately, being careful not to modify existing data. On the other hand, if some parts of the structure can be reused, this is done to gain in performance. Doing a persistent update would return a new list, with some nodes that are duplicates of some previous ones, but with no changes whatsoever to the original list. This can be seen in the following diagram:

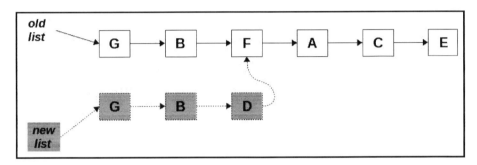

Figure 10.3: The dotted elements show the newly returned list, which shares some elements with the old one

Updating a structure in this way requires duplicating some elements to avoid modifying the original structure, but part of the list is shared.

Of course, we will also deal with updates or deletions. Starting again with the list shown in the following diagram, if we wanted to update its fourth element, the solution would imply creating a new subset of the list, up to and including the fourth element, while keeping the rest unchanged:

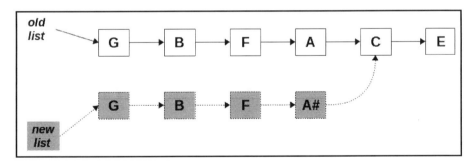

Figure 10.4: Our list, with a changed element

Removing an element would also be similar. Let's do away with the third element, **F**, in the original list, as follows:

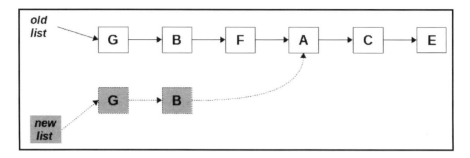

Figure 10.5: The original list, after removing the third element in a persistent way

Working with lists or other structures can always be solved to provide data persistence. For now, focus on what will probably be the most important kind of work for us: dealing with simple JavaScript objects. After all, all data structures are JavaScript objects, so if we can work with objects, we can work with other structures.

Updating objects

This kind of method can also be applied to more common requirements, such as modifying an object. This is a very good idea for, say, Redux users: a reducer can be programmed so that it will receive the old state as a parameter and produce an updated version with the minimum needed changes, without altering the original state in any way.

Imagine you had the following object:

```
myObj = {
  a: ...,
  b: ...,
  c: ...,
  d: {
    e: ...,
    f: ...,
    g: {
      h: ...,
      i: ...
    }
  }
};
```

Let's assume you wanted to modify the value of the `myObj.d.f` attribute, but working in a persistent way. Instead of copying the full object (with the `deepCopy()` function that we used earlier), we could create a new object that has several attributes in common with the previous object, but new ones for the modified ones. This can be seen in the following diagram:

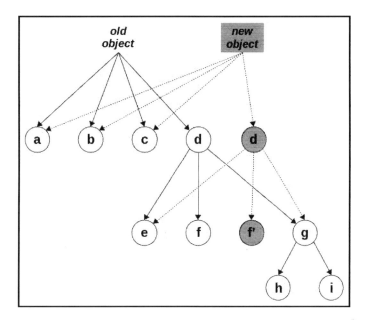

Figure 10.6: A persistent way of editing an object, that is, by sharing some attributes and creating others

The old and new objects share most of the attributes, but there are new **d** and **f** attributes, so you managed to minimize the changes when creating the new object.

If you want to do this by hand, you would have to write, in a very cumbersome way, something like the following. Most attributes are taken from the original object, but **d** and **d.f** are new:

```
newObj = {
  a: myObj.a,
  b: myObj.b,
  c: myObj.c,
  d: {
    e: myObj.d.e,
    f: the new value,
    g: myObj.d.g
  }
};
```

We saw some code similar to this earlier in this chapter when we decided to work on a cloning function. Here, let's go for a different type of solution. In fact, this kind of update can be automated:

```
const setIn = (arr, val, obj) => {
  const newObj = Number.isInteger(arr[0]) ? [] : {};

  Object.keys(obj).forEach(k => {
    newObj[k] = k !== arr[0] ? obj[k] : null;
  });

  newObj[arr[0]] =
    arr.length > 1 ? setIn(arr.slice(1), val, obj[arr[0]]) : val;
  return newObj;
};
```

The logic is recursive, but not too complex. First, we figure out, at the current level, what kind of object we need: either an array or an object. Then, we copy all the attributes from the original object to the new one, except the property we are changing. Finally, we set that property to the given value (if we have finished with the path of property names) or we use recursion to go deeper with the copy.

 Note the order of the arguments: first the path, then the value, and finally the object. We are applying the concept of putting the most *stable* parameters first and the most variable last. If you curry this function, you can apply the same path to several different values and objects, and if you fix the path and the value, you can still use the function with different objects.

Let's give this logic a try. We'll start with a nonsensical object, but with several levels and even an array of objects for variety:

```
let myObj1 = {
  a: 111,
  b: 222,
  c: 333,
  d: {
    e: 444,
    f: 555,
    g: {
      h: 666,
      i: 777
    },
    j: [{k: 100}, {k: 200}, {k: 300}]
  }
};
```

We can test this by changing myObj.d.f to a new value:

```
let myObj2 = setIn(["d", "f"], 88888, myObj1);

/*
{
  a: 111,
  b: 222,
  c: 333,
  d: {
    e: 444,
    f: 88888,
    g: {h: 666, i: 777},
    j: [{k: 100}, {k: 200}, {k: 300}]
  }
}
*/

console.log(myObj.d === myObj2.d);       // false
console.log(myObj.d.f === myObj2.d.f);   // false
console.log(myObj.d.g === myObj2.d.g);   // true
```

The logs at the bottom verify that the algorithm is working correctly: myObj2.d is a new object, but myObj2.d.g is reusing the value from myObj.

Updating the array in the second object lets us test how the logic works in those cases:

```
let myObj3 = setIn(["d", "j", 1, "k"], 99999, myObj2);
/*
{
  a: 111,
  b: 222,
  c: 333,
  d: {
    e: 444,
    f: 88888,
    g: {h: 666, i: 777},
    j: [{k: 100}, {k: 99999}, {k: 300}]
  }
}
*/
console.log(myObj.d.j === myObj3.d.j);       // false
console.log(myObj.d.j[0] === myObj3.d.j[0]); // true
console.log(myObj.d.j[1] === myObj3.d.j[1]); // false
console.log(myObj.d.j[2] === myObj3.d.j[2]); // true
```

We can compare the elements in the myObj.d.j array with the ones in the newly created object. You will see that the array is a new one, but two of the elements (the ones that weren't updated) are still the same objects that were in myObj.

This obviously isn't enough to get by. Our logic can update an existing field, or even add it if it wasn't there, but you'd also need to eliminate and attribute. Libraries usually provide many more functions, but let's work on the deletion of an attribute for now so that we can look at some of the other important structural changes we can make to an object:

```
const deleteIn = (arr, obj) => {
  const newObj = Number.isInteger(arr[0]) ? [] : {};

  Object.keys(obj).forEach(k => {
    if (k !== arr[0]) {
      newObj[k] = obj[k];
    }
  });

  if (arr.length > 1) {
    newObj[arr[0]] = deleteIn(arr.slice(1), obj[arr[0]]);
  }
  return newObj;
};
```

The logic here is similar to that of setIn(). The difference is that we don't always copy all the attributes from the original object to the new one: we only do that if we haven't arrived at the end of the array of path properties. Continuing with the series of tests after the updates, we get the following:

```
myObj4 = deleteIn(["d", "g"], myObj3);
myObj5 = deleteIn(["d", "j"], myObj4);

// {a: 111, b: 222, c: 333, d: {e: 444, f: 88888}};
```

With this pair of functions, we can manage to work with persistent objects by making changes, additions, and deletions in an efficient way that won't create new objects needlessly.

The most well-known library for working with immutable objects is the appropriately named *immutable.js*, which can be found at https://facebook.github.io/immutable-js/. The only weak point about it is its notoriously obscure documentation. However, there's an easy solution for that: check out *The Missing Immutable.js Manual with all the Examples you'll ever need* at http://untangled.io/the-missing-immutable-js-manual/ and you won't have any trouble!

A final caveat

Working with persistent data structures requires some cloning, but how would you implement a persistent array? If you think about this, you'll realize that, in that case, there would be no way out apart from cloning the whole array after each operation. This would mean that an operation such as updating an element in an array, which took a constant time, would now take a length of time proportional to the size of the array.

 In algorithm complexity terms, we would say that updates went from being an O(1) operation to an O(*n*) one. Similarly, access to an element may become an O(*log n*) operation, and similar slowdowns might be observed for other operations, such as mapping and reducing.

How do we avoid this? There's no easy solution. For example, you may find that an array is internally represented as a binary search tree (or even more complex data structures) and that the persistence library provides the necessary interface so that you'll still able to use it as an array, not noticing the internal difference.

When using this kind of library, the advantages of having immutable updates without cloning may be offset in part by some operations that may become slower. If this becomes a bottleneck in your application, you might have to go so far as changing the way you implement immutability or even work out how to change your basic data structures to avoid the time loss, or at least minimize it.

Summary

In this chapter, we looked at two different approaches (used by commonly available immutability libraries) to avoiding side effects by working with immutable objects and data structures: one based on using JavaScript's *object freezing* plus some special logic for cloning, and the other based on applying the concept of persistent data structures with methods that allow all kinds of updates without changing the original or requiring full cloning.

In Chapter 11, *Implementing Design Patterns – The Functional Way*, we will focus on a question that's often asked by object-oriented programmers: how are design patterns used in FP? Are they required, available, or usable? Are they still practiced but with a new focus on functions rather than on objects? We'll answer these questions with several examples, showing where and how they are equivalent or how they differ from the usual OOP practices.

Questions

10.1. **Freezing by proxying**: In the *Chaining and fluent interfaces* section of `Chapter 8`, *Connecting Functions – Pipelining and Composition*, we used a proxy to get operations in order to provide automatic chaining. By using a proxy for *setting* and *deleting* operations, you may do your own *freezing* (if, instead of setting an object's property, you'd rather throw an exception). Implement a `freezeByProxy(obj)` function that will apply this idea to forbid all kinds of updates (adding, modifying, or deleting properties) for an object. Remember to work recursively in case an object has other objects as properties!

10.2. **Inserting into a list, persistently**: In the *Working with lists* section, we described how an algorithm could add a new node to a list, but in a persistent way, by creating a new list. Implement an `insertAfter(list, newKey, oldKey)` function that will create a new list but add a new node with `newKey` just after the node with `oldKey`. Here, you'll need to assume that the nodes in the list were created by the following logic:

```
class Node {
  constructor(key, next = null) {
    this.key = key;
    this.next = next;
  }
}

const node = (key, next) => new Node(key, next);

let c3 = node("G", node("B", node("F", node("A", node("C", node("E"))))));
```

10.3. **Composing many lenses**: Write a `composeLenses()` function that will allow you to compose as many simple lenses as you want, instead of only two as in `composeTwoLenses()`, along the same lines as what we did in `Chapter 8`, *Connecting Functions – Pipelining and Composition*, when me moved from `composeTwo()` to a generic `compose()` function.

10.4. **Lenses by path**: In this chapter, we created lenses using `getField()` and `setField()`. Then, we used composition to access deeper attributes. Can you create a lens by giving a path and allow shorter code?

10.5. **Accessing virtual attributes**: By using lenses, you can view (and even set) attributes that don't actually exist in an object. Here are some tips to let you develop that. First, can you write a getter that will access an object such as `author` and return the author's full name in LAST NAME, FIRST NAME format? Second, can you write a setter that, given a full name, will split it in half and set its first and last names? With those two functions, you could write the following:

```
const fullNameLens = lens(
  ...your getter...,
  ...your setter...
);

console.log(view(fullNameLens, author));
/*
  Kereki, Federico
*/

console.log(set(fullNameLens, "Doe, John", author));
/*
{ user: 'fkereki',
  name: { first: ' John', middle: '', last: 'Doe' },
  books:
    [ { name: 'GWT', year: 2010 },
      { name: 'FP', year: 2017 },
      { name: 'CB', year: 2018 } ] }
*/
```

10.6. **Lenses for arrays?** What would happen if you created a lens like so and applied it to an array? If there's a problem, could you fix it?

```
const getArray = curry((ind, arr) => arr[ind]);

const setArray = curry((ind, value, arr) => {
  arr[ind] = value;
  return arr;
});

const lensArray = ind => lens(getArray(ind), setArray(ind));
```

10.7. **Lenses into maps**: Write a `lensMap()` function that will create a lens that you can use to access and modify maps. You may want to look into cloning maps at `https://developer.mozilla.org/en-US/docs/Web/JavaScript/Reference/Global_Objects/Map` for more information. Your function should be declared as follows. You'll have to write a couple of auxiliary functions as well:

```
const lensMap = key => lens(getMap(key), setMap(key));
```

11
Implementing Design Patterns - The Functional Way

In Chapter 10, *Ensuring Purity – Immutability*, we saw several functional techniques to solve different problems. However, programmers who are used to employing OOP may find that we have missed some well-known formula and solutions that are often used in imperative coding. Since design patterns are well known, and programmers will likely already be aware of how they are applied in other languages, it's important to take a look at how a functional implementation would be done.

In this chapter, we shall consider the solutions implied by *design patterns*, which are common in OOP, to see their equivalences in FP. This will help you to transition from OOP to a more functional approach and to learn more about the power and methods of FP, by seeing an alternative solution to problems you already knew.

In particular, we will study the following topics:

- The concept of *design patterns* and to what they apply
- A few OOP standard patterns and what alternatives we have in FP if we need one
- In particular, the *observer* pattern, which leads to *reactive programming*, a declarative way of dealing with events
- A discussion about FP design patterns, not related to the OOP ones

Understanding design patterns

One of the most relevant books in software engineering was *Design Patterns: Elements of Reusable Object-Oriented Software*, 1994, written by the **Gang of Four** (**GOF**): Erich Gamma, Richard Helm, Ralph Johnson, and John Vlissides. This book presented about two dozen different OOP *patterns* and has been recognized as a highly important book in computer science.

 Patterns are actually a concept from architectural design, originally defined by an architect, Christopher Alexander.

In software terms, a *design pattern* is a generally applicable, reusable solution to a commonly-seen problem in software design. Rather than a specific finished and coded design, it's a description of a solution (the word *template* is also used) that can solve a given problem that appears in many contexts. Given their advantages, design patterns are on their own *best practices* that can be used by developers working with different kinds of systems, programming languages, and environments.

The GoF book obviously focused on OOP, and some of the patterns within cannot be recommended for or applied in FP. Other patterns are unnecessary or irrelevant because functional languages already provide standard solutions to the corresponding object-oriented problems. Even given this difficulty, since most programmers have been exposed to OOP design patterns and usually try to apply them even in other contexts such as FP, it makes sense to consider the original problems and then take a look at how a new solution can be produced. The standard object-based solutions may not apply, but the problem can still stand, so seeing how to solve it is still valid.

Patterns are often described in terms of four essential, basic elements:

- A simple, short *name* that is used to describe the problem, its solutions, and its consequences. The name is useful for talking with colleagues, explaining a design decision, or describing a specific implementation.
- The *context* to which the pattern applies: specific situations that require a solution, possibly with some extra conditions that must be met.
- A *solution* that lists the elements (classes, objects, functions, relationships, and so on) that you'll need to solve the given situation.
- The *consequences* (results and trade-offs) if you apply the pattern. You may derive some gains from the solution, but it may also imply some losses.

In this chapter, we will assume that the reader is already aware of the design patterns that we will be describing and using, so we won't be providing many details about them. Rather, we will focus on how FP either makes the problem irrelevant (because there is an obvious way of applying functional techniques to solve it) or solves it in some fashion. Also, we won't be going over all of the GoF patterns; we'll just focus on those for which applying FP is more interesting, bringing out more differences to the usual OOP implementations.

Design pattern categories

Design patterns are usually grouped into several distinct categories, according to their focus. The first three in the following list are the ones that appeared in the original GoF book, but more categories have been added. They are as follows:

- **Behavioral design patterns**: These have to do with interactions and communications between objects. Rather than focusing on how objects are created or built, the key consideration is how to connect them so that they can cooperate when performing a complex task, preferably in a way that provides well-known advantages, such as diminished coupling or enhanced cohesiveness.
- **Creational design patterns**: These deal with ways to create objects in a manner that is suitable for the current problem. With it, you can decide between several alternative objects, so the program can work differently depending on parameters that may be known at compilation time or runtime.
- **Structural design patterns**: These have to do with the composition of objects, forming larger structures from many individual parts and implementing relationships between objects. Some of the patterns imply inheritance or implementation of interfaces, whereas others use different mechanisms, all geared toward being able to dynamically change the way objects are composed at runtime.
- **Concurrency patterns**: These are related to dealing with multithreaded programming. Although FP is generally quite appropriate for this (given, for example, the lack of assignments and side effects), since we are working with JavaScript, these patterns are not very relevant to us.
- **Architectural patterns**: These are more high-level oriented, with a broader scope than the previous patterns we've listed, and provide general solutions to software architecture problems. As is, we aren't considering such problems in this book, so we won't deal with these either.

Coupling and cohesiveness are terms that were in use even before OOP came into vogue; they date back to the late '60s when *Structured Design* by Larry Constantine came out. The former measures the interdependence between any two modules, and the latter has to do with the degree to which all components of a module really belong together. Low coupling and high cohesiveness are good goals for software design because they imply that related things are close by and unrelated ones are separate.

Following along these lines, you could also classify design patterns as *object patterns* (which concern the dynamic relationships between objects) and *class patterns* that deal with the relationships between classes and subclasses (which are defined statically at compile time). We won't be worrying much about this classification because our point of view has more to do with behaviors and functions rather than classes and objects.

As we mentioned earlier, we can now readily observe that these categories are heavily oriented toward OOP, and the first three directly mention objects. However, without the loss of generality, we will look beyond the definitions, remember what problem we were trying to solve, and then look into analogous solutions with FP, which, if not 100% equivalent to the OOP ones, will in spirit be solving the same problem in a parallel way. Let's move on and start by considering *why* we want to deal with patterns at all!

Do we need design patterns?

There is an interesting point of view that says that design patterns are only needed to patch shortcomings of a programming language. The rationale is that if you can solve a problem with a given programming language in a simple, direct, and straightforward way, then you may not need a design pattern at all. (An example: if your language doesn't provide recursion, we would have to implement it on our own, but otherwise, you can just use it without further ado.) However, studying patterns lets you think about different ways of solving problems, so that's a point in their favor.

In any case, it's interesting for OOP developers to really understand why FP helps to solve some problems without the need for further tools. In the next section, we shall consider several well-known design patterns and take a look at why we don't need them or how we can easily implement them. It's also a fact that we have already applied several patterns earlier in the text, so we'll point out those examples as well.

We won't try, however, to express or convert all design patterns into FP terms. For example, the *Singleton* pattern basically requires a single, global, object, which is sort of opposed to everything that functional programmers are used to. Given our approach to FP (remember **Sorta Functional Programming (SPF)**, from the initial part of the first chapter of this book?), we won't mind either, and if a Singleton is required, we may consider using it, even though FP doesn't have an appropriate equivalent.

Finally, it must be said that our point of view may affect what is considered a pattern and what isn't. What may be a pattern to some may be considered a trivial detail for others. We will find some such situations, given that FP lets us solve some particular problems in easy ways, and we have already seen examples of that in previous chapters.

Object-oriented design patterns

In this section, we'll go over some of the GoF design patterns, check whether they are pertinent to FP, and study how to implement them. Of course, some design patterns don't get an FP solution. As we said, for example, there's no equivalent for a *Singleton*, which implies the foreign concept of a globally accessed object. Additionally, while it's true that you may no longer need OOP-specific patterns, developers will still think in terms of those. Also, finally, since we're not going fully functional if an OOP pattern fits, why not use it?

We will be considering the following:

- *Façade* and *Adapter*, to provide new interfaces to other code
- *Decorator* (also known as *Wrapper*) to add new functionality to existing code
- *Strategy*, *Template*, and *Command*, to let you fine-tune algorithms by passing functions as parameters
- *Observer*, which leads to reactive programming, a declarative way of dealing with events
- Other patterns that do not so fully match the corresponding OOP ones

Now, let's begin our study by analyzing a couple of similar patterns that let you use your code in somewhat different ways.

Facade and adapter

Out of these two patterns, let's start with the *Facade* or, more correctly, *Façade*. This is meant to solve the problem of providing a different interface to the methods of a class or to a library. The idea is to provide a new interface to a system that makes it easier to use. You might say that a Façade provides a better control panel to access certain functionalities, removing difficulties for the user.

Façade or facade? The original word is an architectural term meaning the *front of a building* and comes from the French language. According to this source and the usual sound of the cedilla (ç) character, its pronunciation is something like *fuh-sahd*. The other spelling probably has to do with the lack of international characters in keyboards and poses the following problem: shouldn't you read it as *faKade*? You may see this problem as the reverse of *celtic*, which is pronounced as *Keltic*, changing the *s* sound for a *k* sound.

The main problem that we want to solve is being able to use external code more easily (of course, if it were your code, you could handle such problems directly; we must assume you cannot—or shouldn't—try to modify that other code. This would be the case when you use any library that's available over the web, for example). The key to this is to implement a module of your own that will provide an interface that better suits your needs. Your code will use your module and won't directly interact with the original code.

Suppose that you want to do Ajax calls, and your only possibility is using some hard library with a really complex interface. With modules, you might write something like the following, working with an imagined, hard-to-use Ajax library:

```
// simpleAjax.js

import * as hard from "hardajaxlibrary";
// import the other library that does Ajax calls
// but in a hard, difficult way, requiring complex code

const convertParamsToHardStyle = params => {
  // do some internal steps to convert params
  // into whatever the hard library may require
};

const makeStandardUrl = url => {
  // make sure the url is in the standard
  // way for the hard library
};
```

```
const getUrl = (url, params, callback) => {
  const xhr = hard.createAnXmlHttpRequestObject();
  hard.initializeAjaxCall(xhr);
  const standardUrl = makeStandardUrl(url);
  hard.setUrl(xhr, standardUrl);
  const convertedParams = convertParamsToHardStyle(params);
  hard.setAdditionalParameters(params);
  hard.setCallback(callback);
  if (hard.everythingOk(xhr)) {
    hard.doAjaxCall(xhr);
  } else {
    throw new Error("ajax failure");
  }
};

const postUrl = (url, params, callback) => {
  // some similarly complex code
  // to do a POST using the hard library
};

export {getUrl, postUrl}; // the only methods that will be seen
```

Now, if you need to do GET or POST, instead of having to go through all of the complications of the provided hard Ajax library, you can use the new façade that provides a simpler way of working. Developers would just do `import {getUrl, postUrl} from "simpleAjax"` and could then work more reasonably.

However, why are we showing this code that, though interesting, doesn't show any particular FP aspects? The key is that, at least until modules are fully implemented in browsers, the internal implicit way to do this is with the usage of an IIFE (Immediately Invoked Function Expression) as we saw in the *Immediate invocation* section of Chapter 3, *Starting Out with Functions – A Core Concept*, using a *revealing module* pattern. The way to implement this would then be as follows:

```
const simpleAjax = (function() {
  const hard = require("hardajaxlibrary");

  const convertParamsToHardStyle = params => {
    // ...
  };

  const makeStandardUrl = url => {
    // ...
  };

  const getUrl = (url, params, callback) => {
```

```
      // ...
    };

    const postUrl = (url, params, callback) => {
      // ...
    };

    return {
      getUrl,
      postUrl
    };
  }) ();
```

The reason for the *revealing module* name should be now obvious. With the preceding code, because of the JavaScript scope rules, the only visible attributes of `simpleAjax` will be `simpleAjax.getUrl` and `simpleAjax.postUrl`; using an IIFE lets us implement the module (and hence, the façade) safely, making implementation details private.

Now, the Adapter pattern is similar, insofar it is also meant to define a new interface. However, while Façade defines a new interface to old code, Adapter is used when you need to implement an old interface for a new code, so it will match what you already had. If you are working with modules, it's clear that the same type of solution that worked for Façade will work here, so we don't have to study it in detail. Now, let's continue with a well-known pattern, which you'll recognize we've already seen earlier in this book!

Decorator or wrapper

The *Decorator* pattern (also known as *wrapper*) is useful when you want to add additional responsibilities or functionalities to an object in a dynamic way. Let's consider a simple example, which we will illustrate with some React code. (Don't worry if you do not know this framework; the example will be easy to understand. The idea of going with React is because it can very well take advantage of this pattern. Also, we have already seen pure JavaScript higher-order function examples, so it's good to see something new.) Suppose we want to show some elements on the screen, and for debugging purposes, we want to show a thin red border around the object. How can you do it?

If you were using OOP, you would probably have to create a new subclass with the extended functionality. For this particular example, you might just provide some attribute with the name of some CSS class that would provide the required style, but let's keep our focus on OOP; using CSS won't always solve this software design problem, so we want a more general solution. The new subclass would *know* how to show itself with a border, and you'd use this subclass whenever you wanted an object's border to be visible.

With our experience of higher-order functions, we can solve this in a different way using *wrapping*; wrap the original function within another one, which would provide the extra functionality.

Note that we have already seen some examples of wrapping in the *Wrapping functions – keeping behavior* section of Chapter 6, *Producing Functions – Higher-Order Functions*. For example, in that section, we saw how to wrap functions to produce new versions that could log their input and output, provide timing information, or even memorize calls to avoid future delays. On this occasion, for variety, we are applying the concept to *decorate* a visual component, but the principle remains the same.

Let's define a simple React component, ListOfNames, that can display a heading and a list of people, and for the latter, it will use a FullNameDisplay component. The code for those elements would be as seen in the following fragment:

```
class FullNameDisplay extends React.Component {
  render() {
    return (
      <div>
        First Name: <b>{this.props.first}</b>
        <br />
        Last Name: <b>{this.props.last}</b>
      </div>
    );
  }
}

class ListOfNames extends React.Component {
  render() {
    return (
      <div>
        <h1>
          {this.props.heading}
        </h1>
        <ul>
          {this.props.people.map(v =>
            <FullNameDisplay first={v.first} last={v.last} />
          )}
        </ul>
      </div>
    );
  }
}
```

The `ListOfNames` component uses mapping to create a `FullNameDisplay` component to show data for each person. The full logic for our application could then be the following:

```
import React from "react";
import ReactDOM from "react-dom";

class FullNameDisplay extends React.Component {
  // ...as above...
}

class ListOfNames extends React.Component {
  // ...as above...
}

const GANG_OF_FOUR = [
  {first: "Erich", last: "Gamma"},
  {first: "Richard", last: "Helm"},
  {first: "Ralph", last: "Johnson"},
  {first: "John", last: "Vlissides"}
];

ReactDOM.render(
  <ListOfNames heading="GoF" people={GANG_OF_FOUR} />,
  document.body
);
```

 In real life, you wouldn't put all of the code for every component in the same single source code file—and you would probably have a few CSS files. However, for our example, having everything in one place, and going with inline styles is enough, so bear with me and keep in mind the following saying: *Do as I say, not as I do.*

We can quickly test the result in the online React sandbox at `https://codesandbox.io/`; Google `react online sandbox` if you want some other options. The interface design isn't much to talk about (so please don't criticize my poor web page!) because we are interested in design patterns right now; refer to *Figure 11.1*, given as follows:

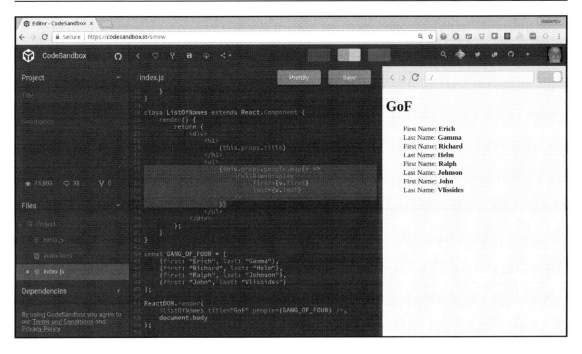

Figure 11.1: The original version of our components shows a (not much to speak about) list of names

In React, inline components are written in JSX (inline HTML style) and are actually compiled into objects, which are later transformed into HTML code to be displayed. Whenever the `render()` method is called, it returns a structure of objects. So, we will write a function that will take a component as a parameter and return a new JSX, a wrapped object. In our case, we'd like to wrap the original component within `<div>` with the required border:

```
const makeVisible = component => {
  return (
    <div style={{border: "1px solid red"}}>
      {component}
    </div>
  );
};
```

If you wish, you could make this function aware of whether it's executing in development mode or production; in the latter case, it would simply return the original component argument without any change, but let's not worry about that now.

We now have to change ListOfNames to use wrapped components; the new version would be as follows:

```
class ListOfNames extends React.Component {
  render() {
    return (
      <div>
        <h1>
          {this.props.title}
        </h1>
        <ul>
          {this.props.people.map(v =>
            makeVisible(
              <FullNameDisplay
                first={v.first}
                last={v.last}
              />
            )
          )}
        </ul>
      </div>
    );
  }
}
```

The decorated version of the code works as expected: each of the ListOfNames components is now wrapped in another component that adds the desired border to them; refer to *Figure 11.2*, given as follows:

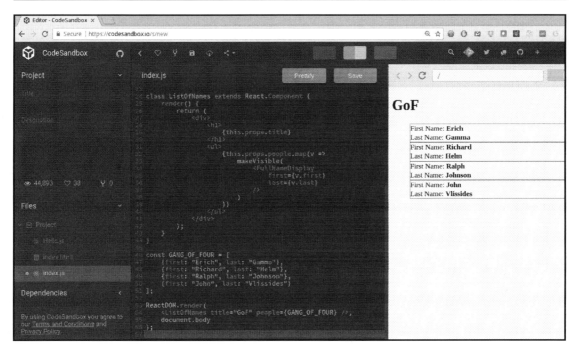

Figure 11.2: The decorated ListOfNames component is still nothing much to look at, but now it shows an added border

In earlier chapters, we saw how to decorate a function, wrapping it inside of another function, so it would perform extra code and add a few functionalities. Now, here, we saw how to apply the same style of the solution to provide a *higher-order component* (as it's called in React parlance) wrapped in an extra `<div>` to provide some visually distinctive details.

 If you have used Redux and the *react-redux* package, you may note that the latter's `connect()` method is also a decorator in the same sense; it receives a component class, and returns a new component class, connected to the store, for usage in your forms; refer to `https://github.com/reactjs/react-redux` for more details.

Let's move to a different set of patterns that will let us change how functions perform.

Strategy, Template, and Command

The *Strategy* pattern applies whenever you want to have the ability to change a class, method, or function, possibly in a dynamic way, by changing the way it actually does whatever it's expected to do. For example, a GPS application might want to find a route between two places by applying different strategies if the person is on foot, rides a bicycle, or goes by car. In that case, the fastest or the shortest routes might be desired. The problem is the same, but different algorithms must be applied, depending on the given condition.

By the way, does this sound familiar? If so, it is because we have already met a similar problem. When we wanted to sort a set of strings in different ways, in Chapter 3, *Starting Out with Functions – A Core Concept*, we needed a way to specify how the ordering was to be applied or, equivalently, how to compare two given strings and determine which had to go first. Depending on the language, we had to sort applying different comparison methods.

Before trying an FP solution, let's consider more ways of implementing our routing function. You could make do by having a big enough piece of code, which would receive an argument declaring which algorithm to use, plus the starting and ending points. With these arguments, the function could do a switch or something similar to apply the correct path-finding logic. The code would be roughly equivalent to the following fragment:

```
function findRoute(byMeans, fromPoint, toPoint) {
  switch (byMeans) {
    case "foot":
      /*
        find the shortest road
        for a walking person
      */

    case "bicycle":
      /*
        find a route apt
        for a cyclist
      */

    case "car-fastest":
      /*
        find the fastest route
        for a car driver
      */

    case "car-shortest":
      /*
        find the shortest route
        for a car driver
```

```
      */

    default:
      /*
        plot a straight line,
        or throw an error,
        or whatever suits you
      */
  }
}
```

This kind of solution is really not desirable, and your function is really the sum of a lot of distinct other functions, which doesn't offer a high level of cohesion. If your language doesn't support lambda functions (as was the case with Java, for example, until Java 8 came out in 2014), the OOP solution for this requires defining classes that implement the different strategies you may want, creating an appropriate object, and passing it around.

With FP in JavaScript, implementing strategies is trivial: instead of using a variable such as byMeans to switch, you provide a route-finding function (routeAlgorithm() in the following code) that will implement the desired path logic:

```
function findRoute(routeAlgorithm, fromPoint, toPoint) {
  return routeAlgorithm(fromPoint, toPoint);
}
```

You would still have to implement all of the desired strategies (there's no way around that) and decide which function to pass to findRoute(), but now that function is independent of the routing logic, and if you wanted to add new routing algorithms, you wouldn't touch findRoute().

If you consider the *Template* pattern, the difference is that Strategy allows you to use completely different ways of achieving an outcome, while Template provides an overarching algorithm (or *template*) in which some implementation details are left to methods to be specified. In the same way, you can provide functions to implement the Strategy pattern; you can also provide them for a Template pattern.

Finally, the *Command* pattern also benefits from the ability to be able to pass functions as arguments. This pattern is meant to be enabled to encapsulate a request as an object, so for different requests, you have differently parameterized objects. Given that we can simply pass functions as arguments to other functions, there's no need for the enclosing object.

We also saw a similar use of this pattern back in the *A React-Redux reducer* section of Chapter 3, *Starting Out with Functions – A Core Concept*. There, we defined a table, each of whose entries was a callback that was called whenever needed. We could directly say that the Command pattern is just an **object-oriented (OO)** replacement for plain functions working as callbacks.

Let's now move on to a classic pattern that implies a new term, *reactive programming*, that's being thrown around a lot these days.

Observer and reactive programming

The idea of the *observer* pattern is to define a link between entities, so when one changes, all of the dependent entities are updated automatically. The *observable* can publish changes to its state, and its observer (which subscribed to the observable) will be notified of such changes.

 There is a proposal for adding observables to JavaScript (see https:// github.com/tc39/proposal-observable) but as of December 2019, it's still stuck at stage 1; check https://github.com/tc39/proposal-observable/issues/191. Hence, for the time being, it seems that using a library will still be mandatory.

There's an extension to this concept called **reactive programming**, which involves asynchronous streams of events (such as mouse clicks or keypresses) or data (from APIs or web sockets), and different parts of the application subscribing to observe such streams by passing callbacks that will get called whenever something new appears.

 We won't be implementing reactive programming on our own; instead, we'll use RxJS, a JavaScript implementation of Reactive Extensions (*ReactiveX*) originally developed by Microsoft. RxJS is widely used in the Angular framework and can also be used in other frontend frameworks, such as React or Vue, or in the backend with Node. Learn more about RxJS at https://rxjs-dev.firebaseapp.com/ and https://www.learnrxjs.io/.

The techniques we will be showing in these sections are, confusingly, called both **Functional Reactive Programming (FRP)** and **Reactive Functional Programming (RFP)**; pick whichever you want! There is also a suggestion that FRP shouldn't be applied to discrete streams (so the name is wrong) but the expression is seen all over the web, which gives it some standing. But...what makes this functional, and why should we be interested in it? The key is that we will be using similar methods to `map()`, `filter()`, and `reduce()` to process those streams, and pick which events to process and how. OK, this may be confusing now, so bear with me and let's see some concepts first, and after that, some examples of FRP—or whatever you want to call it! We will be seeing the following:

- Several basic concepts and terms you'll need to work with FRP
- Some of the many available operators you'll use
- A couple of examples: detecting multi-clicks, and providing typeahead searches

Let's move on to analyze each item, starting with the basic ideas you need to know.

Basic concepts and terms

Using FRP requires getting used to several new terms, so let's begin with a short glossary:

- **Observable**: This represents a stream of (present or future) values and can be connected to an observer. You can create observables from practically anything, but the most common case is from events. By convention, observable variable names end with `$`; see `https://angular.io/guide/rx-library#naming-conventions`.
- **Observer**: This is either a callback that is executed whenever the observable it's subscribed to produce a new value or an object with three methods: `next()`, `error()`, and `complete()`, which will be called by the observable when a value is available, when there's an error, and when the stream is ended respectively.
- **Operators**: These are pure functions (similar to `map()`, `filter()`, and so on, from Chapter 5, *Programming Declaratively – A Better Style*) that let you apply transformations to a stream in a declarative way.
- **Pipe**: This is a way to define a pipeline of operators that will be applied to a stream. This is very similar to the `pipeline()` function we developed back in Chapter 8, *Connecting Functions – Pipelining and Composition*.
- **Subscription**: This is the connection to an observable. An observable doesn't do anything until you call the `subscribe()` method, providing an observer.

An interesting way of looking at observables is that they complete the lower row of this table; check it out. You will probably be quite familiar with the *Single* column, but maybe not with the *Multiple one*:

	Single	Multiple
Pull	Function	Iterator
Push	Promise	Observable

How do we interpret this table? The rows distinguish between pull (you call something) and push (you get called), and the columns represent how many values you get: one or many. With these descriptions, we can see the following:

- `function` is called and returns a single value.
- `promise` calls your code (a callback in the `then()` method) also with a single value.
- `iterator` returns a new value each time it's called—at least until the sequence is over.
- `observable` calls your code (provided you `subscribe()` to the observable) for each value in the stream.

Observables and promises can be compared a bit more:

- They are both mostly async in nature, and your callback will be called at an indefinite future time.
- Promises cannot be canceled, but you can `unsubscribe()` from an observable.
- Promises start executing the moment you create them; observables are lazy, and nothing happens until an observer does `subscribe()` to them.

The real power of observables derives from the variety of operators you can use; let's see some of them.

Operators for observables

Basically, operators are just functions: creation operators can be used to create observables out of many different sources, and pipeable operators can be applied to modify a stream, producing a new observable: we'll see many families of these, but for complete lists and descriptions, you should access `https://www.learnrxjs.io/operators/` and `https://rxjs.dev/guide/operators`.

 We won't be covering how to install RxJS; see `https://rxjs.dev/guide/installation` for all of the possibilities. In particular, in our examples, meant for a browser, we'll be installing version 6 of RxJS from a CDN, which creates a global `rxjs` variable, similar to jQuery's $ or LoDash's _ variables.

Let's begin by creating observables, and then move on to transforming them. For creation, some of the several operators you can use are explained in the following table:

Operator	Usage
ajax	Creates an observable for an Ajax request, for which we'll emit the response that is returned
from	Produces an observable out of an array, an iterable, or a promise
fromEvent	Turns events (for example, mouse clicks) into an observable sequence
interval	Emits values at periodic intervals
of	Generates a sequence out of a given set of value
range	Produces a sequence of values in a range
timer	After an initial delay, emits values periodically

To give a very basic example, the following three observables will all produce a sequence of values from 1 to 10, and we'll be seeing more practical examples a bit later in this chapter:

```
const obs1$ = from([1, 2, 3, 4, 5, 6, 7, 8, 9, 10]);
const obs2$ = of(1, 2, 3, 4, 5, 6, 7, 8, 9, 10);
const obs3$ = range(1, 10);
```

The available pipeable operators are way too many for this section, so we'll just go over some families and describe their basic idea with one or two particular mentions. The following table lists the most common families, with their most often used operators:

Family	Description
Combination	These operators allow joining information from several distinct observables, including the following: • `concat()` to put observables in a queue one after the other. • `merge()` to create a single observable out of many. • `pairWise()` to emit the previous value and the current one as an array. • `startWith()` to inject value in an observable.
Conditional	These produce values depending on conditions, and include the following: • `defaultIfEmpty()` emits a value if an observable doesn't emit anything before completing. • `every()` emits true if all values satisfy a predicate and emits false instead. • `iif()` subscribes to one of two observables depending on a condition, like the ternary `?` operator.
Error handling	These (obviously!) apply to error conditions, and include the following: • `catchError()` to gracefully process an error from an observable. • `retry()` and `retryWhen()` to retry an observable sequence (most likely, one linked to HTTP requests.)
Filtering	Probably the most important family, providing many operators to process sequences, by selecting which elements will get processed or dismissed, by applying different types of conditions for your selection. Some of the more common ones include the following: • `debounce()` and `debounceTime()` to deal with values too close together in time. • `distinctUntilChanged()` to only emit when the new value is different from the last. • `filter()` to only emit values that satisfy a given predicate. • `find()` to emit only the first value that satisfies a condition. • `first()` and `last()` to pick only the first or last values of a sequence. • `skip()` plus `skipUntil()` and `skipWhile()` to discard values. • `take()` and `takeLast()` to pick a given number of values from the beginning or end of a sequence. • `takeUntil()` and `takeWhile()` to pick values and more.

Transforming	The other very commonly used family, which includes operators to transform the values in the sequence. Some of the many possibilities include these: • buffer() and bufferTime() to collect values and emit them as an array. • groupBy() to group values together based on some property. • map() to apply a given mapping function to every element in the sequence. • partition() to split an observable into two, based on a given predicate. • pluck() to pick only some attributes from each element. • reduce() to reduce a sequence of values to a single one. • scan() works like reduce(), but emits all intermediate values. • toArray() collects all values and emits them as a single array.
Utilities	A sundry collection of operators with different functions, including the following: • tap() to perform a side effect, similar to what we saw in the *Tapping into a flow* section in Chapter 8, *Connecting Functions – Pipelining and Composition* • delay() to delay sequence values some time. • finalize() to call a function when an observable completes or produces an error. • repeat() is just like retry() but for normal (that is, non-error) cases. • timeout() to produce an error if no value is produced before a given duration.

Wow, that's a lot of operators! We have excluded many, and you could even write your own, so be sure to look at the documentation.

Understanding operators is made easier with *marbles diagrams*; we won't be using them here, but read http://reactivex.io/documentation/ observable.html for a basic explanation, and then check out https:// rxmarbles.com/ for many interactive examples of operators and how they function.

Let's finish this section with a couple of examples of the real possibility of application for your own coding.

Detecting multi-clicks

Suppose you decided, for some reason or another, that users should be able to triple-click or four-click on something, and the number of clicks would somehow be meaningful and produce some kind of special result. Browsers do very well detecting single- or double-clicks and let you respond to them, but triple- (or more) clicks aren't available so easily. However, we can make do with a bit of FRP. Let's start with a really basic layout, including a text span that the user should click. The code is given here:

```
<html>
  <head>
    <title>Multiple click example</title>
    <script type="text/javascript" src="rxjs.umd.js"></script>
  </head>
  <body>
    <span id="mySpan">Click this text many times (quickly)</span>
    <script>
      // our code goes here...
    </script>
  </body>
</html>
```

This is as plain as can be; you just get a text onscreen, urging you to multi-click it. See *Figure 11.3*:

Figure 11.3: A very plain screen, to test detecting triple-clicks

To detect these multi-clicks, we'll need some RxJS functions, so let's start with those:

```
const { fromEvent, pipe } = rxjs;
const { buffer, filter } = rxjs.operators;
```

We will use these functions soon enough. How do we detect triple- (or more) clicks? Let's go straight on to the code given here:

```
const spanClick$ = fromEvent(
  document.getElementById("mySpan"),
  "click"
);
```

```
spanClick$
  .pipe(
    buffer(spanClick$.pipe(debounceTime(250))),
    map(list => list.length),
    filter(x => x >= 3)
  )
  .subscribe(e => {
    console.log(`${e} clicks at ${new Date()}`);
  });

/*
  4 clicks at Mon Nov 11 2019 20:19:29 GMT-0300 (Uruguay Standard Time)
  3 clicks at Mon Nov 11 2019 20:19:29 GMT-0300 (Uruguay Standard Time)
  4 clicks at Mon Nov 11 2019 20:19:31 GMT-0300 (Uruguay Standard Time)
*/
```

The logic is simple:

1. We create an observable with `fromEvent()` listening to mouse clicks on our span.
2. Now, a tricky point: we use `buffer()` to join together many events, which come from applying `debounceTime()` to the sequence of clicks—so all clicks that happen within an interval of 250 milliseconds will get grouped into a single array.
3. We then apply `map()` to transform each array of clicks into just its length—after all, we care about how many clicks there were, and not their specific details.
4. We finish by filtering out values under 3, so only longer sequences of clicks will be processed.
5. The subscription, in this case, just logs the clicks, but in your application, it should do something more relevant.

If you wanted, you could detect multi-clicks by hand, writing your own code; see question *11.3* in the *Questions* section. To finish, let's go with an even longer example and do some typeahead searches invoking some external API.

Providing typeahead searches

Let's do another web example: typeahead searches. The usual setup is that there is some textbox, the user types in it, and the web page queries some API to provide ways of completing the search. The important thing is when and how to do the search and trying to avoid unnecessary calls to the backend server whenever possible. A (totally basic) HTML page could be as follows, and see *Figure 11.4* later in this section:

```html
<html>
  <head>
    <title>Cities search</title>
    <script type="text/javascript" src="rxjs.umd.js"></script>
  </head>
  <body>
    Find cities:
    <input type="text" id="myText" />
    <br />
    <h4>Some cities...</h4>
    <div id="myResults"></div>
    <script>
      // typeahead code goes here...
    </script>
  </body>
</html>
```

We have a single textbox in which the user will type and an area below that in which we'll show whatever the API provides. We'll be using the GeoDB Cities API (see http://geodb-cities-api.wirefreethought.com/), which provides many search options, but we'll just use it to search for cities starting with whatever the user has typed. Just to get it out of our way, let's see the getCitiesOrNull() function, which will return a promise for search results (if something was typed in) or a promise that resolves to null (no cities, if nothing was typed in). The results of this promise will be used to fill the myResults division on the page. Let's see how this works out in code:

```
const getCitiesOrNull = text => {
  if (text) {
    const citySearchUrl =
      `http://geodb-free-service.wirefreethought.com/v1/geo/cities?` +
      `hateoasMode=false&` +
      `sort=-population&` +
      `namePrefix=${encodeURIComponent(text)}`;
    return fetch(citySearchUrl);
  } else {
    return Promise.resolve(null);
  }
};
```

The code is simple: if some text was provided, we generate the URL for the cities' search and use `fetch()` to get the API data. With this done, let's see how to generate the needed observable. We will need some RxJS functions, so first, let's have some definitions:

```
const { fromEvent, pipe } = rxjs;
const {
  debounceTime,
  distinctUntilChanged,
  filter,
  map,
  reduce,
  switchMap
} = rxjs.operators;
```

We will be using all of these functions later. Now, we can write the code to do the typeahead:

```
const textInput$ = fromEvent(
  document.getElementById("myText"),
  "input"
).pipe(
  map(e => e.target.value),
  debounceTime(200),
  filter(w => w.length === 0 || w.length > 3),
  distinctUntilChanged(),
  switchMap(w => getCitiesOrNull(w))
);
```

This requires going step by step:

1. We use the `fromEvent()` constructor to observe input events (every time the user types something) from the `myText` input field.
2. We use `map()` to get the event's target value, the complete text of the input field.
3. We use `debounceTime(200)` so the observable won't emit until the user has been 0.2 seconds (200 milliseconds) without typing—what's the use of calling the API if the user isn't done with their query?
4. We then use `filter()` to discard the input if it was only one, two, or three characters long because that's not good enough for our search. We accept empty strings (so we'll empty the results area) and strings four or more characters long.
5. Then, we use `distinctUntilChanged()` so if the search string is the same as before (the user possibly added a character but quickly backspaced, deleting it), nothing will be emitted.
6. We finally change use `switchMap()` to cancel the previous subscription to the observable and create a new one using `getCitiesOrNull()`.

How do we use this? We subscribe to the observable and when we get results, we use them to display values. A possible sample code follows:

```
textInput$.subscribe(async fetchResult => {
  domElem = document.getElementById("myResults");

  if (fetchResult !== null) {
    result = await fetchResult.json();
    domElem.innerHTML = result.data
      .map(x => `${x.city}, ${x.region}, ${x.country}`)
      .join("<br />");

  } else {
    domElem.innerHTML = "";
  }
});
```

An important point: the promise is resolved, and the final value of the sequence is hence whatever the promise produced. If the result wasn't null, we get an array of cities, and we use map() and join() to produce the (very basic!) HTML output; otherwise, we just empty the results area.

Let's try it out. If you start typing, nothing will happen while you haven't reached four characters and pause a bit; see *Figure 11.4*, as follows:

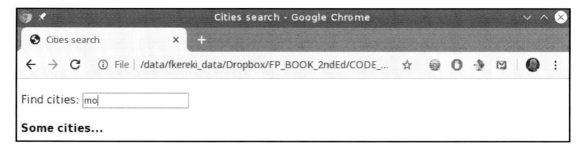

Figure 11.4: Our search for cities doesn't trigger for less than four characters

When you reach four characters and pause a bit, the observable will emit an event, and we'll do a first search: in this case, for cities with names starting with MONT. See *Figure 11.5*, as follows:

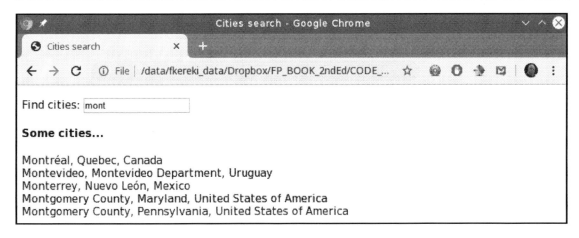

Figure 11.5: After reaching four characters, searches will be fired

Finally, as you add more characters, new API calls will be done, refining the search; see *Figure 11.6*, as follows:

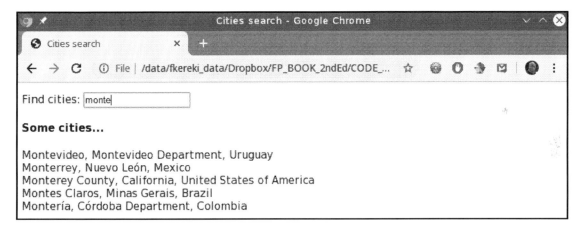

Figure 11.6: Further characters are used to refine the search

What can we learn from these examples? Using observables for events lets us achieve a good separation of concerns as to event production and event consumption, and the declarative style of the stream process makes the data flow clearer. You could even note that the HTML code itself has no reference to click methods or anything like that; the complete code is separate from that.

We have now seen most of the interesting patterns; let's finish with some other ones, which may or may not be exactly equivalent to their classic OOP partners.

Other patterns

Let's end this section by glancing at some other patterns, where the equivalence may or may not be so good:

- **Currying and Partial Application** (which we saw in Chapter 7, *Transforming Functions – Currying and Partial Application*): This can be seen as approximately equivalent to a *Factory* for functions. Given a general function, you can produce specialized cases by fixing one or more arguments, and this is, in essence, what a Factory does, of course, speaking about functions and not objects.
- **Declarative functions** (such as map() or reduce()): They can be considered an application of the *Iterator* pattern. The traversal of the container's elements is decoupled from the container itself. You might also provide different map() methods for different objects, so you could traverse all kinds of data structures.
- **Persistent data structures**: As mentioned in Chapter 10, *Ensuring Purity – Immutability*, they allow for the implementation of the *Memento* pattern. The central idea is, given an object, to be able to go back to a previous state. As we saw, each updated version of a data structure doesn't impact on the previous one(s), so you could easily add a mechanism to provide an earlier state and *roll back* to it.
- A **Chain of Responsibility** pattern: In this pattern, there is a potentially variable number of *request processors* and a stream of requests to be handled, which may be implemented using find() to determine which is the processor that will handle the request (the desired one is the first in the list that accepts the request) and then simply doing the required process.

Remember the warning at the beginning: with these patterns, the match with FP techniques may not be so perfect as with others that we have previously seen, but the idea was to show that there are some common FP patterns that can be applied, and it will produce the same results as the OOP solutions, despite having different implementations.

Now, after having seen several OOP equivalent patterns, let's move on to more specific FP ones.

Functional design patterns

After having seen several OOP design patterns, it may seem a cheat to say that there's no approved, official, or even remotely generally accepted similar list of patterns for FP. There are, however, several problems for which there are standard FP solutions, which can be considered design patterns on their own, and we have already covered most of them in this book.

What are candidates for a possible list of patterns? Let's attempt to prepare one—but remember, it's just a personal view. Also, I'll admit that I'm not trying to mimic the usual style of pattern definition; I'll just be mentioning a general problem and refer to the way FP in JS can solve it, and I won't be aiming for nice, short, memorable names for the patterns either:

- **Processing collections using filter/map/reduce**: Whenever you have to process a data collection, using declarative higher-order functions, such as `filter()`, `map()`, and `reduce()`, as we saw in this chapter and previously in Chapter 5, *Programming Declaratively – A Better Style*, is a way to remove complexity from the problem (the usual `MapReduce` web framework is an extension of this concept, which allows for distributed processing among several servers, even if the implementation and details aren't exactly the same). Instead of performing looping and processing as a single step, you should think about the problem as a sequence of steps, applied in order, doing transformations until obtaining the final, desired result.

  JS also includes *iterators*, that is, another way of looping through a collection. Using *iterators* isn't particularly functional, but you may want to look at them since they may be able to simplify some situations. Read more at https://developer.mozilla.org/en-US/docs/Web/JavaScript/Reference/Iteration_protocols.

- **Lazy evaluation with thunks**: The idea of *lazy evaluation* is not doing any calculations until they are actually needed. In some programming languages, this is built in. However, in JavaScript (and in most imperative languages as well), *eager evaluation* is applied, in which an expression is evaluated as soon as it is bound to some variable. (Another way of saying this is that JavaScript is a *strict programming language*, with a *strict paradigm*, which only allows calling a function if all of its parameters have been completely evaluated.) This sort of evaluation is required when you need to specify the order of evaluation with precision, mainly because such evaluations may have side effects.

In FP, which is rather more declarative and pure, you can delay such evaluation with *thunks* (which we used in the *Trampolines and thunks* section of Chapter 9, *Designing Functions – Recursion*) by passing a thunk that will calculate the needed value only when it's needed, but not earlier.

> You may also want to look at JavaScript *generators*, which is another way of delaying evaluation, though not particularly related to FP at all. Read more about them at https://developer.mozilla.org/en-US/docs/Web/JavaScript/Reference/Global_Objects/Generator. The combination of generators and promises is called an async function, which may be of interest to you; refer to https://developer.mozilla.org/en-US/docs/Web/JavaScript/Reference/Statements/async_function.

- **Persistent data structures for immutability**: Having immutable data structures, as we saw in Chapter 10, *Ensuring Purity – Immutability*, is mandatory when working with certain frameworks, and in general, it is recommended because it helps to reason about a program or debugging it. (Earlier in this chapter, we also mentioned how the *Memento* OOP pattern can be implemented in this fashion). Whenever you have to represent structured data, the FP solution of using a persistent data structure helps in many ways.

- **Wrapped values for checks and operations**: If you directly work with variables or data structures, you may modify them at will (possibly violating any restrictions) or you may need to do many checks before using them (such as verifying that a value is not null before trying to access the corresponding object). The idea of this pattern is to wrap a value within an object or function, so direct manipulation won't be possible, and checks can be managed more functionally. We'll be referring to more of this in Chapter 12, *Building Better Containers – Functional Data Types*.

As we have said, the power of FP is such that, instead of having a couple of dozen standard design patterns (and that's only in the GoF book; if you read other texts, the list grows!), there isn't yet a standard or acknowledged list of functional patterns.

Summary

In this chapter, we have made a bridge from the OO way of thinking and the usual patterns that we use when coding that way, to the FP style, by showing how we can solve the same basic problems (but rather more easily) than with classes and objects. We have seen several common design patterns, and we've seen that the same concepts apply in FP, even if implementations may vary, so now you have a way to apply those well-known solution structures to your JavaScript coding.

In Chapter 12, *Building Better Containers – Functional Data Types*, we will be working with a *potpourri* of functional programming concepts, which will give you even more ideas about tools you can use. I promised that this book wouldn't become deeply theoretical, but rather more practical, and we'll try to keep it this way, even if some of the presented concepts may seem abstruse or remote.

Questions

11.1. Decorating methods, the future way: In Chapter 6, *Producing Functions – Higher-Order Functions*, we wrote a decorator to enable logging for any function. Currently, method decorators are being considered for upcoming versions of JavaScript: refer to https://tc39.github.io/proposal-decorators/ for that (Draft 2 means that inclusion of this feature in the standard is likely, although there may be some additions or small changes). Study the following draft and take a look at what makes the next code tick:

```
const logging = (target, name, descriptor) => {
  const savedMethod = descriptor.value;
  descriptor.value = function(...args) {
    console.log(`entering ${name}: ${args}`);
    try {
      const valueToReturn = savedMethod.bind(this)(...args);
      console.log(`exiting ${name}: ${valueToReturn}`);
      return valueToReturn;
    } catch (thrownError) {
      console.log(`exiting ${name}: threw ${thrownError}`);
      throw thrownError;
    }
  };
  return descriptor;
};
```

A working example would be as follows:

```
class SumThree {
  constructor(z) {
    this.z = z;
  }
  @logging
  sum(x, y) {
    return x + y + this.z;
  }
}

new SumThree(100).sum(20, 8);
// entering sum: 20,8
// exiting sum: 128
```

Following are some questions about the code for the `logging()` decorator:

- Do you see the need for the `savedMethod` variable?
- Why do we use `function()` when assigning a new `descriptor.value`, instead of an arrow function?
- Can you understand why `.bind()` is used?
- What is `descriptor`?

11.2. **Decorator with mixins**: Back in the *Questions* section of `Chapter 1`, *Becoming Functional – Several Questions*, we saw that classes are first-class objects. Taking advantage of this, complete the following `addBar()` function, which will add some mixins to the `Foo` class so that the code will run as shown. The created `fooBar` object should have two attributes (`fooValue` and `barValue`) and two methods (`doSomething()` and `doSomethingElse()`) that simply show some text and properties, as shown here:

```
class Foo {
  constructor(fooValue) {
    this.fooValue = fooValue;
  }
  doSomething() {
    console.log("something: foo... ", this.fooValue);
  }
}

var addBar = BaseClass =>
  /*
    your code goes here
  */
  ;
```

```
var fooBar = new (addBar(Foo))(22, 9);
fooBar.doSomething(); // something: foo... 22
fooBar.somethingElse(); // something else: bar... 9
console.log(Object.keys(fooBar)); // ["fooValue", "barValue"]
```

Could you include a third mixin, `addBazAndQux()`, so
that `addBazAndQux(addBar(Foo))` would add even more attributes and methods to `Foo`?

11.3. **Multi-clicking by hand**: Can you write your own multi-click detection code, which should work exactly as our example?

12
Building Better Containers - Functional Data Types

In Chapter 11, *Implementing Design Patterns – The Functional Way*, we went over how to use functions to achieve different results. In this chapter, we will look at data types from a functional point of view. We'll be considering how we can implement our own data types, along with several features that can help us compose operations or ensure their purity so that our FP coding will become simpler and shorter.

We'll be touching on several themes:

- **Data types** from a functional point of view. Even though JavaScript is not a typed language, a better understanding of types and functions is needed.
- **Containers**, including *functors* and the mystifying *monads*, to structure data flow.
- **Functions as structures**, in which we'll see yet another way of using functions to represent data types, with immutability thrown in as an extra.

With that, let's get started!

Specifying data types

Even though JavaScript is a dynamic language, without static or explicit typing declarations and controls, it doesn't mean that you can simply ignore types. Even if the language doesn't allow you to specify the types of your variables or functions, you still work—even if only in your head—with types. Now, let's learn how we can specify types. When it comes to specifying types, we have some advantages, as follows:

- Even if you don't have compile-time data type checking, there are several tools, such as Facebook's *flow* static type checker or Microsoft's *TypeScript* language, that let you deal with it.

- It will help if you plan to move on from JavaScript to a more functional language such as *Elm*.

- It serves as documentation that lets future developers understand what type of arguments they have to pass to the function and what type it will return. All the functions in the Ramda library are documented in this way.

- It will also help with the functional data structures later in this section, where we will examine a way of dealing with structures, similar in some aspects to what you do in fully functional languages such as Haskell.

 If you want to learn more about the tools that I cited, visit `https://flow.org/` for Flow, `https://www.typescriptlang.org/` for TypeScript, and `http://elm-lang.org/` for Elm. If you want to know more about type checks, the corresponding web pages are `https://flow.org/en/docs/types/functions/`, `https://www.typescriptlang.org/docs/handbook/functions.html`, and `https://flow.org/en/docs/types/functions/`.

Whenever you read or work with a function, you will have to reason about types, think about the possible operations on this or that variable or attribute, and so on. Having type declarations will help. Due to this, we will start considering how we can define the types of functions and their parameters. After that, we will consider other type definitions.

Signatures for functions

The specification of a function's arguments and the result is given by a *signature*. Type signatures are based on a *type system* called **Hindley-Milner**, which influenced several (mostly functional) languages, including Haskell, though the notation has changed from that of the original paper. This system can even deduce types that are not directly given; tools such as TypeScript or Flow also do this, so developers don't need to specify *all* types. Instead of going for a dry, formal explanation about the rules for writing correct signatures, let's work by examples. We only need to know the following:

- We will be writing the type declaration as a comment.
- The function name is written first, and then : :, which can be read as *is of type* or *has type*.
- Optional constraints may follow, with a double (*fat*) arrow ⇒ (or => in basic ASCII fashion, if you cannot key in the arrow) afterward.
- The input type of the function follows, with a → (or ->, depending on your keyboard).
- The result type of the function comes last.

Note that instead of this vanilla JavaScript style, Flow and TypeScript have their own syntax for specifying type signatures.

Now, we can begin with some examples. Let's define the type for a simple function that just capitalizes a word and do the same for the `Math.random` function:

```
// firstToUpper :: String → String
const firstToUpper = s => s[0].toUpperCase() + s.substr(1).toLowerCase();

// Math.random :: () → Number
```

These are simple cases—only take the signatures into account here; we are not interested in the actual functions. The first function receives a string as an argument and returns a new string. The second one receives no arguments (the empty parentheses show this) and returns a floating-point number. The arrows denote functions. So, we can read the first signature as `firstToUpper` *is a function of the type that receives a string and returns a string* and we can speak similarly about the maligned (impurity-wise) `Math.random()` function, with the only difference being that it doesn't receive arguments.

We've already looked at functions with zero or one parameter, but what about functions with more than one? There are two answers to this. If we are working in a strict functional style, we would always be doing currying (as we saw in `Chapter 7`, *Transforming Functions – Currying and Partial Application*), so all the functions would be unary. The other solution is enclosing a list of argument types in parentheses. We can see both of these solutions in the following code:

```
// sum3C :: Number → Number → Number → Number
const sum3C = curry((a, b, c) => a + b + c);

// sum3 :: (Number, Number, Number) → Number
const sum3 = (a, b, c) => a + b + c;
```

Remember that `sum3c` is actually `a => b => c => a + b + c`; this explains the first signature, which can also be read as follows:

```
// sum3C :: Number → (Number → (Number → (Number)))
```

After you provide the first argument to the function, you are left with a new function, which also expects an argument, and returns a third function, which, when given an argument, will produce the final result. We won't be using parentheses because we'll always assume this grouping from right to left.

Now, what about higher-order functions, which receive functions as arguments? The `map()` function poses a problem: it works with arrays of any type. Also, the mapping function can produce any type of result. For these cases, we can specify *generic types*, which are identified by lowercase letters: these generic types can stand for any possible type. For arrays themselves, we use brackets. So, we would have the following:

```
// map :: [a] → (a → b) → [b]
const map = curry((arr, fn) => arr.map(fn));
```

It's perfectly valid to have a and b represent the same type, as in a mapping that's applied to an array of numbers, which produces another array of numbers. The point is that, in principle, a and b may stand for different types, and that's what we described previously. Also, note that if we weren't currying, the signature would have been `([a], (a → b)) → [b]`, showing a function that receives two arguments (an array of elements of type a and a function that maps from type a to type b) and produces an array of elements of type b as the result. Given this, we can write the following in a similar fashion:

```
// filter :: [a] → (a → Boolean) → [a]
const filter = curry((arr, fn) => arr.filter(fn));
```

And now the big one: what's the signature for `reduce()`? Be sure to read it carefully and see if you can work out why it's written that way. You may prefer thinking about the second part of the signature as if it were `((b, a) → b)`:

```
// reduce :: [a] → (b → a → b) → b → b
const reduce = curry((arr, fn, acc) => arr.reduce(fn, acc));
```

Finally, if you are defining a method instead of a function, you use a squiggly arrow such as `~>`:

```
// String.repeat :: String ⤳ Number → String
```

So far, we have defined data types for functions, but we aren't done with this subject just yet. Let's consider some other cases.

Other data type options

What else are we missing? Let's look at some other options that you might use. *Product types* are a set of values that are always together and are commonly used with objects. For tuples (that is, an array with a fixed number of elements of (probably) different types), we can write something like the following:

```
// getWeekAndDay :: String → (Number × String)
const getWeekAndDay = yyyy_mm_dd =>
```

```
/* ... */
return [weekNumber, dayOfWeekName];
```

For objects, we can go with a definition very similar to what JavaScript already uses. Let's imagine we have a `getPerson()` function that receives an ID and returns an object with data about a person:

```
// getPerson :: Number → { id:Number × name:String }
const getPerson = personId =>
  /* ... */
  return { id:personId, name:personName }
```

Sum types (also known as *union types*) are defined as a list of possible values. For example, our `getField()` function from Chapter 6, *Producing Functions – Higher-Order Functions*, either returns the value of an attribute or it returns undefined. For this, we can write the following signature:

```
// getField :: String → attr → a | undefined
const getField = attr => obj => obj[attr];
```

We could also define a type (union or otherwise) and use it in further definitions. For instance, the data types that can be directly compared and sorted are numbers, strings, and Booleans, so we could write the following definitions:

```
// Sortable :: Number | String | Boolean
```

Afterward, we could specify that a comparison function can be defined in terms of the `Sortable` type, but be careful: there's a hidden problem here!

```
// compareFunction :: (Sortable, Sortable) → Number
```

Actually, this definition isn't very precise because you can compare any type, even if it doesn't make much sense. However, bear with me for the sake of this example!

If you want to refresh your memory about sorting and comparison functions, see `https://developer.mozilla.org/en/docs/Web/JavaScript/Reference/Global_Objects/Array/sort`.

The previous definition would allow us to write a function that received, say, a number and a Boolean: it doesn't say that both types should be the same. However, there's a way out. If you have constraints for some data types, you can express them before the actual signature, using a *fat* arrow, as shown in the following code:

```
// compareFunction :: Sortable a ⇒ (a, a) → Number
```

Now, the definition is correct because all occurrences of the same type (denoted by the same letter, in this case, a) must be exactly the same. An alternative, but one that requires much more typing, would have been writing all three possibilities with a union:

```
// compareFunction ::
//    ((Number, Number) | (String, String) | (Boolean, Boolean)) → Number
```

So far, we have been using the standard type definitions. However, when we work with JavaScript, we have to consider some other possibilities, such as functions with optional parameters, or even with an undetermined number of parameters. We can use . . . to stand for any number of arguments and add ? to represent an optional type, as follows:

```
// unary :: ((b, ...) → a) → (b → a)
const unary = fn => (...args) => fn(args[0]);
```

The unary() higher-order function that we defined in the same chapter we cited previously took any function as a parameter and returned a unary function as its result. We can show that the original function can receive any number of arguments but that the result used only the first of them. The data type definition for this would be as follows:

```
// parseInt :: (String, Number?) -> Number
```

The standard parseInt() function provides an example of optional arguments: though it's highly recommended that you don't omit the second parameter (the base radix), you can, in fact, skip it.

Check out https://github.com/fantasyland/fantasy-land/ and https://sanctuary.js.org/#types for a more formal definition and description of types, as applied to JavaScript.

From now on, throughout this chapter, we will be adding signatures to methods and functions. This will not only be so that you can get accustomed to them but because, when we start delving into more complex containers, it will help you understand what we are dealing with: some cases can be hard to understand!

Building containers

Back in Chapter 5, *Programming Declaratively – A Better Style*, and later, in Chapter 8, *Connecting Functions – Pipelining and Composition*, we saw that the ability to be able to apply a mapping to all the elements of an array—and, even better, being able to chain a sequence of similar operations—was a good way to produce better, more understandable code.

However, there is a problem: the `map()` method (or the equivalent, *demethodized* one, which we looked at in `Chapter 6`, *Producing Functions – Higher-Order Functions*), is only available for arrays, and we might want to be able to apply mappings and chaining to other data types. So, what can we do?

Let's consider different ways of doing this, which will give us several new tools for better functional coding. Basically, there are only two possible ways of solving this: we can either add new methods to existing types (though that will be limited because we can only apply that to basic JavaScript types) or we can wrap types in some type of container, which will allow mapping and chaining.

Let's start by extending current types before moving on to using wrappers, which will lead us into the deep functional territory, with entities such as functors and monads.

Extending current data types

If we want to add mapping to basic JavaScript data types, we need to start by considering our options:

- With `null`, `undefined`, and `Symbol`, applying maps doesn't sound too interesting.
- With the `Boolean`, `Number`, and `String` data types, we have some interesting possibilities, so we can examine some of those.
- Applying mapping to an object would be trivial: we just have to add a `map()` method, which must return a new object.
- Finally, despite not being basic data types, we could also consider special cases, such as dates or functions, to which we could also add `map()` methods.

 As in the rest of this book, we are sticking to plain JavaScript, but you should look into libraries such as Lodash, Underscore, or Ramda, which already provide functionalities similar to the ones we are developing here.

A key point to consider in all these mapping operations should be that the returned value is of exactly the same type as the original one: when we use `Array.map()`, the result is also an array, and similar considerations must apply to any other `map()` method implementations (you could observe that the resulting array may have different element types to the original one, but it is still an array).

What could we do with a Boolean? First, let's accept that Booleans are not containers, so they don't really behave in the same way as an array: trivially, a Boolean can only have a Boolean value, while an array may contain any type of element. However, accepting that difference, we can extend `Boolean.prototype` (though, as I've already mentioned, that's not usually recommended) by adding a new `map()` method to it and making sure that whatever the mapping function returns is turned into a new Boolean value. For the latter, the solution will be similar to the following:

```
// Boolean.map :: Boolean ⤳ (Boolean → a) → Boolean
Boolean.prototype.map = function(fn) {
  return !!fn(this);
};
```

The `!!` operator forces the result to be a Boolean: `Boolean(fn(this))` could also have been used. This kind of solution can also be applied to numbers and strings, as shown in the following code:

```
// Number.map :: Number ⤳ (Number → a) → Number
Number.prototype.map = function(fn) {
  return Number(fn(this));
};
```

```
// String.map :: String ⤳ (String → a) → String
String.prototype.map = function(fn) {
  return String(fn(this));
};
```

As with Boolean values, we are forcing the results of the mapping operations to the correct data types.

Finally, if we wanted to apply mappings to a function, what would that mean? Mapping a function should produce a function. The logical interpretation for `f.map(g)` would be applying `f()`, and then applying `g()` to the result. So, `f.map(g)` should be the same as writing `x => g(f(x))` or, equivalently, `pipe(f,g)`. The definition is more complex than it was for the previous examples, so study it carefully:

```
// Function.map :: (a → b) ⤳ (b → c) → (a → c)
Function.prototype.map = function(fn) {
  return (...args) => fn(this(...args));
};
```

Verifying that this works is simple, and the following code is an easy example of how to do this. The `by10()` mapping function is applied to the result of calculating `plus1(3)`, so the result is 40:

```
const plus1 = x => x + 1;
const by10 = y => 10 * y;

console.log(plus1.map(by10)(3));
// 40: first add 1 to 3, then multiply by 10
```

With this, we are done talking about what we can achieve with basic JavaScript types, but we need a more general solution if we want to apply this to other data types. We'd like to be able to apply mapping to any kind of values, and for that, we'll need to create a container. We'll do this in the next section.

Containers and functors

What we did in the previous section does work and can be used with no problems. However, we would like to consider a more general solution that we can apply to any data type. Since not all things in JavaScript provide the desired `map()` method, we will have to either extend the type (as we did in the previous section) or apply a design pattern that we considered in Chapter 11, *Implementing Design Patterns – The Functional Way*: wrapping our data types with a wrapper that will provide the required `map()` operations.

In particular, we will do the following:

- Start by seeing how to build a basic container, wrapping a value
- Convert the container into something more powerful—a functor
- Study how to deal with missing values using a special functor, `Maybe`

Wrapping a value – a basic container

Let's pause for a minute and consider what we need from this wrapper. There are two basic requirements:

- We must have a `map()` method.
- We need a simple way to wrap a value.

To get started, let's create a basic container. Any object containing just a value would do, but we want some additions, so our object won't be that trivial; we'll explain the differences after the code:

```
const VALUE = Symbol("Value");

class Container {
  constructor(x) {
    this[VALUE] = x;
  }

  map(fn) {
    return fn(this[VALUE]);
  }
}
```

Some basic considerations that we need to keep in mind are as follows:

- We want to be able to store some value in a container, so the constructor takes care of that.
- Using a `Symbol` helps hide the field: the property key won't show up in `Object.keys()` or in `for...in` or `for...of` loops, making them more meddle-proof.
- We need to be able to `map()`, so a method is provided for that.

 If you haven't worked with JavaScript symbols, possibly the least known of its primitive data types, you might want to check out `https://developer.mozilla.org/en-US/docs/Glossary/symbol`.

Our basic barebones container is ready, but we can also add some other methods for convenience, as follows:

- To get the value of a container, we could use `map(x => x)`, but that won't work with more complex containers, so we'll add a `valueOf()` method to get the contained value.
- Being able to list a container can certainly help with debugging. The `toString()` method will come in handy for this.
- Because we don't need to write `new Container()` all the time, we can add a static `of()` method to do the same job.

Working with classes to represent containers (and later, functors and monads) when living in a functional programming world may seem like heresy or sin... but remember that we don't want to be dogmatic, and `class` and `extends` simplify our coding. Similarly, it could be argued that you must never take a value out of the container—but using a `valueOf()` method is sometimes too handy, so we won't be that restrictive.

By taking all of this into account, our container is as follows:

```
class Container {
  //
  // everything as above
  //

  static of(x) {
    return new Container(x);
  }

  toString() {
    return `${this.constructor.name}(${this[VALUE]})`;
  }

  valueOf() {
    return this[VALUE];
  }
}
```

Now, we can use this container to store a value, and we can use `map()` to apply any function to that value, but this isn't very different from what we could do with a variable! Let's enhance this a bit.

Enhancing our container – functors

We want to have wrapped values, so what exactly should return the `map()` method? If we want to be able to chain operations, then the only logical answer is that it should return a new wrapped object. In true functional style, when we apply a mapping to a wrapped value, the result will be another wrapped value that we can keep working on.

 Instead of `map()`, this operation is sometimes called `fmap()`, standing for *functorial map*. The rationale for the name change was to avoid expanding the meaning of `map()`. However, since we are working in a language that supports reusing the name, we can keep it.

We can extend our `Container` class to implement this change and get ourselves an enhanced container: a *functor*. The `of()` and `map()` methods will require a small change. For this, we'll be creating a new class, as shown in the following code:

```
class Functor extends Container {
  static of(x) {
    return new Functor(x);
  }

  map(fn) {
    return Functor.of(fn(this[VALUE]));
  }
}
```

Here, the `of()` method produces a `Functor` object, and so does the `map()` method. With these changes, we have just defined what a `Functor` is in category theory! (Or, if you want to get really technical, a *Pointed Functor* because of the `of()` method – but let's keep it simple.) We won't go into the theoretical details, but roughly speaking, a functor is some kind of container that allows us to apply `map()` to its contents, producing a new container of the same type, and if this sounds familiar, it's because you already know a functor: arrays! When you apply `map()` to an array, the result is a new array containing transformed (mapped) values.

There are more requirements for functors. First, the contained values may be polymorphic (of any type), just like arrays. Second, a function must exist whose mapping produces the same contained value—`x => x` does this for us. Finally, applying two consecutive mappings must produce the same result as applying their composition. This means that `container.map(f).map(g)` must be the same as `container.map(compose(g,f))`.

Let's pause for a moment and consider the signatures for our function and methods:

```
of :: Functor f ⇒ a → f a

Functor.toString :: Functor f ⇒ f a ⤳ String

Functor.valueOf :: Functor f ⇒ f a ⤳ a

Functor.map :: Functor f ⇒ f a ⤳ (a → b) → f a → f b
```

The first function, `of()`, is the simplest: given a value of any type, it produces a `Functor` of that type. The next two are also rather simple to understand: given a `Functor`, `toString()` always returns a string (no surprise there!) and if the functor-contained value is of a given type, `valueOf()` produces a result of that same type. The third one, `map()`, is more interesting. Given a function that takes an argument of type a and produces a result of type b, applying it to a functor that contains a value of type *a* produces a functor containing a value of type b—this is exactly what we described previously.

As is, functors are not allowed or expected to produce side effects, throw exceptions, or exhibit any other behavior outside of producing a containered result. Their main usage is to provide us with a way to manipulate a value, apply operations to it, compose results, and so on, without changing the original—in this sense, we are once again coming back to immutability.

 You could also compare functors to promises, at least in one aspect. With functors, instead of acting on its value directly, you have to apply a function with `map()`. In promises, you do exactly the same, but using `then()` instead! In fact, there are more analogies, as we'll be seeing soon.

However, you could well say that this isn't enough since, in normal programming, it's quite usual to have to deal with exceptions, undefined or null values, and so on. So, let's start by looking at more examples of functors. After that, we'll enter the realm of monads so that we can look at even more sophisticated kinds of processing. Let's experiment a bit!

Dealing with missing values with Maybe

A common problem in programming is dealing with missing values. There are many possible causes for this situation: a web service Ajax call may have returned an empty result, a dataset could be empty, an optional attribute might be missing from an object, and so on. Dealing with this kind of situation, in a normal imperative fashion, requires adding `if` statements or ternary operators everywhere to catch the possible missing value in order to avoid a certain runtime error. We can do a bit better by implementing a `Maybe` functor to represent a value that may (or may *not*) be present! We will use two classes, `Just` (as in *just some value*) and `Nothing`, both of which are functors themselves. The `Nothing` functor is particularly simple, with trivial methods:

```
class Nothing extends Functor {
  isNothing() {
    return true;
  }

  toString() {
```

```
            return "Nothing()";
        }

    map(fn) {
        return this;
    }
}
```

The isNothing() method returns true, toString() returns a constant text, and map() always returns itself, no matter what function it's given. Moving forward, the Just functor is also a basic one, with the added isNothing() method (which always returns true, since a Just object isn't a Nothing), and a map() method that now returns a Maybe:

```
class Just extends Functor {
    isNothing() {
        return false;
    }

    map(fn) {
        return Maybe.of(fn(this[VALUE]));
    }
}
```

Finally, our Maybe class packs the logic that's needed to construct either a Nothing or a Just. If it receives an undefined or null value, a Nothing will be constructed, and in other cases, a Just will be the result. The of() method has exactly the same behavior:

```
class Maybe extends Functor {
    constructor(x) {
        return x === undefined || x === null
            ? new Nothing()
            : new Just(x);
    }

    static of(x) {
        return new Maybe(x);
    }
}
```

We can quickly verify that this works by trying to apply an operation to either a valid value or a missing one. Let's look at two examples of this:

```
const plus1 = x => x + 1;

Maybe.of(2209).map(plus1).map(plus1).toString(); // "Just(2211)"

Maybe.of(null).map(plus1).map(plus1).toString(); // "Nothing()"
```

When we applied `plus1()` to `Maybe.of(2209)`, everything worked fine, and we ended up with a `Just(2011)` value. On the other hand, when we applied the same sequence of operations to a `Maybe.of(null)` value, the end result was a `Nothing`, but there were no errors, even if we tried to do math with a null value. A `Maybe` functor can deal with mapping a missing value by just skipping the operation and returning a wrapped `null` value instead. This means that this functor is including an abstracted check, which won't let an error happen.

Later in this chapter, we'll see that `Maybe` can actually be a monad instead of a functor, and we'll also examine more examples of monads.

Let's look at a more realistic example of its usage.

Dealing with varying API results

Suppose we are writing a small server-side service in Node to get the alerts for a city and produce a not-very-fashionable HTML `<table>` with them, supposedly to be part of some server side-produced web page. (Yes, I know you should try to avoid tables in your pages, but what I want here is a short example of HTML generation, and actual results aren't really important.) If we used the *Dark Sky* API (see `https://darksky.net/` for more on this API and how to register with it) to get the alarms, our code would be something like this; all quite normal. Note the callback in case of an error; you'll see why in the following code:

```
const request = require("superagent");

const getAlerts = (lat, long, callback) => {
  const SERVER = "https://api.darksky.net/forecast";
  const UNITS = "units=si";
  const EXCLUSIONS = "exclude=minutely,hourly,daily,flags";
  const API_KEY = "you.need.to.get.your.own.api.key";
  request
    .get(`${SERVER}/${API_KEY}/${lat},${long}?${UNITS}&${EXCLUSIONS}`)
    .end(function(err, res) {
      if (err) {
        callback({});
      } else {
        callback(JSON.parse(res.text));
      }
    });
};
```

The (heavily edited and reduced in size) output of such a call might be something like this:

```
{
  latitude: 29.76,
  longitude: -95.37,
  timezone: "America/Chicago",
  offset: -5,
  currently: {
    time: 1503660334,
    summary: "Drizzle",
    icon: "rain",
    temperature: 24.97,
    .
    .
    .
    uvIndex: 0
  },
  alerts: [
    {
      title: "Tropical Storm Warning",
      regions: ["Harris"],
      severity: "warning",
      time: 1503653400,
      expires: 1503682200,
      description:
        "TROPICAL STORM WARNING REMAINS IN EFFECT... WIND - LATEST LOCAL
FORECAST: Below tropical storm force wind ... CURRENT THREAT TO LIFE AND
PROPERTY: Moderate ... Locations could realize roofs peeled off buildings,
chimneys toppled, mobile homes pushed off foundations or overturned ...",
        uri:
"https://alerts.weather.gov/cap/wwacapget.php?x=TX125862DD4F88.TropicalStor
mWarning.125862DE8808TX.HGXTCVHGX.73ee697556fc6f3af7649812391a38b3"
    },
    .
    .
    .
    {
      title: "Hurricane Local Statement",
      regions: ["Austin", ... , "Wharton"],
      severity: "advisory",
      time: 1503748800,
      expires: 1503683100,
      description:
        "This product covers Southeast Texas **HURRICANE HARVEY DANGEROUSLY
APPROACHING THE TEXAS COAST** ... The next local statement will be issued
by the National Weather Service in Houston/Galveston TX around 1030 AM CDT,
or sooner if conditions warrant.\n",
        uri: "https://alerts.weather.gov/cap/wwacapget.php?..."
```

```
      }
    ]
  };
```

I got this information for Houston, TX, US, on a day when Hurricane Harvey was approaching the state. If you called the API on a normal day, the data would simply exclude the `alerts: [...]` part. Here, we can use a `Maybe` functor to process the received data without any problems, with or without any alerts:

```
const getField = attr => obj => obj[attr];
const os = require("os");

const produceAlertsTable = weatherObj =>
  Maybe.of(weatherObj)
    .map(getField("alerts"))
    .map(a =>
      a.map(
        x =>
          `<tr><td>${x.title}</td>` +
          `<td>${x.description.substr(0, 500)}...</td></tr>`
      )
    )
    .map(a => a.join(os.EOL))
    .map(s => `<table>${s}</table>`);

getAlerts(29.76, -95.37, x =>
  console.log(produceAlertsTable(x).valueOf())
);
```

Of course, you would probably do something more interesting than just logging the value of the contained result of `produceAlertsTable()`! The most likely option would be to `map()` again with a function that would output the table, send it to a client, or do whatever you needed to do. In any case, the resulting output would look something like this:

```
<table><tr><td>Tropical Storm Warning</td><td>...TROPICAL STORM WARNING
REMAINS IN EFFECT... ...STORM SURGE WATCH REMAINS IN EFFECT... * WIND -
LATEST LOCAL FORECAST: Below tropical storm force wind - Peak Wind
Forecast: 25-35 mph with gusts to 45 mph - CURRENT THREAT TO LIFE AND
PROPERTY: Moderate - The wind threat has remained nearly steady from the
previous assessment. - Emergency plans should include a reasonable threat
for strong tropical storm force wind of 58 to 73 mph. - To be safe,
earnestly prepare for the potential of significant...</td></tr>
<tr><td>Flash Flood Watch</td><td>...FLASH FLOOD WATCH REMAINS IN EFFECT
THROUGH MONDAY MORNING... The Flash Flood Watch continues for * Portions of
Southeast Texas...including the following
counties...Austin...Brazoria...Brazos...Burleson...
Chambers...Colorado...Fort Bend...Galveston...Grimes...
```

```
Harris...Jackson...Liberty...Matagorda...Montgomery...Waller... Washington
and Wharton. * Through Monday morning * Rainfall from Harvey will cause
devastating and life threatening flooding as a prolonged heavy rain and
flash flood thre...</td></tr>
<tr><td>Hurricane Local Statement</td><td>This product covers Southeast
Texas **PREPARATIONS FOR HARVEY SHOULD BE RUSHED TO COMPLETION THIS
MORNING** NEW INFORMATION --------------- * CHANGES TO WATCHES AND
WARNINGS: - None * CURRENT WATCHES AND WARNINGS: - A Tropical Storm Warning
and Storm Surge Watch are in effect for Chambers and Harris - A Tropical
Storm Warning is in effect for Austin, Colorado, Fort Bend, Liberty,
Waller, and Wharton - A Storm Surge Warning and Hurricane Warning are in
effect for Jackson and Matagorda - A Storm S...</td></tr></table>
```

The output of the preceding code can be seen in the following screenshot:

Tropical Storm Warning	...TROPICAL STORM WARNING REMAINS IN EFFECT... ...STORM SURGE WATCH REMAINS IN EFFECT... * WIND - LATEST LOCAL FORECAST: Below tropical storm force wind - Peak Wind Forecast: 25-35 mph with gusts to 45 mph - CURRENT THREAT TO LIFE AND PROPERTY: Moderate - The wind threat has remained nearly steady from the previous assessment. - Emergency plans should include a reasonable threat for strong tropical storm force wind of 58 to 73 mph. - To be safe, earnestly prepare for the potential of significant...
Flash Flood Watch	...FLASH FLOOD WATCH REMAINS IN EFFECT THROUGH MONDAY MORNING... The Flash Flood Watch continues for * Portions of Southeast Texas...including the following counties...Austin...Brazoria...Brazos...Burleson... Chambers...Colorado...Fort Bend...Galveston...Grimes... Harris...Jackson...Liberty...Matagorda...Montgomery...Waller... Washington and Wharton. * Through Monday morning * Rainfall from Harvey will cause devastating and life threatening flooding as a prolonged heavy rain and flash flood thre...
Hurricane Local Statement	This product covers Southeast Texas **PREPARATIONS FOR HARVEY SHOULD BE RUSHED TO COMPLETION THIS MORNING** NEW INFORMATION --------------- * CHANGES TO WATCHES AND WARNINGS: - None * CURRENT WATCHES AND WARNINGS: - A Tropical Storm Warning and Storm Surge Watch are in effect for Chambers and Harris - A Tropical Storm Warning is in effect for Austin, Colorado, Fort Bend, Liberty, Waller, and Wharton - A Storm Surge Warning and Hurricane Warning are in effect for Jackson and Matagorda - A Storm S...

Figure 12.1: The output table is not much to look at, but the logic that produced it didn't require a single if statement

If we had called `getAlerts(-34.9, -54.60, ...)` with the coordinates for Montevideo, Uruguay, instead, since there were no alerts for that city, the `getField("alerts")` function would have returned `undefined`—and since that value is recognized by the `Maybe` functor, and even though all the following `map()` operations would still be executed, no one would actually do anything, and a `null` value would be the final result.

We took advantage of this behavior when we coded the error logic. If an error occurs when calling the service, we would still call the original callback to produce a table but provide an empty object. Even if this result is unexpected, we would be safe because the same guards would avoid causing a runtime error.

As a final enhancement, we can add an `orElse()` method to provide a default value when no one is present. The added method will return the default value if `Maybe` is a `Nothing`, or the `Maybe` value itself otherwise:

```
class Maybe extends Functor {
  //
  // everything as before...
  //
  orElse(v) {
    return this.isNothing() ? v : this.valueOf();
  }
}
```

Using this new method instead of `valueOf()`, if you're trying to get the alerts for someplace without them, would just get whatever default value you wanted. In the case we mentioned previously when we attempted to get the alerts for Montevideo, instead of a `null` value, we would get the following appropriate result:

```
getAlerts(-34.9, -54.6, x =>
  console.log(
    produceAlertsTable(x).orElse("<span>No alerts today.</span>")
  )
);
```

With this, we have looked at an example of dealing with different situations when working with an API. Let's quickly revisit another topic from the previous chapter and look at a better implementation of Prisms.

Implementing Prisms

The more common implementations of Prisms (which we first met in the *Prisms* section of `Chapter 10`, *Ensuring Purity – Immutability*) we came across was that instead of returning either some value or `undefined` and leaving it up to the caller to check what happened, we could opt to return a `Maybe`, which already provides us with easy ways to deal with missing values. In our new implementation (which we'll look at soon), our example from the aforementioned chapter would look like this:

```
const author = {
  user: "fkereki",
  name: {
    first: "Federico",
    middle: "",
    last: "Kereki"
  },
  books: [
```

```
        { name: "GWT", year: 2010 },
        { name: "FP", year: 2017 },
        { name: "CB", year: 2018 }
    ]
};
```

If we wanted to access the `author.user` attribute, the result would be different:

```
const pUser = prismProp("user");

console.log(review(pUser, author).toString());

/*
    Just("fkereki")
*/
```

Similarly, if we asked for a non-existant `pseudonym` attribute, instead of `undefined` (as in our previous version of Prisms), we would get a `Nothing`:

```
const pPseudonym = prismProp("pseudonym");

console.log(review(pPseudonym, author).toString());

/*
    Nothing()
*/
```

So, this new version of Prisms is better to work with if you are already used to dealing with `Maybe` values. What do we need to implement this? We need just a single change; our `Constant` class now needs to return a `Maybe` instead of a value, so we'll have a new `ConstantP` (P for Prism) class:

```
class ConstantP {
  constructor(v) {
    this.value = Maybe.of(v);
    this.map = () => this;
  }
}
```

We will have to rewrite `preview()` to use the new class, and that finishes the change:

```
const preview = curry(
  (prismAttr, obj) => prismAttr(x => new ConstantP(x))(obj).value
);
```

So, getting Prisms to work with Maybes wasn't that hard, and now we have a consistent way of dealing with possibly missing attributes. Working in this fashion, we can simplify our coding and avoid many tests for nulls and other similar situations. However, we may want to go beyond this; for instance, we may want to know *why* there were no alerts: was it a service error? Or just a normal situation? Just getting a `null` at the end isn't enough, and in order to work with these new requirements, we will need to add some extra functionality to our functors (as we'll see in the next section) and enter the domain of *monads*.

Monads

Monads have weird fame among programmers. Well-known developer Douglas Crockford has famously spoken of a curse, maintaining that *Once you happen to finally understand monads, you immediately lose the ability to explain them to other people!* On a different note, if you decide to go to the basics and read *Categories for the Working Mathematician* by *Saunders Mac Lane* (one of the creators of category theory), you may find a somewhat disconcerting explanation – which is not too illuminating!

> *"A monad in X is just a monoid in the category of endofunctors of X, with product ×
> replaced by composition of endofunctors and unit set by the identity endofunctor."*

The difference between monads and functors is that the former adds some extra functionality; we'll see what functionality they add soon. Let's start by looking at the new requirements before moving on and considering some common, useful monads. As with functors, we will have a basic monad, which you could consider to be an *abstract* version, and specific *monadic types*, which are *concrete* implementations, geared to solve specific cases.

 If you want to read a precise and careful description of functors, monads, and their family (but leaning heavily to the theoretical side, with plenty of algebraic definitions to go around), you can try the *Fantasy Land Specification* at https://github.com/fantasyland/fantasy-land/. Don't say we didn't warn you: the alternative name for that page is *Algebraic JavaScript Specification!*

Adding operations

Let's consider a simple problem. Suppose you have the following pair of functions, working with `Maybe` functors: the first function tries to search for *something* (say, a client or a product) given its key, and the second attempts to extract *some* attribute from it (I'm being purposefully vague because the problem does not have anything to do with whatever objects or things we may be working with). Both functions produce `Maybe` results to avoid possible errors. We are using a mocked search function, just to help us see the problem: for even keys, it returns fake data, and for odd keys, it throws an exception. The code for this search is very simple:

```
const fakeSearchForSomething = key => {
  if (key % 2 === 0) {
    return {key, some: "whatever", other: "more data"};

  } else {
    throw new Error("Not found");
  }
};
```

Using this search, our `findSomething()` function will try to do a search, return a `Maybe.of()` for a successful call, or a `Maybe.of(null)` (in other terms, a `Nothing`) in case of an error:

```
const findSomething = key => {
  try {
    const something = fakeSearchForSomething(key);
    return Maybe.of(something);
  } catch (e) {
    return Maybe.of(null);
  }
};
```

With this, we could think of writing these two functions to do some searching, but not everything would be fine; can you see what the problem is here?

```
const getSome = something => Maybe.of(something.map(getField("some")));

const getSomeFromSomething = key => getSome(findSomething(key));
```

The problem in this sequence is that the output from `getSome()` is a `Maybe` value, which itself contains a `Maybe` value, so the result we want is double wrapped, as we can see by executing a couple of calls, for an even number (which will return a `"whatever"`) and for an odd number (which will be an error), as follows:

```
let xxx = getSomeFromSomething(2222).valueOf().valueOf(); // "whatever"

let yyy = getSomeFromSomething(9999).valueOf().valueOf(); // null
```

This problem can be easily solved in this toy problem if we just avoid using `Maybe.of()` in `getSome()`, but this kind of result can happen in many more complex ways. For instance, you could be building a `Maybe` out of an object, one of whose attributes happened to be a `Maybe`, and you'd get the same situation when accessing that attribute: you would end up with a double wrapped value.

Now, we are going to look into monads. Monads should provide the following operations:

- A constructor.
- A function that inserts a value into a monad: our `of()` method.
- A function that allows us to chain operations: our `map()` method.
- A function that can remove extra wrappers: we will call it `unwrap()`. It will solve our preceding multiple wrapper problems. Sometimes, this function is called `flatten()`.

We will also have a function to chain calls, just to simplify our coding, and another function to apply functions, but we'll get to those later. Let's see what a monad looks like in actual JavaScript code. Data type specifications are very much like those for functors, so we won't repeat them here:

```
class Monad extends Functor {
  static of(x) {
    return new Monad(x);
  }

  map(fn) {
    return Monad.of(fn(this[VALUE]));
  }

  unwrap() {
    const myValue = this[VALUE];
    return myValue instanceof Container ? myValue.unwrap() : this;
  }
}
```

We use recursion to successively remove wrappers until the wrapped value isn't a container anymore. Using this method, we could avoid double wrapping easily, and we could rewrite our previous troublesome function like this:

```
const getSomeFromSomething = key => getSome(findSomething(key)).unwrap();
```

However, this sort of problem could reoccur at different levels. For example, if we were doing a series of map() operations, any of the intermediate results may end up being double wrapped. You could easily solve this by remembering to call unwrap() after each map()—note that you could do this even if it is not actually needed since the result of unwrap() would be the very same object (can you see why?). But we can do better! Let's define a chain() operation (sometimes named flatMap() instead, which is a bit confusing since we already have another meaning for that; see Chapter 5, *Programming Declaratively – A Better Style*, for more on this) that will do both things for us:

```
class Monad extends Functor {
  //
  // everything as before...
  //
  chain(fn) {
    return this.map(fn).unwrap();
  }
}
```

There's only one operation left. Suppose you have a curried function with two parameters; nothing outlandish! What would happen if you were to provide that function to a map() operation?

```
const add = x => y => x+y; // or curry((x,y) => x+y)

const something = Monad.of(2).map(add);
```

What would something be? Given that we have only provided one argument to add, the result of that application will be a function—not just any function, though, but a *wrapped* one! (Since functions are first-class objects, there's no logical obstacle to wrapping a function in a Monad, is there?) What would we want to do with such a function? To be able to apply this wrapped function to a value, we'll need a new method: ap(). What could its value be? In this case, it could either be a plain number, or a number wrapped in a Monad as a result of other operations. Since we can always Map.of() a plain number into a wrapped one, let's have ap() work with a monad as its parameter; the new method would be as follows:

```
class Monad extends Functor {
  //
```

```
// everything as earlier...
//
ap(m) {
  return m.map(this.valueOf());
}
}
```

With this, you could then do the following:

```
const monad5 = something.ap(Monad.of(3)); // Monad(5)
```

You can use monads to hold values or functions and to interact with other monads and chaining operations as you wish. So, as you can see, there's no big trick to monads, which are just functors with some extra methods. Now, let's look at how we can apply them to our original problem and handle errors in a better way.

Handling alternatives – the Either monad

Knowing that a value was missing may be enough in some cases, but in others, you'll want to be able to provide an explanation. We can get such an explanation if we use a different functor, which will take one of two possible values: one associated with a problem, error, or failure, and another associated with normal execution, or success:

- A *left* value, which should be null, but if present then it represents some kind of special value (for example, an error message or a thrown exception) that cannot be mapped over
- A *right* value, which represents the *normal* value of the functor and can be mapped over

We can construct this monad in a similar way to what we did for Maybe (actually, the added operations make it better for Maybe to extend Monad as well). The constructor will receive a left and a right value: if the left value is present, it will become the value of the Either monad; otherwise, the right value will be used. Since we have been providing of() methods for all our functors, we need one for Either too. The Left monad is very similar to our previous Nothing:

```
class Left extends Monad {
  isLeft() {
    return true;
  }
  map(fn) {
    return this;
  }
}
```

Similarly, `Right` resembles our previous `Just`:

```
class Right extends Monad {
  isLeft() {
    return false;
  }

  map(fn) {
    return Either.of(null, fn(this[VALUE]));
  }
}
```

And with these two monads under our belt, we can write our `Either` monad. It shouldn't be a surprise that this resembles our previous Maybe, should it?

```
class Either extends Monad {
  constructor(left, right) {
    return right === undefined || right === null
      ? new Left(left)
      : new Right(right);
  }

  static of(left, right) {
    return new Either(left, right);
  }
}
```

The `map()` method is key. If this functor has got a *left* value, it won't be processed any further; in other cases, the mapping will be applied to the *right* value, and the result will be wrapped. Now, how can we enhance our code with this? The key idea is for every involved method to return an `Either` monad; `chain()` will be used to execute operations one after another. Getting the alerts would be the first step—we invoke the callback either with an `AJAX FAILURE` message or with the result from the API call, as follows:

```
const getAlerts2 = (lat, long, callback) => {
  const SERVER = "https://api.darksky.net/forecast";
  const UNITS = "units=si";
  const EXCLUSIONS = "exclude=minutely,hourly,daily,flags";
  const API_KEY = "you.have.to.get.your.own.key";

  request
    .get(`${SERVER}/${API_KEY}/${lat},${long}?${UNITS}&${EXCLUSIONS}`)
    .end((err, res) =>
      callback(
        err
          ? Either.of("AJAX FAILURE", null)
          : Either.of(null, JSON.parse(res.text))
```

```
        )
      );
};
```

Then, the general process would be as follows. We use an `Either` again: if there are no alerts, instead of an array, we would return a `NO ALERTS` message:

```
const produceAlertsTable2 = weatherObj => {
  return weatherObj
    .chain(obj => {
      const alerts = getField("alerts")(obj);
      return alerts
        ? Either.of(null, alerts)
        : Either.of("NO ALERTS", null);
    })

    .chain(a =>
      a.map(
        x =>
          `<tr><td>${x.title}</td>` +
          `<td>${x.description.substr(0, 500)}...</td></tr>`
        )
      )

    .chain(a => a.join(os.EOL))

    .chain(s => `<table>${s}</table>`);
};
```

Note how we used `chain()` so that multiple wrappers would be no problem. Now, we can test multiple situations and get appropriate results—or at least, for the current weather situation around the world!

- For Houston, TX, we still get an HTML table.
- For Montevideo, UY, we get a text saying there were no alerts.
- For a point with wrong coordinates, we learn that the AJAX call failed: nice!

```
// Houston, TX, US:
getAlerts2(29.76, -95.37, x =>
console.log(produceAlertsTable2(x).toString()));
Right("...a table with alerts: lots of HTML code...");

// Montevideo, UY
getAlerts2(-34.9, -54.6, x =>
console.log(produceAlertsTable2(x).toString()));
Left("NO ALERTS");
```

```
// A point with wrong coordinates
getAlerts2(444, 555, x => console.log(produceAlertsTable2(x).toString()));
Left("AJAX FAILURE");
```

We are not done with the `Either` monad. It's likely that much of your code will involve calling functions. Let's look at a better way of achieving this by using a variant of this monad.

Calling a function – the Try monad

If we are calling functions that may throw exceptions and we want to do so in a functional way, we could use the `Try` monad to encapsulate the function result or the exception. The idea is basically the same as the `Either` monad: the only difference is in the constructor, which receives a function and calls it:

- If there are no problems, the returned value becomes the right value for the monad.
- If there's an exception, it will become the left value.

This can be seen in the following code:

```
class Try extends Either {
  constructor(fn, msg) {
    try {
      return Either.of(null, fn());
    } catch (e) {
      return Either.of(msg || e, null);
    }
  }

  static of(fn, msg) {
    return new Try(fn, msg);
  }
}
```

Now, we can invoke any function, catching exceptions in a good way. For example, the `getField()` function that we have been using would crash if it were called with a null argument:

```
// getField :: String → attr → a | undefined
const getField = attr => obj => obj[attr];
```

In the *Implementing Prisms* section of `Chapter 10`, *Ensuring Purity – Immutability*, we wrote a `getFieldP()` function that could deal with null values, but here, we will rewrite it using the `Try` monad, so, in addition, it will play nice with other composed functions. The alternative implementation of our getter would be as follows:

```
const getField2 = attr => obj => Try.of(() => obj[attr], "NULL OBJECT");
```

We can check that this works by trying to apply our new function to a `null` value:

```
const x = getField2("somefield")(null);

console.log(x.isLeft()); // true

console.log(x.toString()); // Left(NULL OBJECT)
```

There are many more monads and, of course, you can even define your own, so we couldn't possibly go over all of them. However, let's visit just one more—one that you have been using already, without being aware of its *monad-ness*!

Unexpected monads – promises

Let's finish this section on monads by mentioning yet another one that you may have used, though under a different name: *Promises*! Previously, we mentioned that functors (and, remember, monads are functors) had at least something in common with promises: using a method in order to access the value. However, the analogy is greater than that!

- `Promise.resolve()` corresponds with `Monad.of()`—if you pass a value to `.resolve()`, you'll get a promise resolved to that value, and if you provide a promise, you will get a new promise, the value of which will be that of the original one (see `https://developer.mozilla.org/en-US/docs/Web/JavaScript/Reference/Global_Objects/Promise/resolve` for more on this). This is an *unwrapping* behavior!
- `Promise.then()` stands for `Monad.map()` as well as `Monad.chain()`, given the mentioned unwrapping.
- We don't have a direct match to `Monad.ap()`, but we could add something like the following code:

```
Promise.prototype.ap = function(promise2) {
  return this.then(x => promise2.map(x));
};
```

Even if you opt for the modern `async` and `await` features, internally, they are based on promises. Furthermore, in some situations, you may still need `Promise.race()` and `Promise.all()`, so it's likely you will keep using promises, even if you opt for full ES8 coding.

This is an appropriate ending for this section. Earlier, you found out that common arrays were, in fact, functors. Now, in the same way that *Monsieur Jourdain* (a character in Molière's play *Le Bourgeois Gentilhomme*, *The Burgeois Gentleman*) discovered that all his life he had been speaking in prose, you now know you had already been using monads, without even knowing it! So far, we have learned how to build different types of containers. Now, let's learn how functions can also make do as containers, as well as for all kinds of data structures!

Functions as data structures

So far, we have learned how to use functions to work with or transform other functions to process data structures or to create data types. Now, we'll finish this chapter by showing you how a function can actually implement a data type by itself, becoming a sort of container of its own. In fact, this is a basic theoretical point of the lambda calculus (and if you want to learn more, look up *Church Encoding* and *Scott Encoding*), so we may very well say that we have come back to where we began this book, at the origins of FP! We will start with a detour that considers binary trees in a different functional language, Haskell, and then move on to implementing trees as functions, but in JavaScript; this experience will help you work out how to deal with other data structures.

Binary trees in Haskell

Consider a binary tree. Such a tree may either be empty or consist of a node (the tree *root*) with two sons: a *left* binary tree and a *right* one. A node that has no sons is called a *leaf*.

In `Chapter 9`, *Designing Functions – Recursion*, we worked with more general tree structures, such as a filesystem or the browser DOM itself, which allow a node to have any number of sons. In the case of the trees we are working with in this section, each node always has two sons, although each of them may be empty. The difference may seem minor, but allowing for empty subtrees is what lets you define that all nodes are binary.

Let's make a digression with the Haskell language. In it, we might write something like the following; *a* would be the type of whatever value we hold in the nodes:

```
data Tree a = Nil | Node a (Tree a) (Tree a)
```

In the Haskell language, *pattern matching* is often used for coding. For example, we could define an empty function as follows:

```
empty :: Tree a -> Bool
empty Nil = True
empty (Node root left right) = False
```

What does this mean? Apart from the data type definition, the logic is simple: if the tree is Nil (the first possibility in the definition of the type), then the tree is certainly empty; otherwise, the tree isn't empty. The last line would probably be written as empty _ = False while using _ as a placeholder, because you don't actually care about the components of the tree; the mere fact that it's not Nil suffices.

Searching for a value in a binary search tree (in which the root is greater than all the values of its left subtree and less than all the values of its right subtree) would be written in a similar fashion, as follows:

```
contains :: (Ord a) => (Tree a) -> a -> Bool
contains Nil _ = False
contains (Node root left right) x
         | x == root = True
         | x  < root = contains left x
         | x  > root = contains right x
```

What patterns are matched here? We have four patterns now, which must be considered in order:

- An empty tree (Nil—it doesn't matter what we are looking for, so just write _) doesn't contain the searched value.
- If the tree isn't empty, and the root matches the searched value (x), we are done.
- If the root doesn't match and is greater than the searched value, the answer is found while searching in the left subtree.
- Otherwise, the answer is found by searching in the right subtree.

There's an important point to remember: for this data type, which is a union of two possible types, we have to provide two conditions, and pattern matching will be used to decide which one is going to be applied. Keep this in mind!

Functions as binary trees

Can we do something similar with functions? The answer is yes: we will represent a tree (or any other structure) with a function itself—not with a data structure that is processed by a set of functions, nor with an object with some methods, but by just a function. Furthermore, we will get a functional data structure that's 100% immutable, which, if updated, produces a new copy of itself. We will do all this without using objects; here, closures will provide the desired results.

How can this work? We shall be applying similar concepts to the ones we looked at earlier in this chapter, so the function will act as a container and it will produce, as its result, a mapping of its contained values. Let's walk backward and start by looking at how we'll use the new data type. Then, we'll go to the implementation details.

Creating a tree can be done by using two functions: `EmptyTree()` and `Tree(value, leftTree, rightTree)`. For example, let's say we wish to create a tree similar to the one shown in the following diagram:

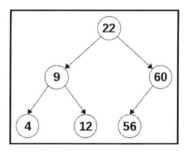

Figure 12.2: A binary search tree, created by the following code

We can create this using the following code:

```
const myTree = Tree(
  22,
  Tree(
    9,
    Tree(4, EmptyTree(), EmptyTree()),
    Tree(12, EmptyTree(), EmptyTree())
  ),
  Tree(
    60,
    Tree(56, EmptyTree(), EmptyTree()),
    EmptyTree()
  )
);
```

How do you work with this structure? According to the data type description, whenever you work with a tree, you must consider two cases: a non-empty tree or an empty one. In the preceding code, `myTree()` is actually a function that receives two functions as arguments, one for each of the two data type cases. The first function will be called with the node value and left and right trees as arguments, while the second function will receive none. So, to get the root, we could write something similar to the following:

```
const myRoot = myTree((value, left, right) => value, () => null);
```

If we were dealing with a non-empty tree, we would expect the first function to be called and produce the value of the root as the result. With an empty tree, the second function should be called, and then a `null` value would be returned.

Similarly, if we wanted to count how many nodes there are in a tree, we would write the following:

```
const treeCount = aTree => aTree(
  (value, left, right) => 1 + treeCount(left) + treeCount(right),
  () => 0
);

console.log(treeCount(myTree));
```

For non-empty trees, the first function would return 1 (for the root), plus the node count from both the root's subtrees. For empty trees, the count is simply 0. Get the idea?

Now, we can show the `Tree()` and `EmptyTree()` functions. They are as follows:

```
const Tree = (value, left, right) => (destructure, __) =>
  destructure(value, left, right);

const EmptyTree = () => (__, destructure) => destructure();
```

The `destructure()` function is what you will pass as an argument (the name comes from the destructuring statement in JavaScript, which lets you separate an object attribute into distinct variables). You will have to provide two versions of this function. If the tree is non-empty, the first function will be executed; for an empty tree, the second one will be run (this mimics the *case* selection in the Haskell code, except we are placing the non-empty tree case first and the empty tree last). The __ variable is used as a placeholder that stands for an otherwise ignored argument but shows that two arguments are assumed.

This can be hard to understand, so let's look at some more examples. If we need to access specific elements of a tree, we have the following three functions, one of which (`treeRoot()`) we've already looked at—let's repeat it here for completeness:

```
const treeRoot = tree => tree((value, left, right) => value, () => null);

const treeLeft = tree => tree((value, left, right) => left, () => null);

const treeRight = tree => tree((value, left, right) => right, () => null);
```

 Functions that access the component values of structures (or *constructions*, to use another term) are called **projector functions**. We won't be using this term, but you may find it being used elsewhere.

How can we decide if a tree is empty? See if you can figure out why the following short line of code works:

```
const treeIsEmpty = tree -> tree(() => false, () => true);
```

Let's go over a few more examples of this. For example, we can build an object out of a tree, and that would help with debugging. I added logic to avoid including left or right empty subtrees, so the produced object would be more compact; check out the two `if` statements in the following code:

```
const treeToObject = tree =>
  tree(
    (value, left, right) => {
      const leftBranch = treeToObject(left);
      const rightBranch = treeToObject(right);
      const result = { value };

      if (leftBranch) {
        result.left = leftBranch;
      }

      if (rightBranch) {
        result.right = rightBranch;
      }

      return result;
    },
    () => null
  );
```

Note the usage of recursion, as in the *Traversing a tree structure* section of Chapter 9, *Designing Functions – Recursion,* in order to produce the object equivalents of the left and right subtrees. An example of this function is as follows; I edited the output to make it clearer:

```
console.log(treeToObject(myTree));
/*
{
  value: 22,
  left: {
    value: 9,
    left: {
      value: 4
    },
    right: {
      value: 12
    }
  },
  right: {
    value: 60,
    left: {
      value: 56
    }
  }
}
*/
```

Can we search for a node? Of course, and the logic follows the definition we saw in the previous section closely. (We could have shortened the code a bit, but I wanted to parallel the Haskell version.) Our treeSearch() function could be as follows:

```
const treeSearch = (findValue, tree) =>
  tree(
    (value, left, right) =>
      findValue === value
        ? true
        : findValue < value
        ? treeSearch(findValue, left)
        : treeSearch(findValue, right),
    () => false
  );
```

To round off this section, let's also look at how to add new nodes to a tree. Study the code carefully; you'll notice how the current tree isn't modified and that a new one is produced instead. Of course, given that we are using functions to represent our tree data type, it should be obvious that we wouldn't have been able to just modify the old structure: it's immutable by default. The tree insertion function would be as follows:

```
const treeInsert = (newValue, tree) =>
  tree(
    (value, left, right) =>
      newValue <= value
        ? Tree(value, treeInsert(newValue, left), right)
        : Tree(value, left, treeInsert(newValue, right)),
    () => Tree(newValue, EmptyTree(), EmptyTree())
  );
```

When trying to insert a new key, if it's less than or equal to the root of the tree, we produce a new tree that has the current root as its own root, maintains the old right subtree, but changes its left subtree to incorporate the new value (which will be done in a recursive way). If the key was greater than the root, the changes wouldn't have been symmetrical; they would have been analogous. If we try to insert a new key and we find ourselves with an empty tree, we just replace that empty structure with a new tree where the new value is its root and it has empty left and right subtrees.

We can test out this logic easily, but the simplest way is to verify that the binary tree that we showed earlier (*Figure 12.2*) is generated by the following sequence of operations:

```
let myTree = EmptyTree();
myTree = treeInsert(22, myTree);
myTree = treeInsert(9, myTree);
myTree = treeInsert(60, myTree);
myTree = treeInsert(12, myTree);
myTree = treeInsert(4, myTree);
myTree = treeInsert(56, myTree);

// The resulting tree is:
{
  value: 22,
  left: { value: 9, left: { value: 4 }, right: { value: 12 } },
  right: { value: 60, left: { value: 56 } }
};
```

We could make this insertion function even more general by providing the comparator function that would be used to compare values. In this fashion, we could easily adapt a binary tree to represent a generic map. The value of a node would actually be an object such as `{key:... , data:...}` and the provided function would compare `newValue.key` and `value.key` to decide where to add the new node. Of course, if the two keys were equal, we would change the root of the current tree. The new tree insertion code would be as follows:

```
const compare = (obj1, obj2) =>
  obj1.key === obj2.key ? 0 : obj1.key < obj2.key ? -1 : 1;

const treeInsert2 = (comparator, newValue, tree) =>
  tree(
    (value, left, right) =>
      comparator(newValue, value) === 0
        ? Tree(newValue, left, right)
        : comparator(newValue, value) < 0
        ? Tree(value, treeInsert2(comparator, newValue, left), right)
        : Tree(value, left, treeInsert2(comparator, newValue, right)),
    () => Tree(newValue, EmptyTree(), EmptyTree())
  );
```

What else do we need? Of course, we can program diverse functions: deleting a node, counting nodes, determining a tree's height, comparing two trees, and so on. However, in order to gain more usability, we should really turn the structure into a functor by implementing a `map()` function. Fortunately, using recursion, this proves to be easy—we apply the mapping function to the tree root and use `map()` recursively on the left and right subtrees, as follows:

```
const treeMap = (fn, tree) =>
  tree(
    (value, left, right) =>
      Tree(fn(value), treeMap(fn, left), treeMap(fn, right)),
    () => EmptyTree()
  );
```

We could go on with more examples, but that wouldn't change the important conclusions we can derive from this work:

- We are handling a data structure (a recursive one, at that) and representing it with a function.
- We aren't using any external variables or objects for the data: closures are used instead.

- The data structure itself satisfies all the requirements we analyzed in Chapter 10, *Ensuring Purity – Immutability*, insofar that it is immutable and all the changes always produce new structures.
- The tree is a functor, providing all the corresponding advantages.

In this section, we have looked at one more application of functional programming, as well as how a function can actually become a structure by itself, which isn't what we are usually accustomed to!

Summary

In this chapter, we looked at the theory of data types and learned how to use and implement them from a functional point of view. We started with how to define function signatures to help us understand the transformations that are implied by the multiple operations we looked at later. Then, we went on to define several containers, including functors and monads, and saw how they can be used to enhance function composition. Finally, we learned how functions can be directly used by themselves, with no extra baggage, to implement functional data structures to simplify dealing with errors.

In this book, we have looked at several features of functional programming for JavaScript. We started out with some definitions, and a practical example, and then moved on to important considerations such as pure functions, side effects avoidance, immutability, testability, building new functions out of other ones, and implementing a data flow based upon function connections and data containers. We have looked at a lot of concepts, but I'm confident that you'll be able to put them to practice and start writing even higher-quality code – give it a try, and thank you very much for reading my book!

Questions

12.1. **Maybe tasks?** In the *Questions* section of Chapter 8, *Connecting Functions – Pipelining and Composition*, a question (8.2) had to do with getting the pending tasks for a person while taking errors or border situations into account, such as the possibility that the selected person might not even exist. Redo that exercise but using Maybe or Either monads to simplify that code.

12.2. **Extending your trees**: To get a more complete implementation of our functional binary search trees, implement the following functions:

- Calculate the tree's height or, equivalently, the maximum distance from the root to any other node
- List all the tree's keys, in ascending order
- Delete a key from a tree

12.3. **Functional lists**: In the same spirit as binary trees, implement functional lists. Since a list is defined to be either empty or a node (head), followed by another list (tail), you might want to start with the following:

```
const List = (head, tail) => (destructure, __) =>
destructure(head, tail);
const EmptyList = () => (__, destructure) => destructure();
```

Here are some easy one-line operations to get you started:

```
const listHead = list => list((head, __) => head, () => null);
const listTail = list => list((__, tail) => tail, () => null);
const listIsEmpty = list => (() => false, () => true);
const listSize = list => list((head, tail) => 1 + listSize(tail),
() => 0);
```

You could consider having these operations:

- Transforming a list into an array and vice versa
- Reversing a list
- Appending one list to the end of another list
- Concatenating two lists

Don't forget the listMap() function! Also, the listReduce() and listFilter() functions will come in handy.

12.4. **Code shortening**: We mentioned that the treeSearch() function could be shortened—can you do that? Yes, this is more of a JavaScript problem than a functional one, and I'm not saying that shorter code is necessarily better, but many programmers act as if it were, so it's good to be aware of such a style if only because you're likely to find it.

Bibliography

The following texts are freely available online:

- *ECMA-262: ECMAScript 2019 Language Specification*, latest edition (currently the 10th) at `http://www.ecma-international.org/ecma-262/`. This provides the official standard to the current version of JS.
- *ELOQUENT JAVASCRIPT, third Edition*, by *Marijn Haverbeke*, at `http://eloquentjavascript.net/`.
- *EXPLORING ES6*, by *Dr. Axel Rauschmayer*, at `http://exploringjs.com/es6/`.
- *Exploring ES2016 AND ES2017*, by *Dr. Axel Rauschmayer*, at `http://exploringjs.com/es2016-es2017/`.
- *Exploring ES2018 AND ES2019*, by *Dr. Axel Rauschmayer*, at `http://exploringjs.com/es2018-es2019/`. This text will let you get up to date with the latest features in JS.
- *Functional-Light JavaScript*, by *Kyle Simpson*, at `https://github.com/getify/Functional-Light-JS`.
- *JavaScript Allongé*, by *Reginald Braithwaite*, at `https://leanpub.com/javascript-allonge/read`.
- *Professor Frisby's Mostly Adequate Guide to Functional Programming*, by *Dr Boolean* (*Brian Lonsdorf*), at `https://github.com/MostlyAdequate/mostly-adequate-guide`

If you prefer printed books, you can go with this list:

- *Beginning Functional JavaScript, Anto Aravinth*, Apress, 2017
- *Discover Functional JavaScript, Cristian Salcescu*, (independently published) 2019
- *Functional JavaScript, Michael Fogus*, O'Reilly Media, 2013
- Functional Programming in JavaScript, *Dan Mantyla*, Packt Publishing, 2015
- Functional Programming in JavaScript, *Luis Atencio*, Manning Publications, 2016
- *Hands-on Functional Programming with TypeScript, Remo Jansen*, Packt Publishing, 2019
- *Introduction to Functional Programming, Richard Bird & Philip Wadler*, Prentice Hall International, 1988. A more theoretical point of view, not dealing specifically with JavaScript.
- *Pro JavaScript Design Patterns, Ross Harmes & Dustin Díaz*, Apress, 2008

- *Secrets of the JavaScript Ninja, John Resig & Bear Bibeault*, Manning Publications, 2012

Also interesting, though with a lesser focus on Functional Programming:

- *High-Performance JavaScript, Nicholas Zakas*, O'Reilly Media, 2010
- *JavaScript Patterns, Stoyan Stefanov*, O'Reilly Media, 2010
- *JavaScript: The Good Parts, Douglas Crockford*, O'Reilly Media, 2008
- *JavaScript with Promises, Daniel Parker*, O'Reilly Media, 2015
- *Learning JavaScript Design Patterns, Addy Osmani*, O'Reilly Media, 2012
- *Mastering JavaScript Design Patterns*, 2nd Edition, *Simon Timms*, Packt Publishing, 2016
- *Mastering JavaScript High Performance, Chad Adams*, Packt Publishing, 2015
- *Pro JavaScript Performance, Tom Barker*, Apress, 2012

On the subject of Reactive Functional Programming:

- *Mastering Reactive JavaScript, Erich de Souza Oliveira*, Packt Publishing, 2017
- *Reactive Programming with Node.js, Fernando Doglio*, Apress, 2016
- *Reactive Programming with RxJS, Sergi Mansilla*, The Pragmatic Programmers, 2015

Answers to Questions

Here are the solutions (partial, or worked out in full) to the questions that were contained within the chapters in this book. In many cases, there are extra questions so that you can do further work if you choose to.

Chapter 1, Becoming Functional – Several Questions

1.1. Classes as first-class objects: As you may recall, a class is basically a function that can be used with `new`. Therefore, it stands to reason that we should be able to pass classes as parameters to other functions. `makeSaluteClass()` creates a class (that is, a special function) that uses a closure to remember the value of `term`. We'll be looking at more examples like this throughout this book.

1.2. Factorial errors: The key to avoiding repeating tests is to write a function that will check the value of the argument to ensure it's valid, and if so call an inner function to do the factorial itself, without worrying about erroneous arguments:

```
const carefulFact = n => {
  if (
    typeof n !== "undefined" &&
    Number(n) === n &&
    n >= 0 &&
    n === Math.floor(n)
  ) {
    const innerFact = n => (n === 0 ? 1 : n * innerFact(n - 1));
    return innerFact(n);
  }
};

console.log(carefulFact(3)); // 6, correct
console.log(carefulFact(3.1)); // undefined
console.log(carefulFact(-3)); // undefined
console.log(carefulFact(-3.1)); // undefined
console.log(carefulFact("3")); // undefined
console.log(carefulFact(false)); // undefined
console.log(carefulFact([])); // undefined
console.log(carefulFact({})); // undefined
```

You could throw an error when an incorrect argument is recognized, but here, I just ignored it and let the function return `undefined`.

1.3. **Climbing factorial**: The following code does the trick. We add an auxiliary variable, f, and we make it *climb* from 1 to n. We must be careful so that `factUp(0)  ===  1`:

```
const factUp = (n, f = 1) => (n <= f ? f : f * factUp(n, f + 1));
```

1.4. **Code squeezing**: Using arrow functions, as suggested, as well as the prefix ++ operator (for more information, see `https://developer.mozilla.org/en-US/docs/Web/JavaScript/Reference/Operators/Arithmetic_Operators#Increment`), you can condense `newCounter()` down to the following:

```
const shorterCounter = () => {
   let count = 0;
   return () => ++count;
};
```

Using arrow functions isn't hard to understand, but be aware that many developers may have questions or doubts about using ++ as a prefix operator, so this version could prove to be harder to understand.

Chapter 2, Thinking Functionally – a First Example

2.1. **No extra variables**: We can make do by using the fn variable itself as a flag. After calling `fn()`, we set the variable to `null`. Before calling `fn()`, we check that it's not `null`:

```
const once = fn => {
   return (...args) => {
      fn && fn(...args);
      fn = null;
   };
};
```

2.2. **Alternating functions**: In a manner similar to what we did in the previous question, we call the first function and then switch functions for the next time. Here, we used a destructuring assignment to write the swap in a more compact manner. For more information, refer to `https://developer.mozilla.org/en-US/docs/Web/JavaScript/Reference/Operators/Destructuring_assignment#Swapping_variables`:

```
const alternator = (fn1, fn2) => {
   return (...args) => {
```

```
      fn1(...args);
      [fn1, fn2] = [fn2, fn1];
   };
};
```

2.3. **Everything has a limit!** We simply check whether the `limit` variable is greater than 0. If so, we decrement it by 1 and call the original function; otherwise, we do nothing:

```
const thisManyTimes = (fn, limit) => {
   return (...args) => {
      if (limit > 0) {
         limit--;
         return fn(...args);
      }
   };
};
```

Chapter 3, Starting Out with Functions – a Core Concept

3.1. **Uninitialized object?** The key is that we didn't wrap the returned object in parentheses, so JavaScript thinks the braces enclose the code to be executed. In this case, `type` is considered to be labeling a statement, which doesn't really do anything: it's an expression (`t`) that isn't used. Due to this, the code is considered valid, and since it doesn't have an explicit `return` statement, the implicit returned value is `undefined`. See `https://developer.mozilla.org/en-US/docs/Web/JavaScript/Reference/Statements/label` for more on labels, and `https://developer.mozilla.org/en-US/docs/Web/JavaScript/Reference/Functions/Arrow_functions#Returning_object_literals` for more on returning objects. The corrected code is as follows:

```
const simpleAction = t => ({
      type: t;
});
```

3.2. **Are arrows allowed?** There would be no problems with `listArguments2()`, but with `listArguments()`, you would get an error since `arguments` is not defined for arrow functions:

```
listArguments(22,9,60);
Uncaught ReferenceError: arguments is not defined
```

3.3. **One-liner**: It works! (And yes, a one-line answer is appropriate in this case!).

3.4. **Spot the bug!** Initially, many people look at the weird `(console(...)`, `window.store.set(...))` code, but the bug isn't there: because of how the comma operator works, JavaScript does the logging first, and then the setting. The real problem is that `oldSet()` is not bound to the `window.store` object, so the second line should be as follows instead:

```
const oldSet = window.store.set.bind(window.store);
```

Reread the *Working with methods* section for more on this, as well as question *11.1* for another way of doing logging, that is, with decorators.

3.5. **Bindless binding**: If `bind()` wasn't available, you could use a closure, the `that` trick (which we saw in the *Handling the this value* section), and the `apply()` method, as follows:

```
function bind(context) {
  var that = this;
  return function() {
    return that.apply(context, arguments);
  };
}
```

We could do something similar to what we did in the *Adding missing functions* section. Alternatively, just for variety, we could use a common idiom based on the `||` operator: if `Function.prototype.bind` exists, evaluation stops right there, and the existing `bind()` method is used; otherwise, our new function is applied:

```
Function.prototype.bind =
  Function.prototype.bind ||
  function(context) {
    var that = this;
    return function() {
      return that.apply(context, arguments);
    };
  };
```

Chapter 4, Behaving Properly – Pure Functions

4.1. **Minimalistic function**: It works because $fib(0)=0$ and $fib(1)=1$, so it's true that for $n<2$, $fib(n)=n$.

4.2. A cheap way: Basically, this algorithm works the same way as you'd calculate a Fibonacci number by hand. You'd start by writing down *fib*(0)=0 and *fib*(1)=1, adding them to get *fib*(2)=1, adding the last two to get *fib*(3)=2, and so on. In this version of the algorithm, a and b stand for two consecutive Fibonacci numbers. This implementation is quite efficient!

4.3. A shuffle test: Before shuffling the array, sort a copy of it, JSON.stringify() it, and save the result. After shuffling, sort a copy of the shuffled array and JSON.stringify() it as well. Finally, two JSON strings should be produced, which should be equal. This does away with all the other tests since it ensures that the array doesn't change length, nor its elements:

```
describe("shuffleTest", function() {
  it("shouldn't change the array length or its elements", () => {
    let a = [22, 9, 60, 12, 4, 56];
    let old = JSON.stringify([...a].sort());
    shuffle(a);
    let new = JSON.stringify([...a].sort());
    expect(old).toBe(new);
  });
});
```

4.4. Breaking laws: Some of the properties are no longer always valid. To simplify our examples, let's assume two numbers are close to each other if they differ by no more than 0.1. If this is the case, then we have the following:

- 0.5 is close to 0.6, and 0.6 is close to 0.7, but 0.5 is not close to 0.7.
- 0.5 is close to 0.6, and 0.7 is close to 0.8, but 0.5+0.7=1.2 is not close to 0.6+0.8=1.4; with the same numbers, 0.5*0.7=0.35 is not close to 0.6*0.8=0.48.
- 0.5 is close to 0.4, and 0.2 is close to 0.3, but 0.5-0.2=0.3 is not close to 0.4-0.3=0.1.
- 0.6 is close to 0.5, and 0.9 is close to 1.0, but 0.6/0.9=0.667 is not close to 0.5/1.0=0.5.

The other cited properties are always true.

4.5. Must return? If a pure function doesn't return anything, it means that the function doesn't do anything since it can't modify its inputs or any other side effect.

4.6. JavaScript does math? If you run the code, you'll (unexpectedly) get the Math failure? message. The problem has to do with the fact that JavaScript internally uses binary instead of decimal, and floating-point precision is limited. In decimal, 0.1, 0.2, and 0.3 have a fixed, short representation, but in binary, they have infinite representation, much like 1/3=0.33333... has in decimal.

If you write out the value of a+b after the test, you'll get 0.30000000000000004 – and that's why you must be very careful when testing for equality in JavaScript.

Chapter 5, Programming Declaratively – a Better Style

5.1. **Filtering... but what?** Boolean (x) is the same as !!x, and it turns an expression from being *truthy* or *falsy* into true or false, respectively. Thus, the .filter() operation removes all falsy elements from the array.

5.2. **Generating HTML code, with restrictions**: In real life, you wouldn't limit yourself to using only filter(), map(), and reduce(), but the objective of this question was to make you think about how to manage with only those. Using join() or other extra string functions would make the problem easier. For instance, finding out a way to add the enclosing <div><ul> ... </ul></div> tags is tricky, so we had to make the first reduce() operation produce an array so that we could keep on working on it:

```
var characters = [
  { name: "Fred", plays: "bowling" },
  { name: "Barney", plays: "chess" },
  { name: "Wilma", plays: "bridge" },
  { name: "Betty", plays: "checkers" },
  { name: "Pebbles", plays: "chess" }
];

let list = characters
  .filter(x => x.plays === "chess" || x.plays == "checkers")
  .map(x => `<li>${x.name}</li>`)
  .reduce((a, x) => [a[0] + x], [""])
  .map(x => `<div><ul>${x}</ul></div>`)
  .reduce((a, x) => x);

console.log(list);
// <div><ul><li>Barney</li><li>Betty</li><li>Pebbles</li></ul></div>
```

Accessing the array and index arguments for the map() or reduce() callbacks would also provide solutions:

```
let list2 = characters
  .filter(x => x.plays === "chess" || x.plays == "checkers")
  .map(
    (x, i, t) =>
      `${i === 0 ? "<div><ul>" : ""}` +
      `<li>${x.name}</li>` +
```

```
        `${i == t.length - 1 ? "</ul></div>" : ""}`
    )
    .reduce((a, x) => a + x, "");
```

We could also do the following:

```
let list3 = characters
    .filter(x => x.plays === "chess" || x.plays == "checkers")
    .map(x => `<li>${x.name}</li>`)
    .reduce(
        (a, x, i, t) => a + x + (i === t.length - 1 ? "</ul></div>" : ""),
        "<div><ul>"
    );
```

Study the three examples: they will help you gain insight into these higher-order functions and provide you with ideas so that you can do independent work.

5.3. **More formal testing**: Use an idea from question 4.3: select an array and a function, find the result of mapping using both the standard map() method and the new myMap() function, and compare the two JSON.stringify() results: they should match.

5.4. **Ranging far and wide**: This requires a bit of careful arithmetic, but shouldn't be much trouble. Here, we need to distinguish two cases: upward and downward ranges. The default step is 1 for the former and -1 for the latter. We used Math.sign() for this:

```
const range2 = (start, stop, step = Math.sign(stop - start)) =>
    new Array(Math.ceil((stop - start) / step))
        .fill(0)
        .map((v, i) => start + i * step);
```

A few examples of calculated ranges show the diversity in terms of the options we have:

```
console.log(range2(1, 10));       // [1, 2, 3, 4, 5, 6, 7, 8, 9]
console.log(range2(1, 10, 2));    // [1, 3, 5, 7, 9]
console.log(range2(1, 10, 3));    // [1, 4, 7]
console.log(range2(1, 10, 6));    // [1, 7]
console.log(range2(1, 10, 11));   // [1]

console.log(range2(21, 10));      // [21, 20, 19, ... 13, 12, 11]
console.log(range2(21, 10, -3));  // [21, 18, 15, 12]
console.log(range2(21, 10, -4));  // [21, 17, 13]
console.log(range2(21, 10, -7));  // [21, 14]
console.log(range2(21, 10, -12)); // [21]
```

Using this new range2() function means that you can write a greater variety of loops in a functional way, with no need for for(...) statements.

5.5. **Doing the alphabet**: The problem is that `String.fromCharCode()` is not unary. This method may receive any number of arguments, and when you write `map(String.fromCharCode)`, the callback gets called with three parameters (the current value, the index, and the array) and that causes unexpected results. Using `unary()` from the *Arity Changing* section of `Chapter 6`, *Producing Functions – Higher-Order Functions*, would also work. To find out more, go to `https://developer.mozilla.org/en-US/docs/Web/JavaScript/Reference/Global_Objects/String/fromCharCode`.

5.6. **Producing a CSV**: A first solution, along with some auxiliary functions, is as follows; can you understand what each function does?

```
const concatNumbers = (a, b) => (a == " " ? b : a + "," + b);
const concatLines = (c, d) => c + "\n" + d;
const makeCSV = t =>
  t.reduce(concatLines, " ", t.map(f => f.reduce(concatNumbers, " ")));
```

An alternative one-liner is also possible, but not as clear – do you agree?

```
const makeCSV2 = t =>
  t.reduce(
    (c, d) => c + "\n" + d,
    " ",
    t.map(x => x.reduce((a, b) => (a == " " ? b : a + "," + b), " "))
  );
```

5.7 **Producing better output**: For this, you'll have to do some extra mapping, as follows:

```
const better = apiAnswer
  .flatMap(c => c.states.map(s => ({...s, country: c.name})))
  .flatMap(s => s.cities.map(t => ({...t, state: s.name, country:
s.country})))
  .map(t => `${t.name}, ${t.state}, ${t.country}`);

/*
[ 'Lincoln, Buenos Aires, Argentine',
  'Lincoln, England, Great Britain',
  'Lincoln, California, United States of America',
  'Lincoln, Rhode Island, United States of America',
  'Lincolnia, Virginia, United States of America',
  'Lincoln Park, Michigan, United States of America',
  'Lincoln, Nebraska, United States of America',
  'Lincoln Park, Illinois, United States of America',
  'Lincoln Square, Illinois, United States of America' ]
*/
```

5.8 Old-style code only! One way of doing this is by using `join()` to build a single long string out of the individual sentences, then using `split()` to split it into words, and finally looking at the length of the resulting array:

```
const words = gettysburg.join(" ").split(" ").length;
```

5.9 Async chaining: An article by Valeri Karpov, which can be found at `https://thecodebarbarian.com/basic-functional-programming-with-async-await.html`, provides polyfills for methods such as `forEach()`, `map()`, and so on, and also develops a class for async arrays that allows chaining.

5.10 Missing equivalents: Start by using `mapAsync()` to get the async values and apply the original function to the returned array. An example for `some()` would be as follows:

```
const someAsync = (arr, fn) =>
  mapAsync(arr, fn).then(mapped => mapped.some(Boolean));

(async () => {
  const someEven = await someAsync([1, 2, 3, 4], fakeFilter);
  useResult(someEven);

  const someEven2 = await someAsync([1, 3, 5, 7, 9], fakeFilter);
  useResult(someEven2);
})();
/*
2019-10-13T22:05:32.215Z true
2019-10-13T22:05:33.257Z false
*/
```

Chapter 6, Producing Functions – Higher-Order Functions

6.1. A border case: Just applying the function to a null object will throw an error:

```
const getField = attr => obj => obj[attr];

getField("someField")(null);
// Uncaught TypeError: Cannot read property 'a' of null
```

Having functions throw exceptions isn't usually good in FP. You may opt to produce `undefined` instead, or work with monads, just like we did in the last Chapter 12, *Building Better Containers – Functional Data Types* of this book. A safe version of `getField()` is as follows:

```
const getField2 = attr => obj => (attr && obj ? obj[attr] : undefined);
```

6.2. **How many?** Let's call *calc*(*n*) the number of calls that are needed to evaluate *fib*(*n*). Analyzing the tree that shows all the needed calculations, we get the following:

- *calc*(0)=1
- *calc*(1)=1
- For *n*>1, *calc*(*n*)=1 + *calc*(*n*-1) + *calc*(*n*-2)

The last line follows from the fact that when we call *fib*(*n*), we have one call, plus calls to *fib*(*n*-1) and *fib*(*n*-2). A spreadsheet shows that *calc*(50) is 40,730,022,147 – rather high!

If you care for some algebra, it can be shown that *calc*(*n*)=5*fib*(*n*-1)+*fib*(*n*-4)-1, or that as *n* grows, *calc*(*n*) becomes approximately (1+√5)=3.236 times the value of *fib*(*n*) – but since this is not a math book, I won't even mention those results!

6.3. **A randomizing balancer**: Using our `shuffle()` function from Chapter 4, *Behaving Properly – Pure Functions*, we can write the following code. Here, we remove the first function from the list before shuffling the rest and we add it back at the end of the array to avoid repeating any calls:

```
const randomizer = (...fns) => (...args) => {
  const first = fns.shift();
  fns = shuffle(fns);
  fns.push(first);
  return fns[0](...args);
};
```

A quick verification shows it fulfills all our requirements:

```
const say1 = () => console.log(1);
const say22 = () => console.log(22);
const say333 = () => console.log(333);
const say4444 = () => console.log(4444);

const rrr = randomizer(say1, say22, say333, say4444);
rrr(); // 333
rrr(); // 4444
rrr(); // 333
rrr(); // 22
```

```
rrr(); // 333
rrr(); // 22
rrr(); // 333
rrr(); // 4444
rrr(); // 1
rrr(); // 4444
```

A small consideration: the first function in the list can never be called the first time around because of the way `randomizer()` is written. Can you provide a better version that won't have this small defect so that *all* the functions in the list will have the same chance of being called the first time?

6.4. **Just say no!** Call the original function and then use `typeof` to check whether the returned value is numeric or Boolean, before deciding what to return.

6.5. **Missing companion**: A simple one-line version could be as follows. Here, we use spreading to get a shallow copy of the original object and then set the specified attribute to its new value by using a computed property name. See `https://developer.mozilla.org/en-US/docs/Web/JavaScript/Reference/Operators/Object_initializer` for more details:

```
const setField = (attr, value, obj) => ({...obj, [attr]: value});
```

In `Chapter 10`, *Ensuring Purity – Immutability*, we wrote `deepCopy()`, which would be better than spreading when it comes to creating a totally new object instead of a shallow copy. By using this, we would have the following:

```
const setField = (attr, value, obj) => ({...deepCopy(obj), [attr]: value});
```

Finally, you could also look into modifying the `updateObject()` function, also from `Chapter 10`, *Ensuring Purity – Immutability*, by removing the freezing code; I'll leave it up to you.

6.6. **Wrong function length**: We can solve this problem by using `eval()` – which, in general, isn't such a good idea! If you persist and insist, though, we can write a `function.length` preserving version of `arity()` as follows; let's call it `arityL()`:

```
const arityL = (fn, n) => {
  const args1n = range(0, n)
    .map(i => `x${i}`)
    .join(",");
  return eval(`(${args1n}) => ${fn.name}(${args1n})`);
};
```

If you were to apply `arityL()` to `Number.parseInt`, the results would be as follows (note that the produced functions have the correct `length` property):

```
const parseInt1 = arityL(parseInt, 1);
/*
  (x0) => parseInt(x0,x1)
  parseInt1.length === 1
*/

const parseInt2 = arity(Number.parseInt,2)
/*
  (x0,x1) => parseInt(x0,x1)
  parseInt2.length === 2
*/
```

6.7. **Not reinventing the wheel**: We can use `Math.max()` and `Math.min()` as follows:

```
const findMaximum2 = findOptimum2((x, y) => Math.max(x, y));

const findMinimum2 = findOptimum2((x, y) => Math.min(x, y));
```

Another way of writing this could be achieved by defining the following first:

```
const max = (...args) => Math.max(...arr);

const min = (...args) => Math.min(...arr);
```

Then, we could write in point-free style:

```
const findMaximum3 = findOptimum2(max);

const findMinimum3 = findOptimum2(min);
```

Chapter 7, Transforming Functions – Currying and Partial Application

7.1. **Sum as you will**: The following `sumMany()` function does the job:

```
const sumMany = total => number =>
  number === undefined ? total : sumMany(total + number);

sumMany(2)(2)(9)(6)(0)(-3)(); // 16
```

7.2. **Working stylishly**: We can do currying by hand for `applyStyle()`:

```
const applyStyle = style => string => `<${style}>${string}</${style}>`;
```

7.3. **Currying by prototype**: Basically, we are just transforming the `curryByBind()` version so that it uses `this`:

```
Function.prototype.curry = function() {
  return this.length === 0 ? this() : p => this.bind(this, p).curry();
};
```

You could work in a similar fashion and provide a `partial()` method instead.

7.4. **Uncurrying the currying**: We can work in a similar fashion to what we did in `curryByEval()`:

```
const uncurryByEval = (fn, len) =>
  eval(
    `(${range(0, len)
      .map(i => `x${i}`)
      .join(",")}) => ${fn.name}${range(0, len)
      .map(i => `(x${i})`)
      .join("")}`
  );
```

Earlier, when currying, given an `fn()` function of arity 3, we would have generated the following:

```
x0=>x1=>x2=> make3(x0,x1,x2)
```

Now, to uncurry a function (say, `curriedFn()`), we want to do something very similar: the only difference is the placement of the parentheses:

```
(x0,x1,x2) => curriedFn(x0)(x1)(x2)
```

The expected behavior is as follows:

```
const make3 = (a, b, c) => String(100 * a + 10 * b + c);
const make3c = a => b => c => make3(a, b, c);
console.log(make3c(1)(2)(3));  // 123

const remake3 = uncurryByEval(make3c, 3);
console.log(remake3(4, 5, 6)); // 456
```

7.5. **Mystery questions function**: It implements partial currying; the following is an example of this:

```
const sum3 = (a, b, c) => 100 * a + 10 * b + c;
const alt3 = what(sum3);

console.log(alt3(1, 2, 4));
console.log(alt3(1, 2)(4));
```

```
console.log(alt3(1)(2, 4));
console.log(alt3(1)(2)(4));
/*
  "124", four times
*/
```

A more understandable and better-named version of the `what()` function is as follows:

```
const partial = fn => (...params) =>
  fn.length <= params.length
    ? fn(...params)
    : (...otherParams) => partial(fn)(...params, ...otherParams);
```

7.6. Yet more curry! This is just an alternative version of our `partialCurryingByBind()`. The only difference is that if you provide all the arguments to a function, this new `curry()` directly calls the curried function, while `partialCurryingByBind()` would bind the function to all its arguments first and then recursively call it to return the final result. We can check that the results are exactly the same by using the following code:

```
const make3 = (a, b, c) => String(100 * a + 10 * b + c);

const make3curried = curry(make3);

console.log(make3curried(1)(2)(3));
console.log(make3curried(4, 5)(6));
console.log(make3curried(7, 8, 9));

/*
123
456
789
*/
```

Chapter 8, Connecting Functions – Pipelining and Composition

8.1. Headline capitalization: We can make use of several functional equivalents of different methods, such as `split()`, `map()`, and `join()`. Using `demethodize()` from Chapter 6, *Producing Functions – Higher-Order Functions*, and `flipTwo()` from Chapter 7, *Transforming Functions – Currying and Partial Application*, would have also been possible:

```
const split = str => arr => arr.split(str);
const map = fn => arr => arr.map(fn);
const firstToUpper = word =>
```

```
       word[0].toUpperCase() + word.substr(1).toLowerCase();
const join = str => arr => arr.join(str);

const headline = pipeline(split(" "), map(firstToUpper), join(" "));
```

The pipeline works as expected: we split the string into words, we map each word to make its first letter uppercase, and we join the array elements to form a string again. We could have used `reduce()` for the last step, but `join()` already does what we need, so why reinvent the wheel?

```
console.log(headline("Alice's ADVENTURES in WoNdErLaNd"));
// Alice's Adventures In Wonderland
```

8.2. **Pending tasks**: The following pipeline does the job:

```
const getField = attr => obj => obj[attr];
const filter = fn => arr => arr.filter(fn);
const map = fn => arr => arr.map(fn);
const reduce = (fn, init) => arr => arr.reduce(fn, init);

const pending = (listOfTasks, name) =>
  pipeline(
    getField("byPerson"),
    filter(t => t.responsible === name),
    map(t => t.tasks),
    reduce((y, x) => x, []),
    filter(t => t && !t.done),
    map(getField("id"))
  )(allTasks || {byPerson: []}); //
```

The `reduce()` call may be mystifying. By that time, we are handling an array with a single element – an object – and we want the object in the pipeline, not the array. This code works even if the responsible person doesn't exist, or if all the tasks have been completed; can you see why? Also, note that if `allTasks` is `null`, an object must be provided with the `byPerson` property so that future functions won't crash! For an even better solution, I think monads are better: see question 12.1 for more.

8.3. **Thinking in abstract terms**: The simple solution implies composing. I preferred it to pipelining in order to keep the list of functions in the same order:

```
const getSomeResults2 = compose(sort, group, filter, select);
```

8.4 **Undetected impurity?** Yes, the function is impure, but using it as-is would fall squarely under the SFP **Sorta Functional Programming (SFP)** style we mentioned back in the *Theory versus practice* section of `Chapter 1`, *Becoming Functional – Several Questions*. The version we used is not pure, but in the way we use it, the final results are pure: we modify an array in place, but it's a new array that we are creating. The alternate implementation is pure and also works, but will be slower since it creates a completely new array every time we call it. So, accepting this bit of impurity helps us get a function that performs better; we can accept that!

8.5 **Needless transducing?** If you only had a sequence of `map()` operations, you could apply a single map and pipeline all the mapping functions into a single one. For `filter()` operations, it becomes a bit harder, but here's a tip: use `reduce()` to apply all the filters in sequence with a carefully thought out accumulating function.

Chapter 9, Designing Functions – Recursion

9.1. **Into reverse**: An empty string is reversed by simply doing nothing. To reverse a non-empty string, remove its first character, reverse the rest, and append the removed character at the end. For example, `reverse("MONTEVIDEO")` can be found by using `reverse("ONTEVIDEO")+"M"`. In the same way, `reverse("ONTEVIDEO")` would be equal to `reverse("NTEVIDEO")+"O"`, and so on:

```
const reverse = str =>
    str.length === 0 ? "" : reverse(str.slice(1)) + str[0];
```

9.2. **Climbing steps**: Suppose we want to climb a ladder with n steps. We can do this in two ways:

- Climbing one single step and then climbing an (n-1) steps ladder
- Climbing two steps at once and then climbing an (n-2) steps ladder

So, if we call *ladder(n)* the number of ways to climb an steps ladder, we know that *ladder(n)* = *ladder(n-1)* + *ladder(n-2)*. Adding the fact that *ladder(0)*=1 (there's only one way to climb a ladder with no steps: do nothing) and *ladder(1)*=1, the solution is that *ladder(n)* equals the $(n-1)^{th}$ Fibonacci number! Check it out: *ladder(2)*=2, *ladder(3)*=3, *ladder(4)*=5, and so on.

9.3. Longest common subsequence: The length of the **longest common sequence (LCS)** of two strings, *a* and *b*, can be found with recursion, as follows:

- If the length of *a* is zero, or if the length of *b* is zero, return zero.
- If the first characters of *a* and *b* match, the answer is 1 plus the LCS of *a* and *b*, both minus their initial characters.
- If the first characters of *a* and *b* do not match, the answer is the largest of the following two results:
  - The LCS of *a* minus its initial character, and *b*
  - The LCS of *a*, and *b* minus its initial character

We can implement this as follows. We do memoization "by hand" to avoid repeating calculations; we could have also used our memoization function:

```
const LCS = (strA, strB) => {
  let cache = {}; // memoization "by hand"

  const innerLCS = (strA, strB) => {
    const key = strA + "/" + strB;

    if (!(key in cache)) {
      if (strA.length === 0 || strB.length === 0) {
        ret = 0;

      } else if (strA[0] === strB[0]) {
        ret = 1 + innerLCS(strA.substr(1), strB.substr(1));

      } else {
        ret = Math.max(
          innerLCS(strA, strB.substr(1)),
          innerLCS(strA.substr(1), strB)
        );
      }

      cache[key] = ret;
    }

    return cache[key];
  };

  return innerLCS(strA, strB);
};

console.log(LCS("INTERNATIONAL", "CONTRACTOR")); // 6, as in the text
```

As an extra exercise, you could try to produce not only the length of the LCS but also the characters that are involved.

9.4. **Symmetrical queens**: The key to finding only symmetric solutions is as follows. After the first four queens have been (tentatively) placed on the first half of the board, we don't have to try all the possible positions for the other queens; they are automatically determined with regard to the first ones:

```
const SIZE = 8;
let places = Array(SIZE);
const checkPlace = (column, row) =>
  places
    .slice(0, column)
    .every((v, i) => v !== row && Math.abs(v - row) !== column - i);

const symmetricFinder = (column = 0) => {
  if (column === SIZE) {
    console.log(places.map(x => x + 1)); // print out solution

  } else if (column <= SIZE / 2) {
    // first half of the board?
    const testRowsInColumn = j => {
      if (j < SIZE) {
        if (checkPlace(column, j)) {
          places[column] = j;
          symmetricFinder(column + 1);
        }
        testRowsInColumn(j + 1);
      }
    };
    testRowsInColumn(0);

  } else {
    // second half of the board
    let symmetric = SIZE - 1 - places[SIZE - 1 - column];
    if (checkPlace(column, symmetric)) {
      places[column] = symmetric;
      symmetricFinder(column + 1);
    }
  }
};
```

Calling `symmetricFinder()` produces four solutions, which are essentially the same. Make drawings and check it to make sure it's correct!

```
[3, 5, 2, 8, 1, 7, 4, 6]
[4, 6, 8, 2, 7, 1, 3, 5]
[5, 3, 1, 7, 2, 8, 6, 4]
[6, 4, 7, 1, 8, 2, 5, 3]
```

9.5. **Sorting recursively**: Let's look at the first of these algorithms; many of the techniques here will help you write the other sorts. If the array is empty, sorting it produces a (new) empty array. Otherwise, we find the maximum value of the array (max), create a new copy of the array but without that element, sort the copy, and then return the sorted copy with max added at the end. Take a look at how we dealt with the mutator functions in order to avoid modifying the original string:

```
const selectionSort = arr => {
  if (arr.length === 0) {
    return [];
  } else {
    const max = Math.max(...arr);
    const rest = [...arr];
    rest.splice(arr.indexOf(max), 1);
    return [...selectionSort(rest), max];
  }
};

selectionSort([2, 2, 0, 9, 1, 9, 6, 0]);
// [0, 0, 1, 2, 2, 6, 9, 9]
```

9.6. **What could go wrong?** This would fail if, at any time, the array (or sub-array) to be sorted consisted of all equal values. In that case, `smaller` would be an empty array and `greaterEqual` would be equal to the whole array to sort, so the logic would enter an infinite loop.

9.7. **More efficiency**: The following code does the work for us. Here, we use a ternary operator to decide where to push the new item:

```
const partition = (arr, fn) =>
  arr.reduce(
    (result, elem) => {
      result[fn(elem) ? 0 : 1].push(elem);
      return result;
    },
    [[], []]
  );
```

Chapter 10, Ensuring Purity – Immutability

10.1. **Freezing by proxying**: As requested, using a proxy allows you to intercept changes on an object. (See `https://developer.mozilla.org/en-US/docs/Web/JavaScript/Reference/Global_Objects/Proxy` for more on this.) We use recursion to apply the proxy *all the way down* in case some attributes are objects themselves:

```
const proxySetAll = obj => {
  Object.keys(obj).forEach(v => {
    if (typeof obj[v] === "object") {
      obj[v] = proxySetAll(obj[v]);
    }
  });

  return new Proxy(obj, {
    set(target, key, value) {
      throw new Error("DON'T MODIFY ANYTHING IN ME");
    },
    deleteProperty(target, key) {
      throw new Error("DON'T DELETE ANYTHING IN ME");
    }
  });
};
```

The following is the output of the preceding code. You'd probably require something other than a `DON'T MODIFY ANYTHING IN ME` message, of course!

```
let myObj = {a: 5, b: 6, c: {d: 7, e: 8}};
myObj = proxySetAll(myObj);

myObj.a = 777;  // Uncaught Error: DON'T MODIFY ANYTHING IN ME
myObj.f = 888;  // Uncaught Error: DON'T MODIFY ANYTHING IN ME
delete myObj.b; // Uncaught Error: DON'T DELETE ANYTHING IN ME
```

10.2. **Inserting into a list, persistently**: Using recursion helps out:

- If the list is empty, we cannot insert the new key.
- If we are at a node and its key isn't `oldKey`, we create a clone of the node and insert the new key somewhere in the rest of the original node's list.

- If we are at a node and its key is `oldKey`, we create a clone of the node that's pointing at a list that starts with a new node, with `newKey` as its value, and itself pointing to the rest of the original node's list:

```
const insertAfter = (list, newKey, oldKey) => {
  if (list === null) {
    return null;

  } else if (list.key !== oldKey) {
    return node(list.key, insertAfter(list.next, newKey, oldKey));

  } else {
    return node(list.key, node(newKey, list.next));
  }
};
```

In the following code, we can see this working. The new list is similar to the one shown in *Figure 10.2*. However, printing out the lists (`c3` and `newList`) wouldn't be enough; you wouldn't be able to recognize the new or old nodes from doing this, so I've included several comparisons. The following last comparison shows that from the `"F"` node onward, the list is the same:

```
class Node {
  constructor(key, next = null) {
    this.key = key;
    this.next = next;
  }
}
const node = (key, next) => new Node(key, next);

let c3 = node("G", node("B", node("F", node("A", node("C", node("E")))))); 
let newList = insertAfter(c3, "D", "B");

c3 === newList // false
c3.key === newList.key // true (both are "G")
c3.next === newList.next // false

c3.next.key === newList.next.key // true (both are "B")
c3.next.next === newList.next.next // false

c3.next.next.key === "F" // true
newList.next.next.key === "D" // true
c3.next.next.next === newList.next.next.next.next // true
```

When we implement this, if `oldKey` isn't found, nothing is inserted. Could you change the logic so that the new node would be added at the end of the list?

10.3. Composing many lenses: We want to compose lenses from left to right so that we can use `reduce()` in a direct way. Let's write the `composeManyLenses()` function and apply it to the same example that was shown in the text:

```
const composeManyLenses = (...lenses) =>
  lenses.reduce((acc, lens) => composeTwoLenses(acc, lens));

console.log(view(composeManyLenses(lC, lE, lG, lJ, lK), deepObject));
/*
    11, same as earlier
*/
```

10.4. Lenses by path: Hint: the needed changes would be along the lines of what we did when we went from `getField()` to `getByPath()`.

10.5. Accessing virtual attributes: Using a getter is always viable, and for this question, you'd write something like the following:

```
const lastNameLens = composeTwoLenses(lensProp("name"), lensProp("last"));

const fullNameGetter = obj => `${view(lastNameLens)(obj)},
${view(firstNameLens)(obj)}`;
```

Being able to set several attributes based on a single value isn't always possible, but if we assume the incoming full name is in the right format, we can split it by the comma and assign the two parts to first and last name, respectively:

```
const fullNameSetter = (fullName, obj) => {
  const parts = fullName.split(",");
  return set(firstNameLens, parts[1], set(lastNameLens, parts[0], obj));
};
```

10.6. Lenses for arrays? The `view()` function would work well, but `set()` and `over()` wouldn't work in a pure way since `setArray()` doesn't return a new array; instead, it modifies the current one in place. Take a look at the next question for a related problem.

10.7. Lenses into maps: Getting a value from the map poses no problem, but for setting, we need to clone the map:

```
const getMap = curry((key, map) => map.get(key));

const setMap = curry((key, value, map) => new Map(map).set(key, value));

const lensMap = key => lens(getMap(key), setMap(key));
```

Chapter 11, Implementing Design Patterns – the Functional Way

11.1. **Decorating methods, the future way**: As we've already mentioned, decorators aren't a fixed, definitive feature at the moment. However, by following https://tc39.github.io/proposal-decorators/, we can write the following:

```
const logging = (target, name, descriptor) => {
  const savedMethod = descriptor.value;
  descriptor.value = function(...args) {
    console.log(`entering ${name}: ${args}`);

    try {
      const valueToReturn = savedMethod.bind(this)(...args);
      console.log(`exiting ${name}: ${valueToReturn}`);
      return valueToReturn;

    } catch (thrownError) {
      console.log(`exiting ${name}: threw ${thrownError}`);
      throw thrownError;
    }
  };

  return descriptor;
};
```

We want to add a `@logging` decoration to a method. We save the original method in `savedMethod` and substitute a new method that will log the received arguments, call the original method to save its return value, log that, and finally return it. If the original method throws an exception, we catch it, report it, and throw it again so that it can be processed as expected. A simple example of this is as follows:

```
class SumThree {
  constructor(z) {
    this.z = z;
  }
  @logging
  sum(x, y) {
    return x + y + this.z;
  }
}

new SumThree(100).sum(20, 8);
// entering sum: 20,8
// exiting sum: 128
```

11.2. **Decorator with mixins**: Working along the same lines as in question 1.1, we write an `addBar()` function that receives a `Base` class and extends it. In this case, I decided to add a new attribute and a new method. The constructor for the extended class calls the original constructor and creates the `.barValue` attribute. The new class has both the original's `doSomething()` method and the new `somethingElse()` method:

```
class Foo {
  constructor(fooValue) {
    this.fooValue = fooValue;
  }

  doSomething() {
    console.log("something: foo...", this.fooValue);
  }
}

var addBar = Base =>
  class extends Base {
    constructor(fooValue, barValue) {
      super(fooValue);
      this.barValue = barValue;
    }

    somethingElse() {
      console.log("something added: bar... ", this.barValue);
    }
  };

var fooBar = new (addBar(Foo))(22, 9);
fooBar.doSomething();   // something: foo... 22
fooBar.somethingElse(); // something added: bar... 9
```

11.3. **Multi-clicking by hand**: There are various ways to achieve this with timers and counting, but make sure that you don't interfere with single- or double-click detection! You can also use a common listener and look at `event.detail`; you can find out more at https://developer.mozilla.org/en-US/docs/Web/API/UIEvent/detail.

Chapter 12, Building Better Containers – Functional Data Types

12.1. **Maybe tasks?** The following code shows a simpler solution than the one we looked at in question 8.2:

```
const pending = Maybe.of(listOfTasks)
  .map(getField("byPerson"))
  .map(filter(t => t.responsible === name))
  .map(t => tasks)
  .map(t => t[0])
  .map(filter(t => !t.done))
  .map(getField("id"))
  .valueOf();
```

Here, we apply one function after the other, secure in the knowledge that if any of these functions produces an empty result (or even if the original `listOfTasks` is null), the sequence of calls will go on. In the end, you will either get an array of task IDs or a null value.

12.2. **Extending your trees**: Calculating the tree's height is simple if you do this in a recursive fashion. The height of an empty tree is zero, while the height of a non-empty tree is one (for the root) plus the maximum height of its left and right subtrees:

```
const treeHeight = tree =>
  tree(
    (val, left, right) =>
      1 + Math.max(treeHeight(left), treeHeight(right)),
    () => 0
  );
```

Listing the keys in order is a well-known requirement. Because of the way that the tree is built, you list the left subtree's keys first, then the root, and finally the right subtree's keys, all in a recursive fashion:

```
const treeList = tree =>
  tree(
    (value, left, right) => {
      treeList(left);
      console.log(value);
      treeList(right);
    },
    () => {
      // nothing
    } );
```

Finally, deleting a key from a binary search tree is a bit more complex. First, you must locate the node that is going to be removed, and then there are several cases:

- If the node has no subtrees, deletion is simple.
- If the node has only one subtree, you just replace the node by its subtree.
- If the node has two subtrees, then you have to do the following:
  - Find the minimum key in the tree with a greater key.
  - Place it in the node's place.

Since this algorithm is well covered in all computer science textbooks, I won't go into more detail about this here:

```
const treeRemove = (toRemove, tree) =>
  tree(
    (val, left, right) => {
      const findMinimumAndRemove = (tree /* never empty */) =>
        tree((value, left, right) => {
          if (treeIsEmpty(left)) {
            return { min: value, tree: right };

          } else {
            const result = findMinimumAndRemove(left);
            return {
              min: result.min,
              tree: Tree(value, result.tree, right)
            };
          }
        });

      if (toRemove < val) {
        return Tree(val, treeRemove(toRemove, left), right);

      } else if (toRemove > val) {
        return Tree(val, left, treeRemove(toRemove, right));

      } else if (treeIsEmpty(left) && treeIsEmpty(right)) {
        return EmptyTree();

      } else if (treeIsEmpty(left) !== treeIsEmpty(right)) {
        return tree((val, left, right) => left(() => left, () => right));

      } else {
        const result = findMinimumAndRemove(right);
        return Tree(result.min, left, result.tree);
      }
    },
```

```
      () => tree
  );
```

12.3. Functional lists: Let's add to the samples that have already been provided. We can simplify working with lists if we can transform a list into an array and vice versa:

```
const listToArray = list =>
    list((head, tail) => [head, ...listToArray(tail)], () => []);

const listFromArray = arr =>
    arr.length
        ? NewList(arr[0], listFromArray(arr.slice(1)))
        : EmptyList();
```

Concatenating two lists together and appending a value to a list have simple recursive implementations. We can also reverse a list by using the appending function:

```
const listConcat = (list1, list2) =>
  list1(
    (head, tail) => NewList(head, listConcat(tail, list2)),
    () => list2
  );

const listAppend = value => list =>
  list(
    (head, tail) => NewList(head, listAppend(value)(tail)),
    () => NewList(value, EmptyList)
  );

const listReverse = list =>
  list(
    (head, tail) => listAppend(head)(listReverse(tail)),
    () => EmptyList
  );
```

Finally, the basic `map()`, `filter()`, and `reduce()` operations are good to have:

```
const listMap = fn => list =>
  list(
    (head, tail) => NewList(fn(head), listMap(fn)(tail)),
    () => EmptyList
  );

const listFilter = fn => list =>
  list(
    (head, tail) =>
      fn(head)
        ? NewList(head, listFilter(fn)(tail))
```

```
            : listFilter(fn)(tail),
        () => EmptyList
    );

const listReduce = (fn, accum) => list =>
    list((head, tail) => listReduce(fn, fn(accum, head))(tail), () => accum);
```

The following are some exercises that have been left for you to tackle:

- Generate a printable version of a list.
- Compare two lists to see if they have the same values, in the same order.
- Search a list for a value.
- Get, update, or remove the value at the *n*-th position of a list.

12.4. **Shortening code**: The first thing you would do is get rid of the first ternary operator by taking advantage of the short circuit evaluation of the || operator:

```
const treeSearch2 = (findValue, tree) =>
    tree(
        (value, left, right) =>
            findValue === value ||
            (findValue < value
                ? treeSearch2(findValue, left)
                : treeSearch2(findValue, right)),
        () => false
    );
```

Also, seeing that both alternatives in the second ternary operator are very similar, you could also do some shortening there:

```
const treeSearch3 = (findValue, tree) =>
    tree(
        (value, left, right) =>
            findValue === value ||
            treeSearch3(findValue, findValue < value ? left : right),
        () => false
    );
```

Remember: shorter doesn't imply better! However, I've found many examples of this kind of code tightening, and it's better if you have been exposed to it, too.

Other Books You May Enjoy

If you enjoyed this book, you may be interested in these other books by Packt:

React Projects
Roy Derks

ISBN: 978-1-78995-493-7

- Create a wide range of applications using various modern React tools and frameworks
- Discover how React Hooks modernize state management for React apps
- Develop progressive web applications using React components
- Build test-driven React applications using the Jest and Enzyme frameworks
- Understand full stack development using React, Apollo, and GraphQL
- Perform server-side rendering using React and React Router
- Design gestures and animations for a cross-platform game using React Native

Web Development with Angular and Bootstrap - Third Edition
Sridhar Rao Chivukula, Aki Iskandar

ISBN: 978-1-78883-810-8

- Develop Angular single-page applications using an ecosystem of helper tools
- Get familiar with Bootstrap's new grid and helper classes
- Embrace TypeScript and ECMAScript to write more maintainable code
- Implement custom directives for Bootstrap 4 with the ng2-bootstrap library
- Understand the component-oriented structure of Angular and its router
- Use the built-in HTTP library to work with API endpoints
- Manage your app's data and state with observables and streams
- Combine Angular and Bootstrap 4 with Firebase to develop a solid example

Leave a review - let other readers know what you think

Please share your thoughts on this book with others by leaving a review on the site that you bought it from. If you purchased the book from Amazon, please leave us an honest review on this book's Amazon page. This is vital so that other potential readers can see and use your unbiased opinion to make purchasing decisions, we can understand what our customers think about our products, and our authors can see your feedback on the title that they have worked with Packt to create. It will only take a few minutes of your time, but is valuable to other potential customers, our authors, and Packt. Thank you!

Index

.

.charCodeAt() method
  reference link 85
.filter() method
  URL 136
.forEach()
  URL 133
.map()
  URL 119, 275

A

Adapter patterns 343, 344, 345, 346
Ajax
  detecting 67, 68
altered functions 153
anonymous 20
arguments
  reference link 54
Array.from()
  reference link 245
Array.prototype.sort()
  URL 377
array
  .reduce(), using 116, 117
  average, calculating 113, 114, 115
  filtering 135, 136
  find(), emulating with reduce() 139
  findIndex(), emulating with reduce() 139
  flattening 125, 126, 127, 128
  reducing, to value 110, 111
  reference link 112
  searching 138
  special search case 139
  summing 112, 113
  values, calculating 115, 116
arrays of arrays

  dealing with 125
arrow functions
  about 20, 21, 51
  multiple arguments 56, 57
  using 205
  values, handling 52, 54
  values, returning 52
  working, with arguments 54, 55
async calls
  filtering with 147
  looping over 145, 146
  mapping 146
  reducing 148, 149
async functions
  strange behaviors 143, 144, 145
  working with 142, 143
async-ready
  looping 145

B

Babel
  URL 24
backtracking 281
basic container 381, 382, 383
Bell System Technical Journal
  URL 224
binary 112
binary trees
  using, in Haskell 402, 403
bind() method
  using, for currying 198, 199, 201
bind()
  reference link 62
black-box testing 103

C

callback 18, 65
chaining
  about 223, 238
  method calls 239, 240, 241
cloning 308, 309, 310, 311
closures
  about 19, 20
  using, in partial application 209, 210
  using, in partial currying 216
CodePen
  URL 26
Colossal Cave Adventure Game
  reference link 58
comma operator
  URL 232, 233
command line interface (CLI) 25
Command patterns 343, 352, 353
commutative property 88
compatibility table, ES6
  reference link 23
compatibility tables
  URL 290
complex memoization 166, 167, 168
composing
  about 223, 242
  composed function, testing 250, 251, 252, 253, 254
  examples 242
  files, counting 244
  unary operators 243
  unique words, searching 244, 245, 246
  with higher-order functions 246, 247, 248, 249
constants 305, 306
containers
  about 381
  API results, dealing with 387, 389, 390, 391
  building 378, 379
  data types, extending 379, 380, 381
  enhancing 383, 384, 385
  missing values, dealing with 385, 386
  monads 393
  prisms, implementing 391, 393
continuation-passing style (CPS) 66, 67, 292, 293, 294, 295, 296

continuations 65, 292
currying
  about 56, 191, 192, 193
  curried-by-hand function 196, 197
  parameters 193, 194, 195, 196
  with bind() 198, 199, 201
  with eval() 201, 202

D

D3.js library
  URL 238
Dark Sky API
  URL 387
data types
  about 373, 374
  extending 379, 380, 381
  options 376, 378
data
  extracting, from objects 120, 121
debugging 223
decorator patterns 343, 346, 347, 348, 350
decorators
  reference link 154
demethodizing 184, 185, 186
design patterns
  about 340, 341
  architectural patterns 341
  behavioral design patterns 341
  categories 341, 342
  concurrency patterns 341
  creational design patterns 341
  need for 342, 343
  structural design patterns 341
destructuring assignment
  reference link 95
Don't Repeat Yourself (DRY) 37
dyadic function 112

E

e-commerce, related issues 31, 32
eight queens puzzle 281, 282, 283, 284, 285
Either monad 397, 398, 400
ES6
  reference link 23
eta abstraction 60

eta conversion 60
eta reduction 60
European Computer Manufacturers Association
   (ECMA)
  about 16
  URL 16
eval() method
  using 205
  using, for currying 201, 202

F

Facade patterns 343, 344, 345, 346
Facebook's Flow
  URL 26
Fantasy Land
  URL 393
fetch()
  reference link 70
  references 203
Fibonacci
  reference link 89
first-class objects
  about 17, 57
  functions, using as 17
Fisher-Yates shuffle
  algorithm, reference link 105
  reference link 105
flat()
  emulating 130, 131, 132
flatMap()
  emulating 130, 131, 132
  flattening 128, 129, 130
  mapping 128, 129, 130
flattening 125
Flow
  URL 374
fluent APIs
  examples 238, 239
fluent interfaces 238
foldr 111
freezing 306, 308
functional design patterns 367, 368
functional programming (FP)
  about 9, 10, 77, 109
  characteristics 13

disadvantages 14
extensible functionality 13
misconceptions 11, 12
modular functionality 12
need for 12
program, customizing 11
qualities 12
reusable functionality 13
testable functionality 12
theoretical way, versus practical way 10
understandable functionality 12
Functional Reactive Programming (FRP)
  about 355
  basic concepts and terms 355, 356
  multi-clicks, detecting 360
  observable 355
  observer 355
  operators 355
  operators, for observables 357, 359
  pipeline 355
  subscription 355
  typeahead searches 362, 363, 364, 365
functional solution, e-commerce related issues
  about 37
  higher-order solution 38, 39
  solution, producing 43, 44
  solution, testing automatically 41, 42, 43
  solution, testing manually 39, 40
functions, using in FP ways
  about 62
  callbacks 65
  continuation-passing style (CPS) 66, 67
  continuations 65
  immediate invocation 71, 72, 73, 74
  injection 62, 63, 64
  polyfills 67
  promises 65
  stubbing 70, 71
functions, with side effects 79
functions
  about 47
  arity changing 177, 178
  arrow functions 51
  behavior, altering 171
  common mistake 60

example 171, 173
lambda function 48, 49, 50, 51
logging, adding to 155
methods, turning into 184, 185, 186
modifying 178
negating, logically 174, 175
operations, turning into 178, 179
optimum value, finding 186, 187, 188
React-Redux reducer 58, 59
references 49
results, inverting 175, 176
signatures 374, 375, 376
turning, into promises 181, 182
types, URL 374
URL 51
used, as objects 57, 58
using 219
using, as binary trees 404, 405, 406, 407, 408, 409
using, as data structures 402
using, as first-class objects 17
working, with methods 61, 62
functors 381, 383, 384, 385

G

Gang of Four (GoF) 340
getRandomLetter() function
  reference link 85
getters 312
  writing 312, 313

H

Haskell
  binary trees, using 402, 403
higher-order functions (HOF)
  about 109, 274, 278, 279, 280
  composing with 246, 247, 248, 249
Hindley-Milner 374
hoisting
  reference link 49

I

idempotency 78
immediate invocation 71, 72, 73, 74
Immediately Invoked Function Expression (IIFE)
  36
immutable objects
  references 334
impure functions
  about 93
  avoiding 93
  injecting 95, 96, 97
  purity, ensuring 97, 98
  state usage, avoiding 93, 95
  testing 103, 104, 105

J

Jasmine
  URL 27
JavaScript (JS)
  about 9, 304
  arrow functions 20, 21
  cloning 308, 309, 310, 311
  closures 19, 20
  constants 305, 306
  features 17
  freezing 306, 308
  functionalities 16, 17
  functions, using as first-class objects 17, 18
  lenses 315
  mutating 308, 309, 310, 311
  mutator functions 304, 305
  prisms 324
  recursion 18, 19
  spread operator 21, 22
  testing 27
  transpilers, using 24, 25, 26
  using, as functional language 14
  using, as tool 15, 16
  working with 23
  working, with online tools 26, 27
JavaScript functions
  reference link 178
JavaScript, getters
  about 312
  writing 312, 313
JavaScript, setters
  about 312
  creating 313, 315
JS prettier

reference link 21
JSBin
  URL 26
JSFiddle
  reference link 26

K

Karma
  URL 27

L

lambda function 48, 49, 50, 51
lazy evaluation 296
lenses
  about 315
  implementing, with functions 321, 322, 324
  implementing, with objects 318, 319, 320
  working with 315, 316, 318
Linux
  pipelining, using in 224, 225, 226
lists
  working with 328, 329, 330
localeCompare()
  reference link 64
logging function
  enhancing 157
logging
  adding, to function 155
  in functional way 155, 156
logical higher-order functions
  about 134
  array, filtering 135, 136
  array, searching 138
  filter(), emulating with reduce() 137
  higher-level predicates 140, 141
  negatives, checking 141, 142
  reduce() example 136, 137
looping 132, 134

M

map()
  about 118, 119
  emulating, with reduce() 124
  using, advantages 119
memoization 88

memoization higher-order function
  testing 168, 169, 171
memoizing functions 163
methods
  turning, into functions 184, 185, 186
Mocha
  URL 27
monads
  about 393
  function, calling 400, 401
  operations, adding 394, 395, 396, 397
  promises 401, 402
morphism 118
mutating 308, 309, 310, 311
mutator functions 305
mutator methods
  about 84, 304
  URL 304

N

Node.js
  reference link 23
numbers
  parsing 121, 122

O

Object Oriented Programming (OOP) 10
object-oriented (OO) 354
object-oriented design patterns
  about 343, 366
  Adapter patterns 344, 345, 346
  Chain of Responsibility pattern 366
  Command patterns 352, 353
  currying and partial application 366
  declarative functions 366
  decorator patterns 346, 347, 348, 350
  Facade patterns 344, 345, 346
  observer programming 354
  persistent data structures 366
  reactive programming 354
  Strategy patterns 352, 353
  Template patterns 352, 353
  wrapper patterns 346, 347, 350
Object.freeze()
  URL 307

Object.seal()
  URL 307
objects
  property, obtaining from 182, 183
  updating 330, 331, 332, 334
observables
  creating, with operators 357
  reference link 354
Observer patterns 343
observer programming 354
operations
  implementing 179, 180
  turning, into functions 178, 179

P

parameter order 217, 218
parseInt()
  URL 122
partial application
  about 191, 192, 203
  with arrow functions 205
  with closures 209, 210
  with eval() 205, 206, 208
partial currying
  about 191, 192, 212, 213
  with bind() 213, 215, 216
  with closures 216
persistent data structures
  creating 327
  limitations 335
  lists, working 328, 329, 330
  objects, updating 330, 331, 332, 334
pipelines
  building 227, 228, 229
  constructs, using 229, 230, 231
  creating 227
  debugging 231
  logging wrapper, using 234
  tapping, into flow 233, 234
  tee function, using 231, 232
pipelining
  about 223, 224
  example 226, 227
  pipelines, creating 227
  pipelines, debugging 231

point-free style 235
  using, in Linux 224, 225, 226
  using, in Unix 224, 225, 226
pivot 271
point-free style
  about 223, 235
  converting to 236, 237
  functions, defining 235, 236
pointfree 60
polyfills
  about 67
  Ajax, detecting 67, 68
  missing functions, adding 69, 70
  reference link 69
popularity indices
  reference link 15
prisms
  about 324
  implementing 327
  working with 324, 325, 327
product types 376
Promise.resolve()
  URL 401
promises
  about 65
  functions, turning into 181, 182
  reference link 65
property
  obtaining, from object 182, 183
proxy
  URL 239
pure functions, advantages
  about 87
  memoization 88, 89, 90, 91, 92
  order of execution 87, 88
  self-documentation 92
  testing 92
pure functions
  about 77, 79
  conditions 77
  referential transparency 78, 79, 80
  testing 99, 100
  versus impure function 98
  working in 158, 159, 161
purified functions

testing 100, 101, 102

R

ranges
  working with 122, 123
React sandbox
  reference link 348
React-Redux package
  reference link 351
React-Redux reducer 58
  working 58, 59
Reactive Functional Programming (RFP) 355
reactive programming 354
recursion techniques
  about 288
  continuation-passing style (CPS) 292, 293, 294, 295, 296
  elimination 299
  tail calls, optimization 289, 290, 291, 292
  thunks 296, 297, 298, 299
  trampolines 296, 297, 298, 299
recursion
  about 18, 19
  applying 265, 266
  applying, methods 266
  backtracking 281
  decrease and conquer strategy 266, 267, 268
  divide and conquer strategy 268, 269, 270, 271, 272
  dynamic programming 272, 274
  eight queens puzzle 281, 282, 283, 284, 285
  filtering 275, 276, 277, 278
  higher-order functions 274, 278, 279, 280
  mapping 275, 276, 277, 278
  searching 281
  tree structure, traversing 285, 287, 288
  using 264, 265
reduce()
  map(), emulating with 124
referential opacity 78
referential transparency 78, 79, 80
RxJS Operators
  reference link 357
RxJS
  about 355

installation link 357

S

Sanctuary
  URL 378
searching 281
set()
  reference link 245
setters
  about 312
  creating 313, 315
side effects, pure functions
  about 79, 80
  argument mutation 84
  global state 81
  inner state 82, 83
  troublesome functions 85, 86, 87
  usual side effects 80
simple memoization 164, 165
solutions, e-commerce related issues
  about 32, 33
  button, disabling 35
  global flag, using 33
  handler, modifying 35
  handler, redefining 36
  handler, removing 34
  local flag, using 36, 37
Sorta Functional Programming (SFP) 10, 343
spread operator
  about 21, 22
  reference link 21
Strategy patterns 343, 352, 353
stub 101
stubbing 70, 71
sum types 377

T

tacit 60
tail calls
  about 290
  optimization 289, 290, 291, 292
TC39
  reference link 154
Template patterns 343, 352, 353
testing 223

thunks 296, 297, 298, 299
timing functions 161, 162, 163
Traceur
  reference link 24, 25
trampolines 297, 298, 299
transducing
  about 255, 256, 257, 258
  reducers, composing 258, 259
  reducers, generalizing 259, 260
transformations
  about 110
  array, reducing to value 110, 111
  looping 132, 134
  operation, applying 118, 119
transpilers
  using 24, 25, 26
Try monad 400, 401

TypeScript
  reference link 26
  URL 25, 374

U

unary() higher-order function 378
Unix
  pipelining, using in 224, 225, 226

V

Value-added Tax (VAT) 195

W

white-box testing 103
wrapped functions 153
wrapper patterns 343, 346, 347, 348, 350
wrapping functions 154

Printed in Great Britain
by Amazon